014632

D1764971

The aim of the Oxford Classical Monograph series (which replaces the Oxford Classical and Philosophical Monographs) is to publish books based on the best theses on Greek and Latin literature, ancient history, and ancient philosophy examined by the Faculty Board of Classics.

Child Emperor Rule in the Late Roman West, AD 367–455

MEAGHAN A. McEVOY

OXFORD
UNIVERSITY PRESS

OXFORD
UNIVERSITY PRESS

Great Clarendon Street, Oxford OX2 6DP
United Kingdom

Oxford University Press is a department of the University of Oxford.
It furthers the University's objective of excellence in research, scholarship,
and education by publishing worldwide.

Oxford is a registered trade mark of Oxford University Press in the UK
and in certain other countries

British Library Cataloguing in Publication Data
Data available

Library of Congress Cataloging in Publication Data
Data available

ISBN 978-0-19-966481-8

Preface

This book aims to set in its full context the rule of child-emperors in the late Roman west from the late fourth until the mid-fifth century AD, and to highlight the proliferation of minority governments of this period as a key factor in the transformation of the imperial office in the late Roman world.

The late Roman empire has received considerable attention in recent decades, yet the child-emperors of the period themselves have seldom been considered worthy of notice. Some modern studies have offered extensive coverage and analysis of fourth- and fifth-century history, yet do not identify or investigate the child-emperor as in any way exceptional.[1] Others focus on specific historians or writers of the period, such as Ammianus, Ausonius, or Claudian, or on key political figures, such as Ambrose of Milan, Stilicho, Galla Placidia, or Aetius; or on broader themes, such as aristocracy and senate in the late empire.[2] And immensely valuable though all of these works have been in addressing many developments of the period, none of them view the accessions of a series of infant emperors as in any way surprising.

Even works which have noted the phenomenon of the child-emperor in late antiquity have thus far dealt only with the depiction of young emperors in the *Historia Augusta* and the topos of child-princes in texts of the period.[3] Studies of the so-called 'generalissimos' of the western Roman empire (a term used, not unreasonably, by many modern scholars to describe the generals who frequently dominated the western governments of the period) trace merely the rise of their protagonists rather than the structural and political circumstances that made such a rise possible.[4] And though a number of recent and excellent studies have highlighted the stresses and strains of the late Roman imperial office, changes in the machinery of government in this era, and the development of imperial policy over this period, child-emperor rule has continued to be seen merely as a curiosity, rather than a significant development worthy of attention in its own right.[5]

---

[1] Jones (1964a); Stein (1959); Seeck (1919).

[2] Matthews (1989); Cameron (1970); Sivan (1993); McLynn (1994); Mazzarino (1942) Sirago (1961); Oost (1968a); Sivan (2011); Zecchini (1983); Coulon (2000); Stickler (2002); Matthews (1975).

[3] Hartke (1951); Molè Ventura (1992).

[4] See particularly O'Flynn (1983). Further examples of use of 'generalissimo': Matthews (1975), 302; Holum (1982), 49; Heather (2005), 223.

[5] Lenski (2002); Kelly (2004); Errington (2006); and for the rule of child-emperors as a curiosity, see e.g. Szidat (2011), 54–5.

In view of the absence of any other collective study of the reigns of the four western child-emperors of the Valentinian/Theodosian house—Gratian, Valentinian II, Honorius, and Valentinian III—and the general avoidance of detailed political analysis of the late fourth and fifth centuries by modern scholars, a chronological investigation of the period seemed the best way to proceed. On examining the wide range of sources for the period and the questions they raised in their turn, it quickly became clear that a careful re-examination of each of the reigns of the four emperors in question, an unpicking and reconstruction of the politics of the period, was essential in order adequately to appreciate the gradual evolution of attitudes towards imperial rulership, to the individual rulers themselves, and to the role of those who surrounded and influenced them across this eighty-year period. I have chosen in consequence to examine each reign through a narrative analysis of its politics and in the process to highlight certain important tendencies, to situate the contingent events in their structural context, and in the conclusion to draw out the key changes which were thus revealed, and to offer an explanation which takes into account both the immediate politics of promotion and also longer-term systemic changes. My approach has thus been to try to differentiate between the 'deeper' structural constraints underlying and framing the politics and cultural assumptions of groups and individuals on the one hand, and the conjunctural or short-term decisions or events on the other, but at the same time to pinpoint their 'emergent' characteristics, that is to say, the results of the combination or re-combination of such different levels of social being as reflected and realized in the actual behaviour of individuals—generals, senators, churchmen—or groups—the senate, aristocracy, the army.

Inevitably, this raises the issue of the tension between a narrative account and a structural analysis. While a *histoire événementielle* alone is perhaps an inadequate vehicle on which to carry an analysis of causal relationships, a narrative account of the very complex politics of the period, particularly from *c*.395 onwards, proved to be the best way to bring out and to illustrate various processes of change in cultural attitude and social practice. As a result I have tried to exploit this possibility, while always bearing in mind the different levels of causal relations referred to above. In thus reconstructing from the sources a history of the period, which, for the fifth century especially, has not yet been firmly established by modern scholarship, this focus on political narrative is able both to situate events in their historical context rather than presenting them as isolated eventualities, and in so doing, as the story of the period itself unfolds, to draw out the structural developments.

Acknowledgements

This book would never have been written without the support and encouragement of a great many people, of whom only a handful can be named here.

I must firstly thank the Australian committee of the John Crampton Travelling Scholarships, which so generously supported me throughout my studies at Oxford, and first gave me the chance to pursue this topic as my DPhil. dissertation at New College. In addition, I am immensely grateful to the British School at Rome, which offered me a glorious nine-month stay at the end of my DPhil. to begin revising this thesis for publication, and the Dumbarton Oaks Research Library and Collection, which similarly so generously supported me for a semester in the beautiful surroundings of Georgetown, Washington, DC. Finally, I am sincerely grateful to the British Academy, and to Corpus Christi College, Oxford, which has provided me with such a supportive, congenial, and active community of scholars, both late antique and other, within which to pursue my research as a postdoctoral fellow.

My supervisor, Peter Heather, has provided innumerable valuable insights and constant encouragement over the course of my research in the last few years, and borne with great good humour my lengthy struggles to pull into shape the particularly unwilling Honorius, and I am sincerely grateful. I must also thank my examiners, John Matthews and Neil McLynn, who offered so many thoughtful and constructive suggestions, and Neil in particular, who has done his best to guide my transformation of this work from thesis to book. All errors of judgement, of course, remain my own. My heartfelt thanks go also to two particularly stalwart friends who have shown such determined faith in me for many years now—Paul Tuffin and John Haldon. A number of other scholars also deserve special mention as well for their thoughtful reading of chapters and suggestions made, particularly Fergus Millar, Noel Lenski, Roger Tomlin, and Caillan Davenport; and for their helpful advice and encouragement: Jan Willem Drijvers, Jill Harries, and Donncha O'Rourke. I am also very grateful to those who have generously offered forthcoming work of their own to assist me in my research: Mark Humphries, Andrew Gillett, Claire Sotinel, Hagith Sivan, and Peter Van Nuffelen. Thank you also to the production team at OUP who have patiently seen this project through the various stages of preparation to reach this point.

I owe a great debt of gratitude to the Classics Department of the University of Adelaide in South Australia, which first introduced me to the classical, and then the late antique, world as an undergraduate and encouraged me to go on to further research.

A number of other faithful and patient friends deserve special mention: Anne Carter, Anna Donaghy, Carly de Jonge, and Frances Hansford especially. My particular thanks go also to Roger and Debbie Tebbutt, who have probably long regretted their generous offer that I treat their idyllic home as my own here in the UK, but have nevertheless shown tremendous patience and hospitality throughout my relentless visits. Last but certainly not least, my greatest thanks must go to my family, whose love of all things historical has influenced my outlook for so many years, and whose support for me has been so constant (and so often happily represented by airmail packages of Haigh's chocolates)—to Mum and Dad, Kieran and Bec, and perhaps most importantly of all to my child-emperor model Hunter, for reminding me frequently how a 4- or 6-year-old might really behave (a role which I am sure baby Sebastian will soon fulfil too!). I dedicate this effort to them.

Contents

List of Abbreviations

AE	*L'Année épigraphique* (Paris, 1888–)
AHR	*American Historical Review*
AJAH	*American Journal of Ancient History*
AJP	*American Journal of Philology*
Ant.Tard.	*Antiquité Tardive*
Art Bull.	*Art Bulletin*
BCAR	*Bollettino della commissione archeologica comunale di Roma*
BZ	*Byzantinische Zeitschrift*
CAH	*The Cambridge Ancient History XIII: The Late Empire, AD337–425*, ed. Av. Cameron and P. Garnsey (Cambridge, 1998); *XIV: Late Antiquity: Empire and Successors, AD425–600*, ed. Av. Cameron, B. Ward-Perkins, and M. Whitby (Cambridge, 2000)
CCL	*Corpus Christianorum, series Latina*
CIL	*Corpus Inscriptionum Latinarum*
CJ	*Codex Justinianus*
CJourn.	*Classical Journal*
CLRE	*Consuls of the Later Roman Empire*, ed. R. S. Bagnall, A. Cameron, S. R. Schwartz, and K. A. Worp (Atlanta, Ga., 1987)
CSEL	*Corpus Scriptorum Ecclesiasticorum Latinorum*
CSHB	*Corpus Scriptorum Historiae Byzantinae*
CSirm	*Sirmondian Constitutions*
CTh	*Theodosian Code*
CP	*Classical Philology*
CQ	*Classical Quarterly*
DOP	*Dumbarton Oaks Papers*
EHR	*English Historical Review*
HThR	*Harvard Theological Review*
HSCP	*Harvard Studies in Classical Philology*
ICUR	*Inscriptiones Christianae Urbis Romae*
ILCV	*Inscriptiones Latinae Christianae Veteres*
ILS	*Inscriptiones Latinae Selectae*
JECS	*Journal of Early Christian Studies*

JEH	*Journal of Ecclesiastical History*
JLA	*Journal of Late Antiquity*
JRS	*Journal of Roman Studies*
JThS	*Journal of Theological Studies*
Mus.Helv.	*Museum Helveticum*
NC	*Numismatic Chronicle*
NTh	*Novels of Theodosius II*
NVal	*Novels of Valentinian III*
Opus.Rom.	*Opuscula Romana*
PBA	*Proceedings of the British Academy*
PBSR	*Papers of the British School at Rome*
PL	*Patrologia Latina*
PLRE	*The Prosopography of the Later Roman Empire,* 3 vols., ed. A. H. M. Jones, J. R. Martindale, and J. Morris (Cambridge, 1971–92)
REA	*Revue des études Anciennes*
REB	*Revue des études Byzantines*
RH	*Revue historique*
RHE	*Revue d'Histoire Ecclésiastique*
RIC	*Roman Imperial Coinage, Volume 9: Valentinian I—Theodosius I* by J. W. E. Pearce (London, 1951); *Roman Imperial Coinage, Volume 10: The Divided Empire and the Fall of the Western Parts, AD395-491* by J. Kent (London,1994)
RIL	*Rendiconta dell'Instituto Lombardo*
RPAA	*Rendiconti della pontificia romana di archaeologia*
SC	*Sources Chrétiennes*
TAPA	*Transactions of the American Philological Association*
ZAC	*Zeitschrift für Antikes Christentum*

Gold solidus of Valentinian I issued in AD367 for the accession of Gratian, bearing the legend 'Spes Rei Publicae'. © Dumbarton Oaks, Byzantine Collection, Washington DC.

Introduction

SPES REI PUBLICAE: THE HOPE OF THE STATE?

The numerous child-emperors of the late Roman world make up a strange and unexpected phenomenon which has been entirely neglected by scholars of the period thus far. Yet it is a development which has crucial ramifications for any understanding of the era, and represents a serious omission in the considerable attention accorded to the political and cultural history of late antiquity in the last few decades.

In the summer of 367, the soldier-emperor Valentinian I, ruler of the western Roman empire since 364, fell seriously ill. As he lay on what was believed to be his deathbed, court factions began scheming over who the emperor's successor should be, even, according to Ammianus Marcellinus, coming up with two potential candidates.

But while these designs were being agitated to no purpose, the emperor was restored with the help of numerous remedies; and observing that he was hardly yet rescued from the danger of death, he purposed to bestow the imperial insignia upon his son Gratianus, who had by this time nearly reached the age of puberty.[1]

Valentinian's son Gratian was 8 years of age, and on 24 August 367, the emperor presented the boy to his assembled army as their new co-Augustus, with a speech commending the child as a tie between army and emperor, who would 'secure the public peace on all sides'.[2] Rarely in Roman history had so young a child been promoted to the full rank of Augustus, and yet only eight years later, in 375, Gratian's half-brother Valentinian II, a boy of only 4 years of age, was also proclaimed co-Augustus upon the death of their father.

---

[1] AM 26.6.4: *Sed dum haec cogitantur in cassum, imperator remediis multiplicibus recreatus, vixque se mortis periculo contemplans extractum, Gratianum filium suum, adulto iam proximum, insignibus principatus ornare meditabatur.*

[2] AM 27.6.8: *Gratianum hunc meum adultum, quem diu versatum inter liberos vestros, commune diligitis pignus, undique muniendae tranquillitatis publicae causa, in augustum assumere commilitium paro, si propitia caelestis numinis vestraeque maiestatis voluntas parentis amorem iuverit praeeuntem . . .*

In 393 the eastern emperor Theodosius I made his 8-year-old son Honorius co-Augustus, and in 395, at the age of 10, Honorius would become sole emperor of the west. In 425, Honorius' 6-year-old nephew followed him in the role of emperor after a major eastern military expedition was conducted to set him on the western throne. None of these reigns was short-lived: Gratian was Augustus for seventeen years (367–83), Valentinian II for seventeen also (375–92), Honorius for thirty years (393–423), and Valentinian III another thirty years (425–55). In the east, similar child-emperor accessions occurred with the 6-year-old Arcadius in 383 and the nine-month-old Theodosius II in 402. Though no one (including Valentinian I) would have expected Gratian to be an actively ruling emperor with a separate administration at the age of 8 years in 367, a precedent had been set. In time these boy-emperors would grow to adulthood, yet their accessions at such tender ages and the methods which developed for coping with such youthful imperial leaders through long minority governments continued to have repercussions throughout their time as adult emperors also. Being a child-emperor for many years before reaching adulthood inevitably had implications for the rest of the reign, and the question of whether any of these boys ever embraced the full range of imperial functions upon reaching adulthood or remained, in some sense, forever 'childlike', is a crucial one. This repetition of child-emperor accessions, the survival and the sheer length of their reigns, following one after another, should give pause for thought: a new pattern was emerging in late Roman imperial politics. In the decades following AD 367, the western Roman empire witnessed three more boy-emperors and three periods of prolonged minority government. Such a situation had simply never occurred before in the long history of the Roman empire, east or west. What was happening to the imperial office in the late fourth/early fifth centuries?

It is not that the narrative of these reigns has been overlooked, but that the basic phenomenon and the developments which made it possible have not been adequately examined thus far. As noted in the Preface, the more dazzling activities of emperors like Theodosius I, or the remarkable and romantic adventures of the empress Galla Placidia, have not unreasonably attracted more interest in modern scholarship, with the later descendants of the Theodosian house in the fifth century especially dismissed as feeble and degenerate.[3] Yet as much as these studies have contributed greatly to general knowledge and understanding of the period, the issue of child-emperors deserves to be addressed in its own right. This unexpected phenomenon— four emperors acceding to the western throne as young children, following each other in succession, and 'ruling' over such a long period—essentially from 375 to 455—was entirely without precedent in Roman imperial history.

---

[3] e.g. Jones (1964a), 1. 173; Bury (1923), 1. 107.

Unless we are willing to concede either that this was just an historical accident, or that the phenomenon had no further ramifications, there must be some grounded explanation to account for it. Historical accident is in any case an unconvincing justification, and in fact merely avoids the issue: contingent events, whether the assumed result of a set of circumstances about which something is understood, or the unpredictable outcome of chance, are nevertheless always situated in the contexts in which they occur, hence framed and limited in their effects and the possibilities to which they may give rise. While the range of possible outcomes, which is usually limited, may be predicted, the exact outcome which will occur cannot be. My purpose, therefore, is not to focus solely on these individual child-emperor regimes, but to place them collectively in the broader picture of imperial politics in the late fourth to mid-fifth centuries, to look at the repeated succession of child-emperors in this period as a whole, as part of an overarching, interlinked development in the nature of imperial rule itself in late antiquity. For it is not merely the youth of these emperors that is intriguing, but still more importantly it is the prolonged minority governments that their reigns entailed, following one after the other, that made the rise of child-emperor rule in the late fourth century so qualitatively different from anything that the Roman empire had seen before.

Young emperors before 367

Before the accession of Gratian in 367 there had of course been young emperors: Augustus himself had been a youth of only 18 when Julius Caesar died in 44 BC, while Nero had been a teenager of 16 at the time of his accession. Caracalla had been made Augustus with his father Septimius Severus at the age of 11 in AD 197, while the eccentric Elagabalus (218–22) had come to the throne at the age of about 14, and his cousin Alexander Severus (222–35) at 13; Gordian III (238–44) had also been a teenage ruler. Amidst the tumultuous rise and fall of emperors during the third century, the emperor Macrinus (217–18) had named his young son Diadumenianus as Caesar, and then a year later co-Augustus (probably when the boy was 10 years of age), while Philip the Arab, emperor from 244 to 249, had attempted a similar arrangement, naming his son (another Philip) first Caesar and then co-Augustus when the boy was probably also aged around 9 or 10. Such accessions were unusual, but they did occur. Indeed, the first half of the third century saw a noticeable concentration of accessions of youthful emperors, with Macrinus and Diadumenianus (217–18), Elagabalus (218–22), Severus Alexander (222–35), Maximus Caesar (235–8), Gordian III (238–44), and Philip the Arab and his son Philip II (244–9). Yet it remained unusual for a child to become emperor before his teens, and it should be noted that, aside from the precocious Augustus (who reigned from 31 BC to AD 14), Nero (AD 54–68), and Severus

Alexander (who reigned for thirteen years, 222–35), few of these young emperors enjoyed long reigns, or indeed died natural deaths. In addition, although the second half of the third century would witness the creation of a number of imperial colleges, such as that of Carus (282–3) and his sons Carinus and Numerian, these sons—and indeed the Tetrarchic Caesars of Diocletian—tended to be adults when they were made partners in the imperial office.

With the exceptions of Diadumenianus and Philip II, it was also rare for an emperor's son to be made a full co-Augustus (rather than a Caesar) at a young age, particularly during the lifetime of an older, reigning Augustus. Marcus Aurelius, for example, had named his son Commodus a Caesar when the boy was only 5 years old, but he had remained Caesar only until raised as co-Augustus at 17. In the early fourth century, with the rise of the Constantinian dynasty, Constantine the Great similarly named his sons as Caesars while they were still boys, but it was not until his death in 337 that three of those Caesars achieved the rank of Augustus. Even at this point, however, Constantine's sons were still young: in 337 the eldest new Augustus, Constantine II, was not yet 21; Constantius II was aged 19, and Constans probably 13–15.[4] Constantine's eldest son, the illegitimate Crispus, who was executed in mysterious circumstances in 326, had been Caesar for nine years (he was appointed to the rank in March 317) by the time of his death, was aged over 20, and had served in a number of military campaigns by this point, but there was no indication his father had anticipated elevating him as a full Augustus imminently; though there may have been numerous political reasons to delay such a promotion, this circumstance should remind us that it was only because of Constantine I's death in 337 that his surviving three sons became Augusti at the ages they did.

The difference between making a child-Caesar or a child-Augustus should also be noted at the outset. The two ranks were marked out as distinct in this period, and although, as shall be discussed further in Chapter 3, Gratian and Valentinian II in particular would remain 'sleeping partners' for the first years of their reigns, they did so as co-Augusti, not as Caesars. The term co-Augustus does not necessarily imply less than full imperial power, merely that a number of members of the imperial college held this highest rank, whether adult or child—Valentinian I and Valens were co-Augusti from 364 to 365 for instance, just as Honorius and Arcadius were a few decades later. Seniority in this ultimate rank theoretically depended upon the date at which it had been achieved, and might involve some deference from the junior to senior Augustus (as with Valentinian III towards Theodosius II), and the order in which emperors' names would be given in official documents, but

---

[4] Burgess (2008), 40.

in practice this distinction frequently had little discernible impact upon each emperor's power.[5]

The previous century, with its Tetrarchic and then Constantinian Caesars, had in all likelihood led to confusion over the role a Caesar was in fact meant to take (if indeed it had ever been clear-cut): should he be an active military lieutenant in the manner of Constantius I or Crispus, or undertake the more ceremonial role of young designated heir, as in the cases of the younger sons of Constantine during their father's reign, who were presumably in time expected to take on the active role? All of the Tetrarchic Caesars had been established generals, and all adults, at the time of their appointments; active leaders and administrators, rather than the blood-relation Caesars of the Constantinian house.[6] Indeed, the rank of Caesar had been a common designation of an heir under the Constantinian dynasty, one which had been granted to no fewer than four sons of Constantine, and four of his half-nephews as well at different points (Crispus, Constantine II, Licinius Junior, Constantius II, Constans, Dalmatius, Gallus, and Julian).[7] Of this collection of Constantinian Caesars, four had been summarily executed (Crispus, Licinius, Dalmatius, and Gallus), while Constantine's surviving sons had become Augusti in 337 only after a bloody massacre of almost every remaining male member of the Constantinian house. The Caesar Julian had become a legitimate Augustus (when already in rebellion) through good fortune when his cousin Constantius died, leaving the path to the throne clear.

With this recent history in mind, and indeed the more distant history of the internecine struggles of the Tetrarchic Caesars, perhaps 'Augustus' seemed a more secure rank for the emperor's young son. It should not be supposed that Valentinian I made Gratian co-Augustus accidentally, when he meant in fact to make a Caesar: there must have been a particular purpose behind this decision. It could be argued that Augusti might be more difficult to dispose of than Caesars, who clearly could be removed—although the sons of Macrinus and Philip the Arab could prove the exception here: in each situation when the father-emperor died (in both cases following defeat in a civil-war battle), the sons, despite their status, were simply eliminated so as to make way for the more favoured candidates, Elagabalus and Decius. In each of these cases, no guardian figure—such as that of Stilicho in the case of the orphaned Honorius in 395—came forward to support the claim of the dead emperor's son. As will be explored in detail in this study, dynastic succession, though not a factor to be dismissed lightly, did not automatically carry the day unless politicians

---

[5] See e.g. Theodosius I's elevation of his son Arcadius as co-Augustus in 383 without the permission of the senior emperor Gratian (below, p. 88).

[6] Though dynastic marriages were made with the aim of establishing familial ties: Potter (2004), 288, 347.

[7] Crispus in 317—*PLRE* 1. 233; Constantine II in 317—*PLRE* 1. 223; Licinius Junior in 317—*PLRE* 1. 509–10; Constantius II in 324—*PLRE* 1. 226; Constans in 333—*PLRE* 1. 220; Dalmatius in 335—*PLRE* 1. 241; Gallus in 351—*PLRE* 1. 224–5; Julian in 355—*PLRE* 1. 477–8.

Introduction

6

around the throne believed it, and the individual it devolved upon, worth supporting.[8]

Aside from these isolated and ultimately unsuccessful occasions, the creation of an emperor's son or chosen heir as an Augustus rather than a Caesar during the father's lifetime remained extremely rare. It has recently been suggested that Constantine I must have intended to elevate his two eldest surviving sons (Constantine II and Constantius II) to the rank of Augusti before his death, thereby creating a new 'Tetrarchy' of two Augusti and two Caesars, but that he failed to do so in time. By this argument, it is asserted that Tetrarchic precedent for creating Caesars and Augusti meant that: 'the proclamation of a new member of the imperial college or the promotion of a Caesar required the presence of an Augustus or the active approval of the senior Augustus, as without such approval at the very least, any new candidate would be viewed as a usurper.'[9] Essentially, it is suggested that without a senior Augustus, the Caesars left after Constantine's death had no constitutional means of becoming Augusti. This is an important consideration, one which may even have had bearing on Valentinian I's decision to bypass the rank of Caesar entirely in Gratian's case: at any rate, the elevation of his son immediately to the highest rank in the imperial college must have been intended to try to avoid any difficulties in passing the throne to Gratian without incident when Valentinian I died. Such a creation certainly reinforced a desire on the part of the senior emperor to demonstrate that legitimate Augusti were made only by members of the imperial college. In the late fourth to mid-fifth centuries, the emperors Valentinian I, Theodosius I, Arcadius, and Constantius III, despite dying natural deaths, all left behind them sons and heirs who were still legally minors, yet who in a number of cases already carried the rank of co-Augustus. Roman mortality rates should probably also be borne in mind in this context: many adult emperors might not live to see their sons achieve maturity, and this would certainly be an element in the accessions of later fourth- and fifth-century child-emperors. Indeed, one of the most interesting questions that such a scenario poses is that of why, when child-emperors foreseeably created an unusual and precarious political situation, powerful individuals at court and in the military should choose to support fatherless boys as young as 4 or 6 years of age as their emperor.

Creating sons as full Augusti could also be interpreted as a strident statement of the legitimacy and intended longevity of a new reign, especially when, as we shall see, these creations were frequently made at moments of political crisis. That the ranks of Caesar and Augustus continued to be clearly perceived

---

[8] One interesting case where such support was believed worthwhile, was that of the deceased Decius' son Hostilianus, who in 251 was adopted as his heir by the new emperor Trebonianus Gallus, though Gallus later plotted against Hostilianus (Zosimus 1.25.1–2).
[9] Burgess (2008), 9.

as carrying a different significance can be seen in the fact that while the term Caesar was rarely used by the dynasty of Valentinian/Theodosius, it was still employed upon occasion to emphasize a particular political situation: such as in 424, when the eastern emperor Theodosius II made his then 5-year-old cousin Valentinian a Caesar, before making him Augustus of the west exactly one year later. Theodosius II was responsible for the creation of Valentinian III's entire rule, and by elevating him gradually in this way emphasized the dependence of his younger colleague upon himself.

Scholars who have given passing attention to the boy-emperors of the late fourth and early fifth centuries have been almost uniformly content to put the accessions of these boys down simply to a triumph of the dynastic principle, without any serious consideration of what this means and whether it was a truly plausible reason for the promotion of a 4- or 6-year-old.[10] Yet it is not clear that in the past dynastic claims had been wholly convincing in winning the throne for young emperors, however much their adult predecessors might wish it. Efforts to manufacture such a desire for dynastic succession can be seen in situations such as Marcus Aurelius' parading of his son Commodus before the military in the *toga virilis* upon learning of the revolt of Avidius Cassius; or the timing of the promotion of Diadumenianus and the use of the Antonine name to boost his claim.[11] As noted above, despite a five-year reign, Philip the Arab could not manage to pass the throne successfully to his son in 249, despite the boy's rank: inevitably, what was needed was a powerful individual, or group of individuals, who saw value in supporting the dynastic-ally legitimate claim of a young heir, and there is no obvious reason why this should be any different in the fourth century.

In those cases where we do know of a young son of an emperor who was a potential heir upon his father's death, such boys rarely survived their fathers, or when they did, were discarded entirely. In AD 260, although the details are murky, another imperial child, the Caesar Saloninus, son of Gallienus, was apparently murdered by the general Postumus when the latter rebelled. The 'spontaneous' purge of 337, mentioned above, which left Constantine's sons as the only possible surviving candidates for the throne, saw the massacre of all male members of the imperial house except—significantly—the young chil-dren Gallus and Julian: apparently there was no expectation that they could pose a threat. Finally, the infant son of Jovian, who shared the consulship with his father in 364, is not mentioned by any source after Jovian's death as a potential successor to his father, though a comment in a sermon of John Chrysostom suggests he did survive into adulthood, having been maimed in infancy, presumably to ensure there was no chance of his posing a threat to

---

[10] e.g. Oost (1968a), 194; Drinkwater (1998), 270. More specifically relating to the accessions of Honorius and Arcadius in 395, see Errington (2006), 13, 30.

[11] On Commodus: Campbell (1984), 49–50; for Diadumenianus, see Syme (1972), 272–91.

future imperial establishments.[12] Less than five years before the acclamation of Gratian, a boy-emperor still was clearly not considered desirable—perhaps not even genuinely feasible.

Although the cases of the child-Caesars or child-emperors of the early empire do not provide many successful scenarios of such political constructs prospering in the longer term, they do provide a backdrop against which to set the child-emperors of the later Roman empire. While none of these past imperial candidates was quite as young as the 4-year-old Augustus Valentinian II or the 6-year-old Valentinian III, and the long reigns that these later child-emperors experienced were extraordinary, earlier accessions of teenage emperors, some of whom did survive in office more than a few years, do suggest that there were ways in which imperial ideology sought to cope with such scenarios and power-players who believed supporting such candidates worthwhile. Youthful emperors such as Elagabalus, Gordian III in the third century, and the Constantinian Caesars in the fourth century laid some of the preliminary ideological groundwork for the phenomenon of the late Roman child-emperors which would come to full fruition in this period. Nevertheless, the extreme youth of the later child-emperors, the remarkable longevity of their reigns, and the circumstance of their succeeding one after the other in the west created the possibility of a true institutionalization of minority rule in the later empire which had never before existed.

For the successions and subsequent long reigns of Gratian, Valentinian II, Honorius, and Valentinian III to have been even remotely possible, a fundamental shift must surely have taken place in both the perception and reality of the demands of the imperial office, as well as in the political structures in which it was embedded. That an element of dynasticism always played a role is not in doubt; but on closer inspection, it rarely provides a full answer to this remarkable situation. In this book I seek to address these issues and the questions arising from them by assessing the nature of the functions expected of a late Roman emperor, and identifying the changes which had occurred in late Roman government and rulership which made the accession of child-emperors plausible, and in the longer run, even perceived as desirable in some eyes. I will consider the aspects of an emperor's office which a child could be presented as fulfilling, as well as the key functions which might be lost under a child-emperor, and the ways in which this loss might be cloaked. And over the longer term, as once primarily imperial responsibilities came to be delegated on a semi-permanent basis from the accession of a child-emperor onwards, the broader implications of change in the expected roles and responsibilities of an emperor will also become apparent, as will the limitations this could also eventually impose on the range of activities available to the emperor himself.

---

[12] Although apparently the boy still feared for his life: John Chrys. *ad vid. iun.* 4.

The increasing Christianization of the imperial office, combining with the reigns of these four boy-emperors during such a crucial period of development for the Christian religion under the Roman empire generally, can also be seen as vital to the character that these reigns would take on. One very significant aspect of this was the growing acceptability (in some circles at least) of extreme religiosity of an emperor as his most conspicuous virtue. In addition, I will examine in detail the particular circumstances in which these four young boys became Augusti, along with the roles of key politicians (military or civilian) behind them who saw more advantage in supporting the rule of a minor than in promoting one of their own. The question of how contemporaries learned to deal with a child-emperor reaching adulthood, whether a transition from ceremonial to actual power could be achieved, and how the same key players might maintain their powers (or seek to do so) through such a transition will also be a crucial consideration in determining how the regimes around child-emperors operated in this period. And in this context, the relations of essential groups, such as the elites of the military and aristocracy, with these minority governments and carefully guarded boy-rulers can also provide important insights to the workings of these late Roman governments. In bringing together the results of these investigations, I will suggest new answers to the core questions posed at the outset: how did the accessions of these child-emperors come about, how did their regimes survive—and for so long—in the highly militaristic world of the late fourth century and thereafter, and what long-term ramifications did this phenomenon have for the imperial office?

Although it might seem at first glance that they need no further elaboration, it will be worth considering very briefly how a number of key terms will be employed in the course of the investigation, beginning with the terms 'child-emperor' or 'boy-emperor' themselves. The latter term hardly needs justification: after all, it was clearly used by contemporaries in the fifth century, as we see in Sidonius Apollinaris' panegyric to Avitus in 455, in which he laments the misfortunes that Gaul had suffered 'under a boy-emperor' (*principe sub puero*).[13] Admittedly, Sidonius was not using this term in a complimentary manner, referring to the recently assassinated Valentinian III, who was aged 36 by the time of his death. However, although Sidonius employed the term in a derogatory sense, it need not always carry such implications. In any other situation, we would certainly refer to a 4- or a 6-year-old male as a child or a boy—there seems no reason, therefore, not to call such a young male upon the throne a child- or boy-emperor.

In contrast, terms such as 'regency' or 'regent' are worth a little more consideration. The term 'regent' is one which has been frequently applied in modern scholarship to a number of individuals closely associated with these

---

[13] Sidonius, *Carm.* 7.533.

late Roman child-emperor governments: figures like Justina, Stilicho, and Galla Placidia.[14] Yet as one scholar originally pointed out back in 1903, and as another explored more extensively in 1969, there could be no question of a fully fledged emperor having a protector whose rights extended to control of his government: 'there were no provisions in constitutional law for a period of minority during which an Augustus could not rule in his own right.'[15] This is a crucial point in recognizing the truly unprecedented and paradoxical nature of the succession of child-emperors in the late Roman west. Though many emperors throughout the empire's history had attempted to pass the throne to their sons (real or adopted), and some certainly succeeded, the office had never legally become hereditary.[16] Although it has been pointed out that there was no minimum age requirement for membership of the imperial college, the lack of legal provision for a regency scenario highlights the fact that the accession of an emperor who was a minor was not an expected outcome that had been regularized in any formal way.[17] By definition, the *imperator* was an active, capable leader who still supposedly attained his high office through ability (frequently military) rather than any other qualification.[18] In practice, of course, hereditary succession frequently did play a significant role in imperial accessions, though never before to the extremes of the acclamation of fatherless 4- or 10-year-olds that the late fourth century was to witness. This situation of such immensely young emperors ruling in the late fourth century (especially ruling 'independently' without an adult colleague in the west) was still very much a new phenomenon.

Since there could be no such thing in the late Roman world as a regency, however, there was in consequence simply no official position of regent for anyone to fill.[19] Yet there was an alternative position, one which I would argue was distinctly different from that of regent, but which more accurately reflected the positions of individuals like Stilicho: that of 'guardian'.[20] As a child left parentless at the age of 10, for instance, the emperor Honorius was in

---

[14] e.g. for Justina: Sivan (1996), 200; for Stilicho: Kulikowski (2007), 166; for Galla Placidia: Mathisen (1999), 174.

[15] Mommsen (1903), 101 f. Cf. Straub (1952), 108; Cameron (1969), 276; (1970), 39.

[16] As far back as Augustus and his designation of Gaius and Lucius Caesar as *principes iuventutis* the ruling imperial house had sought to guarantee its desire for hereditary succession: see Rowe (2002), 75–6; Severy (2003), 68–77.

[17] On there being no minimum age for office, see O'Flynn (1983), 45–6.

[18] See in general Campbell (1984), and esp. 59–69; also Matthews (1989), 283.

[19] Admittedly the *Historia Augusta* does refer to a 'regency' (*interregnum*) existing temporarily in situations where an emperor had died and his successor had not yet been appointed (*SHA* Tacitus 1). This is very different from the sort of scenario envisaged by those who write of a 'regency' of Stilicho or Galla Placidia, however, implying a long-term legally defined role of an adult essentially ruling in place of a child-emperor.

[20] On the legal role of the guardian, see *Der kleine Pauly* (1979), 1012–14, s.v. 'tutela', and in comprehensive detail on the history of tutela, and the legal role of *tutores*, see Kaser (1959, repr. 1971), 85 ff., 277 f., and 352 ff.; 2 (Munich, 1959), 158 ff.

need of a guardian, and assuredly this was the legal remit of Stilicho's protective role in relation to the young emperor.[21] However, the role of a guardian was by no means the same as that implied by the term regent: the two terms did not entail the same function simply because the child in need of protection or guidance was an emperor. Under Roman—and indeed modern—law, the term guardian implies protection of a minor's personal property and rights. In contrast, the term 'regent' suggests control or management of a government in a minor's stead. And in addition, under Roman civil law, *tutela* for a Roman boy ceased when he reached the age of 14: even in the guise of a guardian, the extent of the authority of a figure like Stilicho was legally limited.[22] The position of an Augusta in this respect (or perhaps even the positions of the Augustus Gratian in relation to his younger brother Valentinian II, or the Augustus Theodosius II in relation to his cousin Valentinian III) differed from that of an individual like Stilicho or Arbogast, who were not of imperial rank. A co-Augustus or an Augusta did at least share that status which in theory entitled them also to a share in the government. Nevertheless, in the case of a woman—such as Justina with her son Valentinian II, or Galla Placidia with her son Valentinian III—such powers would surely still be greatly limited.[23]

Overall, the key point to emphasize is that while the term regent is frequently used in modern scholarship to describe individuals who held a position of authority in relation to child-emperors, this is not a term that the late Roman world recognized. Usually, if the relationship of such an individual to an emperor is given a term at all (which is rare), the term used is that of *tutor* or *curator* in Latin, or *epitropos* in Greek—that is, guardian.[24] And the Latin word *regens* itself appears to be an invention of medieval Latin, not classical or late antique.[25] This is not to suggest that in reality the powers exercised by such an individual as Stilicho were not those that we would recognize as regency—much like the position of 'Lord Protector' that Edward Seymour held for part of the reign of the child-king of England,

---

[21] Blockley (in relation to Theodosius II) asserts that an emperor, even when a minor, was legally *sui iuris* and could not therefore have a guardian, but it is unclear on what evidence this claim is based: (1992), 51–2.

[22] Cameron (1969) 277. Cf. Cameron (1970) 39. According to the Glossary of the Pharr translation of the *Theodosian Code*, a person under 25 remained a minor, however, and his legal guardian once he reached the age of puberty was termed a *curator*: Pharr (1952), 578, 588, 598.

[23] As Jones points out: 'Women and eunuchs had no official part in the government and owed their power solely to their personal ascendancy over an immature or weak-minded emperor' (1964*a*), 1. 341.

[24] e.g. Eunapius, frg. 62.1; Claudian *III Cons.* 151–3; Olympiodorus, frg. 1.

[25] Latham (1965), s.v. 'regentia', p. 398. The earliest attestation of 'regens' to mean regent is *c.*1343.

Edward VI. And while the role of an emperor's mother might come close to a position of regent, as we shall see, the question of the genuine extent of influence an imperial woman could have over matters of government is an important one. Sources such as Eunapius or Zosimus had no doubts as to where true power lay in these child-emperor governments, describing individuals like Stilicho or Rufinus as running the west and east in the stead of Honorius and Arcadius, or the general Aetius as wielding great power during the reign of Valentinian III.[26] But it is important to recognize that this frequently cited position of regent itself did not exist for the Romans—however convenient a term it might be for us. This realization highlights again the paradox of an emperor too young to rule in his own right; but additionally, it emphasizes the precarious, quasi-legal status of individuals like Stilicho, who as a guardian and *magister militum* only, in fact had no constitutional control over Honorius' government in the emperor's name such as the term regent would imply, even if he managed to exert that control nevertheless. As has been observed, such unofficial regents could provide stability for a government if they maintained their dominance over a long period, but their positions were insecure and vulnerable to intrigue.[27] As noted above, individuals such as Stilicho and Aetius have often been referred to by modern scholars as 'generalissimos', a not unreasonable term to describe their position as supreme commanders; perhaps, as we shall see, the term 'manager' is also appropriate for such individuals who can be seen as the dominant organizing influence of a government, with effective power (exercised through the emperor) to appoint and dismiss other significant individuals.

Two further terms which will arise frequently in the course of the discussion are 'rule' and 'regime'. In this context, without attributing any particular technical sense to these terms, rule is intended to indicate the emperor himself (that is, the rule of the emperor Valentinian, or Honorius). Regime, on the other hand, is intended to designate the system operating around a given emperor, a system of which he may be either the genuine leader or the figurehead. In the late Roman world within which these child-emperor courts operated, the regime which ran them can perhaps best be seen as a set of personal relationships represented by a group of people who are in a position to manage the way in which the empire is governed. Such a group might be made up of different conglomerations of individual ministers and generals who sought to hold sway over the court. Thus regime may be applied to the system established by dominant individuals under the rule of an emperor— such as 'the regime of Stilicho'.[28] It has been noted that the weakness of the

---

[26] Eunapius, frg. 62.1; Zosimus 5.1.1–5.

[27] Jones (1964*a*), 1. 344.

[28] And as we shall see, in the west such regimes were almost always dominated by the holder of the office of *magister militum utriusque militia in praesenti*; see Jones (1964*a*), 1. 341–2.

consistory (the private advisory body of the emperor) was revealed when the emperor was a child (or immature), because it was at such moments that an individual or clique generally came to dominate.[29] But in fact, while the individual/clique who represented the most powerful influence on the emperor could frequently (as we shall see), pack the consistory and main offices of state with his/its supporters, the consistory nevertheless still continued to perform its usual functions, if not perhaps with the same level of independence theoretically attached to the institution. A regime was essentially institutional—making up the recognizable government—and generally comprised of individuals who held specific offices of state.

The rise of political opponents who managed to dislodge the manager of a regime and take their place could also see the emergence of different regimes at different points in time, such as that of Olympius in 408–9, followed eventually by that of Fl. Constantius (from *c*.411 to 421), both of which still operated under the rule of the emperor Honorius. And of course, if the ruler himself upon reaching adulthood should succeed in taking charge of the regime itself, it could then become *his* regime: thus it is possible to speak (albeit briefly) of the regime of Valentinian III in 454. As we shall see, this was a rare eventuality. And as will be discussed more thoroughly in the following chapters, amidst the jostling for power that the rise and fall of different regimes implied, the stability of the system such regimes sought to control, though inevitably affected by such vicissitudes, in the realms of bureaucratic government especially continued to operate in the increasingly professional and institutionalized manner that had developed over the previous centuries. Below the emperor, it was the very highest military commands and administrative posts for which the influential members of the court vied, and the ability of dominant individuals to direct the assignment of such posts allowed the creation of systems such as the regime of Stilicho or that of Aetius.

Problems and evidence

The western Roman empire of the later fourth, and especially the fifth, centuries has long been viewed as problematic in modern scholarship, due to the state of the source material available. With the conclusion of Ammianus Marcellinus' immensely valuable *Res gestae* in 378, followed by the ceasing of the less reliable (though at times surprisingly well-informed) Zosimus in 410, the last half-century or so of Roman rule in the west has traditionally been regarded as something of a 'black hole', an unfocused, hazy period about

---

[29] Ibid. 1. 341.

which our increasingly fragmentary sources can provide only occasional glimpses into the workings of imperial government or the plight of provincials in the face of barbarian invasions. It is true that the nature and extent of our source material changes markedly from the first decade of the fifth century onwards.[30] Nevertheless, those sources which are available still offer considerable scope for historical investigation of the period.

For a study focusing on the emperors, and particularly the child-emperors, of the period, their presentation, and the workings of their government, there is in fact a rich and varied fund of source material available. For each of the boy-emperors there are extant writings either in the form of outright panegyrics, such as those of Gratian's tutor Ausonius and the aristocrat Symmachus, the court poet Claudian, and the fragments of Merobaudes, or in a very similar laudatory style, such as the imperial funeral orations of Ambrose. While great care must be taken in assuming historical accuracy for such compositions (see the discussion on this issue in Chapter 1), and though the purpose of panegyrics has long been a matter of debate among scholars, these works nevertheless provide an immensely valuable picture of how an emperor—or the regime directing him—was presented. Although they fall just beyond the particular chronological scope of this investigation, the panegyrics of the Gallic aristocrat Sidonius Apollinaris are also a valuable source, in providing both a verdict from outside the centre of government on the recent administration of the empire, and also a picture of the continuing expectations of a late Roman emperor. While these sources always carry biases and hidden (or not-so-hidden) agendas, they remain extremely useful resources.

In terms of secular histories of the period, the work of Ammianus Marcellinus, which as noted above halts soon after the battle of Adrianople in 378, is the most important source for information on fourth-century emperors, their campaigns, and their relations with many senatorial aristocrats and military leaders.[31] Thereafter, for a narrative account we are reliant on the less adept and sometimes muddled work of the eastern historian Zosimus, writing in the late fifth century, who can nevertheless provide remarkably detailed reports of western affairs at times—such as the famous senate meeting at Rome of early 408—which are unavailable anywhere else.[32] After Zosimus' account terminates in 410 there is no continuous narrative surviving. Zosimus relied heavily on two other historians for much of his material—Eunapius and Olympiodorus—whose accounts did extend beyond 410, but sadly little of their compositions have survived except through usage by Zosimus and the

---

[30] The work of John Matthews and Andrew Gillett on Olympiodorus' history, the fragments of which are among the few narrative works to extend beyond 410 on western events, and the reliance of other sources upon this history, make this clear: Matthews (1970), 80–2, and Gillett (1993), 1–2.

[31] Matthews (1989), 3 ff.

[32] Lenski (2002), 5; Goffart (1971), 412–41.

ecclesiastical historian Sozomen.[33] Happily for this investigation, several of the
more extensive surviving fragments of Olympiodorus, who ended his history
with the installation of Valentinian III as western emperor in 425, deal with
the campaign to achieve this event. The fragmentary remains of the work of
Priscus of Panium, whose history covered the years 433–73, similarly provide
some lucky survivals in an eyewitness account of an embassy undertaken to
Attila the Hun, while the extant excerpts of the sixth-century work of John
of Antioch include valuable information regarding the downfalls of Aetius
and Valentinian III. Unfortunately, all of these sources, with the exception of
Ammianus, were written outside the western empire. Yet the importance of
not discounting the information they offer is well demonstrated by a modern
study of the writings of Olympiodorus on the downfall of Stilicho, which
revealed the historian not only to have a strong interest in western affairs, but
also access to information from within Stilicho's inner circle of supporters.[34]
In addition to these more extensive sources, a number of surviving chronicles
also deal with the period, starting of course with that of Jerome, but also
including works such as the much later *Chronicon paschale*, the chronicle
of Marcellinus *comes*, and the work of the fifth-century Spanish bishop
Hydatius. While generally bare of detail, these writings can still offer important information.

There is also a considerable number of ecclesiastical histories dating from
this era, and although once more exclusively the work of easterners, these still
often show an interest in western affairs. The works of Rufinus (*c*.403),
Philostorgius (*c*.425), Socrates (*c*.446), Sozomen (*c*.448–9), and Theodoret
(449–50) all provide valuable insights into the period.[35] Despite their eastern
origins, these sources can yield information regarding the west which remains
unavailable elsewhere—such as Socrates and Sozomen attesting to an edict
passed by Gratian shortly after the battle of Adrianople assuring freedom of
worship to his subjects. None of these ecclesiastical historians encompasses
the whole of the period examined here—Theodoret's work stops around 408,
for example, Sozomen's in 425, and Socrates in 439. Thereafter Evagrius is the
only church historian who attempts to deal with the period from *c*.431
onwards, but he was writing a century after events.[36]

The eastern origin of many of these texts—of both secular and ecclesiastical
history—must make any researcher aware of the strong possibility of eastern
bias in respect of western affairs or individuals, such as Stilicho or Aetius.
But this can be seen as a strength of the material as well, in its potential to give
an insight into eastern court attitudes or traditions regarding such major

[33] Jones (1964*a*), 1. 170.
[34] Matthews (1970), 89–2.
[35] Lenski (2002), 5.
[36] e.g. Jones (1964*a*), 1. 170.

western figures; for example, that apart from the somewhat more favourable stance of Olympiodorus, Stilicho was undeniably regarded with suspicion while so far as we can tell, it appears that Aetius was not.

Although ecclesiastical histories of the west from *c.*360 to 460 are few, there are nevertheless substantial sources of information on affairs of the period to be found in other church writings by western personalities. The copious writings of Augustine of Hippo are the best-known, and while his concern was often not with court matters, nevertheless significant information can be gleaned from the *Confessions, City of God*, and his collected letters in relation to his early years as the court rhetor at Milan, his observations on the 'basilicas conflict' of 385/6, and later his own involvements in issues of religious doctrine and authority in Africa and appeals to the emperor—or his manager—for support. A further North African ecclesiastical writer, Orosius, whose *Seven Books Against the Pagans* terminates in 417, offers some intriguing insights (though his account is regarded by some as 'tendentious').[37] One of the other major letter-writers of the period, Symmachus, has also left a mine of information relating to the lifestyle and patronage networks of Roman aristocrats of the late fourth century, as well as government and administrative procedure, including his most famous work, *Relatio 3*, with its measured defence of the privileges of the ancient state cults. The funeral orations of Symmachus' adversary in the Altar of Victory controversy, Bishop Ambrose of Milan, were mentioned above. The letters and orations of this dynamic church leader provide an invaluable source of material for any examination of the western boy-emperors of the late Roman empire, for Ambrose had direct contact with three of the four. And finally, the extensive correspondence of Pope Leo the Great illustrates the extent of the bishop of Rome's contact with both the western and the eastern court during the reign of the western boy-emperor Valentinian III, which has considerable significance for this study, and the relationship between Christian emperor and Christian church which continued to develop across this period. While any collection of statesmen's letters must be approached with the knowledge that they have been carefully selected and edited to reveal only information that the writer or compiler wanted the reader to know, this does not in any way mean that they cannot be very valuable, even if their content may often be self-conscious.

Aside from these major secular and ecclesiastical writers, there are also many other writings from the period which can provide useful information, such as the later (sixth-century) histories of Procopius, Jordanes, and Gregory of Tours. Biographies of holy men, though only just established as a genre at this point, were growing ever more popular during this period, and for the west at least that of Paulinus on Bishop Ambrose gives some valuable material

---

[37] Ibid. 1. 154.

on the relations between imperial court and church. The ninth-century work of Agnellus on the early bishops of Ravenna, and the *Liber pontificalis* on the church at Rome, yield information on church-building and benefactions by the fifth-century imperial family. And the letters of Jerome and extensive sermons of Peter Chrysologos, bishop of Ravenna *c.*426–50, provide moments of insight into major events or imperial attitudes.

The richness of the legislative material of this period is extraordinarily well demonstrated by the *Theodosian Code*, which was completed in 437. This collection of imperial constitutions from the time of Constantine I provides a vast fund of information not only on matters of legal action but on the administration of government, recruiting for the army, the financial difficulties of the state, and the names of many major office-holders, for example.[38] The *Code* cannot tell us whether the laws issued were observed or enforced, and between 432 and 438 there are few laws preserved from the west, 432 presumably being the cut-off point by which western constitutions needed to be submitted to the eastern compilers for inclusion. From 438 to 454 however, the *novels* of Valentinian III survive, the rulings of his government made after the compilation of the *Code*, so that we have a relatively complete picture of imperial legislation overall throughout the whole period. This legislation generally cannot, of course, inform us whether the child-emperor, or child-turned-adult-emperor, as the case may be, was providing the initiative behind the legislation to which he put his name, or indeed whether legislation was issued in response to petitioning rather than as any sort of imperial initiative; nevertheless, the laws can still provide an otherwise largely unavailable illustration of the wide range of areas requiring imperial attention.

Another valuable early fifth-century text to survive is the *Notitia dignitatum*, which in the west seems to have been irregularly updated until around the time of Honorius' death in 423. Uncertain in accuracy as it is (and it has even been claimed that it cannot be used at all as a representative source), the *Notitia* can nevertheless be employed to discover the extent of military losses in the early fifth-century west, among other matters.[39] These official texts certainly do not hold all the answers, and need to be coupled with the other literary and non-literary evidence of the period to try to gain a complete picture, but they remain highly valuable.

Finally, numismatic and epigraphic evidence for the period can also prove extremely useful in developing the picture of the world of the late Roman west that these boy-emperors ruled. Numismatic evidence can be used, for

---

[38] See generally Matthews (2000).

[39] For the claim it cannot be used at all as a representative source, see Kulikowski (2000*a*), 360, 375–6. But for a more positive evaluation, see Hoffman (1969–70). The most comprehensive recent studies are Jones (1964*a*), Appendix 2, and Brennan (1995), 147–78. For discussion of its use to examine military losses in the west, see e.g. Jones (1964*a*), 2. 1325; Heather (2005), 247.

example, in establishing the ways in which the new boy-emperor's accession might be advertised, such as with the *Spes Rei Publicae* legend chosen by Valentinian I upon the elevation of Gratian. Similarly, relations between the eastern and western courts can to some extent be gauged by surviving coin images, such as through Theodosius II's attitude of paternal protectorship over Valentinian III well into the 430s. Epigraphic evidence, such as the inscription set up at Rome in the late fifth century ascribing victory over Gildo to both Honorius and Arcadius, provides illuminating insights into the tone the west, at least, was trying to strike in relations between the empires. And the inscribed statue-base of Aetius in the Atrium Libertatis at Rome helps to establish not only the general's many claimed victories, but also his position of power in the state in the 440s, and the support such tributes might reflect in their being erected by imperial or senatorial impetus. Similarly, the survival of such items of material culture such as the 406 consular diptych of Probus, depicting the emperor Honorius in martial guise, indicates the continuing presentation of an emperor as responsible for the victories of his armies even when he was no longer in the field, while the survival of a similarly imperial-style diptych for Fl. Constantius some years before the latter's accession illustrates his climb to power at court through the 410s.

In addressing the questions, therefore, of how child-emperor reigns came about, how they were presented, and how they functioned and survived, there is in fact a considerable range of information available, despite increasing gaps in the evidence as the fifth century progresses. This great range and variety of written sources for the period has, inevitably, generated a great deal of literature. But the methodological issues associated with the interpretation of the different types of material, as well as the varying views and agendas of those who have exploited these issues, has inevitably led also to many different and often conflicting views of both specific events or developments as well as the period as a whole. In pursuing my own interpretation and evaluation of the material, I have tried to take into account the different biases and hidden agendas of writers of the period, whether they be panegyrists, historians, government officials, or churchmen. Any specific problematic issues arising from these sources with respect to this investigation will be dealt with as they arise.

The following analysis provides a thorough scrutiny of the reigns of the western child-emperors Gratian, Valentinian II, Honorius, and Valentinian III: the politics of the period, the presentation of these boys as plausible late Roman rulers, and the overarching changes which their reigns imposed upon the nature of the imperial office itself in the longer term. For although these four western emperors all came to the throne as children, as their reigns—and their ages—progressed, only rarely were they themselves able to become more than 'childlike' emperors, even in adulthood. This phenomenon of the child-emperor is not merely an odd development in the politics of the period, but also one which prompts many important questions about late Roman governance: who were the political players who brought about such events? Why did such powerful individuals choose repeatedly to invest in such 'figurehead' regimes? How—and under what conditions—could they maintain their interests or even control such regimes in the longer term once they were created? What may originally have been very short-term political calculations (as in the case of the accession of Valentinian II particularly) led ultimately to longer-term outcomes which in themselves permanently shifted the boundaries of the politically possible and acceptable in late Roman imperial government. It was a shift which in many ways amounted to a fundamental transformation of late Roman imperial governance.

Part One

Gratian and Valentinian II

1

The Emperor in the Late Roman World

> You, best of emperors, at the outset of your Principate, still unripe in years
> but already ripe for power, showed that one did not have to await the
> passage of time in the hastening of virtue.[1]

By the time of the accession of the boy-emperor Gratian in 367, there had been
a Roman emperor for nearly four centuries, and a Roman empire for still
longer. Before beginning to examine how the accessions of the child-emperors
of the late fourth century came about, therefore, we should first consider the
nature of the Roman imperial office itself. Considerable work on the role of
the emperor in the Roman world has provided an invaluable guide to the
many functions of the Roman ruler until the time of Constantine I.[2] But how
had things changed by the late fourth century? In seeking to establish a picture
of the baseline of attributes and virtues usually ascribed to a late Roman emperor,
as well as the more practical aspects of his role, there are a number of valuable
sources available, such as panegyrics, secular and ecclesiastical histories, and
numismatic and epigraphic evidence. There are many contemporary writings on
rulership and indeed rulers from this period, and this chapter is by no means a
comprehensive survey of these: it is intended simply to draw upon a variety of
(predominantly literary) sources to establish general patterns of imperial presentation up to the late fourth century, in order to proceed in following chapters
to consider how these general patterns might be disturbed by the accession and
long reign of an emperor who ascends the throne as a child.

The *Basilikos Logos* of Menander Rhetor was a guide to the aspiring orator
facing the task of composing an imperial panegyric, and was composed in
the late third century.[3] It is this text, with its helpful divisions of the various
aspects of the imperial office as indicating what was desirable in the office-
holder, which provides the structure for this first chapter. Naturally this

---

[1] *Pan.Lat. IV.* 16.4: *Tu, imperator optime, inito principatu, adhuc aeui immaturus sed iam
maturus imperio, ostendisti cursum aetatis non exspectandum in festinatione uirtutis.*
[2] See esp. the seminal monograph of Millar (1977).
[3] Russell and Wilson (1981), xxxiv–xl.

does not mean that every, or indeed any, emperor could satisfy the profile Menander drew up; in addition, the imperial office continued to develop and evolve for another hundred years following Menander's composition, to the remarkable point where it was possible to conceive of a child as young as 4 years old filling the position of emperor in the late fourth century. Furthermore, with the imperial adoption of Christianity, new religious expectations of the emperor also developed—expectations, of course, which Menander could not have foreseen. The *Basilikos Logos* is therefore an extremely useful vehicle for exploring the functions of the position, but is not to be considered comprehensive.

A further valuable source of insight is the corpus of speeches known as the *Panegyrici Latini*. This collection of twelve panegyrics addressed to various Roman emperors over a 300-year period begins with Pliny's famous address to Trajan from AD 100, while all of the other speeches of the corpus date either to the third or fourth centuries, starting with the *Panegyric of Maximian* of 289 and ending with Pacatus' address to Theodosius I in 389.[4] These orations therefore offer a practical application of the instructions given by Menander and other teachers of rhetoric on how to write an imperial panegyric. It is virtually certain that the writers of the *Panegyrici Latini* were familiar with manuals such as that of Menander, whose advice was probably very similar to that of other rhetorical teachers of his time generally.[5] In fact, the methods and traditional vocabulary used conventionally for the praise of rulers had been in existence for centuries before the emergence of the Roman imperial cult.[6] These panegyrics need not therefore be assumed to have consciously followed Menander's model, but their presentation of many of the same desirable imperial functions and virtues assists in discovering patterns of presentation. Similarly, the works of the imperial panegyrist Themistius provide some valuable reflections of how late fourth-century imperial regimes sought to present themselves as meeting the demands of their office and offer a further important resource.

The panegyric is arguably the most valuable source available in drawing up a checklist of the functions expected of an ideal late Roman emperor. Yet the questions of the exact purpose of these texts, and of their value in terms of providing the modern historian with trustworthy and credible evidence have caused considerable debate among scholars. It has been argued that the panegyric could be a speech of recommendation to a wayward emperor of the sort of qualities to which he ought to aspire; that such speeches consisted merely of shameless flattery and bids for patronage with no concern for reality; or that the panegyrist acted as a public-relations officer, broadcasting the

---

[4] For the most recent edition and translation of this corpus see Nixon and Rodgers (1994). The orations are mostly anonymous and seem to have been the work of rhetors in Gaul; the compiler of the collection may well have been its final contributor, Pacatus: Nixon and Rodgers (1994), 4–6. Cf. also Whitby (1998), 4; Rees (2002), 6.

[5] Nixon and Rodgers (1994), 11–12.   [6] Cameron, Av. (1991), 125.

emperor's merits to his subjects exactly as he wished himself depicted.[7] And, as impressive ceremonial occasions usually provided the backdrop against which a panegyric was delivered, such as an accession, an imperial *adventus*, or the assumption of a consulship, it has also been claimed that the form and execution of such an oration was more important than its content.[8]

Panegyrics must undoubtedly be approached with caution for use as historical sources, and it is important always to locate both panegyrist and panegyric within their specific historical context when considering their aims.[9] Nor should the values or deeds ascribed to any individual in the context of a panegyric be automatically assumed to have any basis in truth, although equally, some of what they describe may well have had its roots in reality. Yet, while these texts must be treated cautiously as sources for historical facts, nevertheless they provide a rich source of information on how a particular emperor was presented at a particular moment in time, and the 'shameless flattery' panegyrics often contain should not blind us to the adaptability of the genre.[10] Such public orations may only ever have reached a very limited audience: essentially the elite of the senatorial classes, senior bureaucrats and military leaders would be most likely to hear these speeches, and even if their written texts were later circulated, these too must have been available only to the literate upper classes. As one scholar has observed, the panegyric was a highly transient form of public communication.[11] Yet even with their limited audience, that audience was an extremely important one, for fundamentally it made up a significant proportion of those subjects any emperor needed to convince of his legitimacy and suitability to reign: the senatorial and military elite.[12] Moreover, the messages presented through imperial panegyrics would also frequently be echoed in other forms of imperial propaganda and government activity which would reach a far wider audience—such as in legislation and coin mottoes. And in the context of this investigation, there is another significant reason to view late Roman panegyrics as important sources, which is that they are an enduring form of imperial presentation which continued to be employed throughout the reigns of the boy-emperors of the late Roman west as one of the principal forms of presentation and which, as we shall see,

---

[7] For the panegyric as a speech of recommendation, see Born (1934), 20 f.; as shameless flattery, see Macmullen (1964), 437; and for the panegyrist as human-relations officer, see Straub (1939). MacCormack argues that panegyrics were a medium to announce imperial programmes and policies: MacCormack (1976), 160. For further discussion, see Nixon and Rodgers (1994), 28–9; Rees (2002), 26–8.

[8] On panegyrics forming part of the ceremonial of important imperial occasions, see MacCormack (1981), esp. 1–14. Cf also Whitby (1998), 3. On form and execution of the oration, see Cameron (1970), 36–7.

[9] See on this point: Nixon and Rodgers (1994), 34; MacCormack (1981), 3.

[10] Rees (2002), 26.

[11] Ibid. 188.

[12] Cameron (1965), 502.

come to be visibly adapted to meet the different needs of child-emperor governments.

Careful analysis of extant panegyrics thus allows patterns of presentation to be established and the drawing up of a checklist of what functions a Roman emperor of this period was ideally expected to fulfil, even though each surviving panegyric—and of the thousands which must have existed only a handful survive today—was often highly individualized to suit the aims of the panegyrist, the man honoured, or the political moment.[13] Whether or not the practicalities of any emperor's rule measured up to this ideal is not at issue here: it is doubtful any ruler could meet the full criteria, but it is precisely the idealized presentation that is sought at this point. Just what was the late Roman emperor supposed to do, and how did a panegyrist present him as doing it?

Alongside these panegyrics, and as a further illustration of the expectations of a late Roman emperor, we can set the secular history of Ammianus Marcellinus. This important text, with its contemporary (and sometimes quite candid) opinions on the extent to which fourth-century emperors fulfilled their expected functions, acts as a further caution against the idea that panegyrics presented a realistic picture of the practicalities of ruling.[14] And finally, Eusebius of Caesarea's *Life of Constantine* presents a new element in late Roman imperial ideology: the image of the Christian emperor, a ruler chosen by God to rule the earthly kingdom in harmony and order. The *Life* thus brings to the discussion an element of the emperor's function not covered by the other sources—one which would become increasingly important over the remainder of the fourth century and beyond. This work has been described as 'an uneasy mixture of panegyric and narrative history', and while the Eusebian picture contains many of the rhetorical features recommended by Menander, it also presents distinctively Christian attributes required of the late Roman emperor: the Christian construal of traditional imperial ideology.[15] All of these texts—the guidelines of Menander, the *Panegyrici Latini* and the orations of Themistius, Ammianus Marcellinus' secular history, and Eusebius' *Life of Constantine*—in their different ways offer valuable insights into the expectations of the functions that a late Roman emperor ideally should fulfil, though they do not tell us, of course, whether the emperors they deal with truly did fulfil this ideal.

General qualities: family background, youth, and education

In beginning his instructions, Menander wrote that after the *proemion*, the topic of the emperor's native country might be addressed, particularly if it was a distinguished one, or, if his homeland was not conspicuously famous, the

---

[13] Rees (2002), 188.   [14] Matthews (1989), 239.
[15] Cameron and Hall (1999), 1, 30–5. Cf. Baynes (1955c), 168–72.

topic should be omitted, and the prestige of his family considered, though this too might be avoided if it were humble.[16] Any divine signs which occurred at the time of the emperor's birth should be noted, and the orator should go on to consider his nature, commenting on his dazzling beauty.[17] Such a reflection on the physical presence of an emperor can be found in Ammianus' description of Valentinian I: 'His strong and muscular body, the gleam of his hair, his brilliant complexion, his grey eyes, with a gaze that was always sidelong and stern, his fine stature, and his regular features completed a figure of regal charm and majesty.'[18]

Similarly, in the *Panegyrici Latini*, the emperor Maximian's homeland on the Danubian frontier is celebrated for teaching him the tireless habits of toil and patience and the noble native land of Theodosius I is praised as well.[19] Divine origins are claimed for the families of Maximian, Constantius I, and Constantine I.[20] The great deeds and numerous virtues of Constantine's father are emphasized, and the physical beauty of Constantine himself is said to bring security and reassurance to the maidens of Milan.[21] Eusebius takes a similar line on the young Constantine: praising his youthful bloom, handsome physique and nobility, and imitation of his father's many virtues.[22]

Next, Menander instructed the orator to deal with the *princeps'* education: his love of learning, quickness and enthusiasm, and whatever field he excelled in, whether literature, philosophy, language, or the arts of war, must be praised.[23] Educational achievement is something we hear of regularly in Ammianus' writings: that Julian sought out knowledge with great eagerness; that Constantius made pretensions to learning, but suffered from dullness of mind; that Valentinian wrote with a neat hand and was an elegant painter and modeller, and of Valens that 'he had rather an uncultivated mind, and was trained neither in the art of war nor in liberal studies'.[24] According to the *Panegyrici Latini*, Theodosius I spent the summers of his youth in the military

---

[16] On the emperor's native country, see Menander 369.18–24; Also 369.27–32; 370.1–8; on family prestige, see 370.9–28.

[17] Menander 371.3–14; 371.14–17.

[18] AM 30.9.6: *Corpus eius lacertosum et validum, capilli fulgor colorisque nitor cum oculis caesiis, semper obliquum intuentibus et torvum, atque pulchritudo staturae, liniamentorumque recta compago, maiestatis regiae decus implebat.*

[19] Respectively: *Pan.Lat.* X.2.2–5; II.4.1 ff.

[20] For Maximian: *Pan.Lat.* X.2.3; XI.1.3–4; Constantius I: VIII.2.2–3. For Constantine: VI.2.1–5.

[21] For Constantius' deeds and virtues: *Pan.Lat.* IV.5.5–6. For Constantine's beauty: VII.6.3–5; XII.7.5–6.

[22] Eusebius, *VC* I.12.1–18.2.

[23] Menander 371.29–372. 2.

[24] On the abilities of Julian, see: AM 16.5.6. Also 25.4.5–6. For Constantius: 21.16.4. For Valentinian I, see AM 30.9.4, and for Valens 31.14.5: *subagrestis ingenii, nec bellicis nec liberalibus studiis eruditus . . .*

camps of his father, learning the arts of war, while Eusebius praises Constantine I's excellent rhetorical education and youthful, God-given wisdom.[25]

Actions and the virtues

Such matters of family, background, birth, upbringing, and education were part of the process of establishing the picture of the emperor, and it was desirable that he measure up well in these respects; though it is also apparent that if he did not, this might be glossed over. The next issues Menander wrote on, however, were not to be glossed over or simply omitted: after accomplishments should come actions, divided into those of peace and those of war, and there were four cardinal virtues under which the actions to be praised would always fall: courage, justice, temperance, and wisdom.[26] This view of the four fundamental virtues is also found in Ammianus' writings on Julian, and indeed they harked back to the Hellenistic concept of kingship.[27] Ammianus' technique of weighing up the virtues and vices of emperors in his necrologies, as well as the parallels he drew with past emperors, provided a framework within which the author's contemporary readers might thus judge the conduct of emperors of their own day, and also indicate that there were known examples of past behaviour, good and bad, of which emperors were expected to take heed.[28] Ammianus' viewpoint was thus an argument for moral continuity: a classical belief in 'the relevance of historical modes of behaviour, and in knowledge as the source of true moral action'.[29] In this, both he and Menander reflected the grammarians' moral teachings with which the elite of the Roman world was inculcated.

The emperor needed, then, to be the embodiment of these traditional virtues, and it has even been asserted that for the vast majority of the empire's population an emperor's other claims on the throne mattered little if it was believed he possessed these certain virtues.[30] At least in part, the emperor was a 'charismatic' ruler: 'one whose power depends on the conviction of his subjects that he is personally in possession of gifts or talents essential for their well-being, yet beyond the reach of the ordinary mortal.'[31]

---

[25] On Theodosius, see *Pan.Lat.* II.8.1 ff.; similarly on Constantius I: IX.6.1–4. On Constantine, see Eusebius, *VC* I.19.1–2.

[26] Menander 372.25–373.5; 373.5–17.

[27] Dvornik (1966), 276. Cf. Baynes (1955c), 168–72. For Ammianus on Julian, see e.g. AM 25.4.1.

[28] Matthews (1989), 239; AM 30.8.8. For an example of Ammanius' comparisons with past emperors, see his comments on Julian and Marcus Aurelius: AM 16.1.3.

[29] Matthews (1989), 243–4.

[30] Charlesworth (1937), 105 ff.

[31] Wallace-Hadrill (1981), 298.

Military prowess

The first of the virtues stipulated by Menander was courage, demonstrated foremost by military leadership and prowess. Menander explained that in the treatment of war, the rhetor should describe the traps laid by the enemy, and add that through the emperor's wisdom the ambushes were discovered, though the enemy knew nothing of the emperor's plans.[32] Similarly, the emperor's own battles should be described, investing him with all impressiveness and knowledge.[33] War was a reality of the Roman world, and a major preoccupation of its rulers, and to some extent the primary purpose of the Roman state was, quite simply, the financing of combat. It is natural, therefore, to find military expertise among the central virtues advocated by Menander, and also among those Ammianus focuses upon in his writings on the emperors, while the military setting of their lives is clear throughout his narrative.[34]

Menander wrote that in describing the military successes of the emperor: 'You will also have an opportunity here to link up a passage on wisdom, saying that he was himself the planner, the commander, the discoverer of the moment for battle, a marvellous counsellor, champion, general, and orator.'[35] In this, the orator pointed out that the emperor's military function, in practice, might be satisfied via a number of different guises: by battlefield commands, morale-rousing speeches, controlling logistics, and engaging in counsels with generals. His humanity in dealing with conquered foes was to be noted also.[36] In the end, however, an emperor did not have to be the military commander in the field, though in fact all the emperors of the fourth century up until the death of Valentinian I had been, but there were many other ways in which he might fulfil his military function, such as ensuring that the army was well-fed and sufficiently equipped, or even being responsible for tactical decisions without actually leading the soldiers into battle. Yet it was vital for an emperor to maintain the loyalty of his troops, and, indeed, of the generals who led them: the emperor wanted loyal military commanders, not usurpers. If he was not being a battlefield general, therefore, an emperor needed to ensure sufficient distribution of patronage among those who were performing that function on his behalf, in order to maintain their loyalty: as we shall see, this was to become a major issue for the boy-emperors of the late fourth and fifth centuries.

---

[32] Menander 373.17–25. [33] Ibid. 374.3–6, p. 87.

[34] Matthews (1989), 280, 283. On the role of the emperor as a military leader in late antiquity, see Lee (2007), 21–49.

[35] Menander 374.21–5: ἐνταῦθα δὲ καιρὸν ἕξεις καὶ ἐπισυνάψαι περὶ φρονήσεως, ὅτι αὐτὸς ἦν ὁ διαταττόμενος, αὐτὸς ὁ στρατηγῶν, αὐτὸς ὁ τὸν καιρὸν τῆς συμβολῆς εὑρίσκων, σύμβουλος θαυμαστός, ἀριστεύς, στρατηγός, δημηγόρος.

[36] Ibid. 374.25–375.

Ammianus wrote extensively on military leadership and ability among the emperors who figured in his history. The skill of Constantius II in hurling the javelin, use of the bow, and the exercises of the foot-soldiers is noted.[37] In addition, he observes that Julian was a careful commander in his wars against the Alamanni, and inspired his troops to keep up the fight in battle through his personal bravery—though his disregard for his own safety on the Persian campaign ultimately led to his death.[38] And Valentinian I was similarly praised as a skilful and careful veteran, foresighted in council and strict with regard to military discipline, though not severe enough in punishment to-wards higher officers.[39] Many of the works of the *Panegyrici Latini* collection show a similar concern for the military exploits of the emperor: Maximian was described as travelling with great speed through the provinces on campaign, with each new great deed outstripping his last, and Julian praised for spending every summer subduing barbarians.[40]

The emperor's military role was a major function of the imperial ruler; perhaps more so than ever in the era of fourth-century invasions and usurpa-tions.[41] For the moment we shall leave our consideration of it at the level of one of Menander's fundamental virtues to be sought after in the emperor, in the form of courage, yet as we shall see, military prowess and courage in the form of *victory* also played a crucial role in legitimating an emperor's claim to the throne, and thus additionally to the image of divine favour.

Justice

Of the peacetime virtues of an emperor, Menander wrote that they should be divided under the headings of temperance, justice, and wisdom. Under the heading of justice should be considered mildness, humanity, and accessibility to petitioners, and in addition to his legislative activity, it should be noted that he struck out unjust laws and promulgated just ones.[42] The administration of justice was an absolutely essential element of the emperor's function in the Roman state, from the earliest times.[43] The emperors' judicial responsibility might even be seen as their pre-eminent function in non-military affairs, and

---

[37] AM 21.16.7.

[38] AM 16.2.11–13; 16.12.39–41 (and see similarly Pliny on Trajan, *Pan.* 13); AM 25.3.6.

[39] AM 30.9.4; 30.9.1.

[40] For the speed of Maximian, see: *Pan.Lat.* XI.4.1–4; cf. X.3.3–4. For Julian's summer campaigning, see III.4.5–6. See similarly on Constantius I: VI.5.6 ff. and 6.1; cf. VIII.5.1–9.6; and Constantine I: IV.18.3–4 and 19.5; VI.11.1 and 16.3–9; XII.5.2.

[41] Although as Hopkins has pointed out (Hopkins (1978*a*), 180) it is missing from Millar's *The Emperor in the Roman World*: Millar (1977).

[42] Menander 375.5–13; 375.24–376.2.

[43] Millar (1977), 228.

not only was it their role to see that fair and just decisions were made, but it was also their duty to correct shortcomings or gaps in the laws.[44] The concept of the ruler as law incarnate had been handed down from the Hellenistic perception of kingship, and lay at the centre of the autocratic system: once the king was admitted to be the law incarnate and therefore the only source of law in society, he became not only the essence of the state, but in a way the state itself, a point emphasized in Themistius' *Oration* of 364 to the emperor Jovian.[45] It was similarly a belief which came through clearly in the legal codes of the fourth and fifth centuries AD, where Theodosius II proclaimed that his law code permitted no error or ambiguities, and was to be called by his name, while no other constitution might be cited or have legal force other than those contained in his code.[46]

The belief in the emperor as the source of all law also had a crucial ideological function, in the conviction that the emperor was the representative of Christ's justice on earth. Roman law had an immensely important ideological value to society, perhaps even more so than previously in the late Roman world where rising barbarian forces were to be contended with. Law was considered one of the twin pillars of Roman civilization, along with education—Rome's gifts to an uncivilized world. Law separated Romans from barbarians, and embraced the idea of seeking a civilized, rational outcome to disputes, through placing mind above body.[47] And these ideas, as we shall discuss, played a vital role in legitimating the position of the emperor.

The emperor's practical judicial function (his legislative function) was also of fundamental importance. The rescript system, in theory at least, provided a major form of communication between emperor and his subjects: a citizen could present a written complaint or query to the emperor, known as a *libellus*, and the emperor would give written replies: *subscriptiones*.[48] Papyri preserved in Egypt have indicated that an emperor might respond typically to four to five *libelli* per day, translating into several hundred in a year.[49] And while it might be argued that these *libelli* would be requests from the more privileged sectors of society rather than the ordinary citizen, the possible range and depth of the emperor's concerns are indicated by the contents of the *Codex Theodosianus* (the collection of imperial edicts since 312, of which more than 2,500 survive), which legislated on issues as diverse as taxation and property rights, to the price of bread in Ostia, and the care of horses no longer fit for horse-racing.[50] The routine nature of such legislation more than anything else reinforces the

[44] Matthews (2000), 12–13.
[45] Dvornik (1966), 276; Themistius, *Or.* 5.64b–c.
[46] *CTh.* 1.1.5 (26 Mar. 429); *NTh.* 2 (1 Oct. 447).
[47] Honoré (1978), 35.
[48] Millar (1977), 242–5. Also Honoré (1994), 33–5.
[49] Millar (1977), 252.
[50] Kelly (1998), 139.

essential character of the emperor's judicial function, and his subjects' conception of him as the source of legislation and justice.[51]

Nevertheless, Roman law was primarily about property and its protection:
the majority of an emperor's legal actions would relate therefore to the land-
owning classes, and the result was that his high level of involvement in matters
relating to a small proportion of the population made his activity all the more
significant. It was only at the very end of the third century that praetorian
prefects began to take on some of the emperors' jurisdiction.[52] Yet the regular
references of Ammianus to the judicial role of the emperor make the continued
importance of this imperial function in the late Roman world quite plain:
its particular desirability in an emperor is also noted through Ammianus'
frequent references to his ideal emperor, Julian's, careful administration of
justice.[53] And Julian's own comments (according to Ammianus) on one
occasion make his perception of himself as the source of all law quite clear:
'The laws may censure my clemency, but it is right for an emperor of very
merciful disposition to rise above all other laws.'[54] Valens also was praised for
distinguishing clearly between justice and injustice, yet not consistently.[55]
Constantine, in the *Panegyrici Latini*, was lauded for his compassion in the
administration of justice, as well as his mercy, clemency, and prudence.[56]
Eusebius also lauds the legislative reforms of Constantine, and his humane
and generous laws.[57] Yet his comments also indicate a new Christian angle on
the traditional judicial role of the emperor, for Constantine is greatly praised
particularly for his generosity and compassion towards the poor and unfortunate, and his marked care for orphans and widows. According to Eusebius, he
was anxious to show mercy and a fatherly concern for all.[58]

Linked to the emperor's administration of justice was the condemnation of
rapaciousness and envy: Valentinian I in particular was accused on several
occasions by Ammianus of greed for great wealth, and the desire to overthrow
better men than himself.[59] Nor must an emperor be cruel: Ammianus likened
Constantius II to Caligula, Domitian, and Commodus in savagery, and in
ruthlessness claimed he surpassed Gallienus, while Valentinian I's brutality
was similarly criticized.[60]

---

[51] Millar (1977), 240.
[52] Ibid. 270.
[53] AM 22.10.7; also 25.4.8–9; 25.4.7; 16.5.13. Similarly on Julian: *Pan.Lat.* III.4.5–6.
[54] AM 16.5.12: *Incusent iura clementiam, sed imperatorem mitissimi animi legibus praestare ceteris decet.*
[55] AM 31.14.3, 6.
[56] *Pan.Lat.* V.9.1–6; IV.8.1.2 and 9.1–3.
[57] Eusebius, *VC* I.9.1; I.41.3; II.20.1; IV.26.1–3.
[58] Ibid. I.43.1–3; II.13.1–2; IV.1.1.
[59] AM 30.8.8. Also 30.8.10.
[60] For comparison of Constantius to Caligula, Domitian, and Commodus, see AM 21.16.8, and to Gallienus, see 21.16.9. For Valentinian I's brutality, see 30.8.2–3. Also 30.8.6; 30.8.13.

The area of prudent appointments—an administrative function which can be seen to form part of an emperor's judicial function—is also one which comes through in the writings of Ammianus, and regime-building was a vitally important activity of a new emperor. The emperor had in his gift ranks, titles, and posts which became benefits he could confer as rewards or incentives for loyalty, as part of building his support base.[61] The act of conferring prestige could augment, rather than decrease, the power of the giver, and so we find Valentinian I surrounding himself with loyal fellow-Pannonians in official posts, further securing his hold on the throne through their dependence on him for their positions.[62] The emperor's friends, to whom he would grant these prestigious posts, are also important to recognize as key political players in regime-building, similarly to the army.

Ammianus commended emperors for their prudence in appointments, such as Jovian's in making the few promotions he did to official state positions with care, while Valentinian I was praised for being guarded and not corrupt in bestowing high official positions.[63] Further comments made by Ammianus concerning the appointments made by Constantius highlight what has been called 'a central canon of late Roman government': the separation in both central bureaucracy and in provincial administration of civil and military powers.[64] Thus Constantius was praised on the grounds that: 'The governor of a province never officially met a commander of the cavalry, nor was the latter official allowed to take part in civil affairs. But all the military and civil officials always looked up to the praetorian prefects with the old-time respect, as the peak of all authority.'[65] Julian also was praised for seeking out the best and most learned men in making appointments to his court and provincial governorships: choosing those distinguished for military prowess, oratorical ability, or knowledge of the civil law, and all who showed themselves blameless and energetic in the administration of the state, selecting only upright and trustworthy men.[66]

In addition, the appointments an emperor might make were important in terms of the advisers by whom he himself would be surrounded. Intimates of the emperor's *consistory*, his private advisory body, might wield considerable influence, and were often present when the emperor received embassies

---

[61] Millar (1977), 11.

[62] Drake (2000), 43; Cameron (1970), 81.

[63] On Jovian's appointments: AM 25.10.15. Similarly Themistius, *Or.* 5.67a. On Valentinian I's: AM 30.9.3. Similarly Valens': 31.14.2: and Constantius': 21.16.3.

[64] Matthews (1989), 270, 284.

[65] AM 21.16.2: *nec occurrebat magistro equitum provinciae rector nec contingi ab eo civile negotium permittebat. Sed cunctae castrensis et ordinariae potestates, ut honorum omnium apicem, priscae reverentiae more, praefectos semper suspexere praetorio.*

[66] *Pan.Lat.* III.25.2–5.

or petitions, and for all an emperor's powers, he might seek their advice.[67] Ammianus even has Julian accepting correction from his associates.[68] That an emperor might be seen to be unwisely under the influence of bad advisers, whether official or unofficial, is also clear through Ammianus' claim that Constantius was flattered by his courtiers, who encouraged his cruelty.[69]

In the later Roman empire it also remained important that the emperor maintain a relationship with the old senatorial aristocracy. Some have seen the fourth century as a period of great decline for the senate, and indeed it could never have been an effective check on the absolute power of the emperor, yet the efforts of several emperors indicate they still felt the goodwill of the senate to be valuable.[70] Under Constantine I, senators held high office at the imperial court; and when Constantius visited Rome in 357 he addressed the senate-house, and we may be sure when we hear of him walking about amongst his subjects, it was once again the elite with whom he was mingling.[71] An emperor's eloquence might be of particular value in this context as well, at the very least as a reassurance to the landed elite of his sharing in the traditional liberal education that was a common ground for the aristocracy.[72]

The emperor's management of the bureaucracy and dealings with the provinces can also be considered under the heading of his judicial and administrative function. Menander instructed that when writing of the emperor's deeds,

> You should say also that he sends just governors around the nations, peoples, and cities, governors of laws and worthy of the emperor's justice, not gatherers of wealth. Mention also the tribute he imposes and the supply of his forces, pointing out that he is concerned also for his subjects' ability to bear those burdens lightly and easily.[73]

Good relations with the local nobility were important here: they played a crucial role in essential government business, not only in reminding provincials of their distant ruler by their actions in his name, but also through the collection of taxes. They also thus incidentally provided the emperor with an opportunity for granting them privileges both through conferring offices and

---

[67] Matthews (1989), 269; Honoré (2006), 130–1.

[68] AM 25.4.16; Unlike Valentinian I, who would not accept correction: 27.7.9. On the role of the consistory, Jones (1964a), 1. 333–41; also Harries (1999), 38–40.

[69] AM 14.5.4–5. Even Julian was criticized for sometimes acting arbitrarily: 22.10.6.

[70] Drake (2000), 56. For an example of scholarship on the 'decline' of the senate in the fourth century, see McGeachy (1942).

[71] On senators in high office under Constantine I: Barnes (1981), 45. On Constantius' mingling with subjects at Rome: AM 16.10.13.

[72] Brown (1992), 4.

[73] Menander 375.18–24: καὶ ἐρεῖς ὅτι δικαίους ἄρχοντας κατὰ ἔθνη καὶ γένη καὶ πόλεις ἐκπέμπει φύλακας τῶν νόμων καὶ τῆς τοῦ βασιλέως δικαιοσύνης ἀξίους, [οὐ] συλλογέας πλούτου. ἐρεῖς ἔτι καὶ περὶ τῶν φόρων οὓς ἐπιτάττει καὶ τοῦ σιτηρεσίου τῶν στρατευμάτων ὅτι στοχάζεται καὶ τοῦ κούφως καὶ ῥᾳδίως δύνασθαι φέρειν τοὺς ὑπηκόους.

in cancelling fiscal debts, since imperial edicts of indulgence wrote off the unpaid taxes of the rich—the poor were never allowed to amass such arrears in the first place.[74]

Julian was repeatedly commended by Ammianus for his improvement of tax and tribute burdens on the provinces, both as Caesar and as Augustus.[75] Constantius, on the other hand, was criticized for the 'insatiable extortion' he allowed the tax-collectors to practice and his lack of regard for the welfare of the provinces.[76] Valens was lauded for being very just in his rule of the provinces, while Valentinian too was praised for this, although it is also noted in his case that those in trouble found no sympathy from their prince.[77] According to the *Panegyrici Latini*, Maximian too showed his care for the state in observing which of his governors emulated his justice and which commanders maintained the glory of his courage, showing great concern for the safety of all.[78] The judicial function of the emperor was clearly varied and far-reaching, covering areas from the hearing of petitions to avoidance of rapaciousness and greed, regime-building, and seeing to the protection of the provinces from excessive taxation.

Wisdom and temperance

With regard to the virtue of wisdom, displayed no doubt largely by the exercise of his judicial function, Menander wrote that the emperor must be declared to surpass all men on earth in wisdom and understanding.[79] In addition, his temperance, chastity, and high moral standards must be extolled.[80] This was again a matter of comment in Ammianus' assessments of the emperors involved in his history: Julian, as ever the benchmark of the ideal ruler, was praised for his extreme moderation in food and drink.[81] Constantius was noted for the prudent and temperate manner of his life and his moderation in eating and drinking, whilst Jovian was observed to be an immoderate eater and drinker, also given to wine and women.[82] In matters of chastity

---

[74] Brown (1992), 28.
[75] AM 16.5.14; also 18.1.1; 25.4.15. Cf. *Pan.Lat.* III.4.5–6, for Julian's generosity to his subjects.
[76] AM 21.16.17.
[77] For Valens: AM 31.14.2; on Valentinian I: 30.8.14; 30.9.1.
[78] *Pan.Lat.* X.3.3–4.
[79] Menander 376.15–23.
[80] Ibid. 376.2-9.
[81] AM 16.5.3; also 16.5.1; 25.4.4. Although his excessive sacrificing was frowned upon: 22.12.6. Gallus was criticized earlier in a similar tone for his excessive enjoyment of blood-sports: 14.7.3.
[82] On Constantius: AM 21.16.5. On Jovian: 25.10.15, although Ammianus also suggested Jovian might have corrected these faults in time. See also McEvoy and Tuffin (2005), 74–5.

Constantius was noted for being extraordinarily chaste throughout his life, Julian's chastity was 'inviolate', and Valentinian I also was 'pure' at home and abroad, and stringently controlled the wantonness of the imperial court.[83] The *Panegyrici Latini* similarly declared Constantine I the guardian of the state, thanks to whom restraint, strength, and wisdom have become common to all men.[84] He himself was easy of access, patient, kindly, dignified, and cheerful.[85] Theodosius I was reported to take pains to correct gently the vices of others, while himself living simply and frugally on the simple meals and needs of a soldier.[86] Once again, Eusebius provides a slightly different angle on this required virtue of the emperor: for him, Constantine I gave a clear example to all of his subjects on a life of godliness.[87] He subjected himself to fasting and self-deprivation and devoted much time to private prayer, and in this way cared for the general welfare through his own purity of life.[88]

Legitimacy

Menander's *Basilikos Logos* is thus extremely useful in establishing key virtues an emperor ought to be seen to have, and by extension certain functions he ought to fulfil. The profile we can draw up also points towards a vital aspect of any emperor's reign: his claim to be the empire's legitimate ruler. This assertion needed to be made against the ideological framework of the ideal virtues of courage, justice, wisdom, and temperance, and clearly panegyrists such as Menander and those he taught could be of great use in establishing such a claim. It has been observed that in order to maintain the loyalty of its subjects, an empire required certain accepted ideological beliefs which proclaimed the legitimacy of the regime.[89] Yet ultimately, legitimacy was a *post factum* phenomenon: an aspect of a regime which would be measured when it was over, by its successes and failures overall, and particularly by its conclusion. The first evidence of an emperor's legitimacy was in military victory, indicating he was blessed with divine favour: once he could make this claim, all other 'proofs' of legitimacy could be fitted in behind it. Ultimately, the fundamental proof of a regime's legitimacy was whether or not it prospered: claims of its divinely sanctioned status might be made during its lifetime, such as those Themistius made concerning Jovian's administration in 364, but the ultimate measure was the *post eventum* verdict: only one year later

---

[83] On Constantius: AM 21.16.6, Julian: 25.4.2, and Valentinian I: 30.9.2.
[84] *Pan.Lat.* VI.16.3–9.
[85] *Pan.Lat.* IV.34.4. See similarly on Julian: III.13.3; 14.3–4; 12.1–3; 27.3–4; 31.1.
[86] *Pan.Lat.* II.13.1–4 and 14.4.
[87] Eusebius, *VC* I.3.4.
[88] Ibid. II.14.1–2; IV.22.1.
[89] e.g. Ando (2000), 5; Kelly (1998), 145.

in 365, under the new government of Valens and with Jovian dead, Themistius had decided that Jovian's appointment clearly had not been genuinely legitimate, since it had not prospered.[90]

The claim of divine favour was far and away the most important: it lay behind any emperor's assertion to have a legitimate hold on the throne, and appeared often in panegyrics.[91] A belief in this fundamental aspect of kingship came before even claims to the cardinal Hellenistic virtues, since by definition God would not appoint a man who was not virtuous to the throne. And military victory was one of the most patent ways in which this divine favour and corresponding legitimacy could most convincingly be demonstrated: clearly a ruler or potential ruler who was defeated in battle could not be God's chosen: victory was 'an innate imperial quality'.[92] Thus Ammianus claimed of Julian's rise to power through military triumphs that: 'His success was so conspicuous that for a long time he seemed to ride on the shoulders of Fortune herself, his faithful guide as he in victorious career surmounted enormous difficulties.'[93] Eusebius lays even greater emphasis than his pagan counterparts on the link between the emperor's military victories and divine blessing. According to him, it was because Constantine had honoured God, that God himself had stood beside the emperor throughout his long reign and blessed him with so many years, and brought him victory over all his enemies, through the victory of the one true God. Because Constantine confessed himself God's servant, he himself became unconquerable.[94]

The law could also play a major role in the way in which an emperor's legitimacy might be established. Late Roman legal codes dwelt upon the link between the divine and the law-giving emperor.[95] It is noteworthy that Justinian, an emperor of not particularly distinguished background, coming to the throne in the sixth century in an era of trouble and not without the threat of competition and war, would find in legal codification a means of reinforcing the legitimacy of his reign, by claims to be God's chosen.[96] By codifying laws or enacting legislation emperors could legitimate and assert their authority, both in the act itself and by stating this as their aim in the *proemia* to their laws. As discussed above, written law was viewed as a fundamental differentiation between civilization and barbarism: it was thus a psychologically sensitive area, and a popular and legitimating one through which a ruler might demonstrate his concern for the Roman state.

---

[90] In 364: Themistius, *Or.* 5.71b; and in 365: *Or.* 6.73c. Heather (1999), 107.

[91] See e.g. *Pan.Lat.* X.12.6–8; XI.6.1–7.3; VIII.17.1; IV.14.1–6.

[92] MacCormack (1981), 41–2; also Drake (2000), 61; Holum (1982), 8.

[93] AM 25.4.14: *Felicitas ita eminuit, ut ipsis quodammodo cervicibus Fortunae aliquamdiu bonae gubernatricis evectus, victoriosis cursibus difficultates superstaret immensas.*

[94] Eusebius, *VC*, I.4–5.2; I.6; I.8.2–4.

[95] e.g. *Dig.* Praef. i.12; 23.

[96] Ibid. ii.2; 18.

An accession carried out with proper, accepted ceremonial would assist in an emperor's assertions of divine favour and corresponding legitimacy. Furthermore, such an accession could be said to have occurred in accordance with the demands of 'official' state ideology: 'which held that the Roman Empire was God's special vehicle for achieving His will in the world, and that, consequently, He intervened personally to direct its affairs.'[97] Such a view is echoed in the words of Themistius who, eager to emphasize the legitimacy of the rule of Valentinian and Valens after the short reigns of both Julian and Jovian, expounded to his audience the view that the new election was the result of divine consent.[98]

It could be helpful to an emperor's accession if he were a relative of a previous emperor, although the imperial office itself had never legally become hereditary. In theory the accession of a new emperor took place by election, although the role of the people in that election had always been nominal. In the later empire, although the senate continued formally to confer power by decree, the acclamation of the army had become increasingly important, and it is striking that usurpers (such as Magnentius in 350 and Magnus Maximus in 383) usually based their claims on the acclamation of the army.[99]

In the later Roman empire, the division of the ruling power of the state derived essentially from Diocletian and his colleagues in the late third to early fourth century, as a response to challenges to government authority posed by disorders in the third century. The new arrangements entailed the division of the empire, with regional emperors in the east and west, and the areas of Italy, Africa, and the Illyrian provinces as a third region between the two. The result was an increase in the 'incidence' of government: emperors were able to fund and conduct military operations in smaller areas without extended communication lines or the problems of moving troops over vast distances. Under Constantine I there was a further separation of powers, with the military placed under the supervision of the new *magistri militum*, and civilian administration under the praetorian prefects.[100] The multiplication of the imperial office meant late Roman emperors could offer their subjects more of a 'presence' than previously, as Themistius observed, as well as answering concerns about political continuity in the face of human mortality.[101] This action of nominating a co-ruler—or in the case of Constantius II with first Gallus and later Julian, a Caesar—as junior co-emperor, could give a new emperor a strong claim to the legitimacy of his accession on the basis of his bond with the current, or previous (and potentially, at least, divinely favoured)

---

[97] Heather and Moncur (2001), 174.
[98] Themistius, *Or.* 6.73b–c.
[99] Jones (1964*a*), 1. 322, 326.
[100] Matthews (1989), 253–4.
[101] Themistius, *Or.* 6.75b–c; see Heather and Moncur (2001), 175–6. As the reasons prompting Valentinian I to name a colleague emphasized: AM 26.2.4.

emperor. Yet this splitting of the imperial office also brought with it its own problems of balancing relations between the two halves, and presenting a united front in times of crisis. Asserting harmony between imperial colleagues, as panegyrists so often did (as in the case of the *Panegyric to Maximian* and the particular harmony between Diocletian and Maximian emphasized by the orator), can also be seen as a means of asserting an emperor's legitimacy and divine blessing.[102]

Ammianus described a number of accessions in his history, such as Constantius' raising of Julian as Caesar, and Julian's later acclamation as Augustus by his troops—proof of his divine appointment being seen in his military glories.[103] Accessions such as Julian's, and also those of Constantine I and Theodosius I according to the *Panegyrici Latini*, whereby the candidate displayed reluctance to take up the imperial office were represented as further proofs of his suitability and legitimacy for the role.[104] The accession of Jovian was a far more hurried affair, and Ammianus' reference to it occurring at the hands of 'a few hot-headed soldiers' gives the election perhaps an intentionally illegitimate and not divinely sanctioned aura.[105] In contrast, Valentinian's accession was said to occur under the inspiration of heaven and without a dissenting voice, and before an assembly of the whole army: 'wearing the imperial robes and a coronet, with all the praises which the charm of novelty could call forth he was hailed as Augustus...'[106] His speech to the troops displayed an unexpected degree of authority, made surrounded by eagles and standards, completing what seemed to be the ideally performed accession—careful, deliberate, and divinely inspired, with the blessing of heaven and the acclamation of the soldiers.[107] With such a beginning, lack of any familial bond with the preceding emperor became far less important.[108]

The episode of the usurpation of Procopius, on the other hand, provides an instance of the way in which a succession that was not divinely inspired might be identified. No purple robe could be found for him at his acclamation, so he wore a gold-embroidered tunic like a palace-attendant, and waved about a small piece of purple cloth in one hand.[109] The affair, as reported, made a mockery of the process and ceremony of succession, yet it is also an episode which reflects the *post eventum* nature of the assessment of the legitimacy of a

---

[102] See *Pan.Lat.* X.9.1–5 and 11.1–7; similarly XI.7.4–8.5; VII.13.3–7.

[103] AM 15.8.9; 20.4.15; 20.4.17–18.

[104] For Constantine I, see *Pan.Lat.*VI.8.4–5; for Theodosius I: II.11.2.

[105] AM 25.5.4: *tumultuantibus paucis* ... See Heather (1999), 108.

[106] AM 26.1.5; 26.2.3: *Mox principali habitu circumdatus et corona, Augustusque nuncupatus, cum laudibus amplis, quas novitatis potuit excitare dulcedo* ...

[107] AM 26.2.11.

[108] MacCormack (1981), 202. On the unanimity of the army's acclamation in the case of Constantine I also, see *Pan.Lat.* VI.8.1–6, and Eusebius, *VC* I.22.1.

[109] AM 26.6.15–16.

regime: usurpers in Ammianus' history always had trouble with their purple robes, and even Jovian, whose short-lived reign in turn suggested he was not the right man for the job, had difficulty finding imperial robes to fit him.[110] It is a point which also highlights the importance of ceremony in the perception of a regime's legitimacy, as shall be discussed below.

Despite the claim which has sometimes been made, then, that the attachment of the people was to an ideal king rather than a particular one, there was a particular process of assertion and legitimation through which the new ruler had to pass.[111] To assist in establishing a new emperor it could also prove useful to disparage past governments in order to highlight the virtues of the present, as in Themistius' *Oration* to Valens, where he emphasized the blood-letting of the Constantinian dynasty in contrast with the peaceful accessions of the house of Valentinian.[112] This was all the more important a point considering that lesser members of the old ruling family—the usurper Procopius, plus Constantius' widow and posthumous daughter—were still at large at this time and could be potential rival claimants to the throne: the new regime therefore needed to be presented as superior.[113] In this context, dynastic marriages also became increasingly important—such as Valentinian I's marriage to Justina, who was said to have Constantinian connections, and, as will be discussed in Chapter 2, the marriage of Gratian to Constantia.[114] Ultimately, such tactics were aimed at making the positions of the claimants acceptable—legitimating them—in the eyes of the influential, land-owning elite.

Thus, the ideological legitimacy of an emperor rested on a bundle of ideas involving divine favour made manifest through military victory, embracing the concept of the ruler as law incarnate, 'proper' modes of accession, and sometimes delegitimizing other regimes. Put together, it appears that there were three basic criteria for legitimacy which an emperor needed to fulfil: first, the manner of his election; secondly, for his reign to succeed, which thus confirmed its divine sanction; and thirdly, what the *post eventum* verdict on the regime was, itself based largely on the two prior criteria.

Religious role

As the importance of divine favour in legitimating a claim on the imperial throne would indicate, an emperor also had an essential religious function. This aspect was not explicitly dealt with by Menander, perhaps because at

---

[110] AM 25.10.7; Heather (1999), 107; Matthews (1989), 236–7.

[111] e.g. by Hopkins (1978b), 198.

[112] Themistius, *Or.*6.74b–c; Similarly for Jovian: *Or.* 5.65c–d; 66d.

[113] Heather and Moncur (2001), 176. Julian used this tactic himself in discrediting his cousin's regime when on the march against Constantius in 361: Julian, *Ep.* 270c–d.

[114] AM 29.6.7.

the time he was writing, in the late third century, there was no concept of there being any separation between church and state and therefore everything the emperor did was, by implication, religious. The emperor had traditionally been the chief priest of pre-Christian Roman religion, and this did not change once the emperors themselves were Christian, although their conception of that role altered. As the divinely appointed ruler, the emperor came to be seen as the anointed vicegerent of the one God.[115] Eusebius of Caesarea's oration celebrating the thirtieth anniversary of Constantine I's accession in 336 (the *Laus Constantini*) stressed the closeness of the relationship between Christ and the Roman emperor,[116] and matters connected with the emperor continued to be 'sacred', though a deceased emperor could no longer be deified.[117]

It is not surprising that it is in the area of the emperor's religious role that Eusebius' description of desirable imperial attributes adds most to the traditional framework. Eusebius quotes a personal letter of Constantine I himself declaring that he believed his aim should be above all else the promotion of a single faith and unanimity of belief within the church.[118] This was a major innovation in the Roman emperor's religious function. Eusebius writes that Constantine was like a 'universal bishop', convoking councils to settle doctrinal issues, taking his seat at them among the bishops, and promoting the peace of God through his arbitration.[119] Moreover, according to Eusebius, the emperor also took steps to have pagan shrines destroyed, such as those of Asclepius in Cilicia and of Aphrodite at Hierapolis.[120] Yet the religious role of a Christian emperor, continuing a tradition rooted in paganism, was a conflicting one, and would continue to be so throughout the fourth century at least. Despite being a committed Christian, Constantius II on his visit to Rome in 357 nevertheless saw fit to fill vacancies in pagan colleges of priests as part of fulfilling his office of *pontifex maximus*.[121] Ammianus, a pagan himself, implied (rather than specifically stated) the religious role of the emperor. Concerning Constantius, he wrote that:

'The plain and simple religion of the Christians he obscured by a dotard's superstition, and by subtle and involved discussions about dogma, rather than by seriously trying to make them agree, he aroused many controversies; and as these spread more and more, he fed them with contentious words',

indicating the influence the emperor could have on religious disputes.[122] Valentinian was praised for the toleration which distinguished his reign, and

[115] Jones (1964a), 1. 321.   [116] Eusebius, *LC* V.4.3.5.
[117] McLynn (1994), 27.   [118] Eusebius, *VC* III.17.1.
[119] Ibid. I.44.1–3; III.5.3–6.1.
[120] For the temple in Cilicia, see ibid. III.55.5–55.6.1. For the temple at Hierapolis, see III.58.1.
[121] Symmachus, *Rel.* 3; Matthews (1989), 235.
[122] AM 21.16.18: *Christianam religionem absolutam et simplicem anili superstitione confundens, in qua scrutanda perplexius quam componenda gravius excitavit discidia plurima, quae progressa fusius aluit concertatione verborum* . . . On Julian summoning bishops to the palace, see also 22.5.3–4.

Themistius, also a pagan intellectual, had similar appreciation of Jovian's religious policies (naturally in line with the tone the policies were intended to strike).[123]

The Christian emperor's role as God's chosen ruler and representative brought with it a need for relations with the church itself. The modern term 'caesaropapism' has been described by some scholars as an incorrect way to describe the relationship between the late Roman emperor and the Christian church, because state and secular power was so interlinked in the ancient world that a distinction between them would not have been understood.[124] But the adoption of Christianity as the state religion did undeniably see the beginnings of such a distinction emerging, and as both secular ruler and *pontifex maximus*, though he was not technically a member of the clergy and could not administer sacraments, the emperor had tremendous influence over church affairs. He could call church councils—as indeed Constantine I did the first ecumenical council at Nicaea in 325—and he could make decisions about doctrine and how it might be imposed, as Ammianus' writings indicate.[125] He could appoint bishops and exile them—as both Constantine I and Constantius II did.[126] He could put great resources at the disposal of the church, and could hear appeals from councils or religious trials.[127] The emperor could also impose, or attempt to impose, uniformity on church doctrine, and this was a role which emperors such as Constantine I clearly saw as extremely important for the peace and prosperity of the empire itself: it was crucial not to arouse God's wrath by disunity within the church or subscribing to incorrect doctrines. In Constantine I's case, such consciousness of the significance of uniformity even led to persecution in the hope of rooting out wrong-believers.[128] Without the sophisticated church hierarchy which would develop over the following centuries yet in place, in short, the late Roman emperor was, in practice, the head of the Christian church.

The famous conflict between Theodosius I and Bishop Ambrose of Milan in 390 has been seen as an indication of the church's freedom from imperial influence under the helm of a powerful bishop.[129] Recent re-evaluation of the events, however, has provided a convincing picture of the saga of the massacre at Thessalonica and Theodosius' subsequent penance as more of an episode of Bishop Ambrose aiding the emperor to stage a major rehabilitation of his character after a disastrous mistake rather than a stern bishop

---

[123] On Valentinian, see AM 30.9.5. On Jovian: Themistius, *Or.*5.67b–c.

[124] e.g. Drake (2000), 36.

[125] Constantine's calling of Nicaea: Eusebius, *VC* III.5.3–6.1; cf. Jones (1966), 43; Lenski (2002), 234.

[126] Hunt (1998), 6; Lenski (2002), 235.

[127] Barnes (1981), 49.

[128] Lenski (2002), 235.   [129] Brown (1992), 109–13; Matthews (1975), 235.

imposing his will on a humbled ruler.[130] The consequent admiration of Theodosius' Christian subjects at their emperor's submitting himself to the discipline of the church, therefore, became a public triumph which wiped the stain of Thessalonica from Theodosius' political record, and also established a partnership between emperor and bishop.[131]

Emperors might be seen to fulfil their Christian role in a variety of different ways: through issuing anti-pagan laws, as Theodosius I famously did in 391; through benefactions such as the building or decoration of churches, in which the Constantinian dynasty was involved on a large scale in many cities of the empire; through staging church councils to debate and determine matters of doctrine and thereby promote religious unity, as did emperors like Constantine I, Constantius II, and Theodosius I; and through displays of personal piety such as Theodosius' penance at Milan.[132] The emperor's religious role might be embraced to a greater or lesser extent by individual rulers, but was nonetheless a required function of his position; and even conspicuously active military emperors—like Constantine I and Theodosius I—were notorious for their piety, with their military successes seen as inextricably bound up in their Christian personas.

Divine favour and ceremonial majesty

Divine favour made manifest through military victory, general prosperity, and thus closeness to God was the key to an emperor's legitimacy, and this was most clearly displayed through imperial ceremonial. The late Roman empire saw an increase in such ceremonial, viewed as oriental in origin, and ascribed by ancient and modern scholars alike to the reign of Diocletian.[133] Whether or not they are correct, what is more important is that ceremonial was perceived to have increased under the late empire, and that it was believed to be of foreign, Persian origin. It was an understanding which reflected a change in conception of the imperial office from the early

[130] McLynn (1994), 323. Although Liebeschuetz disagrees with this interpretation, suggesting that McLynn has exaggerated the public-relations aspect of the events (2005), 19.

[131] McLynn (1994), 328–30.

[132] For Theodosius' anti-pagan laws see esp. *CTh.* 16.10.10 (16 June 391), which banned all pagan sacrifices, both public and private, and prohibited all access to pagan temples, probably in part aiming to protect the sites from attack for the sake of their artistic heritage, as well as obstructing pagan worship. For Constantinian church-building, see Potter (2004), 435–9. For Constantine I's convening of the council of Nicaea in 325, see Eusebius, *VC* 3.5.3–6.1; also Jones (1966), 43. Constantius II hosted more councils than any other emperor—see generally Barnes (1993); also Lenski (2002), 234–6. On Theodosius I's ruling in favour of orthodoxy and calling of the council of Constantinople in 381, see *CTh.* 16.5.5 (10 Jan. 381); also McLynn (1994), 124.

[133] AM 15.5.18; Aurelius Victor 39.2 ff.; Eutropius 8.26; Matthews (1989), 244 ff.; MacCormack (1981), 8.

empire: no longer was there any pretence of the emperor being an exalted 'civil magistrate', or 'first among equals'—this was a one-party state. Ceremonial is ultimately a form of communication, and an emperor's rightful assumption of the throne was reinforced by his sporting of the appropriate imperial regalia, as noted above.[134]

One of the new forms of imperial ceremonial credited to Diocletian's reign was that of *adoratio*: the ritual kissing of the hem of the emperor's purple robe by his courtiers, which Julian used as a gesture of forgiveness and return to imperial favour for the general Lucillianus in 361.[135] In addition, the preserved minutes of the senate of Rome upon the meeting in 438 for the introduction of the *Theodosian Code* suggest that ritual acclamation had superseded any real political discussion in relations between emperor and senators.[136] On that occasion, upon the announcement of the *Code*, the senate burst into a lengthy series of unanimous and clearly non-spontaneous acclamations of the emperors, the *Code*, and their own land rights.[137] The acclamations must have taken over an hour in total to perform, and yet could have been read in just a few minutes—the specific performance of these acclamations, therefore, was important.[138] It was a theatrical show intended to reflect the unity and perfection of the imperial office, and hence, its legitimacy.[139] One reason for this increased ceremonial may have been that late Roman emperors were being drawn from the new military elite of the frontiers rather than the Roman aristocrats of earlier times, and thus shared little of the traditional background of their senatorial subjects. Ceremonial therefore could have provided a bridging mechanism by which to build a new relationship between autocrat and subjects, and this at least could provide individuals around the throne with a sense of where they fitted in the system by way of imperial gesture and ceremony.[140]

Perhaps one of the most important displays of imperial ceremonial was that of the *adventus*, an emperor's entrance to a city.[141] Certainly one of the most memorable images of the majesty and remote grandeur of the late Roman emperor is Ammianus' description of Constantius' entrance to Rome upon his visit to the city in 357.[142] Constantius' tremendous self-control on the occasion once again reinforced the increasingly oriental-style ceremonial that the

---

[134] Matthews (1989), 244–5, 248.

[135] AM 21.9.8; Matthews (1989), 246.

[136] Matthews (1989), 248.

[137] *Gesta* 5.

[138] Matthews (1989), 248. See for a detailed analysis of the promulgation of the *Code*, Matthews (2000), 31–54.

[139] Roueché (1984), 181–99 on the legitimacy acclamations conferred.

[140] Matthews (1989), 249.

[141] See MacCormack (1981), 17 ff.

[142] Matthews (1989), 231. For a not quite so awe-inspiring, but nevertheless valuable, instance of imperial *adventus*, see Julian's arrival into Vienne, AM 15.8.21.

imperial office embraced in the later empire, and has been seen as entailing that the emperor became merely a distant, godlike persona to observers, entirely remote and unapproachable.[143] Yet Constantius' behaviour once inside the city seems at odds with such a simple conclusion: the emperor addressed the nobles in the senate-house, and the populace from the tribunal, holding equestrian games and even delighting in the sallies of the commons, in a far from distant manner.[144] It seems more likely that it was a case of recognizing the need for different modes of conduct required by the emperor in different contexts—a transition from 'military' to 'civil' behaviour.[145]

That Ammianus himself understood the importance of regulating behaviour in different contexts is apparent from his comment that whilst Jovian was known for his excessive indulgence in wine and women, these were 'faults which perhaps he would have corrected out of regard for the imperial dignity', given time.[146] Constantius was praised by Ammianus for his sense of dignity in keeping with his position, and it was one of Ammianus' main criticisms of Julian that he was not as conscious as he should have been of maintaining a sense of behaviour appropriate to the circumstances.[147] An emperor's sense of due decorum according to the circumstances was important.[148]

Although ceremonies like the *adventus* were certainly very significant in public relations between subjects and emperor, it must also have been true that, in an empire of such immense size, a vast proportion of the population would never have witnessed such an event, and perhaps would never even have laid eyes on their emperor.[149] For many, imperial portraits in temples, public places, and on coinage needed to convey the emperor's majesty and legitimacy, and encourage their belief in his superhuman virtues and God-given power.[150] Here again, Eusebius emphasizes the religious function of a Christian emperor, through the rich gifts he gave to the church for many new buildings throughout the provinces and the embellishment of old ones.[151] Imperial benefactions were one way, then, in which an emperor might convey the message of his interest in his subjects and their sense of belonging to his empire.

Overall, Menander's *Basilikos Logos* provides a valuable list of virtues which can be used as labels for the different functions demanded of a late Roman

---

[143] AM 16.10.9–11; Kelly (1998), 143.
[144] AM 16.10.13.
[145] Matthews (1989), 234.
[146] AM 25.10.15: *quae vitia imperiali verecundia forsitan correxisset*...See also Matthews (1989), 238.
[147] On Constantius, see AM 21.16.1. On Julian, 22.4.1–2; 22.7.1; 22.7.3; 25.4.18.
[148] Matthews (1989), 237.
[149] On the importance of the *adventus*, see MacCormack (1981), 20–1.
[150] Price (1984), 171.
[151] Eusebius, *VC* I.42.2; III.47.4.

emperor. His approach was by no means the only possible way, but for our purposes it is a useful method of breaking down the requirements of the imperial office and beginning to get behind these labels to see how the office had evolved, and was evolving still, in the fourth century. The emperor should be possessed of certain key personal virtues: courage, temperance, justice, and wisdom. He ought to be a strong military leader, although this function might take many forms. He needed to look to the administration of justice and the making of appointments, and in both this area and in his military role, he needed to be conscious of the politics involved in keeping powerful members of both the army and bureaucracy behind him as supporters. Many of these functions had always been present in the presentation of the Roman imperial office, yet some, such as the Christian element of his role, were completely new in the fourth century, and over the course of the third and fourth centuries his military abilities became increasingly emphasized. While the imperial adoption of Christianity had a significant impact and brought with it certain additional expectations of the emperor, such as a fundamental role in promoting unity of doctrine and defending orthodoxy as God's appointed ruler, many central attributes remained unchanged but could be presented with an added Christian emphasis, such as compassion to the poor in the administration of justice. The existence of a common and well-established conception of imperial presentation allowed for both Christian and pagan writers to speak of the virtues of their rulers within the traditional framework.[152] And if an emperor's reign prospered, the *post eventum* verdict would find it to have been a legitimate, divinely favoured regime, illustrated also during the emperor's lifetime by appropriately magnificent ceremonial.

Looking at the key desirable imperial virtues represented in surviving literary depictions of the emperor up until *c.*367 and arising from different contexts provides a useful starting-point for the analysis of the phenomenon of the boy-emperors of the later Roman Empire in the west. One would expect different emperors to fulfil different aspects of their office to a greater or lesser extent, in accordance with their abilities and the needs of their times. It is doubtful whether any emperor could fully satisfy the complete imperial checklist or be presented as doing so (and indeed different aspects of this checklist were clearly emphasized in different situations)—and if an adult emperor would struggle in this, how then would a child fare? Scholars have argued over the 'passivity' of emperors amidst the machinery of government, and how much any emperor might ever really achieve.[153] When the emperor was a child, the level of his activity as head of government was surely going to be severely limited, for some years at least.

---

[152] Cameron, Av. (1991), 131–2.
[153] e.g. Millar (1977), 6; Ando (2000), 140; Hopkins (1978a), 180.

There are three political phases through which these questions can best be examined in relation to the reigns of Gratian and Valentinian II. First, the boys' accessions: the circumstances in which they were proclaimed, and the vital precedent set by Valentinian I's raising Gratian as his co-emperor in 367, and how this was swiftly taken up by political players around the throne with the accession of Valentinian II, only eight years later. Secondly, through the long-term successes and failures of the reigns, which often hinged upon the inability of a child-emperor to be a military leader in the field, and the different means through which management of a child-emperor government was attempted—such as with committee-style support, or the dominance of a single manager. And thirdly, the way in which the sources reveal adjustment taking place in the traditional imperial image explored above, in order to try to cope with boy-rulers, need to be examined, along with the tell-tale signs that, despite efforts to cloak any inadequacies, the practical (as opposed to ideological) expectations of the imperial office were not being met. We begin then, with an in-depth analysis of the intrigues and dramas surrounding the accessions of the first western child-emperors, Gratian and Valentinian II.

2

Gratian and Valentinian II:
Setting the Precedent

> This son of mine, Gratianus, now become a man, has long lived among
> your children, and you love him as a tie between you and me; therefore, in
> order to secure the public peace on all sides, I plan to take him as my
> associate in the imperial power, if the propitious will of the god of heaven
> and of your dignity shall support what a father's love suggests.[1]

With this speech (according to Ammianus) Valentinian I in 367 created his
young son Gratian co-Augustus, and in so doing created a vital precedent for
the elevation of the child-emperors who would follow in swift succession
over the decades to come. The reigns of the half-brothers, and sometime
co-emperors, Gratian and Valentinian II, provide the first case study of
the late Roman child-emperors of the west. As explored in Chapter 1, the
conventional expectations of the 'ideal' emperor were repeatedly declaimed in
writings of the third and fourth centuries, and there was a well-established
baseline of required imperial virtues that any Roman emperor coming to the
throne in the 360s or 370s would be expected to demonstrate. But the novelty
of the accessions of 8-year-old Gratian in 367 and 4-year-old Valentinian II in
375 have long been overlooked in modern studies which fail to recognize that
these acclamations and the long reigns which followed them pushed the
boundaries of what had been previously acceptable in the exercise of the late
Roman imperial office. These accessions do raise the question of how such
young emperors might be presented as adequately fulfilling the established
imperial ideal. First, however, we should examine the particular political crises
which led to the elevations of these young boys in the first place, and who the
individuals or groups involved in these events were. How did the accessions of

---

[1] AM 27.6.8: *Gratianum hunc meum adultum, quem diu versatum inter liberos vestros,*
commune diligitis pignus, undique muniendae tranquillitatis publicae causa, in augustum assu-
mere commilitium paro, si propitia caelestis numinis vestraeque maiestatis voluntas parentis
amorem iuverit praeeuntem . . .

8-year-old Gratian and 4-year-old Valentinian II come about—and perhaps most importantly, why did they?

Accessions

While the nature of the circumstances surrounding the acclamations of these two sons of Valentinian I were very different, both boys experienced two accessions in a sense: one 'phantom' accession—Gratian's elevation by his father in 367 and Valentinian II's proclamation upon Valentinian I's death in 375; and one 'real' one—Gratian's upon Valentinian I's death in 375 and Valentinian II's upon Gratian's death in 383. Ammianus has provided a colourful and detailed account of Gratian's phantom accession at Amiens as an 8-year-old, on 24 August 367, when Valentinian I mounted the tribunal, surrounded by men of high rank, then took his son by the hand and presented him to the gathered army.[2] According to Ammianus, Valentinian I made two lengthy speeches before the assembled troops, both to them and to the boy, expressing the hope that he would fulfil his promise and rise to great heights.[3] Before he had finished his address the soldiers responded joyfully, and Valentinian I adorned Gratian with a crown and with what Ammianus describes as the 'robe of his ranks'.[4]

In 366 Gratian had been named as consul alongside the distinguished general Fl. Dagalaifus, and granted the title of *nobilissimus puer*.[5] But raising an 8-year-old boy to the rank of Augustus was a very unusual event in Roman imperial history: and according to Ammianus, in making first his brother Valens Augustus in 364, and then raising his son Gratian to equal rank in 367, in creating co-Augusti rather than Caesars first, Valentinian I had 'over-stepped' the traditional order.[6] And if making even an adult a co-Augustus

---

[2] AM 27.6.4–5. The date is given at *Cons.Const.* s.a. 364; Socrates 4.11.3; *Chron.pasch.* p. 557.

[3] AM 27.6.8. See similarly on Commodus' presentation to the troops: Campbell (1984), 49–50.

[4] AM 27.6.10–11. The accession is noted in other sources as well: Symmachus, *Or.*1.3; 2.31–2; 3.1–6; Sozomen 6.10.1; Socrates 4.11.3; Ps.-Aurelius Victor 45.4; Zosimus 4.14.4; Jerome, *Chron.* s.a. 367; Prosper 1135; Philostorgius 8.8; Theophanes a.m 5857; Zonaras 13.15; *Cons.Const.* s.a. 364; *Chron.pasch.* p. 557. MacCormack has identified a late fourth-century–early fifth-century western jewel depicting an adult emperor and another adult crowning a child as Valentinian I and Valens investing Gratian: MacCormack (1981), pl. 43. I would suggest that in fact the jewel shows the investiture of Valentinian III as *nobilissimus puer* in the late 410s by the emperor Honorius and Valentinian's father, Fl. Constantius (later Constantius III)—see further below, p. 214—one of the adult figures wears a diadem but the other does not, therefore it seems unlikely it can be Valentinian and Valens in 367 who are depicted (see cover image).

[5] *CLRE* 266–7; *PLRE* 1. 401; AM 26.9.1; Doignon (1966), 1693–5; Lenski (2002), 90. On the origins of the title *nobilissimus*, see Instinksy (1952), 98–103.

[6] AM 27.6.16: *Valentinianus morem institutum antiquitus supergressus* . . . Ammianus in-cludes the elevation of Valens in this statement. Pabst suggests that Valentinian I made his

rather than Caesar was out of keeping with imperial convention, how much more unexpected the elevation of an 8-year-old boy directly to the rank of co-Augustus must have been. Yet as Ammianus noted, the difference between making an Augustus rather than a Caesar was a significant one, and one which presented a novel precedent for following regimes. In theory at least, in making Gratian an Augustus, Valentinian had made his 8-year-old son a full joint ruler of the entire Roman empire.[7] It was to be expected that Gratian would remain a 'sleeping partner' during his father's lifetime, at least while the boy was so young, but the question arises as to why Valentinian I had taken this controversial step in the first place?[8] In 364, Ammianus explains, after his accession, the troops had clamoured for Valentinian to appoint a co-emperor as an 'insurance policy' of sorts following the upheavals of the short reigns and unexpected deaths of the emperors Julian and Jovian, so that if Valentinian I also died suddenly, the empire would still have a ruler, and thus Valentinian had appointed his brother Valens.[9] In 367 the elevation of young Gratian seems to have been prompted by similar fears: both Ammianus and Zosimus report that Valentinian had been ill, and court factions had already begun speculating as to who his successor might be.[10] Therefore: 'On his recovery, his courtiers gathered round him and urged him to declare his successor, to prevent a political crisis if anything happened to him. Thus persuaded, the emperor declared his son, Gratian, co-emperor though he was still a young man and not even yet at the end of his youth.'[11]

The implication is that the courtiers had not even considered Gratian, an 8-year-old child, as a viable successor if Valentinian I died at this point. The two factions who met to discuss the issue clearly felt no innate loyalty to the dynasty, and though such speculation would surely have been considered treasonous in another context, there is no indication in this case that those involved were punished.[12] The lack of any known support for the acclamation of the infant (and consul) Varronianus, son of Jovian, following his father-

---

brother and son Augusti instead of Caesars in order to avoid their rising up against him as Julian had done against Constantius, but in view of the circumstances and Gratian's age, this seems an unlikely motivation: Pabst (1986), 56–7.

[7] As Pabst points out, it was a legal anomaly for the *puer* Gratian to rank alongside his father and uncle as Augustus: Pabst (1986), 94 ff.

[8] On the boy as a 'sleeping partner', see Jones (1964a), 1. 141.

[9] AM 26.4.1–3.

[10] AM 27.6.4. According to Ammianus, the Gauls at court in the emperor's service were favouring Rusticus Julianus, the master of the rolls, while against them others were favouring Severus, the commander of the infantry (27.6.3).

[11] Zosimus 4.12.2: ἐπεὶ δὲ ταύτην διέφυγε, συνελθόντες οἱ περὶ τὰ βασίλεια λόγον αὐτὸν ποιήσασθαι παρεκάλουν τοῦ διαδεξομένου τὴν βασιλείαν, ὡς ἂν μή τινος αὐτῷ συμβαίνοντος σφαλείη τὰ τῆς πολιτείας· πεισθεὶς δὲ τούτοις ὁ βασιλεὺς τοῖς λόγοις ἀνεῖπε τὸν παῖδα Γρατιανὸν βασιλέα καὶ κοινωνὸν τῆς ἀρχῆς, ὄντα νέον ἔτι καὶ οὔπω πρὸς ἥβην ἐλθόντα τελείαν. Also Matthews (1989), 207.

[12] Potter (2004), 540–1.

emperor's death only a few years earlier, and the child's virtual disappearance thereafter, should banish any idea that court factions felt an automatic dynastic loyalty to the family of their emperor so soon after his accession.[13]

Valentinian not only designated his son as his successor, he raised him to a supposedly equal share in his own power. It was a move whereby Valentinian I firmly asserted his own authority at the expense of the advisers around him: in associating in his own power a co-emperor who obviously could not rule effectively at this point, he clearly intimated he would not, and did not need to, associate another plausible person with himself as emperor in the west. But if an 8-year-old could be raised as co-Augustus in response to a political crisis, could so young a child—or one even younger—be raised as sole Augustus? What did such a move mean in the longer term for the imperial office?

Valentinian was clearly determined to keep the role of emperor within his own family, and re-invent it as an imperial dynasty. Perhaps in view of his recent illness, he also hoped to ensure a smooth transfer of power to his son in the case of his unexpected demise, and in that sense his elevation of Gratian differed little from Constantine I's plans for his sons—except in the significant change to a more exalted title.[14] Valentinian's actions suggest that, in view of recent history, he doubted Gratian would have been accepted as ruler while still a minor: Valentinian I's elevation of the child Gratian could also be interpreted as a sign of his regime's insecurity.[15] It certainly indicates that he knew if he died without raising his son to the rank of Augustus, there was a high probability Gratian would never become the next western emperor, and that his courtiers had not previously thought the child a likely successor, at least at that stage. Yet with his adult brother already emperor of the east, Valentinian was perhaps in a stronger position to delegate his own young son as heir to the west than he might otherwise have been. Valentinian's speech, as reported by Ammianus, asked that the young boy be accepted on the grounds of the military record of his family, and his excellent education; not the most reassuring of claims, especially to an audience of soldiers.[16] But at this stage, of course, Gratian was 8 years old, and the idea of the boy-Augustus' youthful promise was to be pushed at all costs: really there was little else which could be said.

As both the new emperor and Valentinian I's heir, Gratian became the focus of the hopes of the new imperial dynasty, and of a belief in its future. In 368 the pagan aristocrat Symmachus, who would play a significant role in the reigns of the first three boy-emperors of the west, presented a panegyric on the new young emperor Gratian at his father's court at Trier. Symmachus hailed

---

[13] On Varronianus, see *PLRE* 1. 946.
[14] Jones (1964a), 1. 323.
[15] Sivan (1993), 108.
[16] AM 27.6.8–9. Cf. Sivan (1993), 101.

Gratian's accession as the dawn of a new and hopeful era, echoing the phrases Ammianus attributed to Valentinian I at Gratian's elevation, and extravagantly asserting that the whole empire was in the child's hands.[17] With both his father and an adult uncle still ruling, there was no need for the young Gratian to provide practical imperial leadership at this point. And in a sense Gratian's child-emperorship matters most in the precedent he created, since he himself would have eight years as a sleeping partner in his father's rule before called upon to take up full imperial duties. But through his accession (and his survival beyond his father's death) Gratian's experience created the possibility of the true child-emperors to follow—and the possibility of a minor ruling—and encompassing all of the traditional imperial virtues and functions—alone.

The coins minted to mark the occasion of Gratian's accession bore a hopeful slogan, associating Gratian with the GLORIA NOVI SAECVLI and the SPES R[ei] P[ublicae].[18] These mottoes harked back to the Constantinian dynasty: *Spes Rei Publicae* was the legend Constantine I had used back in 324 to advertise his sons, and as later developments would show, the Valentinian dynasty proved keen to establish links with the house of Constantine, and through such links to promote the concept of a new imperial dynasty embodied in the house of Valentinian.[19] To justify the accession of the child-emperor, the combination of youthful promise and the idea of continuation of the past regime of the great Constantine was being brought to the fore. Yet the praise of a supposedly fully fledged emperor—as opposed to an imperial heir—on the basis of youthful promise rather than actual deeds was a novel development.

It has been observed that Valentinian I's action in thus raising his young son to the purple initiated the practice which was to become standard in the Byzantine empire, of appointing a child to the full honours of an Augustus.[20] Yet the question of why this practice was initiated—and became so common— remains to be addressed. The prevalence of child-emperors in the later, Byzantine world has tended in modern scholarship to obscure the fact that in the late fourth century the accession of an 8-year-old emperor was a truly extraordinary development. In 364 the emperor Jovian had raised his infant son Varronianus to share his first consulship with him, also naming him *nobilissimus puer*.[21] It has been suggested that this is an indication that Jovian too would soon have named his son a co-emperor.[22] Yet given recent imperial history, it is more likely that it would have been some years before

---

[17] Symmachus, *Or.* 3.2. See similarly AM 27.6.8; Sivan (1993), 113.
[18] Lenski (2002), 90–1. *RIC* 9. xvi; p. 16, no. 13.
[19] Holum (1982), 33 (fig. 4).
[20] Lenski (2002), 90.
[21] Philostorgius 8.8; Lenski (2002), 90.
[22] Lenski (2002), 19.

Varronianus were given an imperial rank, and then that it would have been the rank of Caesar first, before a later elevation as Augustus. And although elevating the infant Varronianus could perhaps be seen as an indication of the security of the new regime, it could also arguably be viewed as a sign of its insecurity, at least while the boy was so very young.[23] That imperial hopes were cherished for Varronianus is not in question: in his *Oration 5* (delivered for the joint consulship of Jovian and his son), Themistius did conclude by expressing the aspiration that the child consul would one day share the purple with his father, but there is no hint that this scenario was imminently expected.[24]

Though there had been youthful imperial consuls, Caesars, and even occasionally Augusti in earlier years of the Roman empire, the accession of Gratian as Augustus in 367 seems to have awakened new ideas about succession to the imperial office under the Valentinian dynasty. In the east, there are signs that Valens may have been planning a similar step for his own young son, Valentinian Galates. Themistius' *Oration 9* was delivered on the occasion of the child's first consulship in 369, when he cannot have been more than 3 years of age, and in it the orator looked forward to '[a] four-part yoke of emperors, two teams composed of members of almost the same age and contemporaneous, each walking the same, thinking the same, equalling the ends of the earth they guard'—of Valentinian I and Gratian in the west, and Valens and Valentinian Galates in the east.[25] But Valens' young son was dead by 372, and his designation as co-Augustus, even if planned, never took place—perhaps given the superior status in the imperial college generally ascribed to Valentinian I, the power of elevation was his prerogative alone, whatever Themistius declared.[26] Or perhaps even following Gratian's elevation as a result of political crisis in 367, Valentinian I still had no intention of making child-emperor accessions the new norm for the dynasty. Nevertheless, in the west the promotion of another child-emperor would soon take place, and the nature of its occurrence confirmed the recognition by certain powers around the throne of the significance of Valentinian I's actions in 367.

---

[23] Ammianus indicates also that the infant Varronianus was only chosen as consul after his grandfather and namesake died: AM 25.10.11; 25.10.16–17; see further on this Errington (2006), 19–20.

[24] Themistius, *Or.* 5.71b. Heather and Moncur also, however, take it for granted that Jovian would shortly raise his son as co-Augustus (p. 167, n. 91; p. 173, n. 119).

[25] Themistius, *Or.* 9.128a; 127c; 121c: οἶον ὄψονται ἐπὶ τῆς παρούσης περιόδου θέαμα ἄνθρωποι, τέτρωρον βασιλέων, ποιητὴς ἂν εἴποι, δύο ξυνωρίδας ὁμηλίκων σχεδὸν ἑκατέρων καὶ ὁμοχρόνων, ἴσα βαινόντων, ἴσα πνεόντων, ἰσαρίθμων τοῖς πέρασι τῆς γῆς ἣν φυλάττουσιν.

[26] On Valentinian Galates, see *PLRE* 1. 381. See also Lenski (2002), 30–2; Errington (2006) 25. Theodosius I's appointment of Arcadius as Augustus in 383 occurred without the permission of the senior Augustus Gratian, and was not recognized by him, though his death occurred only shortly afterwards—see further below, p. 83.

On 17 November 375, Valentinian I died suddenly at Brigetio in Illyricum, bursting a blood vessel in a rage and haemorrhaging fatally while receiving an embassy from the Quadi.[27] The late emperor's co-Augustus in the west, his son Gratian, now aged 16, was at Trier and unaware of the event; Gratian had been married in 374, and it seems likely Valentinian had meant to indicate his elder son's independence at this point by leaving him in charge of affairs at Trier while he went on campaign.[28] It was at this stage that Gratian's real accession took place, although it was clearly not a foregone conclusion: his father's manoeuvring had made him difficult to dispense with, but his acceptance as emperor was not automatic, and Gratian's absence from the scene made the situation all the more uncertain.[29] The general Merobaudes, whom the emperor had sent on ahead in the campaign against the Sarmatians and Quadi, was immediately recalled by Valentinian I's advisers to come with all speed to Brigetio, though the reason was not divulged.[30] Upon his arrival and acquaintance with the events, the secret was maintained and the popular general Sebastianus was sent to a distant post, precisely because it was feared he might be proclaimed Augustus instead of Gratian.[31] There certainly were adult alternatives to boy-emperor rule if those wielding power at court had wished to pursue them; the Frankish general Merobaudes, however, perhaps unable to claim the throne due to his non-Roman lineage, or perhaps simply believing more could be gained by manipulating the accession in other ways, did not pose that sort of a threat. The matter of the succession was then considered, and ostensibly to safeguard Gratian's position in the face of fears of the loyalty of the cohorts serving in Gaul, the plan was unfolded for the phantom accession of Valentinian I's younger son, also called Valentinian, and aged only 4 years of age: for the child to be made co-Augustus with his half-brother Gratian, and his uncle, Valens. Neither emperor was consulted, however. Valentinian II was living 100 miles away from Brigetio with his mother Justina, and: 'When this had been approved by unanimous consent, the boy's uncle Cerealis was immediately sent to the place, put him in a litter, and brought him to the camp; and on the sixth day after the passing of his father he was in due form declared emperor, and after the customary manner was hailed as Augustus.'[32]

---

[27] AM 30.6.3. Also Socrates 4.31; Zosimus 4.17.1–2.

[28] AM 30.10.2; Lenski (2002), 102–3.

[29] AM 30.10.1; McLynn (1994), 83–4.

[30] AM 30.5.13; 30.10.2–3. Also Zosimus 4.19.1; Ps.-Aurelius Victor 46.10; *PLRE* 1. 598–9.

[31] AM 30.10.3. Zosimus writes that Sebastianus had left the west because the youth of the emperors there meant they were not able to think for themselves and were controlled by the slanders of the eunuch chamberlains, which would seem to suggest a later date for his departure, but he does not appear in any sources for the west again after 375, and only turns up again in Ammianus in an eastern context in 378 (AM 31.11.1)—see below. Eunapius, frg. 44.3 also suggests Sebatianus was the victim of court politics.

[32] AM 30.10.5: *Hocque concinenti omnium sententia confirmato, Cerealis avunculus eius ocius missus, eundem puerum lecticae impositum, duxit in castra sextoque die post parentis obitum*

There were fears that these actions, carried out entirely without the consent of the two existing emperors, would displease Gratian and Valens, but according to Ammianus, 'being a kindly and righteous man', Gratian accepted the accession with good grace.[33]

Given their respective ages, we can hardly be surprised to find that the original accessions of both Gratian and Valentinian II were the result of the activity of others, rather than their own efforts: Valentinian I's activity in the case of Gratian; while the accession of Valentinian II, though presented as promoting Gratian's safety, in fact served the purposes of Merobaudes and others. Upon Valentinian I's death the empire was not left without a ruler: both Valens, emperor since 364 with his brother, and Gratian, co-Augustus of the west with his father since 367, were still alive and at 16, Gratian was surely close to an age to rule in his own right, with eight years of his father's guidance behind him. The question of there being any need for a third Augustus may seem surprising, and the answer that this need might be met by the acclamation of a 4-year-old, even more so. It is difficult to imagine that Valentinian II's accession in 375 would even have been contemplated had it not been for that of his brother in 367. The sudden death of Valentinian I during a campaign, at a time when the still relatively young and untried Gratian was at distant Trier and Valens even further away in the east, did create a political emergency, and one which arguably called for a creative solution. Yet the situation was not entirely without a relatively recent parallel: Ammianus informs us that when Jovian had died suddenly in 364, and Valentinian I had been chosen as his successor, the new emperor had been at Ancyra, while the imperial army was in Bithynia, near Nicaea. While Valentinian had made the journey to join them, for a whole ten days the empire was without an acclaimed emperor, and although the commanders needed to pay close attention to the 'fickle' temper of the soldiers, Ammianus notes, and to keep them from acclaiming anyone else, in the end the danger-period passed without incident.[34] Clearly it was feasible, on occasion, to maintain calm among the troops and await the arrival of an emperor for some days without usurpation inevitably occurring.

---

imperator legitime declaratus, Augustus nuncupatur more sollemni. On the boy living at Brigetio: AM 30.10.4. Also on the accession: Socrates 4.31; Zosimus 4.19.1–2; Rufinus 11.12; Aurelius Victor 45.10; Philostorgius 9.16; Ambrose, *De ob. Val.* 59. Ausonius, *Grat.Act.* offers an otherwise unsubstantiated account that Gratian had 'summoned' his half-brother to the purple— perhaps attempting to gloss over the potential attack on Gratian's own position that the accession of his brother represented: 2.7; 10.48.

[33] AM 30.10.6. Similarly Matthews (1975), 64. On the fears regarding Gratian's and Valens' reactions: Socrates 4.31. Van Dam wrongly suspects Ausonius of sarcasm in praising Gratian for accepting Valentinian II 'in the guise of a son' (Ausonius, *Grat.Act.* 2; Van Dam (2007), 105–6); this was surely precisely the guise in which Gratian's advisers hoped to portray Valentinian II— as of junior status to Gratian.

[34] AM 26.1.4–6.

Nevertheless, the importance of having a new, legitimate emperor on the scene as soon as possible should not be underestimated, and such a crisis scenario and solution may well be echoed in the accession of Theodosius I in January 379, a few months after Adrianople. And as scholars have pointed out in the case of Constantine I's 'usurpation' at York after the death of his father in 306, the value of a new emperor who was actually on the scene (or near enough) when the army was in the midst of a campaign should not be overlooked.[35] But beside this emergency situation, the reasons behind the promotion of Valentinian II need to be carefully considered, particularly in light of the question of just who was effecting the promotion, and why. The measure was presented as a means of securing the loyalty of a volatile army and avoiding a usurpation of power by another, which are reasonable and justifiable arguments in the situation.[36] The accession of one of the competent generals who were instead safely put out of the way could conceivably have led to civil war, and the persuasive dynastic legitimacy of the young prince did offer a means of avoiding such turmoil. Nevertheless, the course of events does highlight the tenuousness of the 16-year-old Gratian's position, despite his father's efforts: when the moment of his real accession occurred, and the youth was far from the unfolding events, it was clearly quite plausible to argue that the troops might feel little loyalty towards him, and not inconceivable that Gratian might even simply be killed in favour of an established military commander.

The decision to proclaim young Valentinian II must have been taken within twenty-four hours of Valentinian I's death on 17 November, given that the child was 100 miles from Brigetio at the time, but was fetched to the camp and proclaimed within five days, on 22 November.[37] Several specific protagonists are mentioned in the surviving accounts of Valentinian II's accession, which was in effect a military coup. The general Merobaudes is clearly referred to as a key player in the decisions by Ammianus, whilst both Merobaudes and the *magister militum* in Illyricum, Flavius Equitius, are mentioned by Zosimus.[38] The young emperor's uncle, his mother Justina's brother Cerealis (therefore not a blood-relative of Gratian's), is also explicitly mentioned in the events, and the involvement of the illustrious Petronius Probus, a well-known member of the aristocratic elite of Rome, is indicated by several sources.[39]

As noted above, the popular general Sebastianus was sent away, and is not found again in Ammianus' history until asked for by Valens to serve as

---

[35] Humphries (2008), 83.The major difference remains, of course, that Constantine was an adult with experience in military leadership.

[36] Sivan (1993), 120.

[37] Potter (2004), 543.

[38] AM 30.10.2–3; 30.10.4; Zosimus 4.19.1–2. Also Ps.-Aurelius Victor 46.10; *PLRE* 1. 282.

[39] On Cerealis, AM 30.10.5. On Petronius Probus, Rufinus 11.12. AM 30.5.10; Matthews (1975), 64.

magister peditum in his struggles against the Goths in Thrace, indicating that Sebastianus was not in active service at the time.[40] Another popular and successful general to disappear around this time was the elder Theodosius, father of the future emperor. There has been much written regarding his death, and even its date is not certain, but it is highly likely that the general's arrest and execution at Carthage *c*.375 was linked in some way to politics surrounding the death of Valentinian I, the real succession of his elder son, and the phantom accession of the younger son.[41] The elder Theodosius had campaigned successfully in Britain in the late 360s and held the post of *magister equitum* under Valentinian I, while in 373 he had been sent to North Africa as commander of an expedition to deal with the rebellion of Firmus, in which he had also achieved success.[42] Given Theodosius' past successes, current command of an army in Africa, and thus effective control also of the grain supply to Rome at this point, combined with the fact that Merobaudes was surely the man to profit most from eliminating the rival general, and had arranged for the removal of Sebastianus, he was also the most likely prime mover behind Theodosius' sudden execution.[43] Furthermore, following his involvement in Valentinian II's acclamation as Augustus, Flavius Equitius, formerly the senior regional commander in Illyricum, and holder of the consulate together with Gratian in 374, does not appear again in the sources either.[44]

One key idea emerges from this picture of generals put safely out of the way in 375: competing strong military commanders were not wanted on the scene by those behind the accessions of Gratian and Valentinian II. And yet this was a period when the traditional glories of the Roman armies were being persistently recalled on Roman coinage as a reassurance of Roman might against the barbarian threat.[45] It seems surprising to find scholars describing the promotion of a 4-year-old child as emperor, in order to safeguard the accession of a 16-year-old emperor, whilst competent generals were put safely out of the way, as 'the best [decision] that could have been devised under the circumstances'.[46]

---

[40] AM 30.10.3. Sebastianus was *comes rei militaris* in 375 and had served as *dux Aegypti* under Constantius II and *comes* under Julian: Errington (1996*a*), 441; *PLRE* 1. 812–13. On his return to active service: AM 31.11.1. See Errington (1996*a*), 441.

[41] For primary records of the general's death, see Orosius 7.33.7; Jerome, *Chron.* s.a. 376. See for further discussion: Matthews (1975), 64, and also Demandt (1969), 598–626; Thompson (1947), 94; Rodgers (1981), 82–9; Errington (1996*a*), 441; Barnes (1998), 184; Potter (2004), 544–5.

[42] AM 27.8.1 ff.; 28.3.9. Cf. *PLRE* 1. 902–4; Matthews (1975), 93–4.

[43] Tomlin (1973), 527–8. Rodgers, in contrast, argues strongly against Merobaudes' involvement: (1981), 82–9. Potter argues that Maximinus was behind Theodosius *comes*' execution (2004) 544–5.

[44] Errington (1996*a*), 441. Also Sivan (1993), 120.

[45] Pearce (1951), xv.

[46] Rodgers (1981), 90. Similarly Wardman (1984), 233.

Nor is it entirely correct to claim that by 375 there was a familiar pattern for the public promotion of children of the dynasty.[47] Only one child of the dynasty had as yet been promoted as Augustus, and that in itself had been an extraordinary event—the result of a crisis rather than any apparent long-term planning. At the time of Valentinian I's death in 375, in fact, any role in the imperial college that the father might have envisaged for his younger son had as yet been given little expression: Valentinian I may have nominated his younger son as consul for 376 already before his own death, but Valentinian II does not appear to have been granted the title of *nobilissimus puer* (or any other rank) before 375.[48] In contrast, by the time of Valentinian I's death, Gratian had already held three consulships (in 367, 371, and 374): there could be no doubt he was his father's chosen heir.[49] The accession of child-emperors remained a very new development in 375, and any pattern we might retro-spectively apply to the phenomenon in its earliest stages is questionable at best: the elevation of 4-year-old Valentinian II in 375 must surely have come as a great surprise to many. This is not to say there were not issues of potential usurpation by powerful generals and resultant civil war which needed to be averted, but that the choice of young boys who clearly could not fulfil the military demands inherent in the office of *imperator* over capable and proven military leaders, is both striking and novel against the backdrop of fourth-century imperial politics, and needs careful consideration.

It is easy to dismiss the accession of Valentinian II (and indeed the later accessions of Honorius and Valentinian III—discussed below) as a simple triumph of the dynastic principle. Yet as the intricate political manoeuvring surrounding Valentinian II's sudden elevation reveals, his accession was hardly an automatic or predictable result of his father's death. It occurred as a consequence of the specific political crisis brought about by Valentinian I's sudden expiration, but we need to keep in mind that it also reflected the political opportunism of certain powerful individuals, among the military high command and the senatorial aristocracy, who began to see more advantage in wielding power behind the throne than in claiming the throne itself—in this case, men like Merobaudes and Petronius Probus. The tenuous dynastic claim of a young boy was employed as a useful shield for legitimacy, behind which all sorts of political agendas could be played out.

The period of Valentinian I's death and his sons' accessions was marked by intense court rivalries, with both military politicking and senatorial aspirations to be addressed.[50] It has been suggested that Valentinian II was the only

---

[47] Errington (2006), 26.

[48] Ibid. 25–6. Valentinian Galates was consul in 369 with Fl. Victor, and already titled *nobilissimus puer* by this time: *CLRE* 272–3. Galates died *c.*370: *PLRE* 1. 381.

[49] Gratian held his second consulship in 371 alongside Sextus Petronius Probus, and his third in 374 with Fl. Equitius (*CLRE* 276–7, 282–3).

[50] Sivan (1993), 120.

possible legitimate successor to his father, and one acceptable both to Gratian and Valens: acceptable because he was too young to wield power and could thus be considered a figurehead.[51] But whose figurehead was he? And surely, in fact, Gratian was his father's legitimate heir, while the child Valentinian II was something of a 'spare'. We do not possess any indication prior to 375 that Valentinian I was planning to divide up the west between his sons, and we can only guess at the future the dead emperor might have planned for his younger son. In the end, Valentinian II's claim was not one which must necessarily have been exercised: he was placed on the throne by a group of influential men who sought to use him as leverage against his half-brother Gratian. In reality, Valentinian II's accession was a coup against the former ministers of Valentinian I, whose disposal Merobaudes and Probus could dictate to Gratian through their use of Valentinian II, as we shall see.[52] To make this argument is not to underestimate the political emergency created by the unexpected death of Valentinian I: the danger of military usurpation at this time was in all likelihood a genuine one. Yet this 'need' for an emperor seen as prompting the accession of the child Valentinian II does not mean that the individuals involved in finding a rapid solution to the crisis (and their having acted without any imperial authority whatsoever should not be forgotten) did not also seek to claim advantageous positions for themselves in the new regime they created in response to this crisis.

If this explanation of the events of November 375 is accepted, a sense of the tone of the respective administrations of Gratian and Valentinian II begins to emerge. For Gratian, raised to the rank of Augustus by his father in the hope of securing the family's claim to be the imperial dynasty, the situation upon Valentinian I's death, even with eight years of his father's guidance now behind him, was one of pressures and manipulation by different court factions, whose division of his court itself made it inherently weak and susceptible to such exploitation. For Valentinian II, the boy was clearly already being used as a pawn and, from the start, the very existence of his regime was dependent upon its convenience to others. To aristocrats and important ministers at the imperial court, it could clearly be more advantageous to have a young and malleable, but legitimate, emperor than it might be to be in power themselves; although the need to dispose of potential threats—potential adult alternatives—in the form of successful generals (at least those who were not part of the strategy, like Merobaudes) was great. The accessions of Gratian and Valentinian II, therefore, heralded a new development in the way in which members of the military and senatorial elite of the late empire were coming to view the imperial office: as something over which more control

---

[51] Rodgers (1981), 90.

[52] McLynn (1994), 84. Followed by Errington (2006), 26. Stein also describes Valentinian II's accession as: 'cette apparente usurpation': (1959), 183.

might be exerted through the appointment of a youthful emperor in their power, rather than through the problematic appointment of one of their own. But what would this change in perception do, in turn, to the imperial office itself?

Regime-building: Gratian and the senate

The later years of Valentinian I's reign have been described as a period of 'terror' for the nobility, witnessing a series of trials for magic and misconduct (particularly involving adultery and poisoning) principally among the senatorial aristocracy at Rome, with brutal sentences particularly associated with Maximinus, *vicarius* of Rome in 370–1.[53] Although the extent of these trials should not be exaggerated, it is clear that this was an episode of the emperor's reign which had seriously soured his already uneasy relations with the senatorial aristocracy.[54] The sudden death of Valentinian I and the accessions of his two sons must have left many wondering what they could expect next. The exact contents of Gratian's first address to the Roman senate have not come down to us, but the aristocrat Symmachus' ecstatic description of the period as the dawn of a new era makes it clear that it told the aristocracy, at least, what they wanted to hear.[55] The man seen as Valentinian's main agent in the terror, Maximinus, would not long survive his former master, executed for 'intolerable arrogance' under Gratian.[56] By the end of the summer of 376, none of the supporters of Valentinian I seen as responsible for the trials of the Roman senators remained in office.[57] It was a powerful gesture of goodwill by Gratian to the traditional elite of Rome, and it was just the beginning. Senators who had suffered under the trials were recalled and honoured, and a series of laws favourable to the aristocracy passed during 376–7.[58] And in July 376, the office of *praefectura annonae* (from which Maximinus had risen to the vicariate of Rome) was placed in juridical dependence upon the prefecture of Rome.[59] Furthermore, the urban prefects appointed under Gratian tended to hold office for much shorter periods than had been the case under Valentinian I and, with only three exceptions, those appointed to this coveted post

---

[53] Matthews (1975), 38; see further Zosimus 4.14.2–3; cf. AM 28.1.5 ff.

[54] The suggestion that a senatorial conspiracy against the emperor had been uncovered is dismissed by Matthews (1975), 59; see further on the conflict: Alföldi (1952), 50–1; Jones (1964a), 1. 142; Arnheim (1972), 95; Lizzi Testa (2004), 209–323.

[55] Symmachus, *Ep.*1.13; cf. *Ep.*10.2. Similarly, Ausonius, *Grat.Act.* 1. See also Green (1991), xxix; Lenski (2002), 232; Humphries (1999), 120; Alföldi (1952), 93. On Symmachus, see *PLRE* 1. 865–70.

[56] AM 28.1.57; Symmachus, *Ep.*10.3; *Or.* 4.10–13.

[57] Matthews (1975), 65.

[58] *CTh.* 9.6.1–2 (15 Mar. 376); *CTh.* 9.35.3 = *CJ* 12.1.10 (4 Jan. 377). Those recalled included Julius Festus Hymetius—*ILS* 1256. See Matthews (1975), 66 for further examples.

[59] *CTh.* 14.3.15 (16 Feb. 377); *ILS* 5694. See Matthews (1975), 66; Lenski (2002), 232.

were members of the Roman aristocracy.[60] The rapid turnover in office indicated not only that the new regime was eager to build bridges with the old aristocracy, but that it was eager to do so with as many of its members as possible.[61] And indeed, the first three appointees, men who had all been targeted under Valentinian I, must have been selected to convey the overtly conciliatory attitude of Gratian's administration: Tarracius Bassus, Aradius Rufinus, and Furius Maecius Gracchus.[62]

The coup surrounding the accession of Valentinian II meant that the key players with the child-emperor in their charge—who included the aristocrat Petronius Probus—were in a strong position to press measures such as the conciliation of the senate upon Gratian, with the promise of support for his government in return.[63] But there is more to this issue of Gratian's policy at the outset of his regime: the young emperor's overtures towards the senate represented an attempt at regime-building by attracting broader support for his rule beyond his immediate circle. Courting the support of the powerful senatorial elite was of course not something that only a young emperor needed to do; it was the usual activity of any new imperial administration upon assuming office, but was all the more important when, as in Gratian's case, the emperor could not be certain of commanding the military backing that his father had: as indeed the coup promoting the young Valentinian II had so dramatically confirmed. Valentinian I, who had been unanimously elected and had a network of Pannonian associates to assist in running his government, could afford to upset members of the Roman senate; but Gratian, whose sole claim to the throne was a dynastic right and who had yet to demonstrate the military and administrative ability required of the role, needed all the support he could get—not least from wealthy Roman senators.[64] Gratian's advisers clearly intended that the young emperor's accession should demonstrate a marked change in tone towards the senate in comparison with his father's final years.

The absorption of Valentinian II's sovereignty into Gratian's

Between the time of Valentinian II's accession in 375 and the assassination of Gratian in 383, we possess scarcely a mention of the younger emperor at any of the crucial moments facing the imperial government, aside from his

---

[60] Those three exceptions (Matinianus, Fl. Hypatius, and Arborius) were all aristocrats from other areas.

[61] Errington (2006), 122; Potter (2004), 545–6.

[62] Chastagnol (1962), nos. 77, 78, 79. For details on their treatment under Valentinian I, see Errington (2006), 122.

[63] McLynn (1994), 84. On Probus' involvement, see Croke and Harries (1982), 115; cf. Matthews (1975), 98.

[64] Sivan (1993), 125.

consulships in 376 and 378.[65] There are few surviving sources which offer a comprehensive account of the period 375–83, but nonetheless, Valentinian's non-appearance in the records sends a powerful message about the younger emperor's lack of coherent position during this period.[66] From the start, Valentinian II's 'sovereignty' was something which existed only as it was convenient to others, and the nature of Valentinian II's accession set a tone which would endure throughout the boy's reign, highlighting a major difference between his half-brother's situation and his own: Gratian's, for all its weaknesses, was a real administration; Valentinian's, on the other hand, was not independently sustainable.

Ammianus wrote that Gratian took Valentinian in and saw to his education, which probably entailed the child's residing at least for some time at the court of his elder brother at Trier.[67] According to Zosimus, the western empire was divided between Gratian and Valentinian II, with the Gallic provinces, the whole of Spain, and Britain going to Gratian, and Italy, Illyricum, and Africa to Valentinian II.[68] It seems unlikely, in fact, that there was ever any formal division in 375 (and probably none was ever intended): the child Valentinian was patently unable to govern his allotment at the time of his accession, and Gratian seems to have ruled the whole of the west.[69] Although Gratian accepted his brother's proclamation in theory, in practice the child rapidly became very much a sleeping partner in the imperial college—as Gratian himself had been during his father's lifetime; yet while in Gratian's case he had clearly remained his father's heir during his years in Valentinian I's shadow, Valentinian II's position, despite his rank, was more ambiguous.[70] Contemporaries like Symmachus certainly regarded Gratian alone as the emperor responsible for Italy until 383, and Themistius too, in his *Oration 13* (delivered to Gratian in early 376), did not even mention Valentinian II, but had Gratian ruling the entire empire alongside his uncle.[71] And in practical terms, Gratian must have had the prefecture of Illyricum in his charge, since it was to Gratian that Valens applied for military assistance in 377 and had the

---

[65] *CLRE* 286–7; 290–1.

[66] Ausonius and Ammianus, for example, do write of events up to 378/9 and might conceivably have mentioned the young Augustus after 375, as might the writings of Ambrose of Milan. Admittedly, Arcadius and Honorius are barely mentioned in source material after their acclamations as Augusti before their father's death.

[67] AM 30.10.6. Ausonius, *Grat.Act.* 2; See McLynn (1994), 85: Errington (1996a), 442, n. 24.

[68] Zosimus 4.19.1–2. Disputed convincingly by Errington (1996a), 441–2.

[69] Errington (1996a), 442.

[70] Jones (1964a), 1. 141. Similarly Glaesener (1957), 468.

[71] Symmachus, *Or.* 4; Errington (1996a), 442; Themistius, *Or.* 13.167c, 169b, 177b–c, 179c. As Lenski points out, Themistius' oration addresses the emperors in the dual—i.e. as if Gratian and Valens ruled alone and did not even possess a third colleague (Lenski (2002), 360–1). After the death of Valens and accession of Theodosius, Themistius, *Or.* 15.194d, 196d, 198b still assumes only two Augusti.

comes per Illyricum dispatched in reply.[72] Similarly, in 379, after the accession of Theodosius, it was Gratian who ceded the Illyrican dioceses of Dacia and Macedonia to the new Augustus.[73] Young Valentinian II did share the consulship with his uncle Valens in 376 and 378; however, there are no extant independent imperial directives issued by the youngest emperor before Gratian's death.[74] Essentially, following his acclamation in 375 and up until Gratian's death in 383, Valentinian II's title was a hollow one, and as with the boy's position before his father's death, it is not clear what, if any, role was envisaged for Valentinian II once he reached adulthood.

The coinage for the period also illuminates the situation: on coins issued from the mint in Trier, for example, the two emperors never appeared together as co-emperors until after 378, a point at which Gratian will have wanted to emphasize the dynastic legitimacy and seniority of the western emperors to his new colleague Theodosius, for reasons which will become clear.[75] And at all other western mints, with the exception of that of Sirmium (where the child-emperor may have resided for a time with his mother),[76] coinage depicting Valentinian II included IVN (= 'junior') in their legends, plainly signifying the younger emperor's dependence on his brother.[77]

Gratian's administration did not intend his brother to be seen as an equal partner in his rule of the west. The older emperor's ability to eclipse so completely his younger brother also implies that the demands made by the wielders of power who had originally promoted Valentinian II had been met, and that they had accordingly thrown their support behind Gratian and been content to abandon Valentinian II, his usefulness for the moment, and the immediate political crisis of Valentinian I's death, having passed. There could hardly be a firmer indication of this than the fact that even Merobaudes, who had been such a prime mover in Valentinian II's accession, in 376–7 was acting as Gratian's *magister militum* strengthening defences on the Rhine and

---

[72] Lenski (2002), 359.
[73] Sozomen 7.4.1.
[74] Williams (1995), 131.
[75] Ibid.
[76] Liebeschuetz (2005), 11–12, n. 1. Liebeschuetz suggests that Valentinian II and Justina lived at Sirmium until eastern Illyricum was ceded to Theodosius I in 379 as part of the Gothic war, and that the younger emperor and his mother then joined Gratian's court at Trier, but admits that we cannot be certain of this. The evidence of the coinage, with the unexpected difference of issues in Valentinian II's name produced at Sirmium noted above, suggest that the boy-emperor resided there for some time. Ammianus' indication that Gratian called his mother Severa back to court after Valentinian's death (AM 28.1.57) (she had been discarded in favour of Justina), also suggests that it would have made for a happier arrangement to have separate imperial households than to have both imperial mothers resident at the same court from 375. McLynn argues that Valentinian and his mother did not arrive in Milan from Sirmium until 381 when the western army under Gratian left Illyricum: McLynn (1994), 122.
[77] Williams (1995), 131. Pearce (1951), xxxviii–xxxix.

Danube, and in 377 shared the consulship with Gratian.[78] The abandonment of young Valentinian II by those responsible for his accession, so soon after the event, reflected the paradox of a 4-year-old emperor at this early stage in the development of child-emperor rule: for all the claims of his usefulness in maintaining the loyalty of troops on campaign to the Valentinian dynasty, the boy had been little more than a bargaining-tool.

The role of Merobaudes in the unexpected accession of Valentinian II struck an ominous note for the future of the western imperial office, foreshadowing the even more powerful positions of generals like Stilicho and Aetius in later child-emperor reigns, discussed in the following chapters.[79] Despite his usefulness in 375, however, young Valentinian II dwindled into an imperial redundancy almost as swiftly as he had been thrust into power, and in view of Gratian's marriage in 374 (thus even before Valentinian II was proclaimed) to Constantia, the daughter of Constantius II, he could hardly have been expected to be anything else.[80] With the young imperial couple looking forward to the prospect of heirs who would firmly unite the Valentinian line with that of Constantine, there can have been little place for the 4-year-old titular emperor in plans for the future.[81]

The role of Ausonius

Ausonius is a figure who has often been seen as crucial to the political reaction against Valentinian I's policies, and crucial also to Gratian's early relationship with the senate after 375.[82] The nature of Gratian's education and Ausonius' involvement in it will be discussed further in Chapter 4, but in the 360s, probably around the time of Gratian's elevation in 367, Ausonius, a distinguished Gallic professor of rhetoric, had been called to court by Valentinian I to act as tutor to Gratian.[83] By 375, Valentinian I had advanced Ausonius to the post of quaestor, and by the time of the emperor's death the former tutor was one of Gratian's oldest and most entrenched advisers. The honours which his former pupil would heap upon Ausonius after Valentinian I's death would far outstrip these already prestigious posts, and Ausonius himself celebrated

---

[78] Rodgers (1981), 90; *CLRE* 288–9. Merobaudes held a second consulship in 383, a signal honour for a *privatus* at this stage: O'Flynn (1983), 2–3; also Potter (2004), 545; *PLRE* 1. 599.

[79] Also McLynn (1994), 84.

[80] AM 29.6.7. Cf. McLynn (1994), 85. According to *PLRE* 31.10.6, Augustine records that Gratian and Constantia had a son, but the child predeceased his father (citing Augustine, *Civ.Dei* V.25; also Symm., *Rel.* 3.19; Theodoret, *HE* 5.12), but this is a mistake—it is only Gratian's little brother (i.e. Valentinian II) who is referred to here.

[81] McLynn (1994), 85.

[82] e.g. Matthews (1989), 211; Sivan (1993), 126; Alföldi (1952), 88; Bruggisser (1987), 135; *PLRE* 1. 140–1.

[83] Ausonius: *PLRE* 1. 140–1.

his illustrious appointments in his speech of 379.[84] Prior to his selection as consul for 379, Ausonius had been appointed Gratian's praetorian prefect for Gaul in 378, and Gratian's accession in 375 provided his former tutor with remarkable opportunities for him to make his own family, for a short while, the most powerful in the western empire.[85] The offices heaped upon Ausonius' family are numerous and have been listed many times—stretching from the appointment of his octogenarian father, Julius Ausonius, as *praefectus praetorio*, to Ausonius' son Hesperius' posting as proconsul of Africa, and his sister's grandson's as *comes rerum privatarum*.[86] Friends, too, were rewarded.[87]

If Ausonius' family thus represented the most powerful political faction in the west immediately following Gratian's accession to full power in late 375, the question then arises of what the tutor's role was in the coup which promoted Valentinian II and supposedly forced Gratian's hand in breaking with the policies of his father. Ausonius' transformation into a figure of political importance must have meant he was party, in some respects at least, to the coup, not in the sense of colluding in the acclamation of Valentinian II, but in seeing the value of peaceful overtures to the senate and demoting unpopular officials left over from Valentinian I's reign.[88] The correspondence between Ausonius and Symmachus reinforces the idea of Ausonius' willingness to promote senatorial interests with the young emperor, though any claim that Ausonius and Symmachus 'seized' the government in Gratian's name goes too far.[89] As events would soon prove, Ausonius was not 'in control' of the emperor, or if he was, it was a short-lived control that he could not maintain. Nevertheless, Ausonius' hand can be seen influencing Gratian's measures in favour of the senate, and the purge upon Valentinian I's death must also have increased Ausonius' political value as one of the few acceptable surviving representatives of continuity from the old government to the new, as well as reminding the public of Gratian's most publicized virtue: his excellent education.[90] It was a virtue which, interestingly, Valentinian I himself had emphasized (according to Ammianus) when commending his son to the army as their new Augustus, and which the late emperor's

---

[84] Ausonius, *Grat.Act.* 2; 3. See Hopkins (1961), 243.

[85] Sivan (1993), 118–19. *CLRE* 292–3. For Ausonius as prefect of Gaul, see e.g. *CTh.* 8.5.35 (20 Apr. 378).

[86] For Hesperius, AM 28.6.28; for Ausonius' great-nephew, see Alföldi (1952), 87. For details on the many appointments to Ausonius' family, see Jones (1964a), 1. 160; (1964b), 78; Matthews (1975), 69 ff.

[87] e.g. Gregorius Proculus and the historian Eutropius: Green (1991), xxx; Matthews (1975), 69 ff.

[88] Matthews (1975), 54–5.

[89] On the correspondence between Ausonius and Symmachus, see McLynn (1994), 86. For the claim that they 'seized' control of government: Alföldi (1952), 85.

[90] McLynn (1994), 86.

appointment of Ausonius would suggest a concern with; yet which seems curiously calculated to mark a departure from the sorts of skills Valentinian I himself had brought to the imperial office, and aimed rather at achieving the sort of relationship of equals with the senatorial elite that the late emperor had never seemed concerned with himself.

Scholars have questioned whether Gratian's replacement, under Ausonius' influence, of the professional bureaucrats of Valentinian I's government with men of an entirely different social and cultural background was detrimental to the young emperor's administration. Some have seen it as an ominous triumph 'of the attitudes and vested interests of propertied amateurism over the disinterested professionalism of the functionary class'.[91] Others note that Gratian's government was seen to have been 'colonized' by the aristocracy through Ausonius, and Gratian to be at the mercy of his advisers (as Ammianus suggested).[92] As will be explored in further detail in Chapter 4, the development of a largely self-running bureaucracy in the later empire makes it unlikely these appointments would have seriously affected the efficiency of Gratian's government: they were changes made to personnel in high posts, rather than replacements of the trained professionals who staffed the lower echelons of the bureaucracy.[93] Yet although in practical terms the ascendancy of Ausonius' supporters may not have harmed the administration, the way in which Gratian's regime was perceived may have been a different matter.[94] The domination of his government by Ausonius and the senatorial supporters of the coup promoting Valentinian II, involving the rise of a faction which had few allies in the military, always a key support-base of an emperor, posed a significant risk.[95] And as events would show, even the military support that Gratian's rule did have could not be relied upon.

Valentinian II's real accession and regime-building

The death of Gratian at the hands of the usurper Magnus Maximus in August 383 (discussed in Chapter 3) dramatically altered Valentinian II's situation, bringing about his real accession. It suddenly found him, after eight years in his elder brother's shadow, as the sole legitimate emperor of the western

---

[91] Matthews (1975), 76.

[92] McLynn (1994), 153–4. For similar verdicts on Ausonius, see: Drinkwater (1989a), 146; Alföldi (1952), 18–19; and Green (1991), xxix. Alföldi also sees Ausonius' hand in Gratian's edict of May 376 (CTh.13.3.11; 23 May 376) concerning the liberal pay of professors in Gaul: (1952), 87; see also Kaster (1984), 114.

[93] See below pp. 114–16; also Matthews (1975), 77.

[94] For the argument such appointments did not harm Gratian's administration: Green (1991), xxx.

[95] Sivan (1993), 122.

empire, and thus at the very least a powerful ideological, if not military, threat to the usurper's claims—and he was still only 12 years old. Perhaps surprisingly, since the defection of Gratian's army to the usurper must have left only a skeleton military force at his brother's disposal, a 'loyalist' court rapidly gathered around the child-emperor. The interests of the party which had originally promoted Valentinian II came once more to the fore: it was the active support of members of the senatorial aristocracy that would save Valentinian II from Magnus Maximus in 383.[96] It was very much in the interests of such powerful individuals to maintain an imperial court in Italy if they were to have any influence on the empire's politics, and it is at this point that Petronius Probus reappeared to take up his fourth term as praetorian prefect of Italy and Illyricum.[97] That Probus was entirely prepared to take advantage of his position of influence in the new child-emperor government is confirmed by a law of 26 October 383, informing him specifically that he was not entitled to enjoin anything upon the palatine offices.[98] But Probus was by no means the only distinguished senator to be enlisted in Valentinian II's cause: in the last months of 384; the great pagan senator Vettius Agorius Praetextatus, who had not held public office since 367–8, was appointed praetorian prefect in Italy.[99] Praetextatus was designated consul for 385, dying before he could assume office, but distinguished posts for other Roman aristocrats followed, including the appointment of Symmachus as urban prefect in 384.[100] The loyalist court around the child-emperor strengthened: Valentinian II was not bereft of supporters, however self-interested their motivation, and he could not simply be ignored.

Despite the odds, there was also some military support for Valentinian II. Although Merobaudes, Gratian's prize general, and the man principally credited by Ammianus with the decision to promote Valentinian II back in 375, had defected to Maximus, the Frankish officer Bauto emerged to lead Valentinian II's 'resistance' forces and became a mainstay of the boy-emperor's government.[101] Bauto had led western forces as *magister equitum* to campaign in the Gothic wars alongside Theodosius in 380 or 381, and may have been *comes per Illyricum* under Gratian, potentially providing him with opportunities to recruit troops in Valentinian's cause from Alans and Huns, as well as

---

[96] McLynn (1994), 159.

[97] Socrates 5.11; also Symmachus, *Ep.* 1.58.

[98] *CTh.* 6.30.6 (26 Oct. 383).

[99] Jones (1964*a*), 1. 160–1; *PLRE* 1. 722–4.

[100] On Praetextatus' appointment: *ILS* 1259; for his death, Symmachus, *Rel.* 11–12; Jerome, *Ep.* 23.3; and other aristocratic appointments: Matthews (1975), 179–80.

[101] McLynn (1994), 159–60; *PLRE* 1. 159–60. For discussion on the scholarly debate surrounding Merobaudes' defection, see below pp. 83–4, n. 79. Whether or not in fact Merobaudes did desert Gratian (and I subscribe to the view that he did) he certainly did not form a part of the resistance government of Valentinian II after Gratian's death.

the Goths who later formed a crucial part of Valentinian II's army.[102] He was made consul for 385, and a noteworthy measure of the extent of Bauto's influence—or at least the perception of his influence under Valentinian II—was Maximus' accusation (reported by Ambrose) that he sought the imperial power for himself through the figurehead of a child.[103] From the original 'committee' which had promoted the 4-year-old in 375, and returned to bolster his cause in 383, the running of the boy-emperor's government was increasingly coming to be dominated by a single, powerful military leader.

The anti-pagan measures instituted by Gratian in 382, discussed in Chapter 4, may be seen as an indication that by this time the clique which had prompted Gratian to institute so many measures in favour of the senate early in his reign was no longer so influential. After Gratian's death however, the political balance shifted once more. Valentinian II's fledgling regime was greatly in need of support, and conditions in 384 must have appeared highly favourable for a reopening of the issue of pagan privileges: as prefect of Rome Symmachus was the first pagan to hold the post for several years, at the same time as Praetextatus was praetorian prefect of Italy, and both consuls for the year 384 were pagans as well—Richomeres and Clearchus.[104] The two eastern consuls were presumably the choice of Theodosius I rather than of Valentinian II's administration, but alongside these other appointments presented a picture of receptiveness to paganism and pagan senators at the court of the child-emperor Valentinian II. It must have seemed the perfect opportunity for the pagan party to capitalize upon Valentinian II's need for their support and press to regain the liberties revoked by Gratian (witnessed most famously in the Altar of Victory debate, discussed further in Chapter 4), particularly given that Symmachus had been denied recently even an audience at court when petitioning for these privileges under Gratian.[105] It has been argued that this courting of the Roman aristocracy was an indication of the feebleness and instability of the boy-emperor's rule, with the claim that the stronger governments of Gratian and Valentinian I had felt able to deny such prestige to this group.[106] While this may be partly true, the move was also part of the necessary regime-building at the outset of any new reign, which Valentinian II's essentially was in 384, and which, although more urgent in these particular circumstances, had been even more notable when Gratian succeeded his father. It is also worth noting that the pagan senatorial contingent would approach both the usurper

---

[102] McLynn (1994), 160. Cf. O'Flynn (1983), 6.

[103] Ambrose, *Ep.* 30 [24]. 4: *ille Bauto, qui sibi regnum sub specie pueri vindicare voluit.*

[104] Birley (1983), 27; Also Green (1991), xxxi; *PLRE* 1. 765–6, 211–12. *CLRE* 302–3.

[105] On Gratian's removal of pagan privileges: Bloch (1945), 214. On the extent of these revocations, see discussion below, pp. 122–4, and Lizzi Testa (2007), 251–62; Cameron (2007b), 341–87, and now Cameron (2011), 34–56. On the refusal of an audience to Symmachus: Errington (2006), 125.

[106] Errington (2006), 125.

Eugenius and the emperor Theodosius regarding its privileges over the years to follow: the weak government of Valentinian II was hardly their only target. The Altar of Victory controversy can thus be seen as part of the power-broking taking place in the regime-building after Valentinian II's real accession of 383 as new political alliances were tentatively forged. But the pagan party had not reckoned on the uncompromising position of another power-broker: Bishop Ambrose.

The influence of Ambrose of Milan on the emperor Gratian's fulfilment of his religious role will be discussed below, as will his efforts to take up the position of Gratian's leading authority on orthodoxy.[107] With the death of the Nicene Gratian and the real accession of the homoean Valentinian II, Ambrose's position with regard to the imperial court necessarily changed.[108] In the mid-380s, just as earlier under Gratian, there are indications of Ambrose seeking to gain a firm foothold at court, both through his determined conduct during the Altar of Victory debate, as well as through the conflict of 385–6 over the basilicas of Milan, discussed below. Ambrose's actions in this conflict posed a threat to the child-emperor's plausible fulfilment of his religious function that his advisers could ill-afford: it was a highly damaging episode of Valentinian II's reign, exposing only the impotence of his government.[109] But the letters Ambrose wrote to the young emperor over the Altar of Victory also revealed his recognition of a new strategic factor to his advantage, through pointed references to the orthodoxy not only of Valentinian's father and brother, but also Theodosius I, and most dangerously of all, the usurper Magnus Maximus.[110] If the emperor was meant to be the guardian of true doctrine, but failed to fulfil this role through obstinate adherence to homoean doctrines, while a usurper espoused the true faith, did the legitimate emperor still have God's blessing? Events to follow would illustrate that Maximus too saw the benefit of exploiting this potential route to legitimacy. Yet the murder of Gratian and the very existence of Valentinian's court at Milan would long remain a thorn in Maximus' side, and a serious obstacle to him in the path to legitimation. And although, as we shall see, Ambrose's well-publicized actions in dealing with Valentinian II's homoean court at Milan did serious damage to

---

[107] McLynn (1994), 99.

[108] 'Homoean' Christianity was a moderate semi-Arian brand of belief, which agreed that Christ was 'like' the Father. For an excellent summary of the positions of various Christian semi-Arian and orthodox groups in the fourth century, see Lenski (2002), 235–7. See further below also, pp. 117–18 and n. 72.

[109] McLynn (1994), 170–1.

[110] Ambrose paints a scene of Gratian looking down from heaven on his brother, asking: *Quid mihi plus potuit meus hostis auferre? Abrogasti decreta mea, quod adhuc ille qui contra me levavit arma non fecit*; 'Of what more could my enemy have robbed me? You have abolished my decrees, which so far he who rebelled against me has not done'—i.e. even Maximus had not repealed Gratian's anti-pagan legislation: Ambrose, *Ep.* 72 (Maur. 17). 15. See also Errington (2006), 202; cf. Potter (2004), 562–3.

the young emperor's religious and ceremonial image, the bishop's undertaking of a first embassy to the court of Magnus Maximus on the child-emperor's behalf in autumn 383, and another in late 386, convincingly demonstrated that in the end his loyalty was to the legitimate emperor at Milan.[111]

When the circumstances and individuals involved in the accessions of the first of these late Roman child-emperors, Gratian and Valentinian II, are examined, the details which emerge make it clear that these accessions were not ultimately dependent on a triumph of the dynastic principle alone. The promotion of such young boys as Augusti was an unexpected development in fourth-century politics, and neither child-emperor's elevation—nor survival—as emperor, should be seen as a foregone conclusion. In each case, a specific political crisis prompted the succession of these boys as a novel solution, and it was a solution which powerful individuals among the military high command and the senatorial aristocracy of the west saw value in supporting. Yet as the decades to follow would show, these decisions presented attractive precedents for future generations of politicians and generals, and would in time have long-term repercussions for the nature and function of the imperial office itself.

---

[111] On the first embassy, see: Zosimus 4.37.3; Ambrose, *De ob. Val.* 28; Matthews (1975), 179. On the second: Ambrose, *De ob. Val.* 28; Also Paulinus, *VAmb.* 19; McLynn (1994), 217. See further below, p. 89, n. 109.

3

Long-term Success and Failure

> The elder of the princes, with so many wars in progress, is not equal to the task. The other, although he may be a most valiant man one day, is, however, still a child.[1]

In 367 and 375 two separate political crises had seen individuals with vested interests in the smooth running of the imperial government propel two young boys onto the western throne. Yet the business of the practical running of that government, ostensibly under the sole direction of Gratian and Valentinian II after 375, remained. Engineering their accessions had been a fraught business in itself, but it remained to be seen whether the regimes built around them could survive. The years following the death of Valentinian I and the acclamations of his sons would see their courts face numerous challenges, in the form of relations with adult eastern colleagues, extreme military crises, and the continued manoeuvring of different factions and individuals around the western throne, as the practicalities of child-emperor rule were played out.

GRATIAN

Gratian and Valens

Until 378, the emperor Valens, brother of Valentinian I, was co-emperor with his two nephews, the western emperors Gratian and Valentinian II. Valens had been promoted by Valentinian I as his eastern colleague shortly after his own accession in 364.[2] Throughout his brother's reign, Valens' authority was publicly portrayed as inferior to that of Valentinian I's: according to Ammianus, in making his brother his co-Augustus, Valentinian thereby had a lawful

---

[1] Pacatus, 11.5: *Principum senior in tanta bella non sufficit; alter, etsi futurus sit aliquando fortissimus, adhuc tamen parvus est.*
[2] AM 26.4.1.

partner in his power but one who was effectively a subordinate.[3] Ausonius tells
a similar story, envisaging the imperial college of the three Augusti after 367
as a sort of Holy Trinity, intimating that the two emperors Valentinian I had
created depended upon him and were below him in status.[4] Official propaganda even identified Valentinian I and Valens as senior and junior emperors
from 364, appending these titles to the army units that the two emperors
divided between themselves the same year, when they took on their respective
realms.[5] Valens' submission to Valentinian's seniority was most explicitly
spelled out in inscriptions describing Valens simply as the brother of the
western emperor, who was: 'greatest in all things.'[6] Yet, willing though he
had been to accept junior status beside his brother, there are indications that
Valens was less enthusiastic about accepting the 8-year-old Gratian as a full
imperial colleague, even during Valentinian I's lifetime. Surviving eastern
inscriptions refer to Gratian as 'the nephew of Valens', a description which
mirrored the 'brother of Valentinian' phrasing used to describe Valens' relation to his senior colleague, suggesting an attempt to create a hierarchy among
the imperial college. And as a form of passive resistance Valens appears
to have limited, although not prevented outright, the striking of coinage in
the east proclaiming Gratian's new position after 367.[7]

   The issue must have become even more thorny upon the death of Valentinian I, and the unsanctioned promotion of 4-year-old Valentinian II. Valentinian II's title at this time was essentially a hollow one, and the allotments of
land Zosimus claims were made to the new boy-emperor (of Italy, Africa,
and Illyricum), if they existed in any form at all, surely would have impacted
more on the authority of Gratian than that of the eastern emperor.[8] Yet
according to Eunapius, Valens was unhappy that his nephews had decided
to divide up the west between themselves without reference to him; though in
fact Gratian seems to have had little say in the business either.[9] After 375,
a number of coins and multiples bear the obverse legend: DN VALENS
MAX[imus] AUGUSTVS, echoing the paternalistic title Constantine I had

---

   [3] AM 26.4.3. Ammianus makes various other mentions of Valentinian I and Valens being
partners only in appearance (26.5.1) while Valentinian was clearly the superior (26.5.4). See also
RIC 9. xvii.
   [4] Ausonius, *Versus paschales* II.24–8; with Green (1991), 269–79; Green, however, identifies
the three emperors as Valentinian I, Gratian, and Valentinian II, which as McLynn (1994: 83,
n. 17) points out, cannot be correct since the younger Valentinian was never emperor during his
father's lifetime. See also Lenski (2002), 32.
   [5] Symm, *Or.* 1; Jord., *Get.* 131; Them., *Or.* 6.75b; see in greater detail on this point, Lenski
(2002), 33–4.
   [6] *AE* (1908), 178: Va]LENTEM FRATRE [m Valentiniani omnia] MAXIMI; see Lenski
(2002), 357.
   [7] On Gratian as nephew: as above: e.g. *AE* (1908), 178: NEPOTI VALENTI[S]; Lenski (2002),
357. On limiting the striking of eastern coinage: *RIC* 9. xviii.
   [8] Zosimus 4.19.2; 42.1–2.
   [9] Eunapius, frg. 42.

employed in order to distinguish himself from his sons half a century earlier.[10] Pictorial representations of the imperial college on coinage carried a similar message: one medal reverse shows Valens standing between the two boys, distinguished both by his height and a *nimbus* to indicate his elevated status.[11] Consular solidus issues for 376 or 378 similarly show Valens towering over his colleague Valentinian II, and sometimes simply omit the boy-emperor altogether.[12] Valens' attitude gives the distinct impression that he was not happy to accept either of his youthful nephews as equals in the imperial office. Yet there may be sense in which we need not see Valens' public attitude towards his western colleagues as entirely grudging: his depiction as senior Augustus with his nephews in junior, dependent positions, could also be interpreted as a warning that they were under his protection and could not be challenged without eastern retaliation. And in 376 and 378 Valens would share the consulship with his new child co-emperor Valentinian II, suggesting acceptance, even if with reluctance, of the boy's acclamation.[13]

Even if we consider that Valens' attitude towards his nephews, despite being intent on asserting his senior status, may also have been protective, the events leading up to the disaster of Adrianople do suggest an uneasy and to some extent uncooperative relationship between Valens and Gratian. Valens had previously been engaged in a three-year war with the Goths in the late 360s, and the renewal of conflict in the lead-up to his final battle had resulted from the collapse of the treaty of 369 and a flood of imperially sanctioned Gothic immigration into Roman territory in 376 which rapidly spiralled out of control.[14] In this more recent conflict, Valens had turned to his co-emperor Gratian a number of times for assistance.[15] Already in 377 Valens had requested western aid in dealing with the Gothic crisis, and first the general Frigeridus, and then Richomeres had been ordered to lead troops to join Valens and to take the field on Gratian's behalf.[16] Yet a previous request for assistance had only resulted in Gratian's government sending troops who were apparently too few and of poor quality, and, more seriously, the men Richomeres was supposed to be commanding had largely deserted, apparently at the instigation of the general Merobaudes, who allegedly thought that Gaul would suffer barbarian raiding if the troops left for the east, while the general Frigeridus feigned illness (Ammianus suggests) in order to avoid the conflict.[17] After the combined eastern and western Roman forces fought an inconclusive battle in midsummer 377 (at Ad Salices) with the Goths, resulting in heavy losses on both sides, Richomeres returned to Gratian with a request for further

---

[10] Lenski (2002), 358.
[11] *RIC* 9. 178.28; cf. Lenski (2002), 358.
[12] *Numismatic Chronicle* 150 (1990), pl. 23A; cf. Lenski (2002), 358.
[13] *CLRE* 286–7; 290–1.
[14] For details of Valens' first war against the Goths in the late 360s, see Lenski (2002), 127–37. On the conflict leading up to and including Adrianople, ibid. 320–67.
[15] AM 31.10.2–3.   [16] AM 31.7.3–4.   [17] AM 31.7.3–5.

reinforcements.[18] According to Zosimus the western emperors (which can only really mean Gratian) were reluctant to send troops because they did not view the crisis as particularly significant to the west.[19]

Despite these previous less helpful efforts, in 378 Gratian himself finally set out to lead the western field army to join with Valens in the hope of gaining a decisive victory over the Goths. Yet there was a distraction en route for the young emperor which would ultimately cost precious time: a diversion in the form of a side campaign against the Lentienses, an Alamannic group who attempted to take advantage of the movement of the western army by crossing the Rhine and raiding western territory in Raetia in February 378.[20] Ammianus tells the story of the campaign: that when Gratian heard of their activity, he recalled some Roman cohorts who had already been sent on into Pannonia, and then sent a force against the Lentienses under his generals Nannienus and Mallobaudes.[21] The generals were successful in defeating and driving back the raiders, but this was not enough for Gratian, who determined upon their utter destruction, and was bent upon pursuing them himself.[22] Gratian and his men followed the Lentienses into the mountains and spent some time slaughtering them—Ammianus remarks on Gratian's presence in the front ranks of the fighting.[23] When the barbarians attempted to flee again, the emperor and his men again pursued them, and the remaining Lentienses finally surrendered to the emperor, and were taken on as Roman recruits.[24]

Gratian's determination to gain complete victory over the Lentienses had involved months of delay in his journey to join his uncle in the east.[25] His campaign has been described as 'at best stubborn, at worse perverse', given the circumstances, and Ammianus' description of Gratian conducting this campaign with great energy and rapidity has been seen as ironic.[26] Yet if Ammianus is being ironic in his description, he hides it well, otherwise praising Gratian for a victory 'at once reasonable and profitable', as 'a young man of splendid character, eloquent, self-restrained, warlike, and merciful, and [who] was already on his way to rivalry with the most distinguished emperors while yet a comely down was creeping over his cheeks', and for his great courage in the midst of battle—surely a very traditional view of an emperor's military virtue, and not unlike the sort of praise Ammianus bestows on Julian.[27]

---

[18] AM 31.8.2.   [19] Zosimus 4.22.4.
[20] AM 31.10.2–4. See Lenski (2002), 365–6.   [21] AM 31.10.6.
[22] AM 31.10.11–12.   [23] AM 31.10.13–14.   [24] AM 31.10.15–17.
[25] Lenski points out that the *Theodosian Code* reveals Gratian still in winter quarters at Trier in April: *CTh.* 8.5.35 (20 Apr. 378); see Lenski (2002), 365–6.
[26] Lenski (2002), 365–6.
[27] AM 31.10.18: *praeclarae indolis adulescens, facundus et moderatus et bellicosus et clemens, ad aemulationem lectorum progrediens principum, dum etiam tum lanugo genis inserperet speciosa* . . . The quote does, however, end with Ammianus describing Gratian's intimates

It is easy to view Gratian's delay from the point of view of Valens, facing a far graver threat and anxiously awaiting his colleague's reinforcements, and with the benefit of hindsight, the looming disaster of Adrianople makes Gratian's decision to pursue a minor skirmish on the frontiers of the west look like madness. But it is worth, for a moment, considering the situation from Gratian's point of view also. The young emperor was now 19 years old, and in the flattering position of having aid requested of him by his senior colleague. Moreover, he was leading his army eastwards apparently without the presence of Merobaudes, who had dominated the western military since 375: here was a chance for Gratian himself to achieve a personal victory fighting alongside his own soldiers, and inspiring in them personal loyalty to himself through his feats of courage—we can hardly be surprised that he grasped eagerly at the opportunity.[28] In terms of the well-being of the empire in general, it might have been a short-sighted and selfish choice, but in terms of Gratian's personal standing and hope of establishing himself as a military leader to equal his father and with a personal following to rival Merobaudes, it was surely entirely understandable.

Explicable though Gratian's delay in joining Valens might have been from the younger emperor's point of view, it did not help his already uneasy relations with his uncle, and though potentially it improved his standing with his own army, he may also have aimed at outshining his uncle. Following his victory, Gratian began to move his troops and baggage eastwards, reaching Sirmium but remaining there for only four days, and though he continued on to Castra Martis, he was beset by illness en route, which slowed his progress further. He had also, apparently, sent on a letter to Valens, describing 'with what energy' he had overthrown the Alamanni.[29] Rivalry between Valens and Gratian has certainly been seen as contributing to the disaster at Adrianople, both by ancient and modern scholars: Ammianus writes that Valens was troubled by Gratian's defeat of the Lentienses, and was eager to achieve some glorious deed to equal his young nephew, 'whose valiant exploits consumed him with envy'.[30] Gratian's supporters were already exaggerating the significance of the victory, inflating the numbers of the Lentienses defeated by tens of thousands.[31] In another (or possibly the same) letter, sent on with

---

leading him astray. For similar descriptions of Julian's military prowess, see AM 16.2.11–13; 16.12.39–41.

[28] Merobaudes is not mentioned at all in Ammianus' account of this campaign—only Gratian's generals Nannienus and Mallobaudes are referred to (AM 31.10.6), and given Merobaudes' apparent great concern for the defence of Gaul, it seems most likely he remained there while Gratian led troops eastwards.

[29] AM 31.11.6: *qua industria superaverit Alamanos*; Lenski (2002), 366–7.

[30] AM 31.12.1. See also Lenski (2002), 366–7.

[31] Lenski (2002), 366. For the propaganda, see AM 31.10.5; cf. Ps.-Aurelius Victor 47.2; Jerome, *Chron.* s.a. 377; Orosius 7.33.8.

the western general Richomeres, Gratian urged his uncle to await his arrival and not rashly join battle without him.[32] But at the council meeting, Valens, eager to take the field and flattered by his courtiers into believing that he should do so and claim the victory before Gratian had a chance to share in it (not to mention being misinformed about Gothic numbers, an error that would soon be fatally revealed), decided to engage with the Goths without awaiting the arrival of his colleague.[33] Ammianus' opinion that Valens was spurred on by jealousy of his nephew's minor victory is clear; and how much more this victory may have rankled due to Gratian's youth, we can only imagine.

Adrianople and the advent of Theodosius

The battle of Adrianople, fought on 9 August 378, has been described as marking 'one of the most decisive moments of late Roman history'.[34] A great deal of scholarly attention has justly been paid to this momentous battle, and while the intricacies of the crisis leading up to this event in the east lie beyond the scope of this investigation, the battle and its aftermath nevertheless had serious repercussions for western imperial policies also. As relations between Valens and Gratian before the battle reveal, the western emperor's exploits and distractions en route to the east contributed to the disaster.[35] Valens chose to join battle without the support of the western army under Gratian: the result was a catastrophic defeat for the Romans, and Valens himself was killed, his body never recovered.[36] Gratian's delays had kept Valens waiting a considerable time (at least two months), facing a far more severe crisis than any minor skirmishes in which the western army had engaged upon their journey eastwards.[37] At the time of the battle, Gratian had still only reached Castra Martis, some 400 km from Adrianople, a distance equating to at least two weeks' marching time.[38] Aside from irritation over Gratian's attitude, it is possible Valens simply could afford to wait no longer.[39] Gratian continued

[32] AM 31.12.4–7.

[33] Ibid. See also Lenski (2002), 337–8, 366–7; Errington (1996a), 439–40.

[34] Matthews (1975), 88.

[35] For a full discussion of the battle and events leading up to it, see Lenski (2002), 320-367; also Halsall (2007), 165–80.

[36] For detail on the losses at Adrianople, see AM 31.12ff, who estimates that barely a third of the Roman forces survived. Heather estimates Valens probably had 15 000 men with him (and was expecting the same number from Gratian: (2005), 181. See also Zosimus 4.24.1–2.

[37] Following Lenski's analysis of the evidence, Valens established his camp at Melanthias in late May, and waited there a month and a half before moving to Adrianople at the end of July: Lenski (2002), 365–6.

[38] Although the distances armies could travel in a day varied, dependent upon the condition of roads and type of troops involved, the general consensus of modern studies is that a distance of 400 km could not have been covered in less than 14 days: see Vegetius, *Epit. rei militaris*, i, 9; Elton (1996), 244–5; Watson (1969), 54–5; Haldon (1999), 163–6.

[39] Lenski (2002), 365.

to march eastwards, but upon receiving news of Valens' death, withdrew with his army to Sirmium, and there followed a five-month period of uncertainty before decisions were made about the best way forward after this disaster, while Gratian legislated for both the eastern and western empires.[40]

In January 379, the general Theodosius was promoted to the rank of emperor of the east. According to Zosimus, Rufinus, and Socrates, Gratian recognized the need for a military man of mature age to deal with the barbarians and share the cares of government, thus choosing Theodosius.[41] This Theodosius was the son of a successful general of the same name, and the younger Theodosius had already in 374 achieved an honourable victory in battle himself against the Sarmatians, but upon his father's sudden fall from favour in 375 the son had withdrawn to his estates in Spain, and according to Theodoret it was thence that the imperial messengers fetched him in the autumn of 378, presumably at tremendous speed, to Illyricum (although it is possible he was already back in active service).[42] Theodosius had not, therefore, been involved in the humiliating Roman defeat at Adrianople; according to Themistius, Gratian, in making his choice, acted wisely and like one worthy of grey hairs rather than youth, in that 'he did not assume one of his nearest relations to be the best man, but rather the best man to be his nearest relation'.[43]

There has been a great deal of speculation in recent years concerning the manner of his accession, some arguing for his promotion by a court faction (since, despite his father's fall from grace, Theodosius did have relatives in office in 378), and others arguing for a military usurpation which forced the accession upon Gratian.[44] It may well be that the motivation for Theodosius' acclamation originated with his troops rather than the imperial administration. Given the scale of the Adrianople disaster, it could plausibly have seemed preferable to Gratian and his advisers to accept with as little fuss as possible a usurpation by a competent military leader not tarnished by association with the defeat, and to lend it a vague air of legitimacy rather than to launch a civil

---

[40] Matthews (1975), 91; McLynn (1994), 89–90.

[41] Zosimus 4.24.3–4; Rufinus 11.14; Socrates 5.2; Theodoret 5.6.

[42] For Theodosius' victory against the Sarmatians, see AM 29.6.15; Matthews (1975), 93. For his withdrawal to Spain, see McLynn (2005), 88. Matthews (1975), 91 and Errington (1996a), 453 argue he may have already been back in active service in 378. See also above p. 57 on the death of the elder Theodosius.

[43] Themistius, *Or.* 14, 182b: καὶ σοφῶς Γρατιανὸς καὶ πολιᾶς, οὐ νεότητος ἐπαξίως, ὅτι μὴ τὸν οἰκειότατον ἄριστον, ἀλλὰ τὸν ἄριστον ὑπέλαβεν οἰκειό τατον.

[44] For the argument of Theodosius' promotion by a court faction, see e.g. Alföldi (1952), 90 f.; Ehrhardt (1964), 2. Theodosius' relatives in office in 378 were Fl. Eucherius and Fl. Claudius Antonius: for details, see Errington (1996a), 448–9; (2006), 29. Though as McLynn points out, these relatives hardly seem to be sufficiently influential to have been able to engineer Theodosius' accession: McLynn (2005), 90. Most recently arguing for a usurpation, see McLynn (2005), 91–3. The idea of a military clique forcing the accession was also argued by Sivan (1993), 121 and (1996), 209. Supported by Barnes (1990), 162, and McLynn (1994), 90; Lenski (2002), however, disagrees: 137–8.

war against him at a time when this could hardly be contemplated.[45] It seems likely, given the naming of two westerners (Ausonius and Olybrius) as consuls for 379, that Gratian's administration did not originally envisage creating another Augustus when Theodosius was called to take up command of the Gothic war.[46] Yet the fact that in 380 Gratian's generals appear to have taken back control of the war from Theodosius indicates that the young emperor and his advisers were not so powerless as is sometimes suggested.[47]

It has been argued recently that, while Gratian may have been prepared to accept Theodosius' proclamation by his army, he had little interest in helping his new colleague deal with the Gothic crisis now that Theodosius had cast himself as the new emperor of the east.[48] There are, however, indications of some degree of cooperation between the courts at the outset of Theodosius' reign: the dioceses of Pannonia, Dacia, and Macedonia which made up the prefecture of Illyricum appear to have been transferred to Theodosius in 379, presumably to facilitate tax and recruitment for the Gothic war.[49] Additionally, the transfer of certain key personnel from Gratian's regime to that of Theodosius I also indicates amicable relations and awareness of the need for mutual support between the governments at this point. Theodosius' first eastern praetorian prefect was the western senator (and consul for 379) Olybrius, previously Gratian's praetorian prefect of Illyricum in 378.[50] His successors Fl. Neoterius and Florus were also westerners.[51] Gratian's government also supplied Theodosius I with military aid. It is not clear from the sources that Gratian himself was ever actively involved in the campaigning against the Goths between 379 and 382, although a number of scholars have assumed so, and particularly that he was associated with the peace negotiations in 382.[52] Yet it is known that in 380 or 381 Gratian had sent an army under his generals Bauto and Arbogast to support Theodosius I's campaign in

---

[45] McLynn paints a convincing picture of bored troops in winter quarters fomenting usurpation, drawing parallels with the usurpations of Julian in 360 and Magnentius in 350, both of whom were proclaimed by their armies in winter: McLynn (2005), 93.

[46] Potter (2004), 546.

[47] Heather and Moncur (2001), 259.

[48] McLynn (2005), 94.

[49] Errington places the transfer at the start of the new tax indiction for the year, i.e. on 1 September: (1996*b*), 1. Illyricum was returned to western control in 382 once a peace agreement was reached with the Goths: see ibid. 23–6. Followed by Kulikowski (2000*a*), 364–5 and n. 21. As Kulikowski observes, and as noted above, the assertion that a separate prefecture of Illyricum had been created as the realm of Valentinian II upon his accession appears to be merely a scholarly construct (of Grumel (1951), 11–12). Certainly Valentinian II played no part in the arrangements in 379.

[50] *PLRE* 1. 640–2.

[51] Errington (2006), 30–1; (1996*b*), 2. Also *PLRE* 1. 623, 367–8. Although McLynn argues that these men might have simply been whatever personnel Theodosius could 'scratch together' rather than the pick of Gratian's ministries: McLynn (2005), 94–5.

[52] e.g. Seeck (1919), 254–5 and Heather (1991), 171; argued against by Errington (1996*b*), 4–5.

Macedonia, as already noted, and that the western *comes rei militaris* Vitalian was also active in Illyricum in 380.[53] Ultimately, though it is difficult to assess whether or not Theodosius' accession was the result of usurpation or imperial appointment, in 379 and the few years afterwards, even if not prepared to join him personally in leading forces, Gratian's administration does appear to have offered the new emperor some practical aid in the Gothic war.[54]

The crushing Roman defeat at Adrianople marked a crucial test for the new institution of the child-emperor. Although it has been claimed that upon Valens' death it was clear that a new emperor must be chosen at once, this was not necessarily the case: there were still two Augusti living.[55] Gratian was now 19 years old, and could even boast some personal military success by 378, though Valentinian II was still only 7 years of age, and in fact the imperial administration did not choose a new emperor at once: it was almost five months before Theodosius' accession, whether by appointment or usurpation. The suggestion, made by some scholars, that Valentinian II could have been sent to Constantinople with trustworthy generals and advisers (including Theodosius) to act as eastern emperor while Gratian remained in the west should be viewed with caution, however.[56] Once again, such a suggestion crosses into the realm of an arrangement which would later become acceptable (and even this manifestation of power in the cases of Honorius and Arcadius was still almost twenty years off), but had not yet even been attempted, and the phenomenon of a child-emperor too young to exercise full imperial functions remained a novelty in the 370s.

In the end, a boy-emperor was simply not sufficient: it was not accepted, at least as yet, as a satisfactory arrangement in the event of such a dire situation. Ultimately, a powerful and popular general, of exactly the sort of character the coup surrounding the accession of Valentinian II had sought to prevent coming to power, was seen as necessary: the extent of the military crisis following Adrianople called for a commander, not a child, whatever his promising qualities. As a competent military leader who had not been involved in Adrianople, and who was, furthermore, the son of a highly successful general, Theodosius was a promising candidate if the court was

---

[53] Zosimus 4.33.1; 4.34.1; see Errington (1996*b*), 3.

[54] McLynn argues, in contrast, that Gratian, though prepared to accept the accession as a *fait accompli*, would not strike a blow to assist Theodosius, thus condemning him to a series of embarrassing defeats in the first year of his reign (2005: 94), yet the transfer of the prefecture of Illyricum to Theodosius was a major practical effort in assisting the pursuit of the Gothic war by the eastern emperor; one which might, indeed, have been of considerable assistance if offered to Valens before 378.

[55] For such a claim: Matthews (1975), 91. Errington points out it was not in fact constitution-ally necessary to appoint a new emperor: Errington (2006), 28. See also McLynn (2005), 93.

[56] Errington (1996*a*), 450; Sivan (1996), 200; Errington (2006), 28.

looking for one. Overall, the aftermath of Adrianople saw the institution of child-emperor rule tried and found wanting.

The accession of Theodosius also marked a change in the focus of Gratian's court. The influence of Ausonius was waning, even as he was writing his gushing hymn of thanks to Gratian for his consulship of 379: the urgent activity surrounding Adrianople and the accession of Theodosius took place at Sirmium, while Ausonius was far away at Trier, playing no discernible part in the developments. The time for being applauded by his former tutor for his literary accomplishments and youthful promise had passed: the child-turned-adult emperor Gratian had far more important matters to attend to now.[57]

Gratian and Theodosius

Theodosius' first tasks as military leader of the east were to rebuild the army and subdue the Goths.[58] The new emperor was in his thirties, and with a solid military career already behind him, may have been unwilling from the start to accept Gratian as an equal, still less as a senior, colleague.[59] One of the ways in which we may gain a sense of relations between the two emperors, aside from in military and administrative matters as discussed above, is through the religious politics of their respective realms. Gratian's early religious policies will be discussed in more detail below, but at the outset of his reign, and certainly immediately after Adrianople also, he had promoted tolerance. In contrast, in February 380, Theodosius issued his edict *cunctos populos*, declaring that all people under his rule were to conform strictly to the western orthodoxy exemplified by Damasus of Rome and Peter of Alexandria.[60] Theodosius' pro-Nicene stance from the outset of his reign has often been attributed to his Spanish background, seen as a provincial import which influenced his belief in staunch orthodoxy, yet this view also has been disputed in recent years.[61] Theodosius' years of military service under the Nicene Valentinian I probably also played a role, and most likely it was a combination of influences from the army and his provincial origins which shaped his outlook.[62]

Although Theodosius' law of February 380 marked the new emperor's first statement of his own religious preference, the extent of Theodosius' understanding of the niceties of current theological controversy in the east, and the

---

[57] Matthews (1975), 96–8.   [58] Heather and Moncur (2001), 212.
[59] Ibid. 213; Pearce (1951), xix–xx.
[60] *CTh.* 16.1.2 (27 Feb. 380); Matthews (1975), 121–2; McLynn (1994), 106.
[61] McLynn (2005), 78.
[62] See McLynn (1994), 106–7, who points out that the Nicene Valentinian I was known for his refusal to become embroiled in religious politics.

degree to which the new emperor was influenced by orthodox lobbyists at Thessalonica, where he was based at the time, have been questioned recently.[63] Nevertheless, even if the motivation for Theodosius' law had come as the response to a petition from the orthodox Bishop Acholius of Thessalonica rather than prompted by the emperor himself, its firmly pro-Nicene tone marked a clear departure from Gratian's attitude towards religious politics, demonstrated by the edict of toleration he had issued in the aftermath of Adrianople (discussed further below). And Theodosius' baptism in autumn 380 (performed by Acholius) following a serious illness may also have been intended as a further advertisement of his own piety—and divine blessing of his rule in his survival.[64]

Theodosius' law of 380 may be interpreted as deliberately calculated to mark the eastern emperor's religious policies out as distinct from Gratian's, yet it is the apparent sabotage by Theodosius of his colleague's plans for a church council at Aquileia in the early 380s which most clearly suggests an element of antagonism between the two courts. In the summer of 380, Gratian had announced plans for the general council, to which bishops of both the eastern and western empires were invited.[65] But by the time the council was finally held at Aquileia in September of 381, Theodosius had already held a council at Constantinople, to which he had invited 150 eastern bishops, none of whom consequently travelled to Aquileia for the council planned by Gratian.[66] There is nothing to indicate that the two councils were planned as collaborative efforts, and it is very likely that Theodosius' hard-line orthodox position was undermining—perhaps deliberately—the more tolerant attitude adopted by Gratian's administration early in his reign.[67] Gratian was forced to revise his plans and scale back his council, with the face-saving help of Ambrose of Milan (who had his own agenda, which he then proceeded to impose on the meeting at Aquileia).[68] In part this situation may have been a reflection of the difficulties of trying to coordinate the rule of a divided empire; but

[63] McLynn (2005), 86–7. Additionally, if Theodosius' accession had been somewhat less than legitimate, he will have been all the more open to influential lobbyists early in his reign: ibid. 94. See also on the circumstances in which the law was issued: Ayres (2004), 251.

[64] McLynn (1994), 109–10. Also Ayres (2004), 251. Gratian had apparently been baptized by the time of his death in 383, but we do not know the circumstances in which this occurred: Ambrose, *De ob. Val.* 54, 75–6.

[65] McLynn (1994), 111–12.

[66] Theodosius' conference is foreshadowed by *CTh.* 16.5.6 (10 Jan. 381); see further McLynn (1994), 124.

[67] McLynn (1994), 124; also Williams (1995), 164. As Ayres points out, it seems bishops at Aquileia were in fact unhappy about some of the decisions at Constantinople, again suggesting little unity in the doctrinal purpose of the eastern and western councils: Ayres (2004), 266.

[68] McLynn (1994), 124–5. For a detailed analysis of the proceedings of Aquileia, see ibid. 124–37; also Ayres (2004), 265–6; and Gryson (1980) 121–43. On the council of Constantinople in 381, see Ayres (2004), 253–60. McLynn represents Ambrose's efforts as the bishop stepping in to help Gratian save face as Theodosius demonstrated the western emperor's impotence: (1991), 71.

Theodosius' actions were deeply embarrassing for Gratian, and suggest at the very least inadequate communications between the two courts.[69]

The independent religious policies of the two courts, along with other areas of disagreement (such as over the precedence of consuls in 381 and 382), reveal uneasy relations between Gratian and Theodosius, but we do not know that they necessarily had anything to do with Gratian's age.[70] Theodosius might have resented a supposedly 'senior' colleague who was still only in his early twenties (not to mention the even younger, but still technically senior, Valentinian II), but it might be argued that his behaviour in seeking to establish himself may have been little different if Gratian had been ten years older, particularly if Gratian's administration had been implicated in some way in the execution of Theodosius' father in 375. Yet some comments in the orations of the eastern court poet Themistius do reflect a consciousness of Gratian's youth and some ambivalence about the younger emperor claiming seniority over the elder. In *Oration 14*, probably delivered (to an eastern audience) in mid-379, for example, Themistius declares to Theodosius, that:

Gratian had no qualms about your age when he beheld your virtue, nor did he reckon that as a younger man he was going to crown his elder, thinking rather that a father chosen with judgement is superior to a natural sire. Both men share equal praise, the one for proclaiming his elder, the other because being older he was entrusted with a son's good-will.[71]

Later in the same oration, Themistius describes 'the young man' (Gratian) and Theodosius as sharing in a single purpose, like 'an imperial chariot team', while Valentinian II is merely 'the outrunner'.[72] Even at this very early point in Theodosius' reign, his panegyrist is attempting to cast him as a father-figure to Gratian.

Only a few years later, however, Themistius' *Oration 16* provides a more striking picture of difficult relations between the two emperors. Delivered in January 383 at a major consular ceremony before the senate of Constantinople,

---

[69] McLynn (1994), 124. And as McLynn also points out, the case of the Egyptian Maximus, proclaimed bishop of Constantinople and then rejected by Theodosius, later found applying to Gratian at Milan, reflects the fact that the two imperial courts, far from being united in purpose, were operating essentially as separate spheres of patronage and appeal: ibid. 110–11.

[70] The eastern consul of 381 was Theodosius' uncle Eucherius, and in 382 his cousin Antonius; for details of the dispute see McLynn (2005), 95–6.

[71] Themistius, *Or. 14*, 182b–183a: διδοὺς γὰρ τιμὴν προσλαμβάνει κοινωνίαν φροντίδων. διὰ τοῦτό τοι Γρατιανὸς τὴν ἀρετὴν ὁρῶν οὐχ ὑπείδετο ἡλικίαν, οὐδὲ ὅτι νεώτερος πρεσβύτερον ἀναδήσει λελόγισται, ἀλλ' ὅτι καλλίων ἐστὶ πατὴρ τοῦ τῇ φύσει γεννῶντος ὁ τῇ γνώμῃ προαιρούμενος. καὶ ἀμφοῖν ἴσος ὁ ἔπαινος, τοῦ μέν, ὅτι πρεσβύτερον ἀνεῖπε, τοῦ δέ, ὅτι πρεσβύτερος ὢν παιδὸς εὔνοιαν ἕξειν ἐπιστεύθη. On the dating of the speech, see Heather and Moncur (2001), 218.

[72] Themistius, *Or. 14*, 198c.

Oration 16 does not attempt to cast Theodosius in a father-figure guise towards his western colleagues; rather, it simply does its best to ignore them altogether—Gratian appears only as the herald of God who proclaimed on earth the decision made in heaven to raise Theodosius to the purple.[73] Two weeks after this oration was delivered, Theodosius proclaimed as co-Augustus his 5-year-old son Arcadius, certainly without reference to Gratian.[74] The child Arcadius' accession marked the third such child-emperor acclamation in less than twenty years. For Gratian's part, he never accepted Arcadius' elevation or advertised the promotion on his coinage.[75] While the difficulties of Theodosius' position—coming to the embattled eastern throne following the disaster of Adrianople—must have coloured his relations with Gratian, as well as his own need to establish himself, by 383, when the high point of the Gothic crisis had passed, we might have expected imperial relations to have become more (rather than less) cordial.[76] Yet in effect, Theodosius' actions amounted to a declaration of independence, and his abandonment of his western colleague left Gratian more vulnerable to attack.[77]

The usurpation of Magnus Maximus

In Britain, in the summer of 383, the commander of the troops stationed there, Magnus Maximus, was acclaimed Augustus, crossed the Channel, and established himself and his army near Paris. Gratian's army met with that of the usurper some time in June, and the two forces apparently skirmished for five days,[78] until Gratian's influential general Merobaudes deserted to Maximus, taking with him almost the entire western army.[79] The emperor attempted

---

[73] Themistius, *Or*.16, 207b; Heather and Moncur (2001), 214, and 212 on the dating of the speech.

[74] Heather and Moncur (2001) 214. The accession is surely foreshadowed by Themistius' praise of Theodosius not taking the consulship for the year either for himself or for his son, unlike other recent emperors, Themistius observes, who had clothed their sons in the purple-edged toga of a consul, as a precursor to their future reigns: Themistius, *Or*. 16.204c–d. See Heather and Moncur (2001), 271, n. 217.

[75] *RIC* 9. xx; McLynn (1994), 154.

[76] For the argument that Theodosius' attitude stemmed from his need to establish himself: McLynn (1994),109.

[77] *RIC* 9. xx; McLynn (1994), 154.

[78] Zosimus 4.35.3–6. Gratian's last recorded piece of legislation is *CTh*. 1.3.1. (issued 16 June, Verona). McLynn (1994), 154; also Matthews (1975), 173.

[79] The issue of Merobaudes' defection has been a matter of some debate among scholars, due to an apparently favourable mention by Pacatus in 389 (28.4–5), and an inscription which seems to refer to a third consulship for him in 388 (*ICUR* n.s. 2.5996), which, as Bagnall *et al.* point out (*CLRE* 650–7), would have been unheard-of for a *privatus* at this point. Yet Prosper clearly states his defection (Prosper 1183), Gratian is securely attested as having been deserted by his own army (e.g. Jerome, *Ep*. 60.15) and Merobaudes was certainly not among the loyalist camp which developed around Valentinian II following Gratian's death. For the arguments in favour of his

to flee with the remainder of his forces, but Andragathias, Maximus' *magister equitum*, pursued and slew the emperor on 25 August 383.[80] The ancient sources have reported various reasons for Gratian's downfall. After an apparently golden beginning as the hope of the state in 367, Ammianus' verdict was that this young man of splendid character and great promise was led astray after his father's death, by his evil advisers and the indulgence of his intimates.[81] At the very least, such stories indicate a general view that the young emperor was too easily influenced by those around him.

This one-time child-emperor's rule was not helped by his colleague Theodosius' apparent sabotage of Gratian's religious initiatives and public disregard for Gratian's authority, and indeed seniority, revealed most embarrassingly by his entirely independent appointment of Arcadius as co-emperor.[82] But ultimately Gratian's failure was a political failure in the west: clearly he had not succeeded in winning and maintaining the loyalty of his military. His recruitment of Alan troops, a large group of foreigners not traditionally part of the western forces, is an interesting moment in his path towards downfall, and may have signified his intention, at the age of 24, to begin to build an army with more personal loyalty to himself and to break free from the Gallic domination of his military.[83] According to Zosimus,

> Trusting those courtiers who make a practice of corrupting rulers' characters, he took in some Alan deserters, enrolled them in the army, and rewarded them with lavish gifts; indeed, he considered them worthy of being entrusted with the most important tasks, to the neglect of the other soldiers. This bred a hatred of the emperor in his soldiers, which slowly smouldering and growing, incited them, especially those in the British islands who were the most stubborn and violent, to revolt.[84]

---

defection, see: Rodgers (1981), 103; Nixon and Rodgers (1994), 477–8, n. 79; *CLRE* 650–2. For the argument against: Barnes (1975), 159–60.

[80] Zosimus 4.35.3–6. Also Rufinus 11.14; Socrates 5.11; Jerome, *Ep.* 60.15. Reports of the exact manner of his death vary, from his being treacherously slain at a banquet to being caught and killed on a bridge (Zosimus 4.35.6; Socrates 5.11.7–8; Sozomen 7.13.8–9, for discussion, see Dudden (1935), 1. 221). See also Cameron (2007*b*), 346.

[81] AM 31.10.18.

[82] McLynn (1994), 154.

[83] Ibid. 153; Heather and Moncur (2001), 259.

[84] Zosimus 4.35.2–3: Τῶν δὲ κατὰ Θρᾴκην ἐν τούτοις ὄντων, οὐ μέτριαί τινες, οὐδὲ οἷαι διαφέρειν εὐκόλως, τὸν Γρατιανὸν περιίσταντο τύχαι· τοῖς γὰρ περὶ τὴν αὐλὴν τὰ τῶν αὐτοκρατόρων ἤθη διαφθείρειν εἰωθόσι πειθόμενος, Ἀλανούς τινας αὐτομόλους δεξάμενος καὶ στρατιαῖς ἐγκαταλέξας δωρεαῖς τε ἁδραῖς ἐτίμα καὶ θαρρεῖν ἠξίου τὰ πάντων ἀναγκαιότατα, στρατιωτῶν λόγον ὀλίγον ποιούμενος. Τοῦτο τοῖς στρατιώταις κατὰ τοῦ βασιλέως ἔτεκε μῖσος, ὅπερ ὑποτυφόμενον κατὰ βραχὺ καὶ αὐξανόμενον εἰς νεωτέρων πραγμάτων ἐκίνησε τοὺς στρατιώτας ἐπιθυμίαν, τούς τε ἄλλους καὶ κατ᾽ ἐξαίρετον τοὺς ταῖς Βρεττανικαῖς νήσοις ἐνιδρυμένους οἷα τῶν ἄλλων ἁπάντων πλέον αὐθαδείᾳ καὶ θυμῷ νικωμένους· ἐκίνει δὲ πρὸς τοῦτο πλέον αὐτοὺς Μάξιμος Ἴβηρ τὸ γένος, Θεοδοσίῳ τῷ βασιλεῖ κατὰ τὴν Βρεττανίαν συστρατευσάμενος. This issue is discussed further in Chapter 4, p. 113.

Although Zosimus puts Gratian's recruitment of these Alans down to the ill-intentioned advice of bad advisers, the claim that he entrusted them with 'the most important tasks' suggests Gratian was recruiting them as his bodyguard, and separating them out from the troops who had served under his generals. Ammianus' account of Gratian's campaign against the Lentienses, five years earlier, did suggest that the young emperor had the potential to be an inspiring military commander, given the opportunity. At the same time, this importing and favouring of foreign soldiers also revealed Gratian's lack of understanding of how to maintain the support of existing power-players within his military.

The domination of Gratian's regime by Gallic interests—which, as we have already seen, had been powerful enough even to recall troops dispatched eastwards by the emperor in the late 370s to the defence of Gaul—was something from which the young emperor's administration would never free itself.[85] Yet upheavals caused by the collapse of the Danube frontier and the movement of Gratian's court from Trier to Milan in 381 set off new tensions and also provided opportunities for powerful lobbyists—from the Roman senate to the bishop of Milan—to gain access to the emperor more frequently.[86] Reports from the sources that Gratian was at the mercy of his advisers might well relate especially to this move to Milan—the more frequent contacts, for example, of the senator Symmachus with the imperial court from this time onwards hint at the greater frequency and complexity of relations with influential aristocrats from Rome which resulted from the resettlement of the court in northern Italy.[87] At the same time as Italian aristocrats were gaining greater access to the court, however, the access of Gallic elites—senatorial and military—had been lessened by Gratian's move from Trier to Milan. Gaul had grown used to the presence of a campaigning emperor once more through the reign of Valentinian I, and the court's departure in all likelihood resulted in Gallic feelings of neglect accompanied by a local receptiveness to the usurping regime of Maximus.[88]

The usurpation of Magnus Maximus itself indicated a growing separation between the needs and interests of the military and the provinces, and those of the imperial court. Approximately thirty years earlier, another rebellion of a general (Magnentius) against a youthful emperor (Constans, then aged in his early twenties) had taken place in similar circumstances, when conflict with the eastern emperor left his young western colleague vulnerable to attack.[89] Theodosius I's public disregard for Gratian's authority made the situation all the more ripe for a repeat of such a military rebellion. If the rule of child-emperors was to continue to develop, this sort of weakness of an adult co-emperor refusing to accept a younger colleague as an equal would have to be

---

[85] McLynn (1994), 88, 153.   [86] Ibid. 119–20.
[87] Ibid. 120, 153–4.   [88] Errington (2006), 31, 33.
[89] Frakes (2006), 98–101.

addressed in the reigns to follow, as would the issue of whether a child-emperor upon reaching adulthood could ever truly claim the supreme leadership of his armies from his generals. And first and foremost, Theodosius' interest in supporting the highly vulnerable Valentinian II after Gratian's death, would decide the immediate future of the west.

VALENTINIAN II

Valentinian II, Theodosius, and Magnus Maximus

The death of Gratian brought on the real accession of the then 12-year-old Valentinian II, with the loyalist court described in Chapter 2. The usurper Magnus Maximus did not push on immediately to Italy but remained for the moment in Gaul, establishing himself at Gratian's former capital of Trier, in a move clearly aimed both at asserting his legitimacy and winning local support, while the remnants of Gratian's court regrouped around Valentinian II at Milan.[90] The advisers gathered around the boy-emperor must inevitably have looked towards Theodosius for some demonstration of support at this point, but the emperor of the east was slow to act, although there is no evidence of any conspiracy between Theodosius and Maximus.[91] Many scholars have suggested that Theodosius might well have viewed the usurpation with favour, and certainly that Maximus expected his support, given their shared Spanish origin and military links.[92] Theodosius' attitude towards advancement of his own family as the imperial dynasty, expressed so recently in his elevation of Arcadius, and his disregard for Gratian's authority, make it highly unlikely the eastern emperor would have wished to replace the young western emperor with a more militarily formidable colleague, or that he genuinely would have welcomed the rebellion.[93] Until 387 Theodosius I was much occupied with

---

[90] Palanque (1929), 36.

[91] According to Themistius, they were calling upon Theodosius to: 'avenge the monarch slain in his youth, and to save the only survivor of the dynasty' (Themistius, *Or.* 18, 220d). See Matthews (1975), 176.

[92] e.g. Potter (2006), 550–1.

[93] Errington (2006), 33. Cf. Kulikowski (2000*a*), 365; *RIC* 9. xxii. Even if, as some have suggested, he did blame the house of Valentinian for his father's death: see Williams (1995), 197, 199. In fact, as Barnes has argued, Theodosius may have planned an early campaign against the usurper in 383, which then had to be abandoned due to military concerns closer to home: Barnes (2000), 295–6, on the basis of Themistius, *Or.* 18.220d. Vera (1975), 265–301 argues that Theodosius did in fact lead an expedition to the west in 384, relying on an eastern law apparently issued from Verona in August of 384, but as Seeck and Matthews (Seeck (1919), 265; Matthews (1975), 178, n. 2) demonstrate, Verona should be amended to Beroeae, as from May to September of 384 Theodosius' presence is attested at Heraclea on the Sea of Marmara. Cf. also Errington (2006), 32; Williams (1995), 200.

more direct threats to eastern security (see below), which explains his not having taken decisive action against Magnus Maximus before this point.[94]

Yet Valentinian's supporters were influential men, however self-interested their motives, and they were looking to Theodosius for support and assistance: in 384, Symmachus would write to thank Theodosius for help provided during a crisis in supplies at Rome and also to report the senate's erection of a statue to the elder Theodosius.[95] And other allies of Valentinian's court, like Ambrose, certainly wanted to cast the eastern emperor in the role of a father-figure: during the Altar of Victory crisis, Ambrose called upon the boy-emperor to refer the matter 'to the father of your Piety, the *princeps* Theodosius', whom he consulted in all matters of great importance.[96] Theodosius could not ignore Valentinian's loyalist court forever.[97] In 384 an uneasy agreement seems to have been reached between Theodosius and Maximus' envoys, which both supported Valentinian's position and allowed Theodosius to continue dealing with eastern concerns, namely that Maximus would be recognized as an imperial colleague if he allowed Valentinian II to maintain the territories of Italy, Africa, and Illyricum, and did not insist on the boy joining him at his court.[98]

In 386, as Theodosius I was engaged in negotiations with Persia over Armenia, an invasion of the Greuthungi in Thrace further complicated the situation, and the eastern emperor extended greater recognition to Maximus.[99] The very existence of Valentinian II's regime continued to rely upon its convenience to others, and in some sense, its inconvenience to Magnus Maximus, an unwelcome flaw in his image of cobbled-together legitimacy, and a constant reminder of the ideological superiority that the governments of his sometime opponents/sometime colleagues could claim.[100] The presence of the eastern general Timasius at Milan in 386–7 must have been intended as a warning to Maximus, as well as a sign of support for Valentinian—even if it also emphasized the weakness of the boy-emperor's position and his need for external support.[101] And—if we take Ambrose's word for it—the court of Magnus Maximus was unhappily aware that Valentinian's supporters were

---

[94] See Matthews (1975), 178.

[95] Symmachus, *Rel.* 9; see Vera (1979), 381–403; McLynn (1994), 168. On western appeals to Theodosius, see Themistius, *Or.* 18.220d.

[96] Ambrose, *Ep.* 72 (Maur. 17).12: *Certe refer ad parentum pietatis tuae, principem Theodosium, quem super omnibus fere maioribus causis consulere consuesti.*

[97] McLynn (1994), 163.

[98] Matthews (1975), 178. McLynn (1994), 164; Burns (1994), 93; Errington (2006), 33–4.

[99] Zosimus 4.38-40; Matthews (1975), 178–9; recognition of Maximus' prefect Evodius most clearly reflects the accommodation: *CTh.* 2.33.2 (25 Oct. 386); 3.4.1 (29 June 386); 8.5.48 (4 Mar. 386); 9.44.1 (6 July 386); see also Vera (1975), 270–1.

[100] McLynn (1994), 164.

[101] See Symmachus, *Ep.* 3.72–3 for indications of Timasius' power in the western government; cf. McLynn (1994), 218.

looking to Theodosius for assistance.[102] Yet Valentinian himself clearly did retain a potent symbolic value that was not lost on those around the throne; even if the unhappy young Augustine was thoroughly disillusioned by the task which was assigned to him as rhetor to the boy-emperor's court in 384, complaining of having had to tell lies in praising the supposedly valiant deeds of a child-emperor before an audience who knew the truth.[103]

For Maximus, as long as there was the chance the young emperor might be brought into his power, there was a hope he might thereby lend the usurper some of the legitimacy his regime lacked.[104] For the Roman aristocrats, and for Ambrose, the boy-emperor's regime was worth preserving in the interests of the influence it allowed them to exert through proximity to the government. And for Theodosius, it was desirable both to have a divided west and a weak western colleague, who could not threaten his own position while his attention was needed elsewhere, and indeed, who could be ultimately dependent upon him for survival. The ineffectiveness of Valentinian II's government remained a major part of its appeal for those supporting it.[105]

Theodosius and the restoration of Valentinian II

Besides posing a severe military threat to Valentinian II's position, Magnus Maximus was also threatening Valentinian's religious and ceremonial role, through his self-appointed position as the champion of orthodoxy in the west. As will be discussed in Chapter 4, the conflict between the homoean court of Valentinian II and Ambrose in 385–6 severely threatened the vital ceremonial and religious function of the young emperor. But still more worryingly, news of events at Milan had reached Maximus in Gaul also, and an extant letter dating from 386, written by the usurper and seemingly widely circulated in Italy (surely deliberately), addressed these matters with blatant threats against the boy-ruler, who was accused of plotting not only against the churches of God, but against God himself.[106] Maximus told Valentinian II that he was courting disaster and urged him to mend his ways, while the usurper set himself up as the champion of orthodoxy—and thus also of legitimacy. This was a dangerous claim indeed against the young emperor, and echoed

[102] Ambrose, *Ep.* 30 (Maur. 24), 11.
[103] Augustine, *Conf.* 6.6.9: *cum pararem recitare imperatori laudes, quibus plura mentirer, et mentienti faverentur ab scientibus*; As McLynn points out, unlike Claudian a decade later, who found his patron in Stilicho, Augustine's discontent was probably partly to do with the shifting balance of power at Milan under Valentinian II, and the 'father-figure' of the young emperor reposing in the absent Theodosius I: McLynn (1994), 170.
[104] McLynn (1994), 158; Matthews (1975), 176.
[105] McLynn (1994), 165.
[106] *Coll.Avell.* 39. See also Barnes (2000), 296–7; Williams (1995), 216–17.

Ambrose's comments several years earlier during the Altar of Victory debate, that not even the usurper who had killed Gratian had given way to the pagans and overturned Gratian's religious edicts.[107] The controversial religious stance of Valentinian II's court gave the usurper a moral advantage (even though he had murdered a legitimate orthodox emperor!), and if confirmation of God's blessing for the Nicene cause rather than the homoean were needed, it was surely found in the dramatic discovery by Ambrose of the remains of the martyrs Gervasius and Protasius in Milan itself, under the nose of the homoean court and following the struggle for the basilicas in 385/6.[108]

It was in this climate of Maximus' self-righteous threats and the Nicene triumphalism of Ambrose's successes that Ambrose himself was asked to undertake a second embassy to the usurper's court, on behalf of Valentinian II's government.[109] The bishop's willingness to represent Valentinian II's cause (despite his doctrinal differences with the court) against the orthodox usurper, is a vital reminder of the priorities of the supporters (pagan and Christian) gathered around the child-emperor at this point: access to government remained the paramount concern.[110] While the bishop's embassies reflected a need to try to present a united front at Milan, and he may have needed some powerful persuading to act on behalf of the homoean court, he would also use his services to the young emperor to his own ends and to exalt his connections to the imperial house. In his funeral oration for Valentinian, delivered in 391, Ambrose recalled that in acting as an envoy he had taken the emperor up 'as a small boy' entrusted to him by his mother.[111] The bishop may be recalling a genuine incident here, when the palace made an emotive appeal for help to Ambrose, using the child Valentinian's youth as a powerful tool in securing the bishop's aid.[112] And, according to Ambrose, on his second embassy to Maximus he in turn employed the youth of Valentinian as a useful excuse: when defending himself to the usurper, Ambrose recalled how Maximus had demanded on his previous embassy that the boy-emperor ought to come to join him at Trier 'as a son to his father'; Ambrose had replied

---

[107] Williams (1995), 202.

[108] Paulinus, *VAmb.* 15–16.

[109] Ambrose's first embassy took place in late autumn 383: McLynn (1994), 161–3. Ambrose reports on his second embassy in *Ep.* 30 [24]. Estimated dates for this embassy have ranged from 384 to 387. Matthews (1975), 180 and McLynn (1994), 217 argue for 385/6. Williams argues for summer/autumn 386 (1995), 223–4.

[110] McLynn (1994), 161.

[111] Ambrose, *De ob.Val.* 28.

[112] McLynn (1994), 161. As McLynn points out, the scene Ambrose draws strikingly foreshadows an eastern imperial scene some 20 years later, reported by Socrates, when the empress Eudoxia put her infant son, Theodosius II, in the arms of Bishop John Chrysostom, and urged him to end their feud: Socrates 6.11.

that the boy and his mother could not cross the Alps in winter, nor could Valentinian make the journey alone.[113]

The stalling tactics of Valentinian II's loyalist court, illustrated by the embassies of Ambrose, could only hold Magnus Maximus temporarily, despite Theodosius' distant 'support' and the determination to look to the eastern emperor as the regime's father-figure. In the late summer of 387 the usurper broke through the Alpine passes and invaded Italy.[114] The invasion was apparently bloodless, and Valentinian II's court fled to Thessalonica before Maximus' advance.[115] Magnus Maximus certainly hoped to gain possession of his young co-emperor through the invasion, although the exact reasons why he should have chosen this moment to pass into Italy remain unclear.[116] The usurper now set up his court at Milan, appointing a friend of Symmachus, Sextus Rusticus Julianus, to the prefecture of Rome, while Symmachus himself delivered a panegyric on Maximus' virtues in Milan in 388.[117] Given Maximus' determined emphasis on his staunch orthodoxy, Symmachus' actions are a striking reflection of how disaffected he and other pagan Roman aristocrats were with Valentinian II's administration following the Altar of Victory controversy, and also of the failure of Valentinian II's advisers to recognize the need to maintain the support of such political players for the boy-emperor's government, against the conflicting pressure of perserving his religious and ceremonial function.[118] They also, of course, reflect the essential pragmatism and motives of self-preservation of power-players among the senatorial elite at Rome, more threatened by the enemy on their doorstep than by a distant boy-emperor or an even more distant eastern emperor. While Maximus built bridges at Rome, Valentinian II's court once more called upon Theodosius to come to their aid, and Theodosius at last travelled to Thessalonica to meet with the displaced boy-emperor.[119] With a treaty with Persia signed by 387 and the invasion of the Greuthungi in Thrace defeated, Theodosius was free to turn his attention to Maximus' claims in the west against his 'senior'—but clearly helpless—colleague.[120]

---

[113] Ambrose, *Ep.* 30 (Maur. 24), 7.

[114] Zosimus 4.42.5–7.

[115] Ibid. 4.43.1–2. Also Socrates 5.11; cf. Sozomen 7.13.11. See McLynn (1994), 219.

[116] McLynn suggests a general loss of confidence in Valentinian's rule on the part of western elites at this point (1994), 218–19. Errington points out that the longer Maximus waited, the more chance there was Valentinian would be found an independent role in western government: (2006), 34–5.

[117] Socrates 5.14.6; Matthews (1975), 223. Sadly (though not surprisingly) the panegyric does not survive.

[118] Birley (1983), 14; McLynn (1994), 161.

[119] *CTh.* 9.11.1 (30 Apr. 388, Thessalonica); Zosimus 4.43.1–2; Socrates, 5.12.

[120] On the treaty with Persia (386–7): see Baynes (1955*b*), 207; invasion of Thrace: Zosimus 4.38 f.; Matthews (1971), 1077.

At Thessalonica, Theodosius I married Valentinian II's sister Galla, undoubtedly prompted more by pragmatic considerations than Zosimus' assertion of his uncontrollable passions, and according to the ecclesiastical version of the story, then persuaded Valentinian to abandon his wayward faith and adopt orthodoxy.[121] Maximus' addition of Italy and the upper Danube to the territory he had already claimed had made him a still more serious threat to the balance of power between east and west, so a matrimonial alliance between Theodosius and the house of Valentinian was a shrewd political move, an advertisement of the solidarity of the 'legitimate' eastern and western emperors.[122] While Theodosius set out with the field army, according to Zosimus, Valentinian was sent, along with his mother and sisters, by sea—supposedly bound for Rome, where Zosimus asserts Theodosius believed they would be gladly received by the Romans, and would be safe from Maximus.[123]

Although it is not clear from the historical records that Valentinian II or his family ever disembarked at Rome, one important consequence of Valentinian's returning from Thessalonica in this way, while Theodosius travelled with his army by land, was that the younger emperor could claim no direct share in Theodosius' ultimate victory and capture of Maximus. While inevitably the tradition of this campaign has been thoroughly contaminated by Theodosian propaganda, there survives little indication that Valentinian II was granted much of a public part in the defeat of Magnus Maximus.[124] It is not impossible that Valentinian's voyage from Thessalonica was in fact a naval command: a brief reference in one of Ambrose's letters seems to refer to a victory over Maximus at Sicily, but gives no explicit information (such as who was in command).[125] If Valentinian did lead the expedition which achieved this success at Sicily, his colleague Theodosius certainly did not want it portrayed in contemporary records as a pivotal moment in the defeat of the usurper. Theodosius himself moved swiftly against Maximus, defeating him in two battles at Siscia and Poetovio, and the usurper was executed at Aquileia.[126] Maximus' young son, Victor, who had been made co-Augustus by his father in 383 or 384, in an

---

[121] Zosimus 4.44.2–4; Theodoret 5.15.1; cf. McLynn (1994), 293.

[122] Matthews (1975), 176; McLynn (1994), 293. Cf. Williams (1995), 228. According to the ecclesiastical tradition, Theodosius' help was conditional upon Valentinian entirely renouncing his homoean views and adopting orthodoxy (Theodoret 5.15.1–20).

[123] Zosimus 4.45.4.

[124] McLynn (1994), 294. Followed by Liebeschuetz (2005), 107, n. 4. As McLynn emphasizes, the writings of Sulpicius Severus give a brief glimpse of an alternative tradition from Gaul where Valentinian would reside from 388 until 391: see Sulp. Sev., *St Martin* 20.9.

[125] Ambrose, *Ep.* 74 (Maur. 40), 23; Liebeschuetz interprets this as evidence of Valentinian II leading a naval expedition which achieved the victory at Sicily: Liebeschuetz (2005), 107, n. 4.

[126] The progress of Theodosius' court to the west can be measured in laws issued along the route: *CTh.* 9.11.1 (30 Apr. 388), Thessalonica; 16.5.15 (14 June 388) and 16.4.2 (16 June 388), Stobi; 12.1.119 (21 June 388) at Scupi, as Matthews has highlighted (1971), 1077. On the execution of Maximus: Zosimus 4.46.2–3; Jones (1964a), 1. 159; McLynn (1994), 293.

interesting imitation of recent child-emperor elevations of the house of Valentinian/Theodosius, and for whom Maximus had clearly had dynastic hopes, was eliminated.[127]

Theodosius in Italy

Nine months after the completion of the campaign, Theodosius paid a visit to Rome, staging a spectacular triumphal entrance to the city on 13 July 389, accompanied by his younger son, the 5-year-old Honorius.[128] Here, the orator Pacatus delivered an exultant panegyric on Theodosius, in which the newly restored legitimate ruler of the west, Valentinian II, received merely a cursory mention, described as a small boy at the time of Theodosius' accession.[129] And now, under the rule of the victorious Theodosius (and victory, after all, was the ultimate manifestation of an emperor's divine favour and thus legitimacy to rule as imperial tradition decreed), it was to *his* sons that the empire's future would fall: the 'twin guarantees' of the state, Arcadius and Honorius.[130] Valentinian II, though still Augustus of the west, did not take part in the triumphal visit to Rome, even though at 17 he was of an age to have at least a ceremonial role in commanding troops.[131] In fact, Theodosius may have already sent him off to Gaul—according to Zosimus: 'After incorporating the pick of Maximus' troops in his own force, he sent Valentinian off to organize Italy, Gaul, and the rest of his dominion. His mother went with him, to make up, as far as a woman is able, what he lacked in wisdom owing to his youth.'[132]

Not only did Theodosius choose to present himself as the magnanimous and all-powerful eastern emperor rescuing and restoring the helpless boy-

---

[127] Zosimus 4.47.1; on the dynastic hopes see *RIC* 9. xxiii. As Pearce points out, the extent of Maximus' aspirations for Victor may be gauged by the fact that of coins issued by Magnus Maximus and discovered in coin hoards, those in the name of Victor exceed those in the name of his father. He appears however to have first been raised as Caesar, and then Augustus: see *PLRE* 1. 961.

[128] McLynn (1994), 310–11; Cameron (1970), 382–9.

[129] Pacatus 11.5.

[130] Pacatus 45.3; cf. 16.5.

[131] Zosimus 4.45–46.1. Particularly given that Theodosius had shared the honours of his triumph over the Greuthungi with his 9-year-old son Arcadius (*Cons.Const.* s.a. 386); McLynn (1994), 293–4.

[132] Zosimus, 4.47.1–2: Τὴν μὲν οὖν βασιλείαν Θεοδόσιος πᾶσαν Οὐαλεντινιανῷ παρέδωκεν, ὅσην ἔτυχεν ἔχων ὁ τούτου πατήρ, καὶ τοῦτο περὶ τοὺς εὐεργέτας καθῆκον ἔδοξεν εἶναι· τῶν δὲ ὑπὸ Μαξίμῳ στρατευσαμένων ὅσον ἦν ἐπίλεκτον μετὰ τῶν οἰκείων ἀναλαβών, ἀφῆκε μὲν ἐκεῖνον τὰ περὶ τὴν Ἰταλίαν καὶ Κελτοὺς καὶ ὅσα τῆς ἐπικρατείας ἦν τῆς αὐτοῦ διαθήσοντα· συνῆν δὲ καὶ ἡ μήτηρ αὐτῷ, τὸ ἐλλεῖπον ἐν φρονήσει διὰ τὸ νέον τῆς ἡλικίας, καθ' ὅσον γυναικὶ δυνατὸν ἦν, ἐκπληροῦσα. For Valentinian's presence in Gaul, see *CTh.* 4.22.3 (14 June 389), issued at Trier. Sources suggest Justina died soon after, or around the time, of Valentinian's journey to Gaul: *PLRE* 1. 488–9.

emperor, but he continued after 388, as he had throughout his reign, to represent Valentinian II on his coinage with the undivided obverse legend connoting 'irresponsibility', the same representation that he used for his son Arcadius, portraying both boys as juniors under his protection.[133] The famous Madrid missorium of Theodosius clearly demonstrates his conception of himself as senior Augustus, high above his two junior colleagues—Valentinian II and Arcadius.[134] Valentinian's technical four-year seniority to his eastern colleague clearly meant little to Theodosius, or the image of his own position that he sought to project. Perhaps in the circumstances, given Valentinian's dependence on Theodosius to intervene to rescue his throne, we should not find this surprising; but as in the case of Gratian before him, Theodosius' marginalization of Valentinian left the young emperor appearing weak, isolated, and ultimately vulnerable—and Magnus Maximus would not be the last opportunist to take advantage of such a situation.

For the meantime, however, Theodosius chose to extend his visit to the west, and after leaving Rome in August 389 the eastern emperor re-established his court at Milan, Valentinian II's own capital, where Theodosius would reside until his return to the east in 391. Valentinian II was banished to Gaul, under the oppressively watchful eye of Arbogast, another Frankish general.[135] As discussed in Chapter 2, the general Bauto had been the military commander of Valentinian's resistance forces in the immediate aftermath of Gratian's death, and when he died in 385 or 386, Arbogast had taken on this position.[136] After serving as one of Theodosius I's generals in the 388 campaign, principally suppressing resistance in Gaul, Theodosius stationed him at Trier with the young western emperor.[137] Perhaps unexpectedly, Theodosius was to remain in Italy for three years following his defeat of Magnus Maximus, leaving the east in the hands of his elder son Arcadius and his advisers at Constantinople, while he personally governed the west 'alongside' Valentinian II. Following his victory, the eastern emperor appointed some easterners to important offices in the west, such as Trifolius, who became praetorian prefect of Italy for 388–9, and Constantinianus, appointed to the prefecture of Gaul.[138] Yet Theodosius also made efforts

---

[133] On the presentation of Theodosius as rescuer: Rufinus 11.17; Augustine *Civ.Dei*, 5.26; cf. Zosimus 4.47. On the undivided legend, see *RIC* 9. xx. On the representation of Arcadius under Theodosius, see *RIC* 9. xvii.

[134] MacCormack (1981), pl. 55. The missorium is traditionally dated to 387/8: see Matthews (1975), 112, n. 4.

[135] Croke (1976), 236. Eunapius reports that Arbogast had appeared to Theodosius to be an ideal man to entrust with Valentinian's habits, being firm, incorrupt, and a model of rectitude: frg. 58.1.

[136] Stein (1959), 1. 205, n.81.

[137] O'Flynn (1983), 7. *PLRE* 1.95–7.

[138] For the appointment of Trifolius, see *CTh.* 16.5.15 (14 June 388) and for his past career; *PLRE* 1. 923; for Constantinianus, see *CTh.* 15.14.8 (14 Jan. 389) and his past career: *PLRE* 1.223

to win over influential figures in the west, notably including men who had once formed Valentinian II's loyalist court, such as Petronius Probus, Arbogast, and Symmachus.[139] Even if Theodosius' presence in Italy was merely temporary, these familiar political players were prepared to respond favourably to his overtures.[140] Theodosius' visit to Rome had brought the senators rare imperial attention, which must have been all the more valued following the embarassment of senatorial enthusiasm for Magnus Maximus and the desire for imperial forgiveness, and issues of religion seem to have played no part in his efforts to attract their support.[141]

The leading pagan senator, Virius Nicomachus Flavianus, was invited to Theodosius' court at Milan to take up the post of imperial quaestor; his fellow pagan and relative by marriage Symmachus was pardoned for his panegyric-writing for Magnus Maximus and would even become consul in 391, and similar honours and appointments were made to other senatorial aristocrats.[142] Theodosius' later appointment of Nicomachus Flavianus as praetorian prefect of Italy, Africa, and Illyricum in 390 indicates that this whole central prefecture was now under the eastern emperor's control, while Valentinian seems to have been restricted to Gaul alone.[143] Theodosius' attitude towards Valentinian II during his stay in Italy from 388 to 391 was aimed at marginalizing his 'senior' colleague as much as possible, and winning the loyalty of the western emperor's key supporters away from him, while building a western government favourable to himself.[144] Theodosius' ability to dispense such patronage sent a plain message that Valentinian II remained an imperial redundancy.

When Theodosius returned to Constantinople in 391, a number of westerners even followed him eastwards to take up office there, such as Fl. Pisidius Romulus and Andromachus.[145] Once again, Valentinian was being utterly sidelined in favour of a more powerful figure who was happy to undermine his

---

(his appointment is disputed by McLynn (1994), 309). For modern views on these appointments and others, see Matthews (1975), 226; Croke (1976), 236.

[139] McLynn (1994), 293 f. For Arbogast's loyalty to Theodosius, see Zosimus 4.53.2–3; For Probus' favour under Theodosius, see Symmachus' frustration in 389 at a rescript from Theodosius awarding a suit to Probus, overturning the original verdict in Symmachus' favour, *Ep.* 2.30. For Symmachus' support for Theodosius' regime, see Symmachus, *Ep.* 5.38. Also on Theodosius' efforts to win support among the western aristocracy during this period: Leppin (2003), 135–76.

[140] McLynn (1994), 296.

[141] Errington (2006), 134. Although Zosimus claims Theodosius made an ineffective speech to the senate exhorting the senators to convert to Christianity (Zosimus 4.59.1–4).

[142] Errington (2006), 134–5, 138–9. For Aurelius Victor, who was made urban prefect, see: *PLRE* 1. 960; Flavianus: *PLRE* 1. 347–9.

[143] Errington (2006), 85; *PLRE* 1. 347–9.

[144] Indeed, Errington suggests that Theodosius' prolonged stay in the west following Maximus' defeat indicates he was seriously considering taking on the government of the western empire in person: (2006), 37–8.

[145] For the details of their careers, see Matthews (1975), 259–60. Both men would return to the west and hold office under Honorius and Stilicho in the later 390s.

colleague's authority—and western elites were well aware of it.[146] Theodosius I did not just see himself as a paternal, protective senior emperor and Valentinian II as his junior and largely powerless colleague; he seems to have viewed himself as essentially the only full emperor at this time, with a handful of young subordinates—among whom his own sons were of greater significance (and public prominence) than Valentinian II. Although Theodosius cannot conclusively be shown to have surrounded Valentinian II with officers loyal to himself, the power of Arbogast was surely meant to keep Valentinian II in check after Theodosius returned to the east in the summer of 391.[147] It seems most likely that Theodosius intended to create a political vacuum in Italy, with Valentinian effectively under house-arrest in Gaul, perhaps until Honorius was of an age to rule in his own right.[148]

It is interesting to note that the senators whom Theodosius had wooed during his time in Italy decided upon his departure to try their influence with the younger emperor again, presenting him with another petition concerning the Altar of Victory in 391 while Valentinian was in Gaul, but the young man's Christian piety prevailed.[149] No doubt the senators recognized how much the boy-emperor could do with support and that this could prove a strategic moment to try their luck; once again, the pragmatism of such political players comes through. But by this stage his religious function was virtually all that the hapless Valentinian II had left to him, and upholding the cause of Christianity prevailed over other considerations. Perhaps his recent acceptance of orthodoxy as a condition of Theodosius I's campaign to restore Valentinian II to his throne made demonstration of his spotless piety all the more important.[150]

The death of Valentinian II

The sources provide some alarming stories of the extent of the general Arbogast's control over Valentinian II's court in Gaul: from the general's slaying of the young emperor's close advisers in the palace, to tearing up a dismissal notice handed him by Valentinian II, drawing his sword, and roaring at the emperor that since he had not appointed him, he had no power to dismiss him.[151] But in the absence of Theodosius himself, the

---

[146] McLynn (1994), 295–6.
[147] Matthews (1975), 238.
[148] McLynn (1994), 333–4.
[149] Ambrose, *Ep. extra coll.* 10 [57].5; Paulinus, *VAmb.* 26; Also McLynn (1994), 335. They had also, according to Ambrose, approached Theodosius on this issue, but to no avail, although Theodosius had hesitated some days over his decision: Ambrose, *Ep. extra coll.* 10.4.
[150] Theodoret 5.15.1.
[151] Zosimus 4.53.1–4. Cf. Paulinus, *VAmb.* 30; Eunapius, frgs. 9.58.2.22–9; 9.58.2.29–38; John Ant., frg. 187; Greg.Tur. 2.9.

eastern emperor's attempt to control the west through controlling Valentinian was doomed to failure.[152] One major reason for the division of the imperial office in the late empire was recognition of the need for an emperor to be on the scene in order to carry out the essential distribution of patronage among the army and bureaucracy which would ensure his reign's success.[153] In addition, Theodosius' action in confining Valentinian II to Gaul had effectively demilitarized Italy, and in early spring 392 barbarian raiders were reported in the Alps.[154] At Milan there was uncertainty about how the population was expected to defend itself: the nearest forces were under Arbogast with Valentinian II, now in Vienne.[155]

Bishop Ambrose was delegated to lead an embassy requesting assistance from Gaul, and Valentinian II seems to have been informed of the planned appeal before it even eventuated: in his funeral oration Ambrose attested to the young emperor's eagerness to act.[156] Ambrose hesitated over setting out: he claims because it had been announced that Valentinian was already on his way, and even that the imperial insignia had already arrived, suggesting Valentinian would be there any day. He must also have been aware that offering Valentinian II the opportunity to lead a military expedition to repel the invaders might displease Theodosius II.[157] Arbogast seems to have prevented the emperor from leaving Vienne himself, but Valentinian II was clearly utterly determined to try to force this chance of a break for freedom, writing to Ambrose urging his journey and expressing a great desire to receive the sacrament of baptism (specifically from Ambrose), a request the bishop could not possibly refuse.[158] Tellingly, Valentinian also begged Ambrose to come and mediate between Arbogast and himself, confirming that relations between the emperor and his manager were breaking down: Ambrose would later lament that he had not had the chance to restore harmony between them.[159] The sources also suggest that Valentinian had written to Theodosius, pleading for his help against the tyranny of Arbogast.[160]

Ambrose set out, but halfway across the Alps the news reached him that Valentinian II was dead.[161] The exact circumstances of the young man's death

---

[152] McLynn (1994), 335.   [153] Millar (1977), 11; Errington (2006), 79–110.
[154] Ambrose, *De ob. Val.* 2.   [155] McLynn (1994), 335–6.
[156] Ambrose, *De ob. Val.* 2, 24.   [157] Ibid. 23, 24.
[158] Ibid. 23; Croke (1976), 237; McLynn (1994), 336.
[159] Ambrose, *De ob. Val.* 27. It is not clear exactly what Valentinian was asking of Ambrose with regard to his relations with Arbogast—Ambrose declares in his funeral oration for Valentinian that the emperor wanted him to act as a guarantor of his good faith towards the count (ibid. 25). Scholars continue to disagree over exactly what this might mean—see e.g. Palanque (1933), 268; McLynn (1994), 336, n. 153; Liebeschuetz (2005), 19.
[160] Eunapius, frg. 9.58.2.29–38; John Ant., frg. 187; Zosimus 4.53.4.
[161] Ambrose, *De ob. Val.* 27; McLynn (1994), 336–7.

remain unclear: he was found hanged in his quarters at Vienne on 15 May 392, though the verdict of ancient commentators varies on whether this was the result of murder at Arbogast's hands or suicide.[162] Ambrose refused to comment on the matter in his funeral oration on the emperor, which can only have encouraged suspicions of murder.[163] Modern scholars have also been of diverging opinions.[164]

The argument for murder hinges on the claims of Zosimus and Socrates that Arbogast conspired with the grammarian Eugenius to assassinate the young emperor and place the latter on the throne.[165] There are several flaws in this position, however, the most obvious being that it was three months before Arbogast had the usurper Eugenius proclaimed as emperor of the west, at Lugdunum on 22 August 392.[166] This delay surely suggests that the *magister militum* did not have any immediate successor to Valentinian II in mind, and really Arbogast would have had little reason to alter his highly influential position by conspiring in the appointment of a potentially more assertive emperor (unless he truly expected Valentinian II to break free from his domination), making it more likely that the youth had killed himself suddenly and unexpectedly.[167] In fact, Valentinian II's death left Arbogast in a singularly awkward position: the general seems to have waited helplessly for Theodosius to act, and only after three months despaired of this, accepted that he was likely to be blamed for the death regardless of his assertions of loyalty, and committed himself to open rebellion with the proclamation of Eugenius.[168] At Constantinople, on 22 January 393,

---

[162] For the verdict of murder by Arbogast, see Socrates 5.25; Zosimus 4.54.1–4. Rufinus ascribes the death to reasons unknown, Rufinus 11.31. Variant versions are also given by Sozomen 7.22.2 f.; Augustine, *Civ.dei* 5.26.1; Ps.-Aurelius Victor 48; Orosius 7.35.2; Philostorgius 10.1.

[163] Ambrose *De ob. Val.* 33. Valentinian II was buried at Milan: Johnson (1991), 501.

[164] Respectively, arguing murder by Arbogast: Jones (1964*a*), 1. 159; Grattarola (1979), 359–70; and suicide: Croke (1976), 244; Matthews (1975), 238; McLynn (1994), 336–7; Barnes (1990), 165.

[165] Zosimus 4.54.1–4; Socrates 5.25.

[166] For details on the usurpation of Eugenius, see *PLRE* 1.293; also Matthews (1975), 239.

[167] Croke (1976), 244. There was also a two-month delay before Theodosius issued instructions for Valentinian II's burial arrangements, perhaps also suggesting the uncertainty even at Constantinople about how best to proceed: see Lunn-Rockliffe (2008), 197–8.

[168] Matthews (1975), 239; McLynn (1994), 337. As Cameron has most recently argued, it is unlikely that either Arbogast and Eugenius, or their prominent supporters (such as Virius Nicomachus Flavianus), were motivated on religious grounds, even though the usurpation was later described as a pagan one, and has often been seen by modern historians as the last great pagan stand. As seen so often in the politics of the west in the preceding few decades, both pagan aristocrats, Christian aristocrats, and Christian emperors were regularly prepared to make alliances, or attempt to do so, for their own political advantage, and Eugenius and Arbogast were no different in this respect. See, for similar arguments, Salzman (2010*a*), 196 and generally 193–8, against Hedrick (2000), 71. It is surprising, however, to find Salzman asserting that most scholars would probably agree that the usurpation was partly prompted by dissatisfaction with the dynastic succession Theodosius had put in place, in which Salzmann has Theodosius

Theodosius proclaimed his younger son Honorius, then aged 8, co-Augustus, and in 394, Theodosius travelled west once more, defeating Eugenius at the battle of Frigidus on 6 September.[169] Five months later Theodosius himself was dead, leaving his own two sons, the 18-year-old Arcadius and 10-year-old Honorius, as heirs to the entire Roman empire.

The *post factum* verdict on the legitimacy of the reigns of either Gratian or Valentinian II could hardly have been favourable. In Chapter 1, in drawing up the picture of the ideal emperor and the bases for his legitimacy, three key moments in any reign were identified as crucial in evaluating an emperor's fulfilment of the criteria in the eyes of his contemporaries: the manner of his accession, the success of his reign (which confirmed its divine sanction), and the *post eventum* verdict of the reign following the emperor's death. Gratian and Valentinian II both, in their different ways, struggled to fulfil the criteria for a favourable verdict. Their early accessions were phantom ones of dubious legality (4-year-old Valentinian II's accession much more dubious than his brother's), while for both boys, their real accessions were largely supported by self-interested political cliques whose power-struggles throughout their reigns undermined the stability of each regime. Meanwhile, the natural tensions between western and eastern imperial courts were heightened by adult eastern colleagues who consistently aimed to cast themselves as the senior member of the imperial college (whether this was technically the case or not), and who seem to have struggled, not unreasonably, to regard such youthful emperors as Gratian and Valentinian II as viable colleagues. This lack of acceptance by both Valens and Theodosius in turn led to their western co-emperors becoming isolated and vulnerable to attack, and thereby contributed to their miserable ends.

The verdict of contemporary writers was pity rather than endorsement of their legitimacy: Ammianus saw Gratian as a young man of great promise led astray by evil counsellors; for Jerome he was a figure of pathos, deserted by his own army and refused admission by his own cities, the plaything of his enemy; and for Ambrose, a tragic figure of betrayed innocence, who had kept asking for him and seeking his guidance until the end.[170] The wretched Valentinian II evoked similar responses: Theodosius' wife Galla disturbed the court with her

'making' Valentinian II (an 'ineffective, yet headstrong boy') emperor in 391. Valentinian had already held the rank of emperor for sixteen years by 391, but more significantly, the delay between Valentinian's death and Eugenius' usurpation discussed above, again surely indicates that until the emperor's unexpected suicide, no such usurpation was being contemplated, and that when it was, it came about largely as a result of Arbogast's desperation rather than widespread discontent.

[169] For the acclamation of Honorius, see Socrates 5.25, and further below, pp. 138–9. On the battle at the Frigidus, see Jones (1964a), 1. 159.

[170] AM 31.10.18; Jerome, *Ep.* 60.15; Ambrose, *Expl.Ps. 61* 17, 24–5; *Apol.Dav.* 27; *De ob. Val.* 72, 80. Cf. McLynn (1994), 155.

grief for her brother, while Ambrose had even his enemies weeping over the loss of the boy's wisdom and youth, describing his radiant and ruddy countenance as 'bearing a likeness of Christ'.[171] Yet neither boy-emperor's failed reign could, despite the pathos of their situations, compete with the divinely sanctioned legitimacy of their colleague Theodosius, so triumphantly pronounced by Pacatus in 389, which cast them both in the shade: 'What crowds of admiring people, how great an audience, shall surround me when I say: "I have seen Rome; I have seen Theodosius; and I have seen both together; I have seen the father of the ruler himself, I have seen the avenger of the ruler, I have seen the restorer of the ruler!"'[172]

The accessions of Gratian in 367 and Valentinian II in 375 were unexpected and novel events in late fourth-century Roman history. Their reigns represented the first sustained experiments with the opportunities that child-emperor rule could offer, and the possibilities of this phenomenon would continue to shape the western Roman empire for decades to come. Perhaps to describe the accessions as 'experiments' is to attribute too self-conscious a motivation to the individuals involved, and I do not mean to suggest that political crises such as Valentinian I's serious illness in 367, or his death in 375 did not call for some sort of action; or indeed, that the consequences of these child-emperor accessions need to have been expected or foreseen. But it should be borne in mind that these accessions were innovations in Roman imperial tradition—even if only in the seemingly simple shift from making a child-Caesar to making a child-Augustus, and that these innovations paved the way for the longer-term changes in the nature and perception of imperial rule resulting particularly from the lengthy minority governments of Honorius and Valentinian III.

It is important to highlight the differences in the natures of the reigns of Gratian and Valentinian II, convenient as it is to group the half-brothers and co-emperors together, since there were some very real contrasts in their situations. In a sense it was Valentinian II who was truly the first western boy-emperor, since despite Gratian's phantom accession as an 8-year-old, his next eight years were spent in the shadow of a supportive and powerful father, even accompanying him on campaign, learning the arts of war, and perhaps most significantly inheriting the well-established support-base Valentinian I had built up around him over the course of more than a decade in office (even if some among these supporters had to be swiftly removed after 375 to appease

---

[171] Ambrose *De ob. Val.* 58: *Valentinianus meus, iuvenis meus candidus et rubens habens in se imaginem Christi*... For Galla's distress, see Zosimus 4.55.1. See also Lunn-Rockliffe (2008), 205.

[172] Pacatus 47.5: *Quantis stupentium populis, quam multo circumdabor auditore, cum dixero: 'Romam vidi, Theodosium vidi, et utrumque simul vidi; vidi illum principis patrem, vidi illum principis vindicem, vidi illum principis restitutorem!'*

senatorial opinion). Thrust into office as a 4-year-old, though Valentinian II would spend the next eight years also in the shadow of a relative, it was as a 'spare' rather than expected heir. When Gratian was assassinated in 383, bringing Valentinian II once more into the limelight, the boy was still only 12 years old, while most of Gratian's military allies were already in the camp of the usurper Magnus Maximus, and members of the senatorial elite too wavered towards the rival claimant.

Upon his real accession in 375 Gratian's position was a relatively strong one, with all the benefits that his well-established father could bequeath to him, yet across the course of the next eight years Gratian's position deteriorated from promising beginnings to dismal end. In contrast, in 383 Valentinian II had everything to aim for—both a military and political power-base to be built up, and a usurper to be vanquished—yet he too proved unequal to the task, or perhaps rather, the dominant vested interests surrounding him throughout his reign never even allowed him the chance to take up the challenge upon reaching adulthood. Nevertheless, Gratian's acclamation at the age of 8 set a vital precedent for the imperial office, and the potential of such a precedent was rapidly grasped by powers around the throne—such as those involved in Valentinian II's swift elevation in 375, and emperors themselves—as evidenced by Theodosius I's elevation of his own two sons in 383 and 393. These first serious forays into child-emperorship, even if of a largely ceremonial and symbolic nature, had major implications for the continued development of models of emperorship in general.

As the next chapter will go on to explore, there might be ways in which even a child-emperor could be presented as plausibly fulfilling aspects of the imperial ideal, and even structures of the state which had evolved to a point whereby a largely ceremonial emperor could be easily supported; but as the particular politics of the reigns examined in this chapter reveal, there remained problems. The initial accessions of both children—phantom and real— occurred because they were in the interests of particular political parties: Valentinian I in the case of Gratian's phantom accession, and afterwards the political clique or committee headed by Merobaudes and Petronius Probus, with Ausonius and Ambrose also emerging as power-brokers after 375. Yet the weakness of such a political backing for a boy-emperor was highlighted by the defection of Merobaudes and the murder of Gratian: the senatorial party could not ensure the essential support of the military, and so young an emperor struggled wholly to satisfy the traditional military demands of his office. Furthermore, Gratian himself had no model of passive imperial rule before him to provide an example—there had not in recent history been any long-term, successful figurehead emperors, so it was natural that upon his father's death, when he was 16, he would seek an active role in his government as he grew up: that he would seek, in fact, to be a military emperor. The Lentienses campaign, and Ammianus' praise of Gratian's personal conduct and military leadership, show Gratian attempting to pursue this course, rather more than they reveal any particular perversity in Gratian's character in delaying his arrival at Adrianople. In the longer term, however, Merobaudes had other plans.

Valentinian II's original accession, in 375, came as a result of the self-interest of a clique of political players—primarily the general Merobaudes and the senator Petronius Probus—who were then able to use the infant emperor as leverage against his 16-year-old brother. Once their aims were achieved, they quickly abandoned Valentinian II and threw their weight behind Gratian, to emerge again in 383 to form Valentinian II's loyalist support-base against Magnus Maximus, now headed by Petronius Probus and the general Bauto, replaced later by Arbogast. The key players who found promotion of a child-emperor advantageous, therefore, were those who recognized how a young emperor in their power might be used to promote their own interests more effectively than an adult emperor might, such as through Gratian's measures to conciliate the Roman senate following Valentinian I's death. Yet recognition of the essential nature of distributing patronage among important political players of both the army and the bureaucracy as a means of ensuring support and stabilizing regime-building also seems to have been lacking.

These initial, committee-run regimes eventually yielded to the dominance of single, all-powerful military managers, again highlighting one of the key problems emerging from this new type of imperial rule: the child-emperors' inability to fulfil their military function. Though even under a single manager the governments of Gratian and Valentinian II ultimately did not prosper, this development begged the question of which supporting arrangement would allow long-term survival of such a regime. The accession of the proven military commander Theodosius following the disaster of Adrianople only highlighted the young emperors' perceived inability satisfactorily to fulfil the military role required of them, or even to maintain the belief that they could. The usurpation of Magnus Maximus in itself represented discontent and a lack of belief in Gratian's rule on a wider stage, and an indication that it did not satisfy those far from the centre of politics. Maximus' ability to hold on to power for five years following Gratian's death, and the degree of recognition and support that he wrestled from the imperial government during these years, also signified a stumbling-block for the development of the more passive, ceremonial-style rule that Valentinian II represented. Valentinian's helplessness in the face of Maximus' advance, and his subsequent rescue and restoration by Theodosius, once again emphasized the reality that this child-emperor's government only existed insofar as it was convenient to others—and Theodosius' complete marginalization of Valentinian II in favour of his own sons suggests that the younger emperor's rule may not long have remained convenient to his colleague. The weaknesses of the respective administrations of the two brothers were attractive to the self-interest of the power-brokers who promoted and sustained them, but also ultimately led to their downfalls. Yet fascinatingly, the phenomenon of the child-emperor would not die with Valentinian II but would continue to develop, furthered even by Theodosius I himself, through the promotion of his sons as co-Augusti during their childhoods.

4

Adjusting the Imperial Image

O Gratian and Valentinian, lovely and beloved by all! Inseparable in life, even in death you are not divided. The burial mound has not separated, whom love did not separate. The condition of death has not divided whom a shared piety bound together. There was no diversity of virtue to drive you apart. You were simpler than doves, swifter than eagles, milder than lambs, more innocent than calves. The arrow of Gratian did not turn back, and the justice of Valentinian was not in vain, nor his authority empty. How are the mighty fallen, yet not in battle![1]

The last two chapters have been concerned with the politics of the reigns of Gratian and Valentinian II, but in Chapter 1 we examined the traditional expectations of an emperor's function in the later Roman empire, and the question of whether these youthful emperors could be presented in any sense as fulfilling that ideal, remains. At this point, therefore, we can turn back to the writings of Menander, Ammianus, Themistius, Eusebius, and the authors of the *Panegyrici Latini* and the ideal that they presented, and look for answers in the source material available, and particularly in two very important speeches devoted to Gratian and Valentinian II, and delivered at significant and sensitive moments in the late Roman west.

The first of these speeches is the *Gratio actiarum* of Ausonius, former tutor of Gratian and consul for the year 379. This thanksgiving oration elucidating the many virtues of the then 20-year-old emperor was delivered less than six months after the disastrous Roman defeat at Adrianople, and Gratian could not be present to hear it, being fully occupied with the Gothic crisis and military affairs in Thrace at the time of the consular celebrations. The second

---

[1] Ambrose, *De ob. Val.* 79: *O omnibus, Gratiane e Valentiniane, speciosi e carissimi, insepar-abiles in vita et in morte non estis separati. Non vos discrevit tumulus, quos non discernebat adfectus, non causa mortis separavit, quos pietas una iungebat. Non virtutum distantia dispares fecit super columbas simpliciores, super aquilas leviores, super agnos clementiores, super vitulos innocentiores. Gratiani sagitta non est reversa retro, et Valentiniani iustitia non fuit vacua nec inanis auctoritas. Quomodo sine pugna ceciderunt potentes!* This passage contains scriptural references to 2 Sam. 1: 22 and 23 and Matt. 10: 16, as traced by Liebeschuetz: (2005), 398.

speech was delivered at Milan in 392 by Ambrose over the body of Valentinian II: the *De obitu Valentiniani*. The uncertain nature of Valentinian's death, the emperor-less state of the west even as Ambrose delivered his oration, and the bishop's anxiety over relations with Valentinian's absent brother-in-law Theodosius I required Ambrose to draw upon all of his ingenuity in composing a speech which would honour the dead emperor appropriately but avoid dwelling upon any of these sensitive political issues.[2] The delicate political climate surrounding the settings for each of these speeches reminds us of the individuality of each imperial oration and the need to situate it in its specific context. At the same time, with the picture of the traditional late Roman emperor (and his virtues) already developed in Chapter 1, the writings of Ausonius, Ambrose, and others allow us to make some comparisons between the image of these young emperors and their adult predecessors, and to begin to glimpse some of the adjustments to the established imperial ideal which this new phenomenon in Roman rulership required.

PERSONAL VIRTUES

Distinguished background

Returning to Menander's framework, therefore, we turn first to the area of distinguished background. As the sons of an emperor, both Gratian and Valentinian II had dynastic claims in their favour, even if the dynasty was not yet long-lived. The anxiousness of Valentinian I and Valens to emphasize the military valour of their father, Gratianus, betrayed awareness that their family connections were not terribly distinguished, but by the time of Gratian's promotion in 367, according to Ammianus, the carefully primed troops responded to the announcement of the boy's accession with the cry that: 'the family of Gratianus merits this!'[3] Gratian was the child of his father's first marriage, to a woman named Marina Severa, about whom little else is known, and their son was born before his father became emperor, on 18 April 359.[4]

---

[2] The speech was probably delivered in late July or early August 395 (see Liebeschuetz (2005), 386, n. 1), and Eugenius was proclaimed in late August.

[3] AM 27.6.14: *Familia Gratiani hoc meretur*. Similarly Ausonius, *Grat.Act.* 8. Further: Lenski (2002), 90. For emphasis on the military deeds of Valentinian I and Valens, see e.g. Themistius, *Or.* 6.81d and 9.124b. According to Ammianus, the elder Gratianus was of humble origin (originally a rope-seller, Ammianus claims), though possessed of immense strength, who rose steadily through the army to hold the command of the army in Africa as count, and later the same rank in Britain: AM 30.7.2–3.

[4] *PLRE* 1. 401. For some further (speculative) background on Gratian's mother, see Woods (2006), 173–87.

Valentinian I seems to have discarded his first wife after his accession, in favour of a dynastic marriage with Justina, the future mother of Valentinian II (born 2 July 371), who had previously been the wife of the usurper Magnentius, but who more importantly had links with the House of Constantine.[5] The young Valentinian II himself, therefore, could claim a personal blood-tie with Constantine through his mother Justina, even if rather a distant one, though it should be noted that no extant source ever alludes to this.[6] The marriage of Gratian to Constantia, the posthumous daughter of Constantius II, in 374, strengthened this dynastic link to the house of Constantine still further: in 378 Gratian could send Ausonius a consular robe embroidered with the image of Constantius II and refer to him as *parens noster*.[7]

In terms of the qualifications of distinguished birth and family, therefore, both Gratian and Valentinian II easily could be presented well, in accordance with Menander's instructions. As we have already seen, Menander wrote also of the praise to be lavished upon an emperor's personal appearance, and Gratian's physical attributes were praised in just such a way by Ammianus, who wrote of the young emperor recommending himself to the troops by the fiery gleam of his eyes, his delightful charm, and noble nature upon the occasion of his acclamation in 367.[8] Of Valentinian II's appearance we possess only the poetic descriptions of Ambrose in the funeral oration for the young emperor—in which he is praised in scriptural terms as radiant and ruddy.[9] What source material we do possess therefore, indicates that Gratian and Valentinian could be seen to fulfil the imperial ideal of an illustrious background in particular, and Gratian especially was praised for his personal appearance.

---

[5] According to Ammianus, the mother of Gratian was still alive in 376: 28.1.57. On Justina's previous marriage to Magnentius, see Zosimus 4.19; Socrates 4.31, and on her probable links to the house of Constantine: *PLRE* 1. 382; Cf. Lenski (2002), 103–4; Frakes (2006), 59; Woods (2004), 325–7. Both Constantius I and Constantine I had similarly discarded former partners in favour of dynastic marriages after their accessions: see Lenski (2006*b*), 59.

[6] Unless perhaps later references to links with the house of Constantine by Galla Placidia (a niece of Valentinian II, and thus grand-niece of Justina) and her son Valentinian III (see further below on this) relate to this link; though such claims might also refer simply to Gratian's marriage to Constantia.

[7] Ausonius, *Grat.Act.* 11. See also *CTh.* 16.6.2 (17 Oct. 377); Lenski (2002), 103. On sources for Constantia, see *PLRE* 1. 221, and on the marriage, AM 29.6.7 and Themistius *Or.* 13.168a. Constantia died before Gratian, probably in early 383 (he married again before his death) and the marriage was childless.

[8] AM 27.6.15.

[9] Ambrose, *De ob. Val.* 58: *Valentinianus meus*, iuvenis meus candidus et rubens *habens in se imaginem Christi* . . .

Youth and education

Education was the next point Menander advised an imperial panegyrist to deal with, and the writings of Ausonius have left a unique insight into the studies of the youthful Gratian. As noted in Chapter 2, at some point during the 360s, possibly in 367 when Valentinian I established his court at Trier, the distinguished professor Ausonius was called from his chair at Bordeaux to be private tutor to Valentinian I's heir: as we have already seen, Ausonius and his family would then become a dominant faction at Gratian's court for a short period in the immediate aftermath of Valentinian I's death.[10] Ausonius wrote effusively of his pupil's learning and eloquence, claiming the boy outdid the most famous orators of Homer.[11] Ausonius' admiration for Gratian seems excessive, yet this is hardly unexpected in a one-party state with a loyal orator writing on the educational prowess of his own pupil (and at the time of writing, his emperor).[12] In fact there is no real way of knowing what the boy's true capability was. But this is not the key point: ultimately, far more important than Gratian's true ability was the ability he was perceived to possess, and his skill was proclaimed by other writers as well, such as Aurelius Victor, Symmachus, and Themistius.[13]

Ausonius' schooling essentially furnished Gratian with the cultural equipment of a properly trained gentleman, and this is likely to have been a consideration of particular importance to Valentinian I: the sources vary in their accounts of his own level of learning, Zosimus claiming he was quite uneducated, and Ammianus that he wrote neatly and was an elegant painter and modeller.[14] As a military man rather than an aristocrat, however, his eagerness to see his son so highly educated may have reflected a sensitivity to his own shortcomings in meeting this particular demand of the imperial profile, or at least fitting his son to deal on equal terms with, and hopefully be accepted by, the liberal-arts-educated senatorial aristocracy who would make up an influential sector of his subjects.[15] Before his father's acclamation, however, Gratian may simply have been an 'army brat', experiencing the sort of military upbringing that has recently been envisaged similarly befalling the young Theodosius I, as the son of an active military officer: living in the camps and accompanying his father; but Valentinian I clearly was determined that

---

[10] Matthews (1975), 51.

[11] Ausonius, *Grat.Act.* 4; Also 10, 15.

[12] Green is particularly dismissive of Ausonius' excessive praise for Gratian's accomplishments: (1991), xxviii.

[13] Ps.-Aurelius Victor 47.4; Symmachus, *Or.*3.7; *Ep.* 1.20.2; 10.2.5; Themistius, *Or.* 9.125c.

[14] Respectively, Zosimus 3.36.2–3; AM 20.9.4. See Matthews (1975), 84 on the particular purpose of this education of Gratian.

[15] Lenski (2002), 95. Theodosius I, also a military man, would similarly later appoint the philosopher and orator Themistius as tutor to his son Arcadius (Themistius, *Or.*16; 18).

there would be more to Gratian's education than this, once his prospects changed so dramatically after 364.[16] Thus, on Valentinian's promotion of the boy Gratian in 367, he assured his audience that, 'when he enters on the years of youth, since he has been instructed in the liberal arts and in the pursuit of skilful accomplishments, he will weigh with impartial justice the value of right and wrong actions . . .'.[17]

Concerning the education of Valentinian II, there is unfortunately very little available information, other than that after the death of their father, its supervision (though not its teaching) was taken over by Gratian himself.[18] It is difficult to know how much this is truly meant, or whether Valentinian was put through the same rigorous educational training to which Ausonius had apparently subjected Gratian—it would be surprising, however, if he were not. But the survival of Ausonius' writings on Gratian, at least, give a clear impression that this boy-emperor could more than adequately satisfy the requirement of educational attainment in a late Roman emperor.

Wisdom and temperance

The writings of Menander, Ammianus, and Themistius also stressed that an emperor was expected to be conspicuous by his wisdom and temperance. Ausonius insistently asserted that Gratian excelled in gentleness of nature, outstripped even Marcus Aurelius in his wisdom, and was so generous he anticipated the needs of his friends before they knew them themselves.[19] In terms of chastity, a prince whose private life was more seemly than Gratian could not be imagined: his moderate eating and drinking habits were commended also, as was his natural modesty, though this is a quality Rufinus felt the youth possessed in too great a measure for the good of the state.[20] And in contrast to Ausonius' picture, Eunapius wrote that Gratian's qualities were closely guarded palace secrets, 'like some forbidden treasure', and reports about him were full of discrepancies.[21] Ammianus' picture of the young emperor perhaps most persuasively presents the contradiction of Gratian's character and belies Ausonius' account: asserting that, despite his youth, he

[16] On Theodosius' likely upbringing, see McLynn (2005), 102.

[17] AM 27.6.9: *ineunte adulescentia, quoniam humanitate et studiis disciplinarum sollertium est expolitus, librabit suffragiis puris merita recte secusve factorum: faciet, ut sciant se boni intelligi . . .*

[18] AM 30.10.6.

[19] On Gratian's gentleness, see Ausonius, *Grat.Act.*16; his wisdom, ibid. 7; and his generosity, ibid. 1; similarly 6, 8, 11, 15, 17.

[20] On Gratian's chastity, moderation, and modesty see Ausonius, *Grat.Act.* 14, also 15. Similarly Ps.-Aurelius Victor 47.5. For Rufinus' view, Rufinus 11.13.

[21] Eunapius, frg. 5.50.1–19.

was eloquent and self-restrained, but led astray by self-seeking intimates who led him into frivolous pursuits: 'these qualities would have completed an emperor fit to be compared with the choicest rulers of the olden time, had this been allowed by the fates and by his intimates, who, by evil actions, cast a cloud over his virtue, which was even then not firmly steadfast.'[22]

Valentinian II's wisdom in counsel was celebrated by Bishop Ambrose, as was his embracing of duty above pleasure, despite his youth.[23] His chastity, like his brother's, was inviolable, he would not celebrate circus games or hunt wild beasts in case it was said his attention was distracted from matters of state, he corrected his errors before he even learned of them, and practised fasting to an extreme (and rather ostentatious) extent.[24] Indeed, ostentatious moderation and chastity, if we are to believe Ambrose's account, seem to have been a particular feature of young Valentinian's behaviour. When it was reported that all the young men of Rome were infatuated with a young actress, Ambrose asserts that Valentinian invited her to his court, and as an example to his peers, then studiously ignored her and showed no interest in her whatsoever.[25] In addition, when he held elaborate banquets at court, he chose to go without food himself.[26] These comments may have reflected Ambrose's concept of what the habits of an emperor ought to be more than those of the average Roman, perhaps especially a young emperor who had died an untimely death in uncertain circumstances; but they also reflected the need for adaptation of the imperial ideal when the incumbent emperor was still very young and there was little that could be said of his deeds. The ostentatious piety and virtue of Valentinian II reflected the increased emphasis on the young emperor's spiritual worthiness for his position, a theme which would be developed still more noticeably during the reigns of Honorius and Valentinian III.

As with Ausonius' account of Gratian's educational prowess, there is no way of knowing whether these claims of the two boys' wisdom and temperance were in any way accurate. Ausonius' account was written during Gratian's lifetime, and Ambrose's remarks on Valentinian II came as part of the funeral oration he composed on the youth's death: the young men could have been guilty of all manner of greed, folly, and licentiousness, and it was not going to be admitted.[27] But again, the absolute accuracy of these accounts hardly

---

[22] AM 27.6.15: *quae imperatorem implesset cum veterum lectissimis comparandum, si per fata proximosque licuisset, qui virtutem eius etiam tum instabilem obnubilarunt actibus pravis.* Similarly AM 31.10.18: Ammianus' comparison of Gratian with Commodus here is a particular note of anxiety. Cf. Eunapius 9.50.1–19. See also Thompson (1947), 96.

[23] Ambrose *De ob. Val.*3; 9.

[24] On Valentinian II's chastity, see Ambrose *De ob. Val.* 17; his refusal to attend games, ibid. 15; correction of errors, ibid. 14; Similarly 46; 15; and fasting, 16.

[25] Ibid. 17.

[26] Ibid. 16.

[27] As Williams observes, Ausonius' panegyric essentially went to the extent of attributing to Gratian the ascetic virtues of a fourth-century saint: (1995), 131–2.

matters: these were contemporary reports, and their greatest value lies in their picture of the personal virtues Gratian and Valentinian II were presented as possessing rather than those that they really did possess, and the audience to whom this presentation was offered—the imperial court, and the senatorial and military elites. The material point is surely that the theoretical requirement that the late Roman emperor set a good example by his personal conduct was one which both boy-emperors could be (and were) presented as satisfying to a reasonable extent, even if the comments of Eunapius and Ammianus suggest that even in their own times these presentations may not have been wholly convincing.

PRACTICAL ADMINISTRATION

Military prowess and leadership

Boys as young as Gratian and Valentinian II could be portrayed, therefore, as possessing the essential personal virtues required of an emperor in the late Roman world. Yet there was much more to a ruler than his presentation, and even the idealized picture of emperorship established by writers like Menander and Ammianus also demanded practical virtues and abilities from the emperor. The practical administration of the reigns of both child-emperors, the structures in place which could enable them to 'govern', and the reality of how much they could in actual practice fulfil the position of ruler of the empire therefore need to be considered.

The sources provide evidence for the theory, once again, of Gratian's skill in the arts of war. According to Ammianus he was warlike and merciful, while Rufinus wrote that the young emperor was vigorous and physically quick in combat.[28] Ausonius, again, offers the most detail on his pupil's ability, declaring that he was unmatched in athletic pursuits, in running, wrestling, leaping, and hurling the javelin.[29] In addition, his horsemanship was applauded, as was his skill with the bow and his great endurance.[30] In 367, upon presenting the boy to the troops as their new Augustus, Valentinian I had asserted that:

he will so conduct himself that good men will know that he understands them; he will rush forward to noble deeds and cling close to the military standards and eagles; he will endure sun and snow, frost and thirst, and wakeful hours;

---

[28] AM 31.10.18: *bellicosus et clemens*; Rufinus 11.13.
[29] Ausonius, *Grat.Act.* 14. Ausonius' praise is reminiscent of Ammianus' of Constantius II: AM 21.16.7.
[30] Ausonius, *Grat.Act.* 14, 18.

he will defend his camp, if necessity ever requires it; he will risk his life for the companions of his dangers...[31]

This hope was one which Ausonius determinedly presented as realized by Gratian's later deeds, claiming that the titles won by the young emperor's valour and courage were too numerous to list—perhaps an especially important point to make in the aftermath of Adrianople.[32] These were all traditional expectations of an emperor's conduct in war, but the emphasis on the youthful promise of a proclaimed emperor, before he had actually performed any deeds which could be praised, was an innovation in the approach to writing of an emperor's virtues, which mirrored the innovation of the situation. In the past, emperors such as Constantine had often been lauded for their bright promise and signs of greatness in their early years, but though Constantine liked to be portrayed as younger than he was in fact (an interesting attitude reflecting the greater glory and evidence of divine sanction in achieving spectacular feats at as young an age as possible), such praise usually came in the context of a panegyric delivered after such promise had been realized in many impressive deeds (or at least deeds which could be presented as such).[33] Indeed, it was the fulfilment of such promise in the form of mighty feats which marked the man out as the legitimate emperor, even if the greatest victories still came after an emperor had at least made a bid for the throne.[34] With a young child or even a youth on the throne, however, these mighty deeds were all as yet a long way before him, and the heavy emphasis on youthful promise was one way of coping with such a difference, and a method which would be adopted even more enthusiastically by western minority governments which followed.

The actual practice of Gratian's military ability in reality, as opposed to its presentation, is more difficult to assess. As observed in Chapter 1, an emperor's military leadership might take many different forms. As a 9-year-old boy Gratian's father had taken his son and co-Augustus on his Solicinium campaign of 368 against the Alamanni, in which the child can only have played a purely ceremonial role; indeed, Ammianus describes how, when preparing to join battle, Valentinian had Gratian, 'whose youth was even then unequal to battles and toil', kept back with the legion of the Joviani, in

---

[31] AM 27.6.9: *in pulchra facinora procursabit, signis militaribus et aquilis adhaesurus: solem nivesque et pruinas et sitim perferet et vigilias: castris (si necessitas adegerit aliquotiens) propugnabit: salutem pro periculorum sociis obiectabit...*

[32] Ausonius, *Grat.Act.* 2.

[33] On Constantine's youthful depiction, see e.g. *Pan.Lat.IV.16.4*; Cf. *VI.17.1*; *VII.5.2–3*. On Constantine I's preference for being represented as younger than he was, see: Barnes (1982), 38–41; Nixon and Rodgers (1994), 371, n. 71.

[34] As McLynn points out, if, as Theodoret asserts, Theodosius I had really been made emperor on the basis of a victory (over the Sarmatians), he would have been the first legitimate emperor to achieve the throne in this way: McLynn (2005), 91–2.

contrast to his warlike father, who surveyed his troops with uncovered head.[35] Even in 375, when Gratian was 16 and his father setting out on what would prove to be his final campaign, Ammianus reports that Valentinian arranged for Gratian to remain behind at Trier rather than come on campaign with him, although, as noted above, this was probably intended as a demonstration of Gratian's new independence following his marriage.[36] Ammianus does provide a detailed account of a campaign personally undertaken by Gratian as a young man of 19 in 378, however, against the Lentienses, as discussed in Chapter 3. According to the historian, Gratian showed great personal courage, inspiring the soldiers as he fought beside them in the front line, and the barbarians were thoroughly defeated.[37] Ammianus' praise of Gratian during this campaign is particularly interesting—with Gratian's personal leadership of his army in this encounter providing a rare glimpse of the 19-year-old emperor's real potential as a successful military emperor, even if he failed to recognize the grave crisis unfolding in the east at the same time.[38]

Yet despite Gratian's minor victory in the Lentienses campaign in 378, there are indications throughout the young emperor's reign that the extent of his control over his own military was seriously limited, most notably by his *magister militum*, Merobaudes. As discussed in Chapter 3, Valens first had requested western aid against the Goths in 377, and it had not been Gratian, but initially the general Frigeridus and then Richomeres who had been ordered to take the field on behalf of the western emperor.[39] But ominously, most of the troops who were sent under Richomeres, according to Ammianus, were persuaded to refuse to journey eastwards, and even to desert, by Merobaudes, who claimed that Gaul would suffer barbarian raiding if the troops left for the east.[40] Most significant here in the context of Gratian's practical role in his military command is the implication that Merobaudes could behave in such a manner without punishment, surely reflecting the reality that Gratian was far less in command than Ammianus and Ausonius would have us believe. Although Ammianus reported on Gratian holding counsel with his generals on the Lentienses campaign and determining the course of action, he clearly was not always able to enforce his military decisions if Merobaudes opposed them.[41]

---

[35] AM 27.10.6: *quo ita (ut placuit) maturato, Gratianoque apud signa Iovianorum retro detento, cuius aetas erat etiam tum proeliorum impatiens et laborum, Valentinianus ut dux cunctator et tutus, centurias et manipulos capite intecto collustrans...*

[36] AM 30.10.1. See also above, p. 54.

[37] AM 31.10.9–10, 13

[38] See above, pp. 74–6.

[39] AM 31.7.3–4.

[40] AM 31.7.4.

[41] AM 31.10.15. See Rodgers (1981), 90.

Gratian's inability to satisfy the Roman military establishment that he could deal with the Gothic crisis alone in the aftermath of Adrianople is reflected in the appointment of Theodosius as co-emperor (however it came about) in 379.[42] Theodosius' first pressing task was to address the acute problem of the Gothic invasions, and as by early 379 after their victory the Goths were already in Illyricum by early 379, the new emperor was originally given control of all or part of Illyricum, as well as the eastern Balkans and Thrace, even though Illyricum had been under Gratian's control.[43] Theodosius spent 379 rebuilding the eastern army, yet in 380 suffered a serious defeat, and early in September at Sirmium in Pannonia a crisis summit was held between Theodosius and Gratian's generals, possibly involving Gratian himself.[44] The available details are sketchy, but control of the Gothic war seems to have passed back to Gratian's advisers, and Gratian's Frankish generals Bauto and Arbogast succeeded in forcing a Gothic retreat in 381 from Illyricum back into Thrace, while in October 383, following negotiations carried out by the Roman generals Saturninus and Richomeres, a peace treaty was concluded.[45] Yet nowhere was Gratian, or still less his younger half-brother Valentinian II, reported as taking the field against the Goths.

In his writings Ausonius also spent considerable time emphasizing Gratian's empathy with his soldiers, concern for their welfare, and their devotion to him, while on Ammianus' account Valentinian I, on raising his son as Augustus, had urged him always to keep his place beside his soldiers, and to give his life's blood for them.[46] These were stock claims of military loyalty to an emperor, but as events would reveal, they were claims which probably had little grounding in reality, at least by the end of his reign. As noted in Chapter 3, according to Zosimus' account, in *c*.382 Gratian took some Alan deserters into the ranks of his army and showed them excessive favour, thus inspiring the hatred of his other soldiers.[47] It is highly possible that Gratian was taking in Alan troops from the Balkans in the hope of balancing up the Gallic domination of his army under the generalship of Merobaudes.[48] In 383, during the rebellion of Magnus Maximus, Merobaudes deserted Gratian for the usurper, apparently taking with him the bulk of the western army.[49] The ability of the *magister militum* to commit

[42] On the aftermath of Adrianople generally, see Lenski (1997), 131–52.

[43] And, according to Zosimus, Illyricum had been part of Valentinian II's allotment in 375: 4. 19.1–2; see also above, p. 62. On Theodosius I being granted Illyricum, see Errington (1996*b*), 19–22; Heather and Moncur (2001), 206, and also above, p. 78.

[44] Implied by Themistius, *Or.* 15.195a; see Heather and Moncur (2001), 249, n. 139.

[45] Zosimus 4.33.1–2; Heather and Moncur (2001), 207.

[46] Ausonius, *Grat.Act.* 7, 16; AM 37.6.12-13.

[47] Zosimus 4.35.2–3.

[48] Rodgers (1981), 101.

[49] Rodgers (1981), 103. For further discussion of Merobaudes' defection see above, pp. 83–4, n. 79.

such a breathtaking act of treachery makes it overwhelmingly likely that it was he, and not Gratian, who was usually the leader in the field with the troops, earning their personal loyalty and admiration, and suggesting also that Gratian was not perceived as adequately fulfilling his military function in any other manner either.

Not surprisingly, given his years first in Gratian's shadow and then in Theodosius', as well as his early death, there is almost no information concerning Valentinian II's military skill or leadership ability. As discussed above, there is a possibility of the young emperor having a naval command during Theodosius' campaign to recover the west from Magnus Maximus in 388, but little evidence survives to record this command, if it did exist.[50] The only other extant evidence relating even to any planned military activity on the part of Valentinian II comes immediately before the young emperor's death: again in his funeral oration, Ambrose wrote of Valentinian's great eagerness to come to the defence of Italy when Milan was threatened by barbarian raiders.[51] The lack of record of any role for Valentinian in the victory over Magnus Maximus suggests that Theodosius I had little intention of allowing his younger colleague the chance to gain military glory and potentially thereby some independence, and if Valentinian did plan an expedition from Trier to Milan in his final days, it is likely such plans were thwarted by Arbogast. Like Merobaudes dealing with Gratian less than a decade earlier, again Zosimus observed that it was Arbogast who commanded the soldiers' loyalty, rather than the emperor himself; so much so that no one dared to protest against him.[52]

Overall, the impression left by the sources concerning the practical side of Gratian's and Valentinian II's military functions is that the inevitably complimentary picture drawn by writers such as Ausonius could not measure up to the reality. These boy-emperors could be presented as embracing military skill, being full of youthful promise, and inspiring the loyalty of their troops, but they could not practically fulfil the vital military demands made of the emperor in the late Roman world: Gratian because his over-powerful *magister militum* claimed that role for himself, and Valentinian II because he simply was too young, and when he did come of an age for such activity, was not permitted to take part. Yet the record of strong military emperors of the fourth century who had preceded them, and the turbulent times through which these young emperors ruled, makes even their accessions truly remarkable.

---

[50] McLynn (1994), 293–4, and also above, p. 91.
[51] Ambrose *De ob. Val.* 22.
[52] Zosimus 4.54.4.

Justice

As discussed in Chapter 1, the administration of justice was a vital function of the emperor in the Roman world: he was the law incarnate. As we might by now expect, idealizing writers declared the merits of Gratian and Valentinian II in this department as well: according to Ausonius, Gratian's edicts removed all cause for fear, he allowed petitioners easy access, always extended pardon to those who repented, and granted generous arrears of tribute to the provinces, while showing great generosity to his friends.[53] Ambrose similarly described Valentinian II as never listening to the claims of informers, and not permitting any imposition to be visited upon provincials, and demonstrating his extraordinary fairness in judgement in the decision he passed on a matter concerning land belonging to members of his own family.[54] Ausonius praised Gratian for the honour he showed the senators, and both brothers were lauded for their eloquence, and also their thoughtfulness, justice, and maturity in dealing with matters in the consistory.[55] Yet Sulpicius Severus' verdict sounds a note of caution amidst all this praise, casting doubt on the wisdom of Gratian's appointments, asserting of Gratian's court that: 'Everything was for sale there, through the greed and might of a few men'.[56]

So much for the way in which these child-emperors might be presented as fulfilling the judicial and administrative function of their position. What about the reality? A number of scholars have written on the increased centralization of government under the later Roman empire, particularly the massive growth in the bureaucracy from the fourth century onwards. Discussion has focused on the growing powers of praetorian prefects from the time of Diocletian, with their wide range of functions (albeit in the civilian sphere only, following Constantine I's creation of *magistri militum* to command the army) alongside the emperor.[57] The administration of the empire was centralized to a high degree, as was the control of appointments and the administration of justice and finance.[58] According to this view, such 'excessive' centralization led to an

---

[53] Ausonius, *Grat.Act.* 15–16 for access to petitioners, pardons, and grants of arrears, and 1 and 14 for his generosity to his friends.

[54] For Valentinian II's refusal to hear informers, see Ambrose, *De ob. Val.* 18; protection of provincials, ibid. 21, and fair judgement, ibid. 37.

[55] For Gratian's honouring of senators, see Ausonius, *Grat.Act.* 1, 15, 16. For the eloquence of both brothers, see ibid. 15; Ambrose, *De ob. Val.* 62. For dealings in the consistory, Ausonius, *Grat.Act.* 14; Ambrose, *De ob. Val.* 16.

[56] Sulpicius Severus, *Chron.* 2.49.3: *omnia ibi venalia errant, per libidinem ac potentiam paucorum . . .*

[57] Jones (1964a), 1. 371.

[58] Ibid. 1. 403–4.

ever-increasing bulk of paperwork through appeals over conflicting decisions and serious delays piling more routine work onto the emperor and his officials, with the result that the emperor was even more reliant on his ministers and clerks to act on his behalf in dealing with this backlog of official business.[59] By *c*.400, it has been estimated that the number of individuals achieving good bureaucratic jobs was well over 6,000 per generation across the empire, in comparison with the *c*.250 who were thus employed in AD 250.[60] If we understand this growth as indicating an increase not merely in the number of those taking home pay-cheques but in a substantial number of genuine professionals, the impact upon the nature of imperial administration is considerable. This formation of a greatly enlarged and sophisticated bureaucracy meant in some respects a higher degree of control for the central government; at the same time, it also entailed delegation of authority and the empowering of officials to make decisions in their own right.[61]

For the emperor himself, this massive increase in bureaucracy risked his becoming isolated from his government, distant and inaccessible.[62] Beyond this, however, centralization of the government also made the individual emperor's impact on the running of that government less obvious for much of the time. Potentially, whoever the amateurish aristocrat might be who was placed at the head of a bureaucratic department, the effects of such a change on the department need not have been immediately obvious, since the lesser officers would continue to be well-trained civil servants whose careers and duties were unaffected by adjustments at the top.[63] This argument can be taken a step further: with a virtually self-running bureaucracy, what difference would it make to that government machine to have a child as its nominal head? The existence of departments with rules and procedures, heads of offices with semi-independent power-bases, and systems which continued producing the bureaucrats needed to staff the government offices meant that the personal impact of any emperor on his bureaucracy was bound to be reduced (even if the potential for personal intervention still remained). In addition, this new bureaucratic development changed the emperor's judicial role: he no longer needed to know the law himself, there were others around him who could tell him what it was and where to sign his name, as studies tracing the rise of the office of the late Roman legal *quaestor* in the fourth and fifth centuries,

---

[59] Ibid. 1. 410.

[60] Heather (1994), 19–20, defining approximately 3,000 in each half of the empire as achieving 'very good job' through service in palatine ministries, as provincial governors or even higher posts; though also clarifying that many of the higher offices were only held for short periods. Honoré argues that this professionalization was more advanced in the eastern empire than the western: Honoré (2006), 124–5.

[61] Kelly (2004), 186, 190.

[62] Ibid. 192.

[63] Matthews (1975), 77.

and the particular *quaestors* of the period, make clear.[64] Such a degree of sophistication had major repercussions for the judicial demands which would thereafter be made on the emperor.

The surviving laws from the reigns of Gratian and Valentinian II present many of the usual preoccupations of imperial legislation. Besides laws in favour of senatorial rights and regarding ecclesiastical matters, Gratian legislated on rights of appeal in court cases, issues of recruiting and deserters, and the regulation of palatines.[65] Similarly, Valentinian II's laws dealt with the ranking of different dignitaries, punishments for deserters, and the duties of decurions.[66] Nevertheless, a famous and indignant ruling of Valentinian II (addressed to Symmachus) does indicate that the boy-emperor may have been facing some resistance to the appointments of his new administration in 384, reflecting its precarious position at this time: 'There must be no dispute concerning an imperial judgement, for it is a kind of sacrilege to doubt whether the person whom the emperor has selected is worthy.'[67]

More striking still is how little legislation of Valentinian II survives from the entire period of his reign after Gratian's death in 383, and including the period following the arrival of Theodosius I in Italy in 388, and even after the eastern emperor's departure in 391. Before this point, and after, only a handful of laws certainly issued from Valentinian's court—one or two a year—have survived: perhaps an illustration of how little legislation was emanating from the western regime, or perhaps reflecting the priorities of those compiling the *Code* half a century later. In either case, the verdict does not reflect well on perceptions of the young emperor's fulfilment of his judicial function: either he was issuing few laws, or the *Code*'s compilers thought those he did issue rarely worth preserving. In addition, the steady rate of legislation which Theodosius I kept up during his sojourn in the west cannot have helped contemporaries to view Valentinian II as the source of western legislative authority.[68]

---

[64] On the rise of the *quaestor*, see Harries (1988), 148 ff. See generally Honoré's extensive work on the different *quaestors* serving under late Roman government: Honoré (1999), and esp. 11–23. Similarly Harries on the government of Constantinople under Arcadius and Honorius: 'the vagaries of the emperor were no longer important in the formulation of law; he was not a personality, he was an institution': Harries (1999), 47.

[65] e.g. on senatorial rights: *CTh.* 9.1.13 (11. Feb. 376), 9.35.3 (4 Jan. 399); on ecclesiastical issues: 16.5.4 (22 Apr. 376). On rights of appeal, see rights of appeal: 11.36.23 (30 Jan. 378); recruiting: 7.18.2 (2–5 July 379); deserters: 7.18.4 (15 July 380); palatines: 7.12.2 (1 Oct. 379).

[66] e.g. on ranking: *CTh.* 6.5.2 (21 May 384); deserters: 12.1.113 (3 Sept. 386); decurions: *CTh.* 11.16.16 (14 Apr. 385).

[67] *CTh.* 1.6.9 (28 Dec. 384): *Disputari de principali iudicio non oportet: sacrilegii enim instar est dubitare, an is dignus sit, quem elegerit imperator.* Though there are also perhaps echoes of *CSirm.* 1(5 May 333) here, and Constantine I's surprise at having to repeat a ruling on ecclesiastical matters.

[68] For laws from Trier after 388, see e.g. *CTh.* 4.22.3 (14 June 389); 8.5.50 (17 June 390).

Nevertheless, the professionalization which had taken place in the bureaucratic and judicial systems of the later Roman empire by the 370s did allow for the possibility of child-emperors at its head. One scholar has written that the late Roman emperor's purple ink fuelled the engines of the bureaucracy, and therefore 'a child who could not write could not rule'.[69] In fact, as the repeated accessions of child-emperors in the late Roman period must indicate, a child who could write only a little *could* rule: it was not necessary for him to have any thorough understanding of the legal decisions to which he was putting his name: the bureaucratic system had developed beyond that requirement in its emperor. This naturally opened the door to all kinds of abuses of position by bureaucrats, but does not alter the central point: the evolution of the bureaucratic structure of government into a self-sustaining entity in the late Roman empire made it theoretically possible for children like Gratian and Valentinian II to fulfil the judicial and administrative responsibilities of an emperor.

Religious role

As discussed in Chapter 1, from the time of Constantine the religious function of the emperor had been transformed by the adoption of Christianity. On a personal level, the religious role demanded of the emperor piety and devotion— which Ausonius also attested to in Gratian.[70] Bishop Ambrose made repeated assertions as to the piety of both brothers in his writings, claiming as well that, following his restoration, Valentinian II had turned from his mother's homoean beliefs and wholeheartedly embraced orthodoxy.[71] But as noted above, in addition to personal religious commitment, a Christian emperor's duties also involved promoting the unity of the church for the good of his empire and ensuring its peace and prosperity through correct observance of the 'true' faith, thus pleasing God.

The fourth century for the Christian church was a period dominated by the 'Arian' controversy, arising from the presbyter Arius' preaching that God was indivisible, and the Son must therefore be inferior to the Father. Bound up with this was Arius' argument that Christ must have been begotten out of nothing, since the substance of the Father was indivisible; thus Father and Son were not of one, or even the same, substance.[72] This issue requires far too

---

[69] McCormick (2000), 143.

[70] Ausonius *Grat.Act.* 14; Similarly Rufinus 11.13.

[71] On the piety of both brothers, see Ambrose, *De ob. Val.* 6, 19, 74, 79b; *De ob. Theod.* 51; *Ep.* 73 [18].34. On Valentinian's II embracing of orthodoxy, see Ambrose, *Ep.* 25 [53].

[72] Ayres (2004), 15–16. Ayres provides a useful summary of how the original dispute, beginning in the late 310s between the priest Arius, and his bishop Alexander, in Alexandria, grew into the controversy which dominated the church in the centuries to follow: pp. 430–5; also pointing out that the term 'Arian' itself is frequently inappropriately used in modern scholarship:

much detail to be discussed sufficiently here (and continues to receive ample attention from modern scholarship); it must be enough to note that by the time of Valentinian I's accession, the teachings of the church had split in many different directions as a result of repeated attempts to define the issues.[73] Under Constantius II, the homoean (semi-Arian) solution of Christ being of 'like' substance to the Father had been imposed after the councils at Ariminum and Seleukia in 359.[74] Valentinian I and Valens, being natives of Pannonia, may well have been brought up in the belief in homoean Christianity which surrounded them there. Valens was certainly branded as Arian after his accession, although Valentinian I, on the other hand, is usually seen as Nicene, and seems to have pursued a tolerant line of belief, which sought to alienate as few of his subjects as possible—he has even been described as 'indifferent' to religious distinctions.[75]

An emperor's duty to promote the unity of the church might take the practical form of imperial edicts or the calling of councils to settle matters of doctrinal or authoritative dispute, as advocated by Eusebius in his *Life of Constantine*. Early indications of Gratian's attitude to his religious function after 375 suggest that his administration intended originally to continue his father's policy of maintaining a careful balance between different religious parties in the interests of stability, while generally confirming ecclesiastical privileges. In an edict dated to 17 May 376, Gratian legislated to confirm his father's decision to make a distinction between civil and ecclesiastical jurisdiction.[76] Following Adrianople, a number of laws concerning ecclesiastical matters and issued by Gratian indicate that the imperial responsibility of promoting unity within the church—especially at a time of such uncertainty—was coming more to the forefront of his administration's consciousness. A law dating to 379 was directed against heretical assemblies, but appears to have been aimed only at Donatists, once again following Valentinian I's lead.[77] And the

---

pp. 13–14. Ayres's thought-provoking book has been responded to by various scholars in five articles published in *HThR* 100: 2 (2007), 141–75.

[73] Errington (1997), 24–5.

[74] For an excellent summary of the involvement of emperors in Christological controversies in the fourth century up until the Valentinian dynasty, see Lenski (2002), 235–42. See also Errington (1997), 25–6.

[75] Lenski (2002), 240 ff. For the 'Arianism' of Valens, see Theodoret 4.12.1–4; Philostorgius 9.3; Socrates 4.16; Sozomen 6.6.10; Also Errington (1997), 25–6; Lenski (2002), 240–1.

[76] *CTh.* 16.2.23 (17 May 376). On this law, see Williams (1995), 133–4.

[77] The law is *CTh.* 16.5.4 (22 Apr. 376). Although as Williams explains, there is some confusion over the dating of this piece of legislation, due to its being addressed to Hesperius as praetorian prefect, though he was only proconsul of Africa in 376 and not prefect until 378–9. Various scholars have suggested the law therefore belongs to this later date (e.g. Palanque (1931), 87–90), a view which I have followed, but Seeck (1919), 246, followed by Williams (1995), 134, suggests it was simply a mistake in the title of Hesperius. On measures of Valentinian I against Donatists, see Piganiol (1972), 227–8, n. 7; Gottlieb (1973), 77; Williams (1995), 134–5. For a concise explanation of the origins and nature of the Donatist schism in North Africa, see Drake (2006), 116–21.

ecclesiastical historians report that in the immediate aftermath of Adrianople, Gratian issued an edict of toleration for the whole empire, recalling bishops who had been exiled by Valens, and assuring freedom of worship to all religious groups (except those already outlawed).[78] This edict was hardly a surprising action amidst the confusion which must have ensued in the eastern church, especially following the death of the 'Arian' Valens.[79] The rescript of 20 August 379, which may well refer back to this edict, seems to have thought better of it, rescinding those freedoms, though once again it was probably principally the Donatists at whom the withdrawal of freedoms was aimed.[80]

That the early position of Gratian's rule on the issue of his embracing of his religious function was one of tolerance is confirmed also by the emperor's having handed over a basilica in Milan for the use of the homoean community at some point between 378 and 381, probably in connection with the arrival in the city of the homoean empress Justina.[81] The evidence for this action comes in the context of Ambrose's publication of his *De spiritu sancto* in 381, in part celebrating Gratian's subsequent decision to hand back the sequestered basilica to the Nicene community.[82] The fact that it was at Milan that the rescript of August 379 was issued which, as noted, rescinded at least part of an earlier edict of toleration given at Sirmium, has raised claims among some scholars that this move was due to Gratian falling rapidly under the influence of Ambrose, causing the young emperor to abandon immediately his earlier tolerant stance.[83] A change in Gratian's religious policies from an initially tolerant, hands-off approach, much like his father's, is undeniably apparent from the early 380s onwards; Ambrose is unlikely, however, to have been the only individual influencing Gratian in this respect at this time—the actions of his new co-emperor Theodosius I, and the military crises of the time, were also significant.

Ambrose's influence upon the young Gratian's exercise of his religious function has been viewed as crucial, and he has been represented by more than one scholar as the young emperor's 'guide, philosopher, and friend', principally on the basis of the bishop's lengthy treatise, the *De fide*, the first

---

[78] Socrates 5.2.1; Sozomen 7.1.3; Theodoret 5.2.

[79] McLynn (1994), 91.

[80] *CTh.* 16.5.5 (3 Aug. 379). See Gottlieb (1973), 60–1; McLynn (1994), 102.

[81] Maier (1994), 74; Williams (1995), 139, 166; Liebeschuetz (2005), 12. On the empress Justina's probable movements during this period, see above p. 63, n. 76. Errington, however, disagrees that the handover had anything to do with Justina, though he does not suggest an alternative motivation: (2006), 198. For the debate on the relative sizes of the Nicene and homoean congregations of Milan during this era, and homoean leaders, see Barnes (2002), 235–6; Kaufman (1997), 440 ff.; Williams (1997), 441–5; McLynn (1997), 449.

[82] Ambrose, *De spir.sanct.* i.I.19–21.

[83] On the different arguments, see Williams (1995), 157–60. For a recent consideration of Ambrose's influence over Gratian, see Errington (2006), 31.

volumes of which he presented to Gratian in March 380.[84] Many reasons have been suggested as to why the treatise was written, with perhaps the most convincing being that what led to Ambrose's writing *De fide* was not a desire on the part of the young emperor for spiritual guidance, as it has often been portrayed, but an order that Ambrose provide a statement of his own faith, upon which the bishop then chose to put his own gloss.[85] At the time of Gratian's request, which came probably in October 378, the emperor was stationed at Illyricum, trying to deal with the aftermath of the Adrianople disaster.[86] His court was doubtless populated by homoean churchmen, whose views may have been prevalent throughout the emperor's early childhood in the region.[87] He may have been influenced in addition by the arrival at Milan of his stepmother Justina and the young Valentinian II.[88] At any rate, Gratian's request for a statement of faith from Ambrose is likely to have been prompted more from a desire to promote unity within the church at such a troubled time than a desire for doctrinal guidance from a bishop who had not as yet particularly distinguished himself as a defender of orthodoxy.[89]

The degree of Ambrose's influence over Gratian is important here insofar as it influenced the religious policies of the government—and hence the emperor's exercise of his religious function. Yet assertions of Ambrose's early influence over Gratian should be treated with caution, since the evidence for there being any intimacy between Gratian and Ambrose derives almost entirely from the writings of Ambrose himself.[90] And as affairs throughout Gratian's reign, such as the Priscillianist case and the Altar of Victory controversy, reveal, Gratian's court was subject to pressures and lobbying from many different groups and individuals, and Ambrose, though often able to involve himself in the politics of such affairs, was unable to impose his views consistently.[91] Nevertheless, the imperial court's move to Milan from Trier in the

---

[84] On Ambrose as Gratian's 'guide', see Hanson (1988), 795. Similarly Matthews (1975), 187–8; Sivan (1993), 109; Nautin (1974), 229–44. On the date of the presentation of the first volume: Nautin (1974), 238. On early relations between Ambrose and Gratian generally, see also Barnes (1999), 168–74.

[85] McLynn (1994), 102–3. In general, ibid. 79 ff. Also Nautin (1974), 238; Williams (1995), 141–3. For a slightly different view, see Liebeschuetz (2005), 11, n. 3. On *De fide* generally, see Ayres (2004), 262–4. For traditional views on Gratian requesting the work for his own spiritual guidance, see e.g. Palanque (1933), 50; Dudden (1935), 189.

[86] Nautin (1974), 238.

[87] McLynn (1994), 91; also Nautin (1974), 239–40. Ps.-Aurelius Victor notes Gratian's birthplace as Sirmium (47.1) although McLynn argues for Cibalae (1994: 98).

[88] Glaesener (1957), 472.

[89] McLynn (1994), 98; Nautin (1974), 237. Although, see Williams (1995), 142. Ambrose's apparent intervention in the installation of a new bishop at Sirmium may have prompted the accusations of the Arian clergy (McLynn (1994), 99); Glaesener argues Justina, Valentinian II's mother, who may have resided at Sirmium at this point, made the accusations (1957: 472).

[90] McLynn (1994), 80: including several posthumous tributes to their friendship and Gratian's piety: Ambrose, *De ob. Val.* 78, 80; *De ob.Theod.* 52.

[91] McLynn (1994), 149–52.

spring of 381 would have provided increased opportunity for Ambrose to wield greater influence at court, and his counselling of the young emperor from this time is more clearly attested.[92]

As well as legislating for the entire empire in late 378 with his edict of toleration, it was also during this period that, following the council of Rome (378) and a request from Pope Damasus, the young emperor endorsed a new system of ecclesiastical jurisdiction and accepted Rome's claim to authority to hear cases of deposed bishops in all of the western provinces, and possibly metropolitans of the east too.[93] It seems most likely that this was the time when Gratian laid his plans for a council to be held at Aquileia as well, summoning delegates from both halves of the empire, and taking advantage of his ability at this point to claim responsibility for both regions.[94] Yet the council did not eventuate quite as Gratian seems originally to have planned, and the developments provide an insight into the growing influence of Ambrose of Milan over the young emperor's religious policies at this time.[95] Gratian's letter to the praetorian prefect Syagrius confirmed that, by the time the council met in September 381, Ambrose had convinced the emperor to reduce the scope of the meeting considerably, and in the end it had become only a small gathering of bishops from local Italian cities.[96] Rather than an ecumenical gathering for the discussion of issues of doctrine, it became a forum for Ambrose to stage the specific condemnation and deposition of two homoean bishops.[97] By 381, therefore, Ambrose's influence with Gratian— and hence also the pro-Nicene stance of the government—had clearly grown; probably coloured additionally by the staunch orthodoxy of Gratian's eastern colleague from 379 onwards, Theodosius I, discussed earlier. To some extent Ambrose's actions aimed at helping Gratian save face after Theodosius' sabotage of the western council plans: Gratian was, it seems, being manipulated by both Theodosius and Ambrose, for their own ends.[98] Nevertheless, both the calling of this council, as well as Gratian's plans for a general church settlement to be made at a further council at Rome in 382, illustrate the young emperor's attempt to fulfil the traditional religious responsibilities of a Christian emperor.[99]

---

[92] Ibid. 120. Cf. Williams (1995), 166.

[93] *Coll.Avell.* 13; see McLynn (1994), 90–1; Hanson (1988), 794; Liebeschuetz (2005), 244–5.

[94] Errington (1997), 45–6; McLynn argues for the plans being made in summer 380 as part of a move to outbid Theodosius (1994: 112).

[95] On the council generally, see McLynn (1991), 56–72.

[96] *Acta* 3; Errington (2006), 196–7.

[97] Williams (1995), 163, 169–84 on the whole council; also Errington (2006), 197–8; Liebeschuetz (2005), 12–13.

[98] See Heather and Moncur (2001), 215; McLynn (1994) 124.

[99] Heather and Moncur (2001) 215.

Any Christian emperor of the fourth century (regardless of his age) would be expected to take a stance on pagan issues, and would find himself subject to pressures from different Christian factions on the extent to which paganism was to be tolerated. The Altar of Victory saga, played out under the reigns of both Gratian and Valentinian II, reflected just such an instance of lobbying and pressure from different groups and individuals, as each emperor strove to be seen as fulfilling his expected religious function. One area of policy for which Gratian has received most attention in modern scholarship is his anti-pagan legislation, his removal of the Altar of Victory from the senate-house in Rome, and his supposed repudiation of both the pontifical robe and the title of *pontifex maximus*, traditionally borne by every Roman emperor. Gratian's anti-pagan legislation seems to have been issued around 381–2 (the laws themselves do not survive), and at about the same time the removal of the Altar of Victory was ordered.[100]

A delegation was sent from the senate in Rome to protest to Gratian over the new measures, but the emperor never received them.[101] Ambrose had presented Gratian with a *libellus* forwarded to him by Pope Damasus, signed by 'countless' senators, protesting against any restoration of the pagan privileges, and the emperor was thus skilfully prevented from realizing the extent of the opposition to his actions.[102] Ambrose explicitly denied responsibility for initiating the legislation, and some scholars have suggested a Christian aristocrat was behind it—either Anicius Auchenius Bassus, urban prefect in 382, or Valerius Severus, who was both urban prefect and praetorian prefect of Italy in the course of 382.[103] If a Roman aristocrat was responsible for the suggestion, however, it does not follow that the aristocracy in general were pleased with the move, and Gratian's refusal even to grant Symmachus an audience was a most serious snub to the pagan senators, with the potential to sour relations dangerously between the court and many Roman senatorial families.[104]

The extent of Gratian's anti-pagan legislation—and indeed its contemporary significance—has been questioned in two recent studies.[105] The general

---

[100] Ambrose, writing in the summer of 384, writes of the laws being issued almost two years earlier (*Ep.* 72 [17].10). On the legislation, see Jones (1964a), 1. 163; Matthews (1975), 204; and particularly Brown (1972b), 181.

[101] Symmachus, *Rel.* 3.1. McLynn (1994), 151. On the Roman aristocrats involved in upholding the pagan cause generally in the 380s–390s, see Bloch (1963), 193–218, and most recently Cameron (2011), 34 ff.

[102] Ambrose, *Ep.*72 [17]. 10; McLynn (1994), 152.

[103] For Ambrose's denial of responsibility, see Ambrose, *Ep. Extra coll.* 10 [57].2. For suggestions of the involvement of Bassus or Severus, see Errington (2006), 200; Lizzi Testa (2007), 262; McLynn (1994), 151; Potter (2004), 560–1. On the Christian aristocrats among the Roman senatorial elite by the late fourth century, see Brown (1972b), 161–82. Also on the role of the urban prefect in religious affairs generally, see Chastagnol (1960), 137–77.

[104] Liebeschuetz (2005), 13–14; Errington (2006), 124–5; Potter (2004), 560–1.

[105] Lizzi Testa (2007), 251–62; Cameron (2007b), 341–87; and now restated in Cameron (2011), 39–51.

consensus for many years had been that Gratian's legislation had seen the confiscation of public funds used to support the Vestal Virgins and the upkeep and ceremonies of other traditional state-supported Roman priesthoods, including the confiscation of landed property. One recent suggestion, however, is that Gratian's legislation did not in fact apply to all priestly colleges or temples, as is generally claimed, but only to some specific privileges of the Vestals.[106] The precise language used by the urban prefect Symmachus, who wrote an official *relatio* on the subject in 384, focuses only on the particular privileges of the Vestal Virgins that had been revoked.[107] Nevertheless, though hardly as wide-ranging as has been generally assumed, Gratian's actions were clearly still considered severe enough to provoke protests from pagan senators of Rome, particularly when combined with the emperor's removal of the Altar of Victory.[108] It is highly likely that Gratian himself had little understanding of the sort of response his actions might elicit from the pagans of Rome.[109]

The claim of Gratian's repudiation of the pontifical robe and the title of *pontifex maximus* has also come under recent scrutiny.[110] It has been argued that there probably never was a pontifical robe for Gratian to refuse, and certainly, the only mention of such a garment (at all, not merely in relation to Gratian) appears in Zosimus on this one occasion.[111] Regarding the title of *pontifex maximus*, it is suggested that here there is a genuine change taking place around the time of Gratian's reign—but not so much a repudiation of the title, as a slight adjustment and redefinition of it. For it is around the end of the fourth century, it has been pointed out, that *maximus* comes to be replaced by *inclitus* in imperial titulature, which could allow this traditional pagan title to be reinterpreted in a Christian sense.[112]

A less draconian anti-pagan law, and modification, rather than repudiation, of the *pontifex maximus* title, would certainly seem more in keeping with the generally tolerant attitude that Gratian seems otherwise to have pursued in religious affairs. Within the context of the expectations of religious function upon any Christian emperor in the late fourth century, Gratian's actions seem unlikely to have been especially influenced by his youth: he was, after all, a military emperor (even if ultimately an unsuccessful one), who by the time of

---

[106] Lizzi Testa (2007), 260.
[107] Symmachus, *Rel.* 3.40; Lizzi Testa (2007), 252–4, pp. 255, 258.
[108] Lizzi Testa (2007), 260.
[109] McLynn (1994), 151–2.
[110] Cameron (2007*b*), 341–87; and now Cameron (2011), 51–6.
[111] Zosimus 4.36.5. Cameron originally made an argument for the date of 383 for the repudiation of the robe (Cameron (1968*a*), 99) but has now decided the robe itself probably never existed: Cameron (2007*b*), 349–54. Errington also argues that there probably never was a pontifical robe: (2006), 300, n. 119.
[112] Cameron (2007*b*), 364, 366, 375.

these changes in his religious policy was well into his twenties. Yet it is very important to highlight that, although churchmen themselves remained uncomfortable with emperors interfering in church affairs or claiming any kind of 'priestly' capacity themselves, the modification and redefinition of the *pontifex maximus* title emphasized how unwilling emperors themselves were to relinquish their claims to religious authority.[113] As we shall see, Valentinian II's court was prepared to go to extreme (and damaging) lengths in attempting to preserve the aura of the boy-emperor's pious and ceremonial authority. And as child-emperor regimes were repeated and methods of presenting them as appropriately authoritative and plausible continued to develop, this claim to religious authority would carry on growing and become increasingly prominent in imperial presentation.

The follow-up to Gratian's anti-pagan legislation was the famous debate between Symmachus and Ambrose in 384, as the pagan faction petitioned Valentinian II in hope of a revocation of Gratian's law.[114] Symmachus' official *relatio* has come to be regarded as the classic statement of late Roman pagan ideals, but his eloquence was to no avail. Ambrose's hard-line response allowed no compromise, though his impassioned appeal probably would not have been so vehement if there had not been some chance the emperor would give in.[115] Yet we can hardly be surprised, given Valentinian's need to demonstrate his Christian authority, that the then 12-year-old emperor refused the pagan petition.[116] The extent to which the beleaguered regime of Valentinian II in 384 still needed the support of the powerful pagan aristocrats of Rome had to be weighed against his need to be seen as fully embracing his religious function.

It was in the course of 385–6, through the conflict between the homoean court of Valentinian II (supposedly headed by his mother Justina) and the staunchly orthodox Bishop Ambrose, that the centrality of the child-emperor's religious role was demonstrated most clearly. Much has been written regarding this conflict, and only the most relevant points need to be discussed here.[117] The conflict of 385–6 centred around the struggle for possession of certain basilicas of the city which Valentinian II's court wished to claim for use by himself and his fellow-homoeans, and the adamant and public refusal of the orthodox bishop to allow this use.[118] The empress Justina has often been

---

[113] Cameron (2007*b*). 360–1, 365 on church discomfort with imperial claims to religious authority; on imperial reluctance to give up such claims, see pp. 366, 370.

[114] See Symmachus, *Rel.* 3; Ambrose, *Epp.* 72 [17]; 73 [18]. Cf. McLynn (1994), 166; Liebeschuetz (2011), 91–4.

[115] Errington (2006), 126.

[116] Matthews (1975), 205–6.

[117] For detailed analysis of the sources and events, see: Lenox-Conyngham (1982), 353–7; Maier (1994), 85–8; Williams (1995), 210–15; McLynn (1994), 187ff; and most recently, Liebeschuetz (2011), 85–9.

[118] McLynn (1994), 187–8 ff.

viewed as the prime mover on the homoean side, but despite the prevailing opinion of both ancient and modern commentators, the conflict cannot be attributed solely, or even largely, to the religious fervour of Valentinian's mother, but must in fact have had the backing of the boy's advisers, given the constitutional methods which were used by the court in the attempt to prevail over Ambrose.[119] Modern scholarship has often attributed the position of regent to Justina, but as discussed in the Introduction, in fact there simply was no such constitutional office within the Roman government.[120] Justina had therefore no legal power to direct imperial policy, though no doubt her personal influence with her son was a significant factor. The most convincing explanation for the willingness of court advisers of the boy-emperor to embroil the regime in such a damaging episode lay in the vitally important ceremonial and religious function of the young emperor, and the threat posed by Ambrose to that function.[121] Still only just into his teenage years, and under threat from a powerful adult usurper, there were not many functions that Valentinian II could adequately perform at this stage, and Ambrose's unrelenting stance during the Altar of Victory debate, and more specifically his threat to the emperor that he might refuse him entrance to the church if he restored the pagan privileges, had been already a serious assertion of power on the bishop's part.[122] As a 13-year-old boy, in a highly vulnerable situation, with a strong, orthodox usurper (Magnus Maximus) holding a rival court at Trier, Valentinian II had few arenas other than his Christianity in which to display his legitimacy: it was vital that this religious and ceremonial role be maintained.[123] Moreover, the government's desire to annex one of Milan's basilicas for its ceremonies (when presumably such ceremonies could have been held within the palace complex if necessary) also suggests that the young emperor's advisers were well aware that public attendance at church for religious feasts could bolster Valentinian II's civic image and garner public loyalty, and potentially aid in making the emperor's religious preferences seem less covert and more acceptable.

Valentinian II's laws proclaiming that his subjects should not be concerned with workaday matters on Sundays, and that all but the most serious of crimes should be pardoned at Easter, indicate that the boy-emperor and his ministers were anxious for him to be seen to be fully embracing this function.[124] Most

---

[119] Ibid. 171 ff. For the suggestion that there was nevertheless some opposition at court also, see Barnes (2000), 293. For the view of Justina as a key protagonist, see e.g. Rufinus 11.15; Theodoret 5.13; Socrates 5.11; Augustine, *Conf.* 9.7.15; Paulinus, *VAmb.* 12–13; McLynn (1994), 171. Matthews (1975), 188–9; Jones (1964a), 1. 164.

[120] See above, pp. 9–12. Cf. Mommsen (1903), 101 f.; Straub (1952), 108. For an example of Justina described as 'regent', see Sivan (1996), 200.

[121] McLynn (1994), 174.

[122] Ambrose, *Ep.* 72 [17].13. Most recently on this episode, see Liebeschuetz (2011), 83, and more generally on Ambrose's views of the place of the emperor in relation to the church, p. 82.

[123] McLynn (1994), 174.

[124] *CTh.* 9.38.7 (22 Mar. 384); 9.38.8 (25 Feb. 385); 8.8.3 (24 Nov. 386). McLynn points out that the public tone set by Valentinian II's administration through such laws anticipated the

significantly, in January 386 the regime of the 15-year-old Valentinian II decreed freedom of assembly for all who followed the faith as laid down at Constantius II's councils of Ariminum and Constantinople, namely homoeanism. Any who considered such freedom was theirs alone would be guilty of treason and a capital offence—implicitly including even the city's bishop.[125] A perceived threat from Ambrose to the child's ability to demonstrate his majesty could conceivably have caused the emperor's ministers to be willing to favour the homoean clerics attached to the imperial court, whose commitment to the dynasty at least was unconditional.[126] Valentinian II's personal piety, of course, may also have been involved, but he was still very young, and the fact that the advisers around the boy-emperor were prepared to involve the government in such a damaging conflict at a time when it could scarcely afford to reveal its weaknesses only emphasizes the importance of the issues at stake.[127] The court's eventual decision to back down may have been an indication of Ambrose's power, but it was even more a demonstration of the government's weakness. The events surrounding the 'persecution' of Ambrose of Milan starkly emphasized that power-brokers surrounding the child on the throne believed that it was essential he be perceived as fulfilling his religious function, and were prepared to go to extreme lengths to preserve such an image. Ambrose's refusal to comply with the demands of the homoean court unquestionably posed a far greater threat to Valentinian II's authority than it might have done with an adult ruler.

There were many ways in which a Christian emperor might seek to fulfil his religious function at this time: through the issuing of anti-pagan legislation and ecclesiastical laws, through benefactions to churches, through staging councils to settle matters of doctrine and thereby promote unity within the church, and through acts of personal piety. In their different efforts, both Gratian and Valentinian II can be seen to have made attempts in most of these areas to live up to their responsibilities. Yet the specific role of a Christian emperor within the church was by no means clear-cut, and as episodes such as the basilicas controversy confirm, the boundaries between religious and political activity were frequently blurred. The centrality of Christian liturgy in the self-presentation of Theodosius I has been observed to highlight an increased demand in ceremonial services offered by the church, rather than an increase in imperial piety, reflecting less the strength of the emperor's faith than the

---

studied piety of the later boy-emperors Arcadius and Honorius: McLynn (1994), 174. There is also a hint in Ambrose's speech that Valentinian had sought to convene a council of Gallic bishops to resolve their disputes, which Ambrose had been requested to attend: *De ob. Val.* 25.

[125] *CTh.* 16.1.4 (23 Jan. 386); McLynn (1994), 181.

[126] McLynn (1994), 174.

[127] Ibid. 172. Valentinian's personal piety as a factor in the matter is suggested by Ambrose, *Ep.* 76 [20]. 2.

precariousness of his political situation.[128] In the case of Valentinian II, the need for an imperial alliance with the church to bolster a weak and threatened regime was even more clearly demonstrated in the struggles of the young emperor's court to exert his authority in religious politics at Milan.

Adding to the catalogue of imperial virtues; the use of 'youth' to exalt or excuse

When examined in the light of the sort of traditional imperial functions and expectations outlined in Chapter 1, the presentation of both Gratian and Valentinian II, and in many cases these young emperors' attempts at practical fulfilment of these functions, indicate the awareness of their advisers of the need for the emperor to continue to live up to these ideals regardless of his age. Yet these first child-emperor reigns also see some less conventional virtues being introduced to the imperial catalogue, virtues which might be unexpected if applied to adult emperors, and which would come to be further developed in the child-emperor reigns to follow. These new virtues we see particularly emphasized in the funeral oration of Ambrose for Valentinian II, and they are virtues with clearly Christian overtones which, again, may reflect qualities Ambrose wanted to attribute to Gratian and Valentinian II rather than those which their governments would have chosen to emphasize during their lifetimes.[129] Nevertheless, they are virtues worth noting in this early stage of the process of making plausible the rule of a child-emperor, and foreshadow the writings of later commentators on the emperor Honorius, and especially the eastern emperor Theodosius II.

Thus, as Ambrose declared, Gratian was: 'faithful to the Lord, pious and gentle, pure-hearted and chaste.'[130] Perhaps more surprising is Ambrose's description of the two brothers as 'simpler than doves, swifter than eagles, milder than lambs, more innocent than calves'.[131] According to Ambrose, though Valentinian II had died young, he had been 'a veteran in the service of the virtues', immature in years yet mature in judgement, while bearing the heavy yoke of stern self-discipline in his youth.[132] His 'self-control and peace-loving serenity' were credited with ensuring the safety of both Gaul and Italy, while Ambrose asserts that while reproaching Magnus Maximus for his actions, the bishop had told him to note the difference between his (the

---

[128] McLynn (2005), 107.

[129] McLynn (1994), 155.

[130] Ambrose, *De ob. Val.* 74: *Promittit fratri augustae memoriae Gratianus praesto sibi fructus diversarum esse virtutem; fuit enim et ipse fidelis in domino, pius atque mansuetus, puro corde.*

[131] Ibid. 79: *Non virtutum distantia dispares fecit super columbas simpliciores, super aquilas leviores, super agnos clementiores, super vitulos innocentiores.*

[132] Ibid. 46: *Esto tamen, dolendum sit, quod primaeva obierit aetate: gratulandum tamen, quod virtutum stipendiis veteranus decesserit.* See also 3 and 10.

usurper's) threats and 'the mildness of the boy Valentinian Augustus', who had paid Huns and Alans to make peace terms.[133] Praise for mildness and innocence in an emperor is something we would surely not expect were that emperor not a child; such virtues played upon the idea of a boy-emperor's vulnerability, and the emotive idea of the purity of such a boy-ruler invoking greater security for the state precisely through his youth and innocence attracting divine protection—although for both Gratian and Valentinian II, it was rather a struggle to claim that such protection had been successful.

Ambrose was also entirely capable of using Valentinian II's youth to excuse him—as when he protested to Magnus Maximus that the boy-emperor could not possibly have travelled across the Alps in winter to join him at Trier at his age, and without his mother.[134] At the same time, as in the Altar of Victory controversy, Ambrose stridently informed Valentinian himself that his youth was no excuse for action which the bishop believed to be wrong: he should 'Let no one creep upon [his] youthful age', for: 'Every age is mature where Christ is concerned. Every age has the full experience of God. A childhood of faith is not recognized.'[135]

This use of a boy-emperor's age both to exalt or excuse, as the occasion demanded, reflected the complexity of the situation—a paradox also suggested by Ausonius' writings on Gratian, in which he describes him as: 'Gratian, who in virtue of his authority is styled Imperator; of his courage, the Victorious, of his sacred person, Augustus; of his devotion, Pontifex; of his tenderness, a Father; of his age, a Son; and of natural affection, both one and the other.'[136] Fulfilling the role of both Father and Son of the empire was not one which either Gratian or Valentinian II ultimately managed comfortably.[137]

A great deal of the plausibility of the young Valentinian II as presented by his advisers to senatorial supporters relied upon the use of religious ceremonial to justify and bolster his position where possible. After all, on a very basic level, if in many areas of the empire imperial portraits served the purpose of making the ruler's image known to his subjects, being displayed in public

---

[133] On Valentinian II's self-control, see ibid. 68: *Denique moderatione tua et tranquillitate pacifica nec Gallia hostem sensit et Italia hostem reppulit, qui eius finibas imminebat.* On his mildness, see Ambrose, *Ep.* 30 (Maur. 24). 8: *Vide autem, quid intersit inter tuas minitationes et Valentiniani Augusti pueri mansuetudinem.*

[134] Ambrose, *Ep.* 30 (Maur. 24). 7.

[135] Ibid. 72 (Maur. 17).15: *Omnis aetas perfecta Christo est, omnis deo plena. Pueritia fidei non probatur, parvuli etiam Christum intrepido adversus persecutores ore confessi sunt.*

[136] Ausonius, *Grat.Act.* 7: *unus in ore omnium Gratianus, potestate imperator, virtute victor, Augustus sanctitate, pontifex religion, indulgentia pater, aetate filius, pietate utrumque.* Themistius writes similarly of Constantius (who was aged about 30 at the time of the speech) in *Oration 1*, 16c–17a.

[137] Similarly, McLynn points out that Augustine's account of Theodosius' restoration of Valentinian II's throne in the *City of God* portrays the younger emperor as more 'consistently small' than any other: McLynn (1998), 32.

places and carried in processions, this was surely a role a well-behaved child could fulfil.[138] Writings such as those of Ausonius and Ambrose were part of that presentation: they could portray child-emperors as amply satisfying the demands of personal virtue made on the ruler, such as distinguished background, a liberal-arts education, wisdom, temperance, and chastity. They could offer the new emphasis on a proclaimed Augustus' youthful promise, when there were no actual deeds to praise. They could also make claims as to the boys' military skill, and judicial and religious suitability for the position in which they were placed, but the real demands of practical administration in these areas in the later Roman empire made such claims harder to maintain. And of course, we need not suppose that those at court believed all that they were being told of their young ruler, as Augustine's comments in later life on his role as rhetor to the court of Valentinian II in the 380s emphasized.[139]

For Valentinian, the reality must have been limited power in his hands—a situation which did not improve with his age after his restoration by Theodosius I—and a great deal more in the hands of those supporting his rule, particularly the generals Bauto and Arbogast. The case of Gratian is somewhat different, but his ultimate inability to win and maintain the loyalty of his own military similarly suggests that the greatest power lay in the hands of Merobaudes. The development of sophisticated government structures, such as a self-sustaining bureaucratic machine, and an increase in ceremonial made it possible to conceive of having a child-emperor, but as the long-term picture of the reigns demonstrated, such supportive structures and purported possession of imperial virtues were not enough. Aurelius Victor neatly encapsulated the issue in his summary of Gratian:

'He would have been fitted with all good qualities, if he had attended to comprehending the science of ruling the state, from which he was almost a stranger not only by inclination but also by practice.'[140]

Yet it is clear that while some aspects of the emperor's role, such as the judicial and ceremonial function, had evolved to a point where a child could reasonably be argued to fulfil them, his expected military role, around which many of the political problems of these two regimes centred, had not. Furthermore, alongside the evolution of new strategies for managing and presenting boy-emperors, with their first appearance consequent upon the

---

[138] Although admittedly the behaviour of a very young child might not always be reliable: Ammianus notes how, at his consular inauguration, the infant Varronianus, son of Jovian, cried and proved obstinately resistant to being carried in the curule chair, which was later interpreted to have been a bad omen (AM 25.10.11).

[139] Augustine, *Conf.* 6.6.9.

[140] Ps.-Aurelius Victor 47.5: *cunctisque esset plenus bonis, si ad cognoscendam reipublicae regendae scientiam animum intendisset, a qua prope alienus non modo voluntate, sed etiam exercitio fuit.* Ammianus too, notes that Gratian neglected many serious matters while intent on pursuing wild-beast hunts and other amusements: AM 31.10.19.

accessions of Gratian and Valentinian II, new problems had also arisen: in particular, the issue of what happened when the child-emperor grew up. How was the child-emperor's transition from ceremonial to real power to be managed, and how were the power-brokers around them to respond? At the time when both emperors died, they were each apparently attempting military action: in 383, Gratian, aged 24, was taking the field with his army against a usurper, only to be betrayed and deserted by his *magister militum*; while according to Ambrose, Valentinian, aged 21 in 392, was attempting to break free from the domination of Arbogast and ride to the aid of Italy. Both examples suggest that the situation of a child-emperor reaching adulthood could open a whole new range of problems as—and if—he attempted to make the transition from ceremonial to actual power.

It remains the case, however, that methods for coping with the inability of a child-emperor to fulfil certain imperial functions had by this time emerged. Alongside the emphasis on youthful promise came an emphasis also on an increased ceremonial and religious role for the young emperor. This awareness of ceremonial function playing a key role in the plausible presentation of a boy-emperor would carry on into the regimes of Honorius and Valentinian III, but is more discernible in the case of Valentinian II than Gratian at this early stage. As the first child-emperor of the late fourth century, the great significance of Gratian's position lies in the precedent his accession as an 8-year-old created, but nevertheless his reign and his attempt to make a full transition from 'sleeping partner' during his father's lifetime, and military emperor after Valentinian I's death, mark a turning-point in the development of the late Roman imperial office. Unlike Gratian, no fourth- or fifth-century child-emperor (or child-turned-adult emperor) to follow him would even attempt to lead the imperial armies—in fact the only Roman emperors to do so, eastern or western, in the next seventy years would both be military men turned emperors, rather than princes born to the purple—Theodosius I and Constantius III.[141] From Gratian's death onwards, the ceremonial function of an emperor—and indeed his Christian function—was pushed ever more to the forefront of imperial presentation.

The experience of the failures of the respective reigns of these two boy-emperors showed that it was possible to push the political boundaries of the imperial office in the late Roman west into new territory, but that there were still problems to resolve if a new model of figurehead imperial rule, following all of the active military emperors of the fourth century, was to evolve further.

---

[141] And of these two, only Theodosius I is known to have led the armies after his accession: Constantius III's 6-month reign as emperor in 421 was so short he probably never had the opportunity. The next emperor to lead an imperial army was Avitus in 455. See also on non-campaigning emperors, Lee (2007), 30–7.

Among other strategies, the deliberate ceremonialization of the imperial office over the longer term would be one of the keys to that development, and would introduce a fundamental and qualitative contrast with the rule of earlier young emperors of the principate, for example. While the reigns of two boy-emperors might be taken as coincidence, and the political strategies which accompanied them written off as ad hoc, the subsequent reigns of Honorius and Valentinian III make the phenomenon of child-emperors something qualitatively quite different from what had gone before, and entailed real changes in the structure of court politics and imperial government, though they were changes which nevertheless had their roots in the preceding reigns.

Up until this point, a thematic approach has been the most useful way of highlighting the key issues in the overlapping reigns of these first late Roman child-emperors, the brothers Gratian and Valentinian II. Henceforth, a chronological analysis of the long reigns of their successors in the west, Honorius and Valentinian III, will be pursued, in order the better to elucidate the often complex and confusing events of these far less studied emperors.

Part Two

Honorius

5

An Accident of Power?

Their age should not trouble us! The loyal support of his soldiers makes the emperor's age fully grown. For age is fully grown when strength is.[1]

Within two years of Valentinian II's inauspicious death, the full accession of yet another child-emperor of the west, the 10-year-old Honorius, took place. Honorius has commonly been seen by ancient and modern historians alike as an uninspiring mediocrity, even sometimes accused of being intellectually disabled or derided as impotent.[2] His minimal appearances in the sources for the period, and his apparent inertia, certainly present problems for any study of his reign. Yet this only makes Honorius all the more intriguing. From his father's death in 395, Honorius was emperor in the west for almost thirty years, until his death by natural causes in 423. Surviving serious barbarian invasions and sieges, numerous usurpations and rebellions, military crises, family controversies, and financial difficulties, Honorius was the longest-serving Roman emperor since Constantine I. And yet, although he has been dismissed so frequently by modern historians, it is quite clear that powerful political figures in the west saw considerable value in preserving the rule of this child-emperor, or rather this child and then adult emperor, and over a prolonged period. Honorius' survival in spite of the political turmoil of his reign poses important questions about the ways in which the late Roman state and its politicians were adapting to the sovereignty of child-emperors, about the transition from child to adult ruler, and about how, whether such a transition was successful or not, this would impact on the vested interests and political activity of those involved.

The long reign of Honorius in many ways provides a key to understanding the phenomenon of the child-emperors of the period, because it is during

---

[1] Ambrose, *De ob. Theod.* 6: *Nec moveat aetas! Fides militum imperatoris perfecta aetas est; est enim perfecta aetas, ubi perfecta est virtus.* See McLynn (1994), 358.
[2] e.g. Zosimus 5.28.1–3; Cameron (1970), 154; Kulikowski (2007), 2.

this era in particular that the developing framework within which the institutionalization of child-rule took place becomes most apparent. Through an
examination of the different regimes (by which I mean the different conglomerations of individual ministers and generals who sought to hold sway over his
court at various points) surrounding the young ruler, it becomes clear that the
presentation of boy-emperors in the late Roman west was growing increasingly sophisticated, and therefore, although the politics of the period must be
carefully examined, most important is what they reveal about the evolution of
the child-emperor phenomenon itself.[3] Yet it remains essential, nevertheless, to
trace the chronology of the reign carefully in order to come to a clear understanding of this evolution. Honorius and his government have received very
little attention from modern scholarship—apart from excellent general works
which give a broad picture of the period, only studies of the writings of the poet
Claudian tend to approach any analysis of the court of Honorius, and these in
any case end with the poet's presumed death in *c*.404, leaving the next two
decades of Honorius' reign largely untreated.[4] In addition, the sources for the
period are often fragmentary (and become increasingly so in the later years of
the reign): we possess no complete western history of the period, with the nearest
approaches to a full chronology being the fragmentary remains of the eastern
court bureaucrat Olympiodorus' history, and the at times vague and at other
times surprisingly detailed account of Zosimus. For these reasons, it seems all
the more important to provide a narrative account of the reign as a framework
against which the evolution of child-emperor rule in the west can be assessed.
Though fragmentary, enough does survive in our sources to establish a clear
chronology, and we are more in need of one in looking at the reign of Honorius,
especially through the many bewildering usurpations and rebellions of the
period 408–23, than for the reigns of Gratian and Valentinian II, for whom
the political narrative has already been well established and worked upon.

  The case of Honorius raises the central question of what happened when a
child-emperor grew up—both to the child and to his managers. Honorius'
reign was almost twice as long as that of either Gratian or Valentinian II,
which in itself suggests that methods for coping with the difficulties arising
from having a child on the throne were becoming more advanced, and ways
were being found to deal with the ageing of a child-emperor. Indeed, the
institutionalization of this phenomenon could never be complete until this
particular problem was solved, as the fates of Honorius' immediate predecessors illustrated. Yet while the reigns of Gratian and Valentinian II could hardly
be seen as ultimately successful in this respect, they still had an impact on the

---

  [3] On regimes, see Introduction, pp. 12–13.
  [4] For such excellent general studies see e.g. Bury (1923), Stein (1959), and Jones (1964*a*). For
the most comprehensive study of Claudian to date, see Cameron (1970). But see also now for an
excellent literary analysis of Claudian's works, Ware (2012).

perceived possibilities of how the imperial office might now function. This chapter will examine the early years of Honorius, and the political manoeuvring surrounding his accession, as well as the manner in which this accession was first presented, most notably in the funeral oration of Ambrose of Milan for Theodosius I. Overall, the focal issue is how, after the difficulties of the reigns of Gratian and Valentinian II before him, the accession, survival, and lengthy reign of the child-emperor Honorius changed the political culture of the late Roman empire decisively towards accepting the rule of child- (or ceremonial) emperors. The political players of Honorius' reign finally found a working model which firmly established the infantilization of the imperial office in the late Roman west. Henceforth, the occupant of the imperial throne could be treated as a minor, regardless of his age and maturity.

Honorius' early years

Honorius was born to the purple, on 9 September 384, at Constantinople, the second son of Theodosius I and his first wife Aelia Flaccilla. Theodosius I, like his predecessors Valentinian I and Valens, was keen to establish his sons as clearly designated imperial heirs: his elder son Arcadius was already an Augustus by 384.[5] The infant Honorius was immediately styled *nobilissimus*, the rank once awarded to Gratian and Valentinian Galates, and in 386 Honorius entered upon his first consulship, aged only fifteen months.[6] These early impressive titles and honours were clearly part of an overall programme Theodosius I had in mind for his younger son. Following his defeat of Magnus Maximus, Theodosius had sent for Honorius, then only 5 years of age, to make the immense journey all the way from Constantinople to join him for victory celebrations at Rome.[7] Significantly, and as observed above, the then reigning emperor of the west, Valentinian II, was absent from the triumph; significantly also, Theodosius I chose this moment, in 389, to raise Honorius to the rank of Caesar there at Rome.[8] The decision to make Honorius Caesar first, and not propel him directly to the rank of Augustus (like Gratian, Valentinian II, and Arcadius so recently before him), is an

---

[5] See above, p. 83.

[6] For Honorius' bearing of the title *nobilissimus*, see Socrates 12.5; Sozomen 7.14. For his consulship of 386 see *CLRE* 306–7; *RIC* 10. 123.

[7] Oost (1968*a*), 51. A journey the future Valentinian III would in turn make in 424 as part of the campaign to install him as the new western emperor at the age of 6 in 425: see below Ch. 8.

[8] Claudian, *IV Cons.* 169–70 clearly states a short time when Honorius was Caesar before he reached the rank of Augustus. Zosimus (4.59.1), Theophanes (AM 5881), and the *Chron.pasch.* (p. 564) all mistakenly claim Honorius became Augustus at Rome, either in 389 or in 394. Socrates mentions the visit to Rome but no elevation (14.5). Cf. Cameron (1969); also Matthews (1975), 227.

interesting one on Theodosius I's part. It is likely the fact that the legitimate western emperor Valentinian II was still alive, and Theodosius' elder
son Arcadius was already Augustus, played a role in the decision to
advance Honorius more gradually towards the highest rank in the imperial
college.

Claudian, writing some fifteen years after the events for a Roman senatorial
audience, provided a sentimental retrospective picture of the visit: pointing
out to Honorius the imperial palace to which his father had brought him as a
child of tender years, giving him the first taste of triumph, as peoples of every
race came and laid their crowns at his feet.[9] Theodosius I's deliberate display
of Honorius to the people of Rome in 389—whether or not it occurred quite as
Claudian envisaged it, there should be no doubt it did occur—was highly
significant.[10] Through such a display, the young Honorius (rather than the
absent Valentinian II) was presented as the west's future emperor, and the
intentions of the victorious Theodosius I for his 5-year-old son made clear to
the assembled aristocratic audience. A special bronze issue from the mint at
Rome appeared in conjunction with the victory celebrations of 389, bearing a
legend again indicating how conscious Theodosius I was of methods used by
the dynasties of Valentinian and Constantine to designate imperial heirs: *Spes
Rei Publicae*.[11]

These were key steps towards Honorius' future, and Theodosius I was doing
his utmost to secure the boy's prospective accession in the west. Only a few
years later, and prompted more particularly by the usurpation of Eugenius in
the west, Theodosius I made Honorius a full Augustus, before he himself
departed on his campaign to deal with the rebellion. Like Gratian and Valentinian II before him (and also his elder brother Arcadius), Honorius thus had a
phantom accession as a very young child—at the age of 7. The ceremony took
place on 23 January 393, at the Hebdomon outside Constantinople, which by
the late fourth century was becoming the traditional location for such occasions.[12] Claudian again provided a retrospective picture of the events (writing
in 398), describing the senior emperor's pride as he travelled back into the city
with his two sons (like the Dioscuri sitting with Jove), all clothed in gold and
wearing crowns.[13] Claudian's evocation of these Spartan twins may have
been intended particularly to signal to his western audience that, from the

---

[9] Claudian, *VI Cons.* 53–72.

[10] Cameron (1969), 260. See in general on the visit: Claudian, *VI Cons.* 53–64.

[11] *RIC* 9. 113, n. 63; cf. McCormick (1986), 121–2.

[12] For Honorius' accession as Augustus, see Socrates, who also gives the date as 10 January:
25.5; also Philostorgius 11.2; Sozomen 7.24.1; Marcellinus *comes*, s.a. 393; also Seeck (1919), 281;
Ridley (1982), 203. For the Hebdomon as a venue for such occasions: Cf. Cameron (1969), 248–
9; Oost (1968a), 55.

[13] Claudian, *IV Cons.* 203–9. See for analysis of Honorius's accession ceremony: MacCormack (1981), 210–11; Oost (1968a), 55–6.

beginning, Honorius' power was equal to that of his elder brother Arcadius. The ceremonial of the occasion, and the demonstration of the stability of the dynasty in the strength of the older generation and the youthful promise of the younger, must have been impressive. The timing of Honorius' acclamation as co-Augustus was of particular significance to the western campaign: clearly refuting the claims of Eugenius to be the new western emperor through the elevation of a new emperor of the legitimate imperial dynasty. Like Valentinian I before him, raising Gratian after his own serious illness, Theodosius I was making a pointed dynastic statement in a time of political crisis.

Following his victory over Eugenius at the Frigidus in September 394, Theodosius I again sent for his younger son to make the long journey from Constantinople to join him for celebrations in the west. Theodosius would probably have brought Honorius to the west at this point regardless of whether or not he was aware of his own illness: the acclamation of the boy before the campaign had marked him out already as the west's future ruler.[14] The report of Paulinus records that when young Honorius and his half-sister Galla Placidia arrived in the west, Theodosius I welcomed them at the church of Ambrose at Milan and 'entrusted' them to the bishop's care. The inclusion of Galla Placidia in the party potentially also signals the determination of Theodosius to present his son's new administration as a continuation of the rule of the house of Valentinian: Placidia was (unlike Honorius) the grand-daughter of Valentinian I, and niece of Valentinian II through her mother, the recently deceased Galla.[15] At the same time as his children arrived, Theodosius I also supposedly ended his self-imposed abstinence from communion following the blood-letting at Frigidus, providing a liturgically charged welcome for the young Augustus and his sister.[16] Theodosius was well acquainted with the public-relations value of Ambrose's influence, and the emperor's return to communion was presented as a thanksgiving for the divine blessing evidenced by the safe arrival of his children.

It was natural that Theodosius I would originally have planned to return to the East once the western situation stabilized, just as he had after 389, and such plans would have been given greater impetus by the fact that eastern affairs had deteriorated in his absence and there were now barbarian incursions to

[14] The primary sources generally claim that he did realize he was ill: Socrates 26.5; Sozomen 7.29; Philostorgius 11.2; Theodoret 5.25. Cf. Cameron (1969), 267–74; McLynn (1994), 355, n. 222; *RIC* 9. 112–13; McCormick (1986), 121–2.

[15] Galla, Theodosius' second wife, died the day before he launched the campaign against Eugenius: *PLRE* 1. 382. Apparently Arcadius had also come into conflict with his stepmother Galla during Theodosius' time in the west from 389 to 391, so perhaps this history also played a role in Galla Placidia's journey to the west with Honorius, while Arcadius remained in Constantinople: Marcellinus *comes*, s.a. 390.

[16] Paulinus, *VAmb.* 32.1; also Ambrose, *De ob. Theod.* 34. Cf. McLynn (1994), 355.

be dealt with there.[17] Theodosius I had three months between the victory at Frigidus and his death within which to make his plans for the new western regime, and according to Zosimus' report: 'After this success, Theodosius went to Rome, where he proclaimed his son Honorius emperor, and declared Stilicho *magister praesentalis*, leaving him as guardian for his son.'[18] It has been argued forcibly that the full implications of Zosimus' account have not been recognized in the past (though some aspects of this report are clearly muddled), due to reliance instead upon the writings of ecclesiastical historians more interested in presenting a moralizing picture of the emperor's last days than the political implications of Theodosius I's death.[19] It is true that the church historians mention neither Stilicho nor any 'regency', but equally true that, whether Theodosius I knew he was dying or not, the west needed a government.[20] The claim that Theodosius I made an initial arrangement in the immediate aftermath of his victory, whereby he himself would return to Constantinople, while Honorius was established as the western emperor with the general Stilicho (the husband of Theodosius' niece Serena) to guide him, is plausible.[21] The victorious emperor may have announced his plans at Milan, perhaps even before his son arrived, prior to staging a triumphal entrance to the city, accompanied by the new young western emperor.

Claudian provides a lavish picture of the scenes in 394 when Theodosius and Honorius entered the city: the boy-emperor in the embrace of his father, riding in a triumphal chariot decked with laurels and surrounded by plumed warriors with gleaming swords.[22] All the same, plausible as this suggestion is, it is unfortunate that the supposed new mainstay of the western government, Stilicho, was not mentioned also in the triumphal parade—and perhaps somewhat surprising, given Claudian's general exaltation of Stilicho's role in all such occasions.[23] Furthermore, the man who was to be Stilicho's first principal opponent for management of Arcadius in the east had already been granted higher honours in the form of the consulship for 392, which Stilicho never achieved in Theodosius I's lifetime: a fact which Claudian

---

[17] Cameron (1969), 270. Cf. Stein (1959), 1. 228; Demougeot (1951), 116–17.

[18] Zosimus 4.59.1: Τῶν δὲ πραγμάτων ὧδε τῷ βασιλεῖ Θεοδοσίῳ προχωρησάντων, ἐπιδημήσας τῇ Ῥώμῃ τὸν υἱὸν Ὁνώριον ἀναδείκνυσι βασιλέα, Στελίχωνα στρατηγόν τε ἀποφήνας ἅμα τῶν αὐτόθι ταγμάτων καὶ ἐπίτροπον καταλιπὼν τῷ παιδί· See Cameron (1969), 273.

[19] Cameron (1969), 273. Cameron's general argument is for two separate and distinct settlements between September 394 and January 395, which would explain the discrepancies in Zosimus' account. See, in general, Cameron (1969), esp. 269 ff.; also (1970), 38–45.

[20] Neither the account of Philostorgius (at 11.2) nor Rufinus (11.34) mention Stilicho. Cf. Cameron (1969), 272–3.

[21] Cameron (1969), 269. Followed by Kulikowski (2007), 164.

[22] Claudian, *III Cos.* 126–36. Cameron originally argued that Theodosius I returned to Rome for this triumphal entrance following the battle at the Frigidus, but now suggests the location was Milan, which seems more likely: Cameron (1969), 248–65; (2011), 47.

[23] Cameron himself points out that it would have strengthened Stilicho's position as a virtual unknown in the west, to have been presented at Rome officially by Theodosius I. (1969), 266–7.

conveniently omits from all mentions of Rufinus.[24] In addition, very little evidence is available concerning the nature of Theodosius' illness and just how incapacitated he may have been in his final months—and three months is not a very long time—even how fit he might have been to make such arrangements.

If he were capable of planning at this stage, Theodosius might well have hesitated, given the example of Valentinian II's unhappy experience under the thumb of Arbogast, to leave his even younger son in the west in the care of Stilicho. And although it has often been claimed that Stilicho was the obvious choice, since he was not only linked to the imperial house by marriage, but as a part-Vandal could never claim the throne himself, the question arises: just how 'barbarian' did a man have to be to be totally barred from the throne?[25] Stilicho's mother had been a Roman and his father a half-Vandal cavalry officer under Valens; it is worth bearing in mind that, in the 350s, the Frank Silvanus had been considered a viable contender for the throne, while the usurper Magnentius (r. 350–3) is described in the sources as being of barbarian descent.[26] Nevertheless, if Honorius was to be the resident western emperor, at 10 years of age he did need a legal guardian, and Stilicho's ties to the imperial house did make him a natural choice. We cannot know the exact intentions of Theodosius I regarding the powers that Stilicho was to exercise in his stead, but the extent to which the general himself grasped the political possibilities of the situation would shape the early years of the reign of this new child-emperor.

Stilicho's 'regency'

In late 394, Theodosius and Honorius remained in Milan following the victory celebrations. On 17 January 395, while attending the games, the senior emperor fell ill and left his son to officiate on his behalf.[27] Theodosius died later the same day, leaving the 18-year-old Arcadius as emperor in the east and

---

[24] Cameron (1968*b*), 393.

[25] For the claim that Stilicho was too 'barbarian' to rule himself: Cameron (1969), 274; also (1970), 38.

[26] On Stilicho's father as cavalry commander under Valens: Claudian, *Stil.* I.36–99. For Silvanus, see *PLRE* 1. 840–1 and for Magnentius, 1. 532. It was also apparently entirely acceptable for both Arcadius and Honorius to marry women of part-barbarian descent: Arcadius' wife Eudoxia was the daughter of the Frankish general Bauto, and her mother's ethnicity is unknown, while Maria, Honorius' first wife, was Stilicho's daughter. Though never noted in ancient sources and rarely in modern ones, Arcadius and Eudoxia's son Theodosius II, emperor of the east from 402 to 450, was therefore part-Frankish himself. For Eudoxia's background, see *PLRE* 2. 410; Holum (1982), 52.

[27] As Cameron points out, attendance at the games was a highly important imperial activity (1976), 175–6.

10-year-old Honorius as emperor in the west.[28] Whatever Theodosius I's true intentions had been, a new claim emerged upon his death. The 'deathbed' settlement of Theodosius has been a matter of some debate among scholars.[29] After Theodosius' death, it was asserted that his dying words had been to entrust to Stilicho the guardianship of not only Honorius, but also his older brother Arcadius. Though his struggle to claim such guardianship of Arcadius from a distance would never succeed, in the west Stilicho effectively seized the opportunity from the very start to take up a position which vastly outstripped the powers of either Merobaudes or Arbogast before him: to establish the new government as a partnership, whereby the dynastically legitimate young emperor was to rule under the guidance of his loyal guardian, Stilicho. His marriage tie with the imperial house gave him an advantage he was very ready to exploit to make his own position more secure than that of any of the individuals who had attempted to manage boy-emperors before him.

While it is conceivable that Theodosius I had made some sort of dying plea for Stilicho to watch over his sons, it is difficult to believe that he had ever meant him to dominate Honorius' government as completely as he would come to do, well into the emperor's adult years.[30] And although the scenario of a pre-deathbed settlement which had already granted guardianship of Honorius to Stilicho is possible, it is also likely that Stilicho effectively engin-eered a coup upon Theodosius' death, seizing the opportunity to claim the position of Honorius' chief minister. Like the political clique which had elevated Valentinian II in 375, Stilicho could claim he was acting in the best interests of the state, so soon after a bloody civil war, in supporting the full accession of the boy clearly designated as the west's new emperor. Arguably there was no real alternative to Honorius who would not have resulted in further conflict. Stilicho's first claims of his guardianship over both Honorius and Arcadius would not appear until a full year had passed following Honor-ius' accession in the west. For the consulship of Honorius in 396 (which he shared with Arcadius), the poet Claudian penned the first of the many political speeches he would compose for his patron Stilicho. It was here that the story of the dying Theodosius I's plea—witnessed by Stilicho alone—to watch over his sons first emerged.[31] In the meantime, neither the funeral oration of Ambrose for Theodosius nor any surviving laws passed between January 395 and January 396 had told the story of this extraordinary joint guardianship of

---

[28] Theophanes AM 5886; Sozomen 8.1; Socrates 5.26. Cf. McLynn (1994), 356; Matthews (1975), 248.

[29] The most thorough and detailed analysis remains that of Cameron (1969), 247–80.

[30] Cameron (1970), 39. Even if, as some scholars have claimed (e.g. Stein (1959), I. 226; McCormick (1986), 47), Theodosius I had a poor opinion of his sons' abilities—which we cannot possibly know. Demougeot argues that the dying emperor gave Stilicho a 'moral' charge to protect both sons: (1951), 99–102. Followed by O'Flynn (1983), 47.

[31] Claudian, *III Cons.*142–62; cf. Cameron (1969), 247, 275.

two ruling emperors. In the year that had passed, considerable efforts must have been made in the west by Stilicho to manoeuvre court factions in his favour and assert his own position.[32]

As discussed in the Introduction, Stilicho's claims have been conventionally described in modern scholarship as a regency, though in fact no such office existed in the late Roman empire. In effect, the extent of the power that Stilicho would exercise between 395 and 408 certainly does amount to what we would recognize in modern terms as a regency, and it can still be used as a convenient term to describe the situation, as long as we bear in mind that it is a term we use only retrospectively and was unknown in the Roman world. In reality, Stilicho can only have been Honorius' guardian, a legal position which did not entitle him to control of the child-emperor's government. And in relation to the 18-year-old Arcadius, who could hardly be viewed as too young to rule in his own right, Stilicho's position must have been even less secure.[33] The fact that there was no legal position of regent for Stilicho to fill is important to remember in relation to the potential precariousness of Stilicho's situation and authority in the child-emperor Honorius' government.

Stilicho was in a powerful position to make a claim of guardianship, at least. In 384 he had married Serena, the niece of Theodosius I, and *c*.393 had been made a *magister militum*, journeying west on campaign with Theodosius I to fight Eugenius.[34] His wife Serena had brought Honorius and Galla Placidia from Constantinople to Milan at the senior emperor's command, presumably bringing her own three children also.[35] They were the closest relatives in the west with Honorius at the time of his father's death, and Claudian would lay heavy emphasis on the bonds between the family adding weight to Stilicho's claims.[36] Essentially there may well have been little other option than to accept Stilicho's guardianship of Honorius if the house of Theodosius was to continue to rule the west. Nevertheless, the earliest textual evidence from the reign

---

[32] Claims to the guardianship of Arcadius—already aged 18 in 395—would continue to appear in Claudian's poetry for years to come: e.g. *Ruf.* II.4–6; again in 398: *IV Cons.* 437–8, and *Nupt.* 307–8, and in 399: *Eutr.* II.599 f.; still in 400: *Stil.* II.78–87; cf. I.140 f. See Cameron (1970), 49–50. The claim was also reported in other sources, e.g. Zosimus 5.4.3; Eunapius, frg. 63; Olympiodorus, frg. 1.

[33] Cameron (1969), 277.

[34] For Stilicho's marriage to Serena, see Cameron (1970), 56, and Oost (1968a), 51. *CTh.* 7.4.18 (29 July 393) and 7.9.3 (29 July 393) first record Stilicho as *magister militum*. His first attested command seems to have been a mission to try to engage in peace negotiations in 391 with Gothic rebels who had killed the general Promotus (Zosimus 4.50–1; Claudian, *Ruf.* I.350–51), although he was apparently also involved in a diplomatic mission to Persia in 383–4 (Claudian, *Stil.* I.51–8). See Demougeot (1951), 134 ff., who dates his appointment as *magister* to 386–88. Cf. also O'Flynn (1983), 15–16. It was in the aftermath of the victory over Eugenius that Stilicho was named senior western general; Eunapius 9.60.1.1–11. Also Heather (2005), 216; Levy (1971), 236.

[35] For Honorius and Galla Placidia being brought west by Serena: Claudian, *VI Cons.* 88 f.

[36] See e.g. Claudian, *VI Cons.* 92–100; *Stil.* I.140–3.

(the oration of Ambrose, Claudian's panegyric for 396, and early laws) all reflect the anxiety of this tenuous situation.[37]

Regime-building

Ambrose of Milan's funeral oration for Theodosius I, delivered forty days after the emperor's death, is a document of tremendous importance for the insight it provides into the fledgling government of young Honorius.[38] Crucially, in it Ambrose did not explicitly endorse Stilicho's claim to management of the new administration—and did not even refer to Stilicho by name. It is inconceivable that he was not present, and the one phrase of the speech which does appear to refer to Stilicho has occasioned some debate among scholars. One suggestion is that the phrase *praesenti parenti* referred to Theodosius entrusting his sons to a close relative on his deathbed, while another contends that the phrase instead simply implied that Stilicho was visible in Ambrose's audience.[39] Yet, in either case Ambrose's words cannot be construed as a wholehearted endorsement of any claims Stilicho might be making at this point.[40] It could be argued that Ambrose's failure to name Stilicho or make an unquestionable statement of support for him was simply Ambrosian rhetoric at work, and that the overall speech nevertheless does represent the backing of the bishop; yet this seems an unnecessarily complicated argument to try to explain why Ambrose did not simply say he supported Stilicho if that was what he meant—or even better, put his eloquence to good use enlarging upon the benefits to be anticipated from a Stilicho-backed regime. The bishop could have made an explicit assertion and lengthy justification of Stilicho's role as Honorius' guardian, and publicly thrown his weight behind him—but he did not.[41] At this crucial point early in the new boy-emperor's reign, explicit statements of support must have been anxiously sought. This was surely a conscious—and conspicuous—decision on Ambrose's part: it looks rather like he was fence-sitting, diplomatically avoiding endorsing Stilicho publicly until he saw how entrenched the young emperor's guardian would become. This omission alone suggests that Stilicho's position at the outset of Honorius' reign was less secure than has usually been appreciated.

---

[37] For an alternative view, see O'Flynn (1983), 14.

[38] Liebeschuetz (2005), 174.

[39] Ambrose, *De ob. Theod.* 5. For the argument that the phrase refers to Theodosius' sons being entrusted to Stilicho: Liebeschuetz (2005), 180, n. 3. For the argument that it refers instead to Stilicho being visible in the audience: McLynn (1994), 357–8, n. 3, though even so the phrase still suggests his presence in the guise of a father-figure.

[40] Though scholars do contend that it was the first evidence for Stilicho's 'regency' claims: Matthews (1975), 249. Cf. Liebeschuetz (2005), 174.

[41] Cameron (1969), 274–5.

Stilicho was a virtually unknown easterner as far as the western civil and military establishments were concerned, and Ambrose clearly intended that his oration in support of any new regime would be based purely on the appeal of loyalty to Honorius alone. Ambrose's speech was a masterly exercise in public relations in its appeal to different power-groups and its presentation of the 10-year-old Honorius' rule as a viable and divinely-inspired new government. Yet it also revealed the true anxiety surrounding the child's accession. The audience for the oration undoubtedly comprised key representatives of both the eastern and western military establishments, so recently warring against each other but now supposedly united, as well as western civil dignitaries from previous governments—not only that of Valentinian II but probably also of Eugenius.[42] Ambrose's command of ceremonial needed to be deployed in the most impressive manner, therefore. Honorius himself was present, and Ambrose's words are helpful in indicating how the child was singled out: Ambrose referred to him as *assistente sacris altaribus*, a privilege of tremendous significance when Ambrose had previously denied Theodosius access to the altar.[43] The primary purpose of Ambrose's oration in this case was to support Honorius' right to the throne, appealing to the loyalty of both court and army, and the obligation owed to Theodosius I.[44]

Yet Ambrose's oration displayed absolute consciousness throughout of the anxiety afoot over Honorius' age. He chose a number of key motifs on which his speech hinged: the divine blessing of Honorius' accession, the youthful promise of the new emperor and his dynastic legitimacy, as well as the continuation of his father's policies under the new administration—most importantly in the extension of pardons to those who had been involved in the recent usurpation. These were all vitally important messages about the character of the new government, and comprised a concerted bid for support from the west for what was essentially an unknown eastern regime—of not only Honorius and Stilicho, but also a number of eastern office-holders who had travelled west with Theodosius.[45] According to Ambrose, the young emperor's age was augmented by his faith, for the great departed emperor was still to be found in his sons, while their strength was in their soldiers: 'Their age should not trouble us! The loyal support of his soldiers makes the emperor's age fully grown. For age is fully grown when strength is.'[46]

---

[42] McLynn (1994), 357. Also Liebeschuetz (2005), 174.

[43] Ambrose, *De ob. Theod.* 3. Ambrose compares Honorius' filial respect to that of Joseph for Jacob. See also McLynn (1994), 357–8.

[44] Consolino (1995a), 1039–40.

[45] See below, p. 149.

[46] Ambrose, *De ob. Theod.* 6: *Nec moveat aetas! Fides militum imperatoris perfecta aetas est; est enim perfecta aetas, ubi perfecta est virtus.* See McLynn (1994), 358. Also Ambrose, *De ob.Theod.* 8. See MacCormack (1981), 147. Nazarius expresses a similar idea regarding Constantine I, though

Moreover, Theodosius I's victories could leave no doubt that he had won God's favour, and therefore loyalty was due more than ever to the sons of so divinely favoured a ruler.[47] Ambrose went even further in linking both the dynastic and divine legitimacy of Honorius' accession, declaring that the boy had been made emperor by his father, but confirmed in his command by God.[48] A fanciful picture was painted of deceased emperors greeting Theodosius I in heaven: not only Constantine the Great but most importantly Gratian, walking side-by-side with Theodosius I, clad in clothes of glory.[49] The reality of their earthly relations was not important; what was important was emphasizing the bond between young Honorius and the Valentinianic emperors who had ruled the west from 364 to 393, and hence underlining also the legitimacy of the new emperor.[50] It is interesting that Gratian was chosen to aid in this assertion rather than Valentinian II, whom Theodosius I had so recently avenged: in an oration vehemently insistent on young Honorius' age presenting no barrier to his accession, this was hardly the time to remind the audience of the last boy-emperor's fate.[51]

There can be no doubt that emphasis on the legitimacy of Honorius' accession and the absolute loyalty owed to the sons of Theodosius I was aimed very much at the military contingent of Ambrose' audience. In the past decade the western military had supported two usurpers, and only months earlier the western and eastern armies had been locked in civil war. Even if Theodosius I had lived longer, there must have been major efforts required to heal the scars of the conflict, and now with Theodosius dead, and a 10-year-old in his place, there could be no guarantee that civil war would not break out again—why should the western military support a child who could not lead them? Ambrose's repeated appeals for loyalty from the army make it clear just what a fraught time this was: the army must pay to the sons the loyalty it owed to the father, whose victories showed how God avenges treachery.[52] Ambrose's words should not be dismissed as mere rhetoric: he was making a plea for military support which was not as yet assured.

---

depicting him as younger than he was when he came to power (*Pan.Lat.* IV.16.4): see further above, p. 110, n. 33.

[47] Ambrose, *De ob. Theod.* 11. Also 12. Cf. MacCormack (1981), 147.

[48] Ambrose, *De ob. Theod.* 55. Cf. 2.

[49] Ibid. 52; McLynn (1994), 359. See on Christian interpretation of the funeral ceremony/afterlife of late Roman emperors: MacCormack (1981), 145 ff.

[50] Liebeschuetz (2005), 174. Also McLynn (1994), 358.

[51] McLynn (1994), 359. Interestingly, Honoré has noted also that laws of Honorius' government seem to have attempted to distance his government from that of Valentinian II and emphasized instead links with Valentinian I and Theodosius I (Honoré (1999), 212–13).

[52] Ambrose, *De ob.Theod.* 2. Also 11. See also MacCormack (1981), 147. Similarly, Ambrose emphasizes that as the sons of an emperor, it was even more important that the rights of minors were observed than in the case of an ordinary citizen: *De ob. Theod.* 5. See also Lunn-Rockliffe (2008), 192–3.

A further emphasis on the mercy of a pious emperor reveals an appeal for support aimed not only at the military but also the civilian establishment in the west. Ambrose spoke of Theodosius I as a generous emperor, of how on earth he delighted in showing mercy and sparing many, and asserted that none should fear that promises of pardon granted by Theodosius would be rescinded.[53] The reason for these assurances is obvious: the defeat of Eugenius was less than six months past, and many military men, bureaucrats, and senators had supported the usurper's government. Following the battle at Frigidus, Ambrose himself had pleaded for clemency for these men, and promises of pardon had been made by Theodosius, it seems, but not yet enacted.[54] Ambrose was sending a direct message of reassurance that the new government would not renege on the promises, and again pleading for such men to throw their weight behind the boy-emperor.[55]

Ambrose's speech set up both an appeal for support and the assurance of clemency from the new government and an image of the nature of the new administration and the presentation of Honorius. The continued references to the divine blessing of Theodosius, and Honorius as his son, introduced an emphasis on dynasticism and the undoubted merits and youthful promise of the son of such a father which would be perpetuated for many years to come. The repeated claims of the young emperor's piety inspiring the loyalty and victory of his troops also laid emphasis on Honorius' ceremonial role, and combined an excuse for his inability to lead his armies personally at that age with an assurance that they would be victorious nevertheless as long as they remained loyal, due to his divine blessing. Furthermore, the emphasis on Theodosius I as an emperor who could achieve victory through fasting and prayer (as well as military activity) also supported the position of the untried 10-year-old emperor.[56]

The general pardons for those who had been involved in Eugenius' reign, and which had been advertised by Ambrose, were indeed forthcoming: in April 395 a law issued from Milan assured Honorius' subjects that all decisions of judges made under the tyrant were still to be considered valid.[57] In May the emperor issued a further law which promised pardon to all those who had not been specifically mentioned already. Benefits were to be conferred on those

---

[53] On Theodosius I's delight in mercy, see Ambrose, *De ob. Theod.* 52; Also 5, 12–14, 16–17. See McLynn (1994), 359. For reassurance of pardons, see Ambrose, *De ob. Theod.* 4. Raspanti suggests that the motif of the clemency of the dead emperor was also influenced by Seneca's *De clementia*: Raspanti (2009), 50–1.

[54] For Ambrose's pleas for clemency after Frigidus, see Ambrose, *Ep. extra Coll.* 3.4. Ambrose may have been anxious to restore his own credibility as a Theodosian supporter too: see Matthews (1975), 247; Cracco Ruggini (1998), 7–10.

[55] McLynn (1994), 357. Cf. Liebeschuetz (2005), 174.

[56] Consolino (1995a) 1044–104; also Heim (1974), 272–3.

[57] *CTh.* 15.14.9 (21 Apr. 395).

who did not expect them: those who had served in any administrative or honorary post, or as a governor under Eugenius, were to retain the rank they had held prior to the time of the tyrant.[58] Although the new administration was cautious with its immediate appointments, especially to the urban prefecture, these general pardons appealed for support from those among the military and aristocracy who had held office under Eugenius.[59] The regime that Stilicho was establishing for Honorius needed to be seen as trustworthy in promises and incentives to support them if the boy-emperor—and his self-proclaimed guardian—were to survive. The fact that this legislation was needed to bring such key figures on board was also a sign of the new government's weakness.[60] Yet Ambrose's assurances and the legislation which followed are a reminder that the western elites themselves were badly wrong-footed at this point, as a result of Theodosius' death following swiftly upon the defeat of Eugenius. Those among the ruling classes who had supported the rebellion were not yet assured of their full acceptance back into the triumphant imperial establishment. In a sense, this strengthened from the start Stilicho's position as Honorius' key adviser: for the recently embarrassed western elites would be both less able to manoeuvre around the new child-emperor themselves and secure their own interests with him, as had occurred with Valentinian II in 375, and keener to reach a comfortable settlement with a new, dominant manager figure who would accept them back into the fold.

Through imperial pardons to the senatorial aristocracy, therefore, influential figures such as Nicomachus Flavianus (son-in-law of Symmachus and a prominent former supporter of the usurper) were thus placed in a position of debt to Honorius and to Stilicho. Flavianus was even excused from repaying to Honorius' government the salary he had earned in office under Eugenius, and within a few years had gone on to become prefect of Rome in 399.[61] With the imperial court establishing itself once more at Milan, rather than at distant Trier, influential Roman aristocrats like Symmachus became regular visitors and attended major ceremonial occasions, like consular celebrations.[62] The

[58] *CTh.* 15.14.11 (18 May 395). Reiterated in June: *CTh.* 15.14.12 (17 June 395).
[59] On appointments to the urban prefecture in this period, see Matthews (1975), 259–60.
[60] Sogno (2006), 82, 88.
[61] On Flavianus being excused from repaying the salary: Symmachus, *Epp.* 4.19, 51; cf. 6.12; and on Flavianus' prefecture in 399: *CTh.* 14.10.3 (6 June 399). Cf. Matthews (1975), 266; Sogno (2006), 79–83. On the *cursus* and career of the elder and younger Flaviani, see Hedrick (2000), 6–36. Augustine points out that the younger Nicomachus Flavianus aided his recovery of imperial favour by converting to Christianity: Aug. *Civ.Dei* 5.26; also Hedrick (2000), 28; Cameron (2011), 197–204.
[62] On attending the consular celebrations, see Symmachus *Epp.* 6.30, 35–6; also *Ep.* 5.6 (to Manlius Theodorus) and 4.6 (to Stilicho), and relating to other visits at court, *Epp.* 4.20, 36. The majority of Symmachus' surviving letters date to the period from 395 until his death in 402, including letters to Stilicho himself: for details, see Salzman (2006), 354 ff. On his increased contacts with the court in his final years, see further Matthews (1974), 76–80. On Symmachus' last visit to Milan, see *Epp.* 4.9; 7.13–14. Cf. Matthews (1975), 256, 264–6; and Cameron (1970), 232–3; Heather (2005), 217.

correspondence between Symmachus and Stilicho which was published at some point between the former's death (*c.*402–3) and the latter's fall from grace (408) also attests to the eagerness with which Roman senators might pursue cordial relations with the *magister militum*.[63]

The specific individuals found in office under Honorius and who had once served in previous regimes have received detailed attention.[64] These were men like Basilius, the first prefect of Rome after Honorius' accession, who had held office under Gratian in 382, and Hilarius, praetorian prefect for Gaul in 396, who may have been a provincial governor of Gratian's in 383.[65] Another influential and respected public figure called in to support the boy-emperor was Manlius Theodorus, who had been prefect of Gaul under Gratian, and held the prefecture of Italy from 397 to 399 and then the consulship in 399, with similar high offices for his son Theodorus and his brother Lampadius, also in this early stage of Honorius' reign.[66] Officials from the time of Valentinian II turn up also, such as Firminus (at Milan in the 380s and *comes rei privatae* in 398–9), and even individuals who had served in the west in the 380s, and followed Theodosius I to the east after 391, only to return to the west again later in the 390s to hold office (such as Fl. Pisidius Romulus).[67] Some who took office in the new regime clearly had long-standing imperial careers behind them, such as Fl. Peregrinus Saturninus, although the details of their past offices cannot be discerned from surviving sources.[68] Such appointments were valuable in building young Honorius' administration, both for their advertisement of its continuity with past rulers, and also for the assurance that this eastern-born emperor and his eastern manager had a place for western men in their government.

[63] Salzman notes that nowhere in their preserved correspondence does Symmachus make any allusion to Stilicho's non-Roman heritage, and contrasts this with the senator's letters to the non-Roman generals Bauto and Richomeres, which might be interpreted to have a more condescending tone; yet a crucial difference here is that neither of these earlier generals had married into the imperial house (or at least, the marriage of Bauto's daughter into the imperial house occurred after the general was safely dead), nor approached the heights of power in government that Stilicho did: Salzman (2006), 352–67, esp. at 356.

[64] See esp. the careful study of Matthews (1975), 258 ff. Cf. in much less detail: McLynn (1994), 356.

[65] For Basilius, see *CTh.* 7.24.1 (5 Mar. 395); Matthews (1975), 259; *PLRE* 1. 149. Hilarius was also a correspondent of Symmachus: see *Epp.* 3.38–42; cf. *PLRE* 1. 435–6; for Hilarius' earlier office, *CTh.* 6.1.3 (19 Feb. 383); Matthews (1975), 260–1.

[66] *CTh.* 11.16.21, 11.16.22, 16.2.30 (all on 31 Jan. 397). *PLRE* 1.900–1; Matthews (1975) 262.

[67] For Firminus, see *CTh.* 1.11.2 (24 May 398), 12.6.25 (18 Mar. 399); Matthews (1975), 259. Romulus was *consularis* of Aemilia and Liguria in 385, had held office in the east in the early 390s, and was urban prefect in the west in 406: Matthews (1975), 260; Chastagnol (1962), 262–4; *PLRE* 1. 771–2. See similarly the case of Andromachus, who succeeded Basilius as prefect of Rome, and was prefect of Gaul in 401: Matthews (1975), 259.

[68] Saturninus was prefect of Rome twice between 402 and 407, his statue inscription in the Forum of Trajan noted a long career in the imperial service (*ILS* 1275; Matthews (1975), 260).

It is noticeable, nonetheless, that there were also officials serving in the west after 395 whose previous careers or backgrounds had lain in the east. Theodosius I appears to have left the bulk of his government machine behind in Constantinople when he marched west in 394; again indicating that he intended to return.[69] Some officials must have travelled with him nevertheless, and men like Nummius Aemilianus Dexter, born in Barcelona but *comes rei privatae* in 387 in the east and later proconsul of Asia, found as prefect of Italy after Theodosius I's death, may have been among them.[70] Hadrianus, *comes sacrarum largitionum* in 395 and *magister officiorum* in 396–7, was also an eastern official.[71] Such high offices may have been offered to these eastern bureaucrats as an incentive to stay and support the new government; but this too was essentially an admission of weakness of the regime Stilicho was building in 395.[72]

The pardons to which Ambrose and the early legislation of Honorius' reign referred clearly applied equally to the military, but it seems that the western armies had suffered significant losses in the recent conflict, which might explain why no particular laws bestowing military privileges are recorded. The early legislation of the regime showed a great concern for army numbers—raising conscripts even from imperial estates, punishing deserters, and protecting provincials from supposed military men unlawfully demanding supplies, particularly once the eastern field army had returned to Constantinople.[73]

Ambrose had laboured the sentimental appeal to the military of loyalty to Theodosius' son, and this was a motif the court poet Claudian also picked up, as in his panegyric in honour of Honorius' third consulship, delivered in January 396. Claudian fancifully described a baby Honorius crawling among the shields of his father's soldiers, and a toddler Honorius longing to accompany his father on campaigns.[74] But it is indicative of the continuing uncertainty of military matters under the boy-emperor's rule that even in Claudian's poem of 398 on the Gildonic war, almost four years after the battle on the Frigidus, the rousing speech supposedly given by Honorius before the troops embarked on campaign urged them to wash away the stains of civil war through their endeavours.[75] And in describing the lead-up to this war against Gildo, Claudian imagined a scene of Theodosius I visiting Arcadius in a dream and

---

[69] McLynn (1994), 357. Cf. Liebeschuetz (1990), 132–45.

[70] In office by 18 March 395 (*CTh.* 8.5.52); *PLRE* 1. 251; Matthews (1975), 112, 259.

[71] Hadrianus was also prefect of Italy (401–4). *PLRE* 1. 406; Matthews (1975), 263–4.

[72] Matthews (1975), 258–9.

[73] On raising conscripts, *CTh.* 7.13.12 (17 June 395). On punishing deserters, 7.18.9 (26 Apr. 396). On protecting provincials, 7.4.21 (17 Apr. 396); 7.4.22 (30 May 396); 7.4.23 (16 June 396).

[74] Claudian, *III Cons.* 29–38 and 50–82. The image of the infant Honorius crawling among shields seems reminiscent of that of Maximian at *Pan.Lat.* X.2.3–6.

[75] Claudian, *Gild.* I. 427–66.

describing the state of affairs upon his death which may not have been far from the truth:

When I was raised to heaven, disorder—I admit it—and tumult did I leave behind me. The army was still drawing the forbidden sword in that Alpine war, and conquerors and conquered gave alternate cause for dissension. Scarce could this madness have been calmed by my vigilance, much less a boy's rule.[76]

It seems the scars of the past were still apparent.

Efforts were also made early in the new reign to emphasize further the piety and divine blessing of Honorius so eloquently advertised by Ambrose, through religious legislation, a conventional but important action usually undertaken by recently proclaimed emperors by the end of the fourth century. In March 395 it was decreed that the statutes of past emperors regarding the privileges of the church were to continue unimpaired.[77] A similar ruling in early 397 reconfirmed church privileges, and declared those of the bishop of Rome in particular to be inviolable.[78] Once again, the government of this new boy-emperor was not only to be seen as a continuation of previous legitimate reigns, but as even more generous.

Paulinus reported on a further significant episode in 395 involving both Ambrose and the new court of Honorius. Amidst great ceremonial, Bishop Ambrose discovered the miraculously preserved body of the martyr Nazarius in a private garden in Milan, and had the corpse exhumed and reburied in the Basilica Apostolorum.[79] The magnificent benefaction of Libyan marble made by Stilicho's wife Serena provided the martyr's shrine with an appropriate setting, and with a dedication offering prayers for the safe return of Stilicho, then absent on campaign against the Goths.[80] It was an episode which represented an important affirmation of mutually beneficial church–court relations.[81] And although it might seem reminiscent of Ambrose's discovery of the martyrs Protasius and Gervasius in 385/6, this event can be set in direct contrast to that occasion: in that instance, the discovery was potent proof of the divine blessing of Ambrose's cause *against* that of the boy-emperor Valentinian II's court. But how much more significant for the new rule of Honorius this discovery was, as a demonstration of divine blessing falling instead upon the government of this boy-emperor, together with Ambrose. The bishop's cooperation certainly could bring with it enormous clout. Both parties must have seen the value of

---

[76] Ibid. I. 292–7: *cum divus abirem, res incompositas (fateor) tumidasque reliqui. stringebat vetitos etiamnum exercitus enses Alpinis odiis, alternaque iurgia victi victoresque dabant. vix haec amentia nostris excubiis, nedum puero rectore quiesset.*

[77] *CTh.* 16.2.29 (23 Mar. 395).

[78] *CTh.* 11.16.21; 16.2.30 (both 31 Jan. 397).

[79] Paulinus, *VAmb.* 32.2–33.4.

[80] *ILCV* 1801.

[81] Paulinus, *VAmb.* 32.2-33.4; McLynn (1994) 363–4.

cooperating to their mutual benefit: for Ambrose, the imperial court was close at hand once more and his chance to impose his influence upon it was all the greater. For Honorius' managers (Stilicho, and to a lesser extent Serena), Ambrose was a powerful and widely respected figure whose endorsement could bring a sense of legitimacy and links with past emperors and, most importantly, divine blessing for the new child-emperor of the west.[82]

It has been said that: 'During the first years of Stilicho's administration, the alliance between the senatorial aristocrats of Rome, the *viri militares* of the court and the church of Milan worked perhaps better than ever before.'[83] The need for the pardons issued to the former supporters of Eugenius and the tensions revealed by the oration of Ambrose indicate some of the weaknesses and uncertainties which attended the real accession of Honorius, before this smooth-running alliance settled into place. Such measures had come to be part of the pattern of rehabilitation of western elites following serious rebellions in the course of the fourth century (they had also been part of Theodosius I's policies following his defeat of Magnus Maximus). And though repression rather than clemency is not always a sign of strength, for the fragile new government of a child-emperor coping with the aftermath of a civil war won by that child's father, these were anxious times. Ambrose's heavy emphasis on the new boy-emperor's piety, divine blessing, and dynastic legitimacy also revealed how little else there was to be said in his favour; like Ausonius writing of Gratian in 378, a great deal depended upon 'youthful promise'. But these factors attest to Stilicho's success in stepping in to wield the power behind the throne when Theodosius died, and to establish a functional regime with the backing of senatorial, ecclesiastical, and military factions for the new boy-emperor and for himself.

---

[82] For relations between Ambrose and Stilicho in general, see Palanque (1933), 308–12, and Dudden (1935), 486–90.

[83] McLynn (1994), 366. See also Matthews (1975), 264–70.

6

The Regime of Stilicho

> This is the boy who today summons Rome's citizens to the place of
> meeting and from his father's ivory throne tells to the fathers the causes
> and issues of his acts, and, following ancient precedent, directs the deeds
> of empire at the judgement-seat of the Senate.[1]

Through the accession of 10-year-old Honorius in 395, the emperor's guardian Stilicho had succeeded in creating a western regime which he would lead
for the next thirteen years. He would wage wars in the name of the boy-
emperor, achieving some notable victories such as the defeats of the rebel
Gildo and the Goth Radagaisus, would hold two consulships (at this time an
extremely rare honour for anyone below the rank of emperor), and would even
marry two daughters in turn to Honorius, looking forward hopefully to the
day when his grandchild might inherit his son-in-law's throne. Yet, after more
than a decade at the forefront of western imperial government, in 408 Stilicho
submitted quietly to an execution ordered by the same young emperor he had
striven to protect—and to dominate—for so many years. In this chapter the
form that this domination took will be examined—the struggles and triumphs
of Stilicho's regime and his cataclysmic fall, as he attempted to maintain
his position as guardian well into Honorius' adulthood. Crucial to Stilicho's
justification of his role was the way in which the young Honorius was
presented (primarily through the writings of Stilicho's chief propagandist,
Claudian) as he grew to adulthood. These years were to see many challenges
to the western government take shape, in the form of latent eastern hostility
and interference, provincial usurpations, and the long-running dilemma of
how to deal with the Visigoths under Alaric once they arrived on western soil.

Perhaps the most serious challenge of all for Stilicho was the question of
how to maintain his relationship with Honorius and the emperor's dependency upon him as the years passed. As a child-emperor of 10, Honorius' need

---

[1] Claudian, *VI Cons.* 578–91: *hic est ille puer, qui nunc ad rostra Quirites evocat et solio fultus
genitoris eburno gestarum patribus causas ex ordine rerum eventusque refert veterumque exempla
secutus digerit imperii sub iudice facta senatu.*

for a leading general to take his place on the battlefield was undisputed, and could be used to legitimate the absolute power of the guardian who fulfilled this role. And in the meantime, the image of a partnership of government could be projected: of the pious and youthfully promising emperor and his loyally capable guardian. But such an image could surely only remain plausible for a finite period. The ingenuity and success with which Stilicho was able to maintain and reinvent this relationship was the key to his survival over thirteen years of directing the government of the west.

KEEPING CONTROL

The army, Alaric, and the east

Honorius' accession in January 395 to the western throne had seen Ambrose of Milan offering a justification of the boy-emperor's rule on the basis of his father's achievements and the child's youthful promise, and his self-proclaimed protector Stilicho moving in quickly to shore up power and bring in key western support groups behind him. The first few years of this new regime of Stilicho under the rule of Honorius nevertheless saw some challenges for the western administration, in the form of both the Visigoths, and the eastern imperial government. The Visigoths under Alaric had been allies of Theodosius at Frigidus, but had rebelled early in 395 and begun ravaging Greece.[2] In both 395 and 397, Stilicho led military campaigns against them, but in neither instance was he able to secure a victory. In September 395, when he had set out on the first campaign, he had taken with him not only the western field army, but also the eastern military contingent which had travelled west with Theodosius I in 393 and remained there after his death. According to Claudian, Stilicho and his combined armies had the Goths surrounded and on the point of joining battle (which certainly would have led to Alaric's utter defeat) when a message arrived from Arcadius. The nefarious praetorian prefect Rufinus, alleged Claudian, had been alarmed by Stilicho's success and pretentions to eastern as well as western dominance, and

---

[2] On Visigoths fighting at Frigidus, see Socrates 7.10; Zosimus 5.4; Alaric was not the commander of all the Gothic federates however, that post was held by Gainas (Zosimus 4.57; Eunapius, frg. 60; Jordanes, *Get.* 145). See Liebeschuetz (1992), 78. On the rebellion in 395, see Cameron (1970), 156; cf. Heather (1991), 193; Dewar (1996), xxix–xxx. Liebeschuetz writes that the beginnings of Alaric's career are very obscure, but it is unlikely he was the leader of the group he led before the end of 394; also that it was essentially his own unit Alaric was commanding at this time, and not the Goths settled in Moesia in 376 as well: (1992), 76–80; against Wolfram (1988), 139 f.

prevailed upon Arcadius to demand that Stilicho immediately abandon the campaign and return the eastern troops to Constantinople.[3] Torn by his desire to finish the Visigoths and yet to be loyal to Arcadius, his loyalty won out, and Stilicho with much anguish returned the soldiers and was forced to call off the campaign.[4]

Claudian's version is most likely far removed from the truth: more convincing are arguments that the campaign had been aborted due to ill-discipline in Stilicho's army, while the claimed demand from Arcadius for the return of the eastern troops had served as a convenient excuse.[5] After a recruiting drive in 396, Stilicho launched another campaign against Alaric in 397.[6] Once again the campaign was largely inconclusive and the Romans were unable to achieve a decisive victory.[7] Claims that Stilicho was secretly in league with Alaric against the empire and so engineered these mediocre campaign outcomes should be given no credence: these were expensive and embarrassing expeditions, and Stilicho would gain nothing from their failures: it would have been madness to deliberately risk the inevitable resulting damage to his standing with both the army and the aristocracy, particularly when the regime was still in its early days.[8] Lack of discipline and concerns of disloyalty among his soldiers again seem the most likely explanation for the 397 failure.

The regime of Stilicho under Honorius was clearly experiencing some teething problems in terms of the loyalty of the western military, which seems hardly surprising given that they were now serving under a man whom they had been facing across the battlefield only a year earlier; moreover Stilicho's position as head of the (defeated) western army was probably further complicated by memories of the particular ferocity of the battle on the Frigidus.[9] The fact that Stilicho was leading the army in the name of an unseen child-emperor, and trying to follow up the act of the victorious soldier-emperor Theodosius I (even if he had been the eastern emperor) cannot have helped. Most of all, Stilicho's campaigns against the Visigoths greatly

---

[3] Rufinus had been left at Constantinople when Theodosius marched west and the praetorian prefect dominated the first months of Arcadius' reign: Cameron (1970), 63.

[4] Claudian, *Ruf.* 2.50–3; 161–70; 197–205. Also on the campaign, see: Claudian, *IV Cons.* 479 f.; and on the return of the troops to the east: Zosimus 5.4.2; cf. Cameron (1970), 66; 169. Also Matthews (1975), 271.

[5] Cameron (1970), 159, 164–5, 167. Followed by O'Flynn (1983), 28–33.

[6] As suggested by Claudian, *IV Cons.* 439 f.; *Stil.* I.188 f. Cf. Mazzarino (1942), 127, n. 3; Cameron (1970), 168–9. On manpower shortages after sending troops back to the east, see: Zosimus 5.4.2, and also: *CTh.* 7.18.9 (26 Apr. 396); 7.4.22 (30 May 396); 7.4.23 (16 June 396).

[7] Claudian, *IV Cons.* 461 f.; cf. *Get.* 513 f.; cf. the account of Zosimus: 5.7.1 f. Matthews (1975), 271–2; Cameron (1970), 86; McLynn (1994).

[8] Demougeot (1951), 143 ff.; Stein (1959), 1. 231; Cameron (1970), 172, 177–8; Wolfram (1988),142.

[9] See e.g. Philostorgius 11.2.

increased the mounting tide of antagonism that the eastern government of Arcadius was directing at the new western regime. In 395, Stilicho's military numbers had been seriously depleted by the demand to relinquish the eastern troops. In the course of the 397 campaign, the eastern government, now under the sway of the eunuch Eutropius, chose to view Stilicho's activity with even greater animosity, declared him a *hostis publicus* and themselves came to terms with Alaric.[10]

Stilicho and the senate versus Gildo

An even more dangerous manifestation of the hostility of the eastern government was yet to come. Count Gildo, an African prince to whom Theodosius I had granted full military and civil powers in his own province, rebelled over the course of the summer of 397, originally merely reducing the grain shipments to Rome, but eventually halting them altogether, and all apparently at the instigation of the eastern court.[11] Orosius' explanation for Gildo's motivation is a significant one, for he seems to suggest that some thought Gildo expected neither young emperor to last long:

moved by a kind of envy [Gildo] tried to join Africa to the districts of the eastern empire, or even—as another opinion has it—did this thinking that there would be very little prospect [for himself] in the youthful rulers, perhaps because, except for these, nobody before left in power as a youth had reached the maturity of full manhood, and they are found almost alone whom, on account of the father's eminent faith and his own, separated and forsaken, the protection of Christ had advanced, and so he dared to claim it for himself and detached it from its membership of the state . . .[12]

[10] On the east declaring Stilicho *hostis publicus*: Zosimus 5.11.1; Matthews (1975), 272; Cameron (1970), 176. On Alaric's eastern command: Claudian *Eutr.* II.216; *Get.*535 f. See Cameron (1970), 173–4; cf. Dewar (1996), xxix–xxx.

[11] Zosimus 5.11.1–2; Claudian, *Stil.* I.271–3, 277–9. See Cameron (1970), 93, 103. Claudian claimed Gildo had shown disloyalty in the past and Theodosius I had planned to deal with him personally before prevented by his own death (Claudian, *Gild.* I.253–517). There had been doubts about Gildo's loyalty in the late 380s–early 390s: see Matthews (1975), 272-3; also Oost (1962), 27. Most recently on the rebellion, and Gildo's possible association with church factions in Africa: Shaw (2011), 46–50.

[12] Orosius 7.36: [*interia Gildo comes, qui in initio regni eorum Africae praeerat, simul ut defunctum Theodosium comperit*], *siue (ut quidem* [sc. *quidam*] *ferunt) quadam permotus invidia Africam orientalis imperii partibus iungere molitus est, siue (ut alia tradit opinio) minimam in parvulis spem fore arbitratus—praesertim cum absque his non facile antea quisquam pusillius in imperio relictus ad maturitatem virilis aetatis evaserit istique propemodum soli inveniantur, quos ob egregiam patris ac suam fidem et divisos et destitutos Christi tutela provexerit—Africam excerptam a societate reipublicae sibi usurpare ausus est . . .*

Orosius' verdict of divine protection for the young emperors through the faith of their father (and their own) appears to echo Ambrose's words in 395.[13] For the western government, depriving Rome of her single most important source of corn put the regime of Stilicho in grave danger and could potentially undermine his position entirely—which was presumably the eastern government's aim. Even a delay in the arrival of the grain-ships could result in riots at Rome, and this was a highly provocative step by the eastern government, a blatant challenge to Stilicho to defend his position.[14] Once again, only a few years into the reign of Honorius under the guardianship of Stilicho, this was a reminder of the precariousness of the regime, and with two distinctly untriumphant campaigns against the Visigoths in recent years and concerns remaining about western military loyalty, the eastern government's activity could conceivably have brought about Stilicho's downfall.

Stilicho's response to the crisis is well documented: in an ingenious and popular move he showed his deference for the senate by passing over to them the responsibility for declaring war on Gildo by *senatusconsultum*, thus deflecting plebeian anger over corn shortages on to the senators rather than himself and Honorius.[15] But recruits were needed too, and the back-and-forth wrangling between the court and senate as rulings requiring the furnishing of recruits or cash for recruits from senators were first passed, then petitioned against, then renegotiated, have often been discussed.[16] Stilicho was in a precarious position, already an enemy of the state in the eyes of the eastern government, but struggling to gain practical aid from the Roman senators. Nevertheless, a force was somehow put together, sent off on the expedition with a rousing speech by young Honorius, who yearned to lead them personally (according to Claudian), and led instead by Gildo's estranged brother Mascezel.[17] Departing in November 397, the campaign's object was achieved with remarkable rapidity—Gildo was defeated within weeks of the western army's arrival in North Africa in February 398, and committed suicide.[18]

---

[13] See above, p. 146.

[14] Cameron (1970), 93.

[15] The *senatusconsultum* decree is celebrated by Claudian: *Stil.* I.325–32. Cf. Paschoud (1967), 146–9. The meeting at which the decree was passed is described by Symmachus, *Ep.* 4.5. On deflecting plebeian anger towards the senators, see Matthews (1975), 268. Cf. Dewar (1996), xlviii; Cameron (1970), 230–1; Barrow (1973), 13. Symmachus also referred to emergency supplies in 397–8 in *Epp.* 7.38; 4.5.

[16] The laws passed for recruiting or cash payments: *CTh.* 7.13.12 (17 June 397); 7.13.13 (24 Sept. 397); 7.13.14 (12 Nov. 397). See Symmachus, *Ep.* 6.58; 62. For modern accounts: Jones (1964a), 1. 184; Matthews (1975), 268–9; Harries (1999), 51.

[17] For Honorius' desire to lead the expedition, see Claudian, *Gild.* I.374–8. For the speech: I.424 ff. On Mascezel's leadership, see Orosius 7.36. Cf. Cameron (1970), 95.

[18] Claudian, *Gild.* I.9–13. Cf. Cameron (1970), 95. Orosius asserted that the enemy were defeated almost without a fight: Orosius 7.36.12. Mascezel also died soon after the campaign, with Zosimus claiming Stilicho had him drowned so that he did not become a threat to his own position: 5.11.3–4; Orosius alternatively alleges he had desecrated a church in his arrogance over

Rome's corn supply was secure once more, and Gildo's substantial properties and their revenues were confiscated for Honorius' private treasury.[19]

Claudian's poem on the expedition provides valuable insight into Stilicho's policy of conciliation towards the east, despite their provocative interference in western affairs which could well have cost him his position.[20] As in the case of the recall of the eastern troops during Stilicho's 395 campaign against the Goths, Claudian explains, this was not Arcadius' fault, but the fault instead of evil counsellors who had led the young emperor astray.[21] Although it was conventional for all victories in either half of the empire to be credited to all legitimate emperors, still the monument raised in the Roman Forum ascribing the defeat of Gildo to both Arcadius and Honorius may come as a surprise in the circumstances, but similarly signalled the conciliatory attitude of the western government towards the eastern.[22] Stilicho was utterly determined to insist that relations between east and west were stable and harmonious, even if Arcadius would do better to heed his advice.[23]

It has been claimed that the Gildonic crisis drove a wedge between Stilicho and the senate, and caused permanent damage to their previously good relationship, though given Gildo's swift defeat and the ultimate triumph of Stilicho's policy in dealing with the crisis, it is hard to see why.[24] Certainly, Honorius' government had faced a difficult task trying to extract recruits from the senators for the expedition, but recruiting issues were nothing new, and the downfall of Gildo saw the disappearance of such complaints.[25] Claims of deep-seated suspicion and extreme resentment due to Stilicho's barbarian ancestry also seem unfounded: Stilicho was only part-Vandal, and powerful generals of barbarian stock were hardly unprecedented in the west.[26] The fact that anti-barbarianism was used as a justification for Stilicho's downfall after

the victory and his death was divine judgement: 7.36.13. On Gildo's death see: Claudian, *Gild.* I.415 f. (where it is envisaged rather than reported), *Stil.* I.333 f., *IV Cons.* 381–2; Orosius 7.36; Jordanes, *Rom.* 320.

[19] *CTh.* 9.42.16 (1 Dec. [Sept.] 399); 7.8.7 (8 June 400); 7.8.9 (399; 6 Aug. 409); 9.42. 19 (6 Aug. 409); *Not. Dig.Occ.* 12.5; cf. Matthews (1975), 273.

[20] Cameron (1970), 111. For a recent study of the poem, its characterization of Gildo and promotion of the interests of Stilicho, see Ware (2004), 96–103.

[21] Claudian, *Gild.* I.311 f. Cf. Cameron (1970), 110.

[22] McCormick (1986), 117. For the inscription: *CIL* 6. 1187 and 31256.

[23] See e.g. Claudian, *Gild.* I.1–6. On Arcadius' need for Stilicho's guidance, see I.98–9. Cameron (1970), 122.

[24] For claims of such damage to the relationship, see e.g. McLynn (1994), 368. Cf. Mazzarino (1942), 238–9.

[25] Christiansen (1966), 45–6. Cf. Barrow (1973), 14.

[26] For examples of such claims of anti-barbarian feeling against Stilicho, see O'Flynn (1983), 43, 62, 70; and to a lesser extent Matthews (1975), 268. A decree of 397 forbidding the wearing of trousers in the city of Rome may reflect anti-barbarian sentiment, but presumably more specifically about anti-Persian sentiment than any feeling relating to Stilicho: *CTh.* 14.10.2 (7 Apr. 397).

his death need not mean that it was a significant factor in the perception of his regime at this early stage.

Stilicho had treated the senate with deference, leaving the declaration of war to them and being willing to negotiate over the issues of recruiting. The very fact that senatorial concerns regarding recruits were open to negotiation indicates Stilicho's awareness of maintaining the support of key western power-groups. Nevertheless, it is also indicative of the weakness of Stilicho's regime, even several years into its establishment. Negotiation with the senatorial elite had been, as we have seen, a common occurrence under the reigns of Gratian and Valentinian II; yet exceptionally strong military emperors, such as Valentinian I, apparently had shown little concern for courting such aristocratic favour.[27] There can be no doubt that Stilicho recognized the great importance of his relationship with the senate, and the value of the cooperation of the senatorial elite who between them controlled much of the resources of Italy, Gaul, Spain, and Africa.[28] The events of late 397 should serve to confirm this awareness rather than be seen to undermine his value for that relationship.[29] The Gildonic crisis was ultimately a triumph for the western regime of Stilicho—in fact, the first clear victory for the regime.[30] Roman senatorial estates in North Africa had been preserved, as had the corn supply, and in short there seems little reason to believe the negotiations over recruiting had 'permanently damaged' Stilicho's relations with the senate. Indeed, his popularity may even have been still further increased by the unheard-of consulate of the eunuch Eutropius in the east in 399, unrecognized in the west, and cruelly attacked by Claudian in his *In Eutropium* as constituting a travesty of the distinguished office.[31] The contrasting panegyric by Claudian for Manlius Theodorus, the western consul for 399, was a further display of Stilicho's acute awareness and respect for senatorial dignity, and of the powerful supporters the regime was attracting.[32]

Honorius' first marriage

Stilicho had emerged the unexpected victor of the crisis with Gildo and managed to turn a highly dangerous threat to his position into a significant triumph, and a justification of his own position as Honorius' guardian and

---

[27] See generally for Valentinian I's relations with the senate: Lizzi Testa (2004), 381–460.

[28] Matthews (1975), 268–70, who also discusses the billeting of armies on senatorial estates while travelling around Italy, as confirmed by letters of Symmachus. Also Cameron (1970), 233–4.

[29] O'Flynn (1983), 36.

[30] Commemorated by inscriptions at Rome: *CIL* 6. 31256; 1187; 1730.

[31] See esp. Claudian, *Eutr.* I.484–9. Cf. Cameron (1970), 125–9.

[32] Claudian, *Man.Th.* 265–9.

by extension guardian of the state. This justification of his position, and the ways in which these crises—with the Visigoths, Gildo, and especially the east—affected Stilicho's situation and his relationship with Honorius, are the key issues here. The serious challenges Stilicho had faced can only have made him all the more aware of the crucial importance of linking himself, irrevocably if possible, with Honorius, if he were to maintain his own position. His guardianship was a finite relationship, and it must have been with this thought in mind that Stilicho arranged the first marriage of Honorius, then aged 13, to his eldest daughter Maria.[33] The wedding took place very early in 398, before the news of Gildo's defeat could have been known at court. The timing of the marriage could hardly have been more significant. Through it, Stilicho's influence over Honorius, nearing the age of 14 when he might technically be no longer in need of a legal guardian, was preserved. Stilicho was clearly aware not only that his own position was currently under threat but that this was unlikely to be the last time it would be: that as Honorius grew up his guardian would need to reinvent their relationship if he sought to hold on to his own authority—and how better to do that than by becoming the emperor's father-in-law?

Claudian devoted a full-scale *epithalamium* to the occasion of the marriage, as well as fescennine verses. According to the poet, the match had been arranged by Theodosius I before his death, and Stilicho was reluctant to see it take place so early (Maria was aged about 12 in 398), but it was urged on by the ardent young Honorius, burning with 'passion's first fever'.[34] It is even possible that Claudian was speaking the truth here in relation to Theodosius I's wishes—the marriage of Maria to Honorius at least prevented the princess's marriage to anyone else who might one day pose a political threat to the emperor himself.[35] Eventually, Claudian wrote, Honorius' assertion of his honourable intentions won the day, persuading Stilicho, despite his hesitation, to allow the wedding to take place and, as father to them both, uniting the young couple.[36]

Stilicho might have long had this marriage in mind, but the Gildonic crisis brought a new urgency to the situation. As father-in-law to the emperor,

---

[33] Claudian antedates the marriage in his poem on the war against Gildo, but it seems to have taken place between the expedition's departure and victory: Cameron (1970), 109. Cf. on the marriage: Zosimus 5.4.1–2.

[34] On the supposed arrangement of the marriage by Theodosius I: Claudian, *Nupt.* 19–31. For the ardour of Honorius, see ibid. 1–7. See further Cameron (1970), 99.

[35] The unwed state of Maria's younger sister, Thermantia, in 408, when she was married to Honorius after Maria's death, suggests that the marriages of the daughters of the imperial house were difficult to resolve—although Thermantia's date of birth is unknown, if she were close in age to her elder sister, she was probably already in her late teens by 408: *PLRE* 2. 1111–12. In the later fifth-century east, the husbands of the emperor Leo I's daughters would be a source of considerable trouble for the emperor Zeno: see Jones (1964a), 1. 224–30. See further below on the similar issue of the marriage of Valentinian III's sister Honoria, p. 293 and n. 93.

[36] Claudian, *Fesc.* 1–12.

Stilicho's position was strengthened immeasurably.[37] It placed him far above his peers and any potential challengers, and emphasized that whatever tactics the eastern government might try, he was a part of the western dynasty, in a way that his then rival for dominance of Arcadius in the east, the eunuch Eutropius, never could be: he was there to stay.[38] Claudian's words staunchly supported Stilicho's position: he had proved worthy to be entrusted with Theodosius I's child and to hold the reins of government, and now Honorius' subjects would owe the young emperor even greater allegiance due to the heroic deeds of his bride's father.[39] Such an emphasis both exalted Stilicho's position and highlighted Honorius' youth and dependency upon him—emphasizing that his subjects owed their loyalty to the regime not merely due to the emperor's deeds but to those of his guardian and now father-in-law also. But most importantly of all, Claudian's words highlighted the crucial fact that if this union produced an heir to the throne, then Stilicho's role in the western government truly would be unassailable. Claudian's words are an eloquent expression of Stilicho's hopes: 'may Maria's womb grow big and a little Honorius, born to the purple, rest on his grandsire's lap.'[40]

Two years later, upon the occasion of Stilicho's consulship in 400, Claudian's panegyric gave even freer rein to these dynastic hopes, describing a consular robe embroidered with images of the young mother Maria, so realistic one could almost hear the cries of the child: 'And now the babe had grown up, recalling his father in countenance; Stilicho, riper in years, teaches his grandson, the emperor that is to be, the science of war.'[41] Again the emphasis is on Stilicho's knowledge of 'the science of war', not the young emperor's. The poem went on to suggest further dynastic hopes of Stilicho—a betrothal between his son Eucherius and Honorius' sister Galla Placidia: a back-up plan perhaps, in the case of Honorius' death or failure to produce children; also a means of eliminating any potential rival to the power of Stilicho's family who might be created through the marriage of any other party to Galla Placidia.[42]

---

[37] Cameron (1970), 100, 154.

[38] Eutropius' intrigue in 395 to ensure Arcadius did not marry the daughter of the prefect Rufinus was obviously aimed at avoiding the eunuch's being outmanoeuvred by a similar arrangement in the east—Eudoxia, the daughter of the dead general Bauto, with no known surviving relatives, must have seemed a very safe choice in comparison: see Holum (1982), 52–3.

[39] Claudian, *Nupt.* 299–308, 335–41.

[40] Ibid. 335–41: *sic uterus crescat Mariae; sic natus in ostro parvus Honoriades genibus considat avitis.*

[41] Claudian, *Stil.* II.346–61: *iam creverat infans ore ferens patrem: Stilicho maturior aevi Martia recturo tradit praecepta nepoti.* Similarly II.231–40. See further on late Roman consular robes in general and this one in particular: Dewar (2008), 228–32.

[42] Ibid. II.351–61; cf. Cameron (1970), 154. The match never eventuated but it must surely have been Stilicho's plan. See also Harlow (2004), 140–1.

Becoming the father-in-law of a child-emperor as he grew to adulthood was one means by which a shrewd manager like Stilicho could consolidate his own position, enabling him to reinvent and extend that position with the passage of time. It was probably a tactic that Stilicho had been reserving ever since Honorius' accession in 395, to deploy at the moment when he most needed to reinforce his relationship with the emperor and his position in the government, and the genuine threat that Gildo (with his eastern encouragement) posed provided the moment. Instead of leading the campaign against Gildo, through which he might have achieved a personal military victory, Stilicho put his time to even more valuable use. By remaining with Honorius and the court, he ensured that the emperor remained isolated from other potential advisers, and put in place the one arrangement which could bring about the only result with the potential to make his position truly unassailable: the marriage of Honorius and Maria, and the hope of an imperial heir of his own bloodline which would ensure the future of the western imperial house.

Partnership

The first few years following Honorius' accession thus witnessed a number of threats to the regime that Stilicho had established around the young emperor. It is worth pausing at this point to consider the imperial image which was being projected by the court of the child-emperor under Stilicho's direction. Ambrose of Milan had introduced the new reign with an emotive appeal for loyalty to the sons of Theodosius I, coupled with an assertion of the new child-emperor's youthful promise. This youthful-promise motif was one which the court poet Claudian would continue to promote unstintingly, and to work into the picture that his poems consistently presented of the many ways in which Honorius fitted the established imperial ideal—just as Menander had instructed a century before. Yet as one study has recently highlighted, the poetry of Claudian essentially shifted the role of the panegyrist, making him the permanent propagandist of a dominant political figure, rather than one who produced occasional works for a variety of honorands.[43] Claudian's relationship with Stilicho, and the series of works the poet composed under the general's patronage, provide essentially a steady picture of Stilichonian policy from 396 to 404—and thus also a constant image of the way in which Stilicho's regime wished Honorius to be presented. Claudian's poems therefore offer an unusually large corpus of evidence regarding a single emperor, in the form of the three panegyrics he wrote for Honorius' consulships, as well as numerous other poems—such as those for his wedding, those on the Gildonic and Gothic

---

[43] Gillett (2012), 270.

wars, and the panegyric for Stilicho's consulship in 400.[44] It is from all of these texts, therefore, rather than a single panegyric, that our understanding of the presentation of Honorius as emperor and his fulfilment of the traditional ideals can be drawn.

In the matter of his birth and family there could be no doubt that Honorius admirably fulfilled the imperial requirements. As Claudian liked to remind his audience, Honorius was not only the son of an emperor, but one born after his father's accession: a purple-born prince, who had never been a private citizen, unlike even his brother Arcadius. Honorius alone had been born in kingly state, on a golden couch, clothed in ancestral purple as he grew, and raised to the consulship while still in his cradle.[45] Promising omens attended Honorius' birth, and his accession, while he was worthy of comparison with a young Jove.[46] The military exploits of Honorius' father and grandfather could be lavishly praised, again harking back to the youthful promise of the child-emperor through his military pedigree.[47] With regard to Honorius' education, Claudian described Theodosius instructing young Honorius to cultivate the muses and learn of the deeds of the Roman heroes of old.[48] Moreover, as a testament to his education, Claudian's Honorius made eloquent speeches—when sending off the troops of the Gildonic campaign in rousing style, and in 404 respectfully addressing the senate at Rome.[49]

Central to the established imperial presentation were the cardinal virtues. First of all courage, demonstrated through military prowess. Claudian did have much to say on this matter regarding the boy-emperor, yet it is conspicuous that his accounts dwelt either upon sentimental images of the infant prince in military guise, soldierly advice bestowed upon him by his father, or the young Honorius practicing the arts of war. In short, youthful promise must carry the day. Claudian wrote emotively of the infant Honorius in the military camp of his father, his cradle hedged in by standards of war, the baby crawling amongst shields and the freshly won spoils of battle, the nobility of his lineage shining in his face as he grasped his grandsire's spear and wore his sire's helmet.[50] In a comment reminiscent of Ambrose's

[44] Additionally, as Kulikowski points out, Claudian is one of the few sources for the reign not tarnished by knowledge of the events of 410: Kulikowski (2007), 161.

[45] Claudian, *IV Cons.* 122–31, 135–41, 154–60. Cf. *III Cons.* 13–21.

[46] For omens at birth: Claudian, *III Cons.* 7–12; *IV Cons.* 141 ff., 151–3. For omens at the time of his acclamation, see *IV Cons.* 170 ff. For comparisons with the gods: Claudian, *III Cons.* 126–32. Cf. *IV Cons.* 160–70, 197–202, and with his brother Arcadius after Honorius' acclamation as Augustus, 203–9.

[47] Claudian, *IV Cons.* 24 ff.

[48] Ibid. 396–400 ff.

[49] For the speech to send the troops off to fight Gildo, see Claudian, *Gild.* I.424 ff.; for the 404 speech, see *VI Cons.* 585–91.

[50] For the infant Honorius in his father's camp: Claudian, *IV Cons.* 141 ff., 151–3; crawling among shields: *III Cons.* 7–38, and on this Cameron (1970), 40; and on wearing his father's helmet: *IV Cons.* 518–22. See also above, p. 150.

exhortations to the soldiers to show the sons of Theodosius the faith owed to the late emperor, Claudian declares that the troops' loyalty is a lasting one, not bought with gifts but affection, for the army is anxious for Honorius as 'its own child', loving him as its nursling.[51] From Theodosius I himself, Claudian claimed, Honorius received his training in the arts of war: his father forbade him to indulge in 'enervating sloth' or 'luxurious ease', but instead strengthened his young limbs with hard toils and training, taught the prince to bear winter's cold and summer's heat, swim rivers, climb mountains, run over the plains, and keep watch at night.[52] The emperor told his little son great tales of his grandfather's exploits to inspire him and spur him on, cherishing his own hopes of military glory for Honorius.[53]

According to Claudian, Theodosius advised Honorius on handling his soldiers in times of war: to ensure that they were properly trained and prepared, and to learn of proper formations for fighting on different terrain.[54] And, his father told him, Honorius must himself ride with his cavalry and fight beside his infantry on campaign, for they would be inspired to be even bolder through his presence among them.[55] In addition, Claudian described Honorius duly practising the arts of war and showing great skill at riding and hurling spears, decked out handsomely in his golden armour, with waving plumes on his helmet, like a young Mars, hurling his javelin with such vigour and shooting from his bow with great accuracy, foreshadowing his strength in manhood.[56] Claudian wrote also of young Honorius' great eagerness to ride to war—like a restless young lion, chafing against his father's refusal to take him on the campaign against Magnus Maximus (when Honorius was aged 4!), and again for the campaign against Eugenius in 394.[57] The child's desire to defend his people even at such a tender age betrayed his noble spirit, Claudian told his audience.[58]

In the early days of Honorius' reign, the emperor's youth was a reasonable excuse for his failure to take up any active military role. Unfortunately, Claudian's evidence ends with his poem for Honorius' consulship in 404, when the emperor was *c.*18–19: it would have been fascinating to see how Honorius' lack of a military role would be justified after this point. Still, there

---

[51] Claudian, *IV Cons.* 501–3. See similarly *Eutr.* I.371–89.

[52] Claudian, *III Cons.* 39–50. Cf. *IV Cons.* 337–48.

[53] Claudian, *III Cons.* 22–38, 51 ff. See similarly: Prudentius, *CSymm.* 2.7–9.

[54] Claudian, *IV Cons.* 214–22.

[55] Ibid. 349–52. Again, see similarly: Prudentius, *CSymm.* 2.17–30.

[56] For Honorius practising the arts of war, Claudian, *IV Cons.* 539–45 ff. For his javelin and bow skills, ibid. 523–9 (and see similarly, but with a Christian emphasis, Prudentius, *CSymm.* 2.729–32). And for the hope of his future strength: Claudian, *IV Cons.* 518–22. Cf. *Ruf.* 1.372–6.

[57] For Honorius as the young lion, see Claudian, *III Cons.* 63 ff., 73–6. For his desire to go to war against Maximus, see *IV Cons.* 353–68, and against Eugenius, *III Cons.* 83–7.

[58] Claudian, *IV Cons.* 369–85. Cf. similar claims of Honorius' eagerness to lead the campaign against Gildo: *Gild.* I.368–71, 374–87.

were always the other cardinal virtues: wisdom, justice, and temperance. Yet again, Claudian's comments with regard to these essential imperial virtues usually came in the guise of advice from Theodosius I to his very young son. Theodosius urged Honorius to take Trajan as his model, not because of his many victories but for his high principles, his wisdom, justice, and kindness in dealing with his subjects.[59] Moreover, Honorius was told, he must be both a citizen and father to his people and be stirred not by his own desires, but by those of his people.[60] He was not king of Parthia, or some luxurious eastern kingdom, but of Rome, and must remember that it was merit and not blood which earned his throne (despite appearances), and must unite virtue with his power.[61] Such idealizing comments were an espousal of the highly traditional concept of an emperor's *civilitas* and his role as 'first among equals'.[62]

In the matter of the administration of justice, Theodosius I exhorted his son to lead by example, in being the first to submit himself to any new law made for the general good, for his people will shape themselves after his example.[63] In Claudian's invective against Eutropius, he even portrayed Honorius as busy dictating laws to different barbarian tribes, assisted by Stilicho, signing treaties and enlisting allies, and meting out justice.[64] And in the matter of temperance, Theodosius I again advised his son that he must be master of his own passions, and show restraint in personal luxuries: not having a tent overflowing with princely delights or eating lavish meals on campaigns, but sharing the lot of his soldiers, who would love him the better for it.[65] According to Claudian, under Honorius the unholy increase of taxes was at an end, there were no proscription lists, and the emperor was liberal, but not wasteful, with his money.[66]

Although Claudian's evidence is limited to the first decade of Honorius' rule, in many ways the first tenuous years were always going to be the most crucial in developing the image of how the child-emperor Honorius was to be established as acceptable to his senatorial and military audience. Clearly Claudian did manage to find ways of presenting Honorius as able to fulfil the expectations of a late Roman emperor, even if much of that presentation relied on the hope of the adult leader that the child might one day be. In fact, over the course of almost a decade, Claudian's presentation of Honorius does not change significantly. But careful reading of Claudian's poetry also reveals a striking new twist on the imperial presentation. For it was not only Honorius

---

[59] Claudian, *IV Cons.* 315–19.
[60] Ibid. 294–5.
[61] Ibid. 214–22; also 306–12.
[62] Cameron (1970), 377–8. Also (1976), 175. Rather than representing any advocation of constitutional monarchy as Mazzarino once argued: Mazzarino (1942), 232 ff.
[63] Claudian, *IV Cons.* 296–302.
[64] Claudian, *Eutr.* I.377–90.
[65] Claudian, *IV Cons.* 257–62, 337–48.
[66] Ibid. 493–503.

to whom specifically imperial virtues were being ascribed: it was Stilicho, too. What Claudian was presenting was essentially a partnership: a government based on the youthful promise of the dynastically legitimate boy-emperor and the practical, demonstrated virtues of his loyal guardian.

In 400, when Stilicho entered upon his first consulship, Claudian wrote an immense three-book panegyric in honour of the occasion. A careful reading of this panegyric reveals how closely it reproduces a picture of the imperial virtues recommended by Menander's *Basilikos Logos*. It began with Stilicho's promising nature and appearance, signs of a 'loftier estate' shining forth in him from infancy.[67] Stilicho's actual parentage and background were not dwelt upon, naturally, but of course his link with the imperial house through his marriage to Serena was made much of: stressing that Theodosius I had searched long and hard for a suitable husband for his favourite niece, and merit alone decided the matter.[68] On the issue of his military skill and prowess, few could equal Stilicho—he slept beneath the sky through icy winters amidst the snow, with ceaseless toil winning the victories the empire despaired of.[69] He was generous with the soldiers, inflamed their hearts in battle through his personal example, and terrified his enemies, like a maddened lion intent only on protecting his young.[70] He was always with his army, had the unswerving loyalty of the troops, feared no enemy, but could never be accused of taking up his sword against a fellow-citizen.[71] Above all, Stilicho restored glory to Rome through the all-important matter of victory.[72] It has been argued that the only known surviving image of Stilicho, a diptych perhaps issued in the late 390s to mark the admission of his son Eucherius as a *notarius,* also displayed the general in a pose intended to evoke Mars; at any rate, Stilicho is certainly depicted in a military guise, seeming to complement Claudian's words.[73]

In the matter of other cardinal virtues Stilicho was equally impressive. His justice and generosity in dealing with enemy barbarians was noted, as was the wisdom he displayed through his lack of pride and disdain, and value for merit above birth.[74] He was patient, temperate, and prudent.[75] Unsurpassed in counsel and his knowledge of law, he united strength and fortitude, was noble

---

[67] Claudian, *Stil.* I.39–50.
[68] Ibid. I.69–79.
[69] Claudian, *Get.* 359–63; *Stil.* I.122–8.
[70] Claudian, *Ruf.* II.171 ff.; *Get.* 323–9, 373–5; *Stil.* I.188–97.
[71] For Stilicho's presence with his army: Claudian, *Stil.* I.116–22. For the loyalty of the troops: ibid. I.160–9, II.145–9, 152–6. For the army's love for Stilicho, see also *Get.* 404–7; *Ruf.* II.257 ff. For his fear of no enemy: *Ruf.* I.259–67. And for his never taking a sword against a fellow-citizen: *Nupt.* 328–34. Cf. McCormick (1986), 124.
[72] Claudian, *Stil.* I.384–5.
[73] The famous Monza diptych: Kiilerich and Torp (1989), 361–2.
[74] Claudian, *Stil.* I.207 ff.; II.122–131; II.157 ff.
[75] Ibid. II.100–9.

in appearance, modest, and full of dignity.[76] He was respectful of Roman traditions and towards the senate, and devoted to the ancient customs.[77] He worked to instill all of these virtues in young Honorius, teaching him to do his duty by his people, and embrace moral virtues like chastity and moderation.[78] Stilicho was universally loved, incorruptible, and beyond the envy of all those around him, according to Claudian.[79] He was even backed by divine blessings.[80] Overall, Claudian declared, he gave hope to the virtues of a bygone age and restored Rome to her former glory.[81]

The qualities Claudian ascribed to Stilicho were typical heroic virtues, but they were also highly imperial ones, and yet in the late Roman state it was the emperor who was supposed to be the ultimate hero. Panegyrics on non-imperial figures were by no means unknown—Claudian wrote two other non-imperial panegyrics which have survived, for Probinus and Olybrius, the consuls of 395, and for Manlius Theodorus, consul in 399. But the heights to which Claudian was raising Stilicho—as a figure with distinctly imperial-style virtues—were remarkable. Yet in the context of Honorius' youth and Stilicho's guardianship, this lavish treatment makes sense. The government was being 'sold' on the basis of a partnership: on the youthful promise of Honorius and the practical and proven virtues of his guardian, Stilicho. Depicting Stilicho as possessed of conspicuously imperial virtues reminded the audience of who truly wielded power at court and had offices and privileges to distribute to the loyal among the elite. And the description in the panegyric on Stilicho of the general teaching Honorius how to do his duty by his people, noted above, is only one of many examples of this developing language of partnership in Claudian's poetry.

Throughout Claudian's works, this theme of a sort of corporate rule between the young emperor and Stilicho is both prominent and recurrent. The most familiar instances to modern scholars must be those passages which refer to Theodosius I commending his sons to Stilicho on his deathbed (discussed above)—according to Claudian, the power of Rome was 'entrusted' to Stilicho's care, Theodosius I had made him 'sole guardian' of his children, and the dying father's love had chosen a worthy heir to be the protector of his child and hold the reins of government.[82] The marital ties of Stilicho to both Theodosius I and Honorius are repeatedly noted throughout Claudian's works, and upon Honorius' marriage to Maria it is declared that: 'we owe our emperor an ever firmer allegiance for that you, invincible hero, are the father

---

[76] Claudian, *Nupt.* 313–28.
[77] Claudian, *Stil.* III.26–9.
[78] Ibid. II.62–77, III.113–23.
[79] Ibid. II.109–22, 160–8, 173–5; III.39–44.
[80] Ibid. II.208 ff.
[81] Ibid. III.106–12. Similarly *Man.Th.* 159–72.
[82] Claudian, *III Cons.* 142–59; *Ruf.* II.1–10; *Nupt.* 295–308.

of his bride.'[83] Stilicho's role as adoptive father to Honorius is constantly emphasized, and in that capacity his teaching of the young emperor the arts of rulership also reinforces the idea of their teamwork.[84] Thus, when the goddess Roma visits the emperor to express her horror over the appointment of the eunuch Eutropius to the eastern consulate, she comes upon a scene where: 'the august Honorius, assisted by his father-in-law Stilicho, was making answer to the Germans who come of their own accord to sue for peace.'[85] Stilicho is praised for shaping Honorius' mind with both kindness and sternness: 'as a youth you teach him in secret a king's lesson—his duty to his people; as a reverend senior you pay him honour and govern the empire at a father's bidding; to your lord you give humble worship; you guide your master with obedience, your sire with love.'[86]

Once again, the image of a child-emperor as both father and son of his country appears.[87] Stilicho is Honorius' first and greatest defender; moreover, as the active, military side of the imperial partnership he wages war and forges peace on the emperor's behalf: thus, before Stilicho: 'Germany swears allegiance to the absent Honorius and addresses her suppliant prayers to him . . . That which others were enabled to win by long wars—this, Honorius, Stilicho's mere march gives to you.'[88] The efforts of Stilicho, Claudian declares, have secured laurel wreaths for Honorius' brow.[89] In keeping with the picture of Stilicho as the great military hero, as discussed above, there are still moments when Claudian declares that Stilicho's exploits alone have won the day.[90] Yet envy cannot hold sway in a state where Stilicho and his son-in-law direct affairs, the poet insists.[91] When Roma visits Honorius to entreat that he celebrate his sixth consulship at Rome, the emperor points out that he had not disregarded the city's call before: 'I sent you Stilicho to sit in the curule chair to take my place, a consul instead of an emperor, a father instead of a father-in-law. In him your citizens also saw myself.'[92]

---

[83] e.g. Claudian, *Nupt.* 335–41; also *Carm.Min.* I (XIII).1–12.

[84] For Stilicho as the emperor's adoptive father, see e.g. Claudian, *Fesc.* III.1–12.

[85] Claudian, *Eutr.* I.377–80: *tum forte decorus cum Stilichone gener pacem implorantibus ultro Germanis responsa dabat, legesque Caucis arduus et flavis signabat iura Suebis.*

[86] Claudian, *Stil.* II.62–78: *secreto consona regno ceu iuvenem doceas, moles quid publica poscat: ceu sanctum venerere senem patriisque gubernes imperium monitis; dominum summissus adores; obsequiis moderere ducem, pietate parentem.* See similarly ibid. III.113–23; *VI Cons.* 547–59.

[87] See earlier comments in Ch. 4, p. 128.

[88] Claudian, *IV Cons.* 448–59: *iuratur Honorius absens imploratque tuum supplex Alamannia nomen . . . quod longis alii bellis potuere mereri, hoc tibi dat Stilichonis iter.* Also *IV Cons.* 428–38.

[89] Claudian, *VI Cons.* 351–5.

[90] e.g. Claudian, *Stil.* I.160–1; *Get.* 36–49, 267–9.

[91] Claudian, *Man.Th.* 256–66.

[92] Claudian, *VI Cons.* 431–5: *advectae misso Stilichone curules, ut nostras tibi, Roma, vices pro principe consul impleret generoque socer. vidistis in illo me quoque . . .*

When the *adventus* of Honorius to Rome to celebrate this consulship did take place in 404, Stilicho was riding in the same chariot as the emperor (an image surely reminiscent of the 394 *adventus* when Honorius rode into Milan with his father; and perhaps even the *adventus* to Constantinople with Theodosius I and Arcadius, following Honorius' acclamation as Augustus in 393), seeing his son-in-law pass in triumph through the streets, rewarded in that his singleness of purpose had 'made a boy master of the world'.[93]

The manner in which the aristocrat Symmachus addressed Stilicho in his letters is also significant. In one letter Symmachus refers twice to the *magister militum* as *parens publicus*—a term which it has been pointed out can be construed as intended to bring to mind the official *pater patriae* title of emperors.[94] Some of the other remarkable phrases used in Symmachus' letters addressing Stilicho have also been noted, such as 'vir inlustris comes omni virtutum genere sublimissimus' and 'sublimi et magnificentissimo viro'.[95] Such forms of address certainly indicated awareness of Stilicho's true dominance of Honorius' government. Yet they also reflected the lack of a real title for the true position Stilicho held: in effect, so much more than just the *magister militum* or the young emperor's guardian.

This approach of presenting a picture of corporate imperial rule indicates a developing sophistication in the presentation of a child-emperor which had not been apparent under either Gratian or Valentinian II; but then, Stilicho was also the first long-term manager of a boy-emperor, and his marriage ties with the imperial house gave him a far more powerful position than Merobaudes or Arbogast before him had occupied. Furthermore, Stilicho had the examples of the fates of these boy-emperors before Honorius (and those attempting to be their managers) to learn from. As ever, the passage of time presented a problem for the projection of Honorius as a youthful but promising emperor, which could not be maintained indefinitely. At the outset of the reign, and even in the first ten years or so as Honorius grew up, this could remain a reasonable proposition, but as Honorius grew from childhood to manhood it was going to peter out: there was only so long that the presentation of youthful promise could remain convincing. As far as Claudian's evidence extends, however, there is no change in this presentation apparent, and at least until 404 it clearly remained a vital justification of the positions of both Honorius and Stilicho. And while this presentation might reach only a limited audience, essentially the aristocratic and military elites of the empire, this was a vitally important audience for the survival of the regime.

---

[93] Ibid. 578–86. For the entrance to Milan in 394, see *III Cons.* 126–41; and the entrance to Constantinople in 393, see *IV Cons.* 203–11.

[94] Symmachus, *Ep.* 4.12, 14; see Salzman (2006), 355.

[95] Matthews (1975), 265, and n. 7. For these two particular forms of address, see *Epp.* 7.105 and 122.

Stilicho the victor

From the defeat of Gildo and the resolving of the crises with the eastern government (or at least the stalemate situation which seems to have prevailed for a time after Gildo's downfall) until the late summer of 401, matters seem to have gone more smoothly for the partnership government of Stilicho and young Honorius. Legislation for the period dealt with wide-ranging issues like taxation, municipal duties, recruiting, road and building repairs, and the abuses of palatine officials, and revealed the court to be moving around Italy far more than in the first few years of the regime, again a reflection of increasing stability.[96] But in the late summer of 401 the Visigoths under Alaric invaded Italy.[97] The reasons for the invasion remain unclear, although there is no evidence it was directly incited by the eastern government.[98] The details of the early campaign in particular remain hazy: a Roman defeat seems to have been suffered on the Timavus and another in the Alps.[99] The Roman senate was clearly fearful: the city's walls were repaired at this time, and Symmachus was sent to court to plead for the government's assistance.[100] His visit is a telling reflection of Honorius' continuing lack of leadership within his own government: Stilicho was absent when Symmachus arrived, so although he saw the emperor, it was felt that no decision could be taken until Stilicho returned. Honorius was almost 17 years old at this stage.

In the event, it was Milan which was besieged, probably in the spring of 402, with the young emperor behind its walls. Claudian wrote of Stilicho rushing to raise the siege and rescue the emperor, and sometime before December 402 the entire court had decamped to the greater security of Ravenna.[101] Two pitched battles—one at Pollentia and one at Verona—between the Visigoths and the Roman army under Stilicho took place also in 402—probably in April

---

[96] e.g. recruiting: *CTh.* 7.1.18 (19 Mar. 400); deserters: 12.15.1 (13 Sept. 399); taxation: 1.12.7 (29 Sept. 399); municipal duties: 12.1.161 (16 (21) Aug. 399); road repairs: 15.3.4 (29 Apr. 399); building repairs: 15.1.41 (4 July 401); rapacious palatines: 1.5.13 (27 Nov. 400). For the movement of the court in this period, see e.g. *CTh.* 16.10.15 (Ravenna, 29 Jan. (Aug.) 399); 11.30.59 (Verona, 12 June 399); 11.30.61 (Brescia, 19 Aug. 400); 16.11.1 (Padua, 20 Aug. 399); 14.23.1 (Altinum, 27 Mar. (28 Sept.) 400); 6.19.1 (Aquileia, 29 Sept. 400).

[97] Their arrangement with the eastern government may have broken down: Matthews (1975), 273; Heather (1991), 208.

[98] Bayless (1976*a*), 65, against Demougeot (1951), 267; Grumel (1951), 39; and Stein (1959), 1. 247–8.

[99] Claudian, *Get.* 319 f., 562 ff., and esp. 400 f. See Matthews (1975), 273.

[100] On the repairing of Rome's walls at this point, see *ILS* 797; *CIL* 6. 1188–90; cf. Chastagnol (1962), 256; Matthews (1975), 273, and Oost (1968*a*), 70. On Symmachus' visit to court, Symmachus, *Epp.* 5.95–6; 7.13, repeated at 7.14; See Dewar (1996), xxxii–xxxiii.

[101] The first legislation issued from Ravenna appears in December: *CTh.* 7.13.15 (6 Dec. 402); Baynes (1955*d*), 329.

and August respectively.[102] Roman and Gothic sources both claimed victory at Pollentia for their own sides: but as Alaric was able to escape, it seems most likely it was a fairly even contest in which the Romans gained a slight edge, and Verona too seems to have been largely inconclusive.[103] As one scholar has pointed out, the most enduring impact of the invasion of 401 was the removal of Honorius' court to Ravenna.[104] It was a city with formidable natural defences—swampy marshland on one side and the sea on the other—although it was hardly impregnable, as modern scholarship frequently asserts: in fact it was repeatedly captured in the fifth and sixth centuries.[105] But it was well positioned in terms of roads to other cities, food supplies from the nearby northern Italian plains, and crucially, able to supply itself with food and troops by sea, through its access to the fleet.[106] But this was also a move which further isolated young Honorius from the realm he supposedly ruled, and moved the emperor further from the Rhine, potentially prompting a sense of greater isolation among his Gallic subjects. And while Honorius, behind the walls of Ravenna, could still be presented theoretically to his subjects as youthful and promising, once more it was Stilicho who was out in the field as the military leader.

Stabilization

Although once seen as a period of serious deterioration in relations between the eastern and western courts, more recent scholarship has highlighted that the first years of the fifth century, when the eastern government was led by men like Aurelian and Anthemius, in fact show signs of a distinct improvement in relations.[107] The controversial eastern consulship of Eutropius in 399

---

[102] Matthews (1975), 274; Cameron (1970). The dating of Pollentia in particular has been a matter of some debate: see Mazzarino (1942), 279, n. 2; Demougeot (1951), 275–7; Jones (1964a), 1. 184; Stein (1959), 1. 248. For a recent argument for the traditional dating of both battles to 402, see Cesa and Sivan (1990), 361–74, but for an alternative argument for 403, see Hall (1988), 245–57.

[103] On the battle at Pollentia, for the Roman side: Claudian, *Get.* 598 ff., 610 ff. and esp. 635–8. Also *VI Cons.* 127–31. Prudentius also wrote of it as a great Roman victory: *CSymm.* 2.715 ff. For the Gothic side: Cassiodorus, *Chron.* 154; Jordanes, *Get.* 155. Orosius rails against the battle taking place on Easter Sunday under command of the barbarian, 'pagan' general Saul, asserting that it was divine judgement that 'we won the battle, but were vanquished in our victory' (7.37.2–3). See generally Heather (1991), 209. On the battle at Verona, see Claudian, *Get.* 550 f. See also *VI Cons.* 229–37. Cf. Matthews (1975), 274.

[104] Barnes (1976), 373.

[105] As pointed out by Gillett (2001), 161–2, and Deliyannis (2010), 46–7.

[106] Christie and Gibson (1988), 158. Cf. Stein (1959), 1. 249.

[107] For evidence of an improvement in relations, see Bayless (1976b), 74–5; Gillett (1993), 18 and n. 84. See generally on this Cameron and Long (1993), 323–36, and on relations between the eastern and western courts particularly, 165–7, 246–50. For the 'deterioration' argument: Demougeot (1951), 235–6. Similarly Christiansen (1970), 114.

had not been recognized by the west, and following his fall as Arcadius' chief minister, and the eventual rise of Aurelian after the short-lived military regime of Gainas, still Aurelian's consulship in 400 was not acknowledged by Honorius' government. In 401 however, the eastern consulship of the general Fravittas was accepted in the west, and in 402, more significantly still, another joint consulship for Arcadius and Honorius was recorded—their first since 396.[108] These signs of improved relations—and the abandonment of Stilicho's regency claims over Arcadius around this time (indicated by its disappearance from Claudian's poetry)—suggests that Stilicho's regime was enjoying a period of greater stability after the first five years of young Honorius' reign.[109] It was really only once the matter of eastern hostility had been resolved that the government of Stilicho and his son-in-law Honorius could function normally.

In 404 the most dramatic piece of ceremonial on record for Honorius' reign was staged at Rome: a triumphal entrance in celebration of the vanquishing of the Goths, the emperor's sixth consulship, and his *decennalia* (celebrated a year late, but commemorating his accession at Constantinople in 393).[110] Claudian's panegyric to Honorius, delivered on the occasion and to an audience of a far greater number of powerful Roman aristocrats than would ever have been present when the court was at Milan, provides a vivid picture of the celebrations.[111] It has been argued on the basis of Prudentius' *Contra Symmachum*, published late 402/early 403, that the final visit of Symmachus to Milan in 402 had presented a further petition requesting the restoration of the altar of victory.[112] If such a petition was indeed repeated in 402 it was evidently refused, but the appointments of the prominent pagans Decius Albinus as urban prefect in late 402 and Rumorides as western consul for 403 may have been a conciliation effort by the government, and an assurance that pagan aristocrats could nevertheless still hold the very highest offices of state.[113] Against the backdrop of these developments, it was to be expected that the regime of Stilicho would be doing its utmost to play to senatorial interests on this major ceremonial occasion. One reported event of the visit,

---

[108] Heather (1991), 210; also Cameron (1970), 38–51; Bayless (1976a), 66–7. As Cameron and Long point out, the images displayed on the column of Arcadius at Constantinople, erected around this time, also reflect the improvement in relations between the two courts and the emphasis on imperial concordia: (1993), 247.

[109] The claim to guardianship of Arcadius as well as Honorius still appears in the panegyric for Stilicho's consulship of 400 (*Stil.* II.50–62, 78–99), but not in the panegyric for Honorius' sixth consulship of 404.

[110] Cameron (1970), 180–1; Baynes (1955d), 329; Oost (1968a), 70–1.

[111] Dewar (1996), xlv. For detailed analysis of Honorius' 404 *adventus* in Claudian, see MacCormack (1981), 52 ff.

[112] Barnes (1976), 381–6. See particularly Prudentius, II.769–70.

[113] On the appointment of Albinus: *CTh.* 7.13.15 (6 Dec. 402). Cf. Barnes (1976), 386. Rumorides had been present at Valentinian II's court when Symmachus presented his *relatio* on the Altar of Victory, and was *magister utriusque militiae* in 384 (Ambrose, *Ep.* 57). See Cesa and Sivan (1990), 368.

which goes unremarked by Claudian but appears in a homily of St Augustine, and will be discussed further below, is a visit made by Honorius to St Peter's Basilica. According to Augustine, here Honorius reverently knelt before the grave of St Peter and removed his imperial diadem, an action which would both contribute to the particularly pious image of the young emperor's rule and appeal to the sensibilities of the Christian aristocracy of the city.[114]

Claudian's panegyric devoted considerable space to a visit that the goddess Roma supposedly made to the emperor in order to encourage his appearance in the city, with a lengthy enumeration of its many claims on his affections, and its great worthiness through its incomparable tradition and as the true seat of his government.[115] The description of the ceremonial entrance to the city itself dwelt upon the emperor's youthful beauty and dazzling appearance—crowned, and clad in a jewel-studded consul's cloak, with emeralds hung around his neck.[116] A distinctly military feel was given by the armed knights on horseback who surrounded the emperor, with their gleaming weapons; a military flavour which probably aimed to disguise the young man's lack of personal military achievements, and perhaps also to reassure the populace, with Alaric still not decisively defeated, that the government had military matters in hand.[117] As noted above, in 404, when Honorius was nearing 20, the youthful-promise motif was probably starting to become a little less plausible.

As the emperor entered Rome, he returned the salutations of the adoring crowds, and as he met the senators, Claudian claimed, he forbade them to walk before his chariot, and they rejoiced at an emperor so easy of access.[118] An imperial *adventus* offered the opportunity to celebrate relations between emperor and senate.[119] Stilicho was not forgotten either—indeed, the justification of his role in the imperial partnership only became more crucial as Honorius reached adulthood. As noted above, he rode in the same chariot as Honorius, who during the visit of the goddess Roma before he celebrated his consulship in 404 exclaimed to her that he could never sufficiently praise the benefits Stilicho had conferred upon himself and the empire.[120] Stilicho's careful training of his adopted son, Claudian declared, was such that now: 'This is the boy who today summons Rome's citizens to the place of meeting and from his father's ivory throne tells to the fathers the causes and issues of

---

[114] Augustine, *Cum pagani* 26; Liverani (2007), 83. See below for further discussion, p. 211.
[115] Claudian, *VI Cons.* 356–60, 407–24.
[116] Ibid. 560–7.
[117] Ibid. 569; see McCormick (1986), 86–7, 90.
[118] Claudian, *VI Cons.* 543–54, 611–17.
[119] Machado (2010), 291–2.
[120] Claudian, *VI Cons.* 426–40. Also generally: ibid. 356–60, 407–24. Cf. *Stil.* I.325–32. Also MacCormack (1981), 54.

his acts, and, following ancient precedent, directs the deeds of empire at the judgement-seat of the senate.'[121]

The triumph of 404 was a spectacular demonstration of the success and stability of the regime Stilicho had built up around the boy-emperor over the past nine years; nor was it a hollow demonstration. For more than a decade he succeeded in dominating utterly the government of Honorius, isolating the emperor from other major sources of advice and guidance, while the number of officials who would fall with Stilicho when he was finally dislodged testifies to the thoroughness with which his regime-building had packed the adminis-tration with 'his' men. From the 'accident' of the accession of the 10-year-old Honorius, Stilicho had built up a regime which had survived Visigothic attacks, the hostility of the eastern government, and the dangers of the Gildonic crisis, and had successfully throughout the period managed to keep his hold on Honorius. Even at this stage, when Honorius was 19 years old, the regime was still being 'sold' by its public spokesman Claudian on the basis of the emperor's youthful (but unproven) promise, and the current, realized virtues of Stilicho: just how much longer that presentation might be stretched, or how it might be reinvented, remained to be seen. One underlying vulnerability, a chink in Stilicho's armour which could not be repaired, was the failure of his daughter Maria to produce an heir for Honorius. The emperor's childless marriage could, as time went on, undermine the value of Stilicho's reinvention of his guardian-ship role to that of father-in-law. Unless an imperial grandson did appear, and the future of the western ruling house could be assured without any threat to the present, Stilicho could never be entirely safe.

LOSS OF CONTROL

Invasions

Following the triumphal spectacle of the 404 visit of Honorius and Stilicho to Rome, and the easing of tensions between the eastern and western courts, in late 405–early 406 a new crisis struck. The Goth Radagaisus launched a major attack on Italy, crossing the Danube with an army of Gauls and Germans which Zosimus claims numbered as many as 400,000.[122] The struggle to

---

[121] Claudian, *VI Cons.* 578–91: *hic est ille puer, qui nunc ad rostra Quirites evocat et solio fultus genitoris eburno gestarum patribus causas ex ordine rerum eventusque refert veterumque exempla secutus digerit imperii sub iudice facta senatu.*

[122] Zosimus 5.26.3. The number is certainly an exaggeration but it was clearly a large enough group to make a strong impression; Orosius put the number under Radagaisus' command at 200,000 Goths (7.37.2–3). Matthews (1975), 274, argues for the date of 405–6 for the invasion, as against Baynes (1955*d*), 87, who favours 404–5. See further Heather (2005), 194–9.

contain the invaders took up Stilicho's attention for more than a year, but ended in a satisfyingly thorough victory for the *magister militum* before the gates of Faesulae on 8 August 406.[123] Radagaisus was executed, while large numbers of his followers were enrolled in the Roman army as federate troops, and those of lower status, according to Orosius, sold off in droves like cattle for an *aureus* apiece.[124] Monuments were erected in honour of the hero Stilicho, including a statue opposite the entrance to the Curia at Rome, the immense base of which remains *in situ* today.[125] Once again the strength of the imperial partnership was demonstrated.

But the barbarian invasions did not end there, and Stilicho himself seems to have anticipated further trouble, reflected in his decision to enlist the help of Alaric and his Visigothic following in the hope of annexing eastern Illyricum.[126] From 395 the western half of the diocese of Illyricum appears to have been administered by Honorius' government.[127] Given the improvement of relations between the eastern and western courts in recent years, such a decision by Stilicho to invade eastern Illyricum seems surprising, for the hostility it would evoke from Arcadius' government as a result must have been entirely foreseeable.[128] Yet already in 404 signs of tension between east and west had surfaced once more: in a notably aggrieved letter from Honorius to Arcadius which survives from this year, the western emperor presented his brother with a list of complaints.[129] Aside from disgruntlement over the distribution of images to the provinces of the eastern empress Eudoxia as Augusta, to which Honorius took exception, he complained that the previous year eastern Illyricum had been devastated by Alaric and the eastern court had not informed the west of this development. Presumably it was feared in the east that Stilicho might view Alaric's activity as an invitation to intervene in Illyricum once more. Antagonism between the two imperial courts was clearly

---

[123] Muhlberger (1984), 73.

[124] Orosius 7.37; Zosimus 5.26.4–5; Olympiodorus, frg. 9 claims 12,000 were enrolled in the army.

[125] Paul. Nola, *Carm.* 21.1–34; inscriptions collected by Demougeot (1951), 360 f. The statue base inscription is *ILS* 799. Stilicho's name was obliterated from the statue base as part of his *damnatio memoriae* after 408, but as Humphries points out, leaving the base in its prominent position thus only emphasized its political message: Humphries (2003), 40.

[126] On this, see Heather (2009), 26–8.

[127] Cameron (1970), 60–1; cf. Grumel (1951), 22; Heather (1991), 202.

[128] On Stilicho's plans for Illyricum, see Cameron (1970), 59–60; also Demougeot (1950), 33. For a different view on Stilicho's reason for the planned invasion see Mazzarino (1942), 66 ff.; Kulikowski argues that the plan never existed at all, but was an eastern fabrication: Kulikowski (2000*b*), 330.

[129] *Coll. Avell. Ep.* 38. Honorius also complained in this letter of the treatment of John Chrysostom: see further below, pp. 209–10.

on the rise again, and this eastern concealment of Alaric's activity may even have contributed to Stilicho's decision to form an alliance with the Visigoths a few years later.[130]

However, legislation passed in early 406 and before the threat of Radagaisus had been contained attests to the desperate situation of the western army with regard to recruiting. In one famous law, even slaves were exhorted to take up arms in defence of their country, with the reward of their freedom in return, and in another, all freemen were summoned to military service and promised 10 *solidi* each.[131] In the face of such dire recruiting needs, Stilicho was clearly prepared to go to extreme ends, coming to an arrangement with Alaric, and appointing one Jovius as praetorian prefect of Illyricum in *c*.406, apparently with the intention that he and Alaric should together seize eastern Illyricum for the west.[132] If the scheme had come to fruition it would have allowed the western government not only to gain new recruiting grounds but also to enlist Gothic manpower—we know, after all, that Alaric had already been active in eastern Illyricum and may have been stationed there illegally for some time previously.[133] Even after the defeat of Radagaisus and the swelling of western military ranks with some of his followers, this must have seemed a tempting enough incentive for Stilicho to maintain the plan for east Illyricum's annexation.

On the last day of 406, a new wave of barbarian invaders entered the empire—this time Vandals, Alans, and Sueves, who crossed the Rhine into Gaul.[134] The motivations for their arrival on the Roman frontier and their invasion of Roman territory at this particular point have been the subject of considerable argument among modern scholars, though what matters most for our purposes is simply that the invasion took place when it did, allowing it to contribute to a major military crisis that was beginning to spiral out of control in the west.[135] Stilicho's foreboding of some such event may well have been behind his plans for Illyricum, but they were not carried through in time, and in the end no action at all was taken by the government against these new

---

[130] On the deterioration of relations between the courts again after 404, see Cameron and Long (1993), 246–50, and Liebeschuetz (1990), 64–5.

[131] *CTh.* 7.13.16 (17 Apr, (15 Feb.) 406); 7.13.17 (19 Apr. (15 Feb.) 406).

[132] Zosimus 5.26.1–3; Sozomen 8.25.3, 9.4.3. See Matthews (1975), 274; Heather (2009), 26–8.

[133] Heather (1991), 212.

[134] Kulikowski has argued for a mistake in the sources which would have made the date 405 instead and thus explained Stilicho's inaction by his being occupied with Radagaisus, but Birley has restated the case for 406, which remains the more convincing: Kulikowski (2000*b*), 328; Birley (2005), 457–9 and Kulikowski's reconsideration (2007), 171, n. 37. For a recent analysis of the sources reporting the crossing, see Heather (2009), 3–29.

[135] The debates focus on whether the invasion was the result of Roman internal weaknesses or external impetus (such as Hunnic expansion forcing other barbarian groups westwards)—it is difficult to separate out such causal relationships entirely, though it seems unlikely internal problems in the late Roman west were very apparent to those beyond the frontiers: see, for a recent summary and analysis, Heather (2009), 3–29.

intruders, for the other military crises facing the regime were beginning to escalate.[136]

Over the course of 406–7 a series of usurpers had been proclaimed in Britain, and the only source to record a reason for this rash of usurpations, Zosimus, asserts it was in response to fear of barbarians who had escaped after the defeat of Radagaisus, crossed the Alps into Gaul, and were now thought a potential threat to Britain.[137] Whether this truly was the prompt behind the rebellion or not, it soon became an increasingly urgent problem for the central administration in Italy. In 407 the most successful of the British usurpers, calling himself Constantine III, crossed to Bononia with a large force (probably all that remained of the British field army) and succeeded in seizing the prefecture of Gaul.[138] Early in 408 the Ravenna government took the unusual step of sending an army commanded by the Gothic general Sarus against the rebel Augustus in a pre-emptive strike, but after some initial success the imperial army was forced to retreat to Italy.[139] Within the space of a few years, a build-up of different crises had begun to put immense pressure on the government of Honorius.

Problems and solutions: Alaric, the senate, and Honorius' second marriage

Up until the end of 405, Stilicho's star had shown no sign of falling. In 404 he had seen the sixth consulship of Honorius celebrated at Rome in a vivid demonstration of the reign's stability, and he had achieved his own second consulship in 405, followed by a tremendous success against Radagaisus in 406. Until things started to go wrong at the end of 406, with more barbarian invaders who were not dealt with, the arrangement with Alaric falling through and the arrival of Constantine III in Gaul, there is little solid evidence on which to base claims of Stilicho's unpopularity with key players within the

[136] Drinkwater (1998), 275; Matthews (1975), 275; cf. Heather (1991); Demougeot (1951), 376 ff.

[137] The usurpers were first Marcus, then Gratian, and finally Constantine: Olympiodorus, frg. 13.1.7–13; Zosimus 6.2.1–2. For a detailed analysis of the usurpation of Constantine III, see Drinkwater (1998), 269–98. For the date of Constantine III's elevation, see Prosper 1232, and Zosimus 6.2.1–2. For the motivation behind the usurpations, see Zosimus 6.3.1; Paschoud (1986), 3. 2, n. 115; Kulikowski (2000b), 328; Birley (2005), 458–9.

[138] Zosimus 5.27.1–3, 6.2.1–2; Olympiodorus, frg. 13.1.13–21; Orosius 7.40; Sozomen 9.11.3. For the court's establishment at Arles: Zosimus 5.31.4. Cf. Stevens (1957), 322–3; Matthews (1975), 308–9. On the departure of Roman troops from Britain under Constantine III, see Bury (1923), 188–9; Esmonde Cleary (1989), 142; Burns (1994), 251; Drinkwater (1998), 175.

[139] Zosimus 6.2.2–6. See Drinkwater (1998), 278–9; Kulikowski (2000b), 334.

western government or aristocracy: up until this point, the regime he had built up had been notably successful and stable.[140]

At some point in the course of 406–7, Alaric had moved his men out of Epirus and encamped them near the city of Emona, to await the arrival of the Roman army for the planned invasion of Illyricum.[141] When Stilicho proved unable to keep to the agreement, Alaric marched his men into the province of Noricum and sent to Stilicho a demand for recompense for the costs of his efforts. Stilicho decided that Alaric should indeed be paid, and went to Rome in early 408 to have the matter discussed at a senate meeting, described by one scholar as 'perhaps the most crucial single moment in the regime of Stilicho'.[142] The pressure was mounting on Stilicho to find a solution to the compounding military crises now besetting the west: after all, he was the active military side of the imperial partnership, and legitimating his position had depended upon demonstrating that. The emperor himself does not appear to have attended this vital meeting, despite his presence in Rome at the time.[143] The question arises as to whether the emperor would usually attend meetings of the senate when the court was in Rome, and it is a surprisingly difficult one to answer, with few references to actual senate meetings appearing in the sources. One indication that an emperor could attend such meetings should he wish to do so, however, is Ammianus' description of Julian attending meetings of the Constantinopolitan senate in the early 360s.[144] It seems likely that Honorius could have attended a meeting on such an important matter had he, or Stilicho, wished it.

Zosimus gives a detailed report of the meeting: that Stilicho argued that Alaric had been acting on his instruction and should be compensated, but that the senate voted first to wage war against Alaric instead, with Stilicho having to argue his case for conciliation and payment.[145] According to Zosimus: 'Everyone at this thought Stilicho spoke reasonably and the senate voted that four thousand pounds of gold should be paid to Alaric, although most voted that way not from preference but out of fear of Stilicho.'[146] The famous

---

[140] Christiansen (1966), 46.

[141] Olympiodorus, frg. 1.2.1–11; Zosimus 5.26. See Cameron (1970), 158–9, and Jones (1964a), 1. 184–5. Jones states that Alaric was given the rank of *magister militum* at this point, but it is not clear that this was so.

[142] Matthews (1975), 276. Laws dating from 15 Nov. 407 (*CTh*. 16.5.41) to 3 Feb. 408 (*CTh*. 1.20.1) given at Rome suggest a date of late 407–early 408 for the senate meeting.

[143] Zosimus 5.29.5–5.30.3.

[144] AM 22.7.3.

[145] Zosimus 5.29.6–9. Also Olympiodorus, frg. 7.2, and Matthews (1975), 279.

[146] Zosimus 5.29.8–9: Πᾶσι τοίνυν δόξαντος δίκαια λέγειν Στελίχωνος, ἐδόκει τῇ γερουσίᾳ χρυσίου τετρακισχιλίας ὑπὲρ τῆς εἰρήνης Ἀλαρίχῳ δίδοσθαι λίτρας, τῶν πλειόνων οὐ κατὰ προαίρεσιν ἀλλὰ τῷ Στελίχωνος φόβῳ τοῦτο ψηφισαμένων ...

reaction of the influential senator Lampadius, murmuring, 'this is slavery rather than peace', was highly significant: he had held the urban prefecture in 399 and was brother to the celebrated former consul Manlius Theodorus, and his dissatisfaction with the Visigothic payment may have marked the turning-point for some of the early supporters of Stilicho's regime.[147] Here at last is the earliest direct evidence for resentment and unhappiness among the senatorial elite directed towards Stilicho. Senatorial reluctance to give substantial assistance to the imperial government in the form of military conscripts or cash was certainly in evidence long before 407, but there is no reason to believe this reluctance was any greater under Stilicho than it had been under any previous regime, or that they would be any more willing to help once Stilicho was dead.[148] Much of the wealth of the senatorial elite lay in landed property, and was therefore not necessarily accessible, while many senators clearly preferred to hoard their funds to spend on lavish displays—such as Symmachus' praetorian games for his son in AD 400, on which 2,000 pounds were spent.[149] But again, there is no obvious reason to believe senatorial reluctance to provide recruits or funds was a greater problem under Stilicho than under other recent regimes; rather, by 408 the crises were simply more dire, and therefore so too were the consequences.

It is significant that Stilicho consulted the senate at all over the issue of Alaric's payment, since he could surely have had Honorius order legislation to exactly the same effect (even if it had resulted in senatorial petitions and protests)—but this was a pattern of Stilicho's behaviour. Just as in 398 the granting to the senate of the privilege to declare war on Gildo had legitimated Stilicho's position in a time of crisis and deflected blame for subsequent difficulties away from him, so he sought to do the same in 408. But by this stage, with his regime faced by military emergencies on several fronts, and thus far showing no ability to deal with them successfully, the tide of senatorial opinion was turning against him, and even a recourse to his celebrated respect for senatorial tradition could not salvage the situation, though since presumably the senators were being asked to find the money to pay Alaric, their lack of enthusiasm is not entirely surprising.

---

[147] Zosimus 5.29.8–9. See Matthews (1975), 279. For Lampadius, see *PLRE* 2. 656.

[148] For senatorial objection to furnishing cash or recruits in military crises, see e.g *CTh.* 7.13.13 (24 Sept. 397); 7.13.14 (12 Nov. 397), and for reassurances that imperial estates must pay also: 7.13.12 (17 June 397); 6.2.22 (26 Feb. 401). See Matthews (1975), 277.

[149] Symmachus, *Ep.* 6.62, 64. On Symmachus' lengthy preparations for his sons' games, see Sogno (2006), 84–5; also Machado (2010), 301–4. The senator Maximus not long afterwards apparently spent twice as much again as Symmachus on his own son's praetorian games (Olympiodorus, frg. 41.2). Matthews points out that the games were arranged ten years in advance, and senatorial families would save for them for years: Matthews (1975), 277–8 as evidenced by *CTh.* 6.4.13 (3 May 361); 6.4.22 (9 June 373); Symmachus, *Or.* 5.4. For some critics in older scholarship of senatorial attitudes: e.g. Sundwall (1915), 150 ff.; Mazzarino (1942), 238 f. For a traditionally negative view on senatorial selfishness when it came to imperial policy, see McGeachy (1942), 49.

It was also in the course of 408 that another important and revealing event took place, which again reflected Stilicho's awareness of the danger of his position. Honorius' first marriage to Maria had lasted ten years, but she died, childless, probably in 407 or early 408.[150] At some point before August 408, Stilicho married Honorius to his second daughter, Thermantia.[151] By this time, with Honorius now aged 23, the period over which Stilicho could continue to stretch the ideal of the emperor's youthful promise, and his own essential contribution to the government in protecting the child-emperor and carrying out the functions that the emperor could not (yet), must have been limited indeed. With the loss of his elder daughter, and with it his position of father-in-law to the emperor and the hope of an imperial heir, and in the face of massive military crises on several fronts, Stilicho urgently needed to re-invent his relationship with the emperor once again. A repeat of his father-in-law role must have seemed the best option—both for his own position and to avoid any other rival for the emperor's ear seizing the opportunity to take up the role himself—particularly, of course, if a second marriage brought forth a child. If Stilicho was to maintain his hold on the western government, he must, at all costs, maintain his relationship with Honorius.[152]

Downfall

The story of the events surrounding Stilicho's downfall is told in surprising detail by Zosimus, and bears careful reading for some of the more unexpected elements of the tale. Following the tumultuous senate meeting at Rome, Stilicho planned to return to Ravenna to coordinate the various military operations. Yet Honorius (supposedly prompted by Serena, who felt they would all be safer at Ravenna than Rome) decided that he wanted to come too, to review and encourage the army.[153] Although the emperor is not given the initiative for this decision, his apparent interest in military affairs at this point comes as rather a surprise, and apparently an unwelcome one for Stilicho, who went so far as to instigate a minor mutiny among barbarian troops near Ravenna to dissuade the emperor from coming, but Honorius proved adamant in insisting that he would make the journey.[154] Further hints of army unrest follow: according to Zosimus, the troops at Ticinum were known by Justinianus (a legal assistant of Stilicho) to be already disaffected with the *magister militum*, and as Honorius began his journey (Stilicho seems

[150] The empress Maria was buried in St Peter's in Rome: *ILS* 800; see generally *PLRE* 2. 720, and McEvoy (2010), 181–2.
[151] Zosimus 5.28.1; Olympiodorus, frg. 3.
[152] Heather (2005), 218.
[153] Zosimus 5.30.1–2.
[154] Ibid. 5.30.3–5.

to have been a few days ahead of him), soldiers accompanying him quarrelled and Stilicho had to be called back to deal with them at Bononia.[155]

In May of 408 the news reached the west that Honorius' brother Arcadius had died, leaving his throne to his 7-year-old son Theodosius II—who had been his co-Augustus since 402.[156] According to the sources, when Honorius and Stilicho heard the news they both hoped to travel east—separately—to 'support' the new child-emperor. Olympiodorus explained:

> After the death of Arcadius, Honorius, out of concern for his nephew, was eager to visit Constantinople to appoint loyal ministers to ensure the safety of his nephew's person and throne. For Honorius regarded him as a son and was afraid that he might suffer harm, since he was young and liable to fall victim to plotting.[157]

It is not hard to imagine that Honorius had the circumstances of his own accession in mind. Zosimus reports that both Honorius and Stilicho wanted to make the journey to Constantinople and to take on the role of guardian for Theodosius II, and Stilicho eventually prevailed, telling Honorius that the treasury could not afford the expense of an imperial journey, and furthermore, that with Constantine III on their doorstep the usurper would certainly overrun Italy if Honorius left.[158] In the event, neither Stilicho nor Honorius travelled eastwards, but the dispute between them opened up a central tension in the nature of the imperial partnership that Stilicho had created: of whether it could function at all without the presence of the dynastically legitimate figurehead. Despite Honorius' lack of personal leadership in military affairs, it must indeed have remained crucial for Stilicho to keep the emperor in the west: with Stilicho's own position increasingly under threat as the crises mounted and he struggled to deal with them, his position would have been even more insecure if the emperor whose existence gave him that position departed for Constantinople.

Stilicho's stranglehold on the western government seemed at last to be weakening in 408, with senatorial unpopularity, more military problems than he could deal with, and now dissension with young Honorius himself—despite the emperor's second marriage. Yet it is important to note just how extreme

---

[155] Ibid. 5.30.3–5; 5.31.1–3. Matthews suggests that this Justinianus was the likely source of this section of Zosimus' history, since he managed to escape the court before Stilicho's death: Matthews (1970), 89–90.

[156] On the date of news of Arcadius' death reaching Italy: Paschoud (1986), III.1. 222. Also Matthews (1975), 279.

[157] Olympiodorus, frg. 5.2.1–6: ἐπεὶ δὲ ἐτελεύτησεν Ἀρκάδιος, ὥρμησε μὲν Ὁνώριος φειδοῖ τῇ περὶ τὸν ἀδελφιδοῦν ἐλθεῖν εἰς Κωνσταντινούπολιν καὶ πιστοὺς ἄρχοντας καί φύλακας καταστῆσαι τῆς αὐτοῦ σωτηρίας καὶ βασιλείας. ἐν τάξει γὰρ υἱέος αὐτον ἔχων ἐδεδίει μή τι πάθοι διὰ τὸ νέον ἔτοιμος ὢν πρὸς ἐπιβουλήν. Cf. Socrates 1.7.

[158] Zosimus 5.31.3–4. Cf. Sozomen 9.4.

the situation became before Stilicho could be dislodged. Following the decision that Stilicho would travel east after arranging western military matters, the general left court once more to review troops while Honorius continued his journey to Ravenna, pausing at Ticinum. A court functionary named Olympius—who apparently owed his advancement in the civil service to Stilicho—took advantage of the concatenation of circumstances.[159] According to the sources, he spread damaging rumours that Stilicho had a nefarious plan to use Alaric to wear down the state, that he had instigated a plot in which Olympius had been forced to draw his sword in the palace in order to defend Honorius (with echoes of rumours of Arbogast's treatment of Valentinian II which cannot have been accidental), and perhaps most damagingly, that he meant to remove Honorius and make his own son Eucherius emperor in his stead.[160] Stilicho was separated from Honorius at this point, as he prepared different groups of soldiers for military campaigns, and this would prove to be a crucial factor in Olympius' success.

There is no hint in the sources that Honorius was the real force behind the events leading to Stilicho's death. On 13 August a mutiny of soldiers occurred, apparently at the instigation of Olympius, while Honorius was reviewing them at Ticinum.[161] Following a signal from Olympius, the soldiers fell into a frenzy, killing most of the officials in sight. Zosimus' list of the individuals slaughtered is worth considering carefully. First we are told that Limenius, the praetorian prefect of the provinces beyond the Alps (i.e. Gaul), who had escaped when Constantine III invaded, was killed, along with Chariobaudes, the Gallic *magister militum*. Vincentius, the *magister equitum* of Italy, and Salvius, the *comes domesticorum*, were also killed on the spot, while the *magister officiorum* Naimorius, the *comes sacrarum largitionum* Patroinus, the unnamed *comes rerum privatum*, the *quaestor* Salvius, and the praetorian prefect of Italy Longinianus were hunted down and butchered, as well as 'any officials they could find'.[162]

This is a staggering number of imperial officials eliminated in one sustained attack. These deaths were undoubtedly intended to bring about the total

---

[159] Olympiodorus, frg. 5.3.1–6; Philostorgius 12.1; Matthews (1975), 280; Heather (2005), 222; *PLRE* 2. 801–2.

[160] Orosius 7.38; Philostorgius 12.1. For the rumours that Stilicho intended to replace Honorius with Eucherius, see Zosimus 5.32.1–2; Olympiodorus, frg. 5.2.12–21; Philostorgius 12.2; Orosius 7.38; Marcellinus *comes*, s.a. 408. Sozomen suggests it was Theodosius II that Stilicho intended to replace with Eucherius: 9.4. Yet Zosimus also reported that Stilicho had been careful not to promote his son unduly: 5.34.6–7.

[161] Zosimus 5.32.1–2. The troops were about to be sent against Constantine III: Drinkwater (1998), 279.

[162] Zosimus 5.32.3–7. Also Olympiodorus, frg. 5.2.12–21. Cf. Matthews (1975), 280–1. Zosimus adds that Deuterius, the *praepositus sacri cubicula* and Petrus, the *primicerius notariorum* were brought to trial and tortured after the mutiny, and when they failed to provide any damaging information against Stilicho, Olympius had them clubbed to death: 5.35.1–3.

collapse of Stilicho's regime—and the need to kill so many of the key officers of the state in order to bring down Stilicho himself reinforces the idea that this truly was *his* regime.[163] As the man who had dominated the western government for the past thirteen years as Honorius grew to adulthood, these deaths indicate that all appointments to influential posts had been in his hands, and those appointed were his men. But Stilicho's men were also the men on whom Honorius' government depended: they might be Stilicho's appointees, but they were also in all likelihood the office-holders that Honorius himself knew and trusted—he would have been surrounded by Stilicho's men all of his life. Each one of the named officials killed at the start of the mutiny was probably a member of Honorius' *consistorium*: with one stroke he had been deprived of virtually all of the key office-holders and advisers of his government.[164] Incidentally, the list of those killed in this mutiny may also provide one answer to the question of where the apparatus of government resided in the late Roman west when emperors dwelt at more than one capital.[165] On this occasion at least, clearly the apparatus of government was travelling with Honorius from Rome back to the court at Ravenna—providing the perfect opportunity for the ruthless Olympius to do away with all of the key officers in one concerted attack in Stilicho's absence.

Zosimus' description of the chaos at Ticinum, and of all of the killing, much of which took place before Honorius' eyes (it is said that the *quaestor* Salvius had clasped the emperor's feet in desperation, but even this could not save him), surely also presents a scene which was meant to terrify Honorius utterly, as the men upon whom he depended were cut down around him.[166] As the mutiny spread, Honorius is described as retreating to the palace, but later on, donning a short tunic, leaving behind his cloak and diadem, emerging into the

---

[163] On the background and careers of these supporters of Stilicho, see Matthews (1975), 281; also Matthews (1970), 83.

[164] On membership of the consistory in the later Roman empire, see Jones (1964a) I.333.

[165] The surviving source material in general makes it difficult to ascertain whether the bureaucratic administration travelled with the emperor in the west, or established a permanent base at Rome or Ravenna in the way that we can assume the administration must have done around the far more sedentary court at Constantinople: see Jones (1964a), 1. 366–73; Gillett (2001), 133–4; Kelly (2004), 189–93. While some scholars (e.g. Matthews (1975), 359 and Pietri (1976), 645) have argued that the highest officials seem only to have lived in Ravenna during their terms of office, it is difficult to ascertain whether this was the case for those serving in middle- or lower-ranking bureaucratic posts. See also on arguments for the location of the administration in the west: McCormick (2000), 135–42; Deichmann (1989), 70, 108–15. In this instance at least, we do know that the highest court officials were travelling with the emperor between Rome and Ravenna. On the need for the building of administration blocks at Ravenna to deal with bureaucracy potentially based there in the early fifth century, see Deliyannis (2010), 49–56.

[166] Zosimus 5.7.4–6; for the death of the *quaestor* Salvius, see 5.32.5–7. These killings also seem to echo the murder of Rufinus at Arcadius' feet at the instigation of Eutropius back in 397: see Claudian, *Ruf.* II.366–527; Holum (1982), 59–60.

middle of the city and with great difficulty managing to quell the soldiers.[167] It is hard to know what to make of this unusual passage with Honorius taking action to calm the situation himself, but after this moment of courage he seems to have thought better of it and been content to let the mastermind behind the coup, Olympius, take charge.[168]

When news of the mutiny at Ticinum reached Stilicho at Bononia, it was initially unclear whether or not Honorius had been killed, and some of the barbarians in Stilicho's train wanted to set out at once to deal with the mutineers.[169] When it was established he was alive, Stilicho urged calm on his followers and began to make his way to Ravenna, but as rumours came through that Olympius had prevailed upon the emperor to order his arrest, Stilicho was cautious enough to take refuge in a church on the outskirts of the city overnight. Then, according to Zosimus:

At daybreak the soldiers went into the church and swore an oath before the bishop that they were ordered by the emperor not to kill but to arrest him. When, however, he was led out of the church under military guard, the messenger who was sent with the earlier message brought another, punishing Stilicho with death for his crimes against the state.[170]

On 22 August Stilicho submitted quietly to death, forbidding those with him to defend him.[171] The execution of Stilicho's son Eucherius soon followed, and Stilicho's death is supposed to have swollen the ranks of Alaric's followers still further, with the outraged barbarian allies who had been in the dead general's entourage flocking to join him, eager to make war on Rome.[172] These barbarian allies clearly saw their commitment as having been to Stilicho, the commander in the field, rather than the Roman state.

The sheer magnitude of the crises it took to dislodge Stilicho and to destroy the regime he had built up over the past thirteen years should not be

---

[167] Zosimus 5.32.5–7.

[168] On another occasion shortly afterwards, when the soldiers mutinied at Ravenna and demanded the emperor visit them, Honorius was reportedly so terrified that he hid himself and refused to see them: Zosimus 5.47.1–3.

[169] Zosimus 5.33.1–2; 5.34.1–2. Cf. Matthews (1975), 281–2; Southern and Dixon (1996), 52.

[170] Zosimus 5.34.2–4: Ἐπεὶ δὲ ἡμέρα ἦν ἤδη, παρελθόντες εἰς τὴν ἐκκλησίαν οἱ στρατιῶται, καὶ ὅρκοις πιστωσάμενοι τοῦ ἐπισκόπου παρόντος ὡς οὐκ ἀνελεῖν αὐτὸν ἀλλὰ φυλάξαι μόνον παρὰ βασιλέως ἐτάχθησαν, ἐπειδὴ τῆς ἐκκλησίας ὑπεξελθὼν ὑπὸ τὴν τῶν στρατιωτῶν ἦν φυλακήν, ἀπεδίδοτο δεύτερα γράμματα παρὰ τοῦ κεκομικότος τὰ πρότερα, θανάτου τιμώμενα τὰ κατὰ τῆς πολιτείας ἡμαρτημένα Στελίχωνι. Also Sozomen 9.4; Olympiodorus, frg. 5.1; Philostorgius 11.3; Orosius 7.38; Theophanes, p. 123.

[171] Zosimus 5.34.5; Cf. Matthews (1975), 282; McLynn (1994), 368. The date is supplied by the Copenhagen continuation of Prosper: Muhlberger (1984), 74.

[172] Olympiodorus, frg. 7.6.1–8; cf. Zosimus 5.34.5; Philostorgius 12.3; Orosius 7.38; Sozomen 9.4. Zosimus (5.35.4–6) claims they were motivated also by the killing of some of their families quartered in northern Italy, and that they bolstered Alaric's numbers by 30,000 men, but the number is more likely to have been around 10,000 (Heather (1991), 213–14), probably bringing Alaric's total following to c.40,000. Stilicho's wife Serena, Honorius' cousin, was also executed the following year at Rome: Olympiodorus, frg. 7.3; Zosimus 5.38.1.

underestimated. He had defeated the invasion of Radagaisus in triumphant style, but the Rhine crossing of 406/7 remained an unresolved issue. The combination of crises resulting from barbarian invasions, Visigothic payment demands, senatorial opposition, and the usurpation of Constantine III fatally weakened Stilicho's position, and perhaps no regime could have survived such a simultaneous onslaught. Yet it need not have been these particular military crises which triggered the fall of Stilicho either: for all that the Rhine crossing has been frequently presented in modern scholarship as delivering the fatal blow which unseated the *magister militum*, potentially a different combination of crises—for example, a conflict with the eastern government at the same time as usurpation in Gaul—could have brought about the same result. Essentially, Stilicho's downfall was less about the exact nature or location of the military crises of 405–8, and more about their necessitating his absence from the court and separation from the emperor at a moment when his own reputation was under attack by a court opponent ruthless and determined enough to take advantage of the opportunity that Stilicho's distraction provided. It is not inconceivable that, having made arrangements for Alaric's payment, and deploying the Visigoths against Constantine III, Stilicho's regime might have recovered: it was his separation from Honorius at this crucial moment, and the opportunism of Olympius, which was fatal.

Although Stilicho's absolute dominance of Honorius' rule from 395 until 408 had extended far beyond the power and dominance of previous managers of child- or young-emperor governments, an intrinsic weakness remained. Stilicho had managed to entrench himself in Honorius' government to the exclusion of any other potential chief ministers, but he had not succeeded in making himself entirely indispensable by ensuring that regime's future. The only means by which he could do so would have been as grandfather to Honorius' heir, ultimately a role which lay beyond his grasp. An imperial child would provide a long-term future for the west which posed no threat to the current status quo, yet could offer assurance for its supporters—and for himself—that it would last. Stilicho himself clearly knew that until such a hope was fulfilled, retaining the emperor's ear through constant proximity was his best chance of keeping control, as his remaining at court in 397/8 during the crisis with Gildo had reflected. Yet at the same time, Stilicho's role as the emperor's commander-in-chief, a role upon which a great deal of the justification of his position rested—required him to take the field. Though Stilicho had left Honorius' side on campaign numerous times before, the web of alliances his patronage at court had created—the system he had built up from 395—had held firm. But in 408, as increasing military problems and hints of disaffection of Honorius towards Stilicho came to the surface, the bloody massacre at Ticinum finally tore apart the general's painstakingly constructed regime.

It is highly significant that, amidst all of the troubles besetting the west at this time, it was Stilicho, the proven military commander, who was targeted to fall and not Honorius himself. For all the ideals of a partnership of government that pervaded the regime's presentation, clearly there was no doubt where real power lay: not with the emperor himself, but with the head of the regime operating the administration. Yet at the same time, Honorius' survival testified that this presentation had done its job, too: for he remained the dynastically legitimate shield behind which the true power-broking of court politics could take place. Determined though Stilicho's efforts to embed himself in the imperial family and the ideology of divinely blessed rulership built up around it had been, ultimately Honorius was the only indispensable half of the partnership system Stilicho created. The other half could—and would—be taken on by other individuals, from Olympius onwards. Significantly, when contemporaries like Jerome criticized the government for the empire's woes after 410, he blamed them not on the emperors themselves, whom he asserts were religious men, but on Stilicho, accusing him of arming enemies of the state against them through payment.[173]

In the end, Stilicho had exercised supreme power in the west for thirteen years, and successfully maintained his hold on Honorius well into the emperor's adulthood. The direness of the crisis it took to remove him should be seen as a measure of the strength and success of the system he had built for managing the boy-emperor up until this point. But Stilicho's downfall also made apparent the need for such a manager to maintain his relationship with the emperor at all costs—preferably through blood and marriage ties, if at all possible—and suggested that the only way in which such a man might make himself truly indispensable to such an imperial partnership was through producing his heir and ensuring its future without threatening the present: a feat which one of Stilicho's successors would achieve, but which he could not.

[173] Jerome, *Ep.* 123.17.

7

The Interregnum and the Rise
of Flavius Constantius

Honorius ... became the cause of terrible disasters to the state; for
he appointed men who were able to inspire only contempt in the
enemy ... His other arrangements were of the same calibre, so there
was universal despair. The destruction of Italy seemed to stare them in
the face.[1]

INTERREGNUM

Honorius was aged 23 at the time of Stilicho's fall in August 408. His role
in that fall had been minimal, amounting simply to acquiescence with the
demands of the new man aiming to be the power behind the throne. Yet
even though he had not provided the impetus behind Stilicho's fall, Honorius
had the perfect opportunity as a result of it to personally take over 'his'
regime, and to begin to rule in his own right. He did not. It seems that his
desire to rule personally was limited indeed. The death of Stilicho saw no effort
on the part of Honorius to fill the power vacuum himself; instead, he was
content to wait for another strong man to emerge and take Stilicho's place.
Honorius' lack of leadership at this crucial moment led to the rapid rise and
fall of a succession of ambitious chief ministers whose just as rapidly changing
policies only plunged the western Roman empire into further chaos. The
military crises the government was facing had ultimately grown more dire
with the execution of Honorius' most capable manager. One infamous result

---

[1] Zosimus 5.36.3: Ἀλλ' οὔτε τὴν εἰρήνην δεξάμενος οὔτε τὴν Σάρου φιλίαν ἐπισπασάμενος οὔτε
τὸ Ῥωμαϊκὸν συναγαγὼν στρατόπεδον, τῶν δὲ Ὀλυμπίου τὰς ἐλπίδας ἀναρτήσας εὐχῶν,
τοσούτων αἴτιος ἐγένετο τῷ πολιτεύματι συμφορῶν· στρατηγούς τε γὰρ ἐπέστησε τῷ στρατεύματι
καταφρόνησιν ἐμποιῆσαι τοῖς πολεμίοις ἀρκοῦντας, Τουρπιλλίωνα μὲν τοῖς ἱππεῦσιν, Οὐαράνην δὲ
τοῖς πεζοῖς ἐπιστήσας καὶ τῇ τῶν δομεστίκων ἴλῃ Βιγελάντιον, καὶ τὰ λοιπὰ τούτοις ὁμολογοῦντα,
ὧν ἕνεκα ταῖς ἐλπίσι πάντες ἀπεγνωκότες ἐν ὀφθαλμοῖς ἔχειν ἐδόκουν τὴν τῆς Ἰταλίας ἀπώλειαν.

of the court's vacillation and refusal to honour promises made to allies and enemies alike was the sack of Rome by Alaric in 410. But another result of the inertia of Honorius following Stilicho's death was to reveal just how much of a partnership this emperor's rule really had been from 395 until 408, and how much Honorius really had depended upon (and been sheltered by) his manager, even when he reached adulthood. Such a revelation confirmed the belief of those at court that the best way for a child-emperor to be managed, even when he became a man, was through a corporate-style rule with a powerful individual alongside the young emperor as the active member of an imperial partnership. This arrangement, however, would always depend upon the willingness of the emperor himself to continue to accept it.

We know so little of Honorius' true character and abilities that it is not impossible he was in some way genuinely unable to fulfil the imperial office independently, or that the emphasis on ceremonial which had filled his early years and was inherent in dealing with the phenomenon of a child-emperor meant that he simply did not know what to do once Stilicho was gone. But there is another possibility, too. Perhaps Honorius had the sense to look at what had happened in recent Roman history to child-emperors who had attempted to make the transition from ceremonial to actual power upon reaching adulthood—and decided that he was more likely to survive if he simply did nothing and let those around him fight it out to become the head of the new regime.

Olympius and the anti-Stilichonian reaction

The evidence of the sources, particularly the surviving legislative material and its analysis by modern scholars, has made very clear that the anti-Stilichonian reaction led by Olympius following the general's death was both vicious and thorough.[2] Olympius certainly intended to expunge all traces of his predecessors' regime, and Zosimus writes that as the new *magister officiorum* he had all court offices and appointments under his control, just as Stilicho had before him.[3] Searches were made for Stilicho's supporters, with public torture used in an effort to elicit accusations of the dead general's crimes against the state, though such confessions could not be obtained even under pain of death.[4] The man responsible for Stilicho's actual execution, Heraclian, was rewarded with the coveted post of *comes Africae*, previously held by Bathanarius, the husband of Stilicho's sister, who was also executed.[5] The eunuchs responsible for

---

[2] For modern analyses: Jones (1964a), 1. 185; Matthews (1975), 284; Heather (2005), 223.
[3] Zosimus 5.36.2. Cf. Jones (1964a), 1. 175.
[4] Zosimus 5.35.1–2, 5.44.2.
[5] Ibid. 5.37.6; Cf. Matthews (1970), 83–4; Oost (1966), 236. On Bathanarius: *PLRE* 2. 221. On Heraclianus: *PLRE* 2. 539–40.

carrying out the killing of Stilicho's son Eucherius were given offices in the new government as a reward; and Honorius was rapidly induced to put aside his hapless new bride, Thermantia.[6]

The extant legislation for late 408–9 branded Stilicho a 'public brigand', whose supporters were to be proscribed and their properties added to the imperial treasury.[7] Any of the proscribed individuals who sought to enter the imperial court or the Eternal City were to be deported, thus giving them no chance of access to the emperor or to legal recourse: the laws state adamantly that they were to have no avenue open to them for the recovery of their property.[8] Olympius was plainly taking measures to ensure that Honorius was isolated from anyone who had supported Stilicho's regime, increasing the emperor's dependence upon himself and his appointees. Peaceful overtures towards the eastern government were also made—a ruling of December 408 reveals that recently under Stilicho western harbours had been fortified against incoming ships from the east (probably in relation to the Illyricum issue) but that this blockade was to be lifted.[9]

A number of these laws dealing with the fallen regime of Stilicho were addressed to men who had once been Stilicho's supporters, and had held office during the period of his dominance. The new praetorian prefect, Theodorus, was the son of the illustrious Manlius Theodorus, and nephew of that Lampadius who had denounced Stilicho at the senate meeting early in 408.[10] By November 408 a new urban prefect was also in office—none other than Nicomachus Flavianus the younger, who had held the same post under Stilicho in 399. The new *comes rei privatae*, Volusianus, was also in office by this point.[11] Although there is some confusion over the exact dating of the appointment, in January/February another member of an influential aristocratic family, Caecilianus, had succeeded Theodorus as praetorian prefect.[12] The willingness of such men to take office under the new regime was

---

[6] On the reward of Eucherius' killers: Zosimus 5.37.5–6. On Thermantia's fate: Zosimus 5.35. She was the only member of Stilicho's immediate family to escape execution, apparently dying c.415: *PLRE* 2. 1111–12.

[7] *CTh.* 9.42.20 (24 Sept. 408); 9.42.21 (25 Oct. 408); 9.40.20 (22 Nov. 408); also 7.16.1 (10 Dec. 408). For Stilicho's property: *CIL* 6. 1732–4.

[8] *CTh.* 9.40.20 (22 Nov. 408). Cf. Zosimus 5.35.4–6, 5.45.3–4. See Matthews (1975), 284–5.

[9] *CTh.* 7.16.1 (10 Dec. 408). Cf. Gillett (1993), 18, n. 84.

[10] Matthews (1975), 279–85. Theodorus was in office as praetorian prefect by 13 September 408 (*CTh.* 11.28.4).

[11] For Nicomachus Flavianus: *CJ* 2.15.1 (29 Nov. 408); cf. Chastagnol (1962), 243. For Volusianus, *CTh.* 5.16.31 (29 Nov. 408); *PLRE* 2. 1182. Cf. Matthews (1975), 285. Honoré also suggests Volusianus may have served as *quaestor* in the immediate aftermath of Salvius' death: Honoré (1999), 235–6.

[12] There is a confusing overlap between the beginning of his tenure of office and the end of that of Theodorus: the first laws addressed to Caecilianus as praetorian prefect date from 21 January 409 (e.g. *CTh.* 9.2.5, 9.2.6), but *CTh.* 3.10.1, dated to 23 Jan. 409, is still addressed to Theodorus. The appointment of Caecilianus occured in the context of senatorial negotiations with Ravenna over peace terms with Alaric. See Matthews (1975), 292, n. 1.

testament to their disaffection in recent times under Stilicho, but even more so their acceptance of the need to come to terms with the new chief minister and his new regime: presumably if such offices were offered, refusal could be unwise.[13] Like the western senators of the 380s and early 390s who had been happy to abandon Valentinian II for the camp of Theodosius I, western elites continued to take a pragmatic stance with regard to their allegiance and the access to government and privilege that it could offer. In an effort to reassure elite subjects and garner support following aristocratic resentment to some of the financial measures that Stilicho had implemented in order to sustain military activity, Honorius, under Olympius' guidance, granted major tax concessions to Italian landowners.[14]

The new regime of Olympius also aimed to take a stand on religious issues. Stilicho's regime had not been particularly remarkable for tolerance, but his fall saw a greater need to emphasize the divine blessing and authority of Honorius once more, given added impetus through Olympius' apparent Christian ardour.[15] As discussed in Chapter 5, Honorius' accession to the western throne had seen a number of laws issued confirming ecclesiastical privileges and establishing the picture of the young emperor as the traditional pious ruler. Although Honorius did thereafter legislate on religious matters, and a number of laws issued in the early 400s were aimed at dealing with Donatists in North Africa, it is not until after Stilicho's fall that the regularity of religious legislation increases.[16]

The regime-change from Stilicho to Olympius saw the new government legislating frequently on religious matters, staking the claim that despite the turmoil of the western empire (and the court) at this time, Honorius remained a divinely endorsed ruler whose piety protected his realm. Although this religious legislation will be discussed in more detail below, one well-documented incident in late 408 is particularly illuminating on the wide-ranging

---

[13] See for example, Paulinus of Pella's unhappiness at receiving office from the usurper Attalus in 414–5: *Euch.* 291–30.

[14] *CTh.* 11.28.4 (13 Sept. 408). See also Hermanowicz (2008), 170.

[15] Augustine, *Ep.* 97.2 implies the zealous Christianity of both Stilicho and Olympius (rather, in fact, than Honorius). It is possible the large number of non-orthodox Christian soldiers under Stilicho's command could have encouraged a relatively moderate stand on issues of religion under his influence, but there is little evidence to work with on this point. The pagan Zosimus carries a tale of Serena offending pagans by removing a necklace from the statue of Rhea in the temple of the Magna Mater at Rome: Zosimus 5.38.2–4; cf. Grig (2009), 283. Orosius on the other hand, also preserves a tale of Eucherius making promises of freedom of pagan worship to the senate and people of Rome in an attempt to gain their support in the desperate period after his father's death: Orosius 7.38.

[16] For the Donatist laws, see *CTh.* 16.6.4 (12 Feb. 405); See Honoré (1999), 231; also Jones (1964*a*), 1. 209–10; Frend (1985), 227 ff. And on other religious matters: e.g. *CJ* 1.4.7, to Eutychianus, 27 July 398; and 1.27.2 (408); see Harries (1999), 201–2. On the Donatist schism in North Africa and appeals to courts generally, see Humfress (2007), 264–8. See further below, p. 208.

repercussions of Stilicho's death and the public perception of Honorius' government. In June 408, riots had taken place in the North African town of Calama when the local bishop, Possidius, had attempted to disrupt and disperse a 'pagan' procession passing by his basilica, with the ultimate result that a member of his clergy was murdered, and the basilica looted and burned. Appeals to the local administration had proved futile, and the powerful bishop of the neighbouring town, Hippo, weighed in.[17] Augustine's interest in the case and the outrage over local antipathy towards punishment of the offenders and reparations happily coincided with the rise of the apparently committed Christian Olympius at the imperial court, with whom Augustine had already had contact.[18] Thus it was that, as news of Stilicho's death reached North Africa, violence increased as a result of a general belief that laws promulgated under Stilicho's rule were no longer valid, and Possidius travelled to Ravenna bearing a letter from Augustine to Olympius.[19]

Augustine took advantage surprisingly quickly of his contact Olympius' rise, but his letter to Olympius gave an even more surprisingly blunt indication of public perception (even from the distance of North Africa) of how the court of Honorius operated, and a challenge to Olympius to take a stand on religious matters. He wrote that the matter of the riots at Calama, but also religious laws relating to the Donatists, must be made a priority:

> I urge that charity of yours which you have in Christ Jesus, to press on your good work, with the most immediate attention. Thus, the enemies of the church will understand that the laws sent to Africa while Stilicho was still alive about the destruction of idols and the reform of heretics were indeed promulgated at the will of an emperor most God-fearing and faithful. Whether they deceitfully pretend or actually think so, they claim that these were passed without the knowledge and consent of the emperor, and they thereby stir up the ignorant to great violence, and make them so hostile that they are very dangerous to us.[20]

Augustine's letter reflects widespread public awareness that the chief minister— whether he was Stilicho or Olympius—was the true authority at the emperor's court. The imperial response to this religious petition will be discussed more thoroughly below (in January of 409 a law was issued, ruling that judges in

---

[17] On the course of events at Calama, see Hermanowicz (2004), 481–521; also (2008), 156; Shaw (2011), 251–9; also Harries (1999), 88–9.

[18] On Augustine's help to the clergy of Calama: Augustine, *Ep.* 91.10; on the appeal to the local court being ignored: ibid. 91.8. Cf. Harries (1999), 89–91. On the correspondence of Augustine and Olympius, see Mratschek (2001), 224–32, esp. 224, 226.

[19] Hermanowicz (2004), 502, citing Augustine, *Ep.* 105.6; also Hermanowicz (2008), 156.

[20] Augustine, *Ep.* 97.2: *Quo noverint inimici ecclesiae leges illas, quae de idolis confringendis et haereticis corrigendis vivo Stilichone in Africam missae sunt, voluntate imperatoris piissimi et fidelissimi constitutas;quo nesciente vel nolente factum sive dolose iactant sive libenter putant atque hinc animos imperitorum turbulentissimos reddunt nobisque periculose ac vehementer infestos.*

Africa had failed in their duty to uphold the law and must now bring the culprits to justice; further religious rulings were forthcoming in January and February 409).[21] In the meantime the need for Olympius to differentiate his regime from Stilicho's in the matter of Honorius' religious legislation was only one of many problems he faced.

The Visigoths and the sack of Rome

The death of Stilicho had not resolved the compounded crises facing the Roman west, and demonstrations of Honorius' religious devotion were unlikely to change that. Any new regime which sought to take over Stilicho's position still needed to deal with Alaric and the Visigoths, other barbarian invaders, and the usurper Constantine III now ensconced in Gaul. Most pressing, simply because they were within Italy itself, were the Visigoths. Despite ill-feeling relating to the death of Stilicho which had swollen Visigothic numbers with other disaffected barbarian federates, Alaric was still hoping to come to a peace agreement with the western government: for a small sum of money and a couple of noble Roman hostages, he was prepared to take his men back to Pannonia.[22] Under the influence of the anti-barbarian Olympius, this was refused outright.[23] Honorius' government was prepared neither to make peace nor to wage war against the Visigoths, and Alaric consequently turned his army to march on Rome, where his first siege of the city began in late 408.[24]

The catalogue of sieges and negotiations between Alaric and Honorius' government and the Roman senate between the death of Stilicho and the sack of Rome in August 410 reads as an exasperating and depressing example of Roman imperial ineptitude at its most dangerous. The course of the various sieges, embassies, and negotiations is well documented and has been repeatedly analysed.[25] Over two years from the death of Stilicho in August 408, Alaric repeatedly sought to exert pressure on Honorius' administration to grant a settlement, all the while scaling down his demands. From besieging and taking Rome, to forcing the Roman senate to elect its own

---

[21] See *CSirm.* 14 (15 Jan. 409); Harries feels this is almost certainly the response to Possidius' embassy, even though Calama is not mentioned by name: Harries (1999), 89–90. Also *CTh.* 9.3.7 (25 Jan. 409); 9.16.12 (1 Feb. 409).

[22] Olympiodorus, frg. 7.5.1–7; Zosimus 5.35.4–6, 5.36.1. Zosimus reports that one of the hostages requested was the young Aetius, the future *magister militum* of the west.

[23] Zosimus 5.36.2. On the rapid deterioration of Roman relations with the Visigoths, see Matthews (1975), 286; also Heather (2005), 223–4.

[24] Olympiodorus, frg. 7.5.1–7; Zosimus 5.37.2–4. See Matthews (1975), 287.

[25] e.g. Matthews (1975), 286–7; Heather (2005), 224–9; Kulikowski (2007), 170–7.

emperor—Priscus Attalus—so that he had a figurehead ruler of his own through whom to wield power, to then demoting the pretender he had created in the renewed hope of coming to terms with Ravenna—nothing Alaric tried succeeded in gaining an agreement of terms from the western government. In utter frustration, Alaric finally sacked Rome in August 410, carrying off large amounts of treasure and the emperor's sister, Galla Placidia.[26] Alaric himself died soon afterwards, and his brother-in-law Athaulf took over the leadership of the Visigoths, moving the group (and Placidia) to Gaul in 411.[27]

Meanwhile, at Ravenna itself rapid regime-change continued, and Honorius evidently made no attempt to take any active role in the political in-fighting as factions rose and fell. Olympius must have lost power in March 409—his successor in influence is recorded in office as praetorian prefect from 1 April.[28] Those associated with his short-lived regime fell also, and the new man, Jovius, naturally installed his own supporters.[29] Jovius, a former client of Alaric and supporter of Stilicho, after attempts to bring the government and Alaric to terms, in frustration defected to Alaric and his pretender Attalus.[30] Jovius' regime, like that of Olympius, had only lasted a matter of months—the last law addressed to him dates to 26 June 409, and by late July he had been replaced as praetorian prefect.[31] It is interesting that the only four surviving pieces of legislation addressed to Jovius himself between April and June 409 again all concern religious matters, although admittedly the scarcity of evidence in general makes it hard to assess how significant this truly is.[32] At Ravenna, Jovius' role as the dominant adviser was originally taken over by the chamberlain Eusebius, but according to Olympiodorus, he was soon outmanoeuvred by Allobich, the *magister militum* appointed by Jovius.[33] Yet again, it was those squabbling for power around the throne who met often brutal ends, not

---

[26] For sources on the usurpation of Priscus Attalus, see *PLRE* 2.180–1. For sources on the sack of Rome itself, see: Orosius 7.39; Olympiodorus, frg. 11.1.8–16; Sozomen 9.9. Also Jones (1964a), 2. 1408, n.1; Matthews (1975), 301; Heather (2005), 229. On the abduction of Galla Placidia: Olympiodorus, frg. 6.1–9; Prosper 1240; Hydatius 36(44); Jordanes, *Rom.* 323; *Get.* 159; Zosimus 6.12.3; Orosius 7.40. Cf. Oost (1968a), 98, 118.

[27] Jordanes, *Get.* 158; Philostorgius 12.4; Orosius 7.43.2; Heather (2005).

[28] *CTh.* 2.8.25; 16.8.19 (both issued 1 Apr. 409); On Jovius, Olympius' successor, see *PLRE* 2. 623–4. According to Zosimus, Olympius was slandered by court eunuchs and fled to Dalmatia (5.46.1–2).

[29] On the fall of Olympius' regime, see Zosimus 5.47.2. This Jovius was the same man who had been appointed praetorian prefect of Illyricum *c.*406. On the new appointments under Jovius, see Zosimus 5.48.1; cf. Matthews (1975), 293. Given how short-lived these regimes tended to be, we would not expect regime-change to be quite as thorough each time as it had been in the case of Stilicho, who had had years to build up his support-base and to institute his own men in the different offices of state.

[30] Olympiodorus, frg. 14.1–8; 10.1.25–31; 10.2.11–21; 14.8–16; cf. Sozomen 9.8; Philostorgius 12.3; Zosimus 6.8.1–2. See Matthews (1975), 297–8.

[31] The last surviving law addressed to Jovius is *CTh.* 16.5.47 (26 June 409). A month later his successor is in place as praetorian prefect: *CTh.* 8.8.8; 2.8.26 (26 July 409), is addressed to Johannes.

[32] *CTh.* 2.8.25 (1 Apr. 409); 16.8.19 (1 Apr. 409); 2.4.7 (26 June 409); 16.5.47 (26 June 409).

[33] Olympiodorus, frg. 14.8–16.

the emperor. The determination of these successive chief ministers or managers to claim Stilicho's former position is again a testament to the strength of
the system he had established for managing the regime of the child-turned-
adult-emperor.

Though the sack of Rome achieved little for Alaric and the Visigoths, it did
reveal most clearly the divisions between the interests of the Roman emperor
at Ravenna and the senators of Rome at this time. During the various sieges
the senators themselves had been forced to negotiate on the city's behalf with
Alaric, as little practical aid was forthcoming from Ravenna, and in late 408–
early 409 they had sent distinguished, and increasingly desperate, delegations
to the court in the hope of gaining imperial ratification for the treaty they had
made—ratification which never came.[34] Despite the damage the Visigothic
presence was wreaking on the Italian countryside and the lives of Honorius'
subjects, the government at Ravenna still took no decisive action.[35] In 409,
when Alaric returned to Rome, therefore, the senators had rapidly capitulated
and accepted the demand that they elect an emperor from within their
number. Attalus was a powerful and wealthy senator, and Alaric must have
hoped that this would hold a wide appeal for a Rome which had been
abandoned to its enemies by the court at Ravenna. Though it is clear Alaric
intended Attalus to be a purely ceremonial emperor (in much the same way
that Honorius himself was), it may nonetheless have been significant that the
choice of a rival emperor fell upon an adult—thus pointedly not an individual
who had inherited the throne as a young child through dynastic succession.

The continual jostling for power around Honorius following the death of
Stilicho lent no continuity or consistence of policy to the imperial administration, and the divisions between the interests of the powers behind the
throne, and the senatorial aristocracy, became all the more gaping.[36] Although
this was a problem which could arise with any emperor, with an under-age or
largely inactive emperor it became all the more acute: indeed, this was an
inevitable stumbling-block to the institutionalization of child-emperor—or
figurehead—rule: that the aims of court factions behind the throne were

---

[34] Zosimus vividly describes Alaric's siege of Rome and its effects: 5.39.1–2. Also Olympiodorus, frg. 7.5.7–15; Sozomen 9.6. Cf. Matthews (1975), 287–8. Zosimus reports that the emperor
did try to send legions from Dalmatia under the command of a general Valens to defend Rome,
but Alaric attacked and defeated them en route in January 409: 5.45.1–2. A short while later a
Roman force under the *magister officiorum* Olympius took Huns to attack the forces of Athaulf
near Pisa, but despite some minor success, returned to Ravenna when they realized the size of the
Visigothic army: Zosimus 5.45.5–6. On the embassies from Rome to Ravenna, see Zosimus
5.40.4; 5.41.4; 5.42.1–4; cf. Olympiodorus, frg. 7.5.16–18. For details of the appointments the
court at Ravenna made to the men involved in these embassies, see Matthews (1975), 288–9.
Zosimus 5.45.4–5; Cf. Olympiodorus, frg. 8.1.1–5. Also Demougeot (1954), 30–2.

[35] The damage is indicated by several surviving laws: *CTh.* 10.10.25 (10 Dec. 408), 5.7.2 (11
(3) Dec. 408) and 11.18.1 (15 Feb. 409).

[36] Matthews (1975), 302. Cf. Heather (2005), 255–6.

often not the same as those of imperial subjects—even wealthy and powerful ones—in need of protection. But Honorius' failure to take the initiative and claim power for himself when the clear opportunity to do so was at last before him, and he was old enough to take advantage of it, is striking. Striking also is the fact that, while Honorius sat back and was content to remain ceremonial and apparently passive, it was the political players vying for the power behind the throne who fell, while the emperor survived.

The view that the period 395–410 marked a critical era of separation between east and west under the sons of Theodosius I was once a popular one in late Roman scholarship. An attitude of 'hostile indifference' was ascribed to the two realms, with eastern anti-barbarian regimes under Aurelian and Anthemius at Constantinople seen as playing a pivotal role in a breakdown of relations with the west and the regime of Stilicho.[37] Yet surely too much emphasis has been placed on the 'division' of the empire in 395: in recent decades it had only rarely been united under a single emperor, and only for two and a half years under Theodosius I.[38] The attitude of Stilicho towards Arcadius and the campaigns of the late 390s against Alaric and Gildo had undeniably seen some serious cracks appear in the bonds between the two realms, but this was arguably more about the individual advisers dominating each court, rather than the emperors themselves.[39] In 409, in the midst of the factional in-fighting at Honorius' court and the continuing threat of the Visigoths, the government of the eastern boy-emperor Theodosius II sent a much-needed reinforcement of 4,000 soldiers to Ravenna.[40] Despite vicissitudes in the relationship, such an action demonstrates that there was still no decisive split between the two realms by this point.

Constantine III

Besides the chronic problem of dealing with the Visigoths in Italy, naturally the death of Stilicho had not helped the crisis facing Honorius' government in the form of Constantine III. Stilicho may have planned to deploy Alaric against Constantine III, and was assembling a Roman army at Ticinum for the same purpose, in mid-408, but his death and the rapid deterioration of relations between Honorius' court and the Visigoths put an end to such a

---

[37] Demougeot (1951), 493–562, for 'hostile indifference', see 493. On the policies of Aurelian and Anthemius, see 235–6. Followed by Oost (1968a), 180, n. 40. Also Christiansen (1970), 113–14.

[38] Jones (1964a), 1. 182.

[39] Bayless (1976b), 76.

[40] Zosimus 6.8.1–3. Also Olympiodorus, frg. 10.1.31–6; Sozomen 9.8; Cf. Matthews (1975), 286, 298–9; Matthews (1970), 91.

solution.[41] In early 409, Constantine III sent an embassy to Ravenna protesting that he had been proclaimed Augustus against his will by the soldiers, asking pardon, and requesting recognition.[42] Constantine III was in a good bargaining position, and he knew it: Honorius' government had neither the manpower nor the financial resources to launch a campaign against a well-established usurper in Gaul.[43] In early 409, Honorius dispatched imperial insignia to his rival western emperor, and agreed to some sort of honorary consulship for Constantine III for the year: he was in no position to argue.[44]

Over the course of the following year the peace treaty was renewed, but in early 410, Constantine III took the ominous step of embarking upon an expedition to Italy, ostensibly to 'aid' Honorius against the Visigoths.[45] It is not impossible that Constantine's stated intentions were genuine, especially since it must have seemed likely that any attempt to depose Honorius entirely would have resulted in a reaction from the eastern court. But Constantine himself was running into problems: his general Gerontius, who had been dispatched to Spain with the usurper's son and co-Augustus Constans, had rebelled and raised a usurper of his own, his client Maximus.[46] Constantine abandoned his Italian campaign (though he had already crossed the Cottian Alps) and turned back to Arles, at about the time of the fall from favour of Allobich at Honorius' court, suggesting a possible alliance between them.[47]

Honorius was very fortunate in Constantine III's retreat and the division of the usurper's military forces through the rebellion of Gerontius. The rapid turnover of political factions at Honorius' court was effectively paralysing any decisive action in dealing with the political crises that that government faced at this point. Not unreasonably, Honorius' primary aim must have been his own survival, and this he achieved most successfully while those vying for power behind his throne fell, often brutally. But in the long run these court intrigues and a passive, ceremonial emperor also posed serious dangers to the survival of the western empire itself, and the support of both urban and provincial senatorial classes for the throne. And the problems of both the Visigoths, and

---

[41] Zosimus 6.4.1–2. Cf. Stevens (1957), 324–5.

[42] Zosimus 5.43.1–2.

[43] According to the sources, Constantine III had already induced all the troops in Gaul and Aquitania to back him, repaired the Rhine defences, and set a garrison on the Alps between Italy and Gaul: Zosimus, 6.3.1–3; Sozomen 9.11; cf. Olympiodorus, frg. 13.2.1–11. See Drinkwater (1998), 281; Kulikowski (2004), 158.

[44] Olympiodorus, frg. 13.1.1–7; Zosimus 5.43.1–2, also 6.1.1–2. Cf. Matthews (1975), 310–11; Heather (2005), 225. Also Stevens (1957), 326–8.

[45] Zosimus 6.1.1–2; Sozomen 9.12; Olympiodorus, frg. 15.2.1–3.

[46] On Constans and Gerontius travelling to Spain: Sozomen 9.12; Olympiodorus, frg. 13; Zosimus 6.13.1–2. Cf. Jones (1964a), 1. 185 ff.; Matthews (1975), 311. On Gerontius' rebellion, see Sozomen 9.8; Olympiodorus, frg. 17.2.1 ff.; 17.1.1–5. The reasons for Gerontius' revolt remain unclear: Drinkwater (1998), 283–4; Kulikowski (2004), 363, n. 35.

[47] Olympiodorus, frg. 15.1.1–5; 15.2.5–10. Sozomen 9.12. Also Oost (1968a), 94–5; Stevens (1957), 330–1; Matthews (1975), 312.

Constantine III, still faced any new chief minister who tried to claim leadership of Honorius' government. Four years on from Stilicho's death, the military crises that had helped bring about his downfall, remained unresolved.

FLAVIUS CONSTANTIUS

Flavius Constantius and the usurpers in Gaul

Following the extension of recognition to Constantine III and the Visigothic sack of Rome, the political in-fighting and rise and fall of factions at Honorius' court had continued. The power behind the throne passed from Olympius to Jovius to Eusebius to Allobich, and then back to Olympius (who returned to Ravenna for a short while). Honorius seems to have seen the wisdom of safeguarding his own position by simply letting others fight it out, and finally, in late 410 or early 411, a new strong man emerged: Flavius Constantius.[48] Constantius was a soldier from the city of Naissus in the Balkans, who had probably travelled west in Theodosius I's army for the campaign against Eugenius in 394, and then stayed on under Stilicho's command.[49] Exact details of his rise to power at court are unknown, though he allegedly had his predecessor Olympius clubbed to death, and his apparent desire to punish the man who had engineered Stilicho's execution has seen some scholars suggesting he had been a supporter of the dead general; it is certainly possible that Constantius had served under Stilicho's command.[50] Flavius Constantius was made *magister utriusque militiae* and commander of the campaign (along with the Goth Ulfilas) to be waged against Constantine III, probably in 411.[51] The emergence of Constantius as the new commander-in-chief of Honorius' rule spelled the end of the period of cautious acceptance of Constantine III as a colleague. A successful general himself, and one who clearly held dynastic hopes for his sons, Constantine would pose a serious threat to any new manager of Honorius' government who had long-term plans himself. Over the course of 411, Flavius Constantius conducted a tremendously successful military operation in Gaul, destroying not only the regime of Constantine III

---

[48] Matthews (1975), 302. According to Orosius, Flavius Constantius was seen to be exercising power with Honorius in 410: 7.42.16. On the dating of the beginning of Constantius' ascendancy at Ravenna, see Stein (1959), 1. 262.

[49] Heather (2005), 236–7. Oost (1966), 238; (1968a), 112; Lütkenhaus (1998), 17–51.

[50] On the death of Olympius, see Olympiodorus, frg. 8.2.1–6; Zosimus 5.46.1–2. Also Heather (2005), 237. For a different view of the nature of Constantius' conflict with Olympius, see Lütkenhaus (1998), 59–65.

[51] Orosius 7.42. The first law addressed to him appears in early 412: *CTh.* 7.18.17 (29 Feb. 412). Cf. Oost (1968a), 115; Matthews (1975), 354. For Ulfilas, see *PLRE* 2. 1180.

(whom he besieged at Arles), but also the rebel general Gerontius, who had by now invaded Gaul as well and killed Constantine's son Constans shortly before the arrival of Constantius.[52]

According to Orosius: 'It was then that the state finally realized what advantages there were to having a Roman leader', as opposed to the barbarian counts who had recently dominated military leadership in the west.[53] Flavius Constantius had at last recorded a clear victory for Honorius' government, after two years of utter turmoil, although the usurpations in Gaul were not quite over yet. In late 411 yet another pretender was proclaimed, this time a Gallo-Roman noble by the name of Jovinus.[54] Jovinus had considerable barbarian backing from Alans and Burgundians.[55] But difficulties arose in the barbarian alliance when the feuding Visigoths Athaulf and Sarus both came to join the usurpation, and when Jovinus elevated his brother Sebastianus as co-ruler without consultation.[56] Athaulf turned to Ravenna, offering to bring down the usurpers, and then besieging them at Valence, forcing their surrender.[57] Jovinus and Sebastianus were executed at Narbonne by the praetorian prefect for Gaul, Cl. Postumus Dardanus.[58]

The great significance of this postscript of a rebellion by Jovinus, which was on a much smaller scale than that of Constantine III, lies in its insight into the attitudes of Gallo-Roman aristocrats in the early 410s.[59] Nobles like Decimius Rusticus and Apollinaris, the grandfather of Sidonius, had served in the regime of Constantine III.[60] According to the sources, when Jovinus fell, not only Rusticus but also one Agroecius and 'many nobles' besides were executed along with him.[61] And as scholars have observed, the usurpation of Jovinus itself, despite the resounding defeat of Constantine III, suggests Gallo-Romans

---

[52] On the downfall of Constantine III, see Sozomen 9.15; Orosius 7.42; Olympiodorus, frg. 17.1.5–17, 17.2.32 ff.). Cf. Matthews (1975), 313; Stevens (1957), 345–6. Constantine III had himself ordained a presbyter in a bid to save his own life. He and his younger son Julian were executed en route to Ravenna. On Constantius' dealings with Gerontius (his puppet-emperor Maximus escaped), see Olympiodorus, frg. 17.1.17 ff.; Sozomen 9.13. See further Jones (1964a), 1.175, 185 ff.; Matthews (1975), 312–13; Stevens (1957), 344–5. On the campaign of Gerontius and Maximus in Gaul see Drinkwater (1998), 283–5; also Kulikowski (2004), 158–61. On the death of Constans and the sources, see Matthews (1975), 312.

[53] Orosius 7.42.1–3: *Constantio comiti huius belli summa commissa est. sensit tunc demum respublica et quam utilitatem in Romano tandem duce receperit et quam eatenus perniciem per longa tempora barbaris comitibus subiecta tolerarit.*

[54] Drinkwater provides a thorough account of the usurpation: (1998), 269–98.

[55] Olympiodorus, frg. 18.1–13. Cf. Heather (2005), 237–8; Matthews (1975), 314.

[56] On these developments, see Drinkwater (1998), 289–90; Heather (1991), 220.

[57] Drinkwater (1998), 288.

[58] On their deaths: Orosius 7.42; Philostorgius 12.6; Theophanes, AM 5904; Olympiodorus, frg. 20.1–12. Cf. Matthews (1975), 315.

[59] Drinkwater (1998), 287.

[60] Apollinaris: *PLRE* 2. 113; see esp. Zosimus 6.4.2. Decimius Rusticus: *PLRE* 2. 965. See generally Matthews (1975), 310, n. 1; Harries (1994a), 27–8.

[61] Greg.Tur. 2.9.

were by no means well disposed towards to the idea of the reimposition of authority from distant Ravenna (although there is a question, I think, of how possible it might be to refuse positions in the government of a usurper in your own territory without incurring some personal danger).[62] Though Honorius had survived the political turmoil at the imperial court since the death of Stilicho, factional in-fighting had only further damaged Gallo-Roman relations and Gallic loyalties to the central, but increasingly remote, government.

Flavius Constantius' Gallic successes gave him a far more secure standing at Ravenna than any of the prospective imperial managers before him—and it is significant that it took a military man, and military victories, to build such security. Of other chief advisers in the years since Stilicho's death, the evidence suggests that only Olympius had attempted to lead a military campaign—and that unsuccessfully, against Athaulf.[63] While Honorius was content to remain passive, his military function—even if it were delegated—still needed to be exercised, and the man who did so successfully had the greatest chance of securing the power behind the throne. The regime was still functioning—when it did so effectively—on the partnership model that Stilicho had established.

In the course of 413 one further rebellion had to be dealt with—surprisingly, that of the western consul for the year, Heraclian. Appointed *comes Africae* as a reward for carrying out the execution of Stilicho, Heraclian held Africa for Ravenna during the usurpation of Alaric and Attalus at Rome, and his withholding of the grain supply had played a significant role in Alaric's decision to depose Attalus. The consulship of 413 was presumably a reward for this loyalty, but in April of the same year, when grain shipments to Rome usually commenced, Heraclian chose to withhold them once again.[64] Soon afterwards he himself set sail for Italy, apparently with a large fleet, landed, and began to march on Ravenna.[65] He was swiftly intercepted and defeated by imperial forces, and upon his flight back to Carthage was put to death, but his rebellion remains puzzling.[66] It is possible Heraclian acted out of fear of the growing influence of Flavius Constantius, particularly if the latter really were intent on pursuing those who had brought down Stilicho.[67] And essentially, the structure of Honorius' court in these years, the constant rise and fall of

---

[62] Drinkwater (1998), 288. Cf. Wightman (1985), 301. Although admittedly Paulinus of Pella does not say he was forced into office under the usurper Attalus, his report that the office of Count of the Private Largesses was conferred upon him in his absence does not suggest he served altogether willingly: Paul.Pella, *Euch.* 291–301. See also above, p. 190, n. 13.

[63] Zosimus 5.45.6.

[64] *CLRE* 360–1. For Heraclian's consulship of 413 as a reward, see Orosius 7.42. On Heraclian's withholding of the grain fleet, see Oost (1966), 240.

[65] Orosius 7.42; Philostorgius 12.6.

[66] Orosius 7.42. Cf. Heather (2005), 256–7; Oost (1966), 240; Shaw (2011), 50–1.

[67] Oost (1966), 239. Cf. Heather (2005), 237. O'Flynn (1983), 70. Although if Heraclian and Constantius really were enemies at this point then his appointment as consul suggests Constantius was not yet all-powerful at Honorius' court.

different chief ministers, must have turned all of those serious power-players into paranoid Ravenna-watchers: whether or not Heraclian genuinely needed to fear any personal grudge on the part of Constantius, the new *magister militum*'s steady rise was ominous to any others who might have sought such a position themselves. According to Olympiodorus, Constantius was granted Heraclian's estates following the rebel's death, again hinting at the possibility of personal animosity.[68] Even from the distance of North Africa, the temptation to secure the position as the dominant power behind Honorius' throne beckoned, and the authority wielded by the individual who did so, was clear.

Flavius Constantius and the Visigoths

Though the usurpers in Gaul had been decisively dealt with, the problem posed by the Visigoths remained. Athaulf's efforts to bring down Jovinus and Sebastianus had reopened negotiations between his people and Ravenna, but the imperial court could not meet the ransom of grain the Visigoths demanded in return for the emperor's sister, due to the shortages of corn resulting from Heraclian's revolt.[69] In late 413, Athaulf established his followers at Narbonne, and then in January 414 took a daring and radical step: he married Galla Placidia.[70] The descriptions of the wedding have often been noted for the evidence they provide of the Gallo-Roman aristocracy's willingness to fall in with Visigothic demands: the celebrations took place at the house of a leading citizen, wedding songs were provided by none other than the deposed puppet-emperor Priscus Attalus, and significantly, Athaulf was dressed in the cloak of a Roman general.[71] Orosius' report of the occasion preserves Athaulf's famous alleged declaration that he sought for himself the glory of increasing the Roman name by the forces of the Goths, and to be himself the restorer of Rome.[72]

The readiness of Gallo-Roman nobles to accommodate and work with the Visigoths—and indeed with other sources of more accessible authority like Constantine III—has rightly been recognized as one of the most important developments of early fifth-century politics in Gaul.[73] It plainly signifies the

---

[68] Olympiodorus, frg. 23.1–9; cf. Oost (1966), 239; Matthews (1975), 354.

[69] Olympiodorus, frg. 22.1, 22.2. That the problem was caused by Heraclius' revolt, see Orosius 7.42.10 f. Cf. Jones (1964a), 1. 188; Heather (1991), 219; Matthews (1975), 315–16.

[70] Olympiodorus, frg. 24.1–6. Cf. Philostorgius 12.4; Orosius 7.43; Hydatius 49 (57); Prosper 1259. Cf. Matthews (1975), 316. The wedding and its objectives have been a popular topic for discussion among modern historians: see Sivan (2011), ch. 1; Cesa (1992–3), 23–53; Harlow (2004), 140–3.

[71] Olympiodorus, frg. 24.1–6. Several more Roman nobles are also mentioned in connection with the wedding: Candidianus, Phoebadius. and Rusticius (Olympiodorus, frg. 24.1–14).

[72] Orosius 7.43. See further Wallace-Hadrill (1961), 213–37.

[73] Matthews (1975), 320.

local aristocracy's sense of general abandonment by the central government at Ravenna and recognition of the need to come to terms with new powers closer to home if they were to have any hope of maintaining their wealth—most of which was landed—and positions.[74] The question of how periods of prolonged minority governments and closely guarded child-emperors stationed in Italy might have impacted on such developments is one which has thus far been left out of discussions on the so-called 'provincialization' of the aristocracy. It is beyond the scope of this book to deal with the possibilities of such a discourse here. It is nevertheless worth bearing in mind that while the role and function of the Gallic aristocracy was changing in the early fifth century, so too was the role of the late Roman emperor.

Athaulf had overreached himself in marrying the emperor's sister, and in early 414, Constantius set out to deal with him. The stringent naval blockade which he established at Narbonne forced the Visigoths to retreat to Barcelona (after defiantly raising Priscus Attalus as Augustus once more), and it was here that the infant son of Athaulf and Galla Placidia was buried not long after his birth—he had been pointedly named Theodosius.[75] A continued blockade by Constantius placed increasing pressure on Athaulf and his relations with his own followers, however, and *c*.415 he was mortally wounded in a coup.[76] Athaulf's eventual successor, Wallia, decided to try again for terms with the Romans.[77] In 416 a peace agreement was finally settled: Galla Placidia was returned, while the Goths received 60,000 *modii* of wheat and promised to conduct the war against the Vandals and Alans in Spain on the Romans' behalf.[78] Constantius had achieved yet another significant victory, and secured his position as the power behind Honorius' throne still further.

The regime of Flavius Constantius

The achievement of Constantius in dealing with first usurpers and then barbarians as he took over the position of 'active' imperial partner was truly remarkable. His success becomes all the more extraordinary when examined against the evidence available for the seriously depleted resources with which he was working. The *Notitia dignitatum* provides a picture of the western

---

[74] Ibid. 322–4, 328. Also Wallace-Hadrill (1961), 222.

[75] Orosius 7.43.1; Olympiodorus, frg. 26.1.1–6. Also Matthews (1975), 317–18; Heather (1991), 219–20; (2005), 240. At this point, as Honorius' only western male heir the infant Theodosius may not have been as impossible a chance to succeed his uncle as we might assume.

[76] For the blockade, see Orosius 7.43. Cf. Jones (1964*a*), 1. 188; Thompson (1956), 67. For Athaulf's death, Olympiodorus, frg. 26.1.6–12, 26.2.1–7; Philostorgius 12.4; Orosius 7.43.

[77] Orosius 7.43; Olympiodorus, frg. 26.1.13–23. Cf. Matthews (1975), 318–19.

[78] Orosius 7.43; Olympiodorus, frg. 30.1–5. Cf. on the agreement: Heather (1991), 218; Wolfram (1988), 170–1; Burns (1992), 54–6.

military establishment *c.*420, and much-amended and incomplete though it may be, it gives a sobering indication of the limited troops at Constantius' disposal.[79] One major study has pointed out the grave losses that the *Notitia* reveals over the course of Honorius' reign: that by 420 the western field army had been reduced to a staggering one-third of its size prior to 395.[80] Furthermore, the creation of ninety-seven 'new' units to refill the ranks of the *comitatenses* since 395 was merely superficial, for a large number (suggested by one scholar to be ninety-two) of the supposedly new regiments were in fact old frontier units which were recalled and reclassified to become part of the mobile army, with no indication that such garrison troops were themselves replaced. And it was not only depleted military numbers with which Constantius had to deal, but massively reduced financial resources also. Surviving legislation for the period reflects just how dire the damage caused by years of an enemy army's presence in Italy alone had been: in 413 major tax concessions reduced the liability of a large number of areas to a mere one-fifth of their former assessment, and in 418 a further massive concession reduced the liability of Campania to one-ninth and that of Picenum and Tuscany to one-seventh of their previous levels.[81] Years after the conflict had passed, these regions were still struggling to recover from the damage they had sustained—and to provide the government with revenues to fund Constantius' campaigns. In addition, some regions, such as Gaul and Spain, had been beyond imperial control for years as a result of these usurpations, and thus failing to bring in any revenue at all for Ravenna.[82]

Constantius' reconstruction efforts would go far in addressing these territorial losses, but from this time on some regions would be lost forever to the western empire, such as Britain and Armorica.[83] And as part of the business of consolidation of Constantius' achievements, concessions had to be made. In 418 the Visigoths, who for two years had been fighting Vandals and Alans in Spain on Rome's behalf, were recalled and settled in southern Gaul.[84] The

---

[79] On the incomplete picture the *Notitia* provides, see Kulikowski (2000*a*), 360, 375–6.

[80] *Not.Dig.Occ.* 5, 6, 7. Assuming that the size of the eastern field army *c.*395 equalled that of the western: Jones (1964*a*), 2. 1425, also 1. 197 ff. Heather estimates the numbers to be a loss of 47.5% over the 25 years, amounting to *c.*30,000 lives lost: (2005), 247.

[81] *CTh.* 11.28.7 (8 May 413); 11.28.12 (15 Nov. 418). Also 15.14.14 (1 Mar. 416); on abandoned landholdings, e.g: 11.1.31 (31 Jan. 412). On areas unable to meet their tax demands: 13.11.13 (6 June 412).

[82] Jones (1964*a*), 2. 1425; also Heather (2005), 247–8.

[83] Britain entirely fell outside of the Roman system during the 410s, after providing Constantine III with his power-base—he presumably took the bulk of the remaining Roman military there with him when he crossed to Bononia. For details and sources, see: Heather (2005), 244; also Jones (1964*a*), 1. 204; Matthews (1975), 320; Thompson (1982*b*), 461; Esmonde Cleary (1989), 138. On Armorica: Matthews (1975), 320.

[84] Debate continues on the terms of the settlement, whether it involved the grant of land or of tax revenues: for some of the alternative arguments and details on the source material, see: Goffart (1980); Heather (1991), 221–3; Jones (1964*a*), 1.188; Southern and Dixon (1996), 49.

circumstances of the settlement have been the subject of much scholarly debate: the most likely explanation for the move is that Constantius placed them in Aquitaine with the aim of being able to use them in the future against various troublesome groups if needed—whether they be Bacaudae or rebellious Gallo-Romans.[85] This settlement itself reflected the position of strength from which the regime of Constantius now operated: it was not imposed upon the Romans, but designed by them.[86] Nevertheless, it represented another area too which would from now on be lost to the government's revenue base.[87]

Constantius' successes over the course of the 410s demonstrated what an able and dynamic military leader could still achieve, despite the many crises facing Honorius' government at this time. The new active member of the imperial partnership also understood clearly the value of building bridges with the aristocracy in the wake of the cracks in the relationship between court and the senatorial elite which had been exposed particularly by the activity of Alaric in Italy and of Constantine III in Gaul. In some of the appointments of the later 410s a consciousness of the need for overtures towards such groups comes through—such as that of 19-year-old Petronius Maximus, member of a distinguished Roman senatorial family, as *comes sacrarum largitionum* from 415 to 418, and as prefect of Rome in 420.[88] The appointment of the Italian aristocrat Fl. Iunius Quartus Palladius, western consul in 416 and prefect of Italy from 416 to 421, represents a similar case.[89] The appointment of Rutilius Namatianus as *magister officiorum* in 412, and later as urban prefect of Rome in 415, may represent the inclusion of Gallic aristocrats in this rebuilding of ties between court and the senatorial elite.[90] And after the revolt of Heraclian, the younger Nicomachus Flavianus and his fellow-senator Caecilianus were sent to North Africa to investigate complaints of unhappy provincials there.[91]

In Gaul, arguably the most famous of Constantius' efforts at refocusing Gallic loyalties on the central government at Ravenna was the founding—or as it was presented, re-founding—of an annual *concilium* in 418.[92] It was ruled that the provinces and individual cities of southern Gaul were to send delegates for an annual meeting at Arles, held under the auspices of the Gallic praetorian prefect, whereby the landowning classes of the province would have

[85] Thompson (1956), 65–70; Bachrach (1969), 354; Matthews (1975), 329; Kulikowski (2001), 32, (2004), 170.

[86] Thompson (1956), 66; Heather (1991), 222–3.

[87] Matthews (1975), 320–1.

[88] For his career, see Matthews (1975), 359; *PLRE* 2. 749–51.

[89] See also on Palladius: Matthews (1975), 263; *PLRE* 2. 822–4.

[90] On Namatianus, see *PLRE* 2. 770–1.

[91] *CTh.* 7.4.33 (3 Mar. 414); see further Hedrick (2000), 31–2.

[92] For the details, see Matthews (1975), 334; Mathisen (1989), 41–3; Honoré (1999), 242; Van Dam (2007), 66–8.

a forum within which to voice their concerns.[93] Undoubtedly linked to the settlement of the Visigoths in Aquitaine in 418, the council was aimed both at reassuring Gallic elites that they had a political voice, and at tying their loyalties back to Ravenna after their willingness to support rebel, and even barbarian, causes in recent years.[94] It is noticeable too that from this time on it was members of the Gallic aristocracy who were more frequently found filling the office of praetorian prefect of their province, rather than Italian officials being sent out to take up the post.[95] And indeed, the lack of further rebellions or usurpations in Gaul following the downfall of Jovinus attests to Constantius' success in reforging these ties with the Gallic aristocracy.

Honorius: religious and ceremonial presentation

Alongside the political events of Honorius' reign, and the long-term regimes of Stilicho and Flavius Constantius, the religious and ceremonial function of the (by now adult) emperor can be considered. As his lavish descriptions of Honorius' return to Constantinople following his accession at the Hebdomon in 393, the boy's visit to Rome with his father in 389, and his visit of 404 for his consular celebrations make clear, Claudian's presentation of the young emperor laid a heavy emphasis on Honorius' ceremonial role. And as in the case of Valentinian II and the conflict over the basilicas in 385/6, it was essential that this role, at least, remained the province of the boy-emperor if his rule were to remain plausible. A further description by Claudian of another ceremonial occasion also highlights the sacred aura with which the child-emperor was coming to be imbued: at the time of an earlier ceremonial *adventus* of the young Honorius—this time to the city of Milan in 398—the boy-emperor was compared to the infant sun-god of Memphis, clad in triumphal white, and carried aloft by proud warriors, bearing a 'godlike burden'.[96] The significant difference between the 'godlike' image described here and the citizen-prince image of Honorius at Rome in 404 has been highlighted rightly as indicative of the importance of adjusting the emperor's presentation and behaviour according to his context.[97] But the specifically sacred aura attached to the boy-emperor in the 398 description is a striking

---

[93] The date of the transfer of the Gallic prefecture to Arles from Trier has been much debated: see e.g. Palanque (1934), 359 ff.; Chastagnol (1973), 23–40; and more recently: Drinkwater (1998), 274–5; Matthews (1975), 333; Heather (2005), 250.

[94] Matthews (1975), 335–6.

[95] Ibid. 333; Wightman (1985), 302. On the limited opportunities for Gallic aristocrats to hold office in the central government by this point, see Drinkwater (1998), 274. Also Mathisen (1992), 228–32, (1984), 159.

[96] Claudian, *IV Cons.* 565–76. McCormick dates this *adventus* to 398: (1986), 51.

[97] Cameron (1970), 382. As also discussed above in Ch. 1, pp. 44–5.

reminder of how much the regime depended upon the concept of the child's divine blessing as a legitimation of his position—and Stilicho's.

As Honorius grew to adulthood and remained a passive figure, his religious and ceremonial function continued to be just as important in justifying his own position, and that of his manager, whoever that might be. Right from the start of his reign, Ambrose had laboured the point of Honorius' piety bringing divine blessing upon his rule, and this was taken up by other ecclesiastical writers of the period, writing both before and after Honorius' death.[98] Orosius' vision of the reason for the triumph of Honorius' forces against Gildo has been noted above; and according to Sozomen, although many tyrants arose during Honorius' reign: 'Some fell upon one another, while others were apprehended in a marvellous way, and so evidenced that the divine love towards Honorius was not common.'[99] Even for commentators writing far from the western imperial court, the presentation of the emperor's Christian piety as the key to the well-being of his realm was known—perhaps not least because the eastern imperial court of Arcadius and Theodosius II projected similar messages of their own divinely blessed rule.

The enduring importance of the presentation of Honorius' divine blessing throughout adulthood as well as childhood is given a wonderful visual depiction in the diptych of Anicius Petronius Probus, dating to 406. Honorius is displayed in military attire (although at the age of 21 he still had never been near a battlefield), and beside him a banner topped with a *Chi-Rho* declares IN NOMINE *XPI* VINCAS SEMPER—'may you always conquer in the name of Christ'.[100] The Christian victory imagery of this diptych is utterly unique for its time, in an era when iconography of consular diptychs remained solidly secular, as one scholar has recently observed.[101] The significant difference between the religious imagery of this diptych and the surviving Monza diptych portraying Stilicho (probably dating to the late 390s) is also important to note: while Stilicho's image shows him in military dress and with his family alongside him, nothing of a religious nature—no mottoes or symbols—accompany the image. It is unlikely the role of the manager could ever be truly devoid of ceremonial, but it was Honorius whose piety was credited with his armies' successes, even without his presence on the battlefield, and even when he was old enough to take up such a role. The Probus diptych is unique also for its double representation of Honorius as soldier-emperor, rather than the conventional image of the consul himself (Probus, who is named but not portrayed) presiding over games; it has been suggested that this diptych was a

---

[98] See e.g. Ambrose, *De ob. Theod.* 2, 6, 8.

[99] Sozomen 9.11.1: Ὑπὸ δὲ τοῦτον τὸν χρόνον πολλῶν ἐπανισταμένων τυράννων ἐν τῇ πρὸς δύσιν ἀρχῇ, οἱ μὲν πρὸς ἀλλήλων πίπτοντες, οἱ δὲ παραδόξως συλλαμβανόμενοι οὐ τὴν τυχοῦσαν ἐπεμαρτύρουν Ὀνωρίῳ θεοφίλειαν. Cf. Orosius 7.35, 42; Theodoret 5.26.

[100] MacCormack (1981), 221.

[101] Cameron (2007a), 193.

special issue to commemorate a specific victory—that over Radagaisus in the late summer of 406—Stilicho's victory, but in Honorius' name.[102]

On coinage too, similar images appeared: even as a little boy, the emperor had been depicted dressed in military costume, with a cuirass and chlamys, and for his *tricennalia* in 422 he wears a helmet and carries a spear and a small shield emblazoned with a *Chi-Rho*.[103] It is interesting that in 408, probably following the death of Arcadius, a special solidus was issued depicting Honorius in overtly military guise, with a sword and wielding a long staff bearing a Christogram, and trampling a lion with a serpent-tail, while the emperor is crowned by the hand of God.[104] It is not known whether such coins were produced before or after the death of Stilicho, but in either case they were probably aimed at the assertion of Honorius' position as the senior Augustus following his brother's death, and perhaps also a response to the current military crises in the west.

Surviving accounts of great ceremonial occasions of the later years of Honorius' reign are unfortunately rare, though there are still some indications of imperial victory celebrations during the 410s, such as the ceremonial mutilation of Priscus Attalus in 415, for which Honorius apparently journeyed to Rome and signalled his approval of the revival of the city.[105] The traditional portrayal of the emperor as the bringer of victory was maintained, despite Honorius' absence from military campaigns, and perhaps with Honorius stationed for the most part at Ravenna there was little else which could be communicated about him beyond the traditional images.[106] But these portrayals, too, were part of the presentation of the rule of Honorius as a partnership: others might lead the armies in Honorius' name, but he was still emperor, the legitimate figurehead of the regime, whoever else might hold the reins of government alongside him, and his religious function—closely linked with victory in contemporary depictions—was being conscientiously fulfilled, thus bringing God's blessings on his generals and armies. Their victories thus reinforced his divine sanction. If Stilicho—or in turn, Constantius—was the active member of the partnership, then Honorius could not take on that role also, otherwise the guardian/manager no longer had a function. Honorius' continued passivity throughout his reign suggests that both he and his more successful 'managers' understood very well how this system worked.

---

[102] Cameron (2007*a*), 191–202.

[103] For military depictions of the child Honorius on coinage, see *RIC* 10. 46–7. For the *tricennalia*, see *RIC* 10. 48, 133. See similarly the Ravenna solidi of 408: *RIC* 10. 48.

[104] *RIC* 10. 131–2.

[105] Olympiodorus, frg. 26.2, in Blockley, p. 191. For further details and sources, see McCormick (1986), 56–7, who claims there are indications of six such celebrations between 411 and 422, but the evidence is sketchy. On the humiliation of Attalus in particular, see Matthews (1975), 354; also Lejdegård (2002), 137–58.

[106] MacCormack (1981), 221.

Honorius' religious legislation has already been mentioned, but needs further consideration. It has been persuasively argued that an increase can be perceived in religious legislation under Honorius from 407 onwards, as the military situation became increasingly grave, and as scholars have observed it is tempting to see in these laws a reaction against the crises—a determination to assert, nevertheless, that Honorius remained God's chosen ruler and was fulfilling his role as emperor through his religious efforts.[107] Thus, while in 397 Honorius had issued a law which merely confirmed existing privileges of the church, from 408 onwards he legislated increasingly on all sorts of religious matters, such as church discipline and doctrine, as well as property and power.[108] Similarly, in 407 a law of Honorius insisted that strong measures be taken against pagan temples in Africa, and in 415 this decree was extended to the whole of the west, though earlier legislation had been mild.[109] And although Honorius had ruled on ecclesiastical jurisdiction in 398, it was again addressed in 408.[110]

The regime of Olympius, in the immediate aftermath of Stilicho's fall, has been viewed by some scholars as one whereby a whole 'programme for ecclesiastical politics' was realized through the legislation issued at this time.[111] Although the number of religious-oriented laws which survive from Olympius' brief period of dominance is worth noting, religious legislation does seem to have emanated fairly regularly from Honorius' court, particularly from 402 and the move to Ravenna onwards.[112] Amidst the more hard-line policy on religious orthodoxy which emerges around this time, an unexpected edict of 410 allowing freedom of worship to all Christians, though quickly rescinded, is a reminder that, while the desire to present the emperor as ensuring security for the state through guarding the 'true' faith was very much present, the turmoil of events could not but cause confusion.[113] It is also tempting to think that this upsurge in religious laws might have been one means of coping with

---

[107] Honoré (1999), 228.

[108] Ibid.; also Harries (1999), 87. See e.g. *CTh*. 16.2.30 (31 Jan. 397); 14.15.5 (7 Apr. 407); 16.8.20 (26 July 412).

[109] Law of 408: *CSirm*. 12 (5 June); of 415, *CTh*. 16.10.20 (3 Aug.); see Jones (1964a), 1. 208–9. For earlier legislation, see *CTh*. 16.10.15 (29 Jan. 399), 16.10.17–18 (both issued 20 Aug. 399); see Jones (1964a), 1. 208–9. See also the barring of all pagans from imperial service in early 408—withdrawn within the year: *CTh*. 16.5.42 (14 Nov. 408); also Zosimus 5.46. See Jones (1964a), 2. 1110.

[110] *CJ* 1.4.7 (27 July 398); *CTh*. 1.27.2 (13 Dec. 408); see Harries (1999), 201–2.

[111] Mratschek (2001), 231.

[112] Honoré (1999), 228. Ten religious-oriented laws survive from September 408 until March 409, the period of Olympius' domination of the court: *CTh*. 16.5.42 (14 Nov. 408); 16.5.43 (15 Nov. 408); 16.10.19 (15 Nov. 408); 16.5.44 (24 Nov. 408); 16.2.39 (= *CSirm*. 9) (27 Nov. 408); 16.5.45 (27 Nov. 408); 16.5.46 (= *CSirm*. 14) (27 Nov. 408); 9.3.7 (= *CJ* 1.4.9) (25 Jan. 409); 9.16.12 (= *CJ* 9.18.3) (1 Feb. 409).

[113] The edict itself does not survive, but is rescinded by *CTh*. 16.5.51 (25 Aug. 410); see also Shaw (2011), 552–3. Gratian of course issued a similar edict of toleration following the battle of Adrianople: see above, pp. 118–19.

the fact that Honorius continued to be a civilian emperor—despite the troubles besetting his realm, and despite his no longer having the excuse of childhood— and that this was one tangible way of asserting that he still had a function beyond youthful promise. Perhaps this was all the more important with the rise of a long-term military manager again in Flavius Constantius, who was conspicuously taking on the more active elements of the imperial office.[114] Even before imperial Christianity, the ideology of imperial victory promoted the idea that an emperor's victories fundamentally came from God. Through his attention to Christianity—and, as we shall see in his rulings on Donatism and Pelagianism, his insistence on orthodoxy—Honorius could be seen to be ensuring divine support, and hence military success: a crucial point to be able to make when the emperor himself was not appearing on the battlefield.

Yet as the letter of Augustine to Olympius quoted earlier in the chapter illustrates, Honorius' laws on religious matters (as on other matters) might frequently be responses to petitions rather than spontaneous imperial initiatives.[115] Two recent and detailed studies on the religious affairs of Roman North Africa through this period reveal that both Catholics and Donatists were regularly sending embassies to the imperial court seeking rulings or restatements of previous laws.[116] In fact such expeditions had become so regular that it was probably in response to their constant embassies that Pope Innocent ruled to try to limit the traffic by insisting that such delegations must travel to him at Rome for their case to be heard there, before they might be permitted to go on to the imperial court.[117] Such a ruling suggests cooperation between the interests of both the imperial court and the bishop of Rome: Honorius' court would be spared being presented with some, at least, of the religious disputes arising thereafter, while the influence of Innocent over other churches in the region was enhanced by his taking on such power over ecclesiastical access to the emperor.[118] Although North Africa's Catholic–Donatist disputes may have raised greater numbers of cases than was usual in a region, doubtless representatives of other churches also sent embassies to Honorius' court seeking rulings.

---

[114] Hardly any other generals are mentioned in the surviving source material for the 410s at all—other than Ulfilas, who shared with Constantius the command of the campaign against Constantine III in 411, but disappears after this point. See O'Flynn (1983), 64, 70.

[115] Such as e.g. *CTh.* 16.5.42 (14 Nov. 408).

[116] See generally, Merdinger (1999), 88–110; Hermanowicz (2004), 481–521, esp. 283–95, and (2008), 85–6, 149. For the suggestion that the timing of these appeals and related religious legislation may not always reveal such laws as the direct response to these petitions, see, however, McLynn (2009).

[117] *Concilia Africae* 94; see Hermanowicz (2008), 149, n. 47.

[118] Merdinger (1999), 100.

Even if many of Honorius' religious laws had been solicited by different lobbyists, however, it is worth remembering that responding to—indeed, giving priority to—such cases requiring action through religious legislation may well have suited the court just as much as the lobbyists; and it may even have been widely known that the emperor or his administration was particularly interested in hearing such cases. Thus the Calama incident, the attempt to resolve the Donatist dispute, and the disputed papal election following the death of Pope Zosimus in 418 all gave Honorius opportunities to be seen embracing his religious function.[119] In February 405, Honorius' government issued the 'Edict of Unity', the first law to classify Donatists as heretics, and finally the emperor instructed that a council of all Catholic and Donatist bishops be summoned to Carthage in 411 to debate the issues.[120] Unsurprisingly, the council ruled against the Donatists, reclassified them as Catholics, and followed up the ruling with a number of penal laws against those who continued to practice the Donatist faith.[121] Similarly, Honorius ruled against the teachings of Pelagius and his supporters in 418, after some conflicting judgements from bishops of the African church and successive popes.[122]

In Honorius' surviving letter of 404 detailing various grievances against his brother Arcadius, prominent among his list of complaints was criticism of the treatment of the exiled bishop of Constantinople, John Chrysostom.[123] Again, this letter must have been the result of petitioning on Chrysostom's behalf, probably by Innocentius, the bishop of Rome at the time. Honorius' protests that he must faithfully admonish his brother for this and other misdeeds did little to aid Chrysostom, and formed part of a downturn in relations between the two imperial courts once more after this point.[124] Nevertheless, it gave the

---

[119] On Calama, see Hermanowicz (2008), 157–79. On the attempt to resolve the Donatist dispute, see Honoré (1999), 231; also Jones (1964a), 1. 209–10; Frend (1985), 227 ff.; Bonner (1963), 266–7. On the disputed papal election, see *Lib.Pont.* 44, c. 60, I.227; Jones (1964a), 1. 210–11. For details of Honorius' rulings on the matters, see Honoré (1999), 245. Also Chastagnol (1960), 172–7 and Mathisen (1989), 60–1. Honorius' sister Galla Placidia and her husband Constantius also became involved in the disputed papal election, though their actions essentially amounted to voicing support for Honorius' decisions: Consolino (1995b), 479; Cristo (1977), 165–6.

[120] *CTh.* 16.6.4 (12 Feb. 405); also 16.5.38 (12 Feb. 405) and 16.11.2 (5 Mar. 405). On the council specifically, which was clearly only ever expected to rule against the Donatists, see Brown (2000), 330–9, and most recently Shaw (2011), 544–86. A collection of letters between African bishops, Marcellinus (who convened the council), the emperor Honorius, and Pope Innocent survive in the correspondence of St Augustine concerning these rulings: see *Epp.* 128, 129, 133, 175, 176, 177, 181, 182, 183, 201 with dates ranging from 411 to 419. Cf. Jones (1964a), 1. 209–10; Frend (1985), 269–74.

[121] e.g. *CTh.* 16.5.52 (30 Jan. 412); 16.5.54 (17 June 414); 16.5.55 (30 Aug. 414). Honorius also ruled in 412 that priests could only be accused before bishops: *CTh.* 16.2.41 (11 Dec. 412). See Humfress (2007), 267.

[122] See Brown (2000), 340–66, and esp. 362–3; Honoré (1999), 242; also Jones (1964a), 1. 209; Mathisen (1989), 37–41.

[123] *Coll.Avell. Ep.* 38.

[124] Cameron and Long (1993), 249–50.

western emperor the chance to pontificate to his elder brother on correct imperial treatment of churchmen, an opportunity which the tone of Honorius' letter suggests he rather relished. According to Honorius, Arcadius should remember that the interpretation of divine matters ought to be left to the bishops, while the emperor's concern was compliance with religion.[125]

One further area to consider as part of Honorius' religious and ceremonial function is that of ecclesiastical building and benefaction. It is likely that a considerable amount of building of government and administrative offices took place at Ravenna when the court moved there in 402, along with palace building, even though our sources generally attribute this to the reign of Valentinian III.[126] It is difficult to trace with certainty secular building at Rome during Honorius' reign, although the city walls were repaired in the first years of the fifth century, some restoration work on the Colosseum and Forum Romanum apparently took place after 410, and recent excavations have uncovered what may have been a new imperial palace built on the Pincian hill in the 410s.[127] No church-building is recorded at Ravenna under Honorius' rule.[128] Yet there was one major Christian foundation under Honorius which deserves more attention that it has generally received, and this was the imperial mausoleum attached to St Peter's basilica in Rome.[129] The construction of the mausoleum is difficult to date precisely, but appears to have taken place at some point between 400 and 408.[130] It was a very long time since an emperor (even a pre-Christian emperor) had been buried at Rome, and in fact up until this point, unlike the east with its Church of the Holy Apostles at Constantinople, the western empire did not possess an extra-dynastic Christian imperial mausoleum.[131] Valentinian II and Gratian were probably buried at Milan in the chapel attached to the basilica of San Lorenzo, now known as Sant'Aquilino, but when Valentinian I died in 375, though he was a western emperor, his

---

[125] *Coll.Avell. Ep.* 38.4: *ad illos (viz. episcopus) enim divinarum rerum interpretatio, ad nos religionis spectat obsequium.*

[126] Deliyannis (2010), 51.

[127] On restoration of the city wall undertaken between 401 and 403 by the prefect Longinianus, see *CIL* 6. 1188–90; on the Colosseum and Forum Romanum work, see Humphries (2007), 36–7, and on the potential imperial palace, Sotinel and Jolivet (2012).

[128] Although Deliyannis suggests that another reason why Ravenna may have seemed an appealing site for a new imperial capital was its state of disrepair and the fact that it supposedly had no 'strong pagan core' and could therefore serve as a 'blank slate' upon which a new Christian city could be re-founded: Deliyannis (2010), 48–50.

[129] For a fuller discussion of the mausoleum and its significance, see now McEvoy (2010), 178–85; and (forthcoming), 131–49.

[130] Maria is generally assumed to have been the first burial in the mausoleum after her death in c.407–8. The building was presumably at least partially complete by this date: Johnson (2009), 171).

[131] Much has been written on the structure and intent behind the building of Constantine's Apostoleion; for the most recent analysis, see Johnson (2009), 119–28. Members of Constantine's family had been laid to rest in or near Rome in the fourth century, however, such as his mother Helena, and daughters Constantina and Helena: see also ibid. 110–18, 139–56.

body was transported across the empire for burial in the Apostoleion at Constantinople.[132] There may even have been a sense that only emperors whose deaths were something of an embarrassment to the imperial college were buried in the west, where they could be safely forgotten, rather than granted all the ceremonial of a journey back to Constantinople and solemn processional entrance to the city for burial in Constantine's church. Or perhaps there was as yet no clear plan as to the appropriate place of burial of a fourth-century Christian emperor, although Theodosius I's apparent reorganization of the imperial burials at the Apostoleion in the 380s suggests that he at least had a clear idea of the potential prestige of the site, and burial of eastern emperors there was certainly entrenched by the end of the century.[133]

The building of Honorius' mausoleum at Rome may be interpreted as a statement of renewed commitment to the old imperial capital—and indeed, the idea for it may have come on Honorius' 404 visit as he knelt at the shrine of St Peter. Members of the highest Christian elite of the city had already been laid to rest at the basilica—such as Junius Bassus, the urban prefect of 359, and Petronius Probus, who had had a mausoleum attached to the basilica for his burial in *c*.388.[134] But the timing of the construction of Honorius' mausoleum may also reveal an element of competition with the eastern court at this point too. For in the first decade of the fifth century, Honorius' brother Arcadius was attaching his own personal mausoleum to the Church of the Holy Apostles at Constantinople.[135] It would hardly be surprising if the western emperor's ability to link his dynastic mausoleum with the shrine of St Peter was in some way a reassertion of the equality—or even superiority—of Rome and the west.[136]

[132] We do not know if Gratian's body was ever recovered for burial, though Ambrose did request it upon his first embassy to the court of Magnus Maximus (see Ambrose, *Ep.* 30 [24]; also McLynn (1994), 161–3 on the embassy); Ambrose also communicated with Theodosius I over arrangements for Valentinian II's burial at Milan: Ambrose, *Ep.* 53 [= 25, ed. Faller].4; and seems to indicate in the funeral oration for Valentinian II that the brothers had been buried alongside one another: *De ob. Val.* 72, 78, 80. On their burials and Sant'Aquilino, see Johnson (1991), 503–5, and now also (2009), 156–67. For the burial of Valentinian I at Constantinople, see AM 30.10.1. The body of Gratian's first wife Constantia (posthumous daughter of Constantius II) was transported to Constantinople for burial when she died in 383 (*Chron.pasch.* p. 563).

[133] Croke (2010), 252–4.

[134] On Junius Bassus, and also members of the high-profile Probi-Anicii family being buried at St Peter's, see Paolucci (2008), 246–9. The sarcophagus of Junius Bassus was discovered in 1597 (*CIL* 6. 1737; *PLRE* 1. 155). On the mausoleum of Petronius Probus, see Krautheimer (1964). As Machado points out, Christianity offered aristocrats the chance to be buried in monuments which allowed them to essentially be honoured through the religious ceremonial performed there: Machado (2011), 498–9.

[135] The so-called 'South Stoa', built *c*.404: see most recently Johnson (2009), 127; Grierson (1962), 26, 36–7.

[136] Alchermes (1995), 8.

Our information about the mausoleum is sadly incomplete: we know of it from accounts of the discovery of the burial of Maria, Stilicho's daughter and Honorius' first wife, who died probably c.407–8.[137] It was in the course of the demolition of the Old St Peter's and the building of the new in the fourteenth and fifteenth centuries that this discovery took place.[138] Although no inscription survived (if there ever was one), when opened her sarcophagus contained lavish jewellery and other treasures which identified her by name; at least two other late Roman burials discovered around the same time in the mausoleum could not be identified but must certainly have also been imperial.[139] No record in our surviving sources notes Maria's burial in the mausoleum; in fact, the first imperial burial mentioned there is not until 450, but clearly the structure was being used for the interment of members of the imperial family well before this, and the eighth-century source Paul the Deacon records that Honorius was buried there when he died in 423.[140] The rich treasures buried with Maria hint at the grandeur of the funerary ceremonial which must have accompanied her interment (an estimated 180 precious items are recorded in our sixteenth-century source), with all of the impressive theatrical potential that St Peter's basilica could offer such an occasion. And it is interesting to note that these imperial burials were taking place on the Vatican Hill well before the papal tradition of burial there evolved—the first securely attested burial of a pope at St Peter's would be that of Leo the Great in 461.[141] The building of Honorius' mausoleum at such a significant martyr-shrine in Rome was surely a clear statement of the conception of the centrality of imperial Christianity under this child-turned-adult emperor.

---

[137] On the little available evidence regarding the mausoleum, see Koethe (1981), 10–11; Gem (2005), 13, 36–7. Also Alchermes (1995), 8–9. For the most recent scholarly studies, see Paolucci (2008), 225–52; Johnson (2009), 167–74, and McEvoy (forthcoming).

[138] The discovery of late antique sarcophagi beneath the chapel of St Petronilla occurred in three phases, with the first find of a marble sarcophagus in 1458, several more being unearthed in 1519, and finally the finding of Maria's sarcophagus in 1544. The discoveries are discussed in Johnson (2009), 171–4, and Paolucci (2008), 225–31.

[139] The item which has survived to the present day and allowed positive identification of Maria was a bulla, now in the Louvre in Paris, which was inscribed with the names of Maria, Honorius, Stilicho, Serena, Thermantia, and Eucherius: see Johnson (2009), 173–4; Paolucci (2008), 223, 232.

[140] The first burial recorded in surviving sources is that of the infant Theodosius, son of Galla Placidia and the Visigoth Athaulf, who seems to have been re-interred in this mausoleum at Rome in 450, according to the Reichenau addition to the chronicle of Prosper (*Add.* 12. I. 489); cf. Olympiodorus, frg. 26.1, and Oost (1965), 7–8. See *PLRE* 2. 1100 for this Theodosius. For the burial of Honorius, see Paul the Deacon, *Hist.Rom.*13.7, and Johnson (2009), 202. For an estimate of all those members of the imperial family likely to have been interred in this mausoleum in the fifth century, see McEvoy (2010), 183, n. 154.

[141] For further discussion on this point, see McEvoy (2010), 182–5; for the attestation of Leo's burial, see Alchermes (1995), 12.

It has been pointed out that by the end of the fourth century, Christianity had come to represent the ultimate reassurance of security, continuity, and imperial respectability for the Roman emperor.[142] But this demonstration of imperial respectability through piety became infinitely more important when the emperor was a child, or a child-emperor reaching adulthood but apparently continuing to take little active role in the workings of the regime his chief minister established. And although admittedly, when it comes to instances of Honorius actually being seen at public church services, he seems to vanish after Ambrose's funeral oration in 395, there were other means of making public demonstrations of imperial piety and commitment to orthodoxy—such as through legislation, ceremonial occasions, and building projects, which Honorius did embrace throughout his reign.[143]

Constantius Augustus

In the space of a few years Constantius had achieved great success in tackling the many crises which had beset the western government since before the death of Stilicho, and in taking on the 'active' role which Stilicho's death, and the continued passivity of Honorius, had left vacant in the imperial partnership. His heritage as a 'Roman' might eventually allow him to push his role in that partnership a little further than Stilicho had done, but essentially their means of embedding themselves in the imperial structure were very similar: through military leadership and marriage into the imperial family. Following his successful campaign against Constantine III and Gerontius in 412–13, Constantius was rewarded with his first consulship in 414.[144] By 415 he had acquired the title of *patricius*, at this point an unusual title for a general, and a surviving consular diptych dating to the 410s depicts Constantius in a distinctly imperial pose, above subject barbarians.[145]

In 417, Constantius was granted his second consulship and a still more conspicuous honour: the hand of Galla Placidia in marriage.[146] Olympiodorus provides a hint of the ceremonial which must have accompanied this occasion.[147] If reports of her previous lavish wedding to Athaulf had reached

---

[142] MacCormack (1981), 150.

[143] For Honorius' absence from church services after 395, see McLynn (2004), 265.

[144] *CLRE* 362–3; Heather (2005), 251.

[145] On Constantius as *patricius*, see Jones (1964a), 1. 176. On the consular diptych, see MacCormack (1981), pl. 56. Cf. Shelton (1983), 8.

[146] On the consulship of 417, see *CLRE* 368–9.

[147] Olympiodorus, frg. 33.1.1–7. Cf. Sozomen 9.16; Prosper 1259. Also Matthews (1975), 354–5, 377.

Ravenna, no doubt it would have been important to ensure that this event suitably eclipsed the other in splendour—as a demonstration of its greater legitimacy, above all. The sources reinforce the idea of Constantius' personal determination to achieve this marriage—despite the reported unwillingness of his bride—and given the lesson of Stilicho's rise and fall, this is no surprise.[148] Galla Placidia was, in the first place, far too dangerous a marital prize to leave available for any potential rival to seize upon, and thereby deprive Constantius of his dominance in government by gaining private access to the emperor. But secondly, given Honorius' lack of heirs and his unwed state from 408 onwards, with Placidia still only in her twenties in the 410s and thus of childbearing age, the princess presented the one obvious route to producing a dynastically legitimate heir for the western empire. Constantius was understandably determined to be the father of that heir: Stilicho's fate had made it clear that whatever the heights of office to which an emperor's manager might climb, actually managing to become indispensable to the emperor was almost impossible—but this might be the one way to achieve it.

Constantius' marriage to Galla Placidia did produce children: their first child was a girl, Justa Grata Honoria, born *c.*418, but in 419 a boy—Placidus Valentinianus—was born.[149] The birth of this heir for Honorius was another aspect of the new stability Constantius was able to bring to Honorius' rule, and allowed the general to reinvent his position yet again. In 420, Constantius was western consul for a third time, an unheard-of honour for a civilian.[150] Finally, on 8 February 421 the emperor Honorius declared Constantius his co-Augustus (albeit grudgingly, according to Olympiodorus).[151] That Honorius was at this point elbowed aside seems hardly surprising, but Constantius clearly recognized the value of a wholly legitimate accession: he must have had the military backing to engineer his own acclamation, but far better to prevail upon Honorius to put his elevation through peacefully, and by so doing, extend the divine blessing for Honorius' reign which had been emphasized from 395 to his new co-emperor.

At the same time as Constantius' elevation, the title of Augusta was granted to Galla Placidia, and the significant name of *nobilissimus* bestowed upon the infant Valentinian.[152] Flavius Constantius—now Constantius III—had worked his way steadily into the imperial partnership arrangement that Stilicho had established many years before at the time of Honorius'

---

[148] Olympiodorus, frg. 33.1.

[149] Ibid. 33.1.7–12, 3.2.1–10; Sozomen, 9.16. Cf. Matthews (1975), 354–5.

[150] *CLRE* 374–5.

[151] Olympiodorus, frg. 33.1.13–18, 33.2.1–10; Sozomen 9.16; Philostorgius 12.12. Cf. Heather (2005), 251.

[152] Olympiodorus, frg. 33.1, 33.2; also Philostorgius 12; Sozomen 9.16 (with less detail). Also Matthews (1975), 377; O'Flynn (1983), 74; Holum (1982), 128; Bury (1919), 1–2.

accession, and over ten years of court dominance had made himself indispens-able. Honorius could no longer be depicted as brimming with youthful promise—but his inactivity following Stilicho's death revealed him to be content to remain largely passive, which perhaps was the only prudent course of action open to him. And if he could no longer be convincingly hopeful and promising, he could still serve a ceremonial and religious function, while Constantius took over the active—and predominantly military—side of the partnership and, like Stilicho before him, tied himself to the imperial house, this time truly irrevocably, with the birth of Honorius' heir.

Stabilized by the military victories of Constantius in the 410s, with two middle-aged emperors who might both be expected to have many years of their reigns still ahead of them, and a young heir with an impeccable dynastic claim, the future must have seemed secure and even bright. There was no need to expect another lengthy minority government for the child Valentinian either, with the back-up of two adult reigning emperors as a safeguard. Unfortunately this promising state of affairs did not last: in September 421, less than seven months after his accession, Constantius fell ill and died, supposedly regretting the constraints his accession had placed upon him, and planning a campaign against the eastern government for its refusal to recognize his elevation.[153]

After Constantius

With Flavius Constantius died also the stability he had brought to the western government over the last ten years. Like any political player in a one-party state who had reached such a pinnacle of power, he had taken care that there should be no successor-in-waiting other than his infant son—all those in office in 421 should reasonably be considered his appointees, just as those who fell with Stilicho in 408 had been.[154] Constantius' death did not reveal Honorius stepping in to take control, any more than Stilicho's had: instead it saw the court fall back into the 'old' system of cut-throat political factions fighting it out for power behind the throne, while again Honorius remained quietly in the background, and survived. When the perfect opportunity presented itself, Honorius was unable (or perhaps chose to be unable), even at the age of 37, having been emperor for almost thirty years, to make the transition essentially from child to adult emperor.

---

[153] Olympiodorus, frg. 33.1.18–25, 33.2.1–10; Philostorgius 12.12. Cf. Matthews (1975), 377–8. As Van Nuffelen points out, Constantius' transformation from virtuous general to greedy tyrant through marriage to the imperial house, as presented by Olympiodorus, may well represent eastern views of appropriate marriage policies for the imperial family: Van Nuffelen (forthcoming); see similarly, Harlow (2004), 147.

[154] Heather (2005), 257.

The sources indicate that his sister Galla Placidia was well able to recognize the dangers of the situation, and made an effort to monopolize the affections of the emperor for the next year, in a manner which gave rise to scandal.[155] Yet she was outmanoeuvred in her efforts to protect her own interest and that of her son. Her enemies poisoned the emperor against her, while the Visigothic bodyguard she retained from her years with the barbarians were blamed for riots in Ravenna, with the rift reaching such a peak of animosity that both she and her children—thus including Honorius' only heir, Valentinian—were sent away to Constantinople in late 422 or early 423.[156]

The history of the political factions vying in their attempts to establish some sort of power behind the throne in the last year of Honorius' rule is even more complicated to disentangle than in the years following Stilicho's death, and the chief ministers more difficult to identify. The *comes Hispaniarum* Asterius, who led a campaign against the Vandals in Gallaecia in 420 and managed to capture the former usurper Maximus, was probably one of the more influential figures.[157] He may have received the title of *patricius* for his efforts, but disappears from the sources by 422.[158] Another general, the *magister militum* Castinus, who was also sent on campaign against the Vandals in 422, is a possible chief minister, as is the influential general Boniface, who had originally set out on the campaign with him but decamped to Africa when they quarrelled, and who remained loyal to Galla Placidia, sending funds for her support in Constantinople.[159] Castinus may have been among the enemies of Galla Placidia who engineered her exile from Honorius' court, given his later involvement in the 424 usurpation of John.[160] That these military men are the most obvious candidates attempting to claim the position of chief minister at this time once again confirms the strength and success of the system established by Stilicho, and followed so successfully by Constantius. But the triumph of Galla Placidia's enemies was short-lived, for Honorius himself died in August 423, reportedly of dropsy, at the age of only 39.[161]

---

[155] e.g. Olympiodorus, frg. 38.1–8.

[156] Ibid. 38.1–16; Matthews (1975), 378.

[157] On Asterius, see Kulikowski (2004), 173, (2000c), 123; *PLRE* 2. 171. On the war between the Vandals and Sueves, see Hydatius 63(71), 66(74). Kulikowski argues Maximus had launched a further usurpation in 418 or 419: (2004), 173–4; also (2000c), 125–6. Maximus had been raised as the puppet-emperor of Gerontius, the former general of the usurper Constantine III (see above, p. 196 and n. 46). On Maximus being paraded at the celebrations: *Chron.Gall.452*, 85; Marcellinus *comes*, s.a. 422.

[158] Kulikowski (2000c), 127–8.

[159] For Boniface quarrelling with Castinus on the expedition to Spain and departing for Africa: Prosper 1278. Cf. Kulikowski (2004), 174, (2000c), 135. Boniface had already been in Africa as *comes* from 417, and in receipt of letters from St Augustine: *Epp.* 185, 185A, 189. On his support for Galla Placidia: Olympiodorus, frg. 38.1–8; also Prosper 1286. On Castinus, *PLRE* 2. 269–70; on Boniface, *PLRE* 2. 237–40.

[160] See below, p. 227.

[161] Olympiodorus, frg. 39.1.1–6; 39.2; Philostorgius 12.13. Cf. Matthews (1975), 379.

Analysis of Honorius' reign and the key political events of the thirty years he ruled contributes significantly to the picture of the institutionalization of child-rule which was taking place in the late Roman west, and the ways in which the coping—or cloaking—mechanisms for dealing with the rule of a figurehead emperor were continuing to develop after the experience of the reigns of Gratian and Valentinian II. A boy-emperor's accession could never be as simple as the triumph of the dynastic principle alone: at the age of 10, Honorius was in no position to exercise his own dynastic right to the throne and relied upon others to do so upon his behalf, and they had their own agendas in turn. It has been suggested that Ambrose's funeral oration for Theodosius I, and its pleas for loyalty to the young Honorius, recalled the tensions of the year 383 as powerful interests arranged themselves around a boy-emperor in the promotion of their own interests.[162] This is quite true. But by 395 the methods for advancing those interests in such a situation were becoming increasingly sophisticated, and the outcomes were very different. There is no doubt that the succession of a dynastically legitimate child-heir to a dead emperor provided the opportunity for the Roman state to avoid civil war through rival generals battling for the throne, if enough support for the child could be garnered. By the same token, the accession of a boy of Honorius' age meant that political conflict became increasingly focused on factional in-fighting at court (rather than on generals leading armies in the provinces), as ambitious individuals clamoured to become the dominant influence upon the minority government. In prolonged periods of relative stability, as under the regimes of Stilicho or Constantius III, such jostling was minimized by the extent of their control of offices and patronage; but during the interregnum—the years between these regimes—such inwardly focused politics led to a chaotic inconsistency in imperial policy and the neglect of matters essential to the survival of the western empire itself.

When Honorius became emperor in 395, the structural changes within the Roman imperial system which had enabled young children like Gratian and Valentinian II to be presented as plausible emperors also held good for him. He could be presented as fulfilling, at least to some extent, the expectations of his office, and the structural evolution of the late Roman bureaucracy and judiciary meant that the accession of a 10-year-old need not affect their normal functioning. And as ever, given the difficulties of assessing the input of any emperor in the legislation issuing from his government, it is entirely possible that as Honorius reached adulthood he did have an active involvement in legal matters: as discussed above, the religious laws produced during his reign may reflect a means of compensating for his non-military role, although many of his laws also pay close attention to army affairs, as we might expect.[163]

---

[162] McLynn (1994), 363.   [163] Honoré (1999), 213.

From the very start of the reign of Honorius, however, Ambrose set a particular tone for the child-emperor's presentation, with his stressing of Honorius' own piety and the divine endorsement of his accession, and perhaps most significantly, of his youthful promise, and of course the heavy emphasis on dynastic loyalty to the son of a pious and victorious emperor. As the new regime under Stilicho made appeals for support to key power-groups, this youthful-promise motif was seized upon by Claudian, and developed still further. The rule of this child-emperor was to be a partnership, based on the dynastic legitimacy and youthful promise of the child, and the actual virtues of the man truly running the empire: Stilicho. As the young emperor's guardian he was immensely influential, and as Honorius' father-in-law he found a way of not only embedding himself still further in the child-emperor's government, but also isolating Honorius from other potential sources of influence. With victories in the Gildonic crisis, as well as, up to a point, over Alaric and Radagaisus, the strength of the system Stilicho had established for managing the child-emperor's government and justifying his own position was great indeed.

That contemporary historians were convinced that the sons of Theodosius were rulers in name only is very clear through the reports of Eunapius, Zosimus, Philostorgius, and Orosius, reporting on Rufinus and Stilicho in particular enriching themselves at the expense of their subjects.[164] It was not until a combination of severe crises on different fronts came together, in the form of the Visigothic demands, further barbarian invasions, and a usurper in Gaul—with a consequent loss of senatorial support at Rome and the opportunism of an enemy at court—that Stilicho's regime showed any sign of weakening. But there must inevitably also have been a point at which the presentation of the partnership upon which Stilicho had built his own power would run into difficulties. Just how long was it going to remain plausible for Honorius to be youthful and promising? And if he did become an active emperor, how would Stilicho retain his own power and justify his position any longer? When Stilicho died in 408, Honorius had reached the age of 23. Yet still, the initiative for Stilicho's downfall had not come from the emperor, and now with the ideal opportunity before him to take up the power which had been wielded on his behalf for so long, he made no attempt to do so. Instead, while different political players vied for the power behind the throne rather than the throne itself, Honorius remained shrewdly passive while they toppled each other—often brutally. The young emperor provided a shield behind which political players manoeuvred, while Honorius presented a front of continuity, and perhaps even, beyond the immediate circle of court politics, of stability. It was a prudent choice: for unlike the two young emperors before him, he would survive the political turmoil to eventually die a natural death after a long reign. It seems that Honorius understood how the system worked.

---

[164] e.g. Eunapius, frg. 9.62.1.1–10; Zosimus 5.1.3, 5.12.1–2; Philostorgius 11.3; Orosius 7.37.

The rapid rise and fall of political factions at the imperial court had the potential for considerable damage to the empire, however—most conspicuously attested through the tortuous negotiations with the Visigoths and their eventual sack of Rome in 410. It was only with the rise of Flavius Constantius that the situation began to stabilize once more, with decisive military victories over usurpers, peace terms with the Vandals, and efforts to reconstruct relations between the court and the senatorial aristocracies of Italy and Gaul. Flavius Constantius' steady climb to absolute power through carefully legitimated means once again followed the model Stilicho had constructed—an evident indication of its efficacy—but he was able to push the model still further. Having established his military credentials, he became the 'active' member of the partnership presentation—leading the emperor's armies in the field, while Honorius' role had moved from being youthful and promising to demonstrations of his religious devotion and his fulfilment of his ceremonial role. This partnership moved beyond ideological presentation, for Constantius was able to do what Stilicho had been unable to: not only to marry into the imperial house, but to produce an heir for Honorius, and finally to become co-Augustus himself.

When Constantius died unexpectedly in middle age, yet again Honorius remained inactive, allowing political players to fight for power behind the throne once more, which they were doubtless still doing when he died in 423. Throughout his reign Honorius had been essentially another figurehead emperor who could be presented as able to fulfil the ideal demands of his position, while his religious and ceremonial functions had also been emphasized as a cloaking mechanism for those functions he could not be seen carrying out. With the fates of Gratian and Valentinian II before him, it seems likely that Honorius was well aware that one of the few ways he might survive to adulthood was by remaining passive. Yet as the need for strong military men to carry out the active requirements of his office demonstrated, this policy also meant that effectively Honorius never made the transition from child to adult emperor, from ceremonial to actual ruler.

The question arises of what the benefits of divorcing the ceremonial and actual power of the emperor might be, and for whom? But a stable, divinely endorsed, and passive child-turned-adult emperor must have provided a valuable front of continuity behind which Stilicho—and later Constantius—could exercise absolute power, while that emperor's acceptance of this, as long as it lasted, insulated such dominant figures from potential threats. Perhaps the job of emperor really was getting too big: there are indications from Olympiodorus that Constantius at least was not very adept at the ceremonial side (and even with Honorius taking the lead in ceremonial matters, as co-emperor Constantius could not have entirely avoided them), looking sullen and downcast in public processions, and though lively enough at banquets, regretting the limitations imperial office placed on him.[165] Perhaps separate ceremonial and military leaders were needed, as the political and military situation of the west became increasingly precarious in the fifth century. It was the long reign of Honorius, however, which transformed the political culture of the late Roman west and created the acceptance of child-emperor and figurehead-emperor rule as a viable option where it had not been before. The examples of the reigns of Gratian and Valentinian II had provided the vital precedent, but the reign of Honorius truly made the difference, for it was during this thirty-year period that the problems which had led to the failures of these previous child-emperor reigns were resolved. Through the efforts of Stilicho, pursued later by Constantius, it was demonstrated that such a government could survive—so long as the figurehead at its centre remained passive. That is not to say that the active model of imperial leadership disappeared, for if Constantius had lived longer the clock could have been turned back and a long-term, active *imperator* might have continued at the helm of government. The active imperial model always remained a possibility: but now the ceremonial, passive rule of a child-emperor, or later a child-turned-adult emperor, with an active partner fulfilling his military function, had become a fully acceptable possibility too.

---

[165] Olympiodorus, frg. 23.10–16.

Part Three

Valentinian III

8

The Struggle for Power

> After the usurper's death, the emperor Theodosius became very anxious
> as to whom he should proclaim emperor of the west. He had a cousin
> then very young named Valentinian; the son of his aunt Placidia, daugh-
> ter of Theodosius the Great, and sister of the two Augusti Arcadius and
> Honorius, and of that Constantius who had been proclaimed emperor by
> Honorius, and had died after a short reign with him. This cousin he
> created Caesar, and sent into the western parts, committing the adminis-
> tration of affairs to his mother Placidia.[1]

When the emperor Honorius died in August 423, his only heir was far from
Ravenna, at Constantinople with his mother and sister. If 4-year-old Valentinian was to become the next in the line of western child-emperors,
someone would have to invest considerable effort in both men and resources
in getting him there. Despite the extraordinary circumstances in which this last
of the Theodosian child-emperors came to the throne, like his uncle Honorius
before him Valentinian has rarely been accorded much attention—or indeed
respect—from modern scholarship. Sidonius' scathing dismissal of him in
rather perplexing terms as a 'mad eunuch', along with later rumours from
Procopius and John of Antioch of Valentinian's supposed degeneracy and
seduction of the wife of Petronius Maximus, seem to have stuck determinedly,
and few modern scholars are prepared to ascribe any redeeming qualities to this
young emperor.[2] One damning verdict was that Valentinian was 'weak and
worthless . . . spoiled by his mother, and grown up to be a man of pleasure who
took no serious interest in his imperial duties', while another similarly described
the young emperor as 'idle, irresponsible and dissolute', and the substantial

---

[1] Socrates, 7.24: Τοῦ δὲ τυράννου ἀναιρεθέντος ἔμφροντις ἦν ὁ αὐτοκράτωρ Θεοδόσιος, τίνα
⟨ἂν⟩ ἀναδείξειε τῶν ἑσπερίων μερῶνβασιλέα. 2. Ἦν δὲ αὐτῷ ἀνεψιὸς κομιδῇ νέος Οὐαλεντινιανὸς
ὄνομα, ἐκ Πλακιδίας τῆς αὐτοῦ θείας γενόμενος, ἥτις θυγάτηρ μὲν ἦν Θεοδοσίου τοῦ μεγάλου
βασιλέως, Ἀρκαδίου δὲ καὶ Ὀνωρίου τῶν δύο Αὐγούστων ἀδελφή· πατρὸς δὲ ἦν ὁ Οὐαλεντινιανὸς
Κωνσταντίου, ὃς ὑπὸ Ὀνωρίου βασιλεὺς ἀναδειχθεὶς καὶ βραχὺν αὐτῷ χρόνον συμβασιλεύσας
εὐθὺς ἐτελεύτησεν. Τοῦτον τὸν ἀνεψιὸν Καίσαρα καταστήσας ἐπὶ τὰ ἑσπέρια μέρη ἀνέπεμψεν, τῇ
μητρὶ αὐτοῦ Πλακιδίᾳ τὴν φροντίδα τῶν πραγμάτων ἐπιτρέψας.
[2] Sidonius, Carm. 7.359; Procopius, Bell. 3.3.9–13; John.Ant., frg. 200(1).

tax remissions granted by Valentinian's government over the course of his reign as signs of 'culpable weakness', given the crises the west faced from 425 to 455.[3]

But perhaps the reign of Valentinian III deserves another chance. The chapters which follow are by no means intended as an attempt to rehabilitate the character of the emperor himself. What they do aim to achieve, however, is a reassessment of the reign which situates Valentinian more thoughtfully within the context of the imperial system which had developed during the rule of his predecessor child-turned-adult emperors, and in particular the infantilization of the imperial office which had staunchly taken hold during the long reign of Honorius. Against this backdrop, the potential for Valentinian to be the sort of active, intervening emperor that modern scholars might have wished for contracts significantly, while the imperial initiatives in which the emperor himself may have been genuinely involved—such as legislation or involvement in ecclesiastical politics at Rome—take on a greater importance. As emperor from the age of 6, throughout a lengthy minority reign and his eventual bloody push for full independence in 454, twenty-nine years after his accession, Valentinian was operating within a severely curtailed system, a construct of the imperial office which had undergone a substantial transformation from the imperial office of a century earlier.

With all of this in mind—the lack of modern scholarship on this period, and especially modern scholarship which takes into account this transformation—it is necessary to trace the course of Valentinian III's reign itself in order to analyse fully the different powers with a stake in the new boy-emperor's government and the continuation of the presentation of the emperor as a civilianized, predominantly religious and ceremonial figure, (again) well into his adult years. The increasingly fragmentary nature of the sources for fifth-century western affairs has always complicated the picture, and make it essential to piece together the available evidence so far as is possible—from the legislative records of the *Theodosian Code* to the fragmentary works of the court poet Merobaudes or the brief entries of the chronicler Prosper. Setting these contemporary sources against the chronological context of the reign also provides a useful reminder that the disgusted verdicts of later sources, such as Procopius or John of Antioch, valuable though their accounts remain, look back on Valentinian's government through an eastern lens which knew that the western Roman empire would disappear as a political entity within three decades of Valentinian's death. Yet as close examination of the events of the period will highlight, despite all of the troubles of the Vandal conquest of North Africa and the growing bankruptcy of the western imperial government, Valentinian himself faced not a single serious rebellion against his rule until his

---

[3] Bury (1923), 1. 250, and Jones (1964*a*), 1. 173 and 206.

death in 455, while outside of Africa, under his powerful general Aetius, the western imperial army remained constantly active and continued to win battles. In some regions of the west at least, the partnership rule of emperor and general under Valentinian and Aetius did provide relative stability.

The reign of Valentinian III was from its beginning a creation of the eastern imperial government, yet within a decade of its establishment western events would bring forth a chief military commander and manager of the boy-emperor's regime once more, a manager whom the government of Theodosius II had not anticipated when it launched the west's new child-emperor. Flavius Aetius' considerable military might, unlike any other *magister militum* of the west before him, derived almost entirely in the 420s from sources beyond imperial control, residing effectively in a personal army loyal to him. A more dangerous figure than either Stilicho or Flavius Constantius because of this, a man just as capable of using his personal following against the state (or other imperial commanders) as for it, by 433 Aetius had made himself the single dominant general of Valentinian III's government. Yet still, it was this position that he sought—that of the prevailing power behind the throne, following the model of Stilicho before him—rather than the throne itself. Acceptance of the structural adaptation of the late Roman state to the phenomenon of child-emperor rule continued.

The accession and events of the reign of Valentinian III were built on a model of managing child-emperors in western government which had evolved by the 420s and which really was radically different from the traditional pattern of imperial rulership. The arrangement of a partnership between emperor and dominant general, now increasingly part of the institutional pattern of power-relations at and around the western imperial court, con-tinued to reassert itself. Yet Aetius' path to the position of Valentinian III's manager was far from smooth, and while the competition for this position between powerful generals was inevitable, given the expectations which had by now developed of how child-emperor administrations were run, the emer-gence of Aetius as the winner of this position was not. The eastern govern-ment's investment in Valentinian III as the future of the west involved not only military commitment but, as we shall see, also bureaucratic commitment to establishing this new government, and the east maintained a vested interest in the fate of the west for many years to come. Thus, while the east had to live with the complication of Aetius, Aetius' dominance in the west would be similarly impinged upon by the interest of the eastern government.

Valentinian III's accession and the east

The very nature of Valentinian III's accession makes it clear that key political figures of the late Roman empire saw real value in the rule of a child-emperor, in both west and east, and underlines yet again that there was far more to the promotion of boy-rulers during this period than blind dynastic loyalty. Despite the investment involved in getting Valentinian onto the western throne, in 424 the eastern government of Theodosius II chose to make that commitment. Eastern intervention or involvement in the affairs of the west was nothing new: in 388 and 393 the eastern government had launched costly military campaigns ostensibly to avenge the deaths of the western emperors Gratian and Valentinian II; in the late 390s it had been bristling on the horizon over the military activities of Stilicho; and in 409 it had sent desperately needed aid to the beleaguered government of Honorius. Now once more, in 424–5, the eastern government weighed into western politics, not to avenge an imperial death, but all for the sake of putting a 5-year-old child (albeit one with an excellent dynastic claim) on the throne of the western empire. What made it worth their while?

It is worth recalling at this point that when Valentinian III became emperor in 425, it was almost sixty years since the accession of 8-year-old Gratian, and fifty years since the acclamation of the 4-year-old Valentinian II. Over these many decades, the bureaucrats and military officers who had served under successive minority governments had spent their lives essentially working with the consequences of these child-emperor accessions, and knew how to manage such situations. Furthermore, the eastern court itself, headed by the now adult Theodosius II, Augustus from the age of nine months and sole eastern emperor from the age of 7, had its own ideas about how effectively the government of a small boy in purple could be managed—and even had the appropriate small boy to hand. Valentinian III's accession as western emperor was more difficult and expensive to achieve than any of the child-emperor accessions previously, yet the decision of the eastern government to undertake the campaign, and the acceptance of the boy as the new emperor in the west, reflects just how far the institutionalization of child-emperor rule had come since 367.

As discussed in Chapter 7, Flavius Placidus Valentinianus, the son of Honorius' sister Galla Placidia and the general (and later emperor) Constantius III, was born on 2 July 419, and had been raised to the rank of *nobilissimus* in early 421.[4] But within a couple of years the infant's father Constantius was dead, and young Valentinian was in exile with his mother and sister at Constantinople. The eastern court, while it took in the western empress and her son, had not acknowledged or accepted the titles conferred upon either her

---

[4] Olympiodorus, frg. 33.1.7–12, 3.2.1–10; Sozomen 9.16; Philostorgius 12; and with less detail: Hydatius 64(72). Cf. Matthews (1975), 354–5, 377; also Oost (1968a), 162–8; O'Flynn (1983), 74. On Galla Placidia becoming Augusta at the same time, see Holum (1982), 128; and Bury (1919), 1–2. A jewel now in the Hermitage museum in St Petersburg but dating to the early fifth-century west may show the occasion of the child Valentinian being made *nobilissimus* at the hands of Honorius and Fl. Constantius: see cover image, also McCormack (1981), pl. 43, and above, p. 49, n. 4.

husband, herself, or the child Valentinian by Honorius, and nor did it do so now.[5] Unsurprisingly, in the total absence of a member of the house of Theodosius in the west, a usurpation arose. The usurper was John, not a military man, but instead the former chief secretary of the western imperial court, and he was proclaimed at Rome, on 23 November 423.[6] Details about John's short-lived rule are sketchy, although it is extremely unlikely this secretary would ever have been able to assume power without military support.[7] Honorius' general Castinus threw his weight behind the usurper, as did Flavius Aetius, the son of one of Honorius' generals and already a man of influence at court.[8]

It has been argued that the decision of the military man Castinus to support the usurpation of a civil servant rather than claim the throne himself indicates awareness that power lay with the soldiery, not the empire, and the recent acclamation of Constantius as emperor had been merely an aberration.[9] In fact, far from being an aberration, Constantius' accession was rather the culmination of a new model of imperial partnership which had been developing for the past three decades. The accession of Constantius was an indication of just how far that partnership arrangement had developed over the past thirty years, and how desirable even military men believed it to be. And, along the same lines as this model, the usurper John must certainly have been a compromise candidate, while the choice to promote him was a means by which civil war between rival generals, who might otherwise resent one among their number claiming the throne, could be avoided. This arrangement was in many ways aimed at achieving a continuation of the very same balance of power which had prevailed under Honorius—of a ceremonial emperor working in partnership with a strong military leader.

The extent to which John was recognized as emperor is difficult to discern: some scholars have claimed he was not supported at Rome, pointing to evidence of this in a dedication there to Valentinian III as Caesar by the *praefectus urbi* Faustus.[10] Though proclaimed at Rome, the usurper's court did

---

[5] Olympiodorus, frg. 33.2; Philostorgius 12, and above, pp. 214–15. Bury mistakenly claims (1919: 2–3) Placidia's rank was recognized upon her arrival in the east, but this did not take place until after the usurpation of John.

[6] For the date and in general on the usurpation: *PLRE* 2. 594–6. Olympiodorus, frg. 39.1, 39.2; Philostorgius 13; Prosper 1282; Socrates 7.23.3; Marcellinus *comes*, s.a. 424 (3); John Ant., frg. 195; Hydatius 74(83); Procopius, *Bell.* 3.3.5–8. For John's rank as *primicerius notariorum*, see Socrates 7.23.3.

[7] Bury (1919), 3; Oost (1968*a*), 180–1.

[8] Prosper 1282, 1288; Philostorgius 12.14; Cf. Matthews (1975), 379.

[9] O'Flynn (1983), 174, n. 5.

[10] *CIL* 6.1677 = *ILS* 805; see Wilkes (1972), 391; also Bury (1919), 3; (1923), 1. 223, n. 1. We cannot guess the exact date of this inscription, however, and it could date from the period between John's death (in June/July 425) and Valentinian's accession as Augustus at Rome in October the same year, during which time he still carried the title of Caesar; the earliest we can certainly date Faustus' prefecture is July 425: *CTh.* 16.5.62 (17 July 425); see also *PLRE* 2. 452–4.

move thereafter to Ravenna.[11] John appears to have elicited even less support outside of Italy: in Gaul his praetorian prefect Exsuperantius was slain in a mutiny at Arles, and it has been claimed that Boniface, the *comes Africae*, withheld the grain shipments to Rome in protest against the usurper for a time.[12] As the conflict between the interests of senatorial and provincial elites and the regime of Honorius had demonstrated, figurehead emperors—children or adults—did not suit all parties.

It would be a mistake, however, to imagine that upon the death of Honorius the eastern court of Theodosius II immediately leapt into action and publicly supported his young cousin against this adult usurper in the west. Socrates reports that Theodosius II delayed making public the news of his uncle's death for some time before announcing it.[13] Honorius' death had left Theodosius II as sole ruler of the Roman empire, and his concealment of the news indicates that he took some time to make up his mind as to what course to take: but the immediate elevation of Valentinian was not his first response.[14] It has been claimed that such a situation might lead Galla Placidia and her children to fear for their lives, but this is a romantic and immensely unlikely view: it would have been much less problematic simply to keep Valentinian in Constantinople and marginalize him entirely, than to incur unnecessarily the public-relations disaster of doing away with a child-prince.[15] Meanwhile, the *Theodosian Code* makes clear that in the interim Theodosius II legislated for the entire empire as sole Augustus.[16] For several months, therefore, Theodosius II ruled alone, and it may be that he hoped to continue doing so indefinitely.[17]

It has also been suggested that Theodosius II originally came to an arrangement with the general Castinus following Honorius' death, whereby Castinus would rule basically as Theodosius II's vicegerent in the west (pointing to Castinus' supposed consulship in 424 as evidence), but that Castinus then

---

[11] Matthews (1975), 379.

[12] On the mutiny at Arles, see Prosper 1285; *Chron.Gall.452* 97. Coins were minted in John's name at Arles however: Hill *et al.* (1960), 54, 57, and possibly also at Trier: Stein (1959), 1. 565. On Boniface's potential action, see Oost (1968a), 180, 187. Oost also claims that John sent an unsuccessful expedition under the general Sigisvult to deal with Boniface, but documentation for this is uncertain. Cf. Matthews (1975), 379; O'Flynn (1983), 76.

[13] Socrates 7.23; also Croke (1995), 76.

[14] Hydatius 73(82).

[15] For the romantic claim of the scenario threatening the lives of Galla Placidia and her children, see Oost (1968a), 176–7. Sensibly argued against by Wilkes (1972), 388.

[16] e.g. *CTh.* 11.20.5 (13 May 424), referring to Honorius as *patricius meus*. On Theodosius II's intentions, see generally Bury (1923), 1. 221–4; Stein (1959), 282–4; Oost (1968a), 179–86; Lippold (1980), 972–3; Kaegi (1968), 19–26; Matthews (1975), 377–81.

[17] On Theodosius II ruling alone: Hydatius 73(82); Prosper 1283; Cassiodorus, *Chron.* 1207; *ILS* 1283. See also Gillett (1993), 19.

went back on the deal.[18] Yet evidence for this consulship is dubious.[19] Castinus, if he was western consul in 424, would have been more likely to owe the appointment to Honorius or the usurper John than to Theodosius II, and if he had been designated the eastern emperor's vicegerent he must have tired of the arrangement very rapidly, given that John's usurpation occurred only three months after Honorius' death.[20] Theodosius' hesitation over backing his cousin's claim was essentially a pragmatic stance: launching a bid to put Valentinian on the throne would involve an expedition of tremendous cost and resources. The fact that Theodosius II did not name the child Valentinian as consul for 424 particularly indicates that he was holding off on any resolution to support the boy's cause in the west. Theodosius seems to have delayed making a decision until John sent envoys to the east in the hope of gaining official recognition and legitimization for his regime. John had already had coins minted in both his and Theodosius II's name at Ravenna, but his embassy did not meet with success in Constantinople, where the eastern emperor refused to make any acknowledgement of the usurper, arrested and then exiled his ambassadors to various locations on the Propontis.[21] It was only at this stage that Theodosius II decided to support the cause of the western branch of his family: when it looked like the west would be lost unless he took action, and when it became clear that he was unlikely to be able to rule the west from Constantinople himself.

In early 424 Theodosius II took the significant steps of recognizing as valid the acts of Honorius which had elevated Galla Placidia to the rank of Augusta and her son to that of *nobilissimus*, issuing *solidi* in Placidia's name, and extending posthumous recognition to Constantius III.[22] At some time in 424 Valentinian was betrothed to Theodosius II's young daughter Licinia Eudoxia, with the marriage to take place when both children reached an appropriate age.[23] This must have been an obvious arrangement to make: once Theodosius II

[18] Oost (1968a), 179; followed by Nagy (1990–1), 86.

[19] It appears only in later sources like Marcellinus *comes* (s.a. 424) and the *Chron.pasch.* (p. 580), and in one law of the *CJ*—the same law in the *CTh.* does not mention Castinus: *CJ* 1.30.1 and *CTh.* 1.8.2 (25 Apr. 424). The *CLRE*, however, does record Castinus as western consul for 424 (382–3).

[20] Stein (1959: 1. 565, n. 152) accepts Castinus' designation as consul by Theodosius II; Matthews ascribes the appointment to John (1975: 379), as does Wilkes (1972: 388–9), and the *PLRE* 2. 269–70. Zecchini (1983: 133) ascribes the appointment to Honorius. Oost claims dubiously that Castinus reneged on his supposed deal with Theodosius II because he knew Galla Placidia would be building a power-base in Constantinople and would turn Theodosius against him: (1968a), 181.

[21] For the coins minted by John, see Hill *et al.* (1960), 43. On the reception of his embassy in Constantinople: Olympiodorus, frg. 39.2; Socrates 7.23; Philostorgius 13; John Ant., frg. 195. Cf. Wilkes (1972), 389; also Oost (1968a), 187.

[22] Marcellinus *comes*, s.a. 424 (1); Olympiodorus, frg. 43.1; 46; also Wilkes, (1972), 389. The *Theodosian Code* confirms the decision to recognize Constantius III, in its recording laws in his name, e.g. *CTh.* 10.10.29 (8 July 421); 10.10.30 (8 July 421); 2.27.1 (28 July 421).

[23] For sources on the life of Licinia Eudoxia, see *PLRE* 2. 410–12; also on the betrothal see Marcellinus *comes*, s.a. 424 (2). Cf. Holum (1982), 129; Oost (1968a), 184–5, and on the marriage in 437, see further below, pp. 256–7.

had decided to push Valentinian's claims, it would have been a natural step to ensure that the new western regime, if ultimately successful, continued to be bound to Theodosius II's own government.[24] Moreover, the marriage of women of the imperial family would pose a constant problem throughout the fifth century in terms of the potential political rivals such marriages might thereby make of their husbands (as the virginity vows of Theodosius II's sisters and the scandals surrounding Justa Grata Honorius—discussed further below—revealed). Valentinian was one of the few suitable candidates for a marriage alliance with the eastern imperial house—one who was already part of the family, who would be an emperor himself, and therefore posed no threat to the position of Theodosius II. It is doubtful a more suitable spouse could ever have been found for the only daughter of the eastern emperor. In financing a campaign to place his young cousin on the throne, Theodosius II (or his advisers) intended to have a powerful role in Valentinian's government, one way or another: if he could not stretch to personal control of the west from Constantinople (an experiment which had already faltered under Theodosius I, thirty years earlier), perhaps installing a dynastically legitimate child-emperor in his stead, surrounded by carefully chosen advisers, and betrothed to his own daughter, was the best way of doing so *in absentia*.

With these formal preparations in place, Theodosius II then launched a major military expedition to deal with the usurper in the west and install the child Valentinian in his place. Led by two Alan generals, Ardaburius and Aspar, and a Roman named Candidianus, the eastern army, taking Galla Placidia and her son and daughter along with them, travelled first to Thessalonica.[25] It was here, on 23 October 424, that the 5-year-old Valentinian was formally invested with the rank and insignia of Caesar, by Theodosius II's *magister officiorum*, Helion.[26] Valentinian was also designated consul for the following year with his cousin, and the mint of Constantinople issued large numbers of coins celebrating the promotion, showing Valentinian and Theodosius II: the young Caesar standing and the Augustus seated, with the legend:

---

[24] Contra Oost (1968a), 184–5, who argues Placidia must have had to push for the betrothal, followed by Connor (2004), 67.

[25] Olympiodorus, frg. 43.1; Socrates 7.23; Procopius, *Bell.* 3.3.8-9. Cf. Jones (1964a), 1. 181; Bury (1919), 3; Holum (1982), 129. This Candidianus has been suggested by some scholars as the same man in whose house at Narbonne Galla Placidia was married to the Visigoth Athaulf in 414, but the evidence does not allow a conclusion on this point: see *PLRE* 2. 257.

[26] Olympiodorus, frg. 43.1; Philostorgius 12.13; Prosper 1286, 1289; Marcellinus *comes*, s.a. 424 (2). Cf. Wilkes (1972), 390. Another fragment of Olympidorus (frg. 43.2) claims that Theodosius himself conferred the dignity of Caesar upon his cousin at Thessalonica, but this seems to be a confusion with Theodosius' later plans to travel to Rome to create Valentinian Augustus, and turning back at Thessalonica due to illness (Socrates 7.24, 25). Socrates also claims incorrectly that Theodosius only decided to make Valentinian Caesar after the defeat of John (Socrates 7.24) while Hydatius has Valentinian being created Caesar in Constantinople (Hydatius 75(84)). On Helion, see *PLRE* 2. 533. Cf. Jones (1964a), 1. 179; Matthews (1975), 380; Oost (1968a), 184.

SALVS REIPVBLICAE; Valentinian has no diadem and wears plain robes, unlike Theodosius.[27] The emphasis on young Valentinian's junior status beside Theodosius II is unmistakable. Indeed, in making Valentinian first a Caesar, and not full Augustus at this point, Theodosius II emphasized his own superior rank still further, and the fact that the junior emperor's rule would be dependent upon the east for its very existence.

Of the following campaign, Olympiodorus and Philostorgius give the most extensive accounts, and Socrates also provides some useful comments. In the spring of 425 the expedition divided in two, Ardaburius taking the infantry by sea and Aspar the cavalry by land towards Aquileia.[28] Disaster seemed near when Ardaburius was shipwrecked and captured by John's men, but through either divine intervention or Ardaburius befriending and winning over his captors to his cause (depending upon the sources), while Candidianus was busy reclaiming northern Italy, Aspar gained entry to Ravenna where his father was imprisoned, took the city, and captured the usurper, whom he sent to Aquileia, where Galla Placidia and her son were waiting.[29] The eastern army's taking of the city was marked by the striking of the Aquileia coin, showing Theodosius II with a nimbus, as Augustus, and Valentinian Caesar, without one.[30]

Following the capture of John, the usurper was paraded on the back of a donkey in the hippodrome at Aquileia before Galla Placidia and her 5-year-old son, was mutilated, and then executed in June or July of 425.[31] A few months later the expedition journeyed on to Rome, where the 6-year-old Caesar was crowned Augustus, again by Theodosius' representative Helion, on 23 October 425.[32] Staging such a major ceremonial event in the old imperial capital was an important move towards gaining the good will of the powerful Italian

---

[27] Kaegi (1968), 20–1; cf. Oost (1968a), 183–4.

[28] Olympiodorus, frg. 43.2; Philostorgius 13; Socrates 7.23; Cf. Bury (1919), 3; Matthews (1975), 380.

[29] Olympiodorus, frg. 43.1; 43.2; Cf. Philostorgius 13; also Marcellinus *comes*, s.a. 425 (1). Cf. Matthews (1975), 380. On the different versions of Aspar gaining entry to Ravenna: Olympiodorus has Ardaburius befriending his captors: frg. 43.1; 43.2; similarly, Philostorgius 13. Socrates has the piety of Theodosius II himself intervening, in the form of an angel guiding Aspar and his troops through the swamps of Ravenna and into the city (7.23); similarly John Ant., frg. 195. One source also reports that Aspar was offered the throne of the west himself at some time, but this is nowhere else recorded, while the *PLRE* suggests a date in the late 450s or early 460s for this: for details see *PLRE* 2.164–9; also Stein (1959), 1. 353–4. But for a different view, see Sivan (2011), ch. 4.

[30] *RIC* 10. 161.

[31] Olympiodorus, frg. 43.1, 43.2; cf. Philostorgius 13; Procopius, *Bell.* 3.3.8–9; John Ant., frg. 195; Hydatius 75(84). Cf. also Matthews (1975), 380.

[32] Olympiodorus frg. 43.1, 33.1; Marcellinus *comes*, s.a. 425 (2); Hydatius 76(85); Socrates 7.25; Philostorgius 12. 13; *Chron.pasch.* p. 580. Theophanes, AM 5916. Cf. also Bury (1919), 3; Holum (1982), 129; Sirago (1961), 249–54; Oost (1968a), 183–93; Matthews (1975), 379–81.

senatorial aristocracy still based there.[33] The ceremonial occasions of Valentinian's accession as Caesar, and the exhibition of the captured usurper John and his execution, followed by the elevation of Valentinian as Augustus at Rome where ceremonial accessions had become unusual by this point, sent a clear message that the new child-emperor's advisers knew the value of ceremonial display, and also betray notable signs of Constantinopolitan influence on this western ceremonial.[34] Theodosius II himself had apparently begun the journey westward to elevate Valentinian as Augustus personally, and the message of his seniority and conferral of *imperium* upon the new boy-emperor would have been all the more emphatically demonstrated if he had, but he had fallen ill at Thessalonica, and then returned home instead.[35] But celebrations were held at Constantinople in honour of the event: it was, after all, an eastern victory.[36]

Though Olympiodorus informs us that Helion placed the diadem on the boy's head, we have almost no other information about the ceremony, such as where in Rome it took place, who else was present, or whether the senate and military were involved (though we may assume they were).[37] Yet the deliberation with which these steps in Valentinian's rise were taken is worth noting: the child could certainly have been proclaimed Augustus at Ravenna or Aquileia—but it was at Rome that the advisers were determined his full accession should take place, exactly one year after his elevation as Caesar. It was a very long time since an emperor (rather than a usurper) had been made at Rome; yet the influence of the eastern advisers of Theodosius II sheds light on the reasons for the decision: in fact, the sequence of ceremonial events from June to October 425 all show signs of eastern input. In the east accessions had begun increasingly to take place amidst ceremonial at Constantinople itself: the Hebdomon had been the place of accession of Valens, Arcadius, and of course Honorius, and the procession following the latter's accession from the parade-ground to the palace through cheering crowds was described in rapturous terms by Claudian.[38] At Constantinople,

---

[33] Jordanes and Marcellinus mistakenly placed the coronation at Ravenna, but the evidence in general points to Rome: see *RIC* 10. 161; and also the fragmentary inscription from Sitifis in Mauretania which Wilkes has noted appears to commemorate the event at Rome: *CIL* 8. 8481 = *ILS* 802; see Wilkes (1972), 391–2, also below p. 235 and n. 51.

[34] On the significance of the use of the hippodrome for the humiliation of John and its derivation from eastern practices, see McCormick (1986), 59–60.

[35] Socrates 7.24, 25. The westward start of Theodosius II's journey is confirmed by *CTh.* 6.10.4, 6.22.8 (22 Sept. 425) given from Topisum in Thrace. Cf. Wilkes (1972), 391–2.

[36] Socrates 7.23. Cf. Kaegi (1968), 22.

[37] Olympiodorus, frg. 43.1, 33.1.

[38] On other late fourth- to mid-fifth-century accessions and their locations, and the Constantinopolitan influence apparent in Valentinian III's accession, see McEvoy (2010), 176–8. On Honorius accession at Constantinople and Claudian's description of the occasion, see above, pp. 138–9.

the context of an imperial capital had come to be seen as a more suitable stage for an imperial accession than the military-camp accessions more common in the west in the late fourth century, such as those of Gratian and Valentinian II. And, whether prompted by the time Galla Placidia and her children had spent in exile at Constantinople and the urban ceremonial that they might have witnessed there, or the presence of Helion (and presumably others) in establishing the new emperor, this eastern attitude towards the appropriate stage for such an occasion was now appearing in the west.

Naturally coins were minted to mark the occasion, showing the two victorious emperors in military dress, standing side by side, but even as Augustus, Valentinian III is a noticeably diminutive figure next to his adult colleague, as we might expect. The young emperor is shown crowned by the hand of God, wielding a cross which he stands on the head of a serpent with a human head.[39] In 426, in another show of imperial solidarity, the boy-emperor Valentinian III was consul for the second consecutive year with Theodosius II as his colleague.[40]

Undoubtedly the installation of Valentinian as emperor of the west was a victory for the Theodosian ruling house.[41] As one scholar has observed, Valentinian III was not restored as the west's legitimate ruler, but rather installed as the eastern nominee.[42] Yet there was much more to these events than Valentinian's lineage.[43] The sources reveal that Theodosius took his time in deciding to back Valentinian's cause, and the campaign was a most serious expense for the eastern government: it must have embarked upon this action for reasons beyond simple dynastic ideology. Attempting to depose an adult ruler with military backing and impose in his place a 5-year-old boy was hardly a project guaranteed of success, despite the familiarity of child-emperor rule in the west by this point. Yet Theodosius II and his advisers must have thought the campaign worth his while.

To justify the investment in Valentinian's cause which Theodosius II made, the eastern administration must have intended and expected to have a continuing influence on the new western government: and indeed, eastern involvement in campaigns against the Vandals in the 430s would confirm this maintained interest. The first *magister militum* of Valentinian's

---

[39] *RIC* 10. 161. The image of coronation by the hand of God was still an unusual one in the fifth century, and more commonly used on coinage celebrating the elevation of an Augusta, as with Eudoxia in 400 (see *RIC* 10. 64) and Pulcheria in 414 (*RIC* 10. 74), but had also been used for Honorius, see above, p. 206. McCormick (1986), 256; Kaegi (1968), 23–4.

[40] *CLRE* 386–7; Oost (1968a), 193.

[41] Heather (2000), 1.

[42] Gillett (1993), 20. Van Nuffelen also points out that Olympiodorus' history, which closes with the installation of Valentinian III as western emperor, presents a picture of the imposition of a tutelage on the west by the east: P. Van Nuffelen (forthcoming).

[43] Contra Oost (1968a), 193–4; Stevens (1933), 21, and Stein (1959), 1. 317.

administration, Flavius Felix, has no known career in the west (or in fact the east) before this point and cannot have been involved in the recent usurpation. While we must be cautious about making an argument from silence, one potential explanation for his sudden appearance in such a high post in the west is that he was an eastern nominee, particularly given his presence from the earliest days of this eastern-backed government.[44] It is not known how long the eastern army remained in the west after the victory, but it must have lingered for some time to ensure that the new government was secure and the leadership of the western military was established. The western consulship of Ardaburius in 427 may even suggest that an eastern military contingent under the general was still stationed in the west at this time.[45] It seems that Helion, the eastern *magister officiorum*, stayed some considerable time in the west after his part in the ceremony of October 425: he is not attested back in Constantinople until December 426, and any other official who may have accompanied him could have remained just as long.[46] But continuing eastern commitments to the western government in the years to come indicate that Theodosius II's court was not about to abandon the administration of Valentinian III to its own devices—not after such a substantial investment in its creation. The triumph of the campaign in favour of the new boy-emperor was a dramatic demonstration of the continuing unity of the eastern and western empires at this point—and of the overall supremacy of the eastern court.

Galla Placidia and Justa Grata Honoria

The new six-year-old Augustus was clearly not of an age to rule independently in any sense, and ancient and modern sources alike have assumed that for the next twelve years at least (until Valentinian's marriage at 18), it was the Augusta Galla Placidia who was truly ruling the west.[47] The appealing picture of the strong-willed empress running the government through the years of her son's minority has repeatedly found favour, and it has been asserted, for example, that Galla Placidia was responsible for western legislation issued from Aquileia before Valentinian became Augustus—such as the imperial constitution of 9 July 425, relating to the acts of the 'tyrant' John and

[44] Sirago (1961), 264–86; Kaegi (1968), 23 ff.; Moss (1973), 715.

[45] Kaegi (1968), 23. See similarly Sirago (1961), 264–6. Also on the east naming western consuls early in Valentinian III's reign: Oost (1968a), 209.

[46] Helion is addressed in a law issued in Constantinople on 23 December 426 (*CTh.* 6.27.20); see Honoré (1999), 255. See further below, p. 242.

[47] e.g. Socrates 7.24; Procopius, *Bell.* 3.3.9–13. Similarly Oost (1968a), 183–4; 197; Demougeot (1985), 196; Connor (2004), 69; Honoré (1999), 251; Neil (2009), 10; Sirago (1961), 248, 341; O'Flynn (1983), 76–8; now also Sivan (2011).

given in the names of Theodosius II and Valentinian Caesar.[48] Yet although this is an attractive idea, there is little evidence to support such an assumption, and it seems likely that the government of Theodosius II deserves more credit here.[49] Given eastern investment in the new western government (which was not even firmly established at this point), it is far more likely that before the campaign set out, Theodosius had decided on certain acts—and appointments to certain offices—which should be made at key moments in the campaign. Like Stilicho before her, Galla Placidia was in a very awkward position officially.[50] However much her rank and relationship to the new emperor might entitle her to the position of regent (and however much modern scholars repeatedly use the term to describe her role), the position itself simply did not exist. And while it has been argued that a very fragmentary inscription from Africa relating to Valentinian III and containing the word *tutela* indicates that Theodosius must therefore have granted an unprecedented but specific legal role to Placidia, once again this cannot be further substantiated.[51] In any case, even if the *tutela* mentioned does refer to Placidia, this term entails only legal guardianship, not control of government in the emperor's stead.

Galla Placidia was clearly a colourful personality, and there can be no doubt she was an important figure in her son's life. Her image frequently appeared on coinage under her son's rule, and during the first five years of Valentinian's reign, mints at Rome and Ravenna were striking both for the emperor and for his mother, whose issues were in the style of those for eastern empresses: she was an Augusta, and this was appropriate.[52] A group of multiples from Ravenna are particularly notable, showing a reverse of Valentinian III enthroned and wearing a diadem, holding his mappa, with the legend SALVS REI-PVBLICAE, and a bust of his mother on the obverse, a *Chi-Rho* on her shoulder.[53] Galla Placidia remained an important reminder of the previous legitimate western ruler, and perhaps also of the military successes of her late husband and the new emperor's father. Yet this degree of

---

[48] *CSirm.* 6 (9 July 425); cf. *CTh.* 16.2.46 (6 July 425), 16.2.47 (8 October 425); 16.5.62 (17 July 425), 16.5.63 (4 Aug. 425), 16.5.64 (6 Aug. 425). See Oost (1968a), 191–2; (1968b), 119–20; Wilkes (1972), 389.

[49] Sivan emphasizes the potential role of Galla Placidia in legislation issued during her son's time as Caesar, due to the unusual use of the term 'pope' in *CTh.* 16.5.62 (17 July 425), a term used by the empress in her extant correspondence: Sivan (2011), ch. 4. See similarly Honoré (1999), 249. The empress' role remains speculative however: the term 'pope', though not yet widespread, is used in other fifth-century western texts to refer to the bishop of Rome: see e.g. Prosper 1350, 1376.

[50] Oost (1968a), 194–5.

[51] *CIL* 8. 8481 = *ILS* 802 (with word *tutela*); Mazzarino (1942), 111, n. 2; Oost assumes the term refers to Galla Placidia (1968a), 194–5, as do Sivan (2011), ch. 2, and Kelly (1999), 175. The exact location of the inscription is disputed: Sivan reports it is from the African town of Lambaesis, and Kelly from Sitifis (Mauretania).

[52] *RIC* 10. 62.

[53] From the Velp hoard: *RIC* 10. 162–3.

advertisement of an Augusta was not unusual for women of the Theodosian house. The Augusta Flaccilla, first wife of Theodosius I, appeared frequently on imperial coinage until her death in 387.[54] Coinage in honour of Arcadius' wife Aelia Eudoxia displayed her being crowned by the hand of God upon the occasion of her elevation to the rank of Augusta.[55] When Pulcheria, the sister of Theodosius II, became Augusta in 414, her official portrait was dedicated in the senate-house at Constantinople, along with her fellow-Augusti, the eastern and western emperors.[56] Similarly, coins would be struck for the Augusta Honoria, Valentinian III's elder sister.[57]

Placidia was a very wealthy woman, with her own imperial household, and the *Notitia dignitatum* recorded the existence of a separate bureau of accounts devoted specifically to her assets.[58] But we know too that her daughter, in turn, had her own household while still a young and unmarried woman, as did the sisters of Theodosius II in Constantinople.[59] Placidia's appearance on her son's coinage and her own wealth undoubtedly marked her as an important figure in the reign: it did not, however, imply that she was the only important figure, or that all new initiatives of the government can be attributed to her. It should be remembered, for a start, that the imperial consistory, where all major decisions of the government were ultimately made, was barred to women: there is no evidence that either Galla Placidia, or indeed her niece Pulcheria in the east, though their influence on a personal level within the imperial household is undoubted, could attend these meetings where the true business of government took place.[60] Though it is indisputable that Galla Placidia was a prominent figure in her son's establishment, it is on a personal level, in the guise of power behind the throne, rather than as a regent with any constitutional rights or powers that her role should be viewed. Nevertheless, as the only adult member of the imperial house in the west throughout the 420s and 430s, and a familiar figure also from the reign of Honorius, we should not be surprised to find her role in Valentinian's rule emphasized, even amplified through coinage and other source materials, including those emanating from the east—as with the quote from Socrates at the beginning of this chapter, where it is asserted that the administration of the west was entrusted to her in 425.[61] Her presence in the new western regime could provide reassurance for

---

[54] Holum (1982), 32.

[55] *RIC* 10. 64; Holum (1982), 65–6.

[56] Holum (1982), 97.

[57] Discussed further below, pp. 238–9.

[58] *Not.Dig.Occ.* 15.

[59] Bury (1919), 9.

[60] Harries (forthcoming). Ambrose does not report on the empress Justina attending such meetings, and we would expect him to do so if she did.

[61] Socrates, 7.24, and above, p. 223. Zosimus makes a similar comment on Justina being sent to Gaul with Valentinian II in 388/9: 4.47.1–2.

western elites, especially if eastern bureaucrats as well as military men were prominent during the first few years of her son's reign.

In the late 420s, only a few years after her son's accession, Galla Placidia caused to be constructed a basilica dedicated to St John the Evangelist at Ravenna, which survives today in a much-altered state from the original fifth-century building.[62] The inscription put up in the church and preserved by Agnellus records that it was built in gratitude for the preservation of the empress and her children from perils at sea, and in fulfilment of a vow made during the tempest which had endangered them (the occasion of their danger is not specified, though presumably it related to their journey to or from Constantinople).[63] In addition to the inscription, Agnellus also describes a cycle of mosaics in the church which depicted a large number of members of the imperial family, both living and dead. Along with an image of Christ handing a book to St John, and scenes of ships sailing the sea (possibly showing Placidia and her children in one of them), no less than ten emperors were displayed on the triumphal arch.[64] On the right-hand side were named Constantinus, Theodosius, Arcadius, Honorius, and Theodosius nep, and on the left, Valentinianus, Gratianus, Constantius, Gratianus nep and Johannes nep. As a number of scholars have pointed out, 'nep' is most likely to have been a misreading of 'nb' (= *nobilissimus puer*)—thus the mosaics showed the emperors Constantine I, Theodosius I, Arcadius, and Honorius, Valentinian I, Gratian, Constantius III, and the dead infant sons of Theodosius I (and Galla Placidia's brothers) Gratian and Johannes, and her own late son Theodosius.[65]

It has been argued that these images indicated a deliberate attempt on the part of Placidia to distance her son's rule from that of Theodosius II, but it is difficult to see how such a view holds up against the fact that both eastern and western emperors were apparently depicted, or the eastern investment in the creation of Valentinian III's regime and his betrothal to Licinia Eudoxia.[66] The more convincing explanation is a simpler one: that it was natural to make the most of the boy-emperor Valentinian's connections to as many past emperors as possible in order to increase the sense of his legitimacy, and all the more natural for the emphasis to be on western emperors, given the context. This need not have involved any alternative motive of insulting

---

[62] For the most recent discussion of the basilica and its architecture and artwork see Deliyannis (2010), 67–9.

[63] The dedication reads: *Galla Placidia Augusta cum filio suo Placido Valentiniano Aug. et filia sua Justa Grata Honoria Augusta liberationis periculum maris votum solvent* (*CIL* 11, 276 = *ILS* 818). Also recorded by Agnellus 42. Cf. Deliyannis (2010), 67; Bury (1919), 3; Wilkes (1972), 390; Muntz (1885), 118–20. Peter Chrysologos' *Sermon* 99 may have been preached for the dedication of the church.

[64] Deliyannis provides a plan of how the cycle may have looked: (2010), 63–70. On the emperors depicted in the mosaics, see also Rebenich (1985), 375–7.

[65] Most recently Deliyannis (2010), 68.

[66] Holum (1982), 128.

Theodosius II's lineage; moreover, there is a further, overtly eastern, aspect of the mosaic depictions which has often been overlooked. In addition to these ten emperors, perhaps appearing as busts in medallions upon the triumphal arch, there were some further imperial images on a wall above the clergy's bench, and these apparently displayed the eastern emperor Arcadius and his wife Eudocia on the right, and their son Theodosius II and his wife Eudoxia on the left.[67] There could scarcely have been a more public statement of the new western government's awareness of its indebtedness to its eastern counterpart, and of the east's continuing influence on Valentinian III's government in the late 420s. Clearly, as many emperors as possible—eastern or western—were being called upon to back up the new western child-emperor's claim. These imperial images in the new church at Ravenna were undoubtedly intended to advertise the impressive dynastic heritage of the new western emperor, and in a striking and novel way, which can only have enhanced the aura of the imperial family's piety and divine blessing.[68]

Aside from the young emperor and his mother, there was yet another member of the western imperial family to take into account in these opening years of the new reign: Justa Grata Honoria, the emperor's older sister. Born between October 417 and September 418, Honoria was thus around the age of 7 or 8 when her brother became Augustus in 425.[69] Not long after Valentinian's accession, or possibly at the same time, a most unusual step was taken: Honoria was made Augusta.[70] The west now had not only a child-emperor, but a child-empress as well. Whether the initiative was taken by Theodosius II or by the new western government itself is unclear: if the elevation took place at the same time as Valentinian's, then presumably it was an eastern decision. It is an event largely overlooked by sources, but the numismatic evidence is convincing: coins minted at Ravenna between 425 and 430 display a bust of Honoria which is smaller than her mother's, but otherwise with the same Victory and Cross type, and the legend: DN IVST GRAT HONORIA PF AVG.[71] In addition, the dedicatory inscription of the Church of St John at

---

[67] Recorded by Rossi (1572), 85–6. See Deliyannis (2010), 68. The Arcadius and Eudoxia figures have been mistakenly identified as Theodosius II's children (Brubaker (1997), 54) but this cannot be the case: if Theodosius ever had a son Arcadius (which is dubious) he was never emperor and thus not entitled to be called 'Dominus' as this Arcadius figure was, while Theodosius II's daughter Eudoxia was not an Augusta (and thus could not be called 'Domina') until 439: it is surely the parents of Theodosius II who are depicted. See also on this point, Holum (1982), 178, n. 14.

[68] Deliyannis (2010), 68.

[69] Bury (1919), 1.

[70] Ibid. 3–4. Stickler mistakenly places the elevation of Honoria as Augusta to 437, the date of Valentinian's marriage: (2002), 126–7.

[71] *RIC* 10. 164. A vicennalian coin of Honoria, very similar to those of Galla Placidia struck at Ravenna, Rome, and Aquileia, has also been found: Bury (1919), 4. Cf. De Salis (1867), 211–12; Oost (1968a), 193.

Ravenna specifically refers to her as 'Justa Grata Honoria Augusta'.[72] It is hard to find any other instance in Roman history of the creation of a child-empress, apart from the elevation of Pulcheria, Theodosius II's sister, to the rank of Augusta at the age of 15 (in 414). One suggestion is that Pulcheria's elevation in the 410s had provided the idea, and that the plan was therefore that if Galla Placidia should die whilst Valentinian III remained a minor, his sister would take over their mother's role.[73] This is certainly one possibility: Honoria was only a year or two older than her brother, but Pulcheria was similarly only slightly older than Theodosius II. A further possibility, however, given child mortality rates, is that if Valentinian himself had died, his sister was already there in the west, a proclaimed Augusta, and could provide a neat back-up plan: she could have been quickly married to a suitable candidate (though, as noted above, these could be hard to find), who could then have been substituted in her brother's place, much as Pulcheria herself would one day be married to Marcian when Theodosius II died.

Regime-building

The nature of Valentinian III's accession as a 6-year-old western emperor, and the early tone of his administration, were heavily influenced by eastern interests which continued to maintain a stake in the new government they had created, and to present the new boy-emperor as junior to, even dependent on, his eastern co-Augustus. But even (or perhaps especially) with his eastern military backing, Valentinian's administration needed to make efforts to gain the support of key local power-groups. That the usurper John had found some support amongst the aristocracy—although not necessarily of a very active kind—is indicated by Olympiodorus' record of Probus, the son of Olybrius, of the illustrious Anicii family, having celebrated his praetorian games at great expense under the usurper's rule.[74] The choice of Rome for Valentinian's formal investiture as Augustus was a highly significant one and, as noted above, unusual by this point, and the pomp and ceremony of the occasion must have been calculated to impress the local population as much as possible with the power of the new government and the might of its eastern backing. The issue of coins for the occasion displaying Roma enthroned and holding a

---

[72] It is interesting to note that the names chosen for Galla Placidia's first child specifically advertised her connections with the houses of both Valentinian and Theodosius: Justa and Grata were the names of the sisters of Valentinian II, Galla Placidia's aunts, whom she may well have known—they were still alive in 393 and we know nothing of them thereafter; the name Honoria must have been intended to mark the princess' blood tie to her uncle Honorius.

[73] Bury (1919), 5.

[74] Olympiodorus, frg. 41.2. Cf. Matthews (1975), 356.

figure of Victory was all part of the show: John had been proclaimed at Rome, so it was important to blot out his memory as far as possible with the new young emperor's presence.[75]

A number of early imperial constitutions were also addressed directly to the senate, in a clear bid for their support. On 3 January 426 a constitution was given at Rome of which an excerpt is preserved in the *Theodosian Code*. Presumably the address began by assuring the senators of the respect which their rights would be accorded under the new regime.[76] The surviving excerpt of the law goes on to declare that informers were to be denounced, senators only to be tried in the court of the city prefect, tenants of imperial estates would be constrained by the same laws which even emperors must observe, and provincial governors were not to impose compulsory services on senators.[77] A further constitution of a similar tone was issued the following month: graciously remitting to the senate a part of the *aurum oblaticium*, the obligatory gift of gold traditionally made by the senators to the emperor at New Year, while another part was to be remitted to the city of Rome itself.[78] Like other governments before his, that of the child-emperor Valentinian III was well aware of the importance of courting senatorial backing—particularly in view of recent events.

Early efforts to establish the young emperor's position in relation to the church, and the appearance of piety and claim to divine blessing (accompanying his triumphant accession), can also be found in early ecclesiastical legislation of his reign. In a law given at Aquileia, under the names of Theodosius II and Valentinian Caesar, on 4 August 425, and addressed to the proconsul of Africa, it was declared that privileges granted to the church and clerics by previous laws were all to be preserved.[79] And similarly, only two days later legislation was issued announcing that, 'with eager devotion', the privileges of the churches which 'the tyrant' had begrudged were all to be restored: namely, that whatever privileges had been established by previous 'sainted emperors' should be confirmed and maintained, while this law also went on to rule against heretics, Jews, and pagans.[80] Further legislation in 426 was concerned with confirming ecclesiastical legislation from previous reigns and the disposal

---

[75] MacCormack (1981), 228; Oost (1968*a*), 207.

[76] Oost (1968*a*), 215–16.

[77] *CTh.* 10.10.33, 10.26.2 (both issued 3 Jan. 426) and similarly 5.1.7 (30 Jan. 426); see Honoré (1999), 249. For similar early laws dealing with judicial matters and asserting the equality of the emperor and his subjects before the law, see *CTh.* 1.4.3 (6 Nov. 426); 11.30.68 (25 Feb. 429); *CJ* 1.14.4(429); *CJ* 11.71.5.1(429); also giving rise to unfounded claims of Galla Placidia's influence: Oost (1968*b*), 114–21. For senatorial privileges, see *CTh.* 10.10.33 (27 Dec. 426).

[78] *CTh.* 6.2.25 (24 Feb. 426). Also likely to have been aimed at senatorial interests: *CTh.* 4.10.3 (30 Mar. 426); *CJ* 11.48.18(426). Honoré (1999), 249; Matthews (1975), 356; also Oost (1968*a*), 216.

[79] *CTh.* 16.2.46 (4 Aug. 425).

[80] *CTh.* 16.2.47 (6 Aug. 425). A fuller version of this law is preserved at *CSirm.* 6. See further: Oost (1968*a*), 186.

of property of apostates from Christianity, and the rights to inheritance of Christian heirs of Jews or Samaritans.[81] As the experience of the legitimate homoean emperor Valentinian II against the orthodox usurper Magnus Maximus had illustrated, being able to claim the moral high ground in religious matters could be a powerful ideological advantage for an emperor. Although such actions might be expected of any new orthodox ruler, it is notable that religious matters were addressed even before Valentinian became an Augustus, with legislation issued in the name of Theodosius Augustus and Valentinian Caesar—setting the tone for the new administration even before the child became emperor.

These provisions for the conciliation of both the senate and the church are much as might be expected at the launch of a new emperor, perhaps especially one established through civil war, and look noticeably similar to the measures of the new government of Honorius and Stilicho in 395. But the legislation of the first few years of Valentinian III's reign has attracted the attention of scholars for a couple of reasons. First, and unusually, after these initial provisions relating to the privileges of the church and senate, in November 426 a so-called 'mini-code' was issued by the new government, addressed to the senate, and focused on systematizing the law in relation to sources of judgements and rules of succession.[82] Secondly, after the initial few years of the reign, the rate of legislation issuing from Valentinian III's court declines rapidly: one detailed study has highlighted that while twelve laws were issued in 425–6 under Valentinian III's name, only a further twelve laws from the west between 427 and 437 are preserved in the *Theodosian Code*.[83] Law codification was an act of asserting legitimacy in itself, so the appearance of the 'mini-code' should not come as a surprise in that respect.[84] But why should the rate of legislation in the west decline from 427 to 437?[85] One suggested answer seems to fit well with the image of a very eastern-influenced and eastern-supported western government in its first few years: that the surviving western laws of 425–6 should be attributed to a single *quaestor*. It is argued that this *quaestor* was an easterner who had travelled with the

---

[81] On apostates from Christianity, see *CTh.* 16.7.7 (7 Apr. 426); there were also provisions that if the kinsman thereafter made sacrifices, they should be deprived of their inheritance. On the inheritance of Christian heirs of Jews and Samaritans: *CTh.* 16.8.28 (8 Apr. 426).

[82] On the 'mini-code', dated to 7 November 426, and the twelve surviving excerpts of it, see Honoré (1999), 249–50; also Harries (1999), 37.

[83] Honoré also notes that seven of these twelve laws are dated to 428–9, when Volusianus was prefect: (1999), 251–2.

[84] Harries (1999), 37.

[85] One factor we may need to take into account is the potential gap in the record of western laws during the 430s between when the bulk of western legislation was sent to Constantinople for inclusion in the *Theodosian Code* prior to its promulgation; however, as Honoré points out, some western legislation from this period does still survive, and indeed any general laws enacted during this period should still have been included in the record: Honoré (1998), 249.

expedition from Constantinople and was appointed to serve the new government of Valentinian III in its first few years before returning to the east. The individual suggested is Antiochus, who would in the 430s be chairman of the *Theodosian Code* project in its first stages.[86]

Although the identity of this *quaestor* cannot be proven, it does not seem unreasonable to assume that there was a team of eastern officials who had travelled from Constantinople with the military expedition—including Helion, the east's *magister officiorum*, perhaps Flavius Felix, the soon-to-be *magister militum*, and a *quaestor* (and possibly others) who were to take responsibility for the establishment of the new government's administration and its earliest legislation. It has also been suggested that the historian Olympiodorus probably also came west with Helion and the military campaign to establish Valentinian III as emperor.[87] Some of these easterners, like Felix (if indeed he was an easterner), could have been expected to stay in the longer term, while others, like Helion, Olympiodorus, and perhaps this *quaestor*, were short-term assignments. Although this theory remains hypothetical, it would at least accord with the picture of eastern investment in the new western government, and provide an explanation for the slowing of legislation after November 426, when the eastern officials may have returned to Constantinople.

The possibility (even likelihood) that some of the officials of the early years of Valentinian III's regime were eastern imports also raises the question of what place the local senatorial aristocracy was given in the new administration, and what efforts at conciliation were made by the new government (apart from the legislation discussed above). A growing involvement of the great Italian senatorial families in imperial office-holding through this period has been observed, which is again indicative of the efforts the new government was making to build bridges with the senatorial aristocracy.[88] From the mid-to-late 420s onwards, the office of praetorian prefect in particular was often in the hands of members of major Italian aristocratic families, such as Anicius Auchenius Bassus in 426, Rufius Antonius Agrypnius Volusianus in 428/9, and Nicomachus Flavianus in 431/2.[89] This was not merely a phenomenon of

---

[86] Honoré (1999), 253–7; Harries also suggests eastern input into the early legislation of the new western government is likely: Harries (1999), 37, and 63, n. 28. The suggestion the *quaestor* was Antiochus is also followed by Sivan (2011), ch. 4.

[87] Matthews (1975), 383; also Cameron (1969), 490–1 and Gillett (1993), 13–14.

[88] Jones (1964a), 1. 177; Sundwall (1915), 22; Matthews (1975), 358–9; Wormald (1976), 218–22.

[89] For Bassus, see *CTh*. 10.26.1 (6 Mar. 426); 16.7.7 (7 Apr. 426); 16.8.28 (7 Apr. 426). He had also been *comes rei privatae* in 424 before his prefecture: *CTh*. 16.2.47; 5.64 (6 Aug. 425); *PLRE* 2. 219–20. For Volusianus, see *CTh*. 7.13.22 (25 Feb. 428); *CJ* 1.14.4 (11 June 429); *PLRE* 2. 1184–5. For Flavianus, see *CTh* 11.1.36 (29 Apr. 431)–6.23.3 (24 Mar. 432); *ILS* 2948; *PLRE* 1.345–7; On Valentinian III's praetorian prefects in general, and the family connections linking some of them, see Weber (1989), 476 ff.

the rule of Valentinian III, of course; it was a continuation of a trend which had already existed in the time of Honorius, and would continue throughout the reign of his nephew. Petronius Maximus, who had already held high office as a very young man under Honorius, went on to hold numerous major offices under Valentinian III, as urban prefect some time before 433, western consul in that year, and praetorian prefect of Italy in *c.*435 and again from 439 to 441.[90] Another senator, Trygetius, who had been praetorian prefect under Honorius in 423, also continued to be prominent under Valentinian III, serving as ambassador to the Vandals in 435 and later on to Attila.[91] While some of these efforts are late to be considered as part of initial regime-building, they do represent the continuation of imperial overtures towards the aristocracy and the consolidation of past efforts.

A particularly pointed attempt to garner the support of aristocratic circles at Rome may be seen in the rehabilitation of the memory of Nicomachus Flavianus the elder, who, as discussed in the material relating to Honorius' accession, had been heavily involved in the usurpation of Eugenius and had committed suicide on the latter's defeat. Yet the younger Nicomachus Flavianus had gone on to hold high office under Honorius, and in 431 and 432 would hold the praetorian prefecture of Italy under Valentinian III, as noted above. Furthermore, in a letter to the senate at around this time the boy-emperor declared the rehabilitation of the elder Flavianus' memory.[92] Flavianus was connected with many aristocratic Roman families, and the rehabilitation may be seen as a bid for continuing wide-ranging senatorial support—perhaps relating to the conflict between the generals Boniface and Aetius in these years.[93] Even at this stage of the reign, the government was still building bridges with allies from among the senatorial aristocracy. The continued prominence of senators like Flavianus and Petronius Maximus reflects the genuine social and political monopoly exercised by such senatorial families at Rome, but also reflects the imperial administration's awareness of that predominance and the need to continue to court it.[94] It has been argued

---

[90] *ILS* 809; and *CTh.* 10.10.26 (25 July 415); see Chastagnol (1962), 281 f.; Matthews (1975), 359; Oost (1968*a*), 231. Panciera also suggests on the basis of an inscription in the Forum Romanum that Petronius Maximus may have been appointed as Valentinian III's tutor early in the reign: potentially as an honorary position only, but such an appointment would certainly be a mark of imperial favour: Panciera (1996), 277–97.

[91] For the details, see Matthews (1975), 359–60.

[92] *ILS* 2948, incorporating an *oratio* of the emperor, cf. Stein (1959), 1. 340; Sirago (1961), 289–90; Matthews (1975), 360; Hedrick (2000), 223–4. It has been argued (by Oost (1968*a*), 231) that Galla Placidia arranged the rehabilitation in the hope of gaining senatorial support against the rising power of Aetius, but as Hedrick points out, it might just as easily be claimed Aetius engineered the rehabilitation to garner such support himself, and most recently Cameron has suggested Flavianus' family itself pushed for the rehabilitation: Cameron (2011), 204–5; we simply cannot make firm conclusions from the available evidence.

[93] Oost (1968*a*), 231. Cf. Weber (1989), 479–80.

[94] Matthews (1975), 360.

that the appointment of men like Volusianus as praetorian prefect of Italy in 428–9 and of Nicomachus Flavianus the younger to the same post in 431–2 was part of an attempt by Galla Placidia to create a cabal of political opponents to the general Aetius at court.[95] Given that Aetius was almost constantly in Gaul throughout the late 420s, the opportunity to create such opposition must certainly have been available; yet again, we cannot know whether Placidia was genuinely responsible for these appointments, or that they were made with any particular aim of causing problems for Aetius.

Aetius and the Huns

Overtures towards key power-groups like the senatorial aristocracy and church leaders were to be expected from any new ruler seeking to build up the support base of his new government: in this case, when the new ruler was not only a child but one imposed upon the throne by the might of the east, approaches to local power-bases were all the more vital. The western military was, of course, the other utterly crucial group who needed to be won over to the support of an emperor for whom a civil war had been fought, and who would be unable to take on the role of active military leader for years—if he ever did. This was bound to be more complicated than simply passing laws and granting privileges. Moreover, it brought to the fore a key player whom the eastern government had not anticipated being part of the picture: Flavius Aetius.

Aetius was a Roman of noble rank, the son of a *magister equitum* (probably under Stilicho), and in his youth he had spent time as a hostage for the Roman government not only for a period of three years in the hands of Alaric and the Visigoths, but also with the Huns—a further testament to his father's prominence under the previous regime.[96] Merobaudes in the 440s would write that Aetius' martial skill had been learnt at the courts of the Goths and Huns themselves, who could not help but marvel at his prowess.[97] Aetius' experience with the Huns in particular, and the contacts he retained with them, were to play a vital role in his own position with regard to the rule of Valentinian III, a

---

[95] Zecchini (1983), 157.

[96] On Aetius as the son of a *magister equitum*, see Greg.Tur. 2.8; Jord, *Get.* 176. On Aetius' background and the sources, see *PLRE* 2. 21–9; Bury (1923), 1. 241; Oost (1968a), 212–14; O'Flynn (1983), 77. On his time as a hostage, see Greg.Tur 2.8; Prosper 1310. Cf. also Merobaudes, *Carm.* IV.35–47, *Pan.* II.127–43. Also Coulon (2000), 29–43; O'Flynn (1983), 77; Frank (1969), 188–9. His period of captivity with the Goths was probably c.405–8, and with the Huns from around 410, probably in the middle Danube area: Heather (1995), 18; although for arguments for alternative years, see Maenchen-Helfen (1973), 68, n. 266, and Coulon (2000), 45–8.

[97] Merobaudes, *Pan.* II.125–42. Cf. Greg.Tur 2.8.

role which the eastern drive of Valentinian's accession had not foreseen. Aetius was one of the military men who had supported John's usurpation, and also held the office of *cura palatii* under the short-lived regime.[98] When the threat of eastern military action against him began to be realized, John had sent Aetius off with funds to seek Hunnic reinforcements, probably from Pannonia, with which to bolster his position: Aetius, with his Hunnic contacts, was the ideal ambassador to send on such a mission, and he seems to have achieved spectacular success.[99] The sources record that Aetius returned leading 60,000 men; while this is (almost certainly) an exaggeration, it is clear he returned commanding a substantial Hunnic force.[100] Unfortunately for the usurper, he arrived at Ravenna three days after John had been executed. After some initial skirmishing between Aetius' Hunnic army and the eastern army of Aspar, the new ministers of the soon-to-be Valentinian III were forced to enter into negotiations with Aetius, who persuaded his Hunnic forces to go home in return for payment in gold. Aetius himself had to be found a role in the young emperor's administration: he was given the rank of *comes*, and sent off to wage the new emperor's campaigns in Gaul.[101]

Aetius' appearance on the scene, and the new western government's need to accommodate him, betrayed a serious weakness in the boy-emperor's hold on power and a new phenomenon in western imperial politics. The barbarian might which Aetius could harness in his own support, which lay entirely outside of imperial control, and could as easily be used for as against the government, was a new and frightening force in western affairs. Aetius posed an unforeseen but genuine challenge to the new emperor: Valentinian III's government, and indeed the eastern generals who were the key players in the establishment of the government, would not have entered into negoti- ations with Aetius if he could have been defeated and executed, and the Hunnic mercenaries absorbed into the existing military establishment or destroyed: it would have been a much neater result, and it seems a mistake to view Aetius as the weaker party in the resolution that was devised.[102] But eastern strategists planning the campaign to impose Valentinian III on the west simply had not bargained for a Roman general with outside sources of support, and the Hunnic might which Aetius was able to call upon for so much of his career would prove to be a serious limiting factor for eastern influence on the western realm. The fact that Aetius' support derived

---

[98] Oost (1968*a*), 187; O'Flynn (1983), 77; Coulon argues this was less a civilian post than that of commander of the palace guards (2000), 53–7.

[99] Greg.Tur 2.8. See Maenchen-Helfen (1973), 77. Cf. Harries (1994*a*), 74.

[100] John Ant., frg. 196; Prosper 1291. Cf. Heather (2000), 4. On the exaggeration of the number, see Thompson (1996), 55, who suggests 6,000 instead of 60,000.

[101] Olympiodorus, frg. 43.2; Philostorgius 14; also Wilkes (1972), 391; Maenchen-Helfen (1973), 77; Oost (1968*a*), 189–90; Matthews (1975), 381.

[102] Contra O'Flynn (1983), 76.

from outside of imperial control made him a far more dangerous figure than any of the generals involved in past child-emperor reigns in the west, and made the potential of a partnership arrangement with him even more potent: he was offering resources and manpower which the state did not possess, and when facing Aspar outside Ravenna had nothing to lose. The settlement of 425 between the new western government and Aetius was only the very beginning of a long struggle to keep one or other of the western generals from gaining control of the young emperor's government.

The three generals

Aetius was not the only western general seeking a stake in Valentinian III's administration. Castinus had fled or been exiled at the time of John's fall, but one of the generals who had been his rival for power under Honorius still remained in place, and moreover had remained staunchly loyal to Galla Placidia: Boniface, who had apparently travelled to Africa after a disagreement with Castinus and from there sent aid to the exiled empress in Constantinople.[103] Yet when young Valentinian III was proclaimed Augustus, it was not Boniface who was the new *magister militum*, but Flavius Felix.[104] This again suggests that the choice for this key role lay not in the hands of Galla Placidia but the eastern government, who may (very possibly with Placidia's agreement) have felt a compromise candidate the best option.[105] While Felix held the highest military rank in the realm, and at some point before 430 also acquired the title of *patricius*, Boniface was merely *comes Africae*, and rapidly ran into conflict with the *magister militum* whose position he had probably expected to occupy.[106] Procopius preserves a colourful tale of court intrigue surrounding the three generals. Though Aetius was apparently in Gaul in the late 420s and Felix was in command of Italy (and the court),

[103] On Castinus' fate, see Wilkes (1972), 387–91; O'Flynn (1983), 75; Oost (1968a), 190; Freeman (1887), 432. On Boniface's activity, see in general: Bury (1919), 2; O'Flynn (1983), 75; Oost (1968a), 172–3. See also above, p. 216.

[104] For Felix, see *PLRE* 2. 461–2; and above, pp. 233–4.

[105] As suggested by Sirago (1961), 265–6; similarly, Stickler (2002), 38; Freeman (1887), 433; Zecchini (1983), 142. Oost disagrees: (1968a), 210, 214–15. Coulon also suggests Felix was Placidia's choice, precisely because he was not an established general, was unknown to the western armies, and might therefore put an end to the rivalries of other generals: Coulon (2000), 94–6. It has been suggested that Felix did have a past career in the west, on the basis of the name of his wife Padusia (see Oost (1968a), 170, with n. 2): a 'Spadusa' was mentioned by Olympiodorus (frg. 38) as a confidante of Galla Placidia during the early 420s: see also *PLRE* 2. 1024. This seems a tenuous basis upon which to ascribe to Felix a western past, however. On the deterioration of relations between the three generals see now also Merrills and Miles (2010), 52–3.

[106] For Felix as *patricius* see Hydatius 84(94). There has been debate over exactly when Felix was granted the rank of 'patrician' however: e.g. Sundwall (1915), n. 170; Oost (1968a), 228; Sirago (1961), 284; O'Flynn (1983), 77–8.

Procopius tells a story of Aetius slandering Boniface to Galla Placidia, while also writing to Boniface himself that the empress was plotting against him, with the result that when Boniface was summoned to court, he refused to come and instead went into rebellion.[107] It is not impossible that Aetius was to blame—he would within a few years be facing Boniface across a battlefield—but just as possible that Flavius Felix was behind these devious machinations, and indeed Prosper, writing much closer in time to the events, attributes blame only to Felix and makes no mention of Aetius at this point.[108] At any rate, when a punitive force was sent against Boniface it came from the court and under Felix's instruction, though it was swiftly defeated by the rebel count.[109] Two embassies to Africa followed, the first led by Sigisvult, the *comes rei militares*, and the second by the *vir illustris* Darius, but further bloodshed was avoided, and in 429, Boniface was reconciled to the western imperial government (though only, according to Procopius, when the devious efforts of Aetius were uncovered).[110]

In 430 the *magister militum* Felix himself, his wife, and a cleric named Grunnitus were assassinated in Ravenna on the steps of the Ursiana Basilica.[111] The precise reasons for the killings remain unknown: though, according to Prosper, Felix had been involved in religious politics for some years, having allegedly in 426 ordered the killing of Bishop Patroclus of Arles, a former client of Constantius III.[112] Felix's death was described as the result of a military riot (although Prosper also says he was accused of conspiring against Aetius)—and although he had been absent in Gaul since 425 and Felix's known conflict to date had been with Boniface, the sources have tended to attribute responsibility for the general's death to Aetius.[113] Yet there were surely two generals who benefited from Felix's death: Boniface was restored to the rank of *comes Africae* which he had been deprived of due to his rebellion,

---

[107] Procopius, *Bell.* 3.15–36.

[108] Prosper 1294; Freeman (1887), 437; also Moss (1973), 715; Coulon (2000), 97–8.

[109] According to Prosper, the campaign was commanded by Mavortius, Gallio, and Sanoeces, all of whom were killed in the course of the conflict: Prosper 1294. For discussion of the accusations against Boniface and the failed expedition to Africa, see O'Flynn (1983), 78–9; Oost (1968a), 222–3; Sirago (1961), 220–2.

[110] Procopius, *Bell.* 3.27–9; on the embassies, see the detailed account of Mathisen, mainly concerned with the role of Sigisvult, and also Maximinus, the Arian bishop who accompanied him: Mathisen (1999), 176–83; also Merrills and Miles (2010), 53; Coulon (2000), 102–5.

[111] Prosper 1303; Hydatius 84(94); John Ant., frg. 201.3; Marcellinus *comes*, s.a. 430, 2; Agnellus 31. Aetius is usually seen as behind the murders, see e.g. Bury (1923), 1. 243; Oost (1968a), 229–30; O'Flynn (1983), 79; Heather (2000), 5.

[112] Prosper 1292; see further Coulon (2000), 96–7; Mathisen (1989), 73; Oost (1968a), 211–12.

[113] Freeman argues against Aetius being responsible, however, on the grounds of his not being even in Italy at the time: (1887), 444; similarly Coulon (2000), 99–101.

and in 429 or 430 Aetius was made *magister militum per Gallias*.[114] Aetius'
achievement of the higher rank may suggest he was complicit in Felix's
removal; however, Felix's power did not devolve automatically upon him.
Despite Boniface having met with little success in his campaigns against the
Vandals (who had crossed to North Africa in 429: discussed further below), in
432 it was nevertheless he who was invited to Ravenna, supposedly through
the influence of Galla Placidia, to be named *magister militum praesentalis*.[115]
Aetius had been granted the consulate for the same year, perhaps in the hope
that he would accept Boniface's supremacy, but his own considerable success
in his Gallic campaigns had ensured that he remained a firm rival for
power.[116]

When Boniface was summoned to Ravenna, therefore, Aetius came too, and
the armies of the two generals clashed near Ariminum. Though Boniface won
the day, he was mortally wounded, with his son-in-law Sebastianus swiftly
named his successor.[117] Aetius again found himself in a position which for
most would surely only have foretold disaster, as a rebel who had waged civil
war against the emperor's supreme commander, and been defeated. Yet once
again Aetius turned to the source of personal support which had been his
salvation in 425 and made him so much more dangerous a general than either
Felix or Boniface: the Huns. First withdrawing to his own estates and then
travelling to Pannonia, Aetius gathered a substantial Hunnic force, marched
back to Italy, and demanded yet another settlement with Valentinian III's
government.[118] By the end of 433 both of Aetius' original military rivals,

---

[114] For Boniface's restoration: Augustine, *Ep.* 229–31; also Procopius, *Bell.* 3.29–30. For
Aetius' elevation as *magister militum per Gallias* after successes against the Goths and Franks
in Gaul: Prosper 1298, 1300; Jordanes, *Get.* 176; Sidonius, *Carm.* 5.212 f. Cf. O'Flynn (1983), 78;
Freeman (1887), 444. Sirago argues that Felix gave up the title of *magister militum* to Aetius in
429 and was granted that of *patricius* instead (1961: 284), but this seems an unlikely contention:
whatever the titular superiority of a *patricius*, the *magister* was the one who would hold real
power.

[115] For Boniface's lack of success against the Vandals, see Augustine, *Ep.* 220; Theophanes,
AM 5931. See Procopius, *Bell.* 3.3.29–32 for one account of the campaign. Procopius alone
preserves a report of Boniface having invited the Vandals to cross from Spain to Africa to join
him against the other generals, but this seems an unlikely story, since as soon as they did cross
they were engaged in fighting with Boniface's army: Procopius, *Bell.* 3.3.26–8. On his being
summoned to Ravenna, see e.g. Marcellinus *comes*, s.a. 432 (2); Hydatius 89(99); with Oost
(1968a), 230–3; O'Flynn (1983), 78–81; Freeman (1887), 448–9.

[116] Stickler (2002), 35, 47–8; Oost (1968a), 227–8. For the primary sources on the rivalry
between Boniface and Aetius, see: Procopius, *Bell.* 3.3.14–15; John Ant., frg. 196; Marcellinus
comes, s.a. 432 (2, 3). Theophanes gives a rather confused account: Theophanes, AM 5931. For
secondary accounts, see: Heather (2000) 6 ff.; O'Flynn (1983), 79 ff.; Freeman (1887), 446–51;
Oost (1968a), 231 ff.

[117] For the sources on Boniface, see *PLRE* 2. 237–40. On the final battle between Aetius and
Boniface, see Coulon (2000), 113–18.

[118] Prosper 1310; *Chron.Gall. 452* 109, 111, 112; John Ant., frg. 201.3. Cf. Freeman (1887), 450–1;
O'Flynn (1983), 80; Coulon (2000), 115–18. Sebastianus seems to have survived only a very short
time in office, fleeing to the east when Aetius and his Huns returned to Ravenna, and seeking refuge

Boniface and Felix, were dead; Aetius himself was the *magister militum praesentalis*, and in 435 he too would gain the title of *patricius*.[119]

Yet again Aetius had proved himself too formidable a figure for the boy-emperor's government simply to overcome or defeat; yet again Aetius had been able to call upon a significant source of support entirely outside the government's control which gave him the military clout to force a settlement in his own favour. Twice in the eight years of Valentinian III's reign thus far Aetius had been the power-player that neither the eastern government nor the western had expected, or wished, to be forced to accommodate. Yet still, with powerful military backing and a child-emperor's government which demonstrably could not suppress him, Aetius was not aiming to be emperor, but merely chief minister and supreme military commander. Why?

It has been claimed that it was a strong feeling for dynastic legitimacy which supposedly protected the emperor himself but made battles for power behind the throne during the reigns of Honorius and Valentinian III possible.[120] But this view overlooks the way in which the reign of Honorius had functioned, and that dynastic reverence alone was not a convincing argument. Claims to dynastic legitimacy had not saved Gratian at the hands of the usurper (and, of course, general) Magnus Maximus. Traditional scholarship has asserted that Galla Placidia was merely trying to play off the competing generals against each other and hold them at bay until her son was of an age to command the western armies himself.[121] Yet, given the precedents of Honorius and Valentinian II, not to mention Theodosius II in the east, was it likely anyone really expected Valentinian III ever to lead his armies personally? In any case, it would be many years before this could even be a possibility.[122] But more importantly, the expectations of the emperor's function had changed under the child-emperors; so too had the amount of power wielded by those now carrying out some of those once imperial roles. Whether or not Galla Placidia had taken any active role in dealing with these competing generals, it was a conflict which was bound to occur. These were men who had grown up—and must even have served—under Stilicho and Constantius. They knew how the rule of a boy-emperor functioned, the methods which by now had been

at Constantinople, possibly eventually returning to Africa in the 440s but being murdered there by the Vandals: see *PLRE* 2. 983–4.

[119] On Aetius becoming *patricius*: Barnes (1975), 155–6, 165–6. On the various holders of the office and its implications, see further below pp. 282–3 for discussion.

[120] Oost (1968a), 202.

[121] e.g. Oost (1968a), 202. For a more measured view, see Sivan (2011), Ch. 4.

[122] Galla Placidia's father, Theodosius I, had died when she was probably 5–6 years old, and though her husband Constantius had been a general, we know of no campaigns he conducted after his elevation as Augustus; it is doubtful that the empress or anyone else at court would have had any memory in their lifetime of an emperor who actually led his armies.

developed to deal with the situation. In the case of Stilicho, his military command at the time of Theodosius I's death, and his imperial connections had made him the obvious—and as he was determined to ensure, the only—candidate to take on personally the active side of the partnership arrangement for rule which he created. Under the rule of Valentinian III the case was not so clear-cut, and the generals were fighting it out for the role of chief minister. Once again, their determination to take up this position, and not the throne itself, testifies to the strength of the system developed by Stilicho, and the adjustment which had taken place in cultural and political expectations of the way in which the imperial office functioned. It also testifies to the fact that these Roman generals understood how the system worked.

9

The Regime of Aetius

Through his alliance with the barbarians he had protected Placidia, Valentinian's mother, and her son while he was a child. When Boniface crossed from Libya with a large army, he outgeneralled him so that he died of disease as a result of his anxieties and Aetius gained possession of his wife and property. Felix, who was his fellow-general, he killed by cunning when he learned that he was preparing to destroy him at Placidia's suggestion. He crushed the Goths of western Gaul who were encroaching on Roman territory, and he brought to heel the Aemorichans who were in revolt against the Romans. In short, he wielded enormous power, so that not only kings but neighbouring peoples came at his order.[1]

The establishment of Valentinian III's rule in 425 had also established the interest of the eastern government in this new western administration, an interest which would be consolidated by active eastern involvement in western affairs during the 430s. During the growing crisis of the Vandal conquest of North Africa, an eastern army would join with a western one to combat the Vandals, and in 437 the marriage of Valentinian to the eastern princess Licinia Eudoxia, and the issuing of the *Theodosian Code*, publicly proclaimed the paternalistic attitude of the eastern court towards the western. Yet amidst all of these statements of eastern supremacy, within the west Aetius continued to win his battles and consolidate his power. One of the key moments in the ultimate fate of the west would come in the form of the fall of Carthage to the Vandals in 439, and the abandonment of the combined eastern–western

---

[1] Priscus, frg. 30.1.27–38: Τὴν μὲν γὰρ Πλακιδίαν, ἥτις τοῦ Βαλεντινιανοῦ μήτηρ ἦν, καὶ τὸν παῖδα, νέον ὄντα, ἐπετρόπευσε, διὰ τῆς τῶν βαρβάρων συμμαχίας· τὸν δὲ Βονιφάτιον, σὺν πολλῇ διαβάντα χειρὶ ἀπὸ τῆς Λιβύης, κατεστρατήγησεν, ὥστε ἐκεῖνον μὲν ὑπὸ φροντίδων νόσῳ τελευτῆσαι, αὐτὸν δὲ τῆς αὐτοῦ γαμετῆς καὶ τῆς περιουσίας κύριον γενέσθαι. Ἀνεῖλε δὲ καὶ Φήλικα δόλῳ, τὴν στρατηγικὴν σὺν αὐτῷ λαχόντα ἀρχήν, ὡς ἔγνω ὑποθήκῃ τῆς Πλακιδίας ἐς τὴν αὐτοῦ ἀναίρεσιν παρασκευαζόμενον. Κατηγωνίσατο δὲ καὶ Γότθους τοὺς ἐν Γαλατίᾳ τῇ πρὸς ἑσπέραν τῶν Ῥωμαίων ἐμβατεύσαντας χωρίοις. Παρεστήσατο καὶ Αἰμοριχιανοὺς ἀφηνιάσαντας Ῥωμαίων· ὡς δὲ συνελόντα εἰπεῖν, μεγίστην κατεστήσατο δύναμιν, ὥστε μὴ μόνον βασιλεῖς, ἀλλὰ καὶ παροικοῦνταμιν, ὥστε μὴ μόνον βασιλεῖς, ἀλλὰ καὶ παροικοῦντα ἔθνη τοῖς ἐκείνου ἥκειν ἐπιτάγμασιν.

expedition intended to recover it in 442. And against this backdrop, the child-emperor Valentinian III grew to adulthood. His willingness—or otherwise—to remain content with a civilian and ceremonial role, like Honorius before him, would become an increasingly important issue in his relationships with both the eastern court and his general Aetius. Significantly, what evidence exists for Aetius aiming to invoke a presentation of imperial rule through partnership, as Stilicho had once done through Claudian, survives in the fragmentary poetry of Merobaudes, dating to the 440s, when Valentinian was aged over 20.

The Dominance of Aetius

Aetius had successfully asserted his supremacy as the chief western power-player in the government of Valentinian III by the end of 433, yet throughout the 430s he continued to be occupied with military concerns outside of Italy. The course of his many campaigns (and many successes) against different barbarian groups in Gaul from 425 to the late 430s have been well documented and analysed.[2] As one scholar has pointed out, the constant campaigning, mobility, and success of the Gallic army under Aetius makes a striking argument for the continued strength and effectiveness of the western Roman military under a capable commander during this period.[3] In the late 440s the campaigns of Aetius' lieutenants extended to Spain as well, from whence, Hydatius recorded, appeals for help against the Sueves and Vandals had been made to Aetius (notably, not to the emperor) in 433 and 438.[4] It was to Aetius also, rather than the central administration, that Britain would make its final recorded appeal for help from the Roman empire in the 440s.[5] According to Priscus, Aetius wielded such power that kings and neighbouring people alike came at his command.[6]

[2] On the campaigns of the late 420s–early 430s in general, see Stein (1959), 1. 321–4, 576, n. 23; Jones (1964a), 1. 189; Matthews (1975), 329–30; Harries (1994a), 72–3; Thompson (1982a), 53–4; Zecchini (1983), ch. 9; Stickler (2002), ch. 3; Heather (1995), 25; O'Flynn (1983), 89–90; Oost (1968a), 214; Clover (1978), 42 ff.; Coulon (2000), 59–86; Traina (2009), 63–79. For primary-source accounts of various campaigns, see: Merobaudes, *Pan.* I, fr. IIB, 11–24; Prosper 1324, 1326, 1333, 1338; Sidonius *Carm.* 7.246–8; Jordanes, *Get.* 34.176–7; Hydatius 98 (107), 99 (108), 101 (110), 102 (110), 104 (112), 108 (116), 109 (117). Peace terms were apparently offered to the Goths in 439 by the then praetorian prefect of Gaul, Avitus: Oost (1968a), 239–40, and Harries (1994a), 68–9. On the *Bacaudae* revolt see *Chron.Gall.452* 117, 119; Prosper 1324; Hydatius 117 (126), 120 (128), 134 (142). Also Jones (1964a), 1. 189; Matthews (1975); 330, 337–8; Harries (1994a), 71–2. On the *Bacaudae* in general, see Drinkwater (1989b), 189–203 and (1992), 208–17.
[3] Elton (1992), 170.
[4] Hydatius 86 (96), 88 (98).
[5] The famous 'groans of the Britons' letter described by Gildas, I.20. Wood suggests Aetius' activity in Gaul may have prompted hopes among the Britons that he could come to their assistance: (1987), 256–7.
[6] Priscus, frg. 30.1.27–38.

During the 430s Aetius' alliance with the Huns and his continued ability to deploy Hunnic troops throughout his major campaigns in Gaul played a major role in his success, as in the Hunnic defeat of the Burgundians and their involvement in the army which fought the Visigoths under Litorius.[7] In the course of the 430s the leadership of the Huns would move from King Rua, who had provided Aetius with support in 432, to a new king, Attila, with whom Aetius maintained contacts.[8] Yet as events would show, relying on a support-base which was outside of imperial control could prove just as dangerous to a general's position within the state as it had been advantageous when he was without it. After the defeat of Litorius and his Hunnic auxiliaries at Toulouse in 439 there are no further Hunnic contingents attested as fighting on behalf of the Romans, in Gaul or anywhere else.[9] In fact, by 440 the ambitious Attila is alleged to have forbidden Huns to fight in the Roman army, thereby depriving Aetius of a source of support which had been key to his hold on power thus far, and of a force which he had been able to use against other barbarian tribes encroaching on Roman territory: essentially, in fact, depriving him of a military resource he had been able to deploy both for, and against, the Roman government.[10] Although his successes in Gaul must have brought him considerable loyalty from the army who fought alongside him, and scholars have suggested he must have built up a substantial personal following within Gaul itself as a result of his long-term campaigning, the loss of the ability to call upon the Huns if needed was a most serious depletion of Aetius' support-base, with far-reaching consequences for his position.[11] Nevertheless, Aetius' ability to absent himself from the court of Valentinian throughout this period, even taking the pressing concerns of Gaul into account, suggests a confidence on his part that those immediately around the boy-emperor would not undermine his position in his absence. After Aetius' triumph over Boniface in 433, it seems reasonable to assume that, like Stilicho before him, appointments to major offices lay primarily in his hands, giving him the confidence to spend time away on campaign himself while trusted men protected his interests at court. Perhaps the sheer extent of his military successes, and his ability to rely on forces beyond imperial control, gave him a greater immunity from the threat of enemies at court than his predecessors

---

[7] On the defeat of the Burgundians, see Prosper 1322, 1335. See in general on Aetius' use of Hunnic troops, Jones (1964a), 1. 199–201; Harries (1994a), 74; Matthews (1975), 329; O'Flynn (1983), 88–9; Heather (1995), 26.

[8] Priscus, frg. 11.2. 144–8, 324–31, 345–9. Also Cassiodorus, *Variae* I.4.11. There are many accounts of the rise and fall of the Hunnic empire from the 430s to the 450s—see esp. Maenchen-Helfen (1973), 108 ff.; Thompson (1996), chs. 4–6; Stein (1959), 1. 334–6; Heather (1995), 4–41; and for Aetius' relations with them in general, Zecchini (1983), ch. 11 and Coulon (2000), 217–61.

[9] Thompson (1996), 137–8; Oost (1968a), 258.

[10] Heather (1995), 28.

[11] Mathisen notes that the sources in general indicate Aetius' good relations with Gallic elites on both secular and ecclesiastical levels: (1989), 75–6.

Constantius or Stilicho could enjoy. And, of course, taking on the role of the 'active' member of the imperial partnership did necessitate taking the field, while military success was the surest way of asserting divine blessing on the regime.

The involvement of the east

It seems reasonable to conclude, from the admittedly limited sources for this period, that once Aetius had triumphed as the single dominant general of the boy-emperor's government, the partnership arrangement which had proved so successful under Stilicho and Honorius was functioning once more. As the active partner, Aetius was leading the imperial armies in the field and winning victories in the name of the young emperor, who was in turn fulfilling his ceremonial and religious role. The role of the Augusta Galla Placidia, so often viewed as powerful and dominant through these years, probably in fact belonged more to the latter part of the equation—of supplementing the religious and ceremonial side of her son's office, in the same way that Stilicho's wife (and Honorius' cousin) Serena can also be seen doing during the early years of the last boy-emperor's reign, or Pulcheria, the sister of Theodosius II, famously did for her younger brother.[12]

Yet for Aetius, his role as the active member of the partnership was not to be as straightforward as Stilicho's. As far as we know, after 425 Aetius did not face the outright hostility of the eastern government, as Stilicho had. What he did face was potentially even more dangerous to his own position: direct eastern intervention. The eastern government had created Valentinian III emperor, and if he was to be depicted as ruling in any kind of partnership, or with any dependence upon another, the coin images and proclamations of the east made it clear that that partner must be Theodosius II, and that demonstrating imperial unity was a major concern. The eastern government was determined to maintain a stake in its western creation, and even if Aetius had been an unexpected power-broker with whom it had been forced to come to terms, it could and did also curtail the limits of Aetius' power. During the early 430s in particular, this took the dramatic form of eastern military intervention yet again in the west—in North Africa, and in a campaign in which Aetius played no part. It may be that the murder of the general potentially planted in the

---

[12] Such as, for example, Serena's involvement in the honouring of the martyr Nazarius in late 395 (see above, pp. 151–2). For Pulcheria's many religious involvements, see generally Holum (1982), 79–111 (though Holum does see Pulcheria as the chief protagonist in affairs at Theodosius II's court).

west by the eastern government—Felix—made military action in the west again more of a priority for the east.

The context in which an eastern army once more weighed into western affairs was undeniably extremely serious, for in May 429 the Vandals under their king Geiseric had crossed from Spain to North Africa, and Boniface had proved unable to deal with them.[13] The security of North Africa and its grain production were always matters of paramount concern, but the Vandal invasion was a far more serious problem than a localized rebellion such as Gildo's in 398: and the government of the boy-emperor Valentinian III was still only five years old. The Vandal penetration posed a serious threat to Roman interests, both western and eastern, and additionally provided the perfect opportunity for the eastern government once more to demonstrate its backing of the rule of Valentinian in the most dramatic way—both to enemies, and to western generals.[14]

By 431 an eastern military expedition under the command of the general Aspar was operating in cooperation with Boniface against the Vandals in North Africa. Initially the combined might of the eastern and western armies does not seem to have met with any greater success, suffering a defeat in the spring of 432.[15] But the mere fact that an army of Theodosius II was there at all was a tremendously striking statement of eastern commitment to the government of Valentinian III and to maintaining the stability of the west.[16] In 432, when Boniface was summoned to Ravenna, Aspar had remained in Carthage in full control, and he presumably continued in this position after Boniface's death.[17] In 434, Aspar was named as consul for the west, and in February 435 he was probably party to negotiations led by the western high court official Trygetius for the first treaty between Rome and Geiseric.[18] This treaty permitted the Vandals to retain northern Numidia and parts of Africa Proconsularis or Mauretania Sitifiensis (lands which they already occupied), while Carthage

[13] For the Vandals' crossing, see Hydatius 80 (90). The most recent discussion of the arrival of the Vandals in North Africa is now Merrills and Miles (2010), 52–4. But see also Courtois (1955), 155–71; Clover (1971a), 51 ff.; Jones (1964a), 1. 90 ff.; Heather (1995), 25 ff.; Oost (1968a), 224–42; Traina (2009), 81–91. On Boniface's failure to deal with them, see Procopius, *Bell.* 3.3.29–32. A rumour appears in Procopius also (*Bell.* 3.3.22 and 30) that Boniface had invited the Vandals to North Africa, intending to use them in his struggle with Aetius, but that his plans backfired; Mathisen goes so far as to suggest that Aetius might have encouraged the Vandals to leave Spain for Africa to fight Boniface for him, but admits that there is no evidence to support this view: (1999), 190. See also above, p. 248, n. 115.

[14] Oost claims that the western government appealed to the east for help, which is quite possible, but it is not clear what the evidence for this is: (1968a), 227.

[15] Procopius, *Bell.* 3.3.34–6. Procopius claims that Aspar went home to Constantinople after the battle, but this is not correct: see Heather (2000), 9.

[16] The eastern source Evagrius clearly perceived it so also: Evagrius 1.19.

[17] Heather (2000), 9.

[18] For Aspar's consulship, see *CLRE* 402–3; *PLRE* 2. 164–9.

and the majority of Africa Proconsularis remained in Roman hands.[19] This had become a common treaty arrangement for accommodating barbarians within the western empire by this point, placing them in a subordinate relationship with obligations of military service in return; but it was a relationship which Geiseric would swiftly outgrow.[20]

From 431 until at least 435, therefore, the eastern Roman general Aspar was stationed in a western province, along with the eastern military contingent that he commanded. This was an immensely significant demonstration both of the eastern government's continuing investment in and support for the western realm of Valentinian III and a reflection of the seriousness of the situation with regard to North Africa. These eastern efforts should not be underestimated: this was a long-term, costly commitment to make, and at a time when the east was itself facing an uncertain situation with Persia and growing aggression from the Huns.[21] Perhaps it was also a warning to presumptuous western generals: a reminder that the east had created this government, and that Theodosius II still saw himself as Valentinian III's guardian. The award of a western consulship to Aspar in 434 may also have been intended to point out that Aetius was not the only powerful general around.

Dynastic marriage and the *Theodosian Code*

These continued demonstrations of eastern vested interests in the west are vital in understanding the balance of power between Theodosius II and Aetius, and the respective positions of both within the government of Valentinian III. The late 430s was to see a still more pointed demonstration of the eastern/western partnership, in the marriage of Valentinian III and Licinia Eudoxia. As noted in Chapter 8, the betrothal had taken place at the time of Theodosius II's decision to back Valentinian III's cause in 424. At this point it had been a compelling gesture of eastern support for Valentinian's cause, and it would be even more so now—Eudoxia had proved to be Theodosius II's only surviving child, and a son born to the marriage of the eastern princess and the western emperor would therefore have a strong claim to succeed to both realms.[22]

---

[19] Procopius, *Bell.* 3.4.13–15; Prosper 1321. On the treaty in general, see now Merrills and Miles (2010), 55–61; Courtois (1955), 169–72, 169, n. 7; Clover (1971a), 52–3. Procopius asserted that Geiseric's son Huneric was handed over in the course of this treaty, a point Sirago accepts (1961: 293), but this was in fact part of a later treaty, as shall be discussed.

[20] Merrills and Miles (2010), 60–1.

[21] Heather (1995), 25–6; Jones (1964a), 1. 193; Thompson (1950), 58–78.

[22] Oost (1968a), 242–3. If Theodosius II had other children (*PLRE* suggests a son, Arcadius, but on this see above p. 238, n. 67), they did not live long enough to be accorded any rank, and barely appear in any source material.

In the late summer of 437, Valentinian Augustus and an entourage of distinguished Roman nobles, who included Anicius Acilius Glabrio Faustus and Rufinus Antonius Agrypnius Volusianus, possibly also the court poet Merobaudes, but probably neither Galla Placidia nor Aetius, set out from Ravenna on the journey to Constantinople.[23] After a formal *adventus* to the city on 21 October, this significant dynastic marriage was celebrated on 29 October 437.[24] The eastern mints struck a *solidus* for the occasion showing three nimbate figures in imperial dress—in the middle the tall, crowned figure of Theodosius II, with the smaller, crowned figure of Valentinian III on his left and Licinia Eudoxia on his right, and the legend: FELICITER–NVBTIIS/CONOB.[25] The occasion was a potent demonstration of eastern and western solidarity, but an even more dominant theme of the occasion was the senior, pre-eminent status of Theodosius II, beside his colleague—and now son-in-law.[26]

The occasion of this dynastic marriage also provided the setting for the handing over of one of the most valuable legal documents of the late antique world, in a further conspicuous demonstration of the eastern emperor's seniority. In 429, Theodosius II had commissioned the great project of the codification of laws for the entire empire from AD 313 onwards, and in 438 the immense task was complete—the eastern emperor presented a copy of his *Code* to the nobles who attended the wedding.[27] Henceforth this collection was to be the cornerstone of Roman law, and further laws passed in each half of the empire were to be valid in the other half if accepted by both emperors.[28]

The *Theodosian Code* project was certainly a revolutionary improvement in clarifying the Roman judicial system, and would be of enduring significance to

---

[23] Clover suggests Merobaudes probably accompanied the party to Constantinople, and composed a poem in celebration of the marriage: (1971*b*: 362–3). Similarly Barnes (1975), 168 thinks Aetius accompanied the party but this cannot be substantiated.

[24] For the date of the *adventus*: Socrates 7.44.3; *Chron.pasch.* p. 582 on the marriage itself: Merobaudes, *Carm.* I.10; *Gesta* 2; Socrates 7.44 (Socrates gives the wrong year); Marcellinus *comes*, s.a. 437; Evagrius 1.20.2; Prosper 1328; *Chron.Gall.* 593; Cassiodorus, *Chron.* 1229; Malalas 14.7; Theophanes, AM 5926. Cf. Oost (1968*a*), 242–5; Holum (1982), 183.

[25] Kaegi (1968), 28. Cf. Holum (1982), 209; for further issues on the occasion, see De Salis (1867), 206. Only thirteen years later a similar coin would be minted for the marriage of Pulcheria and Marcian in 450, showing Christ standing behind them in the same position as Theodosius II in relation to Valentinian and Eudoxia: *RIC* 10. 93 and Holum (1982), 209.

[26] Gillett (1993), 24. Sirmium in Illyricum was also ceded to the east at the time of the marriage: Jordanes, *Rom.* 329; Theophanes, AM 5926. Cf. Stein (1959), 1. 285; Sirago (1961), 248, 264–6; Kaegi (1968), 27–8.

[27] On the handing over of the *Code* to the western delegates, see Matthews (2000), 1–9; and on its promulgation in the west, 31–54; also Matthews (1993), 22 ff.; Gillett (1993), 20–1. There were certain parts of the original legal codification scheme as announced in 429 which were never completed, however: see Matthews (2000), 10.

[28] *NTh.* 2 (1 Oct. 447) recorded Theodosius II sending some of his later laws westwards, while *NVal.* 26 (2 June 448) marked their promulgation there. Cf. Oost (1968*a*), 245.

the Roman and post-Roman world.[29] It is a project which also provides a most valuable insight into eastern/western relations under the young Valentinian III and his cousin Theodosius II. Modern scholars have observed that a majority of the laws codified by the eastern commission were in fact western, and must have been sent from the archives of Italy and North Africa for inclusion in the project, indicating a high degree of administrative cooperation between the two courts from the late 420s onwards.[30] Given the eastern investment in this western government, this does not seem surprising. Even more significant in terms of the stance of Theodosius II towards his cousin's rule is the attitude of seniority the eastern emperor continued to adopt. For while this was a joint project, intended to symbolize the harmony of the two realms, it was still the *'Theodosian'* Code. Moreover, the marriage had given Theodosius the perfect opportunity to advertise his paternal—and thus, by implication, even more senior—attitude to his colleague. It is noteworthy that in the minutes of the senate recording the promulgation of the *Code* in the west, Faustus declared that Theodosius II wished to add this honour to 'his' world—which clearly included the west—and desired the *Code* to be consecrated with his most sacred name. Valentinian, on the other hand, simply approved the plan with the affection and loyalty of a colleague—and son.[31]

The surviving minutes of the senate meeting at which the *Code* was promulgated in the west in December 438 also reveal another intriguing insight into the western government at this stage: that Aetius may have been present at this important occasion, while the western emperor himself clearly was not.[32] The case for the general's attendance is undeniably uncertain: he is not mentioned at the start of the minutes, which note that the consul and praetorian prefect Anicius Acilius Glabrio Faustus (in whose home the meeting took place), the prefect of the city Flavius Paulus, and the vicar of the city Junius Pomponius Publianus, and men of noble rank and members of the senate had assembled. However, Aetius is mentioned specifically in the recorded acclamations of the senators following the promulgation of the *Code*, along with Faustus and Paulus. The senators reportedly shouted 'Hail, Aetius!' fifteen times, followed by: 'A third term for you in the consulship!' (repeated thirteen times), 'Through your vigilance we are safe and secure!' (twelve times), and finally 'Through your vigilance, through your labours!' (fifteen

---

[29] On the nature of the overall project and its stages, see Harries (1999), 59–61.

[30] Gillett (1993), 21–2. Cf. Oost (1968a), 220. As usual Oost is far too certain that this active role in sending the laws east was Galla Placidia's, an involvement for which the evidence will simply never provide confirmation, however desirable.

[31] *Gesta* 2. See similarly *NTh.* 2.1 (1 Oct. 447). See Honoré (1999), 258; and Harries (1999), 64 on the eastern attitude to the west reflected in the *Code*, and 65–9 on the meeting for the promulgation of the *Code* in the west. Also in general on the meeting, see Matthews (2000), 31–54, and on the location of the meeting (in the home of Faustus), see 32–3.

[32] *Gesta* 5.

times).[33] Sandwiched between acclamations for two individuals who clearly were present at the meeting, it does seem possible that Aetius was also there; and if he was not, at the very least these acclamations, which must have been intended to be reported to the emperor, reflect that the general had supporters in the senate. But more importantly, the fact that the senators request Faustus to report their wishes to 'the emperors' make it certain Valentinian was not at this rather rowdy-sounding but celebratory meeting. Yet Valentinian III had returned to the west by this stage following his marriage, and given the splendid ceremonial possibilities that the promulgation of the *Code* offered, his absence seems surprising.[34] Surely this occasion would have been a perfect opportunity to display the young emperor, now an adult, taking up a more active role in 'his' government? Again, as in the case of Honorius' absence from the senate meeting of 408 recorded by Zosimus, the question of whether an emperor would usually attend such meetings remains uncertain, though it seems likely he could if he wished to do so.[35]

Aetius probably had not journeyed to Constantinople for the emperor's marriage, but his likely presence in Rome in December 438 does suggest that he had remained in Italy during Valentinian III's absence. His remaining in the west was surely a matter of pure practicality—he had proved himself far more vital to the region's stability than the emperor. Yet this circumstance also reflects the difference in the position of Aetius in relation to Valentinian III compared with Stilicho in relation to Honorius. In 408 when Honorius had wished to travel to Constantinople, Stilicho would not allow it: his own position depended upon keeping young Honorius under his thumb, and Stilicho was already under siege from the mounting military crises facing the western realm at this point. Aetius, however, had not owed his rise purely to the accession of the boy-emperor, but to his own ability to call on substantial military backing that was beyond imperial control, and to his own victories. When necessary, he had been able to wield these abilities against the state to his own ends in a way that Stilicho would never have dared, or been able, to do. Nevertheless, the dynamics of the situation were bound to change as the largely inactive boy-emperor grew to adulthood, and at 18, now married, the question of whether Valentinian III would be content to remain passive as Honorius had before him, or would seek to claim 'his' power, must have been uppermost in Aetius' mind. In addition, eastern interest in this western

---

[33] *Gesta* 6: *Aeti aveas. Dictum XV. Ter consulem te. Dictum XIII. Excubiis tuis salvi et securi sumus. Dictum XII. Excubiis tuis, laboribus tuis. Dictum XV.*

[34] Matthews suggests that Faustus had probably travelled back from Constantinople with the newlywed imperial couple: (2000), 7.

[35] See above, p. 178. Also, in 454, according to Priscus and John of Antioch, Valentinian apparently convened the senate and addressed the senators following the death of Aetius: Priscus, frg. 30.1.39–51; John.Ant., frg. 201(4): see below, p. 297.

administration also meant that Aetius' position was not the complete dominance that Stilicho had achieved for a time. Within the west itself, however, the
continuing presence of Aetius, and the absence of Valentinian on his matrimonial expedition, could be interpreted as a signal that whatever demonstrations of
solidarity between eastern and western courts Theodosius II engineered, he was
far from Rome, and Aetius remained a force to be reckoned with.

Such a view inevitably raises the question of what the attitude of the eastern
court was to Aetius. The eastern emperor's paternal stance towards his co-
Augustus complicated Aetius' position in a way which previous generals
exercising supreme power at the court of a child-emperor had not faced
(with the possible exception of Arbogast in relation to Valentinian II and
Theodosius I). Any presentation of a partnership of rule which Aetius might
have sought to adopt in the style of Stilicho was complicated by the fact that
the eastern emperor himself clearly intended to be seen as Valentinian III's
only—and senior—partner. While Aetius' role in Valentinian III's government had not been foreseen by the east back in 425 and the eastern government may have kept a close eye on his activity (including through its military
activity in the west in the 430s), Aetius does not seem to have suffered from
any obvious signs of eastern disfavour. His western consulship in 432 had
been recognized in the east, and more significantly, in 437 he held a second
consulship, along with his lieutenant Sigisvult, with both consuls for the year
thus being western. This must have indicated a favourable eastern attitude
towards Aetius' achievements and position (and Sigisvult's also), perhaps
especially so in an auspicious year for the unity of the two empires with the
imperial marriage taking place.[36] Aetius' later third consulship of 446 was also
recognized in the east; and with his focus on purely western military matters,
his activity never posed a direct threat to that realm, as Stilicho's was perceived
to do; there was little reason for Aetius to arouse the direct enmity of
Theodosius II.

The determined efforts of Theodosius II to have himself depicted as
Valentinian III's father-figure and partner in rule, however, may provide a
potential answer to the question of why Aetius did not seek to become co-
Augustus in the west as Constantius had. It was not inconceivable, surely, that
given his military backing he might have sought to marry either Galla Placidia
or her daughter, the Augusta Honoria, and work his way into the imperial
office in this way—indeed, it seems remarkable that he did not. The unmarried
state of Honoria still in the 440s may have been related to such an ambition on

---

[36] See Clover (1971*b*), 362–3, n. 52, who also suggests that Socrates' comment that upon
leaving his realm Valentinian III had made the western region safe may also indicate an eastern
tradition favourable to Aetius. See similarly, Croke (1995), 93, n. 454.2. For further discussion of
the relationship between Aetius and Sigisvult, see below, pp. 283–4.

Aetius' part (or at least, the prevention of any other individual marrying her and thus posing a threat to either her brother or Aetius seems a likely factor in her unwed state).[37] Moreover, the experiences of Stilicho and Constantius earlier in the fifth century must have reinforced for any later generalissimo the imperative nature of linking oneself through marriage to the imperial house, and if at all possible producing an heir to the throne, as the most certain means of truly securing their dominance. But there is one obvious explanation for this, which becomes even more compelling when events in 450 are taken into account (as will be discussed in Chapter 10): that the eastern government was exercising a sort of veto on his taking such a step. That up to a point, Theodosius II's government was prepared to accept the military dominance of Aetius and even to endorse his position (perhaps particularly if Felix really had been an eastern nominee and had failed so conspicuously to win support)—as long as he did not take it too far. This is, of course, a purely hypothetical explanation, which our surviving source material cannot confirm. But it would make sense of both eastern acceptance of Aetius' position in the west, and of there not even being a hint in our available evidence of Aetius attempting to marry into the imperial family before the 450s. And if we accept such an explanation as plausible, continuing eastern military expeditions and military presence in the west in favour of the boy-emperor in the 430s would make it abundantly clear that if Aetius did overstep the mark, and marginalize Valentinian III entirely, he could face serious repercussions.

The Vandal crisis

The treaty of 435 between the Romans and the Vandals negotiated by Aspar was destined to be short-lived. In October 439, in absolute contravention of the treaty, King Geiseric took over Carthage, and from there swiftly took to the seas.[38] Landing in Sicily in spring 440, the Vandals began pillaging the towns and terrorizing the local population.[39] In June 440 the famous novel of Valentinian III, 'De reddito jure armorum' ('Restoration of the Right to Use Weapons') was issued, addressed 'to the Roman people'. In this edict, the emperor explained that, for the safety of all, and because it was not certain

---

[37] Aetius was presumably unmarried in the early 430s when he defeated Boniface, for he is reported to have married Boniface's widow, the Gothic princess Pelagia, who was the mother of Aetius' son Gaudentius. Honoria is often assumed to have taken a vow of virginity like her cousins the eastern princesses, but no source actually states that she did so.

[38] Marcellinus *comes*, s.a. 439 (3); Hydatius 107 (115), 110 (118); Prosper 1339; *Chron.pasch.* p. 583.5-7. See now Merrills and Miles (2010), 55. The defensive walls of Rome were hastily repaired in response: *NVal.* 5.3 (3 Mar. 440). Cf. Thompson (1950), 60.

[39] Hydatius 112 (120); Theophanes, AM 5941; Cassiodorus, *Variae* I.4, 14; cf. Merrills and Miles (2010), 111.

where the Vandals might come ashore in mainland Italy, if the occasion demanded it all men should take up what arms they could to resist the brigands. According to the emperor, Geiseric was believed to have set forth from Carthage with a large fleet, whose depredation must be feared by all. But, the Roman people were assured:

the solicitude of Our Clemency is stationing garrisons throughout various places and the army of the most invincible Emperor Theodosius, Our Father, will soon approach, and . . . We trust that the Most Excellent Patrician, Our Aetius, will soon be here with a large band and the Most Illustrious Master of Soldiers, Sigisvuldus, does not cease to organize guards of soldiers and federated allies for the cities and shores . . . [40]

Late in 440 or early 441, as news of an approaching eastern fleet came in, the Vandals swiftly retreated from Sicily back to Carthage.[41] The eastern government must have made an immense effort to respond as rapidly as possible: by late 440, within a year of the fall of Carthage, a eastern fleet twice the size of that which would retake North Africa a century later under Belisarius had reached Sicily: this was no half-hearted effort, and naval expeditions were prohibitively expensive.[42] In early 441 the forces of the eastern and western empires were preparing to launch a major attack on Carthage, under the leadership of no less than five eastern generals.[43] As with the earlier campaigns in North Africa, Aetius was not involved, though as *NVal.* 9 makes clear,

---

[40] *NVal.* 9 (24 June 440): *Et quamvis clementiae nostrae sollicitudo per diversa loca praesidia disponat atque invictissimi principis Theodosii patris nostri iam propinquet exercitus et excellentissimum virum patricium nostrum Aetium cum magna manu adfore mox credamus cumque vir inlustrissimus magister militum Sigisvuldus tam militum atque foederatorum tuitionem urbibus ac litoribus non desinat ordinare . . .* (also *CJ* 12.8.2; 50.21). On the defences, see Merrills and Miles (2010), 112. For a thorough (but perhaps exaggerated) analysis of the role of Sigisvult in the defence of Italy, see Mathisen (1999), 184–6.

[41] Again, for the best modern account, see Courtois (1955), 171 ff. But also Jones (1964a), 1. 190; Stein (1959), 1. 324–5; Thompson (1950), 61; Kaegi (1968), 28–9; Zecchini (1983), 171 ff.; Oost (1968a), 259. It was surely this threat of an eastern approach, rather than an obscure rumour that Sebastianus (the late Boniface's son-in-law) was preparing to cross from Spain with a force to fight the Vandals, that compelled the Vandal withdrawal (contra Mathisen (1999), 187–8). The Suevi, meanwhile, were busy taking over Spain: see Heather (1995), 27–8; Clover (1971a), 52 ff.

[42] Thompson (1950), 64. Cf. Heather (2005), 288–91. The expedition of 468 would cost over 100,000 lb of gold, leaving the eastern empire's treasury hovering on bankruptcy for the next three decades, according to Bury (1923), 1. 337 and nn. 1 and 2. John the Cappadocian apparently opposed Justinian's plans for the reconquest of North Africa in the 530s on the grounds of the cost: Barnish, Lee, and Whitby (2000), 196. On the expense of naval expeditions generally, see Hendy (1985), 221–2.

[43] The generals are named as Areobindus, Ansilas, Inobindos, Arintheos, and Germanus (Theophanes, AM 5941; also Priscus, frg. 9.4). For details on the campaign arrangements, see Merrills and Miles (2010), 112; Courtois (1955), 173; Kaegi (1968), 28–9; Sirago (1961), 96–300. Areobindus, supreme commander of the eastern forces, still seems to have been in Constantinople on 6 March 441, however, according to *NTh.* 7.4.

towards the end of June 440 the general had been sent for and was expected to arrive in Italy imminently. We know from the chronicle of Prosper that Aetius was still in Gaul in mid-September when Pope Sixtus III died, as the new pope, Leo, was also there arbitrating a dispute between Aetius and Albinus.[44] There is no reason to assume that Aetius did not hurry back to Italy when news of the Vandal crisis reached him, however: it was far too grave a threat to be ignored.[45]

Although Theodosius II had responded quickly, unfortunately the situation in the east itself was far from secure. Theodosius was now facing a crisis of his own in the form of the increasingly aggressive Hunnic king Attila, who launched a major invasion of east Roman territory.[46] According to Priscus, the Persians too were preparing for war at this point, and the fact that the experienced Aspar had not been sent with the fleet to Sicily but remained at Constantinople reinforces the picture of eastern anxiety on these fronts at this time.[47] Indeed, given their own concerns it is astonishing that the east sent a force westwards at all; nor is it surprising that as the situation with the Huns became ever more grave, the eastern fleet was recalled from Sicily in early 442 without ever reaching Africa.[48]

The withdrawal of the eastern military contingent saw the abandonment of any plans for a western campaign against the Vandals also. Given what was at stake, and given also the proven military abilities of Aetius, this seems surprising: it certainly made the western government look inherently weak and militarily dependent on eastern backing. Explanations that Aetius was reluctant to lead an expedition to Africa and thereby abandon his power-base in Gaul are unconvincing, given that Aetius had, according to Valentinian III's novel, been recalled to Italy at this time.[49] Nor is the suggestion that he did not wish to send a lieutenant in his place and thereby risk raising a rival much more plausible, in view of his willingness to send other commanders to Spain in the 440s—it seems unlikely that he would have entrusted an important

---

[44] Prosper 1341. Sixtus III died on 19 August 440: Davis (2000), 34.

[45] Contra Mathisen, who claims Aetius was 'nowhere to be found' (1999: 186); there is no reason to suppose he did not return to Italy as *NVal.* 9 indicates the emperor was expecting; and the *Chron.Gall.* s.a. 440 also mentions his recall; see further Merrills and Miles (2010) 111. Prosper does, however, suggest that Aetius' preoccupation with Gallic affairs gave Geiseric the opportunity to take him unawares and claim Carthage: Prosper 1339; see also Mathisen (1999), 190.

[46] Priscus, frg. 9.4.1–20; 10; Theophanes, AM 5942; *Chron.pasch.* p. 583. See further on this: Maenchen-Helfen (1973), 109–10; Jones (1964a), 1. 193; Blockley (1992), 62–7.

[47] Priscus, frg. 10; also Maenchen-Helfen (1973), 111. In the event Aspar was sent on campaign against Attila, with little success, and a further treaty was made whereby ever more tribute was to be paid to the Hunnic leader: see Priscus, frg. 9.4.7–20.

[48] Priscus, frg. 9.4.1–7. Cf. Kaegi (1968), 28–9; Merrills and Miles (2010), 112.

[49] For the argument Aetius did not wish to leave his Gallic power-base: O'Flynn (1983), 91; Oost (1968a), 262–3.

campaign to any lieutenant who was not his own, picked man.[50] It is most likely that the western empire could not afford to equip a fleet of its own for such a campaign.[51] But this abandonment also made it appear (correctly enough) that if the paternal eastern partner of the west could not save the government by military might, then the western government could not save itself either. Theodosius II's position as the west's protector was reinforced once more— but so too was a new sense of the precariousness of the western government.

The Vandals may have been already suing for peace before the eastern fleet departed, and in 442 negotiations for a further treaty between the Vandals and the western empire began in earnest.[52] The terms which were settled upon allowed Geiseric to keep Byzacena and some adjoining territories, and divide up Africa Proconsularis among his followers, while returning the remaining regions of Roman North Africa (those already damaged by Vandal raiding) to Rome. Geiseric was to pay a yearly tribute, and to hand over his son Huneric as a hostage to the Roman court.[53] It has recently been highlighted that the way in which Prosper describes this treaty (as 'Africa divided into two distinct territories') between the Romans and Vandals suggests that this agreement was of a very different nature to those usually made with barbarian groups. It appears to imply that the Vandals were actually being granted these lands as their own, rather than as federates, a reading also supported by the Vandal payments of tribute to Rome.[54] It has been noted also that from this time on there is little legislative evidence for North Africa—other than major tax remissions such as those of 445 and 451.[55] Prior to the Vandal sack of Carthage, the evidence for legislation for North Africa under Valentinian III is not abundant either, however, and those laws which do survive relating to the plight of Romans in North Africa in the 440s and 450s do appear to show genuine concern for their sufferings and attempt to offer what little relief might be in the government's power through these tax remissions.[56] The loss

---

[50] O'Flynn (1983), 91.

[51] The question of when the western fleet disappeared (and also what sort of fleet Geiseric was able to put together to begin his Mediterranean raids) is extremely difficult to resolve on the basis of our existing evidence, see for a helpful overview: MacGeorge (2002), 306–11.

[52] Merrills and Miles (2010), 112; Blockley (1992), 62. The report of Geiseric making peaceful overtures appears in Theophanes, AM 5941.

[53] On the treaty, see: Prosper 1342, 1344, 1346, 1347. Cf. Jones (1964a), 1. 190; Oost (1968a), 259–61. Also Clover (1971a), 21.

[54] Prosper 1347; Merrills and Miles (2010), 63, 112, and on the treaty of 442 in general, 61–6.

[55] *NVal.* 13 (21 June 445); 34 (13 July 451); cf. Matthews (1975), 357–8. Merrills and Miles point out that this indicates the Roman government still took seriously its responsibilities for the areas of North Africa still under its control, which is true, but there is not a great deal of legislation for the provinces otherwise: (2010), 64.

[56] From 425 until 438 only nine laws directly relating to North Africa affairs survive anyway: *CTh.* 16.2.46 (6 July 425); 16.5.63 (4 Aug. 425); 7.13.22 (26 Feb. 428); 11.1.34 (25 Feb. 429); 11.30.68 (25 Feb. 429); 12.1.185 (25 Feb. 429); 12.1.186 (25 Feb. 429); 12.6.33 (15 Feb. 430), and *NVal.* 1.1 (8 July 438), which relates to all provinces including Africa. Four surviving pieces of

of North Africa to the western Roman empire was utterly disastrous: it was one of the richest regions the government had held, was the location of many vast properties of Roman aristocrats, a vital source of tax revenue for the central government, and the primary supplier of Rome's corn.[57] Nevertheless, the treaty was a success, in that it preserved peaceful relations between the Vandals and Rome until Valentinian III's death in 455, although some of the legislation which does exist relating to Roman North Africa in this period indicates that the imperial government had not entirely given up hope of reclaiming the whole of the province in the future.[58]

The laws of the 440s offer a clear picture of the strain under which the government was consequently placed as a result of this loss of territory. The most famous measure to try to deal with the financial crisis—and the still pressing need to fund the military—was the *siliquaticum*, the sales tax instituted in 444, prompted, so the law declared, by the dire reality that current revenues were insufficient to adequately clothe and feed existing troops, let alone support the new recruits that were needed.[59] A further law of 444 detailed that persons of high rank were to pay cash for the cost of military recruits, according to their status, a measure reminiscent of Stilicho's negotiations with the senators over recruitment for the war against Gildo in the late 390s.[60] And a novel of 445 reveals the truly crippling extent of the financial loss caused by the Vandal activity: that before 429 the taxes of Numidia alone had brought in a revenue of 33,600 *solidi*, 9,600 *annonae*, and 1,600 *capita* for the government, and those of Mauretania Sitifensis 40,000 *solidi* and 400 *capita*: all of this had been lost to Rome since the early 430s.[61] The continuing concern of the western government with raising funds for military recruits also indicates that, even if the treaty with the Vandals had brought some degree of stability in that area, military matters remained a pressing preoccupation of the regime during the 440s. Nevertheless, as with earlier efforts, the original eastern commitment to the campaign should not be underestimated. At a time when its own security was being threatened, the eastern government had again weighed in with an expensive and dramatic backing of western interests and concerns.[62] Even if it was expected that the campaign forces would live off

legislation date to the 440s and 450s: NVal. 2.3 (17 Aug. 443); 12 (19 Oct. 443); 13 (21 June 445); 34 (13 July 451).

[57] Thompson (1950), 59. See on Roman senatorial interests in the province: Matthews (1975), 357–8.

[58] e.g. *NVal.* 13 (21 June 445), which refers to arrangements 'after the recovery of the provinces' (13.6). See further Merrills and Miles (2010), 64–5.

[59] *NVal.* 15 (between 11 Sept. 444 and 18 Jan. 445). See Jones (1964a), 1. 201.

[60] *NVal.* 6.3 (14 June 444).

[61] *NVal.* 13 (21 June 445); see Jones (1964a), 1. 207–8; 2. 1110, n. 83. Cf. generally: Harries (1994a), 245.

[62] Thompson (1950), 64. The east would also have been concerned about the Vandal threat to its own assets, of course.

local resources in the course of the expedition, the costs of equipping the forces and maintaining them in Sicily for a year before the campaign was called off must have been extremely high. Despite the eventual calling-off of the eastern expedition, it still revealed the eastern government of Theodosius II seeking to demonstrate in the 440s its continuing support for the western government it had established in 425.

The betrothal of Huneric and Eudocia

As mentioned above, the treaty of 442 had also included, remarkably, a betrothal between the elder daughter of Valentinian III, and Huneric, the son of Geiseric. Merobaudes, writing *c*.443, attested to the engagement, describing Geiseric as taking off the garb of an enemy, and desiring to bind himself to Rome by joining their offspring in matrimony.[63] Huneric has been identified by some scholars as the *novus exul* that Merobaudes, in a different poem, wrote of weeping at the feet of 'our protector' (presumably Valentinian III, if this identification were correct).[64] The poem appears to be a description of a mosaic cycle at court, although there has been much debate over the identity of this figure, and it would hardly have been a very diplomatic depiction of the Vandal prince (though it would be one which saved face for the Romans).[65] Given overt eastern insistence on acting as the 'protector' of the western realm, however, and the 420s mosaics at St John the Evangelist in Ravenna which constituted a clear public statement of the role of the east in the government of the west, the identification of the exile as the child Valentinian III and the protector as Theodosius II should not be discounted. Despite claims of modern scholars that an emperor, even a child-emperor, would never be depicted weeping, it should be recalled that Ambrose explicitly describes young Honorius doing just that during the funeral oration for Theodosius I.[66] Emphasizing the vulnerability of a child-emperor was not unknown in imperial propaganda in this period, as we know. The suggestion that Merobaudes' description is of a series of tableaux showing scenes from Valentinian III's life is tempting, therefore. Furthermore, this persuasive

---

[63] Merobaudes, *Pan.* II.27–9. See Clover (1971*a*), 23–8, 52–4. Also Procopius, *Bell.* 3.1.4.12–14. Also Oost (1964), 27, n. 8; O'Flynn (1983), 90–4. The betrothal must have been in place by 446, the date of Merobaudes' second panegyric: Clover (1971*a*), 54, nn. 119, 120.

[64] Merobaudes, *Carm.* I.1–10. This identification is argued for by Oost (1965), 5–6, and followed by Clover (1971*a*), 21.

[65] For some of the various identifications, see e.g. Bury, who thinks the exile is young Valentinian III: (1919), 8, and Barnes, who claims the exile is the *Bacaudae* leader Tibatto (1974), 318–19.

[66] Ambrose, *De ob. Theod.* 55. Both Oost and Clover argue an emperor could never be depicted in tears: Oost (1965), 5–6; Clover (1971*a*), 20.

explanation of the figures described would certainly fit with the ongoing eastern emphasis on seniority and protectorship of Valentinian III's regime.[67]

At any rate, Huneric should certainly have been celebrating his situation, for the betrothal was a major coup for the Vandals.[68] The marriage of imperial princesses to political rivals was always a complex and sensitive business, and in fact the offer of voluntary (so to speak) marriage of a princess to a barbarian king was a first for Roman–barbarian relations in this period—made more remarkable still by Valentinian's lack of sons (though there was presumably still the prospect of changing this situation in 442).[69] Geiseric might hope through the marriage to promote the position of his people as Rome's closest ally. Whether or not he might have hoped through the alliance to become a true power behind the throne is more tenuous: he and his son had their own kingdom to rule now, and the Romans would presumably assume they would continue to do so after the marriage took place, while the emperor himself would continue to have his own generals commanding his armies. But for the Romans too, there were many advantages to the betrothal. It was the most persuasive way of keeping Geiseric to the 443 treaty and avoiding major future offensives against him which Valentinian III's administration definitely could not afford. And it worked: Geiseric kept to the terms of the treaty until Valentinian III's death in 455.[70]

The motivating force for the betrothal within the western administration has been a matter of some debate among scholars. Some have asserted that Aetius had to force Valentinian III to accept the terms, that Aetius even intended the arrangement as an insult to the imperial family, or alternatively, that the betrothal was part of a cunning plan by the imperial family to outmanoeuvre Aetius and establish a dangerous rival power to him in the form of Geiseric and Huneric.[71] It is hard to believe that the Vandals would truly have seemed a better option as the western government's main military resource than Aetius. By far the most likely scenario is surely that the treaty aimed at stabilizing the situation in Africa as far as could now be hoped for, buying some time for the

---

[67] Gillett (1993), 27–9. Followed also by Sivan (2011), ch. 5.

[68] An existing Vandal alliance with the Goths was abandoned (unpleasantly) in favour of the imperial betrothal (Priscus, frg. 20.2.1–10; Jordanes, *Get.* 36.184). Also Merrills and Miles (2010), 112–13; Clover (1973), 106–7; O'Flynn (1983), 91–2.

[69] 'Voluntary' in the sense of the father of the bride offering her in marriage, rather than Eudocia herself having any say in the matter. The marriage of Galla Placidia to Athaulf had not, of course, been offered by the imperial house; her capture by the Visigoths simply allowed them to carry it out without asking.

[70] Oost (1964), 27, n. 8; Clover (1971a), 24–8, 52–4; O'Flynn (1983), 90. Merrills and Miles point out that the only known major disturbance during this period was a Vandal attack on Gallaecia in 445, but that this may have been intended to contribute to imperial offensives against the Suevi and *Bacaudae* in Spain: (2010), 113–14.

[71] For the argument that Aetius forced the betrothal: Bury (1923), 1. 25; and that it was intended as an insult to the imperial family: Sirago (1961), 299 f. Alternatively, for the contention that it was planned by the imperial family as a means of outflanking Aetius: Oost (1968a), 262–3.

Roman government, and that little Eudocia was the most tempting bait that could be offered to keep the Vandals loyal.[72] At any rate, far more important than who exactly first had the idea of the betrothal is the surprising fact that it existed at all. That it was probably very much a delaying tactic which the Romans may not ever have intended to eventuate is supported by the fact that by 455 Huneric had been returned to his father, but Eudocia was aged 16–17 and no marriage had yet taken place.[73] The Roman court's reluctance to make firm arrangements may have put a growing strain on relations with Geiseric and his people: legislation dating to the early 450s reveals the government needing to make reparations to subjects whose property had been damaged (presumably recently) by the Vandals.[74]

Merobaudes and the partnership

Despite the crisis period from the fall of Carthage to the treaty of 442, the 430s and 440s had seen the steady and continuous rise of Aetius as the dominant general of the western government, albeit with prolonged and repeated instances of eastern intervention, of both a military and ideological nature, to deal with. Such interventions potentially threatened Aetius' ability to establish an unassailable partnership of rule between the young emperor Valentinian and himself, even after he triumphed over his last real military rival in 432. In addition, time was not on Aetius' side: in 425 the emperor was only 6 years old, but by the time Aetius emerged victorious from civil strife in 432 he was 13, and by 438 he was married, to a bride of the eastern emperor's choosing (unlike the marriages of Honorius, arranged by Stilicho). Valentinian was reaching an age where the all-important question of whether nor not he would be content to remain passive or would try to make the transition to active, adult emperor was coming to the fore. Aside from numismatic images, depictions of Valentinian III or writings about him are very rare, which makes the fragmentary remains of the poetry of Flavius Merobaudes, dating to the 440s, all the more valuable.[75] But so too does their timing: although it is an accident

[72] As O'Flynn concludes: (1983), 92–3.

[73] For Huneric's return to his father, see Procopius, *Bell.* 3.4.14; cf. Oost (1968a), 260–1. Eudocia was probably 4 or 5 when the betrothal took place: as Clover points out, betrothal was not even legal at such an age under Roman law, whereby a child should be at least 7, but as in the case of Valentinian III and Licinia Eudoxia back in 424, this was ignored if political needs required it: (1971a), 24. Oost claims that it was Aetius who delayed the marriage: (1968a), 262–3. O'Flynn however argues that both Aetius and Valentinian III probably held back on the formal alliance: (1983), 92–3.

[74] *NVal.* 34.4 (13 July 451); cf. O'Flynn (1983), 93. Clover notes strains in the relationship from 450, when Eudocia reached the marriageable age of about 12: (1973), 108.

[75] For a thorough study of the fragments of Merobaudes, see Clover (1971a), 1–178; and on the figures depicted, see also Barnes (1974), 314–19.

of survival, these poems allow us a glimpse of the presentation of Valentinian III and Aetius at a point when the emperor was no longer a child. Merobaudes was the court poet, though much like Claudian, on whose work he modelled his own, he seems to have written far more in praise of the *magister militum* of the regime than the emperor himself.[76] Following the case of Claudian at the court of Honorius, the attachment of a poet principally to the retinue of a powerful general as a long-term propagandist of his policies and services to the state seems to have become the norm in the fifth-century west.[77]

In one of the surviving fragments of his poetry, from *c*.440–3, Merobaudes describes what seems to be a mosaic cycle depicting different scenes involving the entire imperial family (including the mysterious 'new exile' mentioned above), perhaps from the palace at Ravenna.[78] The scene presented is of a banquet, apparently depicted on the ceiling of a room:

The emperor himself in full splendour occupies with his wife the centre of the ceiling, as if they were the bright stars of the heavens on high; he is the salvation of the land, and worthy of veneration. In the presence of our protector a new exile suddenly weeps for his lost power. Victory has restored the world to the one who has received it from nature, and an illustrious court has furnished a bride from afar.[79]

Next, we hear that the emperor's 'sacred' mother seeks the kisses of her 'peaceful son', and his sister stands nearby, shining in reflection of her brother's glory.[80] The daughters of Valentinian III and Eudoxia are also depicted, and according to Merobaudes:

The court flourishes, after obtaining its master's beautiful offspring, and the ceiling itself, set on fire by the chariot of Phoebus and the purple of the emperor, shines with youthful light and holds united the stars of heaven and earth.[81]

Merobaudes' description of the emperor, and his family, is in a highly ceremonial and ideologically charged guise. The poet's writing of the shining,

---

[76] Merobaudes also, like Claudian, received a statue in the Forum of Trajan at Rome, from the Roman senate and dedicated in 435: *CIL* 6.1724; Clover (1971*a*), 9 and n. 21; Hedrick (2000), 232.

[77] Gillett (2012) 271-6. Gillett notes that Sidonius mentions another panegyrist of Aetius, named Quintinianus (Sidonius, *Carm.* 9.290–5) and that Boniface and Sebastianus were followed by a Gallic poet (ibid. 9.277–88).

[78] Clover (1971*a*), 16–19.

[79] Merobaudes, *Carm.* I.5–10: *ipse micans tecti medium cum coniuge princeps | lucida ceu summi possidet astra poli, | terrarum veneranda salus: pro praeside nostro | amissas subito flet novus exul opes; | cui natura dedit, victoria reddidit orbem | claraque longinquos praebuit aula toros.*

[80] Ibid. I.11–24.

[81] Ibid. II.1–4: *aula uiret pulchram domini sortita iuventam | ipsaque primaevo lumine tecta nitent quae Phoebi flammata rotis et principis ostro | aetheris ac terrae sidera mixta tenent.* On the emperor's daughters, see ibid. I.11–24. The younger daughter seems to have been depicted as recently baptized: Clover (1971*a*), 27; Bury (1919), 7, n. 2. Valentinian and Eudoxia had two daughters, Eudocia and Placidia, who were both born in the late 430s. Licinia Eudoxia was made an Augusta after the birth of Eudocia, in 439, as *solidi* for the empress struck at Ravenna indicate: *RIC* 10. 165. Cf. Oost (1968*a*), 247.

flourishing court, on fire with the sacred light and youthful promise of the imperial family, is reminiscent of the sort of descriptions favoured by Claudian when writing of Honorius at the start of his reign (for example, after Honorius' coronation outside Constantinople, or when described as the Egyptian sun-god at Milan).[82] But this poem was not written at the start of Valentinian III's reign: this one-time boy-emperor was now in his early twenties, not only married but with two daughters born. With this in mind, both the highly ceremonial depiction of the emperor and the manner of Merobaudes' descrip-tion of Aetius are enlightening evidence of the continuing presentation of the government even during Valentinian's adulthood. In a sense, Merobaudes' depiction of the adult Valentinian III picks up where Claudian's image of the child Honorius leaves off.

The surviving fragments of Merobaudes' work reveal that he also composed two panegyrics. One of these appears to have been something akin to a *gratiarum actio* in thanks for an honorific title granted to Merobaudes by Theodosius II, and which the poet felt he owed to Aetius' recommendation (again possibly an indication of eastern acceptance of the western general's influence).[83] The other panegyric was clearly in honour of Aetius—possibly upon the occasion of his taking up a third consulship in 446, a highly distinguished and unusual honour.[84] The fragments remaining from both of these speeches reveal them to have been vehicles for fulsome praise of Aetius, in a manner strikingly reminiscent of Claudian's writings on Stilicho.

All rejoiced in Aetius' great deeds, according to Merobaudes. He was credited with restoring peace to the western empire—along the Danube, the Rhine, and even in the Caucasus; taming the wild Armoricans and bringing their lands under cultivation; causing barbarians to bow to Roman laws; while the lands of southernmost Gaul and of Spain which had slipped from Roman hands had all been reclaimed by the 'warlike avenger'.[85] The war-goddess Bellona wept because she could no longer rule the land, and Aetius had brought peace to all.[86] From his childhood onwards, claimed Merobaudes, Aetius had shown his warlike qualities, and through the years of his captivity with Goths and Huns he had impressed all with his prowess in the martial arts,

[82] See above, p. 204.

[83] Merobaudes, *Pan.* I, frg. IIA, 1–10. On the award of the honour, see Clover (1971*a*), 33 ff.; also (1971*b*), 355–6; and Barnes (1975), 161 ff., 168.

[84] As Clover points out, the general Merobaudes praises is not named, but there can be no doubt it is Aetius (1971*a*), 33 ff. The most recent private citizen to achieve such an honour had been Fl. Constantius, who held the consulship in 414, 417, and 420 (*CLRE*: 362–3, 368–9, 374–5) before his elevation as Augustus in 421.

[85] Merobaudes, *Pan.* II.19–20. On Aetius' struggles in Gaul, cf. ibid. II. On the campaigns Merobaudes refers to or describes, see Clover (1971*a*), 42 ff.

[86] Merobaudes, *Pan.* II. 39–40, 190–5.

while his endurance was well known and all throughout the empire rejoiced in celebrating his achievements.[87]

Merobaudes' praise for Aetius immediately recalls both the depiction of Stilicho, and consequently also the recommendations of Menander Rhetor that military ability was the virtue which would most reveal an emperor.[88] One line of Merobaudes' *Panegyric I* on Aetius has particular resonance here: 'You rely on yourself, you look to yourself, you seek no model which you might wish to imitate beyond yourself.'[89] It was not the young emperor but Aetius himself who had become the ideal, to be looked up to and admired throughout the empire—presumably even by Valentinian III. Once again, the leading general of the government of a one-time child-emperor was being depicted in an imperial manner—indeed, as possessed of the essential imperial virtue of military prowess which the available evidence does not show Merobaudes attributing to the emperor himself. Like Stilicho before him, Aetius was aiming to present a partnership of rule—even if his position was limited by the involvement of the eastern emperor—with himself as the active partner and Valentinian III, though now no longer a child-emperor, playing the ceremonial and religious role. But this arrangement did, of course, hinge on the young emperor himself being content to remain passive and to accept this exercise of his military function by another. Furthermore, the degree to which the young emperor was now presented as a purely ceremonial figure reflects the major shift which had taken place in perceptions of the imperial office since the days of Menander and the fourth-century emperors who were expected to fulfil—to some degree at least—a range of functions on the imperial 'checklist'.

Aside from his third consulship in 446, at some point before this year the Roman senate had erected a statue to Aetius in the Atrium Libertatis, recognizing his contributions to the state and his many military victories.[90] It has been claimed Aetius was increasingly in Italy from c.438, and that this was due to Vandal activity from 439 onwards, which must certainly have been a

---

[87] As well as warlike qualities since childhood, Merobaudes also praises Aetius for living up to his soldierly lineage: *Pan.* II.140–5. For his martial skills in captivity, see *Pan.* II. For praise of Aetius' personal combat see e.g. *Pan.* I, frg. IIB. For his endurance and celebrations of his achievements, see *Pan.* I, frg. IIB. Merobaudes also appears to describe something like a triumph for Aetius, but as Clover points out, we know that no such event occurred: it is more likely Merobaudes is actually describing Aetius' *processus consularis* on 1 January 446 (see *Pan.* II; Clover (1971a), 55).

[88] Menander 373.17–25.

[89] Merobaudes, *Pan.* I, frg. IIA, 19–20: *tu tibi inniteris, ad te respicis nec ullum quod | imitari velis exemplar extra te quaeris.*

[90] *CIL* 6.41389; and see Bartoli (1946–7), 267–73; Degrassi (1946–8), 33–44; Clover (1971a), 38 f.; O'Flynn (1983), 81; Oost (1968a), 258; Stickler (2002), 271–2. On the dating (preferable to the 440s), see Sirago (1961), 367.

concern.[91] The general's willingness to absent himself frequently from court in order to campaign in Gaul during the 430s suggests that he was not concerned that rivals would undermine his position while he was away, and there is no obvious reason to think this situation had changed in the 440s: presumably the chief officers at court remained Aetius' appointees. Yet we have more evidence for Aetius' whereabouts over the course of the late 430s and into the 440s than has been noted generally. In 438 he may have been present in Rome for the promulgation of the *Theodosian Code*, but in 439 he was again occupied in Gaul, although according to one source he again returned to Italy over the course of that year.[92] We know that in July of 440 he was in Gaul, engaged in a dispute with Albinus, though he was recalled to Italy at this point and there is no reason to assume he did not return.[93] In 441 or 442 Aetius may have been at court to hear the verses Merobaudes composed in honour of his son Gaudentius' birthday.[94] But again in 442 he was back in Gaul, arranging the settlement of Alans in Armorica, and may have been present in 443 also, overseeing the settlement of Burgundians in Savoy.[95] Valentinian III's ruling on Hilary of Arles was addressed to Aetius in Gaul in July 445.[96] In early 446 it is highly likely that the general was again at court to celebrate his remarkable third consulship. Yet in 447 or 448 he was again on active campaign in Gaul, where he won a major victory at Vicus Helena.[97]

Although the evidence is fragmentary, therefore, on balance Aetius still seems to have spent the majority of his time in Gaul during the 440s, leading the imperial armies and negotiating settlements with barbarian allies, interspersed with regular visits back to the court in Italy. The general seems to have remained confident his interests and position at court were well represented and well protected during his frequent absences commanding the armies on the emperor's behalf. But the fragmentary poetry of Merobaudes from the 440s provides an important reminder of the state of affairs: namely, that Valentinian was no longer a child—he was an adult, with children himself. Even if Merobaudes was intent on emphasizing a purely and dazzlingly ceremonial role for the emperor and enunciating Aetius' vision of how his partnership with the emperor should continue to operate, it could not be guaranteed that this would remain Valentinian's perception of how his powers should develop as he grew to adulthood.

[91] Zecchini (1983), 239; Oost (1968a), 258–9.
[92] Prosper 1335; Jordanes, *Get.* 176; for his return to Italy in 439, see *Chron.Gall.452*, 123.
[93] Prosper 1341; the law recalling Aetius is *NVal.* 9 (24 June 440), see further above, pp. 262–3.
[94] Merobaudes, *Carm.* 4.
[95] On the Alans, see *Chron.Gall.452*, 127; Constantius, *V.Germani* 28. On the Burgundian settlement, see *Chron.Gall. 452*, 133.
[96] *NVal.* 17 (8 July 445).
[97] Sidonius, *Carm.* 5.210–18.

10

Valentinian III: Child-turned-Adult Emperor?

> When he had been put to death the emperor said to a person able to surmise the truth, 'Was the death of Aetius not well accomplished?' He answered, 'Whether well or not I do not know, but I do know that you have cut off your right hand with your left.'[1]

Following the tumult of the seemingly endless campaigning in Gaul through the 430s, the fall of Carthage, and ominous threat of Vandal attack on Italy in the early 440s, the years following the Vandal treaty of 443 marked a period of relative stability (if not of prosperity) for the western empire until the Huns began to cast their attention westwards. In these years of Valentinian's adulthood, his role as an emperor fulfilling a ceremonial and religious function through church benefactions and cooperation between the imperial court and Leo, bishop of Rome, emerge clearly. Less clear, but still frequent enough to be noticeable, are potential signs of the emperor seeking an independent role in 'his' government, through his frequent presence in the city of Rome and possibly also through his legislation, and of increasing difficulties in the relationship between Valentinian and Aetius. The rise and fall of the Hunnic threat to the west, and the death of Theodosius II, changed the dynamics of power between the emperor and his manager. For both Aetius and Valentinian III, the moment of reckoning came when the emperor finally resolved to break free from his overbearing manager, and attempted to claim the active imperial role for himself, which Honorius had never done. The results of this initiative on the part of the child-turned-adult emperor provides the most compelling evidence for the extent to which the nature of minority rule had become embedded in the western Roman system, and how much the

---

[1] John Ant. frg. 200(1): Ἐπεὶ δὲ ἀνῃρέθη, εἶπεν ὁ βασιλεὺς πρός τινα τῶν στοχάζεσθαι δυναμένων· «Οὐ καλῶς μοι ὁ θάνατος Ἀετίου εἴργασται; »ὁ δέ, «Εἰ καλῶς, φησὶν, ἢ μὴ, οὐκ οἶδα· γιγνώσκω δὲ ὅτι τῇ λαιᾷ χειρὶ τὴν δεξιάν σου ἀπέκοψας.»

expectations of the vested interests around the throne with regard to imperial functions had changed as a result.

Valentinian III: religious and ceremonial presentation

The depiction of Valentinian III by Merobaudes discussed in Chapter 9 raises the question of how the young emperor was fulfilling in practice the highly ceremonial and religious role in which he was being cast. We have already seen that early in the new emperor's reign a conventional claim to his piety and devotion to orthodoxy had been made with legislation confirming the privileges of the church, such as might be expected of any new orthodox ruler. Later laws, such as in 441 when the tax immunities of the clergy were revoked along with those of many others, or in 445 when severe penalties were imposed upon Manichees, also address religious issues—and obviously not always to the advantage of the church.[2] But there was much more to the emperor's religious role than legislation, and many ways in which an emperor might perform this function, along with the ceremonial function so closely tied to it. Valentinian's long reign was to be remarkable for the amount of church benefaction which took place at Rome under imperial auspices—on a level unprecedented since the Constantinian dynasty, and an all the more striking development given shrinking imperial revenues.[3] Furthermore, as a couple of recent studies have highlighted, Valentinian III's rule was also to witness a remarkable resurgence of imperial presence at Rome itself, surely still the most promisingly spectacular venue for imperial ceremonial that the west had to offer.[4]

The eastern advisers of the child Valentinian had showed a marked regard for ceremonial staged at Rome from the earliest days of the reign: as discussed earlier, following the victory of the eastern army over the usurper at Ravenna, and the mutilation and execution of John in the hippodrome at Aquileia in June/July 425, finally in October, upon the anniversary of his elevation as Caesar, Valentinian became Augustus during a ceremony at Rome.[5] Valentinian's accession in the ancient capital set the tone for the reign to follow: although our information regarding imperial ceremonial between 425 and 450 is sparse, those few occasions which we do know of are also likely to have taken place at Rome. What evidence there is indicates that a special effort was made for the young emperor to take up his consulships

---

[2] *NVal.* 10 (14 Mar. 441), also 35 (15 Apr. 452); see Stein (1959), 1. 340. Manichees law: *NVal.* 18 (19 June 445).

[3] Humphries (2007), 43.

[4] Gillett (2001); Humphries (2012); McEvoy (2010).

[5] See also above pp. 231–2.

at Rome itself during the early years of his reign, with all the traditional ceremonial that this would entail, and issues from Roman mints celebrating Valentinian III's consulships in 426 and 430 have survived.[6] And indeed, as has been conclusively demonstrated in recent scholarship, the court itself seems to have spent considerable time at Rome from 425 onwards on numerous visits (some of which lasted years), particularly after 440.[7]

The efforts of Galla Placidia in the area of church benefactions, both at Ravenna and Rome, also assisted in the fulfilment of the young emperor's religious function from the earliest days of his reign: indeed it is in this area that the Augusta can be genuinely regarded as a major force in her son's administration, and as such embracing a very traditional role for imperial women.[8] The building of the church of St John the Evangelist and its extraordinary imperial mosaics has already been discussed above; in addition she is usually credited with funding the creation of the church of the Holy Cross at Ravenna, and the so-called 'mausoleum of Galla Placidia' which was once attached to it.[9] At Rome, a gift of mosaics to the church of the Holy Cross of Jerusalem (the foundation of Helena) is also ascribed to Galla Placidia, a significant choice of benefaction for the mother of an emperor.[10] A more substantial church benefaction still came in the restoration of the great extramural basilica of St Paul's after it was damaged by a major fire. This benefaction is particularly significant in its public assertion of papal and imperial cooperation at Rome, a theme of the emperor's presence in the city which will be developed further below. St Paul's had begun construction in the 380s on imperial orders, and was probably completed c.400, possibly dedicated

---

[6] *RIC* 10. 167–9; also Gillett (2001), 144 and n. 50; Humphries (2012) 166.

[7] Gillett (2001), 142–5; now also Humphries (2012) esp. 162; McEvoy (2010), 152 and n. 10.

[8] Harlow (2004), 138. Cristo points out that Placidia's letter-writing efforts during the disputed papal election in 419 reflected her interest in politics, both ecclesiastical and secular, which may well be the case; nevertheless, religious affairs were still a very traditional area of activity for imperial women: Cristo (1977), 166. It may be significant that Aetius' wife was also apparently remembered for her particular piety and worshipping at St Peter's in Rome, according to Gregory of Tours (2. 7), given the importance of the activities of imperial women in supplementing the religious role of the emperor during this period.

[9] On the Holy Cross at Ravenna, see Oost (1968a), 275 ff. Agnellus writes of her many gifts to the church at Ravenna: Agnellus 27. The purpose of the small chapel known as the empress' mausoleum has long been argued over by scholars; it is certainly possible that Galla Placidia was involved in funding its extraordinarily rich and beautiful interior decoration, and it may have been intended as her mausoleum, but it is most unlikely it ever served as such: Mackie (2003), 174, and Deliyannis (2010), 74–84 and also on the empress' church benefaction efforts at Ravenna generally, 62–3.

[10] On Galla Placidia's activity at Santa Croce in Gerusalemme: *ILS* 817; *Lib.pont.* 34, c. 41, I.179; cf. Krautheimer (1937–77), 1. 167, (1983), 156, n. 22; Oost (1968a), 269–71; Consolino (1995b), 482–3; Brubaker (1997), 61. Galla Placidia's devotion to religion and church-building is attested by Sozomen (9.16.2). The donation of mosaics to Sante Croce was in the name of Galla Placidia, Honorius, and Valentinian.

in the presence of the emperor Honorius during his visit of 404.[11] According to the mosaic inscription preserved on the triumphal arch of the basilica, following fire damage early in the 440s Pope Leo and the empress Galla Placidia jointly contributed to the renewal of the building that her father and brother had created.[12]

Galla Placidia's church-building and decoration efforts, both early in her son's reign in the late 420s at Ravenna, and later during the 440s at Rome, added to the religious image of the imperial house and the fulfilment of Valentinian III's religious function. On coinage minted for her as Augusta, her pious persona was also proclaimed, frequently depicting her with a *Chi-Rho* on her shoulder, sometimes being crowned by the hand of God, or with Victory brandishing a jewelled cross.[13] She was not, however, the only member of the imperial family engaging in such activities: the emperor himself was frequently involved. According to the *Liber pontificalis*, as part of Sixtus III's redecoration of St Peter's basilica in the 430s Valentinian III presented a valuable gold jewelled image to be placed over the shrine. Expensive donations from the emperor are also recorded for the Lateran basilica, in place of items stolen during the Gothic sack of 410. Permission was given by the emperor for the pope to construct a new basilica dedicated to St Laurence at Rome. And in addition to his mother's efforts, Valentinian is credited with the building of a silver *confessio* at St Paul Outside-the-walls.[14]

Similarly, early in the 430s a church dedicated to Saints Peter and Paul (now known as San Pietro in Vincoli) was constructed as part of the building programme of Pope Sixtus III.[15] This church had a particular connection with the eastern imperial princess and wife of Valentinian III, Licinia Eudoxia. An inscription at this church in Rome attests to the empress supporting the new foundation in the names of her parents, Theodosius II and Eudocia, either by contributing to the costs of the building, or possibly, as one legend has it, receiving as a gift from the eastern court one half of the chains of St Peter, which had found their way to Constantinople, reuniting them with the half that had remained at Rome, and donating them to the church.[16]

---

[11] On the building of the church in the 380s, see *Coll.Avell.*3; also Krautheimer (1937–77), 5. 97–8, 161–2. On its potential dedication in Honorius' presence, see Prudentius, *Peristephanon* 12.49.

[12] *ILCV*, 1761, a, b, c; *ICUR* II, 28, 68 note; see also Krautheimer (1937–77), 5. 99.

[13] Deliyannis (2010), 62; also *RIC* 10. 164. Germanus of Auxerre's visit to Ravenna in 446 also gave the empress in particular a chance to display her piety and reverence in her treatment of the elderly bishop: see Constantius, *V.Germani* 35–42, and Mathisen (1989), 169.

[14] *Lib.pont.* 46, c. 65, I.233. On the basilica to St Laurence's likely attribution as San Lorenzo in Lucina, see Krautheimer (1937–77), 2. 6–9.

[15] Krautheimer (1937–77), 3. 181. Pope Leo's *Sermon* 84b was given on the anniversary of the dedication of this church, dwelling on saints Peter and Paul, the Christian patrons of Rome: Salzman (2010*b*), 354.

[16] *ILS* 819; Krautheimer (1937–77), 3. 181.

Modern scholarship has traditionally argued that already by the fifth century popes had taken over the role of emperors within the city of Rome in authority, patronage, and church benefaction, yet the evidence of the activities of Valentinian III and his family suggests a different picture.[17] Although the disappearance of a western emperor would in time see all of these functions devolving upon the bishop of Rome, that time had not come yet. Valentinian— or his advisers—clearly saw such activities as a major aspect of his function as a Christian emperor. And although his long reign coincided with the pontificates of two popes known for their extensive activity in this area, Sixtus III (432–40) and Leo I (440–61), the imperial family itself was frequently involved.[18] Indeed, such papal activities, and the rise of the claim of papal primacy which undoubtedly became increasingly evident during this time, should be seen as taking place with the support of the western imperial court, rather than occurring at its expense.[19]

The expanding efforts of the emperor and his family to contribute to church benefaction and the Christian life of the ancient capital were surely part of an intensifying emphasis on the Christian piety of emperors in evidence during this time. At Ravenna, a substantial church-building programme had also been part of fifth-century imperial involvement in the city; but to some extent such activity must have remained partially hidden from view—at least inaccessible to the vast majority of a wider audience such as the population of Rome. At Rome itself, such efforts could combine with papal cooperation and display—especially to the senatorial aristocracy—in a particularly potent manner.[20]

Indications of close papal–imperial contact seem particularly apparent in the 440s. In 443, Pope Leo had commissioned an investigation into

---

[17] See e.g. the traditional view expressed in Krautheimer (1983), 99, 121. Scholars such as Humphries have already pointed out this dating is premature: Humphries (2007), 25, 46–7, 54–7. Sotinel's forthcoming article will also examine imperial–church relations at Rome in the fifth century.

[18] Gillett (2001), 145. Sixtus III is credited with the building of the basilica of St Mary (now Sta Maria Maggiore) (*Lib.pont.* 46, c. 63, I.232), and Leo I with renewing St Peter's basilica (*Lib.pont.* 47, c. 66, I.239). For further details see Krautheimer (1961), 291–301; (1983), 96–100; Pietri (1976), 1. 503–14; Green (2008), 5–6. It is tempting to see in the mosaics of Sta Maria Maggiore (dating to the 430s), an image of the child Valentinian III as the child-Christ, and Galla Placidia as the imperially dressed Mary figure, but no evidence allows us to link them conclusively.

[19] As Merdinger demonstrates, assertions of papal primacy during this period did not meet with success everywhere: North African resistance to papal interference in local affairs was common during this period, seen particularly in the case of Apiarius: see Merdinger (1997), esp. 183–99.

[20] Although Deliyannis argues that building under the reigns of Honorius and Valentinian III did much to transform Ravenna into an imperial 'capital' (Deliyannis (2010), 51), as Ward-Perkins has pointed out, imperial patronage of church-building efforts at Rome during the reign of Valentinian III far outstripped the more famous imperial church benefactions at Ravenna during the same period: (1984), 241. This point is emphasized also by Humphries (2012) 166–170.

Manicheism at Rome, led by bishops and senators. This commission had condemned Manicheism utterly in 444, and in June of 445, presumably prompted by Leo's findings and in support of them, Valentinian III issued a law decreeing that Manichees were guilty of a public crime, and were to be deprived of testamentary rights (among other freedoms).[21] This theme of imperial–papal cooperation is still more clearly illustrated by the famous case of Bishop Hilary of Arles.[22] Towards the end of the reign of Honorius, Pope Zosimus had been determinedly seeking to assert the authority of the see of Rome over other western sees, and as part of this push had attempted to create a papal vicariate in Gaul, under the bishop of Arles, Patroclus (who was also a client of Constantius III).[23] At the time the plan had met with opposition, but the affair was reopened in the 440s when the then bishop of Arles, Hilary, had attempted to claim an authority over other Gallic sees along the same lines as Pope Zosimus' original plan back in 418. Accused by fellow-bishops in his province of arrogant interference, Hilary had been brought before Pope Leo in 445, who deprived him of his metropolitan rank and certain privileges of his position.[24] Not content with this, Pope Leo then appealed for support for his ruling from the emperor.[25] The emperor issued a law in response, addressed to Aetius in Gaul, presumably with the intent that he should enforce it, which not only confirmed Pope Leo's ruling, but explicitly confirmed also the primacy of the bishop of Rome—the pope's position as the highest Christian authority in the empire.[26] According to the emperor, the conduct of this wayward Gallic bishop constituted crimes 'committed both against the majesty of the empire and against reverence for the Apostolic See . . .'[27] Even as late as 445, a bishop as powerful as Pope Leo the Great was still looking to the Roman emperor for support.

---

[21] *NVal.* 18 (19 June 445). On Leo's actions against the Manichees, see Green (2008), 168–80, and Neil (2009), 31–2; also Musumeci (1997), 459–61; Jalland (1941), 43–50.

[22] In general on the affair, see Heinzelmann (1992), 239–51 and Wessel (2008), 58–9; Mathisen (1989), 145–66.

[23] Mathisen (1989), 48–60; also Green (2008), 20; Jalland (1941), 114–27.

[24] Leo, *Ep.* 10. In 450, some of the Gallic bishops wrote to Pope Leo to request some of Hilary's forfeited rights be restored to his successor Ravennius, and a compromise was found: Leo, *Ep.* 66.

[25] Pope Leo's appeal to Valentinian III in 445 over the issue does not survive, but his ruling on the case does (Leo, *Ep.* 10), and the surviving law of Valentinian III deals explicitly with the case, making Leo's appeal to the emperor undisputed. In fact, as Green notes, the novel relating to Hilary was dated to only eleven days before the anti-Manichaean decree, suggesting communications between the emperor and the bishop were frequent at this point at least: (2008), 180–1.

[26] Mathisen's argument that the 'armed band' who allegedly accompanied Hilary (according to Valentinian's ruling) must have been supplied by Aetius and that the two were allies, with Valentinian's novel addressed to Aetius constituting a form of rebuke, and also an insistence that he see it carried out, seems difficult to sustain on the basis of the evidence available: (1989), 156, 166.

[27] *NVal.* 17.2: *his talibus et contra imperii maiestatem et contra reverentiam apostolicae sedis admissis . . .* (8 July 445). Cf. Heinzelmann (1992), 239–40.

The addressing of this law to Aetius also illustrates the way in which the partnership of religious and ceremonial emperor and militarily active manager continued to operate: Valentinian could issue legislation on such matters in support of the bishop of Rome, while Aetius could mobilize the resources to put this legislation into action as needed. Such a legal response to a papal request need in no way indicate a weak imperial government: the sort of disturbance that Hilary created in the Gallic church threatened stability in the region as well as within the ecclesiastical hierarchy. It was in the emperor's interest to act, as well as the pope's, and the novel provided the church with the resources it lacked to enforce the decision.[28] And indeed, as one detailed study of the religious legislation of Valentinian's reign has revealed, the emperor's government did not simply acquiesce to the desires of church leaders without hesitation, but showed initiatives of its own in religious affairs, sometimes in ways which might not always have pleased the church hierarchy—such as in 452, when Valentinian issued a law restricting the extent of ecclesiastical jurisdiction where it might impinge on the powers of secular courts.[29]

Only a few years after the Hilary affair, in 450, a further—and even more public—instance of imperial–papal cooperation can be discerned. Returning to Rome in February after a two- or three-year residence at Ravenna, the entire imperial family made a special visit to St Peter's to celebrate the Feast of Peter's Chair; indeed, the emperor's return to the city may well have been timed to coincide with this event.[30] On this particular occasion, Pope Leo and other members of the Roman clergy accosted the imperial family as they entered the basilica, and tearfully the pope entreated the emperor and his family to write to the eastern emperor Theodosius II, requesting that the findings of the 'Robber Synod' at Ephesus in 449 (which had ignored Leo's famous *Tome* and seen the eastern church endorse monophysitism) be overturned and a new synod be convened.[31] Moved by Pope Leo's pleas, the emperor Valentinian III solemnly agreed, and surviving letters testify that he, his mother, and his wife

[28] Musumeci (1997), 451.

[29] *NVal.* 35 (15 Apr. 452); see Musumeci (1997), 455–7; also Humphries (2012), 169. Woods also suggests that a further instance of cooperation between central government and the church may potentially be seen—this time with the aim of general reconstruction of the western empire—in the activities of Pope Celestine's missionaries to Britain coinciding with Aetius' reassertion of military control over Gaul in the 430s (Wood (1987), 252): it is an intriguing idea, though not possible to prove.

[30] Gillett (2001), 147. The family's presence at the feast is recorded in Leo, *Ep.* 55.1. Valentinian's laws place him in Rome until June 447 (*NVal.* 25.1) and then Ravenna from June 448 to September 449 (his last surviving law from Ravenna before returning to Rome was *NVal.* 28.1).

[31] On the controversial 'Robber Synod' and events surrounding it, see Wessel (2008), 40–2, and on Leo's request that the western imperial family intervene, 261–2; also see Seeck (1919), 384; also Oost (1968a), 287–9; Clover (1978), 178–9.

(who was, of course, Theodosius II's daughter) all wrote to the eastern emperor to remonstrate with him as Pope Leo had requested.[32]

Although this episode has generally been seen as an indication of Pope Leo's dominance over a weak western emperor, it seems rather more likely, in fact, that this was a carefully stage-managed confrontation, which once again revealed the underlying cooperation between emperor and pope at this time, as well as the undercurrent of continuing competition between western and eastern imperial courts in displays of piety. Previous instances of collaboration between Pope Leo and the imperial family suggest that the bishop did not in general have difficulty gaining access to the emperor, and that there is no reason to suppose he could not have petitioned him privately about the matter; but that was not the point. Staging the appeal in this manner allowed both emperor and pope to display their authority: at the celebration of a feast which marked the supremacy of St Peter and the papacy over the church, Pope Leo publicly and dramatically urged Valentinian III to step in to uphold the doctrinal position of Rome. And in so turning to the emperor, Leo allowed Valentinian to claim still greater authority and influence even than the pope, as well as moral superiority over his colleague, the wayward eastern emperor. Given his many years as 'junior' to his father-in-law's 'senior' position, and the already much-publicized aura of extreme piety attached to Theodosius II, we may even imagine that Valentinian III rather enjoyed the opportunity to claim the moral and religious high ground for once.

This incident also reflects the growing level of comfort of fifth-century emperors within the church and at public church services. During much of the fourth century Christian emperors seem rarely to have attended services outside of their palaces, allowing them thereby to avoid the public uncertainty and embarrassment that their presence could evoke, and the confusion about where the appropriate place for them might be—whether in the ranks of the clergy or amongst the general congregation.[33] In the east, Theodosius II was far more frequently to be found at such public celebrations than his predecessors, however, and although the evidence is sparse, this may have been increasingly the case for the western emperors also.[34] We know that at the start of his reign Honorius had been present at the funeral oration Ambrose

---

[32] The communications survive in the collected letters of Pope Leo: *Ep.* 55–8. The letter of Galla Placidia in particular refers to Leo's sighs and tears as he delivered his request (*Ep.* 58). See further Consolino (1995b), 483–4. As Sivan observes, the occasion also gave the women of the western imperial house the chance to display their orthodoxy: (2011), ch. 5.

[33] See specifically on this McLynn (2004), 235–70, and particularly in relation to Theodosius I and Ambrose of Milan, see McLynn (1994), 298–309. Also Dagron (2003), 127–57.

[34] On Theodosius II's apparent lack of discomfort at public church services, see McLynn (2004), 267. On imperial church appearances under Valentinian III, see also Humphries (2007), 47.

gave at Milan for his father, and in 404 that he visited St Peter's basilica.[35] Apart from this visit to St Peter's in 450, the sermons of bishop Peter Chrysologos of Ravenna make it clear that he numbered the imperial family among the members of his congregation in the 430s, on at least one occasion referring to the empress Galla Placidia and the imperial family as present before him (though admittedly not the emperor specifically).[36]

In Chapter 7 the foundation of the mausoleum of Honorius was discussed, and it is in relation to this mausoleum that another instance of imperial–papal cooperation and imperial church attendance in 450 arises. For the earliest mention of this mausoleum in our extant sources is recorded for this year, describing the burial there of a Theodosius—surely a re-interment of the infant son of Galla Placidia and Athaulf, originally buried at Barcelona upon his death in 415. According to our source, the interment at St Peter's took place with great ceremony in the presence of the empress, the pope, and senators.[37] The potentially considerable number of imperial burials in this mausoleum during the fifth century is significant, as is the fact of imperial rather than papal burials taking place at St Peter's at this time.[38] Given the record of papal and imperial intermingling of church benefaction and mutually supportive demonstrations of authority under Valentinian III, it should come as no surprise that when he died in 461, Pope Leo would become the first pope certainly buried in St Peter's basilica.[39] Admittedly, it was not unusual for bishops of Rome to be buried in churches to which they had contributed in terms of funding or decoration, and Pope Leo is credited with undertaking restoration at St Peter's, as well as being a determined campaigner for claims to papal primacy. Yet it seems also highly likely to have been a consideration that the basilica was by now the resting-place of the fifth-century western imperial family (as well as other members of Rome's Christian elite), and that his place was at their side.[40]

Challenges to Aetius?

The progression of Valentinian III's age, and the preoccupation of the eastern government with its own concerns during the 440s, also raises the question of

---

[35] For Honorius' presence at his father's memorial service, see Ambrose, *De ob. Theod.* 3, also McLynn (1994), 357–8. See further above, p. 145. On Honorius' visit to St Peter's in 404, see Augustine, *Cum pagani* 26 and above, p. 173. As noted above, Honorius may also have been present at the dedication of St Paul Outside-the-walls at Rome (Prudentius, *Peristephanon* 12.49).

[36] Peter Chrysologos, *Serm. 130*, 3; also *Serm. 85B*, 3. Cf. Oost (1968a), 266–7.

[37] Prosper, *Add.* 12, I. 489; also Oost (1965), 7–8.

[38] McEvoy (2010), 182–5: also McEvoy (forthcoming).

[39] Alchermes (1995), 12; Neil (2009), 49. The *Liber pontificalis* records a tradition of frequent papal burial at St Peter's in the first two centuries after Christ, but in fact the first securely attested papal burial is Leo's: see above, p. 212 and n. 141.

[40] *Lib.pont.* 47. On the growth of the concept of papal primacy under Pope Leo, see Wessel (2008), 285–97.

whether Aetius was finding a way to reinvent or extend his power as Valentinian reached adulthood. As far as the evidence of Merobaudes allows us to conclude, it appears that Aetius was still seeking to present the idea of an imperial partnership in operation, with Valentinian's role focusing on the ceremonial, and Aetius' on the active side. As *patricius*, Aetius was consistently referred to as *parens* in the emperor's legislation (but so too were other *patricii*, such as the praetorian prefect Albinus), and amongst many titles recorded for him in the laws, the most complete is: *comes et magister utriusque militiae et patricius*.[41] The accumulation in titles accorded to Aetius in the legislation harks back to Stilicho's situation, his quasi-legal status, and similar uncertainty then about exactly how the generalissimo should be addressed. In 446, Aetius' assumption of a third consulship was in itself a significant demonstration of his continuing centrality in the western government: multiple consulships for private citizens continued to be rare, and the most non-imperial recent holder of three consulships before Aetius was, of course, Constantius.[42] Such a signal honour could be all the more important in a time when the progression of Valentinian III's age might have called into question Aetius' position at the heart of government and made the need for a public expression of Aetius' continuing dominance of the western administration more pressing.

The 440s have attracted considerable attention from modern scholars, due to fragmentary evidence which indicates some possible senatorial intrigues against Aetius—or the emperor—during these years, though often with little thought as to Valentinian's age at this time and the question of whether he might attempt to take up an active role in 'his' government. The famous novel of March 443 relating to the issue of the precedence accorded to ex-consuls and *patricii*, and the implications of this ruling, have received extensive treatment.[43] The novel appears to have related to a very particular issue of the ranking of specific individuals at the court at this time, and as the individual to whom it was addressed, Petronius Maximus, was consul for the year but not yet *patricius*, it is probable he was the driving force behind the law.[44] The question of whom he sought to outrank has been much debated, but there are strong indications the targeted individual was the Gothic general Sigisvult, who probably held the rank of *magister equitum*.[45]

---

[41] *NVal.* 17 (8 July 445). Cf. on various titles for Aetius: Ensslin (1931), 481 f. and Barnes (1975), 166.

[42] Aetius held the consulship in 432, 437, and 446 (see *CLRE* 398–9, 408–9, 426–7). Fl. Constantius held the consulship in 414, 417, and 420 (see *CLRE* 362–3, 368–9, 374–5).

[43] *NVal.* 11 (13 Mar. 443); see especially Barnes (1975), 158 ff.; See also Clover (1978), 187 ff.; (1971*a*), 36–7; and Barnwell (1992), 44 ff.

[44] *NVal.* 19 (8 Dec. 445) first mentions Petronius Maximus as *patricius*. Cf. Barnes (1975), 158–9; Clover (1978), 187; Sundwall (1915), 105, n. 310.

[45] On Sigisvult, see *PLRE* 2. 1010, and further below. Clover details five possible individuals whom the law was designed to rank: Aetius, Albinus, Petronius Maximus, Merobaudes, and the Goth Sigisvult: (1989), 187–8, but comes down in favour of Sigisvult (p. 190). Twyman

The offices and allegiances of Sigisvult have also been the subject of contrasting views among modern scholars (though not, it should be noted, among ancient commentators). One suggestion has been that Sigisvult was a military rival of Aetius, although they have also been seen as political allies. More recently it has been argued that Sigisvult's long military career pre-dated Aetius' association with the western court, and that at one point between the fall of Boniface and the ultimate rise of Aetius, Sigisvult had held the highest military command in the west, the post of 'patrician and master of both services', from 432 to 435, before Aetius' inexorable ascent led to his demotion to a lesser command.[46] Sigisvult did have a long military career in high offices: he is first attested leading an early campaign against Boniface during the latter's rebellion in 427; and it was to Sigisvult as master of soldiers and in Aetius' absence that Valentinian III addressed Novel 6.1 relating to military recruiting in Italy in 440.[47] He may at some point have achieved the patriciate, and the last mention of him in the sources comes in the context of the visit of St Germanus of Auxerre to Ravenna in 448.[48]

Given Aetius' adeptness in dealing with genuine rivals, it is hard to believe Sigisvult would have enjoyed the long career he did if he had been Aetius' enemy. Their extraordinary joint consulship in 437 is a sign of that relationship—it cannot have been intended to maintain 'parity' between the generals, as sometimes suggested, since Aetius must have been the senior consul and had already held one consulship already, unlike Sigisvult.[49] Though Sigisvult may (or may not) have had pre-existing links of service to the imperial house before Aetius arrived upon the scene, he appears to have served as a trustworthy lieutenant to Aetius from 432 until his disappearance from the sources in the late 440s.

The title of 'patrician and master of both services' is also not one we can be certain denoted an actual office that must be filled at all times.[50] Unlike the rank of 'master of both services', which was a clear military office, the patrician

alternatively argues that the individual over whom Petronius Maximus sought to establish his precedence was Fl. Avitus Marinianus (cos. 423) (1970: 503). Sigisvult's tenure of the post of *magister equitum* remains uncertain: O'Flynn (1983), 83–4.

[46] For Sigisvult as Aetius' military rival, see Twyman (1970), 500; for the two as allies, see Clover (1978), 190–1. For the argument Sigisvult held the highest military command in the west from 432 to 435, see Mathisen (1999), 173–96, esp. 193.

[47] On his leading the expedition against Boniface in 427: Prosper 1294; and see *NVal.* 6.1 (20 Mar. 440), regarding the defence of Italy.

[48] The only source to credit Sigisvult with the title of *patricius* is Constantius of Lyons (see *V. Germani*, 38), and on the question of Sigisvult's patriciate, see Barnes (1975), 158–9. The *V. Germani* also refers to Sigisvult's *cancellarius*, which *PLRE* sees as evidence that he still occupied the post of *magister militum* at this point. The date of Bishop Germanus' visit to Ravenna is debated: *PLRE* 2.1010 dates it to 448, but see also on this Thompson (1984), 68–9.

[49] Contra Mathisen, (1999), 193–4.

[50] Barnes (1975), 156–8; and contra Mathisen (1999), 192–3.

aspect of the title might be little more than a sign of special favour and close relationship to the emperor, rather than a formal position—the fragmentary nature of our sources make it impossible to know. It seems to be an unknown title, in fact, before Felix in the 420s, and it may be that no formal clarification of what it meant—beyond seniority—was ever established. Furthermore, our sources are frequently inconsistent in the fifth century about who possessed the rank of *patricius* at certain points in time: Aetius, for example, is described as a *patricius* in 432 by Marcellinus *comes*, though other sources attest he did not achieve this title until 433.[51] It is possible that the only creditable source to ascribe the title of *patricius* to Sigisvult—that of Constantius of Lyons—simply made a mistake, or accorded him the title as a courtesy.[52] But if Sigisvult were a patrician, there is no real reason to suppose that such high honours for trusted lieutenants of Aetius would have seriously threatened his own position.[53]

Assuming Sigisvult was the man Petronius Maximus was aiming to claim precedence over through *NVal.* II, and in asserting himself over Aetius' lieutenant, to thereby undermine Aetius himself, the attempt nevertheless seems to have had little impact on Aetius' position. Similarly, the recall of another of Aetius' lieutenants, Merobaudes (the same Merobaudes who acted as court poet), from a successful campaigning effort in Spain the same year, due to what Hydatius reported as jealousy at court, has been put down to the same aim.[54] It is certainly possible that these efforts signalled a backlash against Aetius by individuals among the senatorial aristocracy, and perhaps more significantly that Valentinian himself was open to suggestions of ways of undermining Aetius' authority, since he had issued the legislation and must have ordered Merobaudes' recall. One scholar has expounded a similar theory that the high number of *patricii* who can be attested for Valentinian III's reign was all part of a plot by that favourite protagonist Galla Placidia to debase Aetius' position by the deliberate multiplication of such illustrious titles.[55] If this was so—and there is no real way of knowing—once again there is no

[51] Marcellinus *comes*, s.a. 432; for details see *PLRE* 2. 21–9.

[52] *NVal.* 6.1, issued in 440, does not name Sigisvult as *patricius*; see Thompson (1984), 60–1.

[53] For the argument honours for his lieutenants would threaten Aetius' position, see Twyman (1970), 499–502. Ensslin also suggested Sigisvult's ranking as a patrician would make him Aetius' rival, but that Sigisvult never did attain this rank: (1931), 467 f. For the point that such men were Aetius' appointees, see Clover (1978), 190.

[54] Hydatius 120(128). See further O'Flynn (1983), 85; Sirago (1961), 349, n. 2; Clover (1971a), 10, n. 32.

[55] Sirago (1961), 349, n. 2; a view tentatively supported by Oost (1968a), 258 and Clover (1971a), 36. The number of attestable *patricii* for the period is seven: the easterner Helion, Felix, Aetius, Sigisvult, Petronius Maximus, Fl. Albinus, and Firminius: Barnes (1975), 165). Barnes goes into a thorough analysis of the evidence in support of the patriciates of these men, and although admits Boniface and Merobaudes are also possibilities, feels that the evidence is not sufficient to support the often-made claims that they were also *patricii*.

indication that these efforts materially affected Aetius' position. In this respect, and despite the various titles accorded him in surviving legislation, it seemed to matter little what title Aetius carried: his position, whether as a rebellious commander outside the gates of Ravenna in 424, as *magister militum* in Gaul, or as 'patrician and master of both services' after 435, was securely based in his military successes, achievements which no amount of jostling for grandiose titles among those at court could tarnish during these years.

The financial measures implemented by the western government during the 440s have given rise to still more theories of conspiracy at court—either on the part of Aetius or against him. The acclamations that the senate accorded Aetius on the occasion of the promotion of the *Theodosian Code* may indicate his close relations with them.[56] But it has been argued, by the same token, that Aetius and the aristocracy as a whole collaborated against the emperor, with the intention of extorting the utmost in privileges and tax concessions from the government, with Valentinian III left powerless against such a potent alliance.[57] According to this theory, while tax measures were regularly (and cynically) passed, they were never implemented, as Aetius intended to keep the imperial treasuries bankrupt so that troops could not be levied and the dependence upon his own personal military backing would be all the greater.[58] An alternative is that Valentinian III himself was busy trying to grant privileges and tax remissions to the senatorial aristocracy during these years in a bid to win their personal support.[59] In fact, the remissions of taxes such as those in honour of the emperor's marriage in 438, and again in 450, may simply have been grand gestures aimed at writing off bad debts rather than conferring any particular benefits on the aristocracy.[60]

Alternatively, might there have been an aristocratic alliance made up chiefly of the Anicii, Caeionii, and Petronii families who monopolized key high offices against Aetius' will and controlled state finances from *c*.441 to 449?[61] The rapid turnover in holders of the praetorian prefecture of Italy from 439 until 443, followed by the lengthy tenure of Albinus from 443 to 448, it is claimed, is evidence of the intriguing of court factions during this period, and the triumph

---

[56] Chastagnol (1976), 19.

[57] Stein (1959), 1. 337–42.

[58] Stein (1959), 1.

[59] O'Flynn (1983), 95–6.

[60] *NVal.* 1.1 (8 July 438); 3 (28 Aug. 439). Though Jones (1964a), 1. 205–6, 365 sees these remissions as a sign of the 'culpable weakness' of the government in a time of such financial necessity.

[61] Twyman (1970), 482–3; Twyman argues for this (esp. at p. 493) chiefly on the basis of seemingly conflicting laws between these years—e.g. *NVal.*6.3 (14 July 444); 7.3 (25 Apr. 447); 20 (14 Apr. 445)—and also the report of Prosper (1341) of a quarrel between Fl. Albinus and Aetius in 440, to assume that the two remained enemies when the former became praetorian prefect in 443.

of a faction opposed to Aetius, in the appointment of Albinus.[62] But these events need to be situated within the broader spectrum of political developments in the western empire at this time: particularly, the chaotic repercussions of the Vandal taking of Carthage in 439, the planned and abandoned campaign against them, and then the brokering of the treaty of 443. Albinus had strong family ties to North Africa, and the argument that his appointment—which was as praetorian prefect for Italy, Illyricum, and Africa—was linked to the very serious financial problems resulting from the Vandal activity, and his personal knowledge of the region, is far more convincing. The earliest laws addressed to him dealt expressly with Africa, and his lengthy tenure surely related to the need to stabilize the situation, rather than to political intrigue at court.[63] In fact, it seems that these theories of clear antagonistic factions are exaggerated, and reflect too narrow an interpretation of the available evidence, not looking beyond political affairs at the Italian court.[64] The evidence simply does not allow a firm conclusion. Albinus and Aetius might not have always been allies—as noted above, they were known in 440 to be embroiled in a property dispute in Gaul.[65] But this dispute need not mean, either, that they were confirmed enemies, and Albinus' tenure of office therefore a triumph of a substantial faction opposed to Aetius—indeed, Albinus' later lengthy tenure of the prefecture might even indicate the success of his reconciliation with Aetius in 440.[66]

If Aetius did face senatorial—or even imperial—opposition, reflected through the financial legislation of the 440s, it was clearly far from devastating to his immediate position, though over a longer term and combined with external factors it could have an overall undermining effect.[67] It is nevertheless interesting that so many theories of factional court opposition to Aetius should have focused on the 440s, with so little corresponding attention to the age of the emperor at this stage, and whether he was making any attempt to stake a greater claim in 'his' realm. We cannot know if the young emperor was directly involved in any possible intrigues against Aetius during this period, but the knowledge that there appeared to be some senatorial feeling against Aetius could

---

[62] Twyman (1970), 490–1. Cf. Stein (1959), 1. 399. On Albinus, see *PLRE* 2. 53. Coulon also sees Albinus' long tenure of office as an indication of opposition to Aetius gaining the upper hand at court—in his view through Valentinian III's efforts: (2000), 195–6. Petronius Maximus is attested as praetorian prefect from 28 August 439, through to 14 March 441; three successors follow in rapid succession, each only attested once: on 13 August 442, Anicius Acilius Glabrio Faustus (*NVal.* 2.2); on 27 September 442, Paterius (*NVal.* 7.2); on 25 May 443, Quadratianus (*NVal.* 6.2).

[63] *NVal.* 2.3 (17 Aug. 443). Also 12 (19 Oct. 443); 13 (21 June 445). Cf. Weber (1989), 496.

[64] As pointed out by Weber (1989), 492. Cf. Moss (1973), 721; also Stickler (2002), 299.

[65] Prosper 1341.

[66] Jalland (1941), 38.

[67] Weber (1989), 492–3.

conceivably have made it easier for Valentinian to contemplate rebellion in time.[68] Valentinian's increasing age alone may have encouraged senatorial elites to look for means of restricting Aetius' degree of influence more than was possible when the emperor was still a child, and any intrigues which did exist against Aetius need not have plotted his absolute replacement. And if Aetius was indeed suffering the scheming of members of the senatorial aristocracy during this period, it may also be a hint that the general remained unable to achieve the absolute dominance of the court that Stilicho or Constantius had claimed.

Signs of independence?

The activity of Valentinian III himself during the 440s must also be considered, therefore. Aetius might aim, so far as possible given the limitations resulting from eastern interest in this western government, to perpetuate the sort of presentation of a partnership arrangement favoured by Stilicho. But Valentinian was at a critical age, and the continuation of Aetius' powerful position in the west also depended upon whether the emperor—now a young man in his twenties—would be content to remain passive, and confine his activity to the ceremonial, as Honorius had before him. According to the verdict of one scholar, it should be assumed that after 438 (following his marriage and return to the west), Valentinian presided over his consistory alone, and without his mother.[69] In fact we may be doubtful whether Galla Placidia had ever been part of Valentinian's consistory, as noted above.[70] But once again this argument suffers from the assumption that it was Galla Placidia who was the dominant figure in her son's administration up until this point, and ignores the question of Aetius' role, both before, and perhaps even more significantly after, 438. An interesting clue to the continuing—even increasing—involvement of Aetius in Valentinian III's administration is offered in the range of the topics of the legal rulings with which the general's name was associated during the 440s and 450s, though the scarcity of extant legislation necessitates caution in drawing too definite a conclusion here. Surviving legislation from the period reveals the *magister militum* taking action on matters as diverse as the curbing of the activities of Gallic bishops, the rescuing of impoverished children, and meat supplies to Rome.[71] Such

---

[68] Coulon also suggests that Valentinian appointed the pagan Litorius who was 'probably' close to the Caeionii-Decii to assist Aetius in Gaul in order to limit Aetius' success, as well as appointing Albinus to the praetorian prefecture from 443 to 449, and Storacius as prefect of Rome in 443, who would later replace Boethius as praetorian prefect in 454, but this remains a hypothesis: (2000), 195–6.

[69] Oost (1968a), 256.

[70] Harries (forthcoming), and see further above, pp. 236–7.

[71] NVal. 17 (8 July 445); 33 (31 Jan. 451); 36 (29 June 452); cf. Jones (1964a), 2. 703.

involvement by Aetius in matters of civilian jurisdiction in the 440s and beyond, that is, during Valentinian III's adulthood, could be interpreted as signalling a determination on Aetius' part to demonstrate his continuing active role in the imperial 'partnership'.

The issue of *Theodosian Code* had also asserted the dominance of the eastern emperor over judicial matters throughout both eastern and western imperial territories. And with the very low number of preserved western laws during the 430s and in the lead-up to the promulgation of the *Code*, it is only after 438, when Valentinian III had reached the age of 19, that we have the chance—potentially—to see the young emperor in action as a legislator. Careful study of these laws has suggested that they do offer a 'voice' to Valentinian—though not necessarily a very creditable one. Indeed, the laws can be understood to reflect an image of the emperor as 'volatile and opinionated', if surprisingly candid about the crises facing the west. It has also been pointed out that the rate of legislation overall between 438 and 455 is low, suggesting that Valentinian III may have been reluctant to legislate (which has been attributed to 'lethargy'), while those laws which he did pass frequently seemed to betray impatience and unwillingness to hear both sides of a case.[72]

If we accept the argument that the laws of this seventeen-year period reflect Valentinian III's character and words (rather than those of his *quaestor*), we have one of the few indications available from the surviving evidence that, despite Aetius and Theodosius II's activities even in this area, the emperor himself was taking up the traditional legislative function of an emperor in his adult life. And whether or not the 'voice' of Valentinian which emerges from these laws seems wise to us, or impatient and opinionated, what matters most in this context is that he should have a voice at all, and that these laws can be claimed to show the emperor embracing an imperial function in adulthood which he could not undertake fully as a child.[73] This interpretation is based on the language and style of the laws, which, it has been argued, can only have originated with the emperor and not his *quaestor*, an argument which is not made for the laws of Valentinian's predecessor, Honorius.[74] The overall question of the extent of personal involvement of emperors in legislation issued in their name has been much debated by modern scholars, and it is likely that each successive government saw alterations in imperial attitudes towards law-giving.[75] But the most important consideration here is that if we do truly see the personal involvement of the emperor in these laws, it may be a

---

[72] See in detail the discussion in Honoré (1999), 258–63.

[73] Humphries, in contrast to Honoré, suggests that the emperor's laws in relation to the needs of the city of Rome at least, show care and good sense: Humphries (2007), 42.

[74] Honoré (1999), 259.

[75] For a full discussion of the different judicial roles and restrictions of the emperor, see Millar (1977), 203–75.

sign of independence on Valentinian's part, and a sign also that he might not be prepared to remain dependent or inactive upon reaching adulthood.

Another notable feature of Valentinian III's government in the 440s and 450s is the frequent (and from 450 onwards, so far as we know, continuous) presence of the emperor and his court at Rome.[76] It is possible that this development, coming as it does more obviously during Valentinian's adult years, reflects the personal preference of the emperor himself, though inevitably we cannot determine this, and it must be noted that imperial attention to Rome had been on the rise from the time of Theodosius I onwards. The question arises of where the machinery of government itself was to be found— whether it always travelled with the emperor, or resided always in Rome or always in Ravenna by this time. Unfortunately, very little evidence survives to provide clues as to the answer. Most of the extant novels of Valentinian III dating from *c.*440 onwards do not give any indication as to whether or not the officials to whom they were addressed were with the emperor when he travelled to Rome. Yet there are three which do. In March 447 a lengthy ruling regarding tomb violation is recorded as issued from Rome by the emperor, and received in Rome by the praetorian prefect Albinus.[77] In 450 a law regarding fiscal debts was given at Rome and addressed to the senate, where it was read by the proconsul Postumianus.[78] And in January 451 a law regarding *coloni* addressed to the praetorian prefect Firminus is recorded as both given and received at Rome.[79] It is difficult to build a case on such sparse evidence, but these records provide at least an interesting possibility that when Valentinian travelled to Rome, these key members of the apparatus of government may have either travelled with him or still have been resident there. And, thinking back to 408 and the slaughter of Stilicho's adherents in Honorius' government as they travelled from Rome to Ravenna, it may be that this movement of key officials to accompany the emperor was normal practice in the fifth century.[80]

Overall, whether Valentinian's time spent in Rome rather than Ravenna and the personal 'voice' detected in the legislation for the period 438–55 reflected a push for independence and an attempt at the taking up of active imperial functions on Valentinian III's part is difficult to say for certain. Yet, given the emperor's eventual, aggressive actions in self-assertion in 454, it is undeniably tempting to think that they did.

---

[76] The extent of imperial presence in the ancient capital rather than Ravenna in the fifth century was first thoroughly explored by Gillett (2001), 142–8. The residences of Valentinian III's court have been more recently examined by Humphries (2012).

[77] *NVal.* 23.1 (13 Mar. 447).

[78] *NVal.* 1.3 (14 Mar. 450). As Humphries points out, some of Valentinian's legislation was even conducted before the senate of Rome: (2007), 42.

[79] *NVal.* 31.1 (31 Jan. 451).

[80] See above, pp. 281–3.

Imperial Betrothals

The year 450 would prove to be a particularly significant one for the relationship between Valentinian III and Aetius. It was in this year that Galla Placidia
died at Rome, and was buried there, probably in the mausoleum adjacent to St
Peter's where her brother Honorius had been interred.[81] Rather more significant for the relationship between the emperor and his *magister militum*,
however, was the death of Theodosius II in July of the same year.[82] Theodosius' influence on the western government of his cousin and son-in-law had
been both long-term and dominating. From the very creation of the administration, to the endowment of a hopeful future for the dynasty through the
marriage of Valentinian and Licinia Eudoxia, from the North African military
campaigns to the gift of legal codification, Theodosius had been a constant
authority *in absentia*. His attitude to his western colleague had been one of
both partnership and paternalism, and, as argued above, it is highly likely that
he had exercised some kind of veto over the extent to which Aetius was able to
marginalize Valentinian. The eastern emperor's death would fundamentally
change the dynamics of the relationship between the western emperor and his
manager in 450. Theodosius II's successor, Marcian, was not born of the ruling
house but had swiftly married into the imperial family to secure his accession,
and with Valentinian III now senior Augustus, Marcian could not be expected
to claim the same paternal attitude to his western colleague as his predecessor,
especially at the outset of his reign.[83] In fact, Valentinian refused to acknowledge Marcian's accession for some time, viewing himself as Theodosius II's
legitimate heir and feeling that he should at the very least have been consulted
over the elevation of Marcian.[84] In 408 the announcement of Arcadius' death
had sent ripples through the western court, opening up a rift between Honorius and Stilicho as each sought to find a way to exploit the death of the eastern
emperor to his own advantage. In 450 the death of Theodosius II would send
similar shock-waves through the relations between Valentinian III and Aetius:
eastern affairs and politics continued to matter to the west in the fifth century,
even directly to influence the outcomes of political crises. It should come as no
surprise, therefore, that the period 450–4 saw at last undisputed evidence that

[81] On Galla Placidia's death, see: Hydatius 140(148); *Chron.Gall.452*, 136; Procopius, *Bell.*
3.4.15; Agnellus 42.
[82] Theodosius II died from spinal injuries following a fall from a horse, on 28 July 450:
see Marcellinus *comes*, s.a. 450 (1, 2); also *Chron.pasch.* pp. 589, 590; *Chron.Gall.452*, 135;
Theophanes, AM 5942; Evagrius 1.22; Hydatius 138(146).
[83] On Marcian's accession, see Marcellinus *comes*, s.a. 450 (1, 2); also *Chron.pasch.* p. 590;
Procopius, *Bell.* 3.4.7; Evagrius 1.22; Theophanes, AM 5943; Zonaras 13.24.1–3; Hydatius 139
(147). Marcian married Pulcheria, elder sister of Theodosius II, who had declared herself a
dedicated virgin at the age of 14: Holum (1982), 208–9.
[84] Valentinian seems to have refused to acknowledge Marcian until 452, and the eastern
consuls for 451 and 452 were not accepted in the west: see generally Burgess (1993–4), 63–4.

Valentinian III was attempting to free himself from the dominance of Aetius, or that Aetius now began to take steps which perhaps had been unavailable to him before, to secure his position more definitively.

Although the exact date is not certain, it was certainly between 450 and 454, and possibly as early as 450, that Valentinian III hatched a plan to launch a serious challenge to Aetius' power. The sources tell us that the emperor betrothed his younger daughter, Placidia (who was probably aged about 10 at this time) to a young man of senatorial rank who had military connections also (he had actually served under Aetius in his Gallic campaigns), by the name of Majorian.[85] The betrothal of Huneric and Eudocia had not been accompanied by any suggestion that the marriage would give the Vandal prince a claim on Valentinian's throne; it had also been agreed upon when the princess was very young and any eventual marriage a distant prospect. But a marriage between Majorian and Placidia would be quite different: Majorian was a Roman of senatorial rank and military experience—he could be lined up as a suitable heir through marriage, and could thus pose a most serious threat to Aetius, and do so imminently, since Placidia was nearing marriageable age under Roman law. There can be no doubt that the betrothal was a direct challenge to the general's power.[86] Valentinian III had now reached the age of 31; he had been prevented from personally gaining a military reputation thus far through the determined exercise of that imperial function by his manager, but he was now resolutely trying to claim a son-in-law who was on the way to building such a reputation, and who might then have had the power to depose Aetius.

Aetius responded swiftly, breaking the engagement, dismissing Majorian from court, and sending him home to his country estates.[87] That he had the ability to do so is a testament to Aetius' growing power from 450 onwards: ten years earlier he had been apparently unable to prevent his lieutenant Merobaudes being recalled from Spain; now he could break the betrothal of the emperor's daughter and send the prospective son-in-law home like a naughty child. Aetius then betrothed his own son, Gaudentius, to the princess, and according to Prosper, had Valentinian III swear an oath of 'friendship' to him, a sure sign that their relationship was strained.[88] By 452, Aetius' title in

---

[85] The date for the betrothal could range between 450 and 454, but Clover's dating of 450 is plausible: (1971*a*), 25. Cf. *PLRE* 2. 702–3 on Majorian. For Majorian's military exploits under Aetius, see Sidonius, *Carm.* 5.210 ff. Majorian was, of course, the later emperor of the west (457–61).

[86] As observed by Sidonius, *Carm.* 5.203–6; For detailed analysis on the whole affair and the sources, see Oost (1964), 23–9; and more generally O'Flynn (1983), 95; Honoré suggests that the betrothal did not take place until 454: (1999), 258.

[87] Sidonius, *Carm.* 5.119–274.

[88] Prosper 1373. Aetius had two sons, the first named Carpilio, and Gaudentius was the second, born of Aetius' second marriage to a Gothic princess by the name of Pelagia, who seems previously to have been the wife of the general Boniface: Clover (1978), 172, and above, p. 260, n. 36. Gaudentius was born *c*.440—Merobaudes composed a *genethliakon* (*Carmen IV*) in honour of the infant's first birthday in 441/2: Clover (1971*a*), 25. See further on Gaudentius, *PLRE* 2. 494. If

imperial legislation was becoming even grander than before—he was *magnificus vir parens patriciusque noster.*[89]

Aetius' ability in 450 to break the engagement of the emperor's daughter, arranged by the emperor himself, and betroth the princess to his own son was certainly the action of an immensely powerful man; indeed, a man whose powers clearly outstripped those of the emperor, since Valentinian III could not prevent it. It was also an act which showed that something major had changed in the dynamics of the relationship between emperor and manager. Aetius could potentially have forged a marriage alliance with the imperial house at any time in the last few decades—if there was nothing standing in his way—and as argued above, it is little short of astonishing that he had not done so. The fact that Valentinian III tried to take this bold step to outflank Aetius in 450 suggests that the emperor too was aware of the one serious control on the extent of Aetius' power having disappeared upon the death of Theodosius II. If Valentinian was going to make a break for freedom before Aetius extended his power even further, it had to be now. But the eastern veto was no longer in operation, and at last Aetius could take the step he surely would have taken many years before if it had not been for the restraining influence of Theodosius II: he could link himself to the imperial family by marriage. Like Stilicho before him, Aetius hoped to embed himself utterly in the regime by becoming the grandfather of an emperor—of Valentinian III's heir. Such a move would allow him to reinvent his relationship with Valentinian just as Stilicho had needed to do as Honorius grew older—even if for Aetius the ability to take such a step came rather later. The progression of Aetius' own age, too (he must have been near 60 in the 450s) probably also contributed to the feeling that the time had come to secure his position once and for all.[90]

The coming of the Huns

As discussed in Chapter 9, in the early 440s Hunnic aggression towards the eastern Roman empire had prompted the recall of the fleet from Italy, and hence secured North Africa for the Vandals. But by the late 440s the focus of Attila, the leader of the Huns, was shifting to the west. From 449 onwards Attila seems to have been collecting reasons to move against the western empire, the most infamous of these being a supposed engagement to Valentinian III's sister, the Augusta Justa Grata Honoria, who had allegedly appealed for his help against her brother after she was detected in an illicit affair with the

---

both Gaudentius and Placidia were born around 440, by 454 they would have just reached the legal age for marriage: ibid. 30.

[89] *NVal.* 36 (29 June 452).
[90] Coulon (2000), 267–8.

manager of her household. Attila demanded that she be handed over as his bride, along with a dowry of half of the western emperor's territory, and when this was refused, invaded.[91] The scandal of Honoria's activity unsurprisingly has attracted the most scholarly attention as a reason for Attila's invasion, and it is noteworthy that by this point, when the Augusta must have been in her late thirties, she remained unmarried.[92] Since there is no evidence to suggest that she had taken a vow of virginity like her eastern cousins, it is likely that she had not been permitted to marry for fear that her husband (or any children) would pose a political threat—either to Valentinian III or to Aetius. But there were other alleged reasons for the Hunnic invasion, such as the dissension between the sons of the recently deceased Frankish king, in which Attila supported the elder son and the Romans the younger, according to Priscus.[93] Given the increasing financial stresses betrayed by legislation of the 440s, and the concern of such laws with raising recruits in spite of the treaty with the Vandals and the comparative peace in the western regions during this decade, it seems as though the western government had long expected the building Hunnic threat to lead to outright conflict, and that preparations for war were already under way.[94] Indeed, Merobaudes' *Panegyric 2* of 446 implies an expectation that 'Scythian'—that is, Hunnic—warriors would soon be upon them, and Roman soldiers rushing to pick up their glittering arms.[95]

In 451, Attila began his march against the west, and was confronted in the same year in Gaul on the Catalaunian Fields by a large confederation of barbarian forces led by Aetius, but including among its ranks the Visigoths under their king Theoderic.[96] Although the battle resulted in an inconclusive draw rather than a resounding Roman victory, it was nevertheless enough to cause Attila to withdraw from Gaul.[97] In the following summer of 452, Attila launched an invasion of Italy, taking major towns and cities, including

[91] Priscus, frg. 20.1, 20.3, 21.2, 22.2. Cf. also Jordanes, *Get.* 42.222–4; *Rom.* 328; Theophanes, AM 5943; John Ant., frg. 199(2).

[92] Jordanes claims she was not permitted to marry: *Get.* 224; *Rom.* 328. The most extensive examination of the scandals surrounding Honoria remains Bury's: (1919), 5 ff. Honoria's activity is extensively attested in the sources; for further details with analysis of the reports, see Thompson (1996), 145–6. The dating of the sequence of events has been much debated, see: Clover (1971a), 22–3; Croke (1995), 81; Oost (1968a), 283, n. 115; Holum (1982), 1–2.

[93] See, for some further reasons claimed: Priscus, frg. 11.2.313–55 and 20.3. See generally Heather (2000), 14–15.

[94] For financial strain on the administration, see e.g. *NVal.* 15.1 (between 11 Sept. 444 and 18 Jan. 445). Cf. Maenchen-Helfen (1973), 103–4. *NVal.* 6.3 (14 July 444) also deals extensively with recruiting issues; cf. Stein (1959), 1. 508. Comparative peace does seem to have been the state of the provinces still under west Roman control at this point, however, apart from a Frankish attack upon Arras which Aetius had to deal with in *c.*448: Heather (2000), 13.

[95] Merobaudes, *Pan.*II.75–90. See also Maenchen-Helfen (1973), 101 ff.

[96] For the progress of his campaign, see: Priscus, frg. 21.1; Jordanes, *Get.* 16.185–6; Hydatius 142(150); also Greg.Tur. 2.7; Thompson (1996), 143 ff.

[97] The battle took place around 20 June 451, and according to Hydatius 142 (150), 300,000 died. For modern analyses and the sources, see Clover (1973), 114–15; Oost (1968a), 296 ff., and

Aquileia and Milan, and apparently preparing to march on Rome, but eventually withdrew from Italy without a decisive battle taking place, seemingly due to a combination of disease among the invading army and eastern action against the Hunnic homeland in their absence.[98] In another show of ecclesiastical and imperial solidarity, Pope Leo had allegedly headed an embassy to Attila which so impressed the Hunnic king that he decided to withdraw without taking Rome—or at least provided a very convenient reason for a strategic retreat from Italy.[99] Things clearly had grown desperate for the western government as the Huns swept southwards, however: Prosper asserts that Aetius had not expected or prepared for the attacks on Italy, and contemplated evacuating the emperor to Gaul.[100] Yet the eastern emperor Marcian's decision to refuse all payment of Hunnic tribute in 452, and then to send forces against the small garrison which Attila had left on the Danube to guard the heartland of the Hunnic territories, was in fact a major action in support of the west, and a further reminder that the concept of unity between the two realms was not yet dead.[101] Hydatius even appears to suggest that Marcian made eastern forces directly available to the west in the defence of Italy, under an eastern general also confusingly named Aetius, though it is difficult to know if this was really the case or simply a muddling of the western Aetius' campaign and Marcian's sending of forces into Hunnic territory in support of the west.[102]

Aetius' achievement in putting together the barbarian confederation which he led against the Huns in 451 was a major one. It was a critical moment, at which the only option was to put to the test the web of uncertain alliances forged with different barbarian groups in Gaul over the last few decades: the

Täckholm (1969), 259–76. On the different treatments of the battle in the sources, see Barnish (1992), 38.

[98] On the invasion of Italy and particularly the siege of Aquileia, see: Priscus, frg. 22.1; Greg. Tur. 2.7; Jordanes, *Get.* 42.219 ff.; Marcellinus *comes*, s.a. 452(3); Prosper 1365; Procopius, *Bell.* 3.4.29–35; Agnellus 42; *Chron.Gall.511*, 617; *Chron.Gall. 452*, 139, 141; Theophanes, AM 5945; Hydatius 145(153). On the capture of Milan see Priscus, frg. 22.1.1–26, 22.3.

[99] Prosper 1367; Priscus, frg. 22.1; Jordanes, *Get.* 223; *Lib.pont.* 47, c. 66, I.239. Jordanes also reports that Attila's followers did not wish him to go to Rome due to a superstitious belief that it would result in their leader's death, since Alaric had died soon after the sack of 410.

[100] Prosper 1367.

[101] For Marcian's activity, see Priscus, frg. 20.1 and 23.1. On Marcian's stance in general, see Thompson (1950), 58–75, and Kaegi (1968), ch. 1. Marcian's action brought down dire Hunnic threats against the east, but Attila died before the next campaigning season: Priscus, frg. 24.2.1 ff.; 25.1–6; Jordanes, *Get.* 254–8; *Chron.pasch.* p. 588.; Marcellinus *comes*, s.a. 454 (1); Hydatius 146 (154); Malalas 14.10; Theophanes, AM 5946; see generally Maenchen-Helfen (1973), 141–3; Thompson (1996), 163; Heather (1995), 20 ff.; Hohlfelder (1984), 54–69.

[102] Hydatius 146(154). An Aetius received the consulship in 454, but this man seems to have been an eastern *comes domesticorum* named Aetius rather than the western *magister militum*: *CLRE* 442–3; also *PLRE* 2. 29–30; Thompson (1996), 163. Blockley also suggests cooperation between the two imperial courts in dealing with the Hunnic threat, and perhaps also the offering of east Roman troops to the west: (1992), 68; Maenchen-Helfen (1973), 138.

Ripuarian and Salian Franks on the middle and lower Rhine; the Alans in Valentia and Civitas Aurelianorum; the Burgundians of Sapaudia; and most importantly the Visigoths of Aquitania Secunda, who had to be persuaded to fight by a special envoy, according to Jordanes.[103] And when tested, these alliances did hold: the force Aetius drew up behind him was a testament both to his diplomatic skill and the extent to which his military successes over the previous two decades had impressed themselves on these different barbarian groups—some of whom, like the Visigoths, had on an earlier occasion been subdued by Hunnic auxiliaries at Aetius' command. But as allies of the active representative of the imperial partnership, were these men supporting the cause of Aetius, or the emperor? And, perhaps more crucially, would they remain loyal if Aetius himself were removed?

Aetius' downfall

The last few years of the lives of both Aetius and Valentinian III provide little in the way of source material, although what little there is has again given rise to theories of political intriguing at court. According to one view, the unexpected appearance of two Gallic aristocrats in high office in Italy between 450 and 454 represented Aetius finally wresting control of the court from the Italian senators who had supposedly opposed him through the 440s, and manoeuvring his own allies (assumed to be such simply because they were Gallic and Aetius had campaigned there) into key positions.[104] The appearance of Firminus as praetorian prefect from 450 to 454, and Opilio as *magister officiorum*, then *praefectus urbi*, and finally consul through the same years, is remarkable: no men of Gallic origin had held these posts in Italy since the death of Honorius.[105] It is certainly possible that these men were Aetius' appointees: as discussed above, even if the emperor were already attempting to outmanoeuvre his manager, Aetius was clearly still extremely powerful, perhaps ever more so since the death of Theodosius II, and it is unlikely he would have allowed such key offices to go to men who did not support him. Yet it is also possible that the appointment of Gallic nobles to these posts was in recognition of the depredations suffered in Gaul as a result of Attila's invasion.

While the death of Theodosius II may have given Aetius the freedom to extend his power and influence at the western court as never before, the rise and fall of the Huns had also had its impact on the dynamics of power at the court of

---

[103] Jordanes, *Get.* 16.186–90. See further Clover (1973), 112–13. Cf. Stein (1959), 1. 323–4. On all of Aetius' barbarian auxiliaries, see: Jordanes, *Get.* 16.191–3; also Hydatius 150(158).

[104] Oost (1968a), 237–8; Twyman (1970), 486–7. Zecchini also concludes that Aetius' relations with the Gallic aristocracy were significantly better than those with the Italian senatorial elite (1983), 249.

[105] ibid.

Valentinian III. When the Huns had been content to provide Aetius' personal military backing they had made him immensely powerful, and even during the 440s, when the prospect of war with them seemed imminent, their very aggression provided a reason for Aetius' position, as in 451 he put together the Roman–barbarian confederation he led personally in battle against Attila. Yet the Huns had been such a major underlying factor in Aetius' success over the past few decades that once both their previous support for Aetius, and then their aggression towards the west had died away, Valentinian III finally felt that his chance to rid himself of Aetius and reclaim the imperial functions which had so long been delegated, had come.[106]

On 21 or 22 September 454, the now 36-year-old emperor Valentinian III personally murdered Aetius. The accounts of both Priscus and John of Antioch report that the general had come to the palace for a planning meeting with the emperor and to evaluate new proposals for the raising of money:

As Aetius was explaining the finances and calculating the tax revenues, with a shout Valentinian suddenly leapt up from his throne and cried out that he would no longer endure to be abused by such treacheries. He alleged that, by blaming him for the troubles, Aetius had wished to deprive him of power in the west, as he had done in the east, insinuating that only because of Aetius did he not go to remove Marcian from his throne. While Aetius was stunned by this unexpected rage and was attempting to calm his irrational outburst, Valentinian drew his sword from his scabbard and, together with Heracleius, who was carrying a cleaver ready under his cloak (for he was head chamberlain), fell upon him.[107]

Valentinian III and his eunuch Heracleius then killed Boethius, the praetorian prefect and a supporter of Aetius, and had both bodies exposed in the Forum as traitors. According to Priscus, the emperor then immediately summoned the senate, making many charges against the dead men out of fear the senate might otherwise support a revolt against him.[108]

Both the manner of Valentinian's attack upon Aetius and the actions he took immediately following the general's death are significant for our understanding of the emperor's position and aims at this point. Possibly due to the extent of his

---

[106] Heather (1995), 29. Also Oost (1964), 25.

[107] Priscus, frg. 30.1.13–27: ὡς δὲ τὰ περὶ των πόρων Ἀέτιος προύθηκε καὶ ἀναλογισμὸν ἐποιεῖτο τῶν ἐκ τῆς εἰσφορᾶς ἀθροισθέντων χρημάτων, ἀθρόον ὁ Βαλεντινιανὸς ἀνακραγὼν ἀνέθορέ τε τοῦ θάκου καὶ οὐκέτι ἔφη οἴσειν τοσαύταις ἐμπαροινούμενος μοχθηρίαις· ἐπ' αὐτὸν γὰρ φέροντα τὴν κακῶν αἰτίαν παρελέσθαι αὐτόν, ὥσπερ τῆς ἑῴας βασιλείας, καὶ τοῦ τῆς ἑσπέρας βούλεσθαι κράτους, παραδηλῶν ὡς δι' ἐκεῖνον οὐκ ᾔει τὸν Μαρκιανὸν ἐκβαλὼν τῆς ἀρχῆς. τὸ δὲ παράδοξον τῆς ὀργῆς ὡς ἀπεθαύμαζεν ὁ Ἀέτιος καὶ ἐπειρᾶτο τῆς ἀλόγου κινήσεως ἀπαγαγεῖν αὐτόν, σπασάμενον ὁ Βαλεντινιανὸς τοῦ κολεοῦ τὸ ξίφος σὺν τῷ Ἡρακλείῳ ὥρμησεν, ἤδη καὶ αὐτοῦ τὴν κοπίδα εὐτρεπῆ ὑπὸ τὴν χλαμύδα φέροντος· πριμικήριος γὰρ τῶν κοιτώνων ἦν. Also briefly at Priscus, frg. 30.2.1–3. Cf. John Ant., frg. 201(2); Hydatius 152(160).

[108] Priscus, frg. 30.1.39–51. Similarly: John Ant., frg. 201(4). Cf. in much less detail: Marcellinus *comes*, s.a. 454(2); Prosper 1373; Sidonius, *Carm.* 7.359; Theophanes, AM 5946; Greg.Tur. 2.8.

personal resentment, but also potentially because there were few among his household whose primary allegiance was to him and not to Aetius, the emperor had carried out the killing himself, relying only upon his personal chamberlain for assistance. As he killed the general, Valentinian allegedly accused him of preventing him from leading a campaign to remove Marcian, a grievance which must have been festering for several years by this point, and which, if not verifiably part of Valentinian's accusations against Aetius, must have been rumoured as a reason for the emperor's anger. Furthermore, this desire of a western emperor to march eastwards upon the death of a senior eastern colleague harks back to Honorius' disagreement with Stilicho in 408 over who should travel to Constantinople upon Arcadius' death. The immediate killing of Boethius, the praetorian prefect, identified explicitly as Aetius' supporter, again is a reminder of the extent to which Valentinian's government must have been filled with the general's men. Perhaps surprisingly (or indeed dangerously), no wholesale slaughter of further members of the government or military high command followed—not even the killing of Aetius' son Gaudentius, for whom more concrete claims of plans to make the boy emperor through his betrothal to Placidia could be found than in the case of Stilicho's murdered son Eucherius.[109]

The fundamental difference between the deposition of Aetius in 454 and that of Stilicho in 408, however, is the identity of the primary actor. In 408 the ruthless bureaucrat Olympius, in the midst of multiple military crises, accompanying a disgruntled army and at a moment when Stilicho and Honorius were separated, had instigated a bloody military coup which removed at a stroke all of the key personnel of the imperial government and left a frightened and isolated emperor with little choice but to sign the order for the absent Stilicho's execution. In contrast, in 454, in a time of peace, Valentinian apparently acted as a lone assassin, unable to rely on any support but that of his chamberlain, and certainly not on the backing of the military Aetius had led so successfully and for so long. Such independent activity left him unable to follow though the full bloodletting that fifth-century regime-change had frequently entailed, and he must be content with dispatching only his *magister militum* and the praetorian prefect. Unlike Honorius after 408, however, Valentinian's unexpectedly brutal activity after so many years in Aetius' shadow did away with any idea that henceforth he would be a ceremonial emperor only. This event had certainly never been part of the script that Aetius had written for him.

---

[109] Hydatius 152 (160) does state that after Aetius was murdered a number of *honorati* were also killed, but can be no more specific, and other sources mention only Boethius.

Valentinian Augustus

At last the child-turned-adult emperor, who had spent twenty-nine years under the thumb of his eastern colleague or his western manager, had broken free. And, again in contrast to Honorius upon the death of Stilicho, Valentinian III clearly had no intention of sitting back and waiting for another strong man to take over Aetius' position: this time, he would be the strong man. According to some sources, the powerful senator Petronius Maximus had influenced Valentinian to act against Aetius, but if this were the case, Valentinian III nevertheless then flatly refused to allow Maximus to take over Aetius' former position.[110] According to the sources, Maximus demanded that Valentinian III grant him a third consulship, as a sign of extreme imperial favour, but the emperor would not, agreeing with Heracleius that having freed himself of Aetius, he should not transfer his power to another.[111]

Valentinian clearly had other plans. His immediate summoning of the senate to denounce Aetius following the murder indicates that Aetius certainly did have some substantial support among the senators and his death could potentially provoke a reaction against the emperor, but also that Valentinian III was shrewd enough to realize this, and to take immediate action to try to prevent it. It also appears that he immediately set about trying to build up his own personal links with the senatorial aristocracy. Sidonius reports that Valentinian III swiftly recalled the senator Majorian out of his country retirement following Aetius' death, and made him *comes domesticorum*.[112] It has been argued that Valentinian III also reinstated Majorian's previous engagement to Placidia (whose betrothal to Gaudentius no doubt had been terminated with Aetius' death), but this is doubtful, even though Majorian was back at court and in favour.[113] There is some evidence to suggest that by the time of Valentinian III's death in 455 Placidia had become engaged not to Majorian but to another senator, Olybrius, whom she did eventually marry. One detailed study of Anicius Olybrius' career and connections has highlighted that the senator not only boasted family connections to numerous fellow-Roman senators, and belonged to the main line of the immensely illustrious Anicii family, but that members of his family had also been Aetius supporters.[114] It seems likely that while Valentinian III recalled Majorian and

---

[110] For accounts of Petronius Maximus urging the murder of Aetius, see Procopius, *Bell.* 3.4.16 ff.; 3.4.24–8; John Ant., frg. 200(1); Priscus, frg. 30.1.1–8; Greg. Tur. 2.8.

[111] Priscus, frg. 30.1.39–51; similarly John Ant., frg. 201(4). On Maximus' request for Aetius' title and position, see Barnes (1975), 156–7.

[112] Sidonius, *Carm.* 5. 305–11. Cf. John Ant., frg. 201.4–5; Prosper 1375. See Oost (1968*a*), 286–7.

[113] Oost (1968*a*), 302–3. There is no evidence a marriage ever actually took place: Clover (1971*a*), 29.

[114] See generally Clover (1978), 169–96. Olybrius would in time become western Roman emperor in 472: also *PLRE* 2. 796–8.

was prepared to bestow a high appointment upon him, now that he had removed Aetius, Valentinian had thought better of lining up a son-in-law who might boast a substantial military following which the emperor himself could not match—at least at this point.[115] Furthermore, the betrothal of Placidia to Olybrius had the potential to bring over a considerable section of the Roman elite to Valentinian III's cause through Olybrius' connections, and perhaps even to placate some of those among the senate who had supported Aetius.[116]

Majorian's major responsibility, at least according to Sidonius, was to win over Aetius' private army, his *bucellarii*, to the cause of the emperor, a task in which he seems to have been conspicuously unsuccessful.[117] Indeed, the very existence of Aetius' *bucellarii* and the absence of one attached to Valentinian himself is a reminder both of how thoroughly Aetius must have managed the emperor's immediate entourage, and of how far removed the emperor had been from any association with military affairs during Aetius' dominance.[118] Yet in his appointment of Majorian, Valentinian III was being proactive in attempting to establish links with his military and recognizing that it needed to be done if he was to take on the active imperial role which Aetius had previously exercised on his behalf. In addition to his appointment of Majorian, Valentinian III himself apparently took to participating in military exercises with the troops stationed at Rome, presumably in the hope of encouraging personal loyalty through his presence and belief in his ability to fulfil the role of military leader.[119] And when Valentinian III took up the consulship for 455, the martial imagery of one type of *solidi* issued at Rome for the occasion similarly suggests the emperor's courting of the favour of the military.[120]

Valentinian III was shrewd enough to realize that the barbarian allies acquired through Aetius' victories and diplomatic efforts over the years might, upon his death, consider their agreements to be void on the basis that they had allied with Aetius rather than the empire, as appeals directly to the general during the 430s and 440s would certainly suggest. According to Hydatius, Valentinian III took great care to send envoys to the many barbarian groups with whom agreements had been made under Aetius, to assure them

---

[115] Clover (1971a), 29.

[116] Clover (1978), 191–2. Clover also suggests that, as Petronius Maximus was a relative of Anicius Olybrius, this move may have been aimed at satisfying his ambitions also in drawing a closer link with the imperial house. Mommaerts and Kelley alternatively claim that Anicius Olybrius was really Petronius Maximus' younger son and propose an alternative chronology for the engagement, which seems less likely: (1992), 119–20.

[117] Sidonius, *Carm.* 5.306–8; cf. John Ant., frg. 201.4–5; Prosper 1375. Also Oost (1964), 24–5.

[118] On the origins and development of *bucellarii*, see Jones (1964a), 2. 666–7; Diesner (1972), 321–50; Haldon (1984), 101.

[119] John Ant., frg. 201.5; cf. Oost (1968a), 303–4; (1964), 25.

[120] *RIC* 10. 163–4.

that the terms still stood.[121] Despite these efforts, there is no indication that the western emperor was any more eager after Aetius' death to see his daughter married to the Vandal prince Huneric, however.[122]

Valentinian III's initiatives in seeking to build his own regime and to establish his own links with senatorial and military powers are quite impressive, given the short time he was to survive Aetius. Clearly this child-turned-adult emperor was no fool, even if he was not prepared to heed the warning of the fate that had befallen Gratian and Valentinian II before him—or had simply decided that the risk was worth it. Yet he was working against a system of rulership which had become increasingly entrenched over the past century, within which there was little room for such activity on the part of the emperor himself, and over the past thirty years he had had little opportunity to develop any personal loyalty among his military. Potentially, had Valentinian found a way to dispose more thoroughly of the remnants of Aetius' regime— had he been more brutal and removed more of Aetius' supporters from the government and the military—his own regime might have survived longer. But it was not to be: on 16 March 455, only six months after the murder of Aetius, Valentinian was assassinated while engaging in military exercises. The plot against the emperor is ascribed by the sources to none other than Petronius Maximus, disgruntled at his inability to take over after the fall of Aetius as the strong man of the government. Maximus apparently recruited a couple of former Hunnic supporters of Aetius to do the deed (perhaps some of the former members of Aetius' *bucellarii*), urging them to take vengeance.[123] According to Priscus, Valentinian III was struck down on the Campus Martius, while the attackers removed his diadem, stole his horse, and rode off to Petronius Maximus, who then claimed the throne. None of those present made any attempt to defend the emperor or to retaliate against his attackers.[124]

Valentinian III's murder of Aetius, followed by his own death by assassination within six months of making this break for freedom, are highly significant events in tracing the gradual institutionalization of child-emperor rule in the late Roman west. For as long as the emperor himself was prepared to accept that the government functioned as a partnership, made up of the ceremonial figure of the emperor himself (even as an adult), and the active figure of his

---

[121] Hydatius 153(161).

[122] Contra Oost (1968a), 302; now also Merrills and Miles, who claim that Valentinian may have been increasingly sympathetic to the Vandal cause (2010: 116)—there is no discernible sign of this supposed attitude.

[123] Priscus, frg. 30.1.51–7; John Ant., frg. 201(4). As Frank points out, the fact that supporters of Aetius had apparently been assigned to Valentinian's bodyguard after the general's death suggests that the emperor had no personally loyal escort himself, and Aetius had controlled even his immediate entourage: Frank (1969), 190.

[124] Priscus, frg. 30.1.58–72; 30.3.1–9; John Ant., frg. 201(5); 200(2); Evagrius 2.7; Marcellinus *comes*, s.a. 455(1); Hydatius 154(162); Jordanes, *Rom.* 334; Prosper 1375. Also briefly: Malalas 14.14; Theophanes AM 5947; *Chron.pasch.* pp. 591–2; Agnellus 42.

most powerful general, and that this was the way that those around the throne expected the system to function, Valentinian III remained an acceptable emperor. This was the pattern which had been employed throughout the reign of Honorius, and had been developed and honed from the less successful attempts to establish such a system under the boy-emperors Gratian and Valentinian II. It was how those around the throne now expected the system to work—how even the eastern court of Theodosius II now anticipated the western rule of the boy-emperor as functioning in 425. And as long as the emperor remained passive—content, effectively, to remain a child—it did function. But Valentinian III was not prepared to accept a lifelong ceremonial role. It is significant that as he murdered Aetius he alluded to plans he had had to take a military campaign to the east to depose Marcian, suggesting that these had been thwarted by Aetius: like Gratian and Valentinian II before him, it seems Valentinian III was struggling to develop an independent military function and believed he was being prevented from doing so by his manager. Yet when Valentinian III sought to claim an active role by removing that manager, even his dynastic legitimacy could not save him. For twenty-nine years he had been an entirely acceptable, largely passive emperor. Within six months of asserting himself and attempting to exercise imperial functions which a century earlier would have been expected of him, he was dead at the hands of his own subjects.

The sources report that when Valentinian III had killed Aetius, flushed with success, he turned to a brave (or foolhardy) courtier and demanded of him whether the deed had been well accomplished, and was told in response simply that he had cut off his right hand with his left.[125] However much Valentinian III refused to recognize it, or struggled to change it, the system of partnership rule which had developed and become increasingly sophisticated over the past century of repeated minority governments had now come to be seen as a norm in western imperial politics. Valentinian III's cause was more complicated in some ways than those of his immediate predecessors, with more serious competition for the role of 'partner' in his government than the accession of Honorius had produced, yet the course of his reign nevertheless serves to confirm the emergent patterns of the Roman imperial government coping with child-rulership which had developed through the preceding reigns of Gratian, Valentinian II, and Honorius.

  Valentinian III's government was an eastern creation, and this substantial eastern commitment to establishing and continuing to support the new boy-emperor's rule was an investment that Theodosius II was not prepared to forget—or to let others forget. From the start he was determined that his

---

[125] John.Ant., frg. 200(1); cf. Procopius, *Bell.* 3.4.25–8.

6-year-old colleague should be portrayed as under his protection, and that he should be the only partner in Valentinian's rule, and the picture of imperial unity perpetuated. Continuing investments in western security, in particular through the lengthy campaigns of Aspar and his eastern army in North Africa during the early 430s, made such a message very clear to any who sought to take over this partnership role for themselves. Yet western generals had inherited an expectation of the way in which the rule of a child- or ceremonial-emperor functioned with the recent examples of Stilicho and Constantius III and, alongside the eastern interest in the western government, still sought the establishment of a dominant general behind the throne.

From the earliest days of the reign, Aetius had proved an unexpected force to be reckoned with. His ability and his willingness to call up substantial Hunnic backing, whose commitment was to him and not to the state, made him far too powerful to be marginalized. While pursuing his own agenda he too adopted the pattern evident from previous regimes, seeking to present himself as the active partner of a ceremonial child-emperor, even when that child-emperor had become a young man in his twenties, as the poetry of Merobaudes indicates. Yet the insistence of Theodosius II that he was the younger emperor's partner in rule complicated Aetius' position and placed limits upon his power, in all likelihood preventing him from establishing a marriage-tie with the imperial house before 450, for example, a move which would have further strengthened Aetius' position by enabling him to reinvent his relationship with the western emperor in the way that Stilicho, and most successfully Constantius, had done.

This external limitation on his power left Aetius more open to attacks on his authority than other imperial partners before him. At the same time, however, the complication of having two partners to his rule also left Valentinian III in a difficult position, especially as he grew to adulthood. For while Aetius aimed to be presented as the active partner of the young emperor's rule in the west, particularly in the sphere of military activity, as Valentinian reached adulthood Aetius' efforts not only involved continuing a dynamic role as the west's military commander, but as the legislation for the period indicates, saw his activities extend into civilian as well as military arenas. In addition, Valentinian's patronizing father-in-law Theodosius II, through his eponymous legal code, presented himself as the supreme source of judicial authority in east and west.[126] In his religious activity and cooperation with the bishop of Rome, as well as in the 'voice' of Valentinian which potentially may be detected in his later legislation, it appears that in the 440s and 450s the emperor was still

---

[126] Barnwell argues that as the active military role of the emperor disappeared his judicial role increased, but such an arrangement potentially became more complicated in a case of two non-military emperors seeking to advertise the exercise of their judicial function at the same time.

striving to be allowed some role beyond the purely ceremonial. And in 454 he would break free from the mould in which Aetius, reflected through the words of the court poet Merobaudes, had cast him, moving from the splendid, majestic, and immobile emperor to a brutal actor in events shaping the fate of his realm. When it came to the ideal virtues Menander prescribed as vital to any praise of the emperor, before this point if he had done little to demonstrate such qualities, he had also done nothing to dispel the appearance of them. Valentinian's personal killing of Aetius, however, lost him the sympathy of the ancient commentators forever, and despite his religious initiatives, from this point on, even his private life was damned by the sources as immoral and degenerate.[127]

The example of Honorius had shown that the strategy of restricting a one-time child-emperor to a purely ceremonial function once he had reached adulthood could work, if the emperor remained passive. Once Theodosius II had died, the most plausible explanation for what occurred in the west is that the eastern limitation of Aetius' powers had ceased, and this, combined with the disappearance of the Huns as a threat to the west, changed crucially the balance of power between Valentinian and Aetius. Yet it is a testament to the continuing institutional strength of the partnership system established by Stilicho and adopted by Constantius and Aetius, that by this time it was so much a part of the way things were done that it was no longer expected that a western emperor would take on the active roles Valentinian so determinedly sought following the murder of Aetius. Ultimately Valentinian fell at the instigation of a disgruntled subject who had hoped to be the new regime manager. Yet subjects of the western emperor were by no means blind to the difficulties of such a system of rule, and given the invasions of the fifth century, perhaps provincials were more than ever aware that this system could not always meet their defence needs as a strong military emperor once would have done. Sidonius Apollinaris, writing only a few years after Valentinian III's death and addressing Avitus when entreating him to take the throne, declared:

Of the cruel fortune that has long harassed us with divers hardships under a boy-emperor, tearing our prosperity to shreds, it would be tedious to relate, O mighty leader, since truly you were the chiefest figure among the mourners, lamenting ever your country's wounds and tortured by uncontrollable anxieties. Amid those calamities, that universal destruction, to live was death. But as we, taught by our fathers' words, paid homage to idle laws and deemed it a hallowed duty to cling to the old order even through disasters, we endured that shadow of empire, content to bear even

---

[127] e.g. Cassiodorus, *Variae* XI.1.9–10; Theophanes, AM 5947; Procopius, *Bell.* 3.4.16 ff.; 3.4.24–5.

the vices of an ancient stock and to tolerate, more from custom than by reason of just claim, a house that had been wont to be invested with the purple.[128]

The refusal of the vested interests around the throne to allow the emperor to take up an active role was to have major implications for all who followed Valentinian III to the throne in the last twenty years of the western Roman empire. The institutionalization of the type of power-relationships at the centre of government which had attended almost a century of child-emperor rule would be a factor with which even adult emperors now coming to the throne would have to contend.

---

[128] Sidonius, *Carm.* 7. 531–43: *quam nos per varios dudum fortuna labores | principe sub puero laceris terat aspera rebus, | fors longum, dux magne, queri, cum quippe dolentum | maxima pars fueris, patriae dum vulnera lugens | sollicitudinibus vehementibus exagitaris. | has nobis inter clades ac funera mundi | mors vixisse fuit. sed dum per verba parentum | ignavas colimus leges sanctumque putamus | rem veterem per damna sequi, portavimus umbram | imperii, generis contenti ferre vetusti | et vitia ac solitam vestiri murice gentem | more magis quam iure pati.*

Conclusion

> May the gods forfend that we should give the title of prince to a child or of father of his country to an immature boy, whose hand a schoolmaster must guide for the signing of his name and who is induced to confer a consulship by sweetmeats or toys or other such childish delights. What wisdom is there – a plague upon it! – in having as emperor one who has not learned to care for fame, who knows not what the commonwealth is, who stands in dread of a guardian, who looks to a nurse, who is in subjection to the blows or the fear of a schoolmaster's rod, who appoints as consuls or generals or judges men whose lives, whose merits, whose years, whose families, whose achievements he knows not at all?[1]

Thus wrote the anonymous author of the *Historia Augusta*, that infamous late Roman collection of scandalous imperial biographies. Probably composed in the 390s, the creator of these writings on the lives and lusts of earlier emperors might well have looked at the past few decades and voiced these opinions with particular vigour.[2]

This book set out to examine certain key assumptions within the established modern historiography on the governance of the late Roman empire, about the nature and function of the imperial office, and more particularly about the ways in which emperors who came to the throne as children came to dominate that position in the west for almost a century, from the 360s to the late 450s. In the process of this examination, however, the investigation of the evidence available for the political history of the period posed a number of other questions which the focus of current research on the late Roman empire has neglected. It became clear that a resort to the dynastic principle, so often seen as the sole reason for the promotion of these boy-emperors, was in no way an adequate explanation for this phenomenon, given the history of the imperial

---

[1] SHA Tacitus VI.4–7: *di avertant principes pueros et patres patriae dici impuberes et quibus ad subscribendum magistri litterarii manus teneant, quos ad consulatus dandos dulcia et circuli et quaecumque voluptas puerilis invitet. quae (malum) ratio est habere imperatorem, qui famam curare non noverit, qui quid sit res publica nesciat, nutritorem timeat, respiciat ad nutricem, virgarum magistralium ictibus terrorique subiaceat, faciat eos consules, duces, iudices quorum vitam, merita, aetates, familias, gesta non norit.*

[2] For a recent comprehensive discussion of the debates over dating and authorship of the *Historia Augusta*, see Cameron (2011), 743–82.

office and more particularly given the circumstances of the boys' accessions and rule. An overarching question thus presented itself: why was the late Roman world able to tolerate boy-rulers across this period, and how did this phenomenon originate? Through a number of key themes running throughout the different regimes of each of these boy-emperors' reigns, short- and long-term patterns can be observed, and we can see how the short-term results of court and aristocratic power-politics could have a long-term impact on the ways in which the Roman state came to be ruled, and hence on its whole system of government.

In the first chapter the background against which the politics and consequences of these long imperial minorities were played out was examined, drawing on the writings of Menander Rhetor, Ammianus, and Themistius (among others) to construct a picture of the functions and expectations of the ideal late Roman emperor. This ideal involved not only the possession of certain cardinal virtues, but also military prowess and success, judicial and administrative responsibilities, and religious and ceremonial roles which helped promote recognition of an emperor's legitimacy. Yet with this imperial checklist in mind, the acclamation of boy-emperors only became all the more puzzling. How could a child possibly fulfil the desired criteria, or be plausibly presented as doing so? Indeed, what reality actually lay behind these symbolic and idealized versions of rulership?

One approach to this issue was to interrogate the writings of idealizing orators such as Ausonius and Ambrose on Gratian and Valentinian II, which provided some valuable insights into how these boys could be presented as fulfilling the imperial ideal. Yet a detailed study of the reigns of these two young emperors also provided some clues as to the manner in which structures around the office of emperor (that is to say, sets of institutionalized practices or ways of doing things, determined in a particular context) had evolved to a point where real demands on imperial ability had diminished. The professionalization of the bureaucracy and the judicial system which had taken place over the previous century made these particular structures essentially self-sustaining entities—which could, therefore, have heads who truly were nominal, without any necessary subsequent damage to the smooth running of the imperial government system. But there was much more to the nature of these boys' governments than this—for while structural developments could allow the accession of boy-emperors, the politics surrounding the accessions, and the very nature of the accessions themselves, contributed to the ways in which their rulership was perceived. Gratian's accession at his father's hand certainly occurred with a dynastic motivation, but it was also in response to a specific political crisis, and set an important precedent which, as we have seen, would not even have been considered only a few years earlier. In the case of the opportunistic acclamation of Valentinian II, it took the recognition by self-interested individuals of how the precedent of Gratian's accession could be used to their own advantage, by men like Merobaudes and Petronius Probus, to bring the child's accession about at all. Having gained their aims—including personal power and conciliation of the Roman senate (though this was also in imperial interests anyway)—by exerting pressure on Gratian through possession of the person of his infant brother, such power-players then accepted the total marginalization of Valentinian II, until Gratian's death in 383 gave them cause to unite behind the younger emperor once more. This was a key difference in the nature of the regimes of Gratian and Valentinian II: while Gratian enjoyed eight years of ceremonial 'authority' during his father's lifetime, thus giving him both some training and a power-base, Valentinian II's rule was only ever invented to serve the aims of others. The emperor was becoming increasingly a symbol of power and authority behind and through which individual and factional ambitions could be realized, and a child-emperor was all the more useful in such a context. Yet this development could present difficulties for the incumbent boy-emperor himself as he grew to adulthood, in the clash between the reality of what those around the throne expected the imperial office to be, and the active model of imperial power embodied by emperors like Valentinian I and Valens—and Theodosius I as well.

The governments built around both Gratian and Valentinian II were not accepted without overcoming some substantial difficulties, in particular over the issue of joint rule between an adult eastern emperor—whether Valens or Theodosius I—and a youthful western ruler. The usurpation of Magnus Maximus and the crucial defection of Merobaudes illustrated both the inexperience of Gratian as well as the lack of acceptance of his leadership by some of his own military. By the same token, these events highlighted Valentinian II's inability to defend his territory and his need to have recourse to the military assistance of Theodosius I. Yet the same events pointed up another difference between the governments of Gratian and Valentinian II: Gratian did personally lead his forces and attempt to fulfil the military function of an emperor, even if not ultimately successfully. He was in fact the last western Roman emperor to do so (apart from Constantius III, whose short reign as emperor did not see him in action militarily) until Avitus in 455. It was a role which Valentinian II was never permitted to take up. After Theodosius restored his 'senior' colleague Valentinian to the throne, carefully making sure that he had no share in the victory over Magnus Maximus, the boy-emperor's actual, practical function was even more reduced, both during Theodosius' residence in Italy and beyond.

As factional interests at the imperial court pushed for greater acceptance of the accessions of these child- or figurehead-emperors, and with it an increasing ceremonialization of the imperial office, they ran into problems with the young emperors themselves. In the case of Gratian in particular, with the active imperial model of his father before him, and in spite of his own accession as a child, he had no example of a similar ceremonial-style rule to follow as a model. Instead of being content, therefore, to allow his active functions to be delegated as those around the throne wished, he was, within a few years of his father's death, (and thus still at a very young age), struggling to take on the traditional active functions of an emperor, a step which his dominant manager Merobaudes was ultimately not prepared to accept. Furthermore, a reluctance to see a continued development of the phenomenon of the child- or figurehead-emperors is also reflected in the usurpation of Magnus Maximus—although it is entirely possible that Maximus would have 'adopted' Valentinian II had he been able to act as his manager in the way that Theodosius later did. As a military usurper raised in the provinces as a rival to two young emperors created at the centre of government, the rebellion indicated not only resistance to this new imperial model but also the difference between the priorities of those seeking power at court through the promotion of a system which suited their own ends, and those of provincial armies, and indeed provincials themselves, in need of active leadership and defence.

The reigns of Gratian and Valentinian II can be seen very much as a learning-curve for political elites surrounding the throne, the first exploration of the possibilities that the long-term rule of a child-emperor might present. The death of Valentinian II, as he too struggled to reclaim some of the supposed powers of his position, brought these early experiments to a close, but as developments over the years to follow would show, they had set a vital precedent, even though the reigns were ultimately unsuccessful. The original beginnings of the child-emperor phenomenon in the late Roman west were a political and strategic education (though not necessarily a premeditated one) for those around the throne who sought to use the figurehead of a child as a front for their own exercise of power. Certain mechanisms for cloaking the child's inability to fulfil some of the expectations of his role were developed, such as the increase in ceremonial and particularly Christian ceremonial. In the end, the critical period came as the child-emperor grew to adulthood, and the exercise of his military function in particular became a sticking-point. It was natural that this role had been entirely delegated when the child was clearly too young to take it up, but could this continued delegation be justified—and would the child-turned-adult emperor continue to accept it—in later years? And was this why both the governments of Gratian and Valentinian II, following their real accessions, moved from initial domination by committee—the Ausonian clique in 375 and the loyalist court in 383 (as detailed in Chapter 2)—to being run by a single, powerful military commander by the end of their reigns?

While the experiments of the accessions of Gratian and Valentinian II had provided the basic precedent for minority rule, it was the long reign of Honorius which truly changed the political culture of the late Roman west. As discussed in Part II, the character of this new boy-emperor's government was shaped by the failures of those which preceded it, and if Honorius and the powers behind him were to survive, coping mechanisms for minority rule must be further developed. Theodosius I had followed the Valentinianic pattern of early promotion for both of his young sons, but the senior emperor's death occurring when it did presented the difficulty of constructing a regime around young Honorius in the west, not only in the wake of civil war, but in a context where both he and Stilicho were virtually unknown. It is significant that from the start Honorius was dominated by a single military figure—there was no early committee promoting the child-emperor in this case, and Stilicho's takeover of power was quite conceivably a coup, like that surrounding Valentinian II in 375. From the start, Stilicho brought a new dynamic to the phenomenon, with his claim to the guardianship of the boy-emperor: a claim that his marriage-ties with the imperial house allowed him to make in a way that Merobaudes and Arbogast before him could not, but which brought a new element to the picture, and a strengthening of the presentation of Honorius' position. The prolific works of Claudian provide the most helpful and extensive picture of just how the rule of a child-emperor and his self-styled guardian could be sold. Crucial in this process was the presentation of the government as a partnership—the heavy emphasis on the youthful promise of the boy-emperor, and the realized virtues of the general Stilicho, reinforced by the very conscious and quite deliberate invention of dynastic loyalty to back up the claims in order to justify both of their positions. Where a writer like Ausonius had brought out the youthful promise and many virtues of Gratian alone, Claudian instead justified both child-ruler and the manager who already dominated the set-up: the 'selling' of a minority rule to elites around the throne was becoming more sophisticated.

Yet there was still a problem—for there could only ever be a limited period during which such a presentation of the boy-emperor's great potential could remain plausible, while not resulting in any actual deeds as he reached adulthood. Although this innovation in presentation of a child-ruler was a response to the original failures in the longer term of the reigns of Gratian and Valentinian II, the essential obstacle of how to cope with the progression of the child-emperor's age endured. As long as Honorius was content to remain passive, the situation was still workable. The heavy emphasis on dynasticism which Stilicho had promoted so skilfully from 395 could continue to insulate Honorius from potential threats, while the cloaking mechanism—highlighting his ceremonial function—was embraced through spectacular occasions like the 404 triumph. In order, however, to maintain his own hold on the emperor, Stilicho needed to reinvent his own position too, since his original claims of guardianship would become far less tenable as Honorius grew older. In a moment of genuine danger to his position in 398, Stilicho found a solution in marrying Honorius to his daughter, taking up an even closer position as the emperor's father-in-law, and thus also being able to isolate Honorius further from potential rival advisers and to continue to justify his own power.

In spite of his loss of senatorial and palace support and fall from grace in 408, the success of Stilicho's regime until that point played a crucial and enduring role in normalizing a particular form of relationship between (boy-) emperor and guardian. While the sheer magnitude of the extent of military pressures finally began to undermine Stilicho's hitherto all-powerful influence, and these pressures were ruthlessly exploited by a determined enemy at court ultimately to bring down the general, it should not be under-estimated just how severe the crises had to become before his stranglehold on Honorius' government was shaken. As the situation grew more precarious, once again Stilicho invoked the marriage policy to try another solution and to stabilize his own position. But the difficulties shown up by the famous senate meeting of early 408 over the payment to Alaric indicated a serious loss of senatorial support, while the death of Arcadius finally brought about conflict between Stilicho and Honorius himself. The *magister militum*'s separation from the emperor at this crucial moment, and the presence of an enemy determined to capitalize on the situation, led to the final collapse of Stilicho's regime. Stilicho's position was surprisingly strong up until 408, given the precariousness of his situation legally and the failure of either of his daughters to provide Honorius with an heir. His method for justifying his position and that of the boy-emperor he ruled through had become increasingly sophisti-cated and novel, and the military and political crises had to become truly severe before he was seriously undermined. The emperor's active partner needed both to maintain access to the emperor's ear, and to be a military success.

Of key significance to the nature of the child-emperor phenomenon is the absolute inertia of Honorius after Stilicho's fall, his limited involvement in that fall, and his lack of interest in actually pursuing the model of active imperial rule now potentially available to him. While Honorius sat back and waited for another strong man to emerge, rival court factions brutally slaughtered each other in their struggle to secure power behind the throne, and the emperor himself survived. All the evidence of his actions—or lack of them—suggests that Honorius clearly understood what was at stake, and how the system now worked. The resilience and strength of that set-up was borne out by the persistence of this model under Flavius Constantius, as well as by the less successful attempts of the subsequent regimes between 408 and 411. Stilicho's emphasis on dynasticism as both the justification for Honorius' rule and at the same time the shield behind which those manipulating power could shelter in a partnership—of a ceremonial and divinely endorsed emperor, accompanied and 'supported' by an active, all-powerful manager—was clearly highly suc-cessful and attractive. Constantius came to employ the same system, as he steadily rose to power and manipulated the model to his own ends: dealing with usurpers and barbarians, rebuilding the western state, marrying the emperor's sister, producing an heir, and finally forcing Honorius to make him co-Augustus. Yet in this Flavius Constantius was able to push the model even further than Stilicho, in becoming emperor himself. Now the partnership entered new territory again, as he embraced the active imperial model as emperor, rather than manager, while Honorius continued in the ceremonial role.

Essentially, Honorius persisted in the guise of a child-ruler despite reaching adulthood, maintaining his ceremonial role while delegating his more active functions. With Constantius III on the scene, however, an active model of imperial rule was back in play once more. This is important, because it clearly demonstrates that the proliferation of child-emperors in the late Roman empire did not mean that the concept of a politically and militarily active ruler had simply disappeared. It remained an available option, although only in the right circumstances, that is, if a strong individual had the power, support, and determination to pursue it. If Constantius had lived longer, outlived Honorius, and even lived to see his own son reach adulthood, the clock could have been turned back. But this would not have been because the structures which had allowed the phenomenon of child-emperor rule to develop so extensively had disappeared; rather, the active model of imperial rule remained one option, an alternative model alongside the viable and now accepted model of child-emperor rule. Interestingly, of the different generals of the fifth century who would attempt to hand their dominance of government on to their sons through marriage alliances—Stilicho to Eucherius, or Aetius to Gaudentius—only Constantius would ultimately succeed, with his son Valentinian crowned emperor less than five years after he had achieved that rank himself. Yet the power that Constantius did manage to transfer to his son was also ultimately the power of the ceremonial, rather than the active, component in the imperial partnership. This was still some years down the track, however; and with Constantius' death in 421 the western imperial government reverted once more to what had, over the previous thirty years, become the normalized system: of court factions vying for the power behind the throne, while the emperor himself remained passive, and survived.

That 'dynastic loyalty' was a sentiment to be created, rather than being somehow structurally inherent in the system, is confirmed by the circumstances (examined in detail in Chapter 8) surrounding the accession of Valentinian III, in particular the usurpation of John and the hesitation of Theodosius II over the decision to impose the new child-emperor upon the west by force. The stake which the eastern government continued to have in the western administration and the careful choice of ceremonial beginnings for Valentinian III, with its continued emphasis on the value of Roman senatorial support, shaped the early character of the new government. These factors are far more important than the influence of Galla Placidia, too often romantically viewed as the regent and governing force of the new boy-emperor's government. But the character of the new reign was also shaped by another, unexpected development, which indicated the extent to which child-emperor or ceremonial rule had become an accepted structure of the late Roman state in the west. Flavius Aetius, with his own private power-base entirely outside of imperial control, was a figure with whom the eastern expedition to install Valentinian had not anticipated having to deal, but whose power was such that they were forced to accommodate him. Yet, as discussed in detail in Chapter 8, he was still prepared to be sent to Gaul and to lead the armies of the emperor on the battlefield, rather than to make any push to take the throne himself.

The fight for the real power in the realm was between the western generals, a struggle conditioned by the institutionalization of child-rule which had taken place up until this point, and which created the expectation that a single military leader behind the throne would be the true wielder of power. But while it was Aetius who eventually triumphed, his degree of absolute control was probably restricted in a way that neither that of Stilicho nor Constantius before him had been—by an eastern veto. Despite the dominance of this western general, it can be argued plausibly that the eastern government of Theodosius II continued to influence affairs in the west and to exercise a restraint over the extent of Aetius' activities, preventing him from establishing marriage-ties with the imperial family which would have shored up his position further, as his predecessors had done, until after the death of Theodosius II.

The determination of Theodosius II to maintain his vested interest in the western emperor whom he had created is vividly evidenced by the eastern campaigns in North Africa during the 430s, which were an impressive demonstration of eastern military commitment to the west, imperial unity, and also a warning to any western generals who might otherwise overstep the mark that the east was a continued presence. The paternal role Theodosius II had adopted from 424 towards his young cousin was further underlined by the dynastic and ceremonial significance of the marriage of Valentinian III and Licinia Eudoxia in 437, and the promulgation of the *Theodosian Code*. In this scenario, it was the eastern emperor Theodosius II, rather than a western manager, who was reinventing his relationship with the western boy-emperor as Valentinian grew up, moving from protector to father-in-law, and thus again curtailing the extent of Aetius' authority. Theodosius II's insistence on presenting himself as the partner of his colleague meant that Aetius' position was more vulnerable to potential challengers within the western realm, as some of the possible murky court intrigues of the 440s may indicate.

Nevertheless, the fragmentary remains of the poetry of Merobaudes reveal that Aetius still steadfastly pursued the presentation of western imperial rule as a partnership as developed by Stilicho—despite Valentinian III being married with children by the time the poems were written. There could no longer be an argument for Valentinian being too young to take on the traditional functions of his position. Yet the surviving descriptions of him from the 440s are overwhelmingly ceremonial in tone, and focused only on his divine authority, coupled with the tremendous military prowess of his commander, Aetius. Aetius clearly intended to restrict Valentinian, even as a child-turned-adult emperor, to the limits of a predominantly ceremonial and religious role.

As with the child-emperors before him, the issue of the progression of young Valentinian III's age presented a key question: would this passive role be one in which he was content to remain? In the case of Valentinian, his judicial authority could be perceived as under threat due to the extensive legal activity of Theodosius II and his empire-wide, but pointedly 'Theodosian', legal code, and the involvement of Aetius in matters of civilian jurisdiction from the 440s. Nevertheless, if the personal 'voice' that can be detected in the legislation of Valentinian's adult years really is that of the emperor, it would seem that Valentinian was aware of the possibilities for exerting his independence in this area. In addition, the extensive involvement of the imperial family in church benefaction, and Valentinian's close communication with Pope Leo during this period, reflect the emperor's taking up of the religious function of his office, and in several cases connecting such activity with political initiatives.

Valentinian had before him the alternative examples of the fates of Gratian and Valentinian II, and of Honorius: to try to reclaim 'his' power and risk his life in so doing, or to be content to remain passive in the likelihood of surviving, and push the ceremonialization of the imperial office even further. Before 450 there are some hints that he was already growing impatient with his lack of genuine power, but after that year, with the death of Theodosius II and the subsequent shifting of dynamics at the western court, Valentinian made an outright attempt to set up a rival to Aetius with the betrothal of Majorian and Placidia. The attempt failed, but the determined emperor, in increasing desperation as Aetius' influence at court showed no sign of waning, saw his chance again following the disintegration of the Hunnic empire. Valentinian's own assassination, following so soon after his murder of Aetius, is a compelling indication that dynastic legitimacy had played a minimal role in keeping him on the throne for thirty years. The rule of child-emperors, the political arrangements that accompanied their governments, and the difficulty of coping with the child's growth to adulthood had necessarily entailed the emperor remaining ceremonial, a mere figurehead. This had by now become an accepted—even at this point, the expected—model of imperial rule among powerful factions in the west. For twenty-nine years, therefore, while Valentinian III remained docile and passive, he also remained entirely acceptable as emperor. As soon as he attempted to effect a full transition from child to adult—and from ceremonial to actual power—he ceased to be an acceptable emperor.

The results of this analysis can be summarized under several key points. First, it becomes clear that what we may, with good reason, refer to as the institutionalization of boy-emperors had little to do, at the outset, with notions of dynastic loyalty. On the contrary, it had everything to do with important shifts in the structures of power at court, shifts which followed from changes in the relationship between emperor and military high command, between military high command and senatorial aristocracies, and between eastern and western governments. More importantly, it had to do with just what all of these groups expected of the western emperor. Each of these elements needs to be examined in the context of the others in order to understand their combined, or emergent, effects. The detailed analysis of the reigns of the four boy-emperors also allows for overall comparisons and contrasts to be drawn, for although all four rulers came to the throne while very young, neither the circumstances in which they did so nor the individuals or groups who promoted or supported them were the same. The moment of accession for each of the boys always involved a period of intense political activity and manoeuvring to get the child on the throne, and was always a case of the intersection of the contingent or 'accidental' (including also the opportunism of individual political players) with the structural or systemic.

The accessions of Gratian, Valentinian II, Honorius, and Valentinian III were all reactions to particular political crises—but might never have taken place without this combination of circumstances. The accession of Gratian at the age of 8 set a vital precedent and clearly presented attractive new possibilities to political opportunists at court—but it was really Valentinian II whose accession constituted that of the first independent child-emperor government, particularly after 383. Yet if Valentinian I had not died when he did, would Valentinian II ever have been proclaimed at the age of 4? His accession was the result of a rapid decision by a political clique which saw it as a means of furthering its own interests, but Valentinian II's elevation in 375 strengthened the precedent of Gratian's extraordinary accession—only eight years later Theodosius I made his eldest son Arcadius emperor at the age of 6, as a demonstration of independence from Gratian. Only twenty years before, such a move was practically unheard of. But spur-of-the-moment decisions—like the acclamation of Valentinian II— could have long-term ramifications. For while they are always to be understood within the prevailing structural constraints imposed by accepted norms of behaviour, political practice, and ideology, moves like the elevation of Gratian in 367 caused shrewd and ambitious politicians to recognize new possibilities within that practice, and to begin pushing the boundaries of the politically acceptable. In the west, the accession of an 8-year-old was thus followed by that of a 4-year-old, then of a 10-year-old, then of a 6-year-old: child-emperor rule in itself came to be a norm of the imperial system. And as the various vested interests represented at court took the rule of child-emperors increasingly for granted, indeed began to see such arrangements as part of their expectations and to exploit the possibilities they offered, so too the whole set of arrangements and political practices associated with them became increasingly part of the institutional scenery of western Roman governance. Under the early reigns of Gratian and Valentinian II the concept of the boy-emperor—in the institutionalized sense defined here—was new. Under the longer and more successful reign of Honorius, and the subsequent rule of Valentinian III, the idea of child or ceremonial rule took firm hold and began to dictate further possible outcomes in imperial politics.

The second point is that it is important to keep in view that, even when the rule of a child or ceremonial emperor had become a viable and accepted model, it was never inevitable, and remained only one of several possible options. While these boy-rulers were obviously not random children but sons of emperors, nevertheless only the last, Valentinian III, belonged to an imperial dynasty of long standing, and western court politicians had shown little inclination to acclaim him in his absence when Honorius died. It was the contingent circumstances of the deaths of the boys' fathers occurring when they did, and the opportunism of shrewd political players that made these children potential candidates for the throne. Valentinian I, Theodosius I, and Constantius III all clearly indicated their intentions that their sons should succeed them, and did their best to make it difficult to dispense with them. Yet blood had never been enough to secure a succession in the Roman imperial system, and it would be a mistake to think that there were no adult alternatives available. When Valentinian I had fallen ill in 367, the court had speculated freely as to the succession, even coming up with two rival candidates, without any thought that the 8-year-old Gratian was an option—and why would they, when only years earlier the infant son of Jovian had been passed over entirely as a potential successor when his father died? As we have seen in Chapter 2, when Valentinian I expired in 375, a number of popular and successful generals, and thus potential rivals for the throne, were carefully put out of the way before or soon after the 4-year-old Valentinian II was proclaimed—Sebastianus and Theodosius *comes*, and perhaps Flavius Equitius also. There is no doubt that avoidance of civil war was an important factor in promoting the young son of a dead emperor, rather than an adult general such as one of these men. Nevertheless, dynasticism alone simply is not a convincing explanation for what became the boy-emperor phenom-enon: these accessions took place because they suited the aims of court politicians, who grasped the potential possibilities raised by Valentinian I's actions in 367. Furthermore, in the longer term the acclamation of very young emperors did not ultimately prevent military usurpations occurring—as the rebellions led by Magnus Maximus and Constantine III make abundantly clear.

Thirdly, the other adult possibilities who arose over the period nevertheless are a clear indication that there was a degree of resistance to the child-emperor phenomenon, and that there was a growing divergence in what different power-players, most conspicuously those at the centre of government and those in the provinces, desired from the imperial office. The genuine possibility that usurpers like Magnus Maximus and Constantine III offered of a return to active, adult imperial rule should not be underestimated. Both had substantial military backing, gained a high degree of imperial recognition over a matter of some years, and were a reminder also that the model of active imperial rule remained a powerful and attractive one for many, and had not been forgotten. But the difference between even the usurpers who were raised at the centre of government and those in the provinces during these years also reveals a vital contrast in the varied aims of those seeking to wield power. For while Magnus Maximus and Constantine III were powerful and proven military commanders, able to offer protection to the provinces, Eugenius and John, and even Priscus Attalus, by contrast, were non-military, compromise candidates who were clearly expected to embrace the ceremonial model of imperial rule developed through the child-emperors, while a dominant general—Arbogast or Alaric or Castinus—led the imperial armies. Even adult alternatives raised at the centre of government during this eighty-year period were therefore expected to reign as ceremonial—virtually as child—emperors. In the provinces, however, where subjects faced repeated barbarian threats and the military was stretched in both numbers and resources, this model was inadequate. In 455 the Gallic *concilium* would demonstrate provincial resistance to figurehead rule once more, through the acclamation of the proven military commander Avitus.

The rise to power of Constantius III demonstrates that the active model of imperial rule was still a potential option, even at the centre of government. Indeed, the active model need not be seen as having been replaced by the ceremonial, child-emperor phenomenon. Rather, the early experiments with child-rule, followed by the long reign of Honorius in particular, meant that the ceremonial option now became a viable and acceptable possibility, where it had not been before. The active model did not disappear, but the political developments of the late fourth century offered attractive possibilities for separating out the functions of the imperial office. The development of two alternative but practical models of imperial rule also raised the question of whether a ceremonial ruler could still exercise some of the more active functions of his office, even while the military role remained delegated. It is inevitably difficult, given the professionalization of the imperial bureaucracy by this point, to determine how much the boy-emperors might have been involved in the day-to-day running of their governments, or were truly behind the legislation to which they put their names. The fact that they did still need to authorize such laws argues for at least the potential of personal impact, as does the evidence that even the 12-year-old Valentinian II still presided over meetings of his consistory, and the assumption that a God-appointed ruler remained a part of the natural order of things.[3] The extent of the frustration of Valentinian III and the involvement of both Theodosius II and Aetius in judicial matters in the west under his rule may, however, suggest that this child-turned-adult emperor was being obstructed by his ruling partners in attempts to step far outside of his ceremonial role. And indeed, whether a child-emperor himself in growing to adulthood could ever have successfully reclaimed the active functions—particularly the military function—which were delegated throughout his minority remains doubtful. Flavius Constantius had won his way through to the throne through military victory—and thereby also claimed the personal loyalty of his armies. For a child-turned-adult emperor like his son, attempting to put the active model of rule into operation meant removing the general who had won victories in his name and com-manded the imperial armies—and their loyalty—for decades. Valentinian's experience suggests that there were no guarantees of success for an emperor who sought to force his own transition from ceremonial to actual power, even after a very long reign.

A key element of the child-emperor phenomenon, therefore, remained the problem of how to cope with the progression of the child's age, and the question of whether or not he was prepared to remain passive as he grew up, as the ceremonial model demanded. With regard to this problem, the reigns of Gratian in particular, but Valentinian II's as well, provided the early experimentation which again presented new options for what was politically possible, but also indicated where the major stumbling-block with these options would always lie. Gratian had no example before him of how a child-emperor reaching adulthood might reinvent his role, but rather a long line of active emperors, including his father, with whom he had travelled on campaigns. It was only natural that he should himself aim to pursue the active model. Even Valentinian II, whose period of minority rule was considerably longer than his half-brother's, in time struggled impotently against the passive role which had been forced upon him. The failures of these two governments ultimately meant that if the new rule of the 10-year-old Honorius in 395 was to survive, the problems of these previous reigns needed to be resolved and, crucially, Honorius needed to remain passive as he grew to adulthood.

The value of remaining passive, as a child-emperor reaching adulthood, was starkly demonstrated by the fact that of all of these four boys, Honorius alone died a natural death. Gratian, Valentinian II, and most conspicuously Valen-tinian III in the killing of Aetius, all made attempts to reclaim some of their own delegated functions—to push for a transition from ceremonial to actual power—and died for it. Honorius alone, even after the downfall of Stilicho or the death of Constantius III, when the opportunity so clearly presented itself,

---

[3] On Valentinian II at his consistory meetings: Ambrose, *Ep.* 72 (Maur. 17).10.

made no attempt to force such a transition, and survived. It is a distinct possibility that Honorius simply had the sense to look at the fates of his two predecessors and learn from their mistakes. Through thirty years of rule, he remained content for others to wield power on his behalf and to remain aloof from the brutal court struggles that went on around him. In this context, a comment from Suetonius' *Life of Claudius* comes to mind—that after his accession, this emperor 'did not even keep quiet about his own stupidity, but in certain brief speeches he declared that he had purposely feigned it under Gaius, because otherwise he could not have escaped alive and attained his present station. But he convinced no one . . .'[4]

Ancient and modern interpretations have held similarly derogatory views of Honorius' abilities, and have ascribed his inactivity to dimness or lethargy, but in the overall picture of the child-emperor phenomenon he alone seems to have understood the workings of the system which had consolidated around him. If Valentinian III, too, recognized the risks of forcing a transition to the active model of imperial rule, he was obviously desperate enough to accept them.

Fourthly, it is clear that presentation, with particular emphasis on the ceremonial and symbolic functions of the ruler, played a crucial role in legitimizing the rule of the child-emperors. As the chapters examining the individual reigns of Gratian, Valentinian II, Honorius, and Valentinian III have illustrated, such presentation developed and became increasingly sophisticated over the eighty-year period. In fact, it was essential to overcoming the problems which arose when an emperor reached adulthood. The reign of Honorius once again proved the most decisive in this development. From the 'Hope of the State' motto of 367 and the youthful promise claimed for Gratian, the presentation of the child-emperor was increasingly refined, to encompass a legitimation of the position of his chief manager also, with such additional legitimation through marriage into the imperial family bringing about a hope for the future that would bond both manager and emperor forever, as a child born to Honorius and Maria would have done. With the writings of Claudian, the weight of dynasticism was thrown much more heavily behind young Honorius than had been the case with his predecessors, and in a sense 'invented', not simply in order to legitimate young Honorius' position, but critically that of Stilicho's also. Through Claudian, a 'partnership' arrangement became the basis on which the reign was sold to the elite: the youthful promise, dynastic claim, and divine blessing of the boy-emperor, and along with it the loyal guardianship of Stilicho and the actual abilities—such as military leadership—that he

---

[4] Suetonius, *Life of Claudius* 38.3: *Ac ne stultitiam quidem suam reticuit simulatamque a se ex industria sub Gaio, quod aliter evasurus perventurusque ad susceptam stationem non fuerit, quibusdam oratiunculis testatus est; nec tamen persuasit . . .*

could actively demonstrate on the young emperor's behalf. As far as the evidence of the poet Merobaudes indicates, this was also the presentation adopted under Valentinian III: a partnership with Aetius as the active general in the field and Valentinian the ceremonial figurehead. The traditional profile of the ideal emperor and his expected functions was still being presented as met—but no longer by the emperor alone: the demands of the office were now shared with a single, dominant figure, in an arrangement that grew directly out of the original committee-run administrations which had backed Gratian and Valentinian II.

It is quite apparent that a vital part of this presentation was the increased emphasis on the ceremonial and religious role of the emperor. This had already been seized upon as a coping mechanism in the early experiments with child-emperor rule, and had only become increasingly important as the phenomenon developed. And in this emphasis, the Christianization of the imperial office which was such a conspicuous aspect of the period proved of enormous value, in a context where traditional pagan religion might have struggled. For while the extreme religiosity and fervour for pagan cults of an Elagabalus—or even a Julian—had led to ridicule and bemusement, by the later fourth century promotion of the religious piety of a Christian child-emperor could be viewed, in contrast, as a key to ensuring the security of his empire and the success of his armies. Gratian's convocation of the council of Aquileia and his removal of the Altar of Victory from the senate-house at Rome indicated a recognition of the importance placed upon the young emperor's religious role, while Theodosius I's actions in outdoing Gratian in public displays of orthodoxy highlighted the eastern emperor's recognition of the central role that religious function was playing in the western government. The 'basilicas controversy' of 385/6 between the court of Valentinian II and Ambrose was a particularly striking indication of just how keenly the importance of the boy-emperor's religious and ceremonial function was felt by court advisers.

The regime built around Honorius by Stilicho, and with it the sophisticated new presentation of imperial rule as a partnership, also laid heavy emphasis on the boy-emperor's religious and ceremonial role, for, like his predecessors, it was the one function which the child could convincingly and usefully fulfil while his active partner took care of other concerns. The child-emperor at the centre of the regime always remained a potent symbol, and public exposure through lavish ceremonial, such as the triumph of 404, could have tremendous propaganda value. As Honorius grew to adulthood, and even as the regimes attempting to run his government rose and fell, the emperor's religious and ceremonial function only grew in significance, as the increase in religious legislation from ca. 408 onwards demonstrates. Now, with the emperor no longer either a child or embracing an active role, the continued emphasis on this function underlined the association between his armies' military victories and the security of the realm on the one hand, and the all-important imperial piety on the other.

From the earliest stages of the rule of Valentinian III, the child-emperor's ceremonial role and his piety were emphasized through his coronation at Rome and the early ecclesiastical legislation of the new government. The many church benefactions of the reign also demonstrated the imperial government's awareness of meeting expectations of this important virtue, while the growth of claims of papal primacy over this period, often viewed as occurring at the expense of imperial authority, can in fact be seen as taking place with the support of Valentinian and his government, reflected especially through imperial legislation mirroring and restating papal directives. Moreover, the highly ceremonial descriptions of the imperial family and court by Merobaudes reflected the emphasis on Valentinian's role as a pious and divinely blessed figurehead, doubtless the image that Merobaudes' patron Aetius, in the style of Stilicho and Honorius before him, aimed to project.

Increased emphasis on the piety of the child-emperors in particular added a new element to the imperial profile: the emergence of innocence and mildness or meekness as potential imperial traits. Mentioned by Ambrose in his orations relating to Gratian and Valentinian II, Peter Chrysologos, the bishop of Ravenna during the reign of Valentinian III, also referred to innocence as one of the virtues of the imperial family.[5] This is a virtue with specifically Christian overtones, attributed to the boys by Christian writers—it is a quality also implied by Ambrose's emphasis on the age of Honorius being augmented by his faith (and his father's), and in the declarations of writers like Orosius and Sozomen that the faith of the young emperors called down divine protection upon them.[6] The mildness of the boy-emperor Valentinian II is contrasted by Ambrose with the warlike focus of Magnus Maximus, while the 'meekness' of the young Theodosius II would be lauded in the east by Socrates.[7] These indications that the pious innocence of a child-emperor might be used to justify his reign also lead naturally to one of the most obvious areas into which to expand this investigation: the child-emperors of the eastern Roman empire, and particularly Theodosius II. The church historian Sozomen dedicated his work to this child-turned-adult emperor, and in his preface declared that under the rule of Theodosius II:

the eastern empire was free from wars, and contrary to all opinion, its affairs were conducted with great order, for the ruler was still a youth. It seems as if God openly manifested this favour towards the present emperor, not only by disposing of warlike

---

[5] Ambrose, *De ob. Val.* 6, 19, 74; *De ob. Theod.* 51; Peter Chrysologos, *Sermon* 85B, 3.

[6] Ambrose, *De ob. Theod.* 6; Orosius 7.36; Sozomen 9.11.1.

[7] Ambrose, *Ep.* 30 (Maur. 24).8; Socrates 7.42.

affairs in an unexpected way, but also by revealing the sacred bodies of many persons who were of old most distinguished for piety . . . [8]

Sozomen's comments immediately call to mind the discovery of martyrs' bodies in the west during the reigns of Valentinian II and Honorius, and the ways in which Ambrose of Milan, and the imperial court, were able to use such dramatic events as evidence of divine favour. According to Sozomen, while young Theodosius II cultivated every desirable virtue, it was his piety which made him the true ornament of the empire.[9] The pious innocence of the young eastern emperor was also precociously displayed in the famous incident following his baptism in 402, when the procession escorting the infant was halted by religious petitioners from Gaza and, by discreet manipulation, Theodosius II was seen to grant their request.[10] Increased ceremonialization and the Christianization of the imperial office have long been recognized as important themes of this period, but they have not previously been linked to the phenomenon of the child-emperors. The examination of the western phenomenon therefore provides some insight into these developments, while the possibilities of the eastern aspect remain to be explored.[11]

Finally, it is very clear that just as the symbolic role became integral to the rule of the western child-emperors over this eighty-year period, so it impacted directly on the expectations of the emperor's military role, and the power which might be wielded by his *magister militum*. Until the accession of the 8-year-old Gratian, all the emperors of the fourth century had been strong military leaders, or had been required at least to demonstrate their military potential. In the 370s and thereafter, military threats to the empire did not suddenly disappear, and nor did the need for military leadership or the perception, in the provinces at least, that this remained a function that the emperor was expected to fulfil, as the usurpation of Magnus Maximus confirmed. Yet at the centre of imperial politics the new model of child-rulership was being explored, and the delegation of the boy-ruler's military function also came to determine the way in which this model could most successfully be run. The real accession of Gratian, and both the phantom and real accessions of Valentinian II, had been engineered and supported by 'committees' which

---

[8] Sozomen 9.16.3–4: ἐν τούτῳ δὲ τὰ μὲν πρὸς ἕω τῆς ἀρχομένης πολεμίων ἀπήλλακτο καὶ σὺν κόσμῳ πολλῷ τὰ τῇδε ἰθύνετο παρὰ τὴν πάντων δόξαν· ἦν γὰρ ἔτι νέος ὁ κρατῶν. ἐδόκει δὲ ὁ θεὸς περιφανῶς ἥδεσθαι τῇ παρούσῃ βασιλείᾳ, οὐ μόνον ἐξ ἀπροσδοκήτου τὰ περὶ τοὺς πολέμους ὧδε διατιθείς, ἀλλὰ καὶ πολλῶν ἐπ' εὐσεβείᾳ πάλαι εὐδοκιμηκότων τὰ ἱερὰ σώματα ἀναφαίνων·— Theodosius was in his forties at the time of the dedication.

[9] Sozomen, *Dedication*. See briefly on this: Harries (1994b), 38–9.

[10] Marc.Diac. *V.Porph.* 33–50.

[11] On the nature of Theodosius II's rule in the east, see most recently Millar (2006) generally and esp. 1–38, and Harries (1994b), 35–44. The eastern child-emperor reigns are the focus of my ongoing research.

were made up of alliances of senatorial and military powers, but, as we have seen, within a few years this system for managing the child-emperors gave way to the dominance of a single military commander. This development was directly associated with the military necessities of the period, as indicated by the events surrounding the disaster of Adrianople, the usurpation of 383, and the intervention of Theodosius I in the west in 388. But the need for a dominant general to lead the armies in the name of a child-emperor opened up new possibilities for the power that such an individual might exercise, as long as the child remained passive when he reached adulthood.

In the cases of both Gratian and Valentinian II recognition of the potential for the wielding of great power behind the throne was still growing, but in those of Honorius and Valentinian III the situation moved into a new realm entirely. For while the reigns of Gratian and Valentinian II had presented the possibility of an entirely new model of imperial rulership, the collapse of the regimes which had managed them compelled those who followed to address the situation they inherited if they were to survive. Contingency was undeniably a significant part of the picture—middle-aged emperors dying unexpectedly—and dynasticism proved a useful justification in promoting the interests of their infant successors. Yet by Honorius' time there were structures—that is to say, sets of inherited practices and assumptions—regarding how to manage the new situation, and expectations of the emperor himself were changing. Stilicho set himself up from the start as the single dominant figure at the helm of the new boy-emperor's government: there would be no committee-run administration this time.

The development of this child-emperor phenomenon in the late Roman west, the institutionalization of ceremonial-style rule, the infantilization of the imperial office (the process by which even emperors who attained adulthood continued to be treated effectively as powerless minors, incompetent in the field of adult duties and responsibilities), all owed a great deal to the efforts of Stilicho during the crucial first decade of Honorius' reign. Stilicho's adoption of the position of guardian and quasi-regent, the use of marriage-ties to bind him closer still to the emperor, and the all-important partnership approach to meeting the imperial ideal, all contributed to building up a sophisticated model; while the ever-increasing emphasis on the emperor's ceremonial role played an integral part. Of course, the dominant manager needed to placate powerful figures at court who might otherwise have sought a return to the committee-run system, but the evidence of his early regime suggests that Stilicho was aiming to do just that. Moreover, the particular political situation in 395, with powerful but recently rebellious Roman aristocrats seeking a return to imperial favour, allowed Stilicho to take full advantage of the situation to establish his own position, obviating any chance of being outmanoeuvred by the wrong-footed senatorial power-players. That Stilicho, like Merobaudes, Bauto, and Arbogast before him, was of barbarian extraction, certainly indicates the extent to which such men were rising to the highest commands in the imperial army by the late fourth century, and such developments within the military itself should not be overlooked in the general picture. But in relation to the military function of the emperor himself, until recently such an integral aspect of the imperial office, the pre-eminence of barbarian/semi-barbarian or non-Roman *magistri militum* cannot itself explain the model of ceremonial child-rule that was developing, a model which Roman generals also, like Constantius and Aetius, and even Castinus and Felix, were content to accept and promote.

The extent to which the ceremonial and military functions of the emperor had been separated, and were perceived to have been so, was demonstrated by the fact that in the midst of the political and military crises of 408 it was Stilicho who fell, and not Honorius. This was surely a testament to the strength of the dynastic stability and divine support which Stilicho had built up as a shield for Honorius, and to the public perception of who truly ran the regime. In the early years of this new imperial model, of the drive towards child- or ceremonial rule, the impact of the exogenous shock of a usurpation or invasion could still dislodge the emperor himself, as with Gratian in 383. By contrast, in the case of the strong regime built up by Stilicho, a dire combination of usurpations, invasions, loss of senatorial support, and separation from Honorius at a crucial moment now brought down the manager, but not the emperor. The position of the child-emperor had become entrenched.

In 425, once more, unpredictable events framed by the structural constraints and political context and practice within which they could have an effect—historical accident coinciding with structures and politics—produced the new 6-year-old emperor of the west. Once again the struggle for power behind the throne eventually generated the corporate presentation of the active military leader and the passive ceremonial ruler. When warring barbarian groups or native provincial populations needed aid, it was Aetius to whom they applied, not Valentinian III. Positions around the throne were bitterly fought over, but the expectations of the young emperor upon the throne himself were of a passive, ceremonial exercise of office. The success of this arrangement, essentially still Stilicho's model of a single, all-powerful, military-based individual (especially one who actively campaigned in Gaul) running the regime around the child-emperor can be seen in the fact that there was not one single usurpation in the west during the thirty-year reign of Valentinian III—until that which brought about the emperor's death in 455. And, as with Stilicho, it was a combination of external events and court intrigue which essentially allowed the removal of Aetius, with the disintegration of the Hunnic empire following the invasions of 451 and 452. Yet the ultimate inability of Valentinian III to break free from the system which had operated around him since his childhood, and the refusal of powers around the throne to allow him to do so, once again reinforces the impression of the degree to which child-emperor or ceremonial rule had become entrenched in the late Roman west. The system relied not only on the continuing passivity of the emperor himself, but also on the expectations of those around the throne as to what was now acceptable in the exercise of the imperial office.

The long-term phenomenon of child-emperor rule in the late Roman west could not but have had an enduring impact upon the office of the emperor and the expectations of others surrounding that office. From the death of Gratian, none of the three child-emperors to follow him to the throne ever led the imperial armies. Before the accession of Gratian every emperor of the fourth century had been an active military leader. This was a tremendous transformation. Writing in the sixth century, John Lydus would attribute this immense change to a ruling of Theodosius I that his sons should be forbidden from setting out to war, yet such a law seems unlikely ever to have existed: if such an excuse for the non-military activities of Honorius and Arcadius (even in adulthood) and the constant military activity of Stilicho had been available, commentators like Claudian would undoubtedly have used them.[12] As an inherently military emperor himself, one whose legitimacy had only been more emphatically endorsed by personal victories such as those over Magnus Maximus and Eugenius, it is simply inconceivable that Theodosius I would not have seen the importance of military leadership in an emperor. And indeed, the transformation of the imperial office in this period had begun even before Theodosius' death in 395, even if it came to full fruition under the rule of his sons. The growing divorce of the emperor from military leadership from *c.*360 to 460 had a crucial significance for rulership in the late Roman west, and beyond. The arrangements developed earlier by Stilicho were pushed further still by Flavius Constantius. They had relied a great deal on the willingness of the emperor himself to be confined to a ceremonial role, but the experience of Constantius confirmed that an active model of imperial rule still remained an option. Both his regime and those which followed make it abundantly clear that the system of child-emperor, or ceremonial, rule relied not only on the continuing passivity of the emperor himself, but also on the expectations of those around the throne as to what was now acceptable in the exercise of the imperial office. What we observe across this century of ceremonial rule is, in effect, the infantilization of the imperial office, the incremental growth and consolidation of the powers of the *magister militum*, and the effective limitation of the functions of the emperor himself.

While the active model of imperial rule remained an option, ceremonial rulership had now become an acceptable model where once it had not been, and this development had implications—and complications—for all of the emperors who followed Valentinian III to the western throne after 455.[13]

---

[12] John Lydus, *De magistratibus* 11.18–29.
[13] See generally on these emperors Jones (1964*a*), 1. 238–45; Bury (1923), 1. 323–47. For an excellent study of the role of dominant generals in particular in the west after 455, see MacGeorge (2002).

Petronius Maximus, who had engineered Valentinian's death and then claimed the throne, made no attempt to lead the imperial armies during his admittedly very short reign and, when the Vandals approached Rome, attempted to flee, only to be killed by the populace. The Gallic emperor Avitus, essentially another provincial military usurper, attempted a return to the active model, only to be toppled within months by an alliance of a new powerful military leader, Ricimer, and the first of the men he sought to use as a ceremonial puppet, Majorian. Majorian had ideas of his own, and initially experienced some success in reinvigorating the active imperial model, but this was hardly in accordance with the plans of Ricimer, who had intended to exercise the supreme power of Stilicho or Aetius, but could not achieve this without a passive emperor. A far more satisfactory puppet—or virtual child—emperor was found in the elderly Libius Severus, whom the patrician Ricimer had proclaimed at Ravenna in 461.

The reigns of all the so-called 'shadow' emperors who would occupy the throne for short periods from 455 down to 476 bear the marks of governments which struggled to follow on from the child-emperor phenomenon that had dominated the west for eighty years since the death of Valentinian I. From the eastern nominees adopted by Ricimer: Anthemius, and to a lesser extent Olybrius and Julius Nepos, to the puppets of further powerful generals: Glycerius the candidate of Gundobad, and finally the child Romulus Augustulus, son of the general Orestes, the conflict between generals vying for management of the emperor on the one hand, and emperors attempting to exercise the theoretical authority of their position on the other, is apparent. A comparable situation arose in the east following the death of Marcian in 457 and the accession of Leo, the nominee of the powerful general Aspar, with the subsequent fourteen-year struggle by the emperor to rid himself of the overbearing power behind the throne, once again signalling the wide-ranging influence of the infantilization of the imperial office which the past century had wrought.[14] Western numismatic evidence from the short reign of Libius Severus provides the most compelling evidence that the partnership presentation of imperial rule remained potent and effective: his coins displayed the image of the emperor alongside the monogram of the patrician Ricimer.[15] This graphic demonstration of Ricimer's role as the true partner in rule of the emperor was, in effect, a visual representation of Claudian's descriptions of Stilicho and Honorius.

An integral part of the politics and presentations of these boy-emperors' reigns was, inevitably, the structures—the political arrangements and ideas within which they operated—which sustained them. It is unlikely that when

---

[14] Jones (1964*a*), 1. 221–4; Bury (1923), 1. 314–23.
[15] *RIC* 10. 188–92. Cf. also an inscription at Rome on a bronze weight: *salvis dd.nn. et patricio Ricimere*: 'with the blessing of our Lords and Masters and the Patrician Ricimer' (*CIL* 10. 8072).

Valentinian I made his 8-year-old son co-Augustus he expected the boy to succeed him fully at a young age, still less that he expected his younger son to be catapulted to the position of co-emperor at the age of 4, although admittedly normal mortality rates in the fourth century made it difficult for any emperor ultimately to pass power on to an adult son. It is also unlikely that the political clique which elevated Valentinian II was looking much beyond the satisfaction of its immediate goals in playing the infant off against his older brother, as demonstrated in Chapter 2. But Gratian's elevation had revealed that a child as young as 8 could be presented and accepted as a plausible emperor; so why not a child of 4? If imperial ideology could be manipulated to support the new situation, and certain traditional functions like the judicial could in fact be virtually self-sustaining, while others, like the military, could be delegated, the imperial office could thereby provide a shield of reassuring continuity and divine sanction behind which the real politics—for the power behind the throne—could be played out.

Very young rulers were not entirely unknown in the classical, or even the Roman, world. The Sassanian king Shapur II (AD 309–79) had been famously crowned *in utero*, following the death of his father and the killing or maiming of his older brothers at the hands of Persian magnates.[16] Ammianus, writing of the usurper Procopius carrying around the posthumous infant daughter of Constantius II to bolster his own cause, mentioned a Macedonian infant-king who was taken into battle with his army to inspire them to greater heights of courage.[17] And in the Roman empire, young rulers like Augustus himself or Severus Alexander had come to the throne before. But never before had there been such an extraordinarily prolonged period of repeated minority rule in the Roman empire, never before had the contingent situation been so propitious for the evolution of such governments, and never before had the methods for dealing with child-rule been able to develop and evolve to the extent that an effective infantilization of the office of the ruler himself had taken place.

This institutionalization of child-emperor rule in the Roman empire had its impact on other magistracies of the late Roman system of government also, as well as on the ruling culture of the barbarian successor kingdoms which would unfold in the west after 476. In addition to the consulships held by infant princes—such as the young Varronianus, Gratian, Valentinian Galates, Valentinian II, and later Honorius, Arcadius, Theodosius II, and Valentinian III—we know of other extremely youthful consuls of the later Roman empire, whose appointments to the highest magistracy in the empire might arguably never have occurred were it not for the phenomenon of the child-emperors. In 395, for instance, the consuls for the year were the teenagers Probinus

---

[16] For sources see *PLRE* 1. 803.
[17] AM 26.9.3; also *Pan.Lat.* IV.20.1–3.

and Olybrius, scions of an illustrious Roman house, upon whom Claudian delivered his first court panegyric.[18] In the fifth century, the appointment of the (at most) 13-year-old Olybrius, son of the princess Anicia Juliana and the general Areobindus, as consul in 491 represented another such precocious magistrate.[19] While the appointment of consuls for each year and the dominance of the office by emperors, generals, and other aristocrats to some extent prevented too great a proliferation of child consuls, the appointment of some of these young candidates could nevertheless be argued to contribute to the increasing ceremonialization of an already largely symbolic office.

Child-emperors were to become common in the following centuries of the Byzantine empire, with the short-lived reign of Leo II in the last half of the sixth century, Constans II from 641, and Constantine VII in the tenth century, among others, who frequently faced similar challenges to the boy-emperors of the late Roman world, in terms of domination by powerful generals or other members of the elite. In the barbarian successor kingdoms of the post-Roman west, the impact of the infantilization of the Roman imperial office may also be discerned, with fiercely warrior-based groups such as the Franks coming to accept child-kings like Clovis II.[20] But the most immediate impact of the transformation of the Roman imperial office on barbarian ruling culture can arguably be seen in the succession crisis of the Ostrogothic kingdom of Italy in the 520s.[21] Theoderic the Ostrogoth had ruled Italy successfully as a soldier-king for three decades, maintaining largely peaceable relations with the remaining Roman elite of his kingdom and bringing a measure of stability to the region once more. Yet in the early 520s, Theoderic's adult heir Eutharic died suddenly, leaving as next in line for the throne his young grandson Athalaric. The Ostrogothic kingdom remained a relatively recent political entity, its leadership dictated by military needs rather than ceremonial (though Theoderic had shown himself keen to adopt as much traditional Roman ceremonial as he could), and its presence in Italy largely justified to its Roman subjects and to the imperial government at Constantinople through its military might.

After many years of peaceful coexistence, a mysterious crisis blew up between members of the Roman senatorial elite and the Ostrogothic government following Eutharic's death. Two of the most prominent aristocrats to have served at Theoderic's court, the philosopher Boethius and his father-in-law Symmachus, were accused of treasonous plotting with Constantinople,

[18] Claudian, *Prob. et Olyb.*; CLRE 324–5.
[19] CLRE 516–17; PLRE 2. 795. Fl. Probus, a nephew of the emperor Anastasius, was also appointed consul at a very young age in 502: CLRE 538–9; PLRE 2. 192–3.
[20] On Clovis II (king of Neustria and Burgundy 639–55, aged around 2 upon his accession), other Frankish child-kings, and the seventh-century Frankish monarchy generally, see Fouracre (2005), 371–96.
[21] For what follows, see Moorhead (1992), 212–51.

and executed. The episode is one which continues to receive attention from modern scholarship, and the full reasons behind it may never be known. Yet one distinct possibility is that some members of the Roman elite were alarmed at the prospect of the child Athalaric succeeding Theoderic—an Ostrogothic child-king who could not lead his armies in the field and personally defend Italy. Such an accession would dispel the illusion that many Romans may still have held that the Ostrogothic kingdom was a temporary arrangement dictated by military necessity; an illusion which the reign of a non-military, ceremonial Gothic ruler could not sustain. Despite this crisis, when Theoderic died in 526 Athalaric did become the new Ostrogothic king of Italy, at the age of perhaps 8. And, like the reigns of Roman child-emperors before him, the young king's reign was a troubled one. Athalaric never led his army, and fellow-Ostrogoths were reportedly unhappy that at his mother's (Amalasuintha's) instigation, their king was receiving an 'effeminate' Roman-style education rather than learning to be a soldier; with accusations of his having become idle and dissolute in consequence. Athalaric died in his late teens, allegedly as a result of a wasting disease brought on by excessive drinking.[22]

King Athalaric's youthful accession and ultimately unsuccessful reign bears a striking resemblance, in some respects, to the early child-emperor governments of the late Roman world—those of Gratian and Valentinian II particularly. But although the institutionalization of child-emperor rule in the previous century must have had its influence upon the Ostrogothic succession in the 520s, this was not a transformation Ostrogothic kingship had undergone, and with no child-kings following on from Athalaric, it would not do so. The predominantly military nature of the Ostrogothic leadership would be reinforced both by the failure of Athalaric's reign, and the reconquest campaign of the eastern emperor Justinian which would soon spread to Italy. Nevertheless, the succession crisis of the 520s and the reign of Athalaric bear signs of the impact of the development and institutionalization of Roman child-emperor rule.

Many different societies and civilizations throughout the centuries have seen the accession of child-rulers: it is, of course, not a phenomenon confined to the late Roman world. Perhaps the most recent examples are offered by the intensely ceremonial imperial houses of Japan and China, and many possibilities exist for comparative studies of the transformation of a predominantly military office into an overwhelmingly religious, symbolic, and increasingly distant position.[23] Although I would not wish to suggest that the developments I have traced here in the fourth- and fifth-century Roman world had a

---

[22] Procopius, *Bell.* 5.2.6–21; 5.4.4.

[23] Morris (1964) provides an invaluable starting-point for looking at ceremonial rulership in Japan.

direct relationship to such developments centuries later in the Far East, intriguing possibilities for comparison and contrast remain.

The appearance and consolidation of child-emperor reigns is a fundamental, and hitherto largely unrecognized, aspect of the evolution of late Roman government. It entails a great deal more than dynastic continuities or mere happenstance. Politics and contingent developments made child-emperors a possibility; the potential this possibility opened up for court factions made child-emperors desirable. The subsequent institutionalization of the arrangements which then evolved around the boy-rulers from 395 onwards transformed them in turn into a new exemplar for imperial rule. The range of potential roles available to any ruler—child or adult—who followed, and along with it the emphases on and expectations of the functions an emperor might perform, were thus changed forever. Child-emperors became, so to speak, a systemic element in late Roman government. True, the extent to which ceremonial rule might succeed as a child-emperor reached adulthood did depend upon the individual ruler being prepared to remain passive. But the successful institutionalization of this style of rule during the reign of Honorius, in particular, marked a turning-point in the political culture of the later Roman empire, and ensured that the ceremonial model remained a viable, acceptable, and indeed desirable possibility. Yet in addition, the phenomenon of the child-emperors of the late Roman west has implications far beyond the limits of its region and period: for the western emperors who followed, for the conception of styles of rulership in the eastern empire, for the expectations of kingship in the western successor kingdoms, and for the medieval world to come.

Bibliography

Primary Sources and Abbreviations

Acta   *Gesta concili Aquileiensis* (*Epp.* 1–3; *Acta*): CSEL 82.3: 313–68, ed. M. Zelzer (1982).

Agnellus   *Liber pontificalis ecclesiae Ravennatis*, ed. O. Holder-Egger, in MGH (SS. Langobard. et Italic.) (Hanover, 1878), 265–391, text 275 ff. English translation: *Agnellus of Ravenna: The book of the pontiffs of the church of Ravenna*, trans. D. M. Deliyannis (Washington, DC, 2004).

Ambrose, *Apol. Dav.*   *De apologia David*: SCh 239 (*Apologie de David*), ed. P. Hadot (1977).

Ambrose, *De ob. Val.*   *De obitu Valentiniani*: CSEL 73: 327–67, ed. O. Faller (1955). English translation: *De consolatione Valentiniani, a text with a translation and commentary*, by T. A. Kelly (Washington, DC, 1940). Also translated by J. H. W. G. Liebeschuetz, in *Ambrose of Milan: political letters and speeches* (Liverpool, 2005), 364–99.

Ambrose, *De ob. Theod.*   *De obitu Theodosii*: CSEL 73: 39–401, ed. O. Faller (1955). English translation by R. J. Deferrari, in *Fathers of the Church*, 22 (Washington, DC, 1953), 307–32. Also translated by J. H. W. G. Liebeschuetz, in *Ambrose of Milan: political letters and speeches* (Liverpool, 2005), 177–203.

Ambrose, *Ep.*   *Epistulae*: CSEL 82.1, ed. O. Faller (1968): books 1–6; CSEL 82.2, ed. M. Zelzer (1990): books 7–9; CSEL 82.3, ed. M. Zelzer (1982): book 10 and *Epistulae extra collectionem*. Selected letters translated in J. H. W. G. Liebeschuetz, *Ambrose of Milan: political letters and speeches* (Liverpool, 2005).

Ambrose, *Ep. extra coll.*   *Epistulae extra collectionem*: CSEL 82.3, ed. M. Zelzer (1982), 141–311. Also translated by J. H. W. G. Liebeschuetz, in *Ambrose of Milan: political letters and speeches* (Liverpool, 2005), 215–345.

Ambrose, *De fid.*   *De fide*: CSEL 78, ed. O. Faller (1962).

Ambrose, *De spir. sanct.*   *De spiritu sancto*: CSEL 79, ed. O. Faller (1964), 15–222.

Ambrose, *Expl. Ps.*   *Explanatio psalmorum*: CSEL 64, ed. M. Petschenig (1919)

AM   Ammianus Marcellinus, *Works*, ed. and trans. J. C. Rolfe, 3 vols. (London and Cambridge, Mass., 1935–9).

Augustine, *Conf.*   *Confessions*, ed. J. J. O'Donnell (Oxford, 1992).

Augustine, *Civ.Dei*
De Civitate Dei: *CSEL* 40, 2 vols., ed. E. Hoffman (1899–1900). English translation by H. Bettenson, *St Augustine: concerning the city of God against the pagans* (London, 1972; repr. 2003).

Augustine, *Ep.*
Epistulae: *CSEL* 34, 44, 57, 58, ed. Al. Goldbacher (1895–1923). English translations in *St Augustine: letters*, in *Fathers of the Church*, 12, 18, 20, 30, 32, trans. Sr. W. Parsons (New York, 1951–6), and 81, trans. R. B. Eno (Washington, DC, 1989).

Augustine, *Cum pagani*
Cum pagani ingrederentur 26, in *Vingt-six sermons au people d'Afrique*, ed. F. Dolbeau (Paris, 1996).

Aurelius Victor
Liber de caesaribus, ed. F. Pichlmayr (Liepzig, 1961). English translation by H. W. Bird, *Aurelius Victor: De Caesaribus* (Liverpool, 1994).

Ps.-Aurelius Victor
Epitome de caesaribus, in *Sexti Aurelii Victoris Liber de Caesaribus*, ed. F. Pichlmayr (Liepzig, 1966).

Ausonius, *Grat.Act.*
Gratiarum Actio ad Gratiarum, in *Ausonius*, ed. and trans. H. G. Evelyn-White, 2 vols. (Cambridge, Mass., 1919–21), 2. 218–69. Also in *The works of Ausonius*, ed. R. P. H. Green (Oxford, 1991), text at 146–52, commentary at 537–54.

Ausonius, *Versus Paschales*
In R. P. H. Green (Oxford, 1991), text at 15–16, commentary at 269–79.

Blockley
The fragmentary classicising historians of the later Roman empire: Eunapius, Olympiodorus, Priscus and Malchus, with text, translation, and notes by R. C. Blockley (Liverpool, 1983).

Cassiodorus, *Chron.*
Cassiodori Senatoris chronica ad. a DXIX, in *Chronica Minora*, ed. Th. Mommsen, 3 vols. (Berlin, 1892–8), 2. 109–61.

Cassiodorus, *Variae*
In *Magni Aurelii Cassiodori variarum libri XII*, ed. A. Fridh (Brepols, 1973), in *CCL* 96: 1–499. Selected letters translated into English by S. J. B. Barnish, *The Variae of Magnus Aurelius Cassiodorus Senator* (Liverpool, 1992).

Chron. Gall.
Chronica Gallica a. CCCCLII et DXI in *Chronica Minora*, ed. Th. Mommsen, 3 vols. (Berlin, 1892–8), 1. 615–66.

Chron.pasch.
Chronicon paschale, in *CSHB* 16, ed. L. Dindorf (Leipzig, 1832). English translation by M. and M. Whitby, *Chronicon paschale 284–628AD* (Liverpool, 1989).

CIL
Corpus Inscriptionum Latinarum, ed. G. Reimerum, 36 vols. (Berlin, 1862–93).

CJ
Codex Justinianus, in *CJC* 2.

CJC
Corpus Juris Civilis, ed. P. Krüger (Berlin, 1892–5; repr. 1945–63).

Claudian	*Claudian*, ed. and trans. M. Plautnauer, 2 vols. (Cambridge, Mass., 1972–6).
Claudian, *III Cons.*	*Panegyricus de Tertio Consulatu Honorii Augusti*, in *Claudian*, 1. 268–85.
Claudian, *IV Cons.*	*Panegyricus de Quarto Consulatu Honorii Augusti*, in *Claudian*, 1. 286–335.
Claudian, *VI Cons.*	*Panegyricus de Sexto Consulatu Honorii Augusti*, in *Claudian*, 2. 70–123. (Also *Panegyricus de Sexto Consulatus Honorii Augusti*, ed. M. Dewar (Oxford, 1996)).
Claudian, *Stil.*	*De Consulatu Stilichonis*, in *Claudian*, 1. 364–93, 2. 3–69.
Claudian, *Ruf.*	*In Rufinum*, in *Claudian*, 1. 24–97.
Claudian, *Eutr.*	*In Eutropium*, in *Claudian*, 1. 138–229.
Claudian, *Gild.*	*De Bello Gildonico*, in *Claudian*, 1. 98–137.
Claudian, *Get.*	*De Bello Gothico*, in *Claudian*, 2. 124–73.
Claudian, *Nupt.*	*Epithalamium de Nuptiis Honorii Augusti*, in *Claudian*, 1. 240–67.
Claudian, *Fesc.*	*Fescennina de Nuptiis Honorii Augusti*, in *Claudian*, 1. 230–9.
Claudian, *Man.Th.*	*Panegyricus dictus Manlio Theodoro Consuli*, in *Claudian*, 1. 336–63.
Claudian, *Prob. et Olyb.*	*Panegyricus dictus Probino et Olybrio Consulibus*, in *Claudian* 1. 2–23.
Claudian, *Carm.Min.*	*Carminum Minorum Corpusculum*, in *Claudian* 2. 174–291.
CTh.	*Theodosiani libri xvi cum constitutionibus Sirmondianis*, edd. Th. Mommsen, P. Meyer, *et al.* (Berlin, 1905). English translation: *Codex Theodosianus: The Theodosian Code and Novels and the Sirmondian Constitutions* (including the *Minutes of the Senate: Gesta Senatus urbis Romae*), trans. C. Pharr (New York, 1952).
CSirm.	*Sirmondian Constitutions*, in *CTh.* (Mommsen), 1. 907–21. English translation in *CTh.* (Pharr), 477–86.
Coll.Avell.	*Collectio Avellana*: CSEL 35, ed. W. Günther (1895–8).
Concilia Africae	*Concilia Africae, A.345–A.525*, in *CCL* 149, ed. C. Munier (Turnhout, 1974).
Constantius, *V.Germani*	Constantius of Lyons, *Vita Germani episcopi Autissiodorensis*, ed. R. Borius (Paris, 1965), in *Sources chrétiennes* 112.
Cons.Const.	*Consularia Constantinopolitana*. *The chronicle of Hydatius and the Consularia Constantinopolitana: two contemporary accounts of the final years of the Roman empire*, ed. and trans. R.W. Burgess (Oxford, 1993).
Dig.	*Justiniani Digesta*, in *CJC* III.
Eunapius	*Fragments*, in Blockley, 2–150.

Eusebius, *LC*   *Eusebius. Oratio de laudibus Constantini*, in *Eusebius Werke*, 1, ed. I. A. Heikel (Berlin, 1902), 195–223. English translation by H. A. Drake, in *In praise of Constantine* (Berkeley, 1975).

Eusebius, *VC*   *Eusebius. Vita Constantini*, in *Eusebius Werke* 1.1, *Über das Leben des Kaisers Konstantin*, ed. F. Winkelmann (Berlin, 1975). English translation by Av. Cameron and S. G. Hall, in *Eusebius, Life of Constantine* (Oxford, 1999).

Eutropius   *Breviarum ab urbe condita*, ed. C. Santini (Leipzig, 1897).

Evagrius   *The Ecclesiastical History of Evagrius*, ed. J. Bidez and L. Parmentier (London, 1898; repr. Amsterdam, 1964). English translation by M. Whitby, *The ecclesiastical history of Evagrius Scholasticus* (Liverpool, 2000).

Gesta   *Gesta Senatus urbis Romae*, in *CTh.* (Pharr), 3–7.

Gildas   *De Excidio Britanniae* I.20, ed. Mommsen, MGH AA XIII (Berlin, 1898).

Greg.Tur.   Gregory of Tours, *History of the Franks*, in *Gregorii Turronensis Opera*, ed. W. Arndt and Br. Krusch (Hanover, 1884), in MGH. English translation by L.Thorpe, *Gregory of Tours, History of the Franks* (London, 1974).

Hydatius   *The chronicle of Hydatius and the Consularia Constantinopolitana: two contemporary accounts of the final years of the Roman empire*, ed. and trans. R. W. Burgess (Oxford, 1993).

ICUR   *Inscriptiones Christianae Urbis Romae*, ed. G. B. de Rossi, 2 vols. (Rome, 1857–61).

ILCV   *Inscriptiones Latinae Christianae Veteres*, ed. E. Diehl (Berlin, 1925).

ILS   *Inscriptiones Latinae Selectae*, ed. H. Dessau (Berlin, 1892–1916).

Jerome, *Chron.*   *Chronicon*, in: *Eusebius Werke* 7, ed. R. Helm and U. Treu, 3rd edn. (Berlin, 1984).

Jerome, *Ep.*   *Epistulae*, in: *CSEL* 54–6, ed. I. Hilberg (1910–18).

John.Ant., frg.   John of Antioch, Fragments, in: *Fragmenta Historicorum Graecorum*, ed. C. and Th. Müller, 5 vols. (Paris, 1874–85), 5. 27–38. English translation in *The age of Attila: fifth century Byzantium and the barbarians*, by C. A. Gordon (Ann Arbor, Mich., 1961), 27–30, 50–4, 113–23.

John Chrys. *Ad. vid. iun.*   John Chrysostom, *Ad viduam iuniorem: À une jeune veuve sur le mariage unique* in *Sources Chrétiennes* 138, ed. and trans. B. Grillet and H. Ettinger (1968).

John Lydus, *De mag.*   John Lydus, *De magistratibus*, in *Ioannes Lydus:
                                 On Powers, or the Magistracies of the Roman State:
                                 introduction, critical text, translation, commentary
                                 and indices*, by A. C. Bandy (Philadelphia, 1983).

Jordanes, *Get.*   *Getica*, in: *Iordanes Romana et Getica*, ed. Th.
                                 Mommsen (Berlin, 1961), 53–138. English translation
                                 by C. C. Mierow, *The Gothic history of Jordanes*
                                 (Cambridge, 1915; repr. 1960).

Jordanes, *Rom.*   *Romana*, in: *Iordanes Romana et Getica*, ed. Th.
                                 Mommsen (Berlin, 1961), 3–52.

Julian, *Ep.*   *Letter to the Senate and People of Athens*, in *The Works
                                 of the Emperor Julian*, ed. and trans. W. C. Wright,
                                 3 vols. (Cambridge, Mass., 1913), 2. 242–91.

Leo, *Ep.*   Leo the Great, *Epistolae*, in *PL* 54. 581–1213. English
                                 translation by Br. E. Hunt, *St Leo the Great: Letters*, in
                                 Fathers of the Church, 34 (New York, 1957).

Leo, *Serm.*   Leo the Great, *Sermons*, in *Sources Chrétiennes* 74, ed.
                                 R. Dolle (1961).

Lib.pont.   *Liber pontificalis*. Texte, introduction et commentaire,
                                 ed. L. Duchesne, 2 vols., Bibliothèque des Écoles
                                 Françaises d'Athènes et de Rome, II sér., 3. (Paris,
                                 1886–92; repr. 1955); vol. 3: *Additions et corrections*,
                                 ed. C. Vogel (Paris, 1957). English translation
                                 by R. Davis, *The book of pontiffs (Liber Pontificalis)*
                                 (Liverpool, 1989).

Malalas   *Ioannis Malalae Chronographia*, ed. L. Dindorf, in
                                 CSHB (Bonn, 1831). English translation in *The chron-
                                 icle of John Malalas: a translation*, by E. Jeffreys,
                                 M. Jeffreys, R. Scott *et al.* (Melbourne, 1986).

Marc.Diac. *V.Porph.*   *Vie de Porphyre, évêque de Gaza [par] Marc le Diacre*.
                                 Texte établi, traduit et commenté par Henri Grégoire
                                 et M.-A. Kugener (Paris, 1930). English translation by
                                 G. F. Hill, *Mark the Deacon, Life of Porphyry, Bishop of
                                 Gaza* (Oxford, 1915).

Marcellinus   *The chronicle of Marcellinus*, ed., trans., and commen-
                                 tary by B. Croke (Sydney, 1995).

Menander   *Basilikos Logos*, in *Menander Rhetor*, ed. and trans.
                                 D. A. Russell and N. G. Wilson (Oxford, 1981), 76–95.

Merobaudes   *Flavius Merobaudes: a translation and historical
                                 Commentary*, ed. and trans. F. M. Clover, in *TAPA*,
                                 NS 61, no. 1 (1971), 1–78.

Merobaudes, *Carm.*I   *Carmina* I, in Merobaudes, text at p. 60, translation at
                                 p. 11.

Merobaudes, *Carm.*II   *Carmina* II, in Merobaudes, text at p. 60, translation at
                                 p. 11.

Merobaudes, *Carm*.IV   *Carmina* IV, in Merobaudes, text at pp. 61–2, translation at pp. 11–12.

Merobaudes, *Pan*.I   *Panegyricus* I, in Merobaudes, text at pp. 62–4, translation at pp. 12–13.

Merobaudes, *Pan*.II   *Panegyricus* II, in Merobaudes, text at pp. 64–8, translation at pp. 13–15.

Not.Dig.Occ.   *Notitia Dignitatum in partibus Occidentis*, in *Notitia Dignitatum*, ed. O. Seeck (Berlin, 1876), 103–225.

NTh.   *Leges novellae Theodosii II*, in *CTh.* (Mommsen), 2. 1–68. *The Novels of Theodosius II*, English translation in *CTh.* (Pharr), 487–514.

NVal.   *Leges novellae Valentiniani III*, in *CTh.* (Mommsen), 2. 69–154. *The Novels of Valentinian III*, English translation in *CTh.* (Pharr), 515–50.

Olympiodorus, frg.   Olympiodorus: Fragments, in Blockley, 152–220.

Orosius   *Orosius: Historiarum adversum paganos libri VII*: CSEL 5, ed. K. Zangemeister (1882). English translation in *Paulus Orosius: the seven books of history against the pagans*, by R. J. Deferrari (Washington, DC, 1964).

Pacatus   Latinus Pacatus Drepanius, *Panegyric of Theodosius (Pan.Lat. II)* in *Pan. Lat.*, text at pp. 647–74, trans. and notes at pp. 437–516.

Pan.Lat.   *In praise of later Roman emperors: the Panegyrici Latini*, ed and trans. C. E. V. Nixon and B. S. Rodgers (Berkeley, 1994).

Pan.Lat.III   *Panegyrici Latini III: Claudius Mamertinus, Speech of thanks to Julian*, in *Pan.Lat.*, text at pp. 629–42, tr. and notes at pp. 386–436.

Pan.Lat. IV   *Panegyrici Latini IV: Nazarius, Panegyric of Constantine*, in *Pan.Lat.*, text at pp. 608–28, tr. and notes at pp. 334–85.

Pan.Lat. V   *Panegyrici Latini V: Speech of thanks to Constantine*, in *Pan.Lat.*, text at pp. 585–93, trans. and notes at pp. 254–87.

Pan.Lat. VI   *Panegyrici Latini VI*: in *Pan.Lat.*, text at pp. 572–84, trans. and notes at pp. 211–53.

Pan.Lat.VII   *Panegyrici Latini VII: Panegyric of Maximian and Constantine*, in *Pan.Lat.*, text at pp. 564–71, trans. and notes at pp. 178–210.

Pan.Lat.VIII   *Panegyrici Latini VIII: Panegyric of Constantius*, in *Pan.Lat.*, text at pp. 543–53, trans. and notes at pp. 104–44.

Pan.Lat. IX   *Panegyrici Latini IX: Eumenius, For the restoration of the schools*, in *Pan.Lat.*, text at pp. 554–63, trans. and notes at pp. 145–77.

Pan.Lat. X	*Panegyrici Latini X: Panegyric of Maximian*, in *Pan. Lat.*, text at pp. 523–31, trans. and notes at pp. 41–75.
Pan.Lat. XI	*Panegyrici Latini XI: Genethliacus of Maximian Augustus*, in *Pan.Lat.*, text at pp. 532–42, trans. and notes at pp. 76–103.
Pan.Lat. XII	*Panegyrici Latini XII: Panegyric of Constantine Augustus*, in *Pan.Lat.*, text at pp. 594–607, trans. and notes at pp. 288–333.
Paul the Deacon, *Hist.rom.*	*Pauli diaconi Historia romana*, ed. A. Crivellucci (Rome, 1850–1914).
Paulinus, *VAmb.*	*Paolino di Milano: Vita di S. Ambrogio*, ed. M. Pellegrino, *Verba Seniorum*, NS 1 (Rome, 1961). English translation: *Paulinus of Milan, Vita Sancti Ambrosii*, trans. Sr. M. S. Kaniecka (Washington, DC, 1928).
Paul. Nola, *Carm.*21	*Carmina* 21, in *Paulinus of Nola: CSEL* 30, ed. W. Hartel (1894), 158–86.
Paul. Pella, *Euch.*	Paulinus of Pella, *Eucharisticus*, in *Ausonius*, ed. and trans. H. G. Evelyn-White, 2 vols. (Cambridge, Mass., 1919–21), 2. 305–51
Peter Chrysologos, *Serm.*	*Opere de San Pietro Crisologo*, ed. G. Banterle *et al.* (*Scrittori dell'area santambrosiana* = *Scriptores circa Ambrosium Scrittori dell'area santambrosiana.* 1. *Sermoni* (1–62 bis); 2. *Sermoni* (63–124); 3. *Sermoni* (125–79) e lettera a Eutiche) (Milan: Biblioteca ambrosiana and Rome: Città nuova editrice, 1996–). English translations: *Saint Peter Chrysologos: Selected Sermons and Saint Valerian: Sermons*, trans. G. E. Ganss SJ, *in Fathers of the Early Church*, 17 (1953). *St Peter Chrysologos: Selected Sermons*, 2, trans. W. B. Palardy, in *Fathers of the Early Church*, 109 (2004).
Philostorgius	*Historia ecclesiastica: Kirchengeschichte*, ed. J. Bidez and F. Winkelmann (Berlin, 1972).
Pliny, *Pan.*	*Panegyricus*, in *Pliny: Letters and Panegyricus*, ed. and trans. B. Radice, 2 vols. (Cambridge, Mass., 1975), 2. 317–547.
Priscus, frg.	*Priscus: Fragments*, in Blockley, 222–400.
Procopius, *Bell.*	Procopius, *History of the Wars*, in *Works*, ed. and trans. H. B. Dewing, 7 vols. (Cambridge, Mass., 1996–2000), vols. 1–5.
Procopius, *Secret History*	Procopius, *The Anecdota or Secret History*, in *Works*, ed. and trans. H. B. Dewing, 7 vols. (Cambridge, Mass., 1996–2000), vol. 6.

Prosper	*Prosper Tironis epitoma chronicon*, in *Chronica Minora*, ed. Th. Mommsen, 3 vols. (Berlin, 1892–8), 1. 341–499.
Prudentius, *CSymm.*	*Contra Symmachum*, in *Prudentius*, ed. and trans. H. J. Thomson, 2 vols. (Cambridge, Mass., 1961), 1. 344–401 and 2. 2–97.
Prudentius, *Peristephanon*	*Peristephanon*, in *Prudentius*, ed. and trans. H. J. Thomson, 2 vols. (Cambridge, Mass., 1961), 2. 98–345.
Rufinus	*Historia ecclesiastica*, in *Eusebii historia ecclesiastica translate et continuata*, ed. Th. Mommsen (Berlin, 1908), 947–1040. English translation by P. Amidon, in *The church history of Rufinus of Aquileia: Books 10 and 11* (Oxford, 1997).
SHA, Tacitus	*Life of Tacitus*, in the *Scriptores Historia Augustae*, ed. and trans. D. Magie, 3 vols. (Cambridge, Mass., 1967–79), 3. 294–333.
Sidonius, *Carm.* 5	*Carmina 5*, in *Sidonius Apollinaris: Poems and Letters*, ed. and trans. W. B. Anderson, 2 vols. (Cambridge, Mass., 1963), 1. 58–113.
Sidonius, *Carm.* 7	*Carmina 7*, in *Sidonius Apollinaris: Poems and Letters*, ed. and trans. W. B. Anderson, 2 vols. (Cambridge, Mass., 1963), 1. 114–71.
Sidonius, *Carm.* 9	*Carmina 9*, in *Sidonius Apollinaris: Poems and Letters*, ed. and trans. W. B. Anderson, 2 vols. (Cambridge, Mass., 1963), 1. 173–97.
Socrates	*Historia ecclesiastica: Kirchengeschichte*, ed. G. C. Hansen (1995).
Sozomen	*Historia ecclesiastica: Kirchengeschichte* (2nd edn.) ed. J. Bidez and G. C. Hansen (1995).
Suetonius	*Life of Claudius*, in *Suetonius*, ed. and trans. J. C. Rolfe, 2 vols. (Cambridge, Mass., 1914; repr. 1997), 2. 2–81.
Sulp.Sev. *Chron.*	Sulpicius Severus, *Chronicon: CSEL* 1, ed. C. Halm (Vienna, 1886). English translation by A. Roberts, in *Nicene and Post-Nicene Fathers* (Oxford, 1844).
Sulp.Sev. *St Martin*	Sulpicius Severus, *Vie de Saint Martin*, ed., trans., and intro. (vol. 1) and commentary (vols. 2 and 3) by J. Fontaine, *Sources Chrétiennes* 133–5, 3 vols. (Paris, 1967–9).
Symmachus, *Ep.*	*Epistulae*, in *Symmaque Lettres: texte établi, traduit et commenté* by J. P. Callu, 3 vols. (Paris, 1972–2002).
Symmachus	*Symmachus*, ed. O. Seeck (Berlin, 1883).
Symmachus, *Or. 1*	*Oration 1*, in Symmachus, 318–23.
Symmachus, *Or. 3*	*Oration 3*, in Symmachus, 330–2.
Symmachus, *Or. 4*	*Oration 4*, in Symmachus, 332–5.
Symmachus, *Or. 5*	*Oration 5*, in Symmachus, 335–6.

Symmachus, *Rel. 3*   *Relationes 3*, in Symmachus, 280–3. Text with English translation in *Prefect and emperor: the Relationes of Symmachus*, by R. H. Barrow (Oxford, 1973), 34–47.

Symmachus, *Rel. 9*   *Relationes 9*, in Symmachus, 287–8. Text with English translation in Barrow, 67–71.

Symmachus, *Rel. 11*   *Relationes 11*, in Symmachus, 289. Text with English translation in Barrow, 76–7.

Symmachus, *Rel. 12*   *Relationes 12*, in Symmachus, 289–90. Text with English translation in Barrow, 78–81.

Themistius, *Orationes*   *Themistii Orationes quae supersunt*, ed. G. Downey and A. F. Norman, 3 vols. (Leipzig, 1965–74). English translation of selected orations in *Politics, philosophy, and empire in the fourth century: select orations of Themistius*, by P. Heather and D. Moncur (Liverpool, 2001 = Heather and Moncur).

Themistius, *Or. 1*   *Oration 1*, in Themistius, *Orationes*, 1. 3–23. English translation in Heather and Moncur, 78–96.

Themistius, *Or. 5*   *Oration 5*, in Themistius, *Orationes*, 1. 91–104. English translation in Heather and Moncur, 159-173

Themistius, *Or. 6*   *Oration 6*, in Themistius, *Orationes*, 1. 105–25. English translation in Heather and Moncur, 180–98.

Themistius, *Or. 9*   *Oration 9*, in Themistius, *Orationes*, 1. 181–94.
Themistius, *Or. 13*   *Oration 13*, in Themistius, *Orationes*, 1. 230–57.
Themistius, *Or. 14*   *Oration 14*, in Themistius, *Orationes*, 1. 259–65. English translation in Heather and Moncur, 225–30.

Themistius, *Or. 15*   *Oration 15*, in Themistius, *Orationes*, 1. 267–86. English translation in Heather and Moncur, 236–54.

Themistius, *Or. 16*   *Oration 16*, in Themistius, *Orationes*, 1. 287–304. English translation in Heather and Moncur, 265–83.

Themistius, *Or. 18*   *Oration 18*, in Themistius, *Orationes*, 1. 311–25.
Theodoret   *Historia ecclesiastica: Kirchengeschichte*, ed. L. Parmentier and G. C. Hansen, 3rd edn. (Berlin, 1998).

Theophanes   *Chronographia*, ed. C. DeBoor (1882; rep., Hildesheim, 1963). English translation by C. Mango and R. Scott, *The chronicle of Theophanes Confessor* (Oxford, 1997).

Vegetius, *Epit. rei militaris*   *Epitoma rei militaris*, ed. C. Lang (Liepzig, 1885). English translation: *Vegetius: Epitome of Military Science*, trans. N. P. Milner (Liverpool, 1993).

Zonaras   *Epitomae historiarum libri XVIII*, ed. T. Büttner-Wobst (Bonn, 1897). English translation by T. Banchich and E. Lane, *The history of Zonaras: From Alexander Severus to the death of Theodosius the great* (London, 2011).

Zosimus   *Histoire nouvelle*, ed. and trans. F. Paschoud, 3 parts, 5 vols. (Paris, 1971–89). English translation by R. T. Ridley, *Zosimus: New History* (Sydney, 1982).

Secondary Sources

Alchermes, J. D. (1995), 'Petrine politics: Pope Symmachus and the rotonda of St Andrew at Old St Peter's', *Catholic Historical Review,* 81: 1–40.

Alföldi, A. (1952), *A conflict of ideas in the late Roman empire,* trans. Mattingly, H. (Oxford).

Amirav, H. and ter Haar Romeny, B. (eds.) (2007), *From Rome to Constantinople: studies in honour of Averil Cameron* (Leuven).

Ando, C. (2000), *Imperial ideology and provincial loyalty in the Roman empire* (Berkeley).

Arnheim, M. T. W. (1972), *The senatorial aristocracy in the later Roman empire* (Oxford).

Ayres, L. (2004), *Nicaea and its legacy* (Oxford).

Bachrach, B. S. (1969), 'Another look at the barbarian settlement in Gaul', *Traditio,* 25: 354–9.

Barnes, T. D. (1974), 'Merobaudes on the imperial family', *Phoenix,* 28, no. 3: 314–19.

——(1975), '*Patricii* under Valentinian III', *Phoenix,* 29, no. 2: 155–70.

——(1976), 'The historical setting of Prudentius' *Contra Symmachum*', *AJP* 97, no. 4: 373–86.

——(1981), *Constantine and Eusebius* (Cambridge, Mass.).

——(1982), *The new empire of Diocletian and Constantine* (Cambridge, Mass.).

——(1985), 'Proconsuls of Africa, 337–392', *Phoenix,* 39: 144–53.

——(1990), 'Religion and society in the age of Theodosius', in Meynell (ed.) (1990), 157–78.

——(1993), *Athanasius and Constantius: theology and politics in the Constantinian empire* (Cambridge, Mass.).

——(1998), *Ammianus Marcellinus and the representation of historical reality* (London).

——(1999), 'Ambrose and Gratian', *Ant.Tard.* 7: 165–74.

——(2000), 'Ambrose and the basilicas of Milan in 385 and 386: the primary documents and their implications', *ZAC* 4: 282–99.

——(2002), 'Valentinian, Auxentius and Ambrose', *Historia,* 51: 227–37.

Barnish, S. (1992), 'Old Kaspars: Attila's invasion of Gaul in the literary sources', in Drinkwater and Elton (eds.) (1992), 38–47.

——Lee, A. D., and Whitby, M. (2000), 'Government and administration', in *CAH* XIV: 164–206.

Barnwell, P. S. (1992), *Emperor, prefects and kings: the Roman west, 395–565,* (London).

Barrow, R. H. (1973), *Prefect and emperor: the* Relationes *of Symmachus, AD 384* (Oxford).

Bartoli, A. (1946–7), 'Il Senator romano in onoredi Ezio', *RPAA* ser. 3, 22: 267–73.

Bayless, W. N. (1976a), 'The Visigothic invasion of Italy in 401', *CJourn.* 72, no. 1: 65–7.

——(1976b), 'Anti-Germanism in the age of Stilicho', *Byzantine Studies/Études Byzantines,* 3.2: 70–6.

Baynes, N. H. (1955a), *Byzantine studies and other essays* (London).

——(1955b), 'Rome and Armenia in the fourth century', in Baynes (1955a), 186–208 (= *EHR* 25 (1910), 625–43).

Barnes, N. H. (1955c), 'Eusebius and the Christian empire', in Baynes (1955a), 168–72 (= *Annuaire de l'institut de philologie et d'histoire orientales* (1933), ii. 13–18).

——(1955d), 'Stilicho and the barbarian invasions', in Baynes (1955a), 326–42 (= *JRS* 12 (1922), 207–29).

——(1955e), 'Symmachus', in Baynes (1955a), 361–6 (= *JRS* 36 (1946), 173–7).

Binns, J. W. (ed.) (1974), *Latin literature of the fourth century* (London).

Birley, A. R. (1983), 'Magnus Maximus and the persecution of heresy', *Bulletin of the John Rylands Library Manchester*, 66, 1: 13–43.

——(2005), *The Roman government of Britain* (Oxford).

Bloch, H. (1945), 'A new document of the last pagan revival of the west, 393–394AD', *HThR* 38: 200–44.

——(1963), 'The pagan revival in the west at the end of the fourth century', in Momigliano (ed.) (1963), 193–218.

Blockley, R. C. (1992), *East Roman foreign policy: formation and conduct from Diocletian to Anastasius* (Leeds).

Bonamente G., and Lizzi Testa, R. (eds.) (2010), *Istituzioni, carismi ed esercizio del potere (IV–VI secolo d.C.)* (Edipuglia).

Bonner, G. (1963), *St Augustine of Hippo: life and controversies* (Norwich).

Born, L. K. (1934), 'The perfect prince according to the Latin panegyrists', *AJP* 55: 20–35.

Bowersock, G. W., Brown P., and Grabar, O. (eds.) (1999), *Interpreting late antiquity: essays on the postclassical world* (Cambridge, Mass.).

Bowes K. and Kulikowski M. (ed. and trans.) (2005), *Hispania in late antiquity: current perspectives* (Leiden).

Brennan, P. (1995), 'The *Notitia Dignitatum*', in *Les Littératures techniques dans l'antiquité romaine* (Geneva), 147–78.

Brown, P. (1972a), *Religion and society in the age of Saint Augustine* (London).

——(1972b), 'Aspects of the christianization of the Roman aristocracy', in Brown (1972a), 161–82 (= *JRS* 51 (1961), 1–11).

——(1992), *Power and persuasion in late antiquity: towards a Christian empire* (Madison, Wisc.).

——(2000; repr. of 1967), *Augustine of Hippo: a biography* (Berkeley).

——and Lizzi Testa, R. (eds.) (2011), *Pagans and Christians in the Roman empire: the breaking of a dialogue (IVth–VIth Century AD)* (Münster).

Brubaker, L. (1997), 'Memories of Helena: patterns of imperial female matronage in the fourth and fifth centuries', in James (ed.) (1997), 52–75.

Bruggisser, P. (1987), '*Gloria novi saeculi*: Symmaque et le siècle de Gratien (Epist. 1.13)', *Mus.Helv.* 44: 134–49.

Burgess, R. W. (1988), 'A new reading for Hydatius *Chronicle* 117 and the defeat of the Huns in Italy', *Phoenix*, 42: 357–63.

——(1993–4), 'The accession of Marcian in the light of Chalcedonian apologetic and Monophysite polemic', *BZ* 86/7: 47–68.

——(2008), 'The summer of blood: the "great massacre" of 337 and the promotion of the sons of Constantine', *DOP* 62: 5–51.

Burns, T. S. (1992), 'The settlement of 418', in Drinkwater and Elton (eds.) (1992), 53–63.

——(1994), *Barbarians within the gates of Rome: a study of Roman military policy and the barbarians ca. 375–425AD* (Indianapolis).

Bury, J. B. (1919), 'Justa Grata Honoria', *JRS* 9: 1–13.

——(1923), *History of the later Roman empire: from the death of Theodosius I to the death of Justinian* (London), 2 vols. (repr. New York, 1958).

Cain, A., and Lenski, N. (eds.) (2009), *The power of religion in late antiquity* (Ashgate).

Cameron, A. (1965), 'Wandering poets: a literary movement in Byzantine Egypt', *Historia* 14: 470–509.

——(1968a), 'Gratian's repudiation of the pontifical robe', *JRS* 58: 96–102.

——(1968b), 'Notes on Claudian's invectives', *CQ* 18: 387–411.

——(1969), 'Theodosius the Great and the regency of Stilicho', *HSCP* 73: 247–80.

——(1970), *Claudian: poetry and propaganda at the court of Honorius* (Oxford).

——(1976), *Circus factions: Blues and Greens at Rome and Byzantium* (Oxford).

——(2007a), 'The Probus diptych and Christian apologetic', in Amirav and ter Haar Romeny (eds.) (2007), 191–202.

——(2007b), 'The imperial pontifex', *HSCP* 103: 341–87.

——(2011), *The last pagans of Rome* (Oxford).

——and Long, J., with a contribution by Sherry, L. (1993), *Barbarians and politics at the court of Arcadius* (Berkeley).

Cameron, Av. (1991), *Christianity and the rhetoric of Empire: the development of Christian discourse* (Berkeley).

——and Hall, S. G. (1999), *Life of Constantine* (Oxford).

Campbell, J. B. (1984), *The emperor and the Roman army, 31BC–AD235* (Oxford).

Cesa, M. (1992–3), 'Il matrimonio di Placidia ed Ataulfo sullo sfondo dei rapport fra Ravenna e i Visigoti', *Romanobarbarica*, 12: 23–53.

——and Sivan, H. (1990), 'Alarico in Italia: Pollenza e Verona', *Historia*, 39: 361–74.

Charlesworth, M. P. (1937), 'The virtues of a Roman emperor: propaganda and the creation of belief', *PBA* 23: 105–33.

Chastagnol, A. (1960), *La Préfectaire urbaine à Rome sous le Bas-Empire* (Paris).

——(1962), *Les Fastes de la prefecture de Rome au bas-empire* (Paris).

——(1973), 'Le Repli sur Arles des services administratifs gaulois en l'an 407 de notre ère', *RH* 505: 23–40.

——(1976), *La Fin du monde antique de Stilicon à Justinien (Ve siècle at début du VIe siècle)* (Paris).

Chevallier, R. (ed.) (1966), *Mélanges d'archéologie et d'histoire offerts à André Piganiol* (Paris).

Christiansen, P. G. (1966), 'Claudian versus the opposition', *TAPA* 97: 45–54.

——(1970), 'Claudian and the east', *Historia*, 19: 113–20.

Christie, N. and Gibson, S. (1988), 'The city walls of Ravenna', *PBSR* 56: 156–96.

Clover, F. M. (1971a), 'Flavius Merobaudes: a translation and historical commentary', *TAPA* ns 61, no. 1: 1–78.

——(1971b), 'Towards an understanding of Flavius Merobaudes' Panegyric I', *Historia*, 20: 354–67; repr. in Clover (1993).

——(1973), 'Geiseric and Attila', *Historia*, 22: 104–17; repr. in Clover (1993).

——(1978), 'The family and early career of Anicius Olybrius', *Historia*, 27: 169–96; repr. in Clover (1993).

——(1993), *The late Roman west and the Vandals* (Aldershot).

Connor, C. L. (2004), *Women of Byzantium* (New Haven).

Consolino, F. E. (1995*a*), 'L'optimus princeps secondo S. Ambrogio: Virtu imperatorie e virtue cristiane nelle orazioni funebri per Valentiniano e Teodosio', *Rivista storica italiana* 96: 1025–45.

——(1995*b*), 'La "santa" regina Elena a Galla Placidia nella tradizione dell'Occidente latino', in Raffaelli (ed.) (1995), 467–92.

Cooper K., and Hillner J. (eds.) (2007), *Religion, dynasty and patronage in early Christian Rome, 300–900* (Cambridge).

Coulon, D. (2000), *Aetius* (Paris).

Courtois, C. (1955), *Les Vandales et l'Afrique* (Paris).

Cracco Ruggini, L. (1998), 'Il 397: l'anno della morte di Ambrogio', in Pizzolato and Rizzi (eds.) (1998), 5–29.

Cristo, S. (1977), 'Some notes on the Bonifacian–Eulalian schism', *Aevum*, 51: 1/2: 163–7.

Croke, B. (1976), 'Arbogast and the death of Valentinian II', *Historia*, 25: 235–44.

——(1995), *The Chronicle of Marcellinus* (Sydney).

——(2010), 'Reinventing Constantinople: Theodosius I's imprint on the imperial city', in McGill, Sogno, and Watts (eds.) (2010), 241–64.

——and Harries, J. (1982), *Religious conflict in fourth-century Rome* (Sydney).

Curran, J. (1998), 'From Jovian to Theodosius', in *CAH* XIII: 78–109.

Dagron, G. (2003), *Emperor and priest: the imperial office in Byzantium*, trans. J. Birrell (Cambridge).

Davis, R. (2000), *The book of the pontiffs (Liber Pontificalis): the ancient biographies of the first ninety bishops to AD715* (Liverpool).

Degrassi, A. (1946–8), 'L'iscrizione in onore di Aezio e l'Atrium Libertatis', *BCAR* 72: 33–44.

Deichmann, F. W. (1989), *Ravenna, Haupstadt des spätantiken Abendlandes* (Wiesbaden).

Deliyannis, D. M. (2010), *Ravenna in late antiquity* (Cambridge).

Demandt, A. (1969), 'Der Tod des älteren Theodosius', *Historia*, 18: 598–626.

Demougeot, E. (1950), 'Note sur la politique orientale de Stilicon, de 405 a 407', *Byzantion*, 20: 27–37.

——(1951), *De l'unité à la division de l'Empire romain 395–410* (Paris).

——(1954), 'A propos des intervention du pape Innocent Ier dans la politique séculière', *RH* 212: 23–38.

——(1985), 'L'Évolution politique de Galla Placidia', *Gerión*, 3: 183–210.

De Salis, J. F. W. (1867), 'The coins of the two Eudoxias, Eudocia, Placidia and Honoria, and of Theodosius II, Marcian, and Leo I, struck in Italy', *NC*, NS 7: 203–15.

Dewar, M. (1996), *Panegyricus de Sexto Consulatus Honorii Augusti*, edited with introduction, translation, and literary commentary (Oxford).

——(2008), 'Spinning the *Trabea*: consular robes and propaganda in the panegyrics of Claudian', in Edmondson and Keith (eds.) (2008), 217–37.

Diesner, H.-J. (1972), 'Das Bucellariertum von Stilicho und Sarus bis auf Aetius (454/5)', *Klio*, 54: 321–50.

Doignon, J. (1966), 'Le Titre de *Nobilissimus Puer* porté par Gratien et le mystique littéraire des origines de Rome à l'avènement des Valentiniens', in Chevallier (ed.) (1966), 1693–1709.

Drake, H. A. (2000), *Constantine I and the bishops: the politics of intolerance* (Baltimore).

—— (2006), 'The impact of Constantine on Christianity', in Lenski (ed.) (2006*a*), 111–36.

Drijvers, J. W., and Hunt, D. (eds.) (1999), *The late Roman world and its historian* (London).

Drinkwater, J. F. (1989*a*), 'Gallic attitudes to the Roman empire in the fourth century: continuity or change?', in Herzig and Frei-Stolba (eds.) (1989), 136–53.

—— (1989*b*), 'Patronage in Roman Gaul and the problem of the Bagaudae', in Wallace-Hadrill (ed.) (1989), 189–203.

—— (1992), 'The Bacaudae of fifth-century Gaul', in Drinkwater and Elton (eds.) (1992), 208–17.

—— (1998), 'The usurpers Constantine III (407–411) and Jovinus (411–413)', *Britannia*, 29: 269–98.

—— and Elton, H. (eds.) (1992), *Fifth century Gaul: a crisis of identity?* (Cambridge).

Dudden, F. H. (1935), *The life and times of St Ambrose* (Oxford).

Duval, Y.-M. (ed.) (1974), *Ambroise de Milan* (Paris).

Dvornik, F. (1966), *Early Christian and Byzantine philosophy: origins and background* (Washington, DC).

Edmondson, J., and Keith, A. (eds.) (2008), *Roman Dress and the Fabrics of Roman Culture* (Toronto).

Ehrhardt, A. (1964), 'The first two years of the Emperor Theodosius I', *JEH* 15: 1–17.

Elton, H. (1992), 'Defence in fifth-century Gaul', in Drinkwater and Elton (eds.) (1992), 167–76.

—— (1996), *Warfare in Roman Europe AD 350–425* (Oxford).

Ensslin, W. (1931), 'Zum Heermeisteramt des spätrömischen Reiches', *Klio*, 24: 467–502.

Errington, R. M. (1996*a*), 'The accession of Theodosius I', *Klio*, 78, 2: 438–53.

—— (1996*b*), 'Theodosius and the Goths', *Chiron*, 26: 1–27.

—— (1997), 'Church and state in the first years of Theodosius I', *Chiron*, 27: 21–72.

—— (2006), *Roman imperial policy from Julian to Theodosius* (Chapel Hill, NC).

Esmonde Cleary, A. S. (1989), *The ending of Roman Britain* (London).

Fouracre, P. (2005), 'Francia in the seventh century', in P. Fouracre (ed.), *The New Cambridge Ancient History*, Volume I: *c. 500–c. 700* (Cambridge), 369–96.

Freeman, E. A. (1887), 'Aetius and Boniface', *EHR* 2, no. 7: 417–65.

Freeman Sandler, L. (ed.) (1964), *Essays in memory of Karl Lehmann* (New York).

Frakes, R.M. (2006), 'The dynasty of Constantine down to 363', in Lenski (ed.) (2006*a*), 91–107.

Frank, R. I. (1969), *Scholae Palatinae: the palace guards of the later Roman empire* (Rome).

Frend, W. H. C. (1985), *The Donatist Church*, 3rd edn. (Oxford).

Fuhrer, Th. (ed.) (2012), *Rom und Mailand in der Spätantike. Repräsentationen städtischer Räume in Literatur, Architektur und Kunst* (Berlin).

Gem, R. (2005), 'The Vatican Rotunda: a Severan monument and its early history, c. 200 to 500', *Journal of the British Archaeological Association*, 158: 1–45.

Gillett, A. (1993), 'The date and circumstances of Olympiodorus of Thebes', *Traditio*, 48: 1–29.

Gillett, A. (2001), 'Rome, Ravenna and the last western emperors', *PBSR* 59: 131–67.
——(2012), 'Epic panegyric and political communication in the fifth-century west', in Grig and Kelly (eds.) (2012), 265–90.
Glaesener, H. (1957), 'L'Empereur Gratien et saint Ambroise', *RHE* 52: 466–88.
Goffart, W. (1971), 'Zosimus: the first historian of Rome's fall', *AHR* 76, no. 2: 412–41.
——(1980), *Barbarians and Romans AD 418–584: the techniques of accommodation*, (Princeton).
Gottlieb, G. (1973), *Ambrosius von Maitland und Kaiser Gratian* (Göttingen).
Grattarola, P. (1979), 'La morte dell'imperatore Valentiniano II', *RIL* 113: 359–70.
Green, B. (2008), *The soteriology of Leo the Great* (Oxford).
Green, R. P. H. (1991), *The works of Ausonius* (Oxford).
Grierson, P. (1962), 'Tombs and obits of the Byzantine emperors (337–1042)', *DOP* 16: 1–63.
Grig, L. (2009), 'Imagining the Capitolium in late antiquity', in Cain and Lenski (eds.) (2009), 279–92.
——and Kelly, G. (2012), *Two Romes: Rome and Constantinople in Late Antiquity* (Oxford).
Grumel, R. P. V. (1951), 'L'Illyricum de la mort de Valentinian Ier (375) à la mort de Stilicon (408)', *REB* 9: 5–46.
Gryson, R. (1980), 'Scolies Ariennes sur le concile d'Aquilée', *SC* 267: 121–143
Haenel, G. F. (1857–60), *Corpus legum ad imperatoribus romanis ante Iustinianum latarum* (Liepzig).
Haldon, J. F. (1984), *Byzantine Praetorians: an administrative, institutional, and social survey of the opsikion and tagmata c. 580–900* (Bonn).
——(1999), *Warfare, state and society in the Byzantine world 550–1204* (London).
Hall, J. B. (1988), 'Pollentia, Verona and the chronology of Alaric's first invasion of Italy', *Philologus*, 132: 245–57.
Halsall, G. (2007), *Barbarian migrations and the Roman west, 367–568* (Cambridge).
Hanson, R. P. C. (1988), *The search for the Christian doctrine of God* (Edinburgh).
Harlow, M. (2004), 'Galla Placidia: conduit of culture?', in McHardy and Marshall (eds.) (2004), 138–50.
Harries, J. (1988), 'The Roman imperial Quaestor from Constantine to Theodosius II', *JRS* 78: 148–72.
——(1994a), *Sidonius Apollinaris and the fall of Rome* (Oxford).
——(1994b), '*Pius Princeps*: Theodosius II and fifth-century Constantinople', in Magdalino (ed.) (1994), 35–44.
——(1999), *Law and empire in late antiquity* (Cambridge).
——(forthcoming), 'Men without women: Theodosius' consistory and the business of government', in Kelly (ed.).
——and Wood , I. (eds.) (1993), *The Theodosian Code: studies in the imperial law of late antiquity* (London).
Hartke, W. (1951), *Römische Kinderkaiser: Eine Strukturanalyse Römischen Denkens und Daseins* (Berlin).
Heather, P. J. (1991), *Goths and Romans* (Oxford).
——(1992), 'The emergence of the Visigothic kingdom', in Drinkwater and Elton (eds.) (1992), 84–94.
——(1994), 'New men for new Constantines? Creating an imperial elite in the eastern Mediterranean', in Magdalino (ed.) (1994), 11–33.

——(1995), 'The Huns and the end of the Roman empire in western Europe', *EHR* 110, no. 435: 4–41.

——(1999), 'Ammianus on Jovian: history and literature', in Drijvers and Hunt (eds.) (1999), 105–16.

——(2000), 'The western empire, 425–76', in *CAH* XIV: 1–32.

——(2005), *The fall of the Roman empire* (London).

——(2009), 'Why did the barbarian cross the Rhine?', *JLA* 2.1: 3–29.

——and Moncur, D. (2001), *Politics, philosophy and empire in the fourth century* (Liverpool).

Hedrick, C.W. Jr. (2000), *History and silence: purge and rehabilitation of memory in late antiquity* (Austin, Tex.).

Heim, F. (1974), 'Le Theme de la "victoire sans combat" chez Ambroise', in *Ambroise de Milan: dix etudes rassemblées par Y. M. Duval* (Paris), 267–81.

Heinzelmann, M. (1992), 'The affair of Hilary of Arles (445) and Gallo-Roman identity in the fifth century', in Drinkwater and Elton (eds.) (1992), 239–51.

Hendy, M. F. (1985), *Studies in the Byzantine monetary economy, c. 300–1450* (Cambridge).

Hermanowicz, E. T. (2004), 'Catholic bishops and appeals to the imperial court: a legal study of the Calama riots in 408', *JECS* 12, no. 4: 481–521.

——(2008), *Possidius of Calama: a study of the North African episcopate at the time of Augustine* (Oxford).

Herzig, H. E., and Frei-Stolba, R. (eds.) (1989), *Labor Omnibus Unus. Gerold Walser zum 70. Gerburtstag* (Stuttgart).

Hill, P. V., Kent, J. P. C., and Carson, R. A. G. (1960), *Late Roman bronze coinage* (London).

Hoffman, D. (1969–70), *Das spätrömische Bewegungsheer und die Notitia dignitatum* (Düsseldorf).

Hohlfelder, R. L. (1984), 'Marcian's gamble: a reassessment of eastern imperial policy toward Attila AD450–453', *AJAH* 9, no. 1: 54–69.

Holum, K. G. (1982), *Theodosian empresses: women and imperial dominion in late antiquity*, (Berkeley).

Honoré, T. (1978), *Tribonian* (London).

——(1994), *Emperors and lawyers* (Oxford).

——(1999), *Law in the crisis of empire, 379–455AD: the Theodosian dynasty and its Quaestors* (Oxford).

——(2004), 'Roman law AD200–400: from Cosmopolis to Rechstaat?', in Swain and Edwards (eds.) (2004) (Oxford), 109–32.

Hopkins, M. K. (1961), 'Social mobility in the later Roman empire: the evidence of Ausonius', *CQ* 11: 239–49.

——(1978*a*), 'Rules of evidence', *JRS* 68: 178–86.

——(1978*b*), *Conquerors and slaves* (Cambridge).

Humfress, C. (2007), *Orthodoxy and the courts in late antiquity* (Oxford).

Humphries, M. (1999), 'The Image of Valentinian I from Symmachus to Ammianus', in Drijvers and Hunt (eds.) (1999), 117–26.

——(2003), 'Roman senators and absent emperors in late antiquity', *Acta ad archaeologiam et Artium Historiam Pertinentia*, 17, NS 3: 27–46.

Humphries, M. (2007), 'From emperor to pope? Ceremonial, space, and authority at Rome from Constantine to Gregory the Great', in Cooper and Hillner (eds.) (2007), 21–58.

——(2008), 'From usurper to emperor: the politics of legitimation in the age of Constantine', *JLA* 1.1: 82–100.

——(2012), 'Valentinian III and the city of Rome', in Grig and Kelly (eds.) (2012), 161–82.

Hunt, D. (1998), 'The successors of Constantine', in *CAH* XIII: 1–44.

Instinksy, H. U. (1952), 'Zur Entstehung des Titels Nobilissimus Caesar', in *Festschrift für Rudolf Egger* (Klagenfurt), 98–103.

Jalland, T. (1941), *The life and times of St Leo the Great* (London).

James, L. (ed.) (1997), *Women, men and eunuchs: gender in Byzantium* (London).

Johnson, M. J. (1991), 'On the burial places of the Valentinian Dynasty', *Historia*, 40: 501–6.

——(2009), *The Roman imperial mausoleum in late antiquity* (Cambridge).

Jones, A. H. M. (1964a), *The later Roman empire 284–602: a social, economic and administrative survey*, 3 vols. (Oxford).

——(1964b), 'Collegiate prefectures', *JRS* 54: 78–89.

——(1966), *The decline of the ancient world* (London).

Kaegi, W. E. (1968), *Byzantium and the decline of Rome* (Princeton).

Kaser, M. (1959), *Römisches Privatrecht* 1 (2nd edn. Munich, 1971).

Kaster, R. A. (1984), 'A reconsideration of Gratian's school-law', *Hermes*, 112: 100–14.

Kaufman, P. I. (1997), 'Diehard Homoians and the election of Ambrose', *JECS* 5: 421–40.

Kelly, C. (1998), 'Emperors, government and bureaucracy', in *CAH* XIII: 138–83.

——(1999), 'Empire building', in Bowersock, Brown, and Grabar (eds.) (1999), 170–95.

——(2004), *Ruling the later Roman empire* (Cambridge, Mass.).

——(ed.) (forthcoming), *Theodosius II: rethinking the Roman empire in late antiquity* (Cambridge).

Kiilerich, B., and Torp, J. (1989), 'Hic Est: Hic Stilicho: the date and interpretation of a notable diptych', *Jahrbuch des Deutschen Archäologischen Instituts*, 104: 319–54.

Koethe, H. (1981), 'Zum Mausoleum der weströmischen Dynastei bei Alt-Sankt-Peter', *Römische Mitteilungen*, 46: 9–26.

Krautheimer, R. (1937–77), *Corpus Basilicarum Christianum Romae*, 5 vols. (Vatican City).

——(1961), 'The architecture of Sixtus III: a fifth-century renascence?', in Meiss (ed.) (1961), 1. 291–301.

——(1964), 'The crypt of Sta Maria in Cosmedin and the mausoleum of Petronius Probus', in Freeman Sandler (ed.) (1964), 173–4.

——(1983), *Three Christian capitals: topography and politics* (Berkeley).

Kulikowski, M. (2000a), 'The *Notitia Dignitatum* as a historical source', *Historia*, 49: 358–77.

——(2000b), 'Barbarians in Gaul, usurpers in Britain', *Britannia*, 31: 325–45.

——(2000c), 'The career of the *comes Hispaniarum* Asterius', *Phoenix*, 54: 123–41.

——(2001), 'The Visigothic settlement in Aquitania: the imperial perspective', in Mathisen and Shanzer (eds.) (2001), 26–38.

——(2004), *Late Roman Spain and its cities* (Baltimore).

——(2007), *Rome's Gothic Wars: from the third century to Alaric* (Cambridge).

Latham, R. E. (1965), *Revised medieval Latin word-list* (Oxford).

Lee. A.D. (2007), *War in late antiquity: a social history* (Oxford).

Lejdegård, H. (2002), 'Honorius and the city of Rome: authority and legitimacy in late antiquity', Diss., University of Uppsala.

Lenox-Conyngham, A. (1982), 'The topography of the basilica conflict of AD385/6 in Milan', *Historia*, 31: 353–63.

Lenski, N. (1997), '*Initium mali Romano imperio*: contemporary reactions to the battle of Adrianople', *TAPA* 127:129–68.

——(2002), *Failure of empire: Valens and the Roman state in the fourth century AD* (Berkeley).

——(ed.) (2006*a*), *The Cambridge companion to the age of Constantine* (Cambridge).

——(2006*b*), 'The reign of Constantine', in Lenski (ed.) (2006*a*), 59–90.

Leppin, H. (2003), *Theodosius der Grosse* (Darmstadt).

Levy, H. L. (1971), *Claudian's In Rufinum: an exegetical commentary* (Cleveland).

Liebeschuetz, J. H. W. G., (1990), *Barbarians and bishops: army, church, and state in the age of Arcadius and Chrysostom* (Oxford).

——(1992), 'Alaric's Goths: nation or army?', in Drinkwater and Elton (eds.) (1992), 75–83.

——(2005), *Ambrose of Milan: political letters and speeches* (Liverpool).

——(2011), *Ambrose and John Chrysostom: clerics between desert and empire* (Oxford).

Lippold, A. (1980), *Theodosius der Grosse*, 2nd edn. (Munich).

Liverani, P. (2007), 'Victors and pilgrims in late antiquity and the early middle ages', *Fragmenta*, 1: 83–102.

Lizzi Testa, R. (2004), *Senatori, popolo, papi: il governo di Roma al tempo dei Valentiniani* (Bari).

——(2007), 'Christian emperor, vestal virgins and priestly colleges: reconsidering the end of Roman paganism', *Ant.Tard.* 15: 251–62.

Lunn-Rockliffe, S. (2008), 'Ambrose's imperial funeral sermons', *JEH* 59, no. 2: 191–207.

——(2010), 'Commemorating the usurper Magnus Maximus: ekphrasis, poetry and history in Pacatus' panegyric of Theodosius', *JLA* 3.2: 316–36.

Lütkenhaus, W. (1998), *Constantius III: Studien zu seiner Tätigkeit und Stellung im Westreich 411–421* (Bonn).

MacCormack, S. G. (1976), 'Latin prose panegyrics: tradition and discontinuity in the later Roman empire', *Revue des études augustiniennes*, 22: 29–77.

——(1981), *Art and ceremony in late antiquity* (Berkeley).

McCormick, M. (1986), *Eternal victory: triumphal rulership in late antiquity, Byzantium, and the early medieval west* (Cambridge).

——(2000), 'Emperor and court', in *CAH* XIV: 135–63.

McEvoy, M. (2010), 'Rome and the transformation of the imperial office in the late fourth- mid-fifth centuries AD', *PBSR* 79: 151–92.

——(forthcoming 2013) 'The mausoleum of Honorius: late Roman imperial Christianity and the city of Rome', in McKitterick *et al.* (eds.) (forthcoming 2013), 131–49.

——and Tuffin, P. (2005), 'Steak à la Hun: food, drink, and dietary habits in Ammianus Marcellinus', in Mayer and Trzcionka (eds.) (2005), 69–84.

McGeachy, J. A. (1942), 'Q. Aurelius Symmachus and the senatorial aristocracy of the west', PhD., University of Chicago.

MacGeorge, P. (2002), *Late Roman Warlords* (Oxford).

McGill, S., Sogno, C., and Watts E. (eds.) (2010), *From the Tetrarchs to the Theodosians: later Roman history and culture, 284–450CE* (Cambridge).

Machado, C. (2010), 'The city as stage: aristocratic commemorations in late antique Rome', in Rebillard and Sotinel (eds.) (2010), 287–317.

——(2011), 'Roman aristocrats and the christianization of Rome', in Brown and Lizzi Testa (eds.) (2011), 493–516.

McHardy F., and Marshall E. (eds.) (2004), *Women's influence on classical civilization* (London).

Mackie, G. (2003), *Early Christian chapels in the west: decoration, function, and patronage* (Toronto).

McKitterick, R., Osborne, J., Richardson C., and Story J. (eds.) (forthcoming 2013), *Old St Peter's Basilica* (Cambridge).

McLynn, N. B. (1991), 'The "Apology" of Palladius: nature and purpose', *JThS* 42: 56–76.

——(1994), *Ambrose of Milan: church and court in a Christian capital* (Berkeley).

——(1997), 'Diehards: a response', *JECS* 5: 446–50.

——(1998), 'Augustine's Roman empire', *Augustinian Studies*, 39, 2: 29–44.

——(2004), 'The transformation of imperial churchgoing in the fourth century', in Swain and Edwards (eds.) (2004), 235–70.

——(2005), '"Genere Hispanis": Theodosius, Spain and Nicene Orthodoxy', in Bowes and Kulikowski (ed. and trans.) (2005), 77–120.

——(2009), 'Possidius of Calama: Review', Ant.Tard. 17:435–7.

MacMullen, R. (1964), 'Some pictures in Ammianus Marcellinus', *Art Bull.* 46: 435–55.

Maenchen-Helfen, J. O. (1973), *The world of the Huns* (Berkeley).

Magdalino, P. (ed.) (1994), *New Constantines* (Aldershot).

Maier, H. O. (1994), 'Private space as the social context of Arianism in Ambrose's Milan', *JThS* 45 (pt 1): 72–93.

Mathisen, R. W. (1979), 'Hilarius, Germanus and Lupus', *Phoenix* 33: 160–9.

——(1981), 'The last year of St Germanus of Auxerre', *Analecta Bollandiana*, 99: 151–9.

——(1984), 'Emigrants, exiles, and survivors: aristocratic options in Visigothic Aquitania', *Phoenix*, 38, no. 2: 159–70.

——(1989), *Ecclesiastical factionalism and religious controversy in fifth-century Gaul* (Washington, DC).

——(1992), 'Fifth century visitors to Italy: business or pleasure?', in Drinkwater and Elton (eds.) (1992), 228–38.

——(1999), 'Sigisvult the Patrician, Maximinus the Arian, and political stratagems in the Western Roman Empire c. 425–40', *Early Medieval Europe*, 8: 173–96.

——and Shanzer, D. (eds.) (2001), *Society and culture in late antique Gaul: revisiting the sources* (Aldershot).

Matthews, J. F. (1970), 'Olympiodorus of Thebes and the history of the west (AD407–425)', *JRS*, 60: 79–97.

——(1971), 'Gallic supporters of Theodosius', *Latomus*, 30: 1073–99.

——(1974), 'The letters of Symmachus', in Binns (ed.) (1974), 58–99.

——(1975), *Western aristocracies and imperial court AD 364–425* (Oxford, repr. 1990).

——(1989), *The Roman empire of Ammianus* (London).

—— (1993), 'The making of the text', in Harries and Wood (eds.) (1993), 19–44.

—— (1997), 'Codex Theodosianus 9.40.13 and Nichomachus Flavianus', *Historia*, 46: 196–213.

—— (2000), *Laying down the law: a study of the Theodosian Code* (London).

Mayer, W., and Trzcionka, S. (eds.) (2005), *Feast, fast or famine* (Brisbane).

Mazzarino, S. (1942), *Stilicone: la crisi imperiale dopo Teodosio* (Rome).

Meiss M. (ed.) (1961), *Essays in honour of Erwin Panofsky (De Artibus Opuscula* XL), 2 vols. (New York).

Merdinger, J. E. (1997), *Rome and the African church in the time of Augustus* (New Haven).

Merrills, A., and Miles, R. (2010), *The Vandals* (Oxford).

Meynell, H. A. (ed.) (1990), *Grace, politics and desire: essays on Augustine* (Calgary, Alberta).

Millar, F. (1977), *The emperor in the Roman world (31 BC–AD 337)* (London).

—— (2006), *A Greek Roman Empire: power and belief under Theodosius II (408–450)* (Berkeley).

Molè Ventura, C. (1992), *Principi fanciulli: legittimismo constituzionale e storiografia Cristiana nella tarda antichità* (Catania).

Momigliano, A. (ed.) (1963), *The conflict between paganism and Christianity in the fourth century* (Oxford).

Mommaerts, T. S., and Kelley, D. H. (1992), 'The Anicii of Gaul and Rome', in Drinkwater and Elton (eds.) (1992), 111–21.

Mommsen, Th. (1903), 'Stilicho und Alarich', *Hermes*, 38: 101–15.

Moorhead, J. (1992), *Theoderic in Italy* (Oxford).

Morris, I. (1964), *The world of the shining prince: court life in ancient Japan* (New York, repr. 1994).

Moss, J. R. (1973), 'The effects of the policies of Aetius on the history of western Europe', *Historia*, 22: 711–31.

Mratschek, S. (2001), '*Te velimus ... consilii participem*: Augustine of Hippo and Olympius—a case study of religious-political cooperation in the fifth century', *Studia Patristica*, 38: 224–32.

Muhlberger, S. (1984), 'The Copenhagen Continuation of Prosper: a tradition', *Florilegium*, 6: 71–95.

Muntz, E. (1885), 'The lost mosaics of Ravenna', *American Journal of Archaeology and History of Fine Arts*, 1, no. 2/3: 115–30.

Musumeci, A. M. (1997), 'La politica ecclesiastica di Valentiniano III', *Siculorum Gymnasium*, n.s.a. XXX-n.2: 431–81.

Nagy, T. (1990–1), 'Transfer of power in the last century of the western Roman empire', *Antaeus*, 19–20: 85–102.

Nautin, P. (1974), 'Les Premières Relations d'Ambroise avec l'empereur Gratien', in Duval (ed.) (1974), 229–44.

Neil, B. (2009), *Leo the Great* (London).

Nixon, C. E. V., and Rodgers, B. S. (1994), *In praise of later Roman emperors: the Panegyrici Latini* (Berkeley).

O'Flynn, J. M. (1983), *Generalissimos of the western Roman empire* (Calgary, Alberta).

Oost, S. I. (1962), 'Count Gildo and Theodosius the Great', *CP* 57: 27–30.

Oost, S. I. (1964), 'Aetius and Majorian', *CP* 59: 23–9.

——(1965), 'Some problems in the history of Galla Placidia', *CP* 60: 1–10.

——(1966), 'The revolt of Heraclian', *CP* 56: 236–42.

——(1968*a*), *Galla Placidia Augusta: a biographical essay* (Chicago).

——(1968*b*), 'Galla Placidia and the law', *CP* 63: 114–21.

Pabst, A. (1986), *Divisio Regni: Der Zerfall des Imperium Romanum in der Sicht der Zeitgenossen* (Bonn).

Palanque, J.-R. (1929), 'Sur l'usurpation de Maxime', *REA* 31: 33–6.

——(1931), 'Sur la date d'une loi de Gratien contre l'hérésie', *RH* 168: 87–90.

——(1933), *Saint Ambroise et l'empire romain: contributions à l'histoire des rapports de l'église et l'état à la fin du quatrième siècle* (Paris).

——(1934), 'La Date du transfert de la préfecture des Gaules de Trèves a Arles', *REA* 36: 359–65.

Panciera, S. (1996), 'Il precettore di Valentiniano III', in Stella and Valvo (eds.) (1996), 277–97.

Paolucci, F. (2008), 'La tomba dell'imperatrice Maria e altre sepolture di rango di età tardoantica a San Pietro', *Temporis Signa: Archeologia della tarda antichità e del medioevo*, III: 225–52.

Paschoud, F. (1967), *Roma Aeterna: études sur le patriotisme romain dans l'occident latin à l'époque des grandes invasions* (Paris).

Pietri, C. (1976), *Roma Christiana: Recherches sur l'église de Rome, son organization, sa politique, son idéologie di Militade à Sixte III (311–440)*, 2 vols. (Rome).

Piganiol, A. (1972), *L'Empire chrétien, 325–395* (Paris, 2nd edn.).

Pizzolato, L. F., and Rizzi, M. (eds.) (1998), *Nec timeo mori: Atti del Congresso internazionale di studi ambrosiani nel XVI centenario della morte di sant'Ambrogio* (Milan).

Potter D. S. (2004), *The Roman empire at bay, AD180–395* (New York).

Price, S. R. F. (1984), *Rituals and power: the Roman imperial cult in Asia Minor* (Cambridge).

Raffaelli, R. (ed.) (1995), *Vincende e figure femminili in Grecia e a Roma* (Amona).

Raspanti, G. (2009), '*Clementissimus Imperator*: power, religion and philosophy in Ambrose's *De Obitu Theodosii* and Seneca's *De clementia*', in Cain and Lenski (eds.) (2009), 45–56.

Rebenich, S. (1985), 'Gratian, a son of Theodosius, and the birth of Galla Placidia', *Historia*, 34: 372–85.

Rebillard É., and Sotinel C. (eds.) (2010), *Les Frontières du profane dans l'antiquité tardive* (Rome).

Rees, R. (2002), *Layers of loyalty in Latin panegyric, AD 289–307* (Oxford).

Ridley, R. T. (1982), *Zosimus: New History* (Sydney).

Rodgers, B. S. (1981), 'Merobaudes and Maximus in Gaul', *Historia*, 30: 82–105.

Roueché, C. (1984), 'Acclamations in the later Roman empire', *JRS* 74: 181–99.

Rossi, G. (1572), *Historiarum Ravennatum libri decem* (Venice).

Rowe, G. (2002), *Princes and political cultures: the new Tiberian senatorial decrees* (Ann Arbor, Mich.).

Russell D. A., and Wilson, N. G. (1981), *Menander Rhetor* (Oxford).

Salway, P. (1981), *Roman Britain* (Oxford).

Salzman, M. R. (2002), *The making of a Christian aristocracy: social and religious change in the western Roman empire* (Cambridge, Mass.).

——(2006), 'Symmachus and the "barbarian" generals', *Historia*, 55, no.3: 352–67.

——(2010*a*), 'Ambrose and the usurpation of Arbogastes and Eugenius: reflections on pagan–Christian conflict narratives', *JECS* 18, no. 2: 191–223.

——(2010*b*), 'Leo in Rome: the evolution of episcopal authority in the fifth century,' in Bonamente and Lizzi Testa (eds.) (2010), 343–56.

Seeck, O. (1919), *Regesten der Kaiser und Päpste fur die Jahre 311 bis 476 n.Chr: Vorarbeit zu einer Prosopographie der christlicher Kaizerzeit* (Stuttgart).

Severy, B. (2003), *Augustus and the family at the birth of the Roman empire* (New York).

Shaw, B. D. (2011), *Sacred violence: African Christians and sectarian hatred in the age of Augustine* (Cambridge).

Shelton, K. J. (1983), 'The consular muse of Flavius Constantius', *Art Bull.* 65, no. 1: 7–23.

Sirago, V. A. (1961), *Galla Placidia e la transformazione politica dell'occidente* (Louvain) (= Université de Louvain, *Recueil de travaux d'histoire et de philologie*, 4th ser., 25).

Sivan, H. (1993), *Ausonius of Bordeaux* (London).

——(1996), 'Was Theodosius I a usurper?', *Klio*, 78, 1: 198–211.

——(2011), *Galla Placidia: the last Roman empress* (Oxford).

Sogno, C. (2006), *Q. Aurelius Symmachus: a political biography* (Ann Arbor, Mich.).

Sotinel, C. and Jolivet, V. (2012), 'Die domus Pinciana: eine kaiserliche Residenz in Rome', in Fuhrer (ed.), 137–60.

Southern, P., and Dixon, K. R. (1996), *The late Roman army* (London).

Stein, E. (1959), *Histoire du Bas-Empire*, Vol. 1: *De l'état romain à l'état byzantin (284–476)*, trans. J. R. Palanque (Paris).

Stella C., and Valvo A. (eds.) (1996), *Studi in onore di Albino Garzetti* (Brescia).

Stevens, C. E. (1933), *Sidonius Apollinaris and his age* (Oxford).

——(1957), 'Marcus, Gratian, Constantine', *Athenaeum*, 35: 316–47.

Stickler, T. (2002), *Aetius: Gestaltungsspielrssume eines Heermeisters im ausgehenden Weströmischen Reich* (Munich).

Straub, J. A. (1939), *Vom Herrscherideal in der Spätantike* (Stuttgart).

——(1952), 'Parens Principum', *La Nouvelle Clio*, 4: 94 f.

Sundwall, J. (1915), *Weströmische Studien* (Berlin).

Swain, S., and Edwards, M. (eds.) (2004), *Approaching late antiquity: the transformation from early to late empire* (Oxford).

Syme, R. (1972), 'The son of Macrinus', *Phoenix*, 26, no. 3: 275–91.

Szidat, J. (2010), *Usurpator tanti nominis: Kaiser und Usurpator in der Spätantike (337–476 n. Chr.)* (Stuttgart).

Täckholm, U. (1969), 'Aetius and the battle on the Catalaunian Fields', *Opus. Rom.* 7, 15: 259–76.

Thompson, E. A. (1947), *The historical work of Ammianus Marcellinus* (Cambridge).

——(1950), 'The foreign policies of Theodosius II and Marcian', *Hermathena*, 76: 58–75.

——(1956), 'The settlement of the barbarians in southern Gaul', *JRS* 46: 65–75.

——(1982*a*), *Romans and barbarians: the decline of the western empire* (Madison, Wisc.).

Thompson, E. A. (1982b), 'Zosimus 6.10.2 and the letters of Honorius', *CQ* NS 32, 2: 445–62.

——(1984), *St Germanus of Auxerre and the end of Roman Britain* (Woodbridge).

——(1996; repr. of 1948), *The Huns*, revised and with an afterword by Peter Heather (Oxford).

Tomlin, R. S. O. (1973), 'The Emperor Valentinian the first', DPhil dissertation, Oxford University.

Traina, G. (2009), *428AD: an ordinary year at the end of the Roman empire* (Princeton).

Twyman, B. L. (1970), 'Aetius and the aristocracy', *Historia*, 19: 480–503.

Van Dam, R. (2007), *The Roman revolution of Constantine* (Ann Arbor, Mich.).

Van Nuffelen, P. (forthcoming), 'Olympiodorus of Thebes and eastern triumphalism' in Kelly (ed.).

Vera, D. (1975), 'I rapporti fra Magno Massimo, Teodosio e Valentiniano II nel 383–384', *Athenaeum*, 63: 265–301.

——(1979), 'Le statue del senato di Roma in onore di Flavio Teodosio e l'equilibrio dei potere imperiali in età Teodosiana', *Athenaeum*, NS 57: 381–403.

Wallace-Hadrill, A. (1981), 'The emperor and his virtues', *Historia*, 30: 298–323.

——(ed.) (1989), *Patronage in ancient society* (London).

Wallace-Hadrill, J. M. (1961), 'Gothia and Romania', *Bulletin of the John Rylands Library, Manchester*, 44: 213–37.

Wardman, A. E. (1984), 'Usurpers and internal conflicts in the fourth century AD', *Historia*, 33: 220–37.

Ward-Perkins, B. (1984), *From classical antiquity to the middle ages: urban public building in northern and central Italy, AD 300–850* (Oxford).

Ware, C. (2004), 'Gildo *tyrannus*: accusation and allusion in the speeches of Roma and Africa', *Aetas Claudianea* (Leipzig), 96–103.

——(2012), *Claudian and the Roman epic tradition* (Cambridge).

Watson, G. (1969), *The Roman soldier* (London).

Weber, R. J. (1989), 'Albinus: the living memory of a fifth-century personality', *Historia*, 38: 472–97.

Wessel, S. (2008), *Leo the Great and the spiritual rebuilding of a universal Rome* (Leiden).

Whitby, M. (1998), *The propaganda of power: the role of panegyric in late antiquity* (Leiden).

Wightman, E. M. (1985), *Gallia Belgica* (London).

Wilkes, J. J. (1972), 'A Pannonian refugee of quality at Salona', *Phoenix*, 26, no. 4: 377–93.

Williams, D. H. (1995), *Ambrose of Milan and the end of the Nicene–Arian conflicts* (Oxford).

——(1997), 'Politically correct in Milan: a reply to the "diehard" Homoians and the election of Ambrose', *JECS* 5: 441–6.

Wolfram, H. (1988), *History of the Goths*, trans. T. L. Dunlap, 2nd edn. (Berkeley).

Wormald, P. (1976), 'The decline of the western empire and the survival of its aristocracy', *JRS* 66: 217–26.

Wood, I. (1987), 'The fall of the western empire and the end of Roman Britain', *Britannia*, 19: 251–62.

Woods, D. (2004), 'The Constantinian origin of Justina (Themistius, *Or.* 3.43b)', *CQ* 54: 325–7.

——(2006), 'Valentinian I, Severa, Marina and Justina', *Classica et Mediaevalia*, 57: 173–87.

Zecchini, G. (1983), *Aezio: l'ultima difesa dell'Occidente romano* (Rome).

Index

San Pietro in Vincoli (Saint Peter in chains)
church, Rome, 276
Sant'Aquilino (chapel), Milan. *See* San
Lorenzo (St Laurence), Milan (church)
Sapaudia, 295
Sarmatians, 54, 77
Sarus (Visigothic chieftain), 177, 198
Sassanian Empire, 326
Saturninus (Fl.) (eastern *magister militum*,
cos. 383), 112
Saturninus, Flavius Peregrinus (urban
prefect), 149
Savoy, 272
Scythians. *See* Huns
Sebastianus (*magister peditum*), 54, 56,
57, 315
Sebastianus (western usurper,
AD 412–413), 198, 200
Sebastianus (*magister militum,* son-in-law of
Boniface), 248, 262, 269
Seleukia, 118
senate/senators, 34, 44, 60–61, 156–9, 167,
170, 174, 177–80, 190, 192, 194, 241, 258,
265, 278, 289, 295–6, 298, 310, 312
senate meetings, 14, 44, 158, 178, 180, 189,
258, 259, 310
Septimius Severus (emperor, AD 193–211), 3
Serena (niece of Theodosius I/wife of Stilicho),
140, 143, 151, 152, 166,
180, 254
Severus Alexander (emperor, AD 222–235),
3, 326
Severus, Valerius (praetorian prefect), 122
Shapur II (Sassanian king, AD 309–379), 326
Sicily, 91, 261, 262, 266
Sidonius Apollinaris, *see* Apollinaris, Gaius
Sollius Sidonius
Sigisvult, Fl. (*magister militum*, cos. 437), 247,
260, 262, 282–3, 284
Silvanus (general), 141
Sirmium, 63, 75, 77, 80, 112, 119
Siscia, 91
Sixtus III (pope, AD 432-440), 263,
276, 277
Socrates of Constantinople (historian), 15, 77,
97, 228, 231, 236, 320
Solicinium campaign, 110
Sozomen (historian), 15, 205, 320, 321
Spain, 62, 77, 159, 196, 201, 202, 252, 255, 263,
270, 291
Sparta, 138
Spes Rei Publicae (coin legend) 18, 52, 138
Stilicho, Fl. (*magister militum*, cos. 400, 405),
10–13, 15, 16, 64, 140, 204, 212, 214,
217–18, 220, 225–6, 235, 241,
249–50, 252–4, 259–61, 265, 268, 271,

282, 287, 290, 292, 302–3, 312–13,
317–20, 324–5
and Alaric, 178
death, 182–4, 188, 191–2, 195, 197, 199,
206, 213, 215–16, 297–8
diptych, 205
downfall of, 158, 180–7, 207, 322
generosity, 166
marriage-ties, 309, 310
military prowess, 161, 170–1, 175, 186
partnership with Honorius, 162–9, 173
reaction against, 188–92
as 'regent' for Honorius, 141–4, 172
regime, 153–86, 310, 311,
322: -building, 144–52
religion, 190–1
statue of, 175
supporters of, 289
versus Gildo, 156–9
Storacius (praetorian prefect), 287
Suetonius (historian), 318
Sueves, 176, 252
Sulpicius Severus (historian), 114
Syagrius (Fl.) (praetorian prefect,
cos. 381), 121
Symmachus, Q. Aurelius (urban prefect, cos.
391), 14, 16, 51, 60, 62, 65, 67–8, 85, 87,
90, 94, 106, 116, 122–4, 148–9, 157, 159,
169, 170, 172, 179,
Symmachus, Q. Aurelius Memmius
Symmachus iunior (cos. 485), 327

taxation, 31, 34–5, 78, 165, 170, 265, 296
concessions, 190, 202, 285
immunities, 274
remissions, 224, 264
temperance, as an imperial virtue, 28, 35–6,
46, 107–9, 165
temples, 45, 123, 207
Tetrarchy, 4, 5, 6
Themistius (orator, philosopher, eastern
urban prefect), 24, 26, 31, 36–8, 40, 42,
53, 62, 77, 82, 103, 106–7, 306
Theoderic (Ostrogothic king of Italy,
AD 493–526), 327–328
Theoderic (Visigothic king, AD 418–451), 293
Theodoret of Cyrus (theologian), 15, 77
Theodorus, Fl. Manlius (praetorian prefect,
cos. 399), 149, 159, 167, 179, 189
Theodosian Code, 17, 31, 44, 116, 224, 228,
240–42, 251, 256–61, 272, 285, 288, 290,
302, 312–13
Theodosius (son of Athaulf and Galla
Placida), 201, 237, 281
Theodosius I (Fl.) (emperor, AD 379-395), 6,
24, 27, 102, 104, 130, 143, 155, 161–2,

Lightning Source UK Ltd.
Milton Keynes UK
UKHW021431130919
349710UK00008B/676/P